Left, Right, and Center

VOICES FROM ACROSS
THE POLITICAL SPECTRUM

ROBERT ATWAN
Series Editor, *The Best American Essays*

and

JON ROBERTS
St. Thomas Aquinas College

Bedford Books *of* St. Martin's Press Boston

For Bedford Books

President and Publisher: Charles H. Christensen
General Manager and Associate Publisher: Joan E. Feinberg
Managing Editor: Elizabeth M. Schaaf
Developmental Editor: Jane Betz
Editorial Assistants: Joanne Diaz, John E. Sullivan III
Production Editor: John Amburg
Production Assistant: Maureen Murray
Copyeditor: Barbara Sutton
Text Design: Claire Seng-Niemoeller
Cover Design: Hannus Design Associates

For information, write: St. Martin's Press, Inc.
175 Fifth Avenue, New York, NY 10010

Editorial Offices: Bedford Books *of* St. Martin's Press
75 Arlington Street, Boston, MA 02116

ISBN: 0–312–10200–3

Acknowledgments

Asante, Molefi Kete. "What is Afrocentrism?" originally titled "Afrocentric Systematics"
from *Malcolm X As Cultural Hero and Other Afrocentric Essays*, © 1993, reprinted with
permission from the publisher, Africa World Press, Inc. All rights reserved.

Bennett, William J. "Revolt against God: America's Spiritual Despair." William J. Bennett,
formerly Secretary of Education, is presently a distinguished fellow at the Heritage
Foundation and editor of *The Book of Virtues*. This article is adapted from an address by
Mr. Bennett on the American Heritage Foundation's 20th anniversary. Reprinted from
Policy Review, Winter 1994, by permission; all rights reserved.

*Acknowledgments and copyrights are continued at the back of the book on pages 616–18, which
constitute an extension of the copyright page. It is a violation of the law to reproduce these selections
by any means whatsoever without the written permission of the copyright holder.*

Preface

---◇---

Designed especially for first-year writing classes, *Left, Right, and Center* offers a representative selection of voices from across America's political spectrum. Drawing on the writings and speeches of many of our nation's most prominent political and cultural figures, journalists, and intellectuals from both inside and outside the academy, we have assembled a comprehensive reader that treats, within a practical compositional framework, seven of the United States' most persistent and controversial social and cultural issues. We believe that our thematic organization — the seven chapters focus on multiculturalism, race, class, gender, sexual politics, freedom of expression, and social values — provides an intensive and exciting introduction to American political culture as well as a rich resource for discussion and writing.

Until recently, the idea of a political reader for the composition classroom would have raised many eyebrows. Selections treating electoral and legislative processes, domestic and foreign policy, and the national economy — topics traditionally at the heart of American political discussion — might be useful for a course in political science, but they could hardly be thought a suitable foundation for a first-year writing class. In the last few years, however, the boundaries of political discussion have been redrawn to encompass the broadest range of cultural and social issues. Public as well as personal issues that were not formerly considered political have become so; the ongoing debates over artistic expression and sexuality are just two examples of this trend. This continual broadening of our conception of politics has given rise to the need for the new kind of reader presented here. Even so, neither the reader's themes nor its organization nor even its selections should strike writing instructors as radically different from those of readers already widely used in the first-year writing curriculum. A quick glance at the table of contents will reveal that most of the selections treat issues with which most teachers of composition are already familiar and well-prepared to teach.

In choosing the selections for *Left, Right, and Center*, we have tried to achieve a balance among the diverse political opinions presented in each chapter. Moreover, we have attempted to reflect a more accurate model of American political discourse than the model of polarization often presented in the media. In our view, the state of political opinion in this country might best be compared to a prism, producing a wide array of brilliant yet discrete colors. The book's selections, we hope, mirror this gradual shading of opinion from one political extreme to another. We believe that we have succeeded in bringing together a collection of authors who inspire fruitful discussion even as they defy easy political labels.

To make this reader as useful as possible for the composition classroom, we built into *Left, Right, and Center* several types of instructional material:

1. *An Introduction by Robert Atwan that provides students with a concise overview of the current state of political discourse in America.* The Introduction also treats several of the major stylistic and rhetorical strategies that students are likely to encounter in the individual selections.

2. *Chapter introductions by Robert Atwan that familiarize students with the issue under examination and with the individual selections that follow.* These remarks have been especially designed to help students perceive the range of opinion on each issue and to start thinking productively about the connections between selections.

3. *Headnotes for each selection by Jon Roberts* that provide important contextual information and tentatively position the author of the selection both politically and intellectually within the spectrum of voices. For further study, a list of the writer's notable publications follows each headnote.

It should also be noted that the selections were carefully read for references and topical allusions that seemed beyond the range of information easily available to today's students. We provided footnotes for any item we thought might not be understandable from text or context alone. While there is bound to be some disagreement about what kinds of cultural information instructors can reasonably expect their students to know — recall the controversy inspired by the publication of E. D. Hirsch's *Cultural Literacy* a few years back — we have generally relied on our own classroom experience as a guide and glossed those details that we thought would be unfamiliar to the average first- or second-year student.

4. *Several questions prepared by Jon Roberts after each selection designed to promote understanding and discussion.* The first five questions after each selection are intended to help foster students' understanding of the particular essay, to offer them an opportunity to challenge the author's argument and assumptions, and to cultivate a richer sense of the possibilities of political language. Although some questions ask about content, most are aimed at bringing the student as close as possible to the author's strategy and style. Generally, the questions require students to return to the selection for closer reading and analysis. They are designed to probe the author's assumptions about politics and culture whether they have their source on the left, on the right, or at the center.

5. *Two writing assignments after each selection.* These assignments are of two kinds. The first is intended to test students' analytical ability. The second asks students to draw parallels between the issues of a selection and their own lives. These writing assignments were also prepared by Jon Roberts.

6. *Brief, boxed selections throughout the reader.* Presented without additional apparatus, these selections respond to the selections that immediately precede them or offer additional perspectives on a chapter's topic.

7. *An appendix containing the Constitution of the United States of America with the Bill of Rights and the remaining amendments.*

Finally, it is worth noting that political affiliation in America is a very unstable category. Over the course of their careers, writers on politics and culture in America may sometimes change their core beliefs and values. While teaching these selections, instructors should encourage their students to remain sensitive to those changes even in the course of a single essay or speech.

Acknowledgments

We acknowledge with pleasure and gratitude the splendid staff at Bedford Books. The idea for *Left, Right, and Center* arose from a series of discussions, presided over by Bedford's publisher, Charles H. Christensen, concerning the need for a different kind of college reader. Chuck and Bedford's Associate Publisher, Joan E. Feinberg, then lent the project their usual unerring guidance. We thank our editor, Jane Betz. From the book's inception through its final stages, she displayed remarkable judgment and wit. We could not have asked for a more supportive editor or a more patient one. John Amburg performed a masterly production job at an incredible pace, and Maureen Murray provided ample production assistance.

We especially want to thank several friends and colleagues for their invaluable comments. At St. Thomas Aquinas College, Professors Charles O'Neill, David Keppler, and Gerald McCarthy were always ready with words of support and clarifying suggestions. The staff at Lougheed Library of St. Thomas Aquinas College, especially John Barth, Ken Donohue, and Virginia Dunnigan, offered their indispensible assistance in locating important materials for the book. We also received valuable advice from the Publisher for the Social Sciences and Public Affairs at Princeton University Press, Peter Dougherty.

Lastly, we thank Ms. Stephanie White of Brandeis University for her fine work in preparing the Instructor's Manual for this book. Teachers will find there an abundance of useful suggestions for additional writing assignments as well as insightful strategies for teaching and discussion.

Robert Atwan

Jon Roberts

Contents

⟨1⟩ The Multicultural Challenge: Ethnicity, Diversity, Disunity   1

Arthur M. Schlesinger, Jr.   *One of America's leading historians . . . Two-time Pulitzer Prize winner . . . Special advisor to President John F. Kennedy.*

The Disuniting of America   3

"Watching ethnic conflict tear one nation after another apart, one cannot look with complacency at proposals to divide the United States into distinct and immutable ethnic and racial communities, each taught to cherish its own apartness from the rest. One wonders: Will the center hold? or will the melting pot give way to the Tower of Babel?"

Molefi Kete Asante   *A founder of the Afrocentrist movement . . . Chair of the Department of African American Studies at Temple University.*

What Is Afrocentrism?   11

"Why should an African American see himself or herself through the perspective of a Chinese or white American? Neither the Chinese nor the white American views phenomena from the perspective of the African American and nor should they."

Linda Chavez   *Republican candidate for U.S. Senate . . . Senior fellow at the Manhattan Institute for Policy Research . . . Highest ranking woman in the Reagan administration.*

Demystifying Multiculturalism   17

"Multiculturalism is not a grassroots movement. It was created, nurtured, and expanded through government policy. Without the expenditure of vast sums of public money, it would wither away and die."

Michael Walzer *Professor of social science at the Institute for Advanced Study, Princeton University . . . Editor of the liberal journal* Dissent *. . . Member of the editorial board of* Philosophy and Public Affairs.

"We need to strengthen associational ties, even if these ties connect some of us to some others and not everyone to everyone else."

Dinesh D'Souza *Senior domestic policy analyst in the Reagan administration . . . John M. Olin Fellow at the American Enterprise Institute . . . Recipient of the Society for Professional Journalists Award.*

"Ironically the young blacks, Hispanics, and other certified minorities in whose name the victim's revolution is conducted are the ones least served by the American university's abandonment of liberal ideals. Instead of treating them as individuals, colleges typically consider minorities as members of a group, important only insofar as their collective numbers satisfy the formulas of diversity."

Cornel West *Philosopher and social activist . . . Du Bois Fellow at Harvard University . . . Chair of the African American Commission of the Democratic Socialists of America.*

"We need to see history as in part the cross-fertilization of a variety of different cultures, usually under conditions of hierarchy. That's thoroughly so for the U.S. For example, jazz is the great symbol of American culture, but there's no jazz without European instruments or African polyrhythms. To talk about hybrid culture means you give up all quest for pure traditions and pristine heritages."

Thomas Sowell *Conservative African American economist and policy expert . . . Senior fellow at the Urban Institute in Washington, D.C. . . . Former economist with the U.S. Department of Labor.*

"We need also to recognize that many great thinkers of the past — whether in medicine or philosophy, science or economics — labored not simply to advance whatever particular group they happened to have come from but to advance the human race. Their legacies . . . belong to all people — and all people need to claim that legacy, not seal themselves off in a dead-end of tribalism or in an emotional orgy of cultural vanity."

2

The American Dilemma: Racism, Fairness, Opportunity 65

itability a book whose tone and substance drearily rehashes innuendos and proposals that should long ago have been consigned to the dustbin of history."

"Racial differences exist at a more profound level than is normally considered.
Why do Europeans average so consistently between Africans and Asians in
crime, family system, sexual behavior, testosterone level, intelligence, and brain
size? It is almost certain that genetics and evolution have a role to play."

"In my legal writing, I follow the caveat of James Madison and other early American democrats. I explore decisionmaking rules that might work in a multi-racial
society to ensure that majority rule does not become majority tyranny."

"There is a great existential challenge facing black America today: the challenge
of taking control of our own future by exerting the requisite moral leadership,
making the sacrifices of time and resources, and building the needed institutions
so that black social and economic development may be advanced. No matter how
windy the debate becomes among white liberals and conservatives as to what
should be done in the public sphere, meeting this self-creating challenge ultimately depends on black action."

The Gender Debate: Roles, Rights, Reaction   237

Feminism at the Crossroads   *239*

"The idea that men and women are radically different species of being, which not so long ago struck so many as an indisputable fact of nature, is more and more coming to be revealed as a historical construct, connected to the rise of the bourgeois industrial household, a social form whose end we are living through."

James Q. Wilson   *Professor of management and public policy at UCLA . . . Former member of the U.S. attorney general's task force on violent crime . . . Cited by the* New York Review of Books *as "probably the most influential single writer on crime in America."*

Gender   *245*

"Men are more aggressive than women. Though child-rearing practices may intensify or moderate this difference, the difference will persist and almost surely rests on biological factors. In every known society, men are more likely than women to play roughly, drive recklessly, fight physically, and assault ruthlessly, and these differences appear early in life."

Naomi Wolf   *Leading feminist social critic and journalist . . . A Rhodes Scholar at Oxford from 1984 to 1987 . . . Author of the best-selling book* The Beauty Myth.

Are Opinions Male?   *269*

"Despite women's recent strides into public life, the national forums of debate — op-ed pages, political magazines, public affairs talk shows, newspaper columns — remain strikingly immune to the general agitation for female access. The agora of opinion is largely a men's club."

Deborah Tannen   *Best-selling author of several books on speech and language . . . A popular speaker with frequent appearances on radio and television . . . One of only three university professors at Georgetown University.*

"Put Down that Paper and Talk to Me!":
Rapport-talk and Report-talk   *280*

"The difference between public and private speaking, or report-talk and rapport-talk, can be understood in terms of status and connection. It is not surprising that women are most comfortable talking when they feel safe and close, among friends and equals, whereas men feel comfortable talking when there is a need to establish and maintain their status in a group."

Susan Faludi   *Pulitzer Prize–winning journalist . . . Author of* Backlash: The Undeclared War against American Women, *which won the National Book Critics Circle Award in 1991.*

The Politics of Sexuality: Identity, Bigotry, Violence   325

were patterns of discreet and discrete behavior to follow, there is now only an unnerving confusion of roles and identities."

"If women are human beings, as feminists suspect, then crimes of violence against women are human rights violations that occur on a massive, almost unimaginable scale. These crimes are committed most frequently in private, in intimacy; but they are committed all the time, every day and every night, all over the world, by normal men."

Christina Hoff Sommers   *Philosophy professor at Clark University . . . Editor of two college textbooks on ethics . . . Has written extensively on ethics, moral theory, American culture, and feminism for both scholarly and general audiences.*

"Gender feminists are committed to the doctrine that the vast majority of batterers or rapists are not fringe characters but men whom society regards as normal — sports fans, former fraternity brothers, pillars of the community. For these 'normal' men, women are not so much persons as 'objects.' In the gender feminist view, once a woman is 'objectified' and therefore no longer human, battering her is simply the next logical step."

⟨6⟩ American Speech: Freedom, Censorship, Correctness 417

Michiko Kakutani   *The principal book reviewer for the* New York Times *. . . Frequently covers cultural and literary news for the* New York Times.

"Instead of allowing free discussion and debate to occur, many gung-ho advocates of politically correct language seem to think that simple suppression of a word or concept will magically make the problem disappear."

Ward Churchill   *Native American rights activist . . . Associate professor of American Indian studies and communications at the Center for the Study of Ethnicity and Race in America . . . Editor of the journal* New Studies on the Left.

"Since 1925, Hollywood has released more than two thousand films, many of them rerun frequently on television, portraying Indians as strange, perverted, ridiculous, and often dangerous things of the past. Moreover, we are habitually presented to mass audiences one-dimensionally, devoid of recognizable human motivations and emotions; Indians thus serve as props, little more. We have thus been thoroughly and systematically dehumanized."

---

many people, in such diverse contexts, that it has become part of our national folk language."

<⟨7⟩>   # Social Values: Religion, Family, Responsibility   487

Introduction
CURRENT CONTROVERSY
AND PUBLIC DISCOURSE

---◇---

The State of Public Discourse

We live in politically contentious times. Judging from the vast number of books and magazine articles devoted to current affairs published over the past few years, the 1990s may prove to be among the most intense political periods in American history. One of the many recent books is called, oddly enough, *Why Americans Hate Politics* (1991). A national best-seller, its popularity seems to refute its central premise; E. J. Dionne might just as well have entitled his provocative and insightful book *Why Americans Love Politics.*

A decade ago, no one would have predicted that a three-hour talk radio program devoted to aggressively conservative political commentary would be the most popular talk show on radio, yet the *Rush Limbaugh Show* has broken nearly all broadcasting records and become one of the most controversial political forums in the country. When Limbaugh's first book was released, it surprised both his publishers and America's booksellers by the lightening speed of its sales. The hardcover book remained on the *New York Times* best-seller list for over a year. Perhaps Americans hate politics yet love nothing better than political discussion.

Politics, of course, is a tricky term. If we restrict its meaning to governmental and electoral politics, it may be true that a sizable portion of Americans are fed up with politics. Only 39 percent of eligible voters participated in the 1992 presidential election — a figure that does not argue for robust political enthusiasm on the part of the average citizen. Indeed, public opinion specialists are confronted with what appears to be a paradox: because most Americans seem to have only the slightest information about current issues and events, how is it that they profess to hold so many opinions concerning them? As Shanto Iyengar succinctly concludes in *Is Anyone Responsible?* (1991), "Low levels of citizen awareness do not preclude political opinionation."

A large part of the reason for this conclusion is that the meaning of "politics" has been stretched over the past thirty years. The realm of the political now encompasses many matters formerly considered either cultural, social, or entirely private. In the 1950s, sexuality was hardly an explicit political issue; today sexual orientation (even the phrase is new) is one of the most intensely argued political topics. An individual may not know the name of a single cabinet official or Supreme Court justice but have decided opinions on abortion, gun control, prayer in school, free speech, and welfare. It is those opinions — not knowledge of governmental procedure or the economic system — that will shape his or her politics. Every day in the news Americans are confronted by issues that not so very long ago would have appeared strange and even incomprehensible: child abuse, antismoking regulations, sexual harassment and speech codes in schools and in the workplace, gay rights, animal rights, and family values, to name a few. Although we continue to debate such fundamental issues as racial justice, economic opportunity, the functions of government, foreign affairs, political appointments, and taxes, there can be no doubt that the scope of political discourse has expanded in recent years.

Why this expansion has occurred and how it affects all Americans is one of the dominant themes of this book. We can attribute the widening scope of political discourse to at least four major factors:

1. *The Civil Rights Act of 1964.* One of the most important legislative documents in American history, this act broadened public awareness of individual rights and quickly sensitized Americans to the political dimensions of "race, color, religion, sex, and national origin."

2. *The feminist movement.* This movement has influenced personal, sexual, and familial attitudes. Feminism's popular 1970s slogan "The personal is political" opened up new avenues of discussion and politicized many unspoken social and cultural assumptions.

3. *Identity politics.* Many Americans no longer feel close ties to traditional political parties and tend to identify themselves with group causes — feminist, African American, homosexual, state militias, the religious right, and so on. Group "identity" concerns such as Afrocentrism have led to unprecedented political struggles within the school curriculum, and those of gay rights activists have opened up suppressed areas of discussion within the U.S. military.

4. *The culture wars.* A good deal of today's political discussion centers on social, religious, and moral values rather than old-fashioned bread-and-butter issues. Debates about poverty and welfare, for example, are almost always conducted within the work-ethic framework;

debates about the AIDS virus frequently come down to "guilty" versus "innocent" victims.

The dramatic change in political discourse over the past three decades can be seen in the way Americans now label their own political identities. For nearly a hundred years, people saw themselves as either Republicans or Democrats. Though there are a number of notable exceptions (in 1912 the Socialist party managed to obtain a large percentage of the vote, and in 1992 Ross Perot, running as an Independent, received nearly twenty million votes), for the most part the two-party system has dominated American electoral politics since the 1850s. After the 1964 election, however, more and more people began describing themselves as liberals or conservatives, not Democrats or Republicans. Though these labels often conform to the platforms of the traditional parties, they sometimes importantly do not. A sizable number of working- and middle-class Democrats, for example, voted for Republican Ronald Reagan in 1984 largely because they endorsed his conservative approach to patriotism and traditional values.

The difference between these two sets of labels (Democrats/Republicans versus liberals/conservatives) is highly significant. The older terms represent distinct and intact political parties; the newer terms are more suggestive of global assumptions and moral dispositions. By characterizing themselves as liberal or conservative rather than Democrat or Republican, Americans showed a loosening attachment to the older electoral or party politics and a growing adherence to the newer forms of "values" politics. The older affiliations implied a world of practical politics, with its machinery and compromises; the newer identities are more suggestive of divergent worldviews and competing ideologies.

We have only to glance at direct-mail advertising to see how moral and cultural values currently shape electoral politics. One of the most influential American interest groups, the Christian Coalition, for example, mails out millions of "Congressional Scorecards" covering "issues that are of utmost importance to Christian and pro-family Americans." The "scorecard" lists the voting records of every House member and state senator on issues such as "whether they voted for or against using your tax money to pay for or promote abortion in America" or "whether they voted for or against using your tax money to promote homosexuality to school children or distribute condoms to minors without the consent of parents." The coalition's index lists a total score for each senator and representative; according to a recent index, Senator Bob Dole of Kansas supported the coalition's position on every vote and scored 100 percent, while Senator Daniel Patrick Moynihan of New York scored zero percent because he never once supported a Christian Coalition position.

Mailings like the above are routinely sent out by interest groups on both the Right and Left. A "strategy survey" sent out by the Democratic Congressional Campaign Committee supporting the reelection of

President Clinton refers to Newt Gingrich's "right-wing gang" and its "politics of cruelty." In the direct-mail wars, each side demonizes the other, and each side assumes a higher moral ground. Each side also maintains that it is functioning in a climate of extreme crisis and urgency. Each side also hopes for generous donations.

For anyone paying attention to the state of public discourse, direct-mail advertising and political commercials on radio and television clearly reveal the everyday language of American politics, with its widening ideological rifts and divisions. As many commentators have noted, ours is rapidly becoming a public discourse of polarized positions, popular slogans, and decontextualized "sound bites." Though in certain books and periodicals we find more sophisticated political expression, more nuanced positions, this everyday extremist discourse exerts a powerful and persistent influence on the American public and its elected officials. In the Winter 1995 *American Scholar,* the historians Oscar and Lilian Handlin noted the "petulance infusing public discourse in the 1990s."

The Collision of Opinions

Many people, it seems, prefer to hear what they already know; they would rather have their opinions confirmed than challenged. Anyone in the business of persuasion — from advertising copywriters to political campaign managers — is well aware of this fact. Activists, advocates, commentators, and political candidates often enjoy nothing more than "preaching to the converted." It's far less onerous to do and you get much louder applause. Nearly all the calls taken by Rush Limbaugh are from self-proclaimed "ditto-heads," flattering fans who like to begin their conversation by saying they agree with Limbaugh "one thousand percent." Rarely do talk radio hosts, whether Right or Left, entertain serious and well-reasoned dissenting arguments.

This may be healthy for ratings, but it is not healthy for democratic discussion and debate, which requires a broad tolerance of opposition. The eminent journalist Walter Lippmann, co-founder of one of America's most influential magazines, the *New Republic,* thought opposition should not merely be tolerated but that it was *indispensable* to a democracy: "A good statesman, like any other sensible human being, always learns more from his opponents than from his fervent supporters." Lippmann was popularizing John Stuart Mill's philosophical essay, "Of the Liberty of Thought and Discussion," in which Mill argues for the necessity of a "diversity of opinion." According to Mill, we need to be mentally open to opposing opinions not only because our cherished opinion may be wrong but because even if it is true, "conflict with the opposite error is essential to a clear apprehension and deep feeling of its truth." In short, our existing opinions need to be earnestly, vigorously, and continually challenged.

For Mill, there is yet another reason that we should not silence dissenting opinion: "Since the general or prevailing opinion on any subject is rarely or never the whole truth," he argues, "it is only by the collision of adverse opinions that the remainder of the truth has any chance of being supplied." Mill's point is especially applicable to most political and social issues, where there is widespread disagreement among parties and factions.

Left, Right, and Center was assembled in the spirit of Mill's "collision of adverse opinions" and Lippmann's "indispensable opposition." The book — as its title suggests — represents the widest range of contemporary social and political views that could conveniently be collected in a single volume. Though it would be impossible to represent every nuance of opinion on every significant issue, the book aims to introduce readers to some of the most influential thinkers interpreting American society today. Approximately half the writers are substantially at odds with one another, and even those in general political agreement often disagree over specific policies. The collection, however, is designed to do more than introduce readers to the spacious and clangorous arena of contemporary political thought. There is a larger agenda at work: making readers more sensitive and responsive to the state of public discourse.

The Art of Controversy

The writers and thinkers engaged in the formulation and analysis of today's political ideas and social policy come from many different fields and educational backgrounds: the social and physical sciences, economics, history, law, philosophy, literature, and the arts. This anthology represents the ideas of people from a wide spectrum of careers and disciplines. One of the most respected leftist critics of American society, Noam Chomsky, is a world-renowned linguist; a leading feminist critic of feminism, Christina Hoff Sommers, is a professor of philosophy; Katha Pollitt and June Jordan, two preeminent feminist thinkers, are also award-winning poets; Charles Krauthammer, the winner of a Pulitzer Prize for distinguished political commentary, holds degrees in political science, economics, and medicine and was at one point chief resident in psychiatry at Massachusetts General Hospital. Whatever their specializations, however, the contributors to this volume all need to rely on the same methods of explanation, persuasion, and argument as they variously attempt to affect the outcome of public discussion. And however impressive their credentials, if they want to win people over to their position, they still need to make a persuasive case. They are subjected to the same logical, evidentiary, and rhetorical criteria as anyone else who has a plan to propose, an issue to analyze, a case to make, or an argument to refute.

Most standard rhetorics and writing textbooks contain a great deal of information on the craft of exposition, persuasion, and argument. In fact, so little has changed over the years that Aristotle's *Rhetoric* and Cicero's *Of Oratory* are still useful guides to the elements of persuasion and the art of debate. As they explain their ideas and construct their cases, the thinkers and political figures included in this collection make ample use of time-honored persuasive and argumentative strategies. An exhaustive list of such methods is impossible here; what follows are some of the most important features of our current public discourse.

Words and Values

Perhaps the most pervasive method of persuasion is word choice. Everyone is aware that certain commonly used words can have positive or negative meanings, that some terms are almost always used in a pejorative sense, while others are intended to convey an affirmative point of view.

For example, the word *community* is today almost always used positively; it invariably means something good. In his invaluable *Keywords* (1976), the English critic Raymond Williams writes of this word: "*Community* can be the warmly persuasive word to describe an existing set of relationships, or the warmly persuasive word to describe an alternative set of relationships. What is most important, perhaps, is that unlike all other terms of social organization (*state, nation, society*, etc.) it seems never to be used unfavorably, and never to be given any positive opposing or distinguishing term." Obviously, a word with such positive value can be put to powerful persuasive use. Thus, the term *community* is easily stretched from any literal reference to a specific locality or neighborhood and made to refer to a far broader and more dubious set of relationships, such as the *business community*, the *scholarly community*, the Internet's *online community*, or even, as foreign-affairs journalists say, the *international community*, which one supposes is a closely knit community consisting of every nation on earth. How large can a community get? In a 1995 fundraising letter for the National Space Society, the organization's chairman, Hugh Downs, declares that the United States must "lead the global community into space." As the word-watching columnist William Safire suggests, the word allows us to project positively warm feelings on any impersonal or bureaucratic organization: the CIA has been called the "intelligence community."

As readers, it is useful to picture terms like *community* with little plus signs above them, as Peggy Rosenthal advises in her provocative study of everyday key words and phrases, *Words & Values* (1984). Hovering above other terms we can see little minus signs. As Rosenthal puts it, a word gets its values from our "attitude toward what it stands for." "Such value can be positive or negative," she writes, "and it can be so much a part of a word's meaning that whenever we use the word we practically see a plus or minus sign over it: the sign of our approval or longing or some other positive attitude, or else of some negative attitude like our disapproval or maybe our fear."

Some terms, however, are politically complicated and cannot be invariably labeled positive or negative. Take the term *assimilation,* for example; it carries a plus sign for those critical of today's ethnic separatism and a minus sign for those who support such movements. Because most writers do not explicitly define such terms, the reader must make an evaluation based on the overall content or the immediate context. When Arthur Schlesinger, Jr., writes that "the multiethnic dogma abandons historic purposes, replacing assimilation by fragmentation, integration by separatism" (see p. 7), it is clear that his use of *assimilation* is positive, as its syntactical opposite, *fragmentation,* is so clearly negative. In fact, the plus and minus terms of Schlesinger's sentence can be easily decoded:

$$- \qquad - \qquad - \qquad + \qquad +$$

The multiethnic dogma abandons historic purposes, replacing

$$+ \qquad - \qquad + \qquad -$$

assimilation by fragmentation, integration by separatism.

This collection contains numerous terms with even more complicated connotations. A good example is *underclass.* In attempting to explain why conservatives now dominate the debate on urban poverty, the distinguished sociologist William Julius Wilson places part of the blame on liberal thinkers who studiously avoid the word *underclass* because it is "a destructive and misleading label" that stigmatizes depressed urban neighborhoods (see p. 165). For certain liberal commentators, then, *underclass* always has a negative meaning and has in some circles even become a taboo term. Wilson, on the other hand, believes that the term is valid and that it "aids in the description of ghetto social transformations." Wilson is not afraid to use other terms — *ghetto* and *inner-city,* for instance — also often eschewed by contemporary liberal policymakers. Though Wilson is not placing invisible plus signs over these terms, he is making a deliberate effort to use them with a certain degree of sociological neutrality, as accurately descriptive words that do not obscure unpleasant conditions. Wilson's entire discussion of the term *underclass* (see paragraphs 11–16) provides an excellent insight into the complexities of political language.

Wilson's deliberate use of *ghetto* and *inner-city* illustrates further semantic intricacies. Originally, the term *ghetto* referred to the Jewish district of a town; it was later extended to apply to black neighborhoods. As the word grew increasingly pejorative, the term *inner-city* was coined as a more neutral expression. Both of these terms were considered more flattering than *slum,* though all three terms essentially refer to similar urban conditions. According to what might be called "The Law of Expanding Euphemism," every new term developed to replace a stigmatizing term will itself become a stigmatizing term requiring replacement (e.g., it wasn't so long ago that *handicapped* replaced *crippled*). Thus *inner-city,* as Wilson suggests, may no longer be the euphemism of choice among liberal commentators, some of whom now prefer *central-city*. Of course, adding *community* to either of these terms cushions the negativity. When relying on euphemisms it is important to know whether they are currently fashionable or unfashionable. In 1961 the *New York Times* complained about the new sociological euphemisms in an editorial called "A Slum Is a Slum." But the euphemisms won; the *Times* will almost always avoid the word *slum* today (though the paper might not avoid calling someone a *slumlord*).

Many common terms are neutral and do not carry with them an implicit attitude. Yet given a particular usage or context, neutral terms can take an affirmative or a pejorative spin. For example, we might consider Schlesinger's use of *multiethnic* neutral, though in this context its close connection with dogma (*dogmatic* today always means something bad) tends to cast a negative shadow over the entire phrase. Or consider another neutral term. The noun *crowd*, for example, seems relatively value-free. To say that there was "a big crowd at the restaurant" could be simply descriptive; or, depending on context or inflection, it could suggest a positive ("exciting") or negative ("uncomfortable") meaning. But when Katha Pollitt refers to the "family values crowd" (see p. 243) she is not expressing a neutrality; instead, the word reveals her negative attitude toward "family values" as a conservative political position. In this case, *crowd* has the contemptuous connotation of a restless and noisy swarm (not unlike Newt Gingrich's "right-wing gang" mentioned earlier), and the phrase "family values crowd" should be seen with a minus sign above it. Consider the difference if she had said the "family-values *community*." Similarly, consider the word *industry*. It is neutral if we say the *steel industry* or the *aerospace industry* and positive if we praise someone's dedication and *industry*. But when Wendy Kaminer writes of "the memory-retrieval industry" (see p. 319), the word takes on a decidedly negative edge, suggesting the opportunistic business aspects of the current recovery movement.

Political discourse is glutted with what rhetoricians call "slanted" and "loaded" terms — words that prejudge the situation and logically beg the question. They are terms that disclose the writer's or speaker's conclusions. As the philosopher Arthur Schopenhauer wrote, "A speaker often betrays his purpose beforehand by the names which he gives to things." What someone calls "placing in safe custody," says Schopenhauer, another calls "throwing into prison." Cautious readers need to be on the alert for invidious terms intended to persuade us without facts, reasons, or evidence. Synonyms very often have shadings that range from positive to neutral to negative; think of the differences in referring to someone as an environmental activist as opposed to an environmental fanatic.

There is hardly a paragraph in this book that does not illustrate the persuasive use of plus and minus terminology.

The Rhetoric of Polarization

American public discourse, as many cultural critics have observed, favors the adoption of extreme statements and positions. This has long been the case ("Give me liberty, or give me death"), and the phenomenon has been astutely analyzed by James Davison Hunter in his overview of recent American social conflict, *Culture Wars* (1991). Closely examining our contemporary political dialogue, Hunter notes that the terms of debate have been aggressively monopolized by two sides, which he prefers to call the orthodox and the progressive. Each side is confident that it is operating with the truest definition of American values, and each side does its best to dehumanize the opposing position. We are left with a vicious, hostile, divisive, and extremist rhetoric, according to Hunter, who claims that the "impulse toward polarization in contemporary public discourse is undeniable."

The polarization is further abetted by the news media, with their penchant for sound bites and sensationalism. Moderate or restrained statements do not make headlines, and subtlety and nuance cannot be fitted into ten-second slots. Hunter notes that "the complexity of personal conviction and the subtlety of personal opinion are rarely reflected at the level of public discourse." A serious political side effect of our media coverage is that it essentially *silences* reflective, ambivalent, or conciliatory views. Television panel discussions and talk shows actively encourage aggressive, polarized opinions. Hunter believes that our "public discourse is more polarized than the American public itself." His opinion is shared by such national figures as Colin Powell, who in *An American Journey* (1995) finds that "civility is being driven from our political discourse." Attack ads and negative campaigns produce destructive, not constructive, debate. "Democracy," says Powell, "has always been noisy, but now, on television and radio talk shows, demagoguery and character dismemberment displace reasoned dialogue."

In a very real sense, the media are in the business of provocation and polarization. Newscasters make every attempt to turn public issues into a two-sided shouting match. They usually avoid interviewing individuals whose political views are nuanced or complex. As Susan Estrich writes (*USA Today*, October 19, 1995): the mass media turn "every issue into a yes–no proposition, as articulated by two people representing the furthest extremes and pushing the most emotional buttons." Screaming gets better ratings than moderation, suggests Estrich, who argues that the media perform this way not because of any "ideological bias," but "because it's the easiest way to produce hot television, hot radio, hot talk." Estrich's comments might make us wonder if in their quest for ratings, news and talk shows deliberately cultivate a divisive and angry mood in America. Would we all get along better — men and women, blacks and whites, gays and straights — *without* the daily agitation of Dan Rather and Tom Brokaw, Rush Limbaugh and Howard Stern, Oprah Winfrey and Geraldo Rivera?

The "impulse to polarization" comes from many sources. Some political figures and activists learn that provocation and extreme expressions are far more likely to reach the public forum than discretion and deliberation. There is also a tendency for legislation originally meant to institute sensible reform to be pushed in the courts to extreme interpretations and applications — a process that can cause a backlash of opinion from supporters who were originally willing to back a moderate, but not a radical, change of policy. Some defenders of affirmative action programs, for example, have recently argued that though the programs were solid and widely supported, they were sometimes legally taken too far and that these highly publicized, extreme cases helped instigate the current backlash against the programs in general.

Behind many extremist positions are what lawyers call "slippery-slope" arguments. Consider pornography. Antipornography advocates, a mixed group that embraces both radical feminists and conservative Christian fundamentalists, would like to see tough legislation against sexually explicit material, but they continually run up against free-speech advocates who generally see any prohibition of such material not only a violation of the First Amendment but also the first step down the slope that inevitably leads to total censorship. The debate takes many predictable positions: the antipornography groups point to the most extreme and violent depictions of sex and ask if society should condone such demeaning images, while the free-speech advocates argue that once we prohibit such images the next step is the censorship of much classic art and literature. In other words, if you prohibit *Deep Throat,* Ovid's *Metamorphoses* is next. Thus the debate gets framed as though no middle ground or alternative views are possible.

The polarized framing of positions is so common to political discourse that it usually passes unnoticed. Let's return to Arthur Schlesinger's multiethnic comment. Besides showing a clear use of favorable and unfavorable terms, Schlesinger's remark is also constructed in an antithetical pattern: *assimilation* is directly opposed to *fragmentation, integration* to *separatism.* By gramatically presenting only these "either-or" options and implying that they are indeed direct opposites, Schlesinger apparently leaves no room for other alternatives. That these may not be the only political possibilities, however, is the point of the Afrocentrist scholar, Molefi Kete Asante, who maintains ethnocentricity is not anti-American and is "neither a destructive nor a disuniting behavior" (see p. 9). Asante, in other words, rejects the way Schlesinger has framed the debate.

Closely related to slippery-slope arguments are what might be called "Give an inch and they'll take a mile" arguments. In a recent film, a slumlord yells at his son (a building superintendent) for installing lights in the hallway of their run-down tenement: Now that the tenants have lights, what next? Soon they'll expect air-conditioning, color televisions, the works. The argument is essentially one of extending a proposition to an extreme position: you do nothing or else you do everything. It leaves no room for middle positions. A young fan calls the Rush Limbaugh show to say that although he basically shares Limbaugh's economic opinions, his McDonald's job doesn't help him make ends meet and he supports an increase in minimum wage. Would you be happy with seven dollars an hour? Limbaugh proposes. Sure, the kid happily responds. Well, then what about ten dollars an hour? What about fifteen dollars an hour? What about fifty dollars an hour? Limbaugh asks, his voice rising with each increment. His strategy was intended to silence the opposition. And it worked.

Another significant source of polarization is a result of what some scholars believe is a disproportionate emphasis on individual rights, a post–World War II political trend that has eroded personal responsibility and civic obligations. In *Rights Talk* (1991) the legal scholar Mary Ann Glendon examines the way our "strident language of rights" has resulted in "the impoverishment of political discourse." According to Glendon, "Discourse about rights has become the principal language that we use in public settings to discuss weighty questions of right and wrong, but time and again it proves inadequate, or leads to a standoff of one right against another." The language is often legalistic, individualistic, and absolute. Rights talk, Glendon claims,

> fits perfectly within the ten-second formats currently preferred by the news media, but severely constricts opportunities for the sort of ongoing dialogue upon which a regime of ordered liberty ultimately depends. A rapidly expanding catalog of rights — extending to trees, animals, smokers, nonsmokers, consumers, and so on — not only multiplies the occasion for collisions, but it risks trivializing core democratic values.

She goes on to show that a "tendency to frame nearly every social controversy in terms of a clash of rights (a woman's right to her own body vs. a fetus's right to life) impedes compromise, mutual understanding, and the discovery of common ground." Reasonable public discussion is thwarted by a "penchant for absolute formulations," as competing individuals or groups try to trump each other's inalienable rights. Thus, which right holds the aces: the right not to be subjected by police to a weapons search or the right to safe and secure streets?

Rights talk frequently ushers us down the familiar slippery slope. If someone (a communitarian, say) decides that public safety serves a higher purpose than an individual's right to privacy and opts for greater police surveillance, someone else (a civil libertarian, say) will no doubt respond with the imminent specter of a police state, and within a fraction of a second the argument will move from questions of reasonable search and seizure to storm troopers breaking down doors and arresting law-abiding citizens. "Let me remind you," the conservative Barry Goldwater once said, "that extremism in the defense of liberty is no vice" and that "moderation in the pursuit of justice is no virtue." Adapting Goldwater's terms to political discourse, perhaps we should call extremism in defense of our opinions a rhetorical vice and moderation in pursuit of a more civil society a rhetorical virtue.

Some? Most? All?   Never? Sometimes? Always?

To write of politics, culture, and society is to speak in generalizations. An unavoidable feature of public discourse, generalizations are hastily used and easily abused: they can be enlightening, and they can be fallacious. An attractive generalization can be powerfully persuasive, and readers should be especially suspicious of its appeal. Generalizations are also key elements in the rhetoric of polarization. No current issue, for example, illustrates the way generalizations can be used to establish extreme positions better than the gender debate (see Chapter 4), with its polarizing tendency to view men and women as wholly distinct creatures. As a best-selling book claims, men are from one planet and women from another.

Generalizations take many different forms. Logicians sometimes speak of *uniform generalizations* — statements that include *all* members of a class — and *statistical generalizations* — statements that include *most* or *some* members of a class. Disputes over such generalizations are a common feature of political discourse. Consider again the book title *Why Americans Hate Politics.* Is the author suggesting that *all* Americans hate politics? That would be unlikely, given the very large number of people who, like the author himself, are obsessed by political issues. The title, then, is probably not intended as a uniform generalization; if so, the author would certainly be hard-pressed to prove his case. But what are we to make of the title as a statistical generalization: does he mean that *most* Americans hate politics? That seems more likely, but would most mean 95 percent? 75 percent? 51 percent? Or is it possible that the title means not quite most but merely "a lot" of Americans hate politics, perhaps up to 40 percent?

The book's title was, of course, chosen for emphasis. (Imagine how the reading public would respond to a book more accurately called *Why a Lot of Americans Hate Politics.* Or, as "hate" suggests a disproportionately *extreme* reaction, imagine how they might respond to the title *Why a Lot of Americans Are Uninterested in Politics.*) Though this may sound like quibbling, the point is crucial to understanding public discourse. In this case, the author was not trying to be misleading but was relying on the rhetorical emphasis resulting from the ambiguity inherent in generalizations that are not made explicit. Because book titles, like newspaper headlines, follow their own rhetorical conventions, we expect that they will employ language designed to grab our attention. We can readily agree that by

"Americans" the author does not mean *all*, but the precise proportion or even the "ballpark figure" is what is really at issue. A critic unconvinced by the author's generalization might reasonably conclude that the main idea of the book is exaggerated.

One difficulty with generalizations, therefore, is that we cannot always be certain whether someone intends a general statement to be uniform or statistical or whether someone is using a generalization literally or for rhetorical emphasis. When Thomas Jefferson wrote "all men are created equal," he made his generalization explicit. George Orwell did the same in *Animal Farm* (1946), though with a parodic twist: One of the Farm's commandments reads, "All animals are equal but some animals are more equal than others." But not all generalizations are so explicit; many of those we encounter in the discussion of current affairs are unclear or ambiguous. If someone claims that "Poverty causes crime," we need to establish the limits of the generalization. Do *all* poor people then commit crimes? If not, then to what extent is poverty responsible? Does poverty cause *all* crime? If so, then why are some high-profile multimillionaire Wall Street traders in jail? Or why would an affluent teenager shoplift?

As the above example indicates, a generalization can be an oversimplification of a complex social and political issue. There is even another common type of generalization at work in our example — a causal one. Crimes can undoubtedly be traced to many different kinds of causes — psychopathology, greed, imitative behavior, adventure, religious or political belief, and so on. Why there is a fixation on finding a single or root cause for complex phenomena and social behavior is in itself interesting to speculate about. Nevertheless, reducing problems and events to a single cause can easily lead to distorted and unpersuasive explanations. Usually causal generalizations such as "Poverty causes crime" are accompanied — as are many political slogans — by invisible qualifiers. Unless the speaker truly means to claim that poverty is always the sole cause of every crime, the sentence is actually saying that "Poverty (sometimes) causes (some) crime." The dispute, then, will not be about absolutes and root causes but about less sensational matters of frequency, degree, and extent.

Enter statistics. In the social, political, and legal sciences — as much of this collection demonstrates — writers and researchers devote a great deal of time and energy to gathering statistical data to support or discredit such propositions as "Poverty causes crime." Such "hard" data can keep formulations of political or social policy from being a simple matter of impression or mere opinion. Few candidates support legislation without glancing at public opinion polls. In many policy decisions, statistical data provide the only evidence to support a claim or proposal.

Yet statistical data alone cannot guarantee that accurate opinions will be formed. As Mark Twain reputedly claimed, there are three kinds of lies — "lies, damned lies, and statistics." The same numerical data can be interpreted in different ways for different purposes. In a discussion of homelessness, for instance, a writer argued that homeless people should not be stereotyped as mentally ill, because statistics showed that *only* one-third of the homeless nationally were found to be mentally disabled. Yet another writer argued that with *as much as* 33 percent of the homeless mentally disabled, the condition was quite serious. Thus, the one-third figure was viewed as high by one social commentator and low by another. Reviewing the same data, one person might conclude that "Poverty causes crime," while another might conceivably argue the opposite. As John Lewis, a Democratic congressman from Georgia, maintained in a recent speech, "It is not only poverty that has caused crime. In a very real sense it is crime that has caused poverty, and is the most powerful cause of poverty today" (cited in the *Atlantic Monthly,* July 1995).

The validity and reliability of statistical data depend on a great many factors, and even a sketchy coverage is impossible here. Suffice it to say that in political and social commentary one should look at statistical evidence with a questioning attitude: Where did the figures come from? Whose political purpose do they serve? Was the sample representative? Is the interpretation they supposedly support valid? Though statistics can be a good antidote to forming hasty generalizations, they can occasionally invite such generalizations. In Christina Hoff Sommers's "Noble Lies" (see Chapter 5), readers will find a highly controversial saga of statistics and their political application.

Another common type of generalization that routinely appears in public discourse is analogy: because two things are similar in certain respects, we expect them to be similar in other ways. The greater the number of points of resemblance, the richer the analogy. Like other forms of generalization, analogical reasoning can be a powerful tool, or it can be an unsound and misleading — though nevertheless persuasive — rhetorical device. Some political analogies have struck a national chord: referring to the Kennedy White House as Camelot lent an aura of glamour and idealism to a brief administration. Dwight D. Eisenhower's "domino effect" aptly characterized America's foreign policy in Southeast Asia — if one nation falls to communism, the next will topple, then the next, and so on.

The so-called domino theory reveals, too, how analogies can lead to slippery-slope extremes. For example, one of the more popular political analogies of our time is also one of the most extravagant — the Nazi analogy. If someone advocates greater discipline in our high schools, the individual is suddenly equivalent to Adolf Hitler. If the government seems to be paying insufficient attention to victims of a medical problem, the Unites States is responsible for a Holocaust. If a person enjoys being part of a state militia, he is unquestionably a Nazi; if a woman insists on equal rights, she is surely, in Rush Limbaugh's nomenclature, a "femi-

Nazi." If someone advocates more sensitivity in classroom discussion, the "gestapo" are pounding at the door. Nazi and Holocaust analogies have become so much a part of public discourse and are brought to bear on so many matters that the horrible magnitude of the Third Reich is essentially trivialized.

Within the span of a few weeks in the spring of 1995, for example, the *New York Times* reported several Nazi analogies. A Representative from Alabama claimed that there was "a similarity" between Newt Gingrich and Hitler. Hitler, he said, "started out getting rid of the poor and those he said were a drag on society, and Newt is starting out the same way." A few days earlier, the *Times* also reported that the National Rifle Association "in a recent fund-raising letter called the agents who enforce Federal gun laws jack-booted Government thugs who wear nazi bucket helmets and black storm trooper uniforms to attack law-abiding citizens." And several days earlier the paper profiled a New York Representative who "repeatedly likens what he calls the current apathy to the attitude in Nazi Germany that led to the Holocaust." The *New York Times* columnist A. M. Rosenthal likened the participants in the October 1995 Million Man March on Washington to Nazi rallyists and claimed that the objectives of the march were reminiscent of "Hitler's message." Nazi analogies are hardly rare; they can be easily collected at any time from any newspaper in any part of the country.

One of the most controversial instances of the Nazi analogy emerged during the murder trial of football star O. J. Simpson. In his closing argument, Simpson's attorney, Johnnie Cochran, compared Mark Fuhrman, the Los Angeles detective whose testimony was impugned by racism, to Adolf Hitler. Cochran's remark set off a firestorm of disapproval. Two people who vehemently disapproved of the comparison were Robert Shapiro, himself a member of Simpson's defense team, and Abraham H. Foxman, the national director of the Anti-Defamation League, who said the analogy "was outrageous and an insult to the millions of innocent victims of Nazism" and that it "trivializes this profound historical tragedy" (*Time Magazine,* October 9, 1995).

Nazi imagery has grown so prevalent in American politics that *The New York Times* (which itself has printed many instances of it) ran a small feature (October 23, 1995) listing some of the more extreme examples. According to the *Times*: "With increasing frequency, candidates from both political parties around the country have used comparisons to Nazis, Nazi behavior and the Holocaust to call attention to some perceived political act of horror." The paper quotes Kathleen Hall Jamieson, dean of the Annenberg School of Communication at the University of Pennsylvania, who claims that Nazi themes "have become an element of the normalization of hyperbole" and demonstrate the current "erosion of civil discourse."

What's wrong with the Nazi analogy is not merely that it is rhetorically extreme, but that it is usually logically faulty. The analogy is often based simply on one extreme point of comparison ("x is like Hitler"), but if the analogy is being urged as an argument, its effectiveness demands that it be based on more than a single similarity. For example, in a Virginia county Sheriff's election, one of the candidates ran a commercial picturing his opponent — who allegedly prevented press coverage of a private fundraiser — as Adolf Hitler; the reason: "Hitler had many facets; controlling the media was one of them." Without further parallels ("x is like Hitler because of a, b, c, and d" — and among these might be racial superiority, genocide, military aggression, and a few of the other items on the agenda of the Third Reich); such comparisons are only ludicrous assertions. In "Crimes against Humanity" (see p. 425), the American Indian activist Ward Churchill introduces the Nazi analogy to explain the power of hateful symbols. Whether one finally considers Churchill's analogy valid, the point is that he proceeds fully aware of the analogical pitfalls involved and sets out his comparisons with evidence and caution. He makes an argument, not an assertion.

The three broad areas of public discourse examined here — slanted and loaded terms, polarized rhetoric, and dubious generalizations — are by no means an exhaustive treatment of this topic. They do, however, represent some of the major features of our polemical landscape. If most Americans really do hate politics, perhaps what needs to be reformed is not our democratic system of government but our habitual modes of discourse. In the selections that follow, readers will encounter many of today's outstanding writers, thinkers, and political personalities. This collection invites readers to participate in our major current controversies, as contentious as they sometimes are, with the expectation that the more conscious people become of political language and the strategies of public discourse, the more resistant they will be to the oversimplifications of slogans, stereotypes, and sound bites. To elevate the level of public discourse is to raise the level of our collective political consciousness. This is not only a rhetorical or linguistic issue. As Justice Louis D. Brandeis put it, "Public discussion is a political duty."

Robert Atwan

1

The Multicultural Challenge
ETHNICITY · DIVERSITY · DISUNITY

WHAT DOES IT MEAN TO BE an American? That question has been debated since the founding of the United States, but perhaps never so passionately as today. As waves of immigration introduce different ethnic groups into our society, and as each ethnic group demands recognition and respect, America appears to be losing its cohesiveness and splintering into an unstable nation of separate and competing groups. In one of the most devastating critiques of the multicultural agenda, "The Disuniting of America," the prominent historian Arthur M. Schlesinger, Jr. laments the "fragmentation, resegregation, and tribalization of American life." But Schlesinger seriously misrepresents multiculturalism, argues the African American scholar Molefi Kete Asante, whose essay "What Is Afrocentrism?" attempts to explain why people seem so threatened by "a simple rational position."

Yet not all people proud of their ethnic identities support multicultural ideals, as Linda Chavez reveals in "Demystifying Multiculturalism." A member of Ronald Reagan's administration and a 1986 candidate for the U.S. Senate, Chavez, a Spanish American, sees multiculturalism as elitist propaganda with little connection to the practical ways most Americans think and feel.

If Michael Walzer is right, however, disunity and divisiveness may be exaggerated by both sides. America's problem, as he sees it in "Multiculturalism and Individualism," has to do not with our "decentering" pluralistic principles but with our collective inability to bring those principles into accord with an equally decentering philosophy of individualism.

1

The multicultural debate has been most intense on the American college campus, where its agenda has been firmly aligned with various affirmative action programs. In "Illiberal Education," Dinesh D'Souza, one of the most outspoken conservative critics of such programs, examines how our universities, under the banner of diversity, are setting the national stage for large-scale bigotry, intolerance, and suppression.

One difficulty with multiculturalism, argues the philosopher Cornel West, is that its proponents tend to simplify history and "refuse to recognize the thoroughly hybrid culture of almost every culture we have ever discovered." According to West, to "talk about hybrid culture means you give up all quest for pure traditions and pristine heritages."

Few African American thinkers could be farther apart politically than the Democratic Socialist Cornel West and the free-market conservative Thomas Sowell. In the chapter's final selection, Sowell, like West, examines diversity from a global perspective. Their occasional agreements will help us appreciate the nuance and complexity of this often polarizing issue.

ARTHUR M. SCHLESINGER, JR.

The Disuniting of America

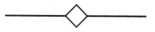

The population of the United States grows more and more ethnically diverse each year. In response to this increasing ethnic diversity, many scholars and educators have rejected the traditional model of a "melting-pot culture" that stressed the value of assimilation. In its place they have proposed a new model, one that they believe preserves and honors the unique cultural values that every ethnic group possesses. The new model's emphasis on ethnic awareness has brought us greater racial sensitivity and the belated recognition of major contributions to American life by minorities.

Despite the new model's successes, however, liberal historian Arthur M. Schlesinger, Jr. sees within it some potentially dangerous and divisive tendencies. According to Schlesinger, the multicultural curriculum being taught in schools can result only in "the fragmentation, resegregation, and tribalization of American life." He sets forth this view most compellingly in the following selection, the foreword to his 1991 study on the effect of multiculturalism on American education, *The Disuniting of America*. The author of fourteen books, Schlesinger has twice received the Pulitzer Prize for his historical studies of American culture. In addition to teaching history at Harvard University and at the Graduate Center of the City University of New York, he served as a special advisor to President Kennedy from 1961 to 1963.

SELECTED PUBLICATIONS: *The Age of Jackson* (1945); *The Politics of Freedom* (1950); *The Politics of Hope* (1963); *A Thousand Days: John F. Kennedy in the White House* (1965); *The Imperial Presidency* (1973); *The Cycles of American History* (1986); *The Disuniting of America* (1991); *Running for President: The Candidates and Their Images* (1994).

The fading away of the cold war has brought an era of ideological conflict to an end. But it has not, as forecast, brought an end to history.[1] One set of hatreds gives way to the next. Lifting the lid of ideological repression in eastern Europe releases ethnic antagonisms deeply rooted in experience and in memory. The disappearance of ideological competition in the third world removes superpower restraints on national and tribal confrontations. As the era of ideological conflict subsides, humanity

[1] Schlesinger alludes to Francis Fukuyama's influential 1989 article "The End of History?" which claims that the end of the cold war would mean the death of traditional ideological conflicts.

enters — or, more precisely, re-enters — a possibly more dangerous era of ethnic and racial animosity.

The hostility of one tribe for another is among the most instinctive human reactions. Yet, the history of our planet has been in great part the history of the mixing of peoples. Mass migrations have produced mass antagonisms from the beginning of time. Today, as the twentieth century draws to an end, a number of factors — not just the evaporation of the cold war but, more profoundly, the development of swifter modes of communication and transport, the acceleration of population growth, the breakdown of traditional social structures, the flight from tyranny and from want, the dream of a better life somewhere else — converge to drive people as never before across national frontiers and thereby to make the mixing of peoples a major problem for the century that lies darkly ahead.

What happens when people of different ethnic origins, speaking different languages and professing different religions, settle in the same geographical locality and live under the same political sovereignty? Unless a common purpose binds them together, tribal hostilities will drive them apart. Ethnic and racial conflict, it seems evident, will now replace the conflict of ideologies as the explosive issue of our times.

On every side today ethnicity is the cause of the breaking of nations. The Soviet Union, Yugoslavia, India, South Africa are all in crisis.[2] Ethnic tensions disturb and divide Sri Lanka, Burma, Ethiopia, Indonesia, Iraq, Lebanon, Israel, Cyprus, Somalia, Nigeria, Liberia, Angola, Sudan, Zaire, Guyana, Trinidad — you name it. Even nations as stable and civilized as Britain and France, Belgium and Spain and Czechoslovakia, face growing ethnic and racial troubles. "The virus of tribalism," says the *Economist*, " . . . risks becoming the AIDS of international politics — lying dormant for years, then flaring up to destroy countries."

Take the case of our neighbor to the north. Canada has long been considered the most sensible and placid of nations. "Rich, peaceful and, by the standards of almost anywhere else, enviably successful," the *Economist* observes: yet today "on the brink of bust-up." Michael Ignatieff (the English-resident son of a Russian-born Canadian diplomat and thus an example of the modern mixing of peoples) writes of Canada, "Here we have one of the five richest nations on earth, a country so uniquely blessed with space and opportunity that the world's poor are beating at the door to get in, and it is tearing itself apart. . . . If one of the top five developed nations on earth can't make a federal, multi-ethnic state work, who else can?"

The answer to that increasingly vital question has been, at least until recently, the United States.

Now how have Americans succeeded in pulling off this almost unprecedented trick? Other countries break up because they fail to give ethnically diverse peoples compelling reasons to see themselves as part of

---

[2] At the time of writing, the Soviet Union and Yugoslavia were in the process of breaking up into independent republics along mainly ethnic lines. South Africa was moving, often violently, toward the full inclusion of black South Africans in the nation's political process.

the same nation. The United States has worked, thus far, because it has offered such reasons. What is it then that, in the absence of a common ethnic origin, has held Americans together over two turbulent centuries? For America was a multiethnic country from the start. Hector St. John de Crèvecoeur emigrated from France to the American colonies in 1759, married an American woman, settled on a farm in Orange County, New York, and published his *Letters from an American Farmer* during the American Revolution. This eighteenth-century French American marveled at the astonishing diversity of the other settlers — "a mixture of English, Scotch, Irish, French, Dutch, Germans, and Swedes," a "strange mixture of blood" that you could find in no other country.

He recalled one family whose grandfather was English, whose wife was Dutch, whose son married a Frenchwoman, and whose present four sons had married women of different nationalities. "From this promiscuous breed," he wrote, "that race now called Americans have arisen." (The word *race* as used in the eighteenth and nineteenth centuries meant what we mean by nationality today; thus people spoke of "the English race," "the German race," and so on.) What, Crèvecoeur mused, were the characteristics of this suddenly emergent American race? *Letters from an American Farmer* propounded a famous question: "What then is the American, this new man?" (Twentieth-century readers must overlook eighteenth-century male obliviousness to the existence of women.)

Crèvecoeur gave his own question its classic answer: *"He is an American, who leaving behind him all his ancient prejudices and manners, receives new ones from the new mode of life he has embraced, the new government he obeys, and the new rank he holds. The American is a new man, who acts upon new principles. . . . Here individuals of all nations are melted into a new race of men."*

E pluribus unum. The United States had a brilliant solution for the inherent fragility of a multiethnic society: the creation of a brand-new national identity, carried forward by individuals who, in forsaking old loyalties and joining to make new lives, melted away ethnic differences. Those intrepid Europeans who had torn up their roots to brave the wild Atlantic *wanted* to forget a horrid past and to embrace a hopeful future. They *expected* to become Americans. Their goals were escape, deliverance, assimilation. They saw America as a transforming nation, banishing dismal memories and developing a unique national character based on common political ideals and shared experiences. The point of America was not to preserve old cultures, but to forge a new *American* culture.

One reason why Canada, despite all its advantages, is so vulnerable to schism is that, as Canadians freely admit, their country lacks such a unique national identity. Attracted variously to Britain, France, and the United States, inclined for generous reasons to a policy of official multiculturalism, Canadians have never developed a strong sense of what it is to be a Canadian. As Sir John Macdonald, their first prime minister, put it, Canada has "too much geography and too little history."

The United States has had plenty of history. From the Revolution on, Americans have had a powerful national creed. The vigorous sense of national identity accounts for our relative success in converting Crèvecoeur's "promiscuous breed" into one people and thereby making a multiethnic society work.

This is not to say that the United States has ever fulfilled Crèvecoeur's ideal. New waves of immigration brought in people who fitted awkwardly into a society that was inescapably English in language, ideals, and institutions. For a long time the Anglo-Americans dominated American culture and politics. The pot did not melt everybody, not even all the white immigrants.

As for the nonwhite peoples — those long in America whom the European newcomers overran and massacred, or those others hauled in against their will from Africa and Asia — deeply bred racism put them all, red Americans, black Americans, yellow Americans, brown Americans, well outside the pale. The curse of racism was the great failure of the American experiment, the glaring contradiction of American ideals and the still crippling disease of American life.

Yet even nonwhite Americans, miserably treated as they were, con-   15
tributed to the formation of the national identity. They became members, if third-class members, of American society and helped give the common culture new form and flavor. The infusion of non-Anglo stocks and the experience of the New World steadily reconfigured the British legacy and made the United States, as we all know, a very different country today from Britain.

The vision of America as melted into one people prevailed through most of the two centuries of the history of the United States. But the twentieth century has brought forth a new and opposing vision. One world war destroyed the old order of things and launched Woodrow Wilson's doctrine of the self-determination of peoples. Twenty years after, a second world war dissolved the western colonial empires and intensified ethnic and racial militancy around the planet. In the United States itself, new laws eased entry for immigrants from South America, Asia, and Africa and altered the composition of the American people.

In a nation marked by an even stranger mixture of blood than Crèvecoeur had known, his celebrated question is asked once more, with a new passion — and a new answer. Today many Americans disavow the historic goal of "a new race of man." The escape from origins yields to the search for roots. The "ancient prejudices and manners" disowned by Crèvecoeur have made a surprising comeback. A cult of ethnicity has arisen both among non-Anglo whites and among nonwhite minorities to denounce the idea of a melting pot, to challenge the concept of "one people," and to protect, promote, and perpetuate separate ethnic and racial communities.

The eruption of ethnicity had many good consequences. The American culture began at last to give shamefully overdue recognition to the achievements of minorities subordinated and spurned during the high noon of Anglo dominance. American education began at last to acknowledge the existence and significance of the great swirling world beyond Europe. All this was to the good. Of course history should be taught from a variety of perspectives. Let our children try to imagine the arrival of Columbus from the viewpoint of those who met him as well as from those who sent him. Living on a shrinking planet, aspiring to global leadership, Americans must learn much more about other races, other cultures, other continents. As they do, they acquire a more complex and invigorating sense of the world — and of themselves.

But, pressed too far, the cult of ethnicity has had bad consequences too. The new ethnic gospel rejects the unifying vision of individuals from all nations melted into a new race. Its underlying philosophy is that America is not a nation of individuals at all but a nation of groups, that ethnicity is the defining experience for most Americans, that ethnic ties are permanent and indelible, and that division into ethnic communities establishes the basic structure of American society and the basic meaning of American history.

Implicit in this philosophy is the classification of all Americans according to ethnic and racial criteria. But while the ethnic interpretation of American history, like the economic interpretation, is valid and illuminating up to a point, it is fatally misleading and wrong when presented as the whole picture. The ethnic interpretation, moreover, reverses the historic theory of America as one people — the theory that has thus far managed to keep American society whole.

Instead of a transformative nation with an identity all its own, America in this new light is seen as preservative of diverse alien identities. Instead of a nation composed of individuals making their own unhampered choices, America increasingly sees itself as composed of groups more or less ineradicable in their ethnic character. The multiethnic dogma abandons historic purposes, replacing assimilation by fragmentation, integration by separatism. It belittles *unum* and glorifies *pluribus.*

The historic idea of a unifying American identity is now in peril in many arenas — in our politics, our voluntary organizations, our churches, our language. And in no arena is the rejection of an overriding national identity more crucial than in our system of education.

The schools and colleges of the republic train the citizens of the future. Our public schools in particular have been the great instrument of assimilation and the great means of forming an American identity. What students are taught in schools affects the way they will thereafter see and treat other Americans, the way they will thereafter conceive the purposes of the republic. The debate about the curriculum is a debate about what it means to be an American.

The militants of ethnicity now contend that a main objective of public education should be the protection, strengthening, celebration, and perpetuation of ethnic origins and identities. Separatism, however, nourishes prejudices, magnifies differences, and stirs antagonisms. The consequent increase in ethnic and racial conflict lies behind the hullabaloo over "multiculturalism" and "political correctness," over the iniquities of the "Eurocentric" curriculum, and over the notion that history and literature should be taught not as intellectual disciplines but as therapies whose function is to raise minority self-esteem.

Watching ethnic conflict tear one nation after another apart, one cannot look with complacency at proposals to divide the United States into distinct and immutable ethnic and racial communities, each taught to cherish its own apartness from the rest. One wonders: Will the center hold? or will the melting pot give way to the Tower of Babel?

I don't want to sound apocalyptic about these developments. Education is always in ferment, and a good thing too. Schools and colleges have always been battlegrounds for debates over beliefs, philosophies, values. The situation in our universities, I am confident, will soon right itself once the great silent majority of professors cry "enough" and challenge what they know to be voguish nonsense.

The impact of ethnic and racial pressures on our public schools is more troubling. The bonds of national cohesion are sufficiently fragile already. Public education should aim to strengthen those bonds, not to weaken them. If separatist tendencies go on unchecked, the result can only be the fragmentation, resegregation, and tribalization of American life.

I remain optimistic. My impression is that the historic forces driving toward "one people" have not lost their power. For most Americans this is still what the republic is all about. They resist extremes in the argument between "unity first" and "ethnicity first." "Most Americans," Governor Mario Cuomo[3] has well said, "can understand both the need to recognize and encourage an enriched diversity as well as the need to ensure that such a broadened multicultural perspective leads to unity and an enriched sense of what being an American is, and not to a destructive factionalism that would tear us apart."

Whatever their self-appointed spokesmen may claim, most American-born members of minority groups, white or nonwhite, while they may cherish particular heritages, still see themselves primarily as Americans and not primarily as Irish or Hungarians or Jews or Africans or Asians. A telling indicator is the rising rate of intermarriage across ethnic, religious, even (increasingly) racial lines. The belief in a unique American identity is far from dead.

But the burden to unify the country does not fall exclusively on the minorities. Assimilation and integration constitute a two-way street. Those who want to join America must be received and welcomed by those who already think they own America. Racism, as I have noted, has

[3] *Mario Cuomo:* Former Democratic governor from New York.

been the great national tragedy. In recent times white America has at last begun to confront the racism so deeply and shamefully inbred in our history. But the triumph over racism is incomplete. When old-line Americans, for example, treat people of other nationalities and races as if they were indigestible elements to be shunned and barred, they must not be surprised if minorities gather bitterly unto themselves and damn everybody else. Not only must *they* want assimilation and integration; *we* must want assimilation and integration too. The burden to make this a unified country lies as much with the complacent majority as with the sullen and resentful minorities.

The American population has unquestionably grown more heterogeneous than ever in recent times. But this very heterogeneity makes the quest for unifying ideals and a common culture all the more urgent. And in a world savagely rent by ethnic and racial antagonisms, it is all the more essential that the United States continue as an example of how a highly differentiated society holds itself together.

A Response to Arthur M. Schlesinger, Jr.

MOLEFI KETE ASANTE
A Defense of Afrocentrism

To be Afrocentric is not to deny American citizenship. Just as to be a Chinese American, live in Chinatown, employ Chinese motifs in artistic expression, and worship Buddha is not anti-American, the person who believes that the African American must be re-centered and relocated in terms of historical referent is not anti-American. This is neither a destructive nor a disuniting behavior. It suggests the strengths of this country compared to other countries. The conviction that we will defend the rights of all cultural expressions, not just Greco-Roman-Hebraic-Germanic-Viking cultures, must be strongly embedded in our political psyches if the nation is to survive. In this way we avoid what I call the Soviet problem, which was the Russification of the empire. Respect for one another's culture must be the guiding principle for a truly remarkable society. Since the American ideal is not a static but a dynamic one, we must constantly reinvent ourselves in the light of our diverse experiences. One reason this nation works the way it does is our diversity. Try to make Africans and Asians copies of Europeans and women copies of men and you will force the disunity Schlesinger fears. This does not mean, as some dishonest writers have written, that black children will be taught black information and white children will be taught white information and so forth. No Afrocentrist has articulated such a view though it has been widely reported in the news.

For more information on MOLEFI KETE ASANTE, *see p. 11.*

PREPARING FOR DISCUSSION

1. Schlesinger believes in the reality of a unified American identity and considers this identity one of America's greatest achievements. How does he establish the historical validity of an American identity? What does he consider to be the single most important institution in shaping an American identity?

2. According to Schlesinger, how has the way we define ourselves as Americans changed? To what extent does he find multiculturalism a disturbing development in American life? Which values does he believe multiculturalism threatens?

3. Why does Schlesinger view assimilation as a positive value? Do you find his historical evidence for a unified "American identity" convincing? Could you argue that Schlesinger's melting-pot ideal might be a convenient myth or mere nostalgia?

4. Schlesinger implies at several points in this selection that certain cultural values are more "American" than others. Which values does he have in mind? In his view, what are the other values that threaten to displace these American values?

5. Consider Schlesinger's use of phrases like "the cult of ethnicity," "the ethnic gospel," and "the multiethnic dogma," as well as his use of the "Tower of Babel" image as a substitute for melting pot. What do these terms have in common? How and why do they invite readers to form a negative view of multiculturalism?

FROM READING TO WRITING

6. Consider the image of the melting pot as Schlesinger presents it. Why do you think this image has endured despite its opponents, may of whom contest the image as antagonistic to cultural pluralism? In an essay, describe your image of a melting-pot society. How does it work? What goes into it, and what comes out? In your opinion, is the melting-pot image outdated and irrelevant to the American experience, or is it still a viable ideal?

7. According to Schlesinger, assimilation offers the best opportunity for social and political harmony. Do you agree with Schlesinger that cultural pluralism poses a serious threat to social stability and cohesion? Write an essay in which you explore the advantages and disadvantages of each position. Where do you find yourself within the spectrum of positions?

MOLEFI KETE ASANTE

What Is Afrocentrism?

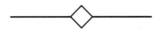

The ideas of the Afrocentrist scholar Molefi Kete Asante stand at the center of the multicultural controversy. Some white scholars, such as Arthur Schlesinger in the previous selection, have singled out Asante for attack on the grounds that Afrocentrism encourages cultural segregation and racial chauvinism. More recently, African American scholars like Cornel West and bell hooks (both of whom are also represented in this book) have joined in the attack. In the following selection from the author's 1993 essay collection, Asante reveals the main tenets of Afrocentricity and the goals of the Afrocentric movement, especially with regard to education. True multicultural education, according to Asante, is not merely a means of raising the self-esteem of minority children; it clears the way to a serious and scholarly revaluation of American history.

Asante is professor and chair of the Department of African American Studies at Temple University. In addition to being regarded as the founder of Afrocentrism, he is credited with developing the first doctoral program in African American studies as well as Afrocentric curricula for several major school districts. He also edits the influential *Journal of African American Studies*. His 1980 book, *Afrocentricity: The Theory of Social Change*, became a best-seller and introduced his ideas to a wider public.

SELECTED PUBLICATIONS: *Afrocentricity: The Theory of Social Change* (1980); *African Culture* (1985); *The Afrocentric Idea* (1987); *Kemet, Afrocentricity and Knowledge* (1990); *The Historical and Cultural Atlas of African-Americans* (1991); *Malcolm X as Cultural Hero and Other Afrocentric Essays* (1993).

Africans owe deference to no people. Those who seek deference from Africans have one goal in mind, the undermining of our confidence and the enthronement of white supremacy. But there is no deference to be given since the history of African-American scholarship, though long ignored by whites in the Western world, is established in the records of numerous books and articles written by excellent critical and reflective thinkers. Nevertheless, we are bombarded by white authors and African Americans who have adopted the vision of whites seeking to challenge our interpretations of our own reality.

Sidney Mintz, a white anthropologist, was quoted in the *Chronicle of Higher Education*, in March 1992, as saying that Afrocentrists would not agree with the conclusions in a paper he wrote on the birth of African-American culture. There have been other such statements expressed mainly in press releases, public relations brochures, and interviews. Most of the comments proceed from ignorance of the concept of Afrocentricity and are stated gratuitously.

Since my works (*Afrocentricity*, first published in 1980; *African Culture*, 1985; *The Afrocentric Idea*, 1987; and *Kemet, Afrocentricity and Knowledge*, 1990) constitute a major corpus in the Afrocentric movement, I have accepted the challenge suggested by my colleagues to write an essay toward the systematics of Afrocentric theory to respond to some of the more unenlightened commentaries. I had hoped that the numerous publications in this emerging tradition would have been engaging enough, but it appears in many cases that those who have commented about Afrocentricity have not read the literature and have therefore reacted to the concept much like Europe reacted to Africa for nearly five hundred years, that is, try to control it, trivialize it, or destroy it, but never truly learn about it or from it. The often flippant responses to Afrocentricity have underscored the point generally made by Afrocentric scholars, namely, that the imposition of the Eurocentric perspective on every subject and theme as if the Eurocentric position is the only human and universal view is the fundamental basis of a racist response to history. That it has affected and infected the Academy should not come as a surprise since it was in the Academy where the ideas of white supremacy were expounded for centuries in Germany, France, England, and the United States by the likes of Hegel, Voltaire, Toynbee, and others.[1] If anything, our contemporary universities are the inheritors of this vicious virus that erodes the very nature of our seeing, our explanations, our methods of inquiry, and our conclusions. Sidney Mintz's conclusion in the *Chronicle of Higher Education* about what Afrocentrists would agree with or not agree with is just such an example. He demonstrates no knowledge in his statement of the Afrocentric position on the question of the origin of African-American culture. I can almost guarantee, however, that if his essay written with Richard Price on "Afro-American" cultural origins does not proceed from an African American perspective it will be highly criticized by Afrocentrists.

Afrocentricity is primarily an orientation to data. There are certainly data and facts which may be used by Afrocentrists in making analyses, but the principal component of the theoretical piece has to do with an orientation, a location, a position. Thus, I have explained in several books and articles that Afrocentricity is *a perspective which allows Africans to be subjects of historical experiences rather than objects* on the fringes of Europe.

---

[1] *G.W.F. Hegel:* Nineteenth-century German philosopher; *Voltaire:* Eighteenth-century French philosopher; *Arnold Toynbee:* Twentieth-century British historian.

This means that the Afrocentrist is concerned with discovering in every case the centered place of the African. Of course, such a philosophical stance is not necessary for other disciplines; it is, however, the fundamental basis for African or African American studies. Otherwise, it seems to me that what is being done in African American studies at some institutions might successfully be challenged as duplicating in content, theory, and method the essentially Eurocentric enterprises that are undertaken in the traditional departments.

African American studies, however, is not simply the study and teaching about African people but *it is the Afrocentric study of African phenomena;* otherwise we would have had African American studies for a hundred years. But what existed before was not African American studies but rather Eurocentric study of Africans. Some of these studies led to important findings and have been useful. So the Afrocentrists do not claim that historians, sociologists, literary critics, philosophers, communicationists, and others do not make valuable contributions. Our claim is that by using a Eurocentric approach they often ignore an important interpretative key to the African experience in America and elsewhere.

This poses a special problem, it seems to me, to those who teach in African American studies because the field is not merely an aggregation of courses on African-American history and literature. Without a fundamental orientation to the data that centers on African people as subjects and agents of historical experiences the African American studies programs are nothing more than extensions of the English, history, or sociology departments. On the other hand, the Afrocentric study of phenomena asks questions about location, place, orientation, and perspective. This means that the data could come from any field or place and be examined Afrocentrically. At Temple University we experiment with materials as varied as literary texts, architectural designs, dance aesthetics, social institutions, and management techniques to teach the concept of centeredness.

Like scholars in other disciplines, Afrocentrists are exposed to the hazards of place and position. We can never be sure that our place is as secure as we want it to be: but we do the best we can with the resources of intellect at our disposal. Our aim is to open fields of inquiry and to expand human dialogue around questions of social, economic, historical, and cultural concern. Everything must be run through the sieve of doubt until one hits the bedrock of truth. Our methods, based on the idea of Afrocentricity, are meant to establish a clear pattern of discourse that may be followed by others. Afrocentricity is not a matter of color but of perspective, that is, orientation to data. The historian, sociologist, psychologist, and political scientist may examine the Gettysburg Battle and see different elements and aspects because of the different emphases of the disciplines. In a similar manner, the Afrocentrist would look at the Civil War or any phenomenon involving African people and raise

5

different questions from the Eurocentrist. These questions are not more or less correct but better in an interpretative sense if the person doing the asking wants to understand African phenomena in context. Since the Afrocentric perspective is not a racial perspective but an orientation to data, anyone willing to submit to the rigid discipline of the field might become an Afrocentrist. There are two general fields in which the Afrocentrist works: cultural/aesthetics and social/behavioral. This means that the person who declares in an intellectual sense to be an Afrocentrist commits traditional discipline suicide because you cannot, to be consistent, remain a traditional Eurocentric intellectual and an Afrocentrist. Of course, there are those who might be bipositional or multipositional under given circumstances. In claiming this posture, I am not dismissing the work that has been done in other fields on Africans and African Americans; some of it has enlarged our understanding, particularly the work that might be considered pre-Afrocentric, such as the works of Melville Herskovits, Basil Davidson, Robert Farris Thompson, and other scholars who have sought to see through the eyes of Africans.

Afrocentric theories are not about cultural separatism or racial chauvinism. Among those who have been quoted as making such a charge are Michele Wallace, Arthur Schlesinger, Miriam Lichtheim, Cornel West, Diane Ravitch, bell hooks, and Henry Louis Gates, Jr. With such a stellar crew in the same bed, one is eager to discover the source of their offhanded remarks about Afrocentricity and separatism or chauvinism. Attempting to give them the benefit of the doubt, I have assumed that they sense in the Afrocentric perspective a pro-African and an anti-white posture. Apart from the fact that one can be pro-African and not anti-white, the concept of Afrocentricity has little to do with pros and cons; it is pre-eminently about how you view phenomena.

I believe that the white scholars who register a negative reaction to Afrocentricity do so out of a sense of fear. The fear is revealed on two levels. In the first place, Afrocentricity provides them with no grounds for authority unless they become students of Africans. This produces an existential fear: African scholars might have something to teach whites. The Afrocentric school of thought is the first contemporary intellectual movement initiated by African-American scholars that has currency on a broad scale for renewal and renaissance. It did not emerge inside the traditional white academic bastions. The second fear is not so much an existential one; it is rather a fear of the implications of the Afrocentric critique of Eurocentrism as an ethnocentric view posing as a universal view. Thus, we have opened the discussion of everything from race theory, ancient civilizations, African and European personalities, the impact of the glaciers on human behavior, and dislocation in the writing of African-American authors. We examine these topics with the eye of African people as subjects of historical experiences. This is not the only human view. If anything, Afrocentrists have always said that our perspective on data is only one among many and consequently the viewpoint, if you will, seeks no advantage, no self-aggrandizement, and no hegemony. The same cannot be said of Eurocentrism.

The African American and African Eurocentrists are a special problem. They represent two cases. The first case is represented by those who have been so well-trained in the Eurocentric perspective that they see themselves as copies of Europeans. These are the Africans who believe they came to America on the *Mayflower* or better yet that classical European music is the only classical music in the world. Their rejection of Afrocentricity is tied to their rejection of themselves. Thus, the inability to see from their own centers or to position their sights on phenomena from their own historical and cultural conditions is related to what Malcolm X used to call "the slave mentality," that is, the belief that their own views can never be divorced from the slave master's. To a large degree these Africans tend to lack historical consciousness and find their own source of intellectual satisfaction in the approval of whites, not in the search for the interpretative key to their own history. I am not suggesting the stifling of this type of imitation in any politically correct way, but rather I want to explain the response to Afrocentricity in a historical manner. The second case is also historical, that is, Afrocentrists find evidences of it in our historical experiences. These are the Africans who seek to be appointed overseers on the plantation. They do not necessarily believe they are the same as whites. They recognize that they did not come here on the *Mayflower* but they aspire to universalism without references to particular experiences. For them, any emphasis on particular perspectives and experiences suggests separatism and separatism suggests hostility. This is a fallacy because neither separatism nor difference suggests hostility except in the minds of those who fear human wholeness.

In an intellectual sense these African Eurocentrists feel inclined to disagree with any idea that has popular approval among the African-American masses. Much like the overseers during the antebellum period they are eager to demonstrate that they are not a part of the rebellion and that they distrust the ideas that are derived from the African masses. Indeed, they might even participate in what Louis Lomax once called "the fooling of white people" by telling white audiences that Afrocentrists represent a new and passing fad.

The point is that Afrocentricity is nothing more than what is congruent to the interpretative life of the African person. Why should an African American see himself or herself through the perspective of a Chinese or white American? Neither the Chinese nor the white American views phenomena from the perspective of the African American nor should they. Thus, to understand the African-American experience in dance, architecture, social work, art, science, psychology, or communication one has to avail one's self of the richly textured standing place of African Americans. In the end, you must ask yourself, why does such a simple rational position threaten so many people?

Notes

1. Sidney Mintz, *Chronicle of Higher Education,* March 15, 1992.
2. Molefi Kete Asante, *The Afrocentric Idea.* Philadelphia: Temple University Press, 1987.
3. Molefi Kete Asante, *Kemet, Afrocentricity and Knowledge.* Trenton: Africa World Press, 1990.

PREPARING FOR DISCUSSION

1. What, briefly, is Asante's primary definition of Afrocentrism? What, according to Asante, accounts for the tendency among many American scholars to misrepresent Afrocentrism? Is the selection aimed only at answering these scholars or is there another audience that Asante hopes to reach?

2. Asante draws an analogy between Europe's historical reaction to Africa and the response of many contemporary scholars to Afrocentrism. How does he describe this reaction? What kinds of evidence does he provide to support his analogy?

3. In paragraph 7 Asante argues that people of any race might become Afrocentrists, because the Afrocentric perspective *"is not* a racial perspective." In the next paragraph he describes his academic discipline as "pro-African." How can a "pro-African" perspective be considered disengaged from the issue of race? Do you suppose Asante believes, for example, that the Arabic cultures of northern Africa and the white culture of South Africa should command as much attention from the Afrocentrist as the continent's black cultures?

4. In describing Afrocentricity as "an orientation to data" (paragraph 4), Asante suggests that Afrocentrists need not concern themselves with a particular field of interest or subject matter. Can you think of other academic disciplines that are defined primarily through the methods they employ rather than their subject matter or field? Why might Asante be hesitant to identify Afrocentrism with a particular field or subject?

5. Consider the way in which Asante attacks African Eurocentrists as possessing an attitude similar to that of those historical "Africans who [sought] to be overseers on the plantation" (paragraph 10). How would you characterize Asante's "overseer" analogy? What kind of response do you think Asante intends it to elicit? What does this analogy imply about the moral position held by the scholars he criticizes? Describe this moral position.

FROM READING TO WRITING

6. In an essay, consider Asante's description of "centeredness" as it relates to Africa and Africans. Does Asante's effort to "center" the African experience and

its values displace the European experience and its values? Why does he think that such displacement need not occur? Do you find his argument valid in this regard? Why or why not?

7. Asante cites Arthur Schlesinger as one of those scholars who believes Afrocentric theories encourage "cultural separatism" and "racial chauvinism." Asante goes on to explain that he finds at the root of Schlesinger's conviction the specious notion that Afrocentrism is "pro-African" and therefore "anti-white." Write an essay in which you describe and examine an instance in which your own position on ethnic or racial identity has been misrepresented.

LINDA CHAVEZ

Demystifying Multiculturalism

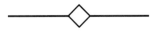

Some of the fiercest criticism of multiculturalism has come from political conservatives who believe that the movement is wholly a creation of liberal politicians and professors and in no way reflects or answers to the educational and cultural needs of ordinary Americans. Conservatives likewise reject the notion held by many multiculturalists that ethnic background is a major determinant of an individual's character and values. In the following selection, a 1994 essay published in the *National Review*, Linda Chavez attempts to explode what she believes to be the central myths of the diversity movement.

While she is proud of her Spanish-American background, Chavez often finds herself at odds with the liberal wing of the Hispanic community in America. After spending most of the 1970s working as a Democrat for a number of liberal causes in Washington, she was appointed to the U.S. Commission on Civil Rights, where she began to question many traditional civil rights measures. Switching her party affiliation in 1985, she became the highest-ranking woman in the Reagan administration as director of the White House Office of Public Liaison. Since her unsuccessful 1986 bid for the U.S. Senate, Chavez has remained a major exponent of English as the official national language and often addresses the need for the rapid assimilation of Hispanics into mainstream American culture. Director of the Center for the New American Community, she is John M. Olin Fellow at the Manhattan Institute.

SELECTED PUBLICATION: *Out of the Barrio: Toward a New Politics of Hispanic Assimilation* (1991).

Multiculturalism is on the advance, everywhere from President Clinton's cabinet to corporate boardrooms to public-school classrooms. If you believe the multiculturalists' propaganda, whites are on the verge of becoming a minority in the United States. The multiculturalists predict that this demographic shift will fundamentally change American culture — indeed destroy the very idea that America *has* a single, unified culture. They aren't taking any chances, however. They have enlisted the help of government, corporate leaders, the media, and the education establishment in waging a cultural revolution. But has America truly become a multicultural nation? And if not, will those who capitulate to these demands create a self-fulfilling prophecy?

At the heart of the argument is the assumption that the white population is rapidly declining in relation to the non-white population. A 1987 Hudson Institute report helped catapult this claim to national prominence. The study, *Workforce 2000*, estimated that by the turn of the century only 15 percent of new workers would be white males. The figure was widely interpreted to mean that whites were about to become a minority in the workplace — and in the country.

In fact, white males will still constitute about 45 percent — a plurality — of the workforce in the year 2000. The proportion of white men in the workforce *is* declining — it was nearly 51 percent in 1980 — but primarily because the proportion of white women is growing. They will make up 39 percent of the workforce within ten years, according to government projections, up from 36 percent in 1980. Together, white men and women will account for 84 percent of all workers by 2000 — hardly a minority share.

But the business world is behaving as if a demographic tidal wave is about to hit. A whole new industry of "diversity professionals" has emerged to help managers cope with the expected deluge of nonwhite workers. These consultants are paid as much as $10,000 a day to train managers to "value diversity," a term so ubiquitous that it has appeared in more than seven hundred articles in major newspapers in the last three years. According to Heather MacDonald in *The New Republic,* about half of Fortune 500 corporations now employ someone responsible for "diversity."

What precisely does valuing diversity mean? The underlying assumptions seem to be that non-whites are so different from whites that employers must make major changes to accommodate them, and that white workers will be naturally resistant to including non-whites in their ranks. Public-opinion polls don't bear out the latter. They show that support among whites for equal job opportunity for blacks is extraordinarily high, exceeding 90 percent as early as 1975. As for accommodating different cultures, the problem is not culture — or race, or ethnicity — but education. Many young people, in particular, are poorly prepared for work, and the problem is most severe among those who attended inner-city schools, most of them blacks and Hispanics.

Nevertheless, multiculturalists insist on treating race and ethnicity as if they were synonymous with culture. They presume that skin color and national origin, which are immutable traits, determine values, mores, language, and other cultural attributes, which, of course, are learned. In the multiculturalists' world view, African-Americans, Puerto Ricans, or Chinese-Americans living in New York City have more in common with persons of their ancestral group living in Lagos or San Juan or Hong Kong than they do with other New Yorkers who are white. Culture becomes a fixed entity, transmitted, as it were, in the genes, rather than through experience. Thus, "Afrocentricity," a variant of multiculturalism, is "a way of being," its exponents claim. According to a leader of the Afrocentric education movement, Molefi Kete Asante, there is "one African Cultural System manifested in diversities," whether one speaks of Afro-Brazilians, Cubans, or Nigerians (or, presumably, African-Americans). Exactly how this differs from the traditional racist notion that all blacks (Jews, Mexicans, Chinese, etc.) think alike is unclear. What is clear is that the multiculturalists have abandoned the ideal that all persons should be judged by the content of their character, not the color of their skin. Indeed, the multiculturalists seem to believe that a person's character is *determined* by the color of his skin and by his ancestry.

Such convictions lead multiculturalists to conclude that, again in the words of Asante, "[T]here is no common American culture." The logic is simple, but wrong-headed: Since Americans (or more often, their forebears) hail from many different places, each of which has its own specific culture, the argument goes, America must be multicultural. And it is becoming more so every day as new immigrants bring their cultures with them.

Indeed, multiculturalists hope to ride the immigrant wave to greater power and influence. They have certainly done so in education. Some 2.3 million children who cannot speak English well now attend public school, an increase of 1 million in the last seven years. Multicultural advocates cite the presence of such children to demand bilingual education and other multicultural services. The Los Angeles Unified School District alone currently offers instruction in Spanish, Armenian, Korean, Cantonese, Tagalog, Russian, and Japanese. Federal and state governments now spend literally billions of dollars on these programs.

Ironically, the multiculturalists' emphasis on education undercuts their argument that culture is inextricable from race or national origin. They are acutely aware just how fragile cultural identification is; why else are they so adamant about reinforcing it? Multiculturalists insist on teaching immigrant children in their native language, instructing them in the history and customs of their native land and imbuing them with reverence for their ancestral heroes, lest these youngsters be seduced by American culture. Far from losing faith in the power of assimilation, they seem to believe that without a heavy dose of multicultural indoctrination, immigrants won't be able to resist it. And they're right, though it remains to be seen whether anything, including the multiculturalists' crude methods, will ultimately detour immigrants from the assimilation path.

The urge to assimilate has traditionally been overpowering in the United States, especially among the children of immigrants. Only groups that maintain strict rules against intermarriage with persons outside the group, such as Orthodox Jews and the Amish, have ever succeeded in preserving distinct, full-blown cultures within American society. (It is interesting to note that religion seems to be a more effective deterrent to full assimilation than the secular elements of culture, including language.) Although many Americans worry that Hispanic immigrants, for example, are not learning English and will therefore fail to assimilate into the American mainstream, little evidence supports the case. By the third generation in the United States, a majority of Hispanics, like other ethnic groups, speak only English and are closer to other Americans on most measures of social and economic status than they are to Hispanic immigrants. On one of the most rigorous gauges of assimilation — intermarriage — Hispanics rank high. About one-third of young third-generation Hispanics marry non-Hispanic whites, a pattern similar to that of young Asians. Even for blacks, exogamy rates, which have been quite low historically, are going up; about 3 percent of blacks now marry outside their group.

The impetus for multiculturalism is not coming from immigrants, but from their more affluent and assimilated native-born counterparts. The proponents are most often the elite — the best educated and most successful members of their respective racial and ethnic groups. College campuses, where the most radical displays of multiculturalism take place, are fertile recruiting grounds. Last May, for example, a group of Mexican-American students at UCLA, frustrated that the university would not elevate the school's 23-year-old Chicano-studies program to full department status, stormed the faculty center, breaking windows and furniture and causing half a million dollars in damage. The same month, a group of Asian-American students at UC Irvine went on a hunger strike to pressure administrators into hiring more professors of Asian-American studies. These were not immigrants, or even, by and large, disadvantaged students, but middle-class beneficiaries of their parents' or grandparents' successful assimilation to the American mainstream.

The protestors' quest had almost nothing to do with any effort to maintain their ethnic identity. For the most part, such students probably never thought of themselves as anything but American before they entered college. A recent study of minority students at the University of California at Berkeley found that most Hispanic and Asian students "discovered" their ethnic identity after they arrived on campus — when they also discovered that they were victims of systematic discrimination. As one Mexican-American freshman summed it up, she was "unaware of the things that have been going on with our people, all the injustice we've suffered, how the world really is. I thought racism didn't exist and here, you know, it just comes to light." The researchers added that "students of color" had difficulty pinpointing exactly what constituted this "subtle form of the new racism. . . . There was much talk about certain facial expressions, or the way people look, and how white students 'take over the class' and speak past you."

Whatever their new-found victim status, these students look amazingly like other Americans on most indices. For example, the median family income of Mexican-American students at Berkeley in 1989 was $32,500, slightly above the national median for all Americans that year, $32,191; and 17 percent of those students came from families that earned more than $75,000 a year, even though they were admitted to the university under affirmative-action programs (presumably because they suffered some educational disadvantage attributed to their ethnicity).

Affirmative-action programs make less and less sense as discrimination diminishes in this society — which it indisputably has — and as minorities improve their economic status. Racial and ethnic identity, too, might wane if there weren't such aggressive efforts to ensure that this not happen. The multiculturalists know they risk losing their constituency if young blacks, Hispanics, Asians, and others don't maintain strong racial and ethnic affiliations. Younger generations must be *trained* to think of themselves as members of oppressed minority groups entitled to special treatment. And the government provides both the incentives and the money to ensure that this happens. Meanwhile, the main beneficiaries are the multicultural professionals, who often earn exorbitant incomes peddling identity.

One particularly egregious example occurred in the District of Columbia last fall. The school system paid $250,000 to a husband-and-wife consultant team to produce an Afrocentric study guide to be used in a single public elementary school. Controversy erupted after the two spent three years and produced only a five-page outline. Although the husband had previously taught at Howard University, the wife's chief credential was a master's degree from an unaccredited "university" which she and her husband had founded. When the *Washington Post* criticized the school superintendent for his handling of the affair, he called a press conference to defend the couple, who promptly claimed they were the victims of a racist vendetta.

D.C. students rank lowest in the nation in math and fourth-lowest in verbal achievement; one can only wonder what $250,000 in tutoring at one school might have done. Instead, the students were treated to bulletin boards in the classrooms proclaiming on their behalf: "We are the sons and daughters of The Most High. We are the princes and princesses of African kings and queens. We are the descendants of our black ancestors. We are black and we are proud." This incident is not unique. Thousands of consultants with little or no real expertise sell feel-good programs to school systems across the nation.

Multiculturalism is not a grassroots movement. It was created, nurtured, and expanded through government policy. Without the expenditure of vast sums of public money, it would wither away and die. That is not to say that ethnic communities would disappear from the American scene or that groups would not retain some attachment to their ancestral roots. American assimilation has always entailed some give and take, and American culture has been enriched by what individual groups brought to it. The distinguishing characteristic of American culture is its ability to incorporate so many disparate groups, creating a new whole from the many parts. What could be more American, for example, than jazz and film, two distinctive art forms created, respectively, by blacks and immigrant Jews but which all Americans think of as their own? But in the past, government — especially public schools — saw it as a duty to try to bring newcomers into the fold by teaching them English, by introducing them to the great American heroes as their own, by instilling respect for American institutions. Lately, we have nearly reversed course, treating each group, new and old, as if what is most important is to preserve its separate identity and space.

It is easy to blame the ideologues and radicals who are pushing the disuniting of America, to use Arthur Schlesinger's phrase, but the real culprits are those who provide multiculturalists the money and the access to press their cause. Without the acquiescence of policy-makers and ordinary citizens, multiculturalism would be no threat. Unfortunately, most major institutions have little stomach for resisting the multicultural impulse — and many seem eager to comply with whatever demands the multiculturalists make. Americans should have learned by now that policy matters. We have only to look at the failure of our welfare and crime policies to know that providing perverse incentives can change the way individuals behave — for the worse. Who is to say that if we pour enough money into dividing Americans we won't succeed?

PREPARING FOR DISCUSSION

1. While Chavez acknowledges that multiculturalism is on the rise, she rejects the popular claim that "whites are on the verge of becoming a minority in

the United States." What evidence does she provide to oppose this claim? How does she account for the widespread acceptance of the claim?

2. At several points in her essay, Chavez asserts that multiculturalism is not "a grassroots movement." Instead, she partly locates the roots of multicultural-ism on college campuses, adding that many entering students have not yet "dis-covered" their ethnic identities when they arrive on campus. What is Chavez's purpose in aligning multicultural ideas with colleges and universities? How would you describe her attitude toward institutions of higher learning?

3. Consider Chavez's statement that "affirmative-action programs make less and less sense as discrimination diminishes in this society" (paragraph 14). She likewise views the improving economic status of many people of color as a sign that discrimination against minorities is gradually disappearing. What reasons does she provide for what she sees as the steady decline of racial discrimination? Does she consider the possibility that the very minority programs she denounces as increasingly unnecessary are in no small way responsible for this decline?

4. Chavez holds that one of the major assumptions underlying multicultur-alism is the notion that racial and ethnic identity determine a person's character. She then maintains that the falseness of this assumption is revealed by the multi-culturalist emphasis on education. On what grounds does she make this case? Do you find it convincing?

5. Chavez often uses words like *indoctrination* and *trained* to describe multi-cultural education. Do you think she uses such words intentionally or uninten-tionally? If the former, what is she implying about the nature of multicultural education? If the latter, what as yet unarticulated assumptions about this kind of education might she possess?

FROM READING TO WRITING

6. Consider the data supplied by Chavez on the median family income of the average Mexican-American student at Berkeley. Does Chavez imply that the relative prosperity of minority students makes those same students' awareness of their ethnic identity unnecessary? Write a response to Chavez that explains your own view of the relationship between ethnic identity and economic security.

7. Chavez's argument assumes that economic opportunity for minorities rather than self-awareness is the best way to combat the effects of discrimination in America. In an essay, trace this assumption through Chavez's argument and then assess its validity in light of your own understanding of the long-term goals of multiculturalism.

MICHAEL WALZER

Multiculturalism and Individualism

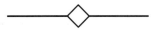

Many Americans have been troubled in recent years by what seems to be a national preoccupation with *difference*. Whether we emphasize the difference between ethnic groups or the difference between individuals, this emphasis threatens, according to some, the common bonds between people living in a democratic society. One important way we are bound together as Americans is through our desire to remain free. And yet without greater social cohesion, some worry, Americans will gradually lose their ability to defend their freedoms as a people. In response to this threat, Michael Walzer looks for a middle ground between the ethnic separatism of multiculturalists like Molefi Kete Asante and the staunch individualism of conservatives like Linda Chavez.

Throughout his career as a political theorist, Walzer has remained a major advocate of communal political involvement. Individual freedoms, he holds, can be preserved only through common purpose and effort, and the way to preserve social cohesion is through greater associational activity. Having served for many years as a professor of government at Harvard, Walzer in 1980 moved to Princeton, where he teaches at the Institute of Advanced Study's School of Social Science. In addition to having written many books and articles on political and moral life, Walzer has edited since 1960 one of the Left's most influential periodicals, *Dissent*, where the following selection originally appeared in 1994.

SELECTED PUBLICATIONS: *The Revolution of the Saints: A Study in the Origins of Radical Politics* (1965); *Radical Principles: Reflections of an Unreconstructed Democrat* (1980); *Spheres of Justice: A Defense of Pluralism and Equality* (1983); *What It Means to Be an American* (1993); *Thick and Thin: Moral Argument at Home and Abroad* (1994).

Two powerful centrifugal forces are at work in the United States today. One breaks loose whole groups of people from a presumptively common center; the other sends individuals flying off. Both these decentering, separatist movements have their critics, who argue that the first is driven by a narrow-minded chauvinism and the second by mere selfishness. The separated groups appear to these critics as exclusive and intolerant tribes, the separated individuals as rootless and lonely egotists. Neither of these views is entirely wrong; neither is quite right. The two movements have to be considered together, set against the background of a democratic politics that opens a lot of room for centrifugal force.

Understood in context, the two seem to me, despite the laws of physics, each one the other's remedy.

The first of these forces is an increasingly strong articulation of group difference. It's the articulation that is new, obviously, since difference itself — pluralism, even multiculturalism — has been a feature of American life from very early on. John Jay, in one of the *Federalist Papers*, describes the Americans as a people "descended from the same ancestors, speaking the same language, professing the same religion, attached to the same principles of government, very similar in manners and customs."

These lines were already inaccurate when Jay wrote them in the 1780s; they were utterly falsified in the course of the nineteenth century. Mass immigration turned the United States into a land of many different ancestors, languages, religions, manners, and customs. Principles of government are our only stable and common commitment. Democracy fixes the limits and sets the ground rules for American pluralism.

Two contrasts can help us grasp the radical character of this pluralism. Consider, first, the (relative) homogeneity of countries like France, Holland, Norway, Germany, Japan, and China, where, whatever regional differences exist, the great majority of the citizens share a single ethnic identity and celebrate a common history. And consider, second, the territorially based heterogeneity of the old multinational empires (the Soviet Union was the last of these) and of states like the former Yugoslavia, the former Ethiopia, the new Russia, Nigeria, Iraq, India, and so on, where a number of ethnic and religious minorities claim ancient homelands (even if the boundaries are always in dispute). The United States differs from both these sets of countries: It isn't homogeneous nationally or locally; it's heterogeneous everywhere — a land of dispersed diversity, which is (except for the remaining Native Americans) no one's homeland. Of course, there are local patterns of segregation, voluntary and involuntary; there are ethnic neighborhoods and places inexactly but evocatively called "ghettoes." But none of our groups, with the partial and temporary exception of the Mormons in Utah, has ever achieved anything like stable geographical predominance. There is no American Slovenia or Quebec or Kurdistan. Even in the most protected American environments, we all experience difference every day.

And yet the full-scale and fervent articulation of difference is a fairly recent phenomenon. A long history of prejudice, subordination, and fear worked against any public affirmation of minority "manners and customs" and so served to conceal the radical character of American pluralism. I want to be very clear about this history. At its extremes it was brutal, as conquered Native Americans and transported black slaves can testify; at its center, with regard to religion and ethnicity rather than race, it was relatively benign. An immigrant society welcomed new immigrants or, at least, made room for them, with a degree of reluctance and resistance considerably below the standards set elsewhere. Nonetheless, all our minorities learned to be quiet; timidity has been the mark of minority politics until very recent times.

I remember, for example, how in the 1930s and 1940s any sign of Jewish assertiveness — even the appearance of "too many" Jewish names among New Deal Democrats or CIO[1] organizers or socialist or communist intellectuals — was greeted among Jews with a collective shudder. The communal elders said, "Sha!" Don't make noise; don't attract attention; don't push yourself forward; don't say anything provocative. They thought of themselves as guests in this country long after they had become citizens.

Today all that is, as they say, history. The United States in the 1990s is socially, though not economically (and the contrast is especially striking after the Reagan years), a more egalitarian place than it was fifty or sixty years ago. No one is shushing us anymore; no one is intimidated or quiet. Old racial and religious identities have taken on greater prominence in our public life; gender and sexual preference have been added to the mix; and the current wave of immigration from Asia and Latin America makes for significant new differences among American citizens and potential citizens. And all this is expressed, so it seems, all the time. The voices are loud, the accents various, and the result is not harmony — as in the old image of pluralism as a symphony, each group playing its own instrument (but who wrote the music?) — but a jangling discord. It is very much like the dissidence of Protestant dissent in the early years of the Reformation: many sects, dividing and subdividing; many prophets and would-be prophets, all talking at once.

In response to this cacophony, another group of prophets, liberal and neoconservative intellectuals, academics, and journalists, wring their hands and assure us that the country is falling apart, that our fiercely articulated multiculturalism is dangerously divisive, and that we desperately need to reassert the hegemony of a single culture. Curiously, this supposedly necessary and necessarily singular culture is often described as a high culture, as if it is our shared commitment to Shakespeare, Dickens, and James Joyce that has been holding us together all these years. (But surely high culture divides us, as it always has — and probably always will in any country with a strong egalitarian and populist strain. Does anyone remember Richard Hofstadter's *Anti-Intellectualism in American Life?*) Democratic politics seems to me a more likely resource than

[1] *New Deal Democrats:* Democrats who believed in the principles of President Franklin D. Roosevelt's New Deal. Introduced during the Great Depression of the 1930s, the New Deal reforms were based on the belief that government must play a major role in alleviating the suffering of poor citizens. *CIO (Congress of Industrial Organizations):* A major American trade union.

the literary or philosophical canon. We need to think about how this resource might usefully be deployed.

But isn't it already deployed — given that multicultural conflicts take place in the democratic arena and require of their protagonists a wide range of characteristically democratic skills and performances? If one studies the history of ethnic, racial, and religious associations in the United States, one sees, I think, that these have served again and again as vehicles of individual and group integration — despite (or, perhaps, because of) the political conflicts they generated. Even if the aim of associational life is to sustain difference, that aim has to be achieved *here*, under American conditions, and the result is commonly a new and unintended kind of differentiation — of American Catholics and Jews, say, not so much from one another or from the Protestant majority as from Catholics and Jews in other countries. Minority groups adapt themselves to the local political culture. And if their primary aim is self-defense, toleration, civil rights, a place in the sun, the result of success is more clearly still an Americanization of whatever differences are being defended. That doesn't mean that differences are defended quietly — quietness is not one of our political conventions. Becoming an American means learning not to be quiet. Nor is the success that is sought by one group always compatible with the success of all (or any of) the others. The conflicts are real, and even small-scale victories are often widely threatening.

The greater difficulties, however, come from failure, especially reiterated failure. It is associational weakness, and the anxieties and resentments it breeds, that pull people apart in dangerous ways. Leonard Jeffries's African-American Studies Department at the City College of New York is hardly an example of institutional strength[2] The noisiest groups in our contemporary cacophony and the groups that make the most extreme demands are also the weakest. In American cities today, poor people, mostly members of minority groups, find it difficult to work together in any coherent way. Mutual assistance, cultural preservation, and self-defense are loudly affirmed but ineffectively enacted. The contemporary poor have no strongly based or well-funded institutions to focus their energies or discipline wayward members. They are socially exposed and vulnerable. This is the most depressing feature of our current situation: the large number of disorganized, powerless, and demoralized men and women, who are spoken for, and also exploited by, a growing company of racial and religious demagogues and tinhorn charismatics.

But weakness is a general feature of associational life in America

10

---

[2] *Leonard Jeffries:* African American scholar whose controversial remarks on the role of Jews in the historical oppression of blacks prompted his removal as chairman of the City College of New York's African-American Studies Department.

today. Unions, churches, interest groups, ethnic organizations, political parties and sects, societies for self-improvement and good works, local philanthropies, neighborhood clubs and cooperatives, religious sodalities, brotherhoods and sisterhoods: This American civil society is wonderfully multitudinous. Most of the associations, however, are precariously established, skimpily funded, and always at risk. They have less reach and holding power than they once did. I can't cite statistics; I'm not sure that anyone is collecting the right sorts of statistics; but I suspect that the number of Americans who are unorganized, inactive, and undefended is on the rise. Why is this so?

The answer has to do in part with the second of the centrifugal forces at work in contemporary American society. This country is not only a pluralism of groups but also a pluralism of individuals. It is perhaps the most individualist society in human history. Compared to the men and women of any earlier, old-world country, we are radically liberated, all of us. We are free to plot our own course, plan our own lives, choose a career, a partner (or a succession of partners), a religion (or no religion), a politics (or an antipolitics), a life-style (any style) — free to "do our own thing." Personal freedom is certainly one of the extraordinary achievements of the "new order of the ages" celebrated on the Great Seal of the United States. The defense of this freedom against puritans and bigots is one of the enduring themes of American politics, making for its most zestful moments; the celebration of this freedom, and of the individuality and creativity it makes possible, is one of the enduring themes of our literature.

Nonetheless, personal freedom is not an unalloyed delight. For many of us lack the means and the power to "do our own thing" or even to find our own things to do. Empowerment is, with rare exceptions, a familial, class, or communal, not an individual, achievement. Resources are accumulated over generations, cooperatively. And without resources, individual men and women find themselves hardpressed by economic dislocations, natural disasters, governmental failures, and personal crises. They can't count on steady or significant communal support. Often they are on the run from family, class, and community, seeking a new life in this new world. If they make good their escape, they never look back; if they need to look back, they are likely to find the people they left behind barely able to support themselves.

Consider for a moment the cultural (ethnic, racial, and religious) groups that constitute our supposedly fierce and divisive multiculturalism. All these are voluntary associations, with a core of militants, activists, and believers and wide periphery of more passive men and women — who are, in effect, cultural free-riders, enjoying an identity that they don't pay for with money, time, or energy. When these people find themselves in trouble they look for help from similarly identified men and women. But the help is uncertain, for these identities are mostly unearned, without depth. Footloose individuals are not reliable members. There are no borders around our cultural groups and, of course, no border police. Men and women are free to participate or not as they please, to come and go, withdraw entirely, or simply fade away into the peripheral distances. This freedom, again, is one of the advantages of an individualist society; at the same time, however, it doesn't make for strong or cohesive associations. Ultimately, I'm not sure that it makes for strong or self-confident individuals.

Rates of disengagement from cultural association and identity for the sake of the private pursuit of happiness (or the desperate search for economic survival) are so high these days that all the groups worry all the time about how to hold the periphery and ensure their own future. They are constantly fund raising; recruiting; scrambling for workers, allies, and endorsements; preaching against the dangers of assimilation, intermarriage, passing, and passivity. Lacking any sort of coercive power and unsure of their own persuasiveness, they demand governmental programs (targeted entitlements, quota systems) that will help them press their own members into line. From their perspective, the real alternative to multiculturalism is not a strong and substantive Americanism, but an empty or randomly filled individualism, a great drift of human flotsam and jetsam away from every creative center.

This is, again, a one-sided perspective, but by no means entirely wrongheaded. The critical conflict in American life today is not between multiculturalism and some kind of cultural hegemony or singularity, not between pluralism and unity or the many and the one, but between the manyness of groups and of individuals, between communities and private men and women. And this is a conflict in which we have no choice except to affirm the value of both sides. The two pluralisms make America what it is or sometimes is and set the pattern for what it should be. Taken together, but only together, they are entirely consistent with a common democratic citizenship.

Consider now the increasingly dissociated individuals of contemporary American society. Surely we ought to worry about the processes, even though these are also, some of them, emancipatory processes, which produce dissociation and are its products:

- the rising divorce rate;
- the growing number of people living alone (in what the census calls "single person households");
- the decline in memberships (in unions and churches, for example);
- the long-term decline in voting rates and party loyalty (most dramatic in local elections);

- the high rates of geographic mobility (which continually undercut neighborhood cohesiveness);
- the sudden appearance of homeless men and women; and
- the rising tide of random violence.

Add to all this the apparent stabilization of high levels of unemployment and underemployment, especially among young people, which intensifies all these processes and aggravates their effects on already vulnerable minority groups. Unemployment makes family ties brittle, cuts people off from unions and interest groups, drains communal resources, leads to political alienation and withdrawal, increases the temptations of a criminal life. The old maxim about idle hands and the devil's work isn't necessarily true, but it comes true whenever idleness is a condition that no one would choose.

I am inclined to think that these processes, on balance, are more worrying than the multicultural cacophony — if only because, in a democratic society, action-in-common is better than withdrawal and solitude, tumult is better than passivity, shared purposes (even when we don't approve) are better than private listlessness. It is probably true, moreover, that many of these dissociated individuals are available for political mobilizations of a sort that democracies ought to avoid. There are writers today, of course, who claim that multiculturalism is itself the product of such mobilizations: American society in their eyes stands at the brink not only of dissolution but of "Bosnian" civil war. In fact, we have had (so far) only intimations of an openly chauvinist and racist politics. We are at a point where we can still safely bring the pluralism of groups to the rescue of the pluralism of dissociated individuals.

Individuals are stronger, more confident, more savvy, when they are 20 participants in a common life, responsible to and for other people. No doubt, this relation doesn't hold for every common life; I am not recommending religious cults or political sects — though men and women who manage to pass through groups of that sort are often strengthened by the experience, educated for a more modest commonality. It is only in the context of associational activity that individuals learn to deliberate, argue, make decisions, and take responsibility. This is an old argument, first made on behalf of Protestant congregations and conventicles, which served, so we are told, as schools of democracy in nineteenth-century Great Britain, despite the intense and exclusive bonds they created and their frequently expressed doubts about the salvation of nonbelievers. Individuals were indeed saved by congregational membership — saved from isolation, loneliness, feelings of inferiority, habitual inaction, incompetence, a kind of moral vacancy — and turned into useful citizens. But it is equally true that Britain was saved from Protestant repression by the strong individualism of these same useful citizens: that was a large part of their usefulness.

So, we need to strengthen associational ties, even if these ties connect some of us to some others and not everyone to everyone else. There are many ways of doing this. First and foremost among them, it seems to me, are government policies that create jobs and that sponsor and support unionization on the job. For unemployment is probably the most dangerous form of dissociation, and unions are not only training grounds for democratic politics but also instruments of economic democracy. Almost as important are programs that strengthen family life, not only in its conventional but also in its unconventional versions — in any version that produces stable relationships and networks of support.

But I want to focus again on cultural associations, since these are the ones thought to be so threatening today. We need more such associations, not fewer, and more powerful and cohesive ones, too, with a wider range of responsibilities. Consider, for example, the current set of federal programs — matching grants, subsidies, and entitlements — that enable religious communities to run their own hospitals, old-age homes, schools, day care centers, and family services. Here are welfare societies within a decentralized (and still unfinished) American welfare state. Tax money is used to second charitable contributions in ways that strengthen the patterns of mutual assistance that arise spontaneously within civil society. But these patterns need to be greatly extended — since coverage at present is radically unequal — and more groups brought into the business of welfare provision: racial and ethnic as well as religious groups (and why not unions, co-ops, and corporations too?).

We need to find other programs of this kind, through which the government acts indirectly to support citizens acting directly in local communities: "charter schools" designed and run by teachers and parents; tenant self-management and co-op buyouts of public housing; experiments in workers' ownership and control of factories and companies; locally initiated building, cleanup, and crime prevention projects; and so on. Programs like these will often create or reinforce parochial communities, and they will generate conflicts for control of political space and institutional functions. But they will also increase the available space and the number of functions and, therefore, the opportunities for individual participation. And participating individuals, with a growing sense of their own effectiveness, are our best protection against the parochialism of the groups in which they participate.

Engaged men and women tend to be widely engaged — active in many different associations both locally and nationally. This is one of the most common findings of political scientists and sociologists (and one of the most surprising: Where do these people find the time?) It helps to explain why engagement works, in a pluralist society, to undercut racist or chauvinist political commitments and ideologies. The same people show up for union meetings, neighborhood projects, political canvassing, church committees, and — most reliably — in the voting booth on election day. They are, most of them, articulate, opinionated, skillful, sure of themselves, and fairly steady in their commitments. Some mysterious combination of responsibility, ambition, and meddlesomeness carries them from one meeting to another. Everyone complains (I mean that all of them complain) that there are so few of them. Is this an inevitability of social life, so that an increase in the number of associations would only stretch out the competent people, more and more thinly? I suspect that demand-side economists have a better story to tell about this "human capital." Multiply the calls for competent people, and the people will appear. Multiply the opportunities for action-in-common, and activists will emerge to seize the opportunities. Some of them, no doubt, will be narrow-minded and bigoted, but the greater their number and the more diverse their activities, the less likely it is that narrow-mindedness and bigotry will prevail.

A certain sort of stridency is a feature of what we may one day come   25
to recognize as *early* multiculturalism; it is especially evident among the newest and weakest, the least organized, groups. It is the product of a historical period when social equality outdistances economic equality. Stronger organizations, capable of collecting resources and delivering real benefits to their members, will move these groups, gradually, toward a democratically inclusive politics. The driving force will be the more active members, socialized by their activity. Remember that this has happened before, in the course of ethnic and class conflict. When groups consolidate, the center holds the periphery and turns it into a political constituency. And so union militants, say, begin on the picket line and the strike committee and move on to the school board and the city council. Religious and ethnic activists begin by defending the interests of their own community and end up in political coalitions, fighting for a place on "balanced" tickets, and talking (at least) about the common good. The cohesiveness of the group invigorates its members; the ambition and mobility of the most vigorous members liberalizes the group.

I don't mean to sound like the famous Pollyanna. These outcomes won't come about by chance; perhaps they won't come about at all. Everything is harder now — family, class, and community are less cohesive than they once were; local governments and philanthropies command fewer resources; the street world of crime and drugs is more frightening; individual men and women seem more adrift. And there is one further difficulty that we ought to welcome. In the past, organized groups have succeeded in entering the American mainstream only by leaving other groups (and the weakest of their own members) behind. And the men and women left behind commonly accepted their fate or, at least, failed to make much noise about it. Today, as I have been arguing, the level of resignation is considerably lower, and if much of the subsequent noise is incoherent and futile, it serves nonetheless to remind the rest of us that there is a larger social agenda than our own success. Multiculturalism as an ideology is not only the product of, it is also a program for, greater social *and economic* equality.

If we want the mutual reinforcements of community and individuality to work effectively for everyone, we will have to act politically to make them effective. They require certain background or framing conditions that can only be provided by state action. Group life won't rescue individual men and women from dissociation and passivity unless there is a political strategy for mobilizing, organizing, and, if necessary, subsidizing the right sort of groups. And strong-minded individuals won't diversify their commitments and extend their ambitions unless there are opportunities open to them in the larger world: jobs, offices, and responsibilities. The centrifugal forces of culture and selfhood will correct one another only if the correction is planned. It is necessary to aim at a balance of the two — which means that we can never be consistent defenders of multiculturalism or individualism; we can never be communitarians or liberals simply, but now one, now the other, as the balance requires. It seems to me that the best name for the balance itself, the political creed that defends the framework and supports the necessary forms of state action for both groups and individuals, is social democracy. If multiculturalism today brings more trouble than hope, one reason is the weakness of social democracy (in this country: left liberalism). But that is another and a longer story.

PREPARING FOR DISCUSSION

1. Walzer writes that two major factors make the American people different from just about every other people in the world. What are these two factors? Does he mention any other factors that contribute to our uniqueness?

2. To what national phenomenon does Walzer attribute the rise of what he labels "early multiculturalism" (paragraph 25)? Why is he confident that greater social organization will lead to greater social cohesion? Does he seem to believe that greater social cohesion will eliminate the need for a multicultural perspective?

3. Consider the manner in which Walzer characterizes traditional minority politics. How, according to Walzer, have the political goals and strategies of minority groups changed in recent years? How does he characterize this new kind of political activity? Do you agree with his characterization of both old and new groups? Can you think of important exceptions to his historical model of American political life among minorities?

4. Describe Walzer's sense of the relation between the multiculturalist and individualist perspectives. Of the two perspectives, which one does he believe poses a greater threat to American social stability? He is clearly presenting a third perspective as a way of resolving the problems associated with the other two perspectives. Can you imagine any problems that might emerge from this third, more "communitarian" perspective? Does Walzer address such potential problems, either directly or indirectly?

5. Walzer generally employs the calm and measured tones of reasoned argument throughout his essay. At certain points, however, he parodies the gestures and vocabulary of social commentators whose ideas about society he wishes to disprove. For example, he describes intellectuals and journalists opposed to multiculturalism as "wring[ing] their hands and [assuring] us that the country is falling apart" (paragraph 8). Why does he use such clearly exaggerated phrasing? What point is he trying to make about the critics of multiculturalism? Does he make a similar point in a similar manner about the advocates of multiculturalism?

FROM READING TO WRITING

6. Consider Walzer's statement: "Becoming an American means learning not to be quiet" (paragraph 9). What does this statement mean within the context of Walzer's essay? Write an essay in which you attempt to prove or disprove Walzer's statement with particular reference to the success or failure of various ethnic groups at entering fully into American life and reaping its economic and social rewards.

7. Walzer believes that only through associational activity can an individual learn how to think, communicate with others, and act responsibly in society. In an essay, consider the validity of this assertion in the context of your own development as a social being. What kinds of activities can you learn on your own? What kinds of activities can only be learned in the presence of others?

DINESH D'SOUZA

Illiberal Education

While Americans generally applaud the educational efforts of those who have opened up our colleges and universities to minorities, some also believe that the diversity movement on campus has gone too far. Included in this latter group is the conservative writer Dinesh D'Souza, who asserts that "the university's quest for racial equality [has produced] a conspicuous academic inequality." In the following selection he argues that in its way the current university model of diversity makes victims of minority students. By granting minorities "preferential treatment," he contends, universities foster the very bigotry and intolerance they had hoped to eliminate.

Born in Bombay, India, D'Souza immigrated to the United States with his family. Before graduating from Dartmouth College in 1983 he edited the school's right-wing student newspaper, the *Dartmouth Review*.

From 1987 to 1988 he served as senior domestic policy analyst under President Ronald Reagan. His book *Illiberal Education,* from which the following selection is excerpted, became a 1991 best-seller and brought D'Souza to national attention as one of the foremost detractors of multiculturalism and its values. He is currently John M. Olin Fellow at the American Enterprise Institute in Washington, D.C.

SELECTED PUBLICATIONS: *Illiberal Education: The Politics of Race and Sex on Campus* (1991); *The End of Racism* (1995); D'Souza's articles have appeared in *Vanity Fair, Forbes, Harper's Magazine,* the *Wall Street Journal,* and the *New York Times.*

Each fall some 13 million students, 2.5 million of them minorities, enroll in American colleges.[1] Most of these students are living away from home for the first time. Yet their apprehension is mixed with excitement and anticipation. At the university, they hope to shape themselves as whole human beings, both intellectually and morally. Brimming with idealism, they wish to prepare themselves for full and independent lives in the workplace, at home, and as citizens who are shared rulers of a democratic society. In short, what they seek is liberal education.

By the time these students graduate, very few colleges have met their need for all-round development. Instead, by precept and example, universities have taught them that "all rules are unjust" and "all preferences are principled"; that justice is simply the will of the stronger party; that standards and values are arbitrary, and the ideal of the educated person is largely a figment of bourgeois white male ideology, which should be cast aside; that individual rights are a red flag signaling social privilege, and should be subordinated to the claims of group interest; that all knowledge can be reduced to politics and should be pursued not for its own sake but for the political end of power; that convenient myths and benign lies can substitute for truth; that double standards are acceptable as long as they are enforced to the benefit of minority victims; that debates are best conducted not by rational and civil exchange of ideas, but by accusation, intimidation, and official prosecution; that the university stands for nothing in particular and has no claim to be exempt from outside pressures; and that the multiracial society cannot be based on fair rules that apply to every person, but must rather be constructed through a forced rationing of power among separatist racial groups. In short, instead of liberal education, what American students are getting is its diametrical opposite, an education in closed-mindedness and intolerance, which is to say, illiberal education.

Ironically the young blacks, Hispanics, and other certified minorities in whose name the victim's revolution is conducted are the ones least served by the American university's abandonment of liberal ideals.

Instead of treating them as individuals, colleges typically consider minorities as members of a group, important only insofar as their collective numbers satisfy the formulas of diversity. Since many of these students depend on a college degree to enhance their career opportunities, their high dropout rate brings tremendous suffering and a sense of betrayal. Even more than others, minority students arrive on campus searching for principles of personal identity and social justice; thus they are particularly disillusioned when they leave empty-handed. Moreover, most minority graduates will admit, when pressed, that if their experience in college is any indication, the prospects for race relations in the country at large are gloomy. If the university model is replicated in society at large, far from bringing ethnic harmony, it will reproduce and magnify the lurid bigotry, intolerance, and balkanization of campus life in the broader culture.

What's Wrong with Diversity

Although university leaders speak of the self-evident virtues of diversity, it is not at all obvious why it is necessary to a first-rate education. Universities such as Brandeis, Notre Dame, and Mount Holyoke, which were founded on principles of religious or gender homogeneity, still manage to provide an excellent education. Similarly, foreign institutions such as Oxford, Cambridge, Bologna, Salamanca, Paris, and Tokyo display considerable cultural singularity, yet they are regarded as among the best in the world.

The question is not whether universities should seek diversity, but   5
what kind of diversity. It seems that the primary form of diversity which universities should try to foster is diversity of mind. Such diversity would enrich academic discourse, widen its parameters, multiply its objects of inquiry, and increase the probability of obscure and unlikely terrain being investigated. Abroad one typically encounters such diversity of opinion even on basic questions such as how society should be organized. In my high school in Bombay, for example, I could identify students who considered themselves monarchists, Fabian socialists, Christian democrats, Hindu advocates of a caste-based society, agrarians, centralized planners, theocrats, liberals, and Communists. In European universities, one finds a similar smorgasbord of philosophical convictions.

By contrast, most American students seem to display striking agreement on all the basic questions of life. Indeed, they appear to regard a true difference of opinion, based upon convictions that are firmly and intensely held, as dangerously dogmatic and an offense against the social etiquette of tolerance. Far from challenging these conventional prejudices, college leaders tend to encourage their uncritical continuation. "Universities show no interest whatsoever in fostering intellectual diversity," John Bunzel, former president of San Jose State University, says bluntly. Evidence suggests that the philosophical composition of the American faculty is remarkably homogenous,[2] yet Bunzel says that universities are not concerned. "When I raise the problem with leaders in academe, their usual response is that [the imbalance] is irrelevant, or that there cannot be litmus tests for recruitment."

But universities do take very seriously the issue of *racial* underrepresentation. Here they are quite willing to consider goals, quotas, litmus tests, whatever will rectify the tabulated disproportion. "What we're hoping," said Malcolm Gillis, a senior official at Duke, "is that racial diversity will ultimately lead to intellectual diversity."

The problem begins with a deep sense of embarrassment over the small number of minorities — blacks in particular — on campuses. University officials speak of themselves as more enlightened and progressive than the general population, so they feel guilty if the proportion of minorities at their institutions is smaller than in surrounding society. Moreover, they are often pressured by politicians who control appropriations at state schools, and by student and faculty activists on campus. As a consequence, universities agree to make herculean efforts to attract as many blacks, Hispanics, and other certified minorities as possible to their institutions.

As we have seen, the number of minority applicants who would normally qualify for acceptance at selective universities is very small; therefore, in order to meet ambitious recruitment targets, affirmative action must entail fairly drastic compromises in admissions requirements. University leaders are willing to use unjust means to achieve their goal of equal representation. In one of the more radical steps in this direction, the California legislature is considering measures to *require* all state colleges to accept black, Hispanic, white, and Asian students in proportion with their level in the population, regardless of the disparity in academic preparation or qualifications among such groups.[3]

The first consequence of such misguided policies is a general mis-   10
placement of minority students throughout higher education. Thus a student whose grades and qualifications are good enough to get him into Rutgers or Penn State finds himself at Tufts or the University of Michigan, and the student who meets Tufts's or the University of Michigan's more demanding requirements finds himself at Yale or Berkeley. Many selective universities are so famished for minority students that they will accept virtually anyone of the right color who applies. In order to fulfill affirmative action objectives, university admissions officers cannot afford to pay too much attention to the probability of a student succeeding at the university.

For many black, Hispanic, and American Indian students who may have struggled hard to get through high school, the courtship of selective universities comes as a welcome surprise. They receive expenses-paid trips to various colleges, where they are chaperoned around campus, introduced to deans and senior faculty, and most of all assured that their presence is avidly desired, indeed that the university would be a poorer place if they chose to go somewhere else. These blandishments naturally enhance the expectations of minority students. These expectations are reinforced by such focused events as the minority freshmen orientation, where black, Hispanic, American Indian, and foreign students are given to understand that they are walking embodiments of the university's commitment to multiculturalism and diversity. Universities emphasize that they are making no accommodations or compromises to enroll affirmative action students; on the contrary, they insist that these students will make a special contribution that the university could not obtain elsewhere.

Their lofty hopes, however, are not realized for most affirmative action students. During the first few weeks of class, many recognize the degree to which they are academically unprepared, relative to other students. At Berkeley, for instance, admissions office data show that the average black freshman's GPA and test scores fall in the 6th percentile of scores for whites and Asians; anthropology professor Vincent Sarich remarks, "As we get more and more selective among Asians and whites, the competitive gap necessarily increases."[4] Yet once these students get to class, professors at demanding schools such as Berkeley take for granted that they know who wrote *Paradise Lost,* that they are capable of understanding Shakespearean English, that they have heard of Max Weber and the Protestant ethic, that they can solve algebraic equations, that they know something about the cell and the amoeba. Students are expected to read several hundred pages of literature, history, biology, and other subjects every week, and produce analytical papers, appropriately footnoted, on short notice.

Unfortunately the basic ingredients of what E. D. Hirsch terms "cultural literacy" are by no means uniformly transmitted in American high schools, nor are regular intellectual habits of concentration and discipline. Thus in the first part of freshman year, affirmative action students with relatively weak preparation often encounter a bewildering array of unfamiliar terms and works. Coping with them, says William Banks, professor of Afro-American Studies at Berkeley, "can be very confusing and frustrating." While they wrestle with the work load, affirmative action students also notice that their peers seem much more comfortable in this academic environment, quicker in absorbing the reading, more confident and fluent in their speech and writing. Even if affirmative action students work that much harder, they discover that it is not easy to keep pace, since the better prepared students also work very hard.

For many minority students, especially those from disadvantaged backgrounds, these problems are often complicated by a difficult personal adjustment to a new environment. It is not easy going from an inner-city high school to a college town with entirely new social routines, or settling into a dormitory where roommates have a great deal more money to spend, or cultivating the general university lifestyle that is familiar to prep schoolers and sons and daughters of alumni but alien to many minority and foreign students.

University leaders have discovered how displaced and unsettled minority freshmen can be, and typically respond by setting up counseling services and remedial education programs intended to assure blacks and Hispanics that they do belong, and that they can "catch up" with other students. Neither of these university resources is well used, however. Students who are struggling to keep up with course work hardly have time to attend additional classes in reading comprehension and algebra. If they do enroll in these programs, they run the risk of falling further behind in class. Relatively few minority students attend counseling because they correctly reject the idea that there is something wrong with them. Nor would the therapeutic assurances of freshman counselors do much to solve their academic difficulties. For many minority undergraduates, therefore, the university's quest for racial equality produces a conspicuous academic inequality.

Separate and Unequal

As at Berkeley, Michigan, and elsewhere, many minority students seek comfort and security among their peers who are in a similar situation. Thus many sign up for their campus Afro-American Society or Hispanic Students Association or ethnic theme house or fraternity, where they can share their hopes and frustrations in a relaxed and candid atmosphere, and get guidance from older students who have traveled these strange paths. The impulse to retreat into exclusive enclaves is a familiar one for minority groups who have suffered a history of persecution; they feel there is strength and safety in numbers, and tend to develop group consciousness and collective orientation partly as a protective strategy.[5]

But when minority students demand that the college recognize and subsidize separatist institutions, the administration is placed in a dilemma.[6] The deans know that to accede to these demands is problematic, given their public commitment to integration of students from different backgrounds — indeed the promise of such interaction is one of the main justifications for the goal of diversity sought through affirmative action. At the same time, university leaders realize how dislocated many minority students feel, and how little the university itself can do to help them. Further, the administration does not know how it could possibly say no to these students, and harbors vague and horrific fears of the consequences.

Virtually every administration ends by putting aside its qualms and permitting minority institutions to flourish. The logical extreme may be witnessed at California State University at Sacramento, which has announced a new plan to establish an entirely separate "college within a college" for blacks.[7] To justify this separatist subsidy, university leaders have developed a model of "pluralism," which they insist is not the same thing as integration. Since integration implies the merging of various ethnic groups into a common whole, it does not really contribute to diversity. By contrast, pluralism implies the enhancement of distinct ethnic subcultures — a black culture, Hispanic culture, American Indian culture, and a (residual) white culture — which it is hoped will interact in a harmonious and mutually enriching manner.

There is a good deal of camaraderie and social activity at the distinctive minority organizations. Most of them, especially ethnic residence halls and fraternities, help to give newly arrived minority students a sense of belonging. They do not, however, offer any solution to the dilemma facing those students who are inadequately prepared for the challenges of the curriculum. Virtually none of the minority organizations offers study programs or tutorials for affirmative action students. Indeed, some separatist institutions encourage anti-intellectualism, viewing it as an authentic black cultural trait. As researchers Signithia Fordham of Rutgers and John Ogbu of Berkeley describe it, "What appears to have emerged in some segments of the black community is a kind of cultural orientation which defines academic learning as 'acting white,' and academic success as the prerogative of white Americans."[8] Thus many minority freshmen who are struggling academically find no practical remedy in the separate culture of minority institutions.

What they do often find is a novel explanation for their difficulties. Older students tell the newcomers that they should be aware of the pervasive atmosphere of bigotry on campus. Although such racism may not be obvious at first, minority freshmen should not be deceived by appearances. Racism is vastly more subtle than in the past, and operates in various guises, some of them as elusive as baleful looks, uncorrected mental stereotypes, and the various forms of deceptively "polite" behavior.[9] In addition to looking out for such nuances, minority freshmen and sophomores are further warned not to expect much support from the university, where "overt racism" has given way to "institutional racism," evident in the disproportionately small numbers of minorities reflected on the faculty and among the deans and trustees.[10] Everywhere, forces of bigotry are said to conspire against permitting minority students the "racism-free environment" they need to succeed.

Typically, minority beneficiaries are strong supporters of preferential treatment, although their natural pride requires that its nature be disguised. They may speak more freely about it among themselves, but among white students and in the mainstream campus discussion, they understandably refrain from admitting that academic standards were adjusted to make their enrollment possible. Instead, these students assert, often under the banner of their minority organization, that the view that blacks, Hispanics, and American Indians benefit at the expense of over-represented students is itself evidence of pervasive bigotry. Consequently, in the minds of minority students, affirmative action is not a cause of their academic difficulties, but an excuse for white racism, which is the real source of their problems.

Once racism is held accountable for minority unrest, it is now up to students to find, expose, and extirpate it. Here the university leadership steps in with offers of assistance. Eager to deflect frustration and anger from the president's office, the administration seeks to convince minority activists that the real enemy is latent bigotry among their fellow students and professors, and that their energies are best invested in combating white prejudice.

Meanwhile, feminists and homosexual activists typically seek to exploit the moral momentum of the race issue. Just as blacks and Hispanics are victimized by arbitrary race discrimination, they assert, women are subjugated by gender bigotry and homosexuals are tyrannized by similar prejudice in the area of sexual orientation. Feminists, for instance, associate themselves with the black cause by insisting that marriage has always been a form of "domestic slavery." These groups promote the idea that they suffer the oppression of a common enemy. Many administrators believe in their cause and agree to link it with the campaign against white racism. Thus while women comprise between 40 and 60 percent of most university populations, they are routinely classified as vulnerable "minorities." Seeking to eradicate the various species of bigotry, the university's reeducation effort narrows to target the white, male, heterosexual element. As at Penn State, Wisconsin, and Michigan, universities set up committees and task forces to investigate the problem of latent and subtle bigotry. Minority students and faculty typically dominate these committees. Surveys are drawn up. Hearings are scheduled. In a Kafkaesque turn of events, the academic inequality of minority students is blamed on the social preferences of their white male peers.

The New Racism

Most white students do not take gender and homosexuality very seriously as political issues. Even the most sympathetic find it hard to believe that the female condition has historically been the moral equivalent of Negro slavery, nor do they equate ethnicity, which is an arbitrary characteristic, with homosexuality, which is a sexual preference. The race question, however, places white students in a very uncomfortable situation. Many of them arrive on campus with tolerant, but generally uninformed, views. They may not have known many blacks or Hispanics in the past, yet they are generally committed to equal rights regardless of race or background, and they seem open to building friendships and associations with people who they know have been wronged through history.

Since the time they applied to college, many students know that cer-   25
tain minorities have benefited from preferential treatment in admission.
It is possible that some minority classmates did not need affirmative action to get in, but it is not possible to know which ones, and the question
seems somewhat superfluous anyway. Even students who support the
concept of affirmative action in theory are discomfitted when they see
that it is now more difficult for them to get into the universities for which
they have studied hard to prepare. Moreover, even if they win admission, many have friends who they believe were denied admission to
places like Berkeley in order to make room for minority students with
weaker scores and grades.

This seems unfair to many white and Asian students, and it is little
solace to tell them that they must subordinate their individual rights to
the greater good of group equality via proportional representation.
Asian American students, unembarrassed by any traditional group advantages in American society, vehemently reject the idea that they
should suffer in order to create space for underrepresented black and
Hispanic groups who suffered no maltreatment or disadvantage at the
hands of Asians.

White and Asian students are reminded of these concerns when they
see the obvious differences in preparation and performance among various groups in the classroom. Black and Hispanic academic difficulties
confirm the suspicion that universities are admitting students based on
different sets of standards — a sort of multiple-track acceptance process.
Yet this may not be stated in public, partly because most universities continue to deny that they lower admissions requirements for select minorities, and partly because favored minorities would take offense at such
"insensitivity." Consequently, white and Asian students talk about affirmative action only in private. But since students live and study in close
quarters, it is impossible to conceal these sentiments for long, and soon
affirmative action students begin to suspect that people are talking behind closed doors about the issue that is most sensitive to them. White
and Asian students frequently attempt to prevent confrontation with
blacks and Hispanics by making passionate public proclamations of their
fidelity to the causes of civil rights, feminism, and gay rights. But for
many, a gap opens up between their personal and public views.

When minority students develop separatist cultures on the campus,
white students tend to have a mixed response. For those who are actually
prejudiced, minority self-segregation comes as a relief, because it removes blacks and Hispanics from the mainstream of campus life, and because it reinforces bigoted attitudes of racial inferiority. Many whites,
however, are merely puzzled at minority separatism, because it goes so
sharply against what they have heard from the university about integra-

tion and cultural interaction. As students at Berkeley, Michigan, and Harvard asked earlier, where is the "diversity" that is supposed to result from the interaction of racial and gender "perspectives"? What affirmative action seems to produce instead is group isolation. Eleanor Holmes Norton, former head of the Equal Employment Opportunity Commission under President Carter and now a professor at Georgetown Law School, complains that the new separatism is "exactly what we were fighting against — it is antithetical to what the civil rights movement was all about. It sets groups apart, and it prevents blacks from partaking of the larger culture." Historian Arthur Schlesinger adds that "the melting pot has yielded to the Tower of Babel," and with the loss of a common multiracial identity, "We invite the fragmentation of our culture into a quarrelsome spatter of enclaves, ghettos, and tribes."[11] Somehow the intended symphony has become a cacophony.

White students generally have no desire to set up their own racially exclusive unions, clubs, or residence halls. But, as we have repeatedly heard, they cannot help feeling that the university is practicing a double standard by supporting minority institutions to which whites may not belong and many agree with *Washington Post* columnist William Raspberry that "you cannot claim both full equality and special dispensation."[12] Separatist institutions irritate many whites on campus not because they are separate, but because in most cases they become institutional grievance factories. Many of these groups are quick to make accusations of bigotry, to the point where any disagreement with the agenda of the Afro-American Society or the Third World Alliance is automatic evidence of racism. Antiwhite rhetoric goes unchecked on campus, evoking at best an eerie silence. Thus, while it is possible to ignore minority self-segregation in principle, such indifference becomes harder when the groups serve as base camps for mounting ideological assaults against everyone else. "Pluralism" becomes a framework for racial browbeating and intimidation.

When they discover resentment among students over preferential treatment and minority separatism, university administrators conclude that they have discovered the latent bigotry for which they have been searching. Consequently, many universities institute "sensitivity" training programs, such as Harvard's notorious AWARE week, to cure white students of their prejudice. As at Michigan, the University of Connecticut, Stanford, and Emory, some schools go so far as to outlaw racially or sexually "stigmatizing" remarks — even "misdirected laughter" and "exclusion from conversation" — which are said to make learning for minorities impossible. On virtually every campus, there is a de facto taboo against free discussion of affirmative action or minority self-segregation, and efforts to open such a discussion are considered presumptively racist. Thus measures taken to enhance diversity have instead created a new regime of intellectual conformity.[13]

Notes

1. In 1988, there were 10.3 million whites, 1.1 million blacks, 680,000 Hispanics, 497,000 Asian Americans, 93,000 American Indians, and 361,000 foreign students enrolled in American colleges. See "1988 College Enrollment," U.S. Department of Education, table reprinted in *Chronicle of Higher Education,* April 11, 1990, p. A-1.

2. A recent Carnegie Foundation report shows that the number of philosophically liberal professors is more than double the number of conservative professors. In humanities departments, where presumably ideology is most likely to manifest itself in the classroom, the ratio is almost four to one. For faculty under the age of forty, the ratio is almost three to one, suggesting that the imbalance is likely to become greater in the future. See *The Condition of the Professoriate,* Carnegie Foundation, Washington, D.C., 1989, p. 143.

3. See Assembly Bill 462, introduced by member Tom Hayden (February 2, 1989) and Assembly Bill 3993, introduced by member Willie Brown (March 2, 1990) in the California legislature, 1989–90 session. Copies obtained from office of Assemblyman Hayden. Although the wording of these bills is somewhat ambiguous, some critics believe that their effect will be to require not only admission, but also passing grades, promotion, and graduation, at the same rate for all racial groups. See John Bunzel, "Inequitable Equality on Campus," *Wall Street Journal,* July 25, 1990; Abigail Thernstrom, "On the Scarcity of Black Professors," *Commentary,* July 1990.

4. See Bunzel, "Inequitable Equality on Campus."

5. The long history of segregation and discrimination has produced a "heightened sense of group consciousness" among blacks, and a "stronger orientation toward collective values and behavior" than exists among whites. See Gerald Jaynes and Robin Williams, eds., *A Common Destiny: Blacks and American Society.* National Academy Press, Washington, D.C., 1989, p. 13.

6. For example, Cornell president Frank Rhodes remarks, "We face an unresolved conflict between the natural impulse toward proud, separate racial and ethnic identity on the one hand and the genuine desire, on the other, for meaningful integration that transcends differences of background." See Frances Dinkelspiel, "In Rift at Cornell, Racial Issues of the 60s Remain," *New York Times,* May 3, 1989.

7. California State University officials, led by faculty member Otis Scott, are planning to establish Cooper-Woodson College as a special adjunct to the university. "Is it separatist?" Scott asked. "No more than the separation that already exists between [black] students and the institution. We are committed to creating a comprehensive support network for African-American students." Cited by Karen O'Hara, "Sacramento State May Try Black University Structure," *Black Issues in Higher Education,* May 10, 1990, p. 13.

8. Seth Mydans, "Black Identity vs. Success and Seeming White," *New York Times,* April 25, 1990, p. B-9. Although the study by Fordham and Ogbu focused on black high schools, Fordham said in an interview that her findings also apply to black culture on college campuses.

9. This view even claims some scholarly support. One study concluded that "research on nonverbal behavior shows that white college students often sit further away, use a less friendly voice tone, make less eye contact, and more speech errors, and terminate the interview faster when interacting with a black rather than a white." See Thomas Pettigrew, "New Patterns of Racism: The Different Worlds of 1984 and 1964," *Rutgers Law Review* 37, 1985, pp. 673, 689.

10. At the University of Virginia, for instance, minority students demanded to know why a larger proportion of blacks than whites were charged with honor code violations, and many called for the abolition of the allegedly bigoted and discriminatory honor system. See Darryl Brown, "Racism and Race Relations in the University," *University of Virginia Law Review* 76, 1989, pp. 295, 334. See also Editorial, "Dishonorable Schoolboys," *Washington Times,* April 9, 1990.

11. Arthur Schlesinger, "When Ethnic Studies Are Un-American," *Wall Street Journal*, April 23, 1990.

12. William Raspberry, "Why the Racial Slogans?" *Washington Post*, September 20, 1989.

13. A vivid recent example of this is the case of Linda Chavez, former staff director of the U.S. Civil Rights Commission, who was invited to be the commencement speaker at the University of Northern Colorado in May 1990. When a campus Hispanic group and several other students and faculty protested, however, President Robert Dickeson rescinded Chavez's invitation. "The intent of the university in inviting Linda Chavez was to be sensitive to cultural diversity and the committee making the decision intended to communicate the importance of cultural pluralism," the university explained in a press release. "It is clear that the decision was both uninformed and gave the appearance of being grossly insensitive." Although Chavez's role as a prominent Hispanic woman apparently accounted for her selection, the problem turned out to be her conservative views, in particular, her opposition to preferential treatment and bilingualism. As Chavez herself observed in the *Chronicle of Higher Education*, "The problem with the cultural pluralist model is that not all blacks, Hispanics or women think alike." Diversity, Chavez charged, was invoked in this instance "to keep out certain ideas and certain people, to foreclose debate, to substitute ideological catechism for the free inquiry usually associated with a university." See "The Importance of Cultural Pluralism," press release by University of Northern Colorado, reprinted in *Wall Street Journal*, May 9, 1990; Linda Chavez, "The Real Aim of the Promoters of Cultural Diversity Is to Exclude Certain People and to Foreclose Debate," *Chronicle of Higher Education*, July 18, 1990, p. B-1; Carol Innerst, "Chavez Encounters Big Chill," *Washington Times*, May 4, 1990, p. 1.

PREPARING FOR DISCUSSION

1. D'Souza holds that most American college students seek a "liberal education." How does he define "liberal education" and what special use of the word *liberal* is being made here? Why does D'Souza feel that "liberal education" is threatened by recent ideas about diversity?

2. D'Souza argues that the push for greater diversity at American colleges and universities ultimately hinders minorities instead of helping them to achieve their education and career goals. On what grounds does he make this argument? According to D'Souza, at what point in the higher educational process do the efforts designed to help minorities begin to work counterproductively?

3. D'Souza suggests that affirmative action programs were originally designed to promote racial diversity at institutions of higher learning. Can you think of other reasons that these programs might have been designed? Could these programs be less a response to the call for diversity than to the persistence of racial inequality?

4. D'Souza suggests that it is the responsibility of colleges and universities to oversee not only their students' intellectual but their moral development as well. Do you agree? What kind of ethical values do you think he has in mind? How much are such values liable to change from college to college?

5. In the second paragraph D'Souza enumerates the "lessons" taught recent college students either "by precept or example." He writes that college students commonly learn "that debates are best conducted not by rational and civil exchange of ideas, but by accusation, intimidation, and official prosecution." Do

you think students are taught these techniques in these terms? Would faculty and administrators describe their methods of debate in these terms? To the extent that such "precepts" can be said to be taught at all in colleges and universities, why had D'Souza articulated them in the way he has?

FROM READING TO WRITING

6. According to D'Souza, most white students "arrive on campus with tolerant, but generally uninformed views. . . . [T]hey are generally committed to equal rights regardless of race or background." Do you agree? Write an essay in which you explore your views on race before and after you arrived at college. If your views have changed, to what experiences do you attribute that change? If not, what in your experience at college has reinforced your original views?

7. D'Souza worries that administrators frequently create a college environment that encourages what he calls "minority self-segregation." Have you witnessed this phenomenon at your college or university? Write an essay in which you consider the causes of this kind of separatism, to the extent that it exists at all, at your school. If you have not witnessed this phenomenon among the minority groups at school, why do you think it has not occurred?

CORNEL WEST

Diverse New World

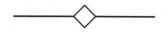

Even among intellectuals who embrace "multiculturalism" as a fitting response to America's ethnic diversity, there remains debate over the word's definition. While the proponents of multicultural education concur that the predominance of Eurocentric history has led to a deeply skewed account of our nation's past and present, some, such as Afrocentrist Molefi Kete Asante, would virtually discount the European perspective altogether. Scholars such as Cornel West, on the other hand, insist on the need for the continual interplay among many cultural perspectives. Without such interplay, West implies, we cannot arrive at an accurate picture of American society.

During the 1990s West has made his presence known as an inspiring speaker in lecture halls, places of worship, and political rallies as well as on such television programs as *The MacNeil/Lehrer Newshour* and William F. Buckley's *Firing Line*. As a scholar and author, he has fought persistently for the continuing relevance of Christianity and Marxism as means for battling white racism and oppression. Just as persistently, he has fought against what he calls "the closing of ranks" among African Americans who place racial allegiances before moral principles. A professor of religion at Princeton and the director of that university's Afro-American Studies Program for several years, West now teaches at Harvard. The selection that follows was originally delivered as a talk at the Socialist Scholars Conference.

SELECTED PUBLICATIONS: *Prophetic Fragments* (1988); *The American Evasion of Philosophy: A Genealogy of Pragmatism* (1990); *Breaking Bread: Insurgent Black Intellectual Life* (with bell hooks) (1991); *The Ethical Dimensions of Marxist Thought* (1991); *Race Matters* (1993); *Keeping Faith: Philosophy and Race in America* (1993).

We are grappling with the repercussions and implications of what it means to live now forty-six years after the end of the age of Europe. This age began in 1492, with the encounter between Europeans and those who were in the new world, with the massive expulsion of Jews in Spain, and with the publication of the first Indo-European grammar books in 1492. It continued through World War II, the concentration camps, and the shaking of the then fragile European maritime empires. Forty-six years later is not a long time for that kind of fundamental glacier shift in civilizations that once dominated the world.

Analyzing multiculturalism from a contemporary philosophical perspective, and looking at its roots especially among the professional managerial strata, in museums, in galleries, in universities and so forth, it is an attempt to come to terms with how we think of universality when it has been used as a smokescreen for a particular group. How do we preserve notions of universality given the fact that various other particularities — traditions, heritages, communities, voices and what have you — are moving closer to the center of the historical stage, pushing off those few voices which had served as the centering voices between 1492 and 1945?

The United States has become the land of hybridity, heterogeneity, and ambiguity. It lacks the ability to generate national identity and has an inferiority complex vis-à-vis Europe, and the U.S. must deal with indigenous people's culture, including the scars and the dead bodies left from its history. Expansion across the American continent trampled the culture and heritages of degraded, hated, haunted, despised African peoples, upon whose backs would constitute one fundamental pillar for the building of the United States and for the larger industrializing processes in Europe.

Within the multiculturalist debate, leading Afrocentric and Africanist thinkers Leonard Jeffries and Molefi Asante articulate a critical perspective that says they are tired of the degradation of things African. On this particular point, they're absolutely right. However, they don't have a subtle enough sense of history, so they can't recognize ambiguous legacies of traditions and civilizations. They refuse to recognize the thoroughly hybrid culture of almost every culture we have ever discovered. In the case of Jeffries, this lack of subtlety slides down an ugly xenophobic slope — a mirror image of the Eurocentric racism he condemns.

We need to see history as in part the cross-fertilization of a variety of different cultures, usually under conditions of hierarchy. That's thoroughly so for the U.S. For example, jazz is the great symbol of American culture, but there's no jazz without European instruments or African polyrhythms. To talk about hybrid culture means you give up all quest for pure traditions and pristine heritages.

Yes, black folk must come up with means of affirming black humanity. Don't just read Voltaire's great essays on the light of reason — read the "Peoples of America," in which he compares indigenous peoples and Africans to dogs and cattle. Don't read just Kant's *Critique of Pure Reason,* read the moments in *The Observations of the Sublime,* in which he refers to Negroes as inherently stupid. It's not a trashing of Kant. It's a situating of Kant within eighteenth-century Germany, at a time of rampant xenophobia, along with tremendous breakthroughs in other spheres. An effective multicultural critique recognizes both the crimes against humanity and the contributions to humanity from the particular cultures in Europe.

We have to demystify this notion of Europe and Eurocentrism. Europe has always been multicultural. Shakespeare borrowed from Italian narratives and pre-European narratives. When we think of multiculturalism, we're so deeply shaped by the American discourse of positively valued whiteness and negatively valued blackness, that somehow it's only when black and white folk interact that real multiculturalism's going on. The gradation of hybridity and heterogeneity is not the same between the Italians and the British, and the West Africans and the British. But "Europe" is an ideological construct. It doesn't exist other than in the minds of elites who tried to constitute a homogeneous tradition that could bring together heterogeneous populations — that's all it is.

In looking at history with a subtle historical sense, I also have in mind the fundamental question: What do we have in common? By history, I mean the human responses to a variety of different processes over time and space — various social structures that all human beings must respond to. In responding to these circumstances, the problem has been that most of us function by a kind of self-referential altruism, in which we're altruistic to those nearest to us, and those more distant, we tend to view as pictures rather than human beings. Yet, as historical beings, as fallen and fallible historical beings, we do have a common humanity. We must not forget our long historical backdrop. The present is history — that continues to inform and shape and mold our perceptions and orientations.

On the political level, multiculturalism has much to do with our present-day racial polarization — which is in many ways gender polarization, especially given the vicious violence against women, and sexual-orientation polarization with increased attacks on gays and lesbians. These conflicts, mediated or not mediated, reverberate within bureaucratic structures, and within the larger society.

Certain varieties of multiculturalism do have a politics. Afrocentrism   10
is an academic instance of a longer black nationalist tradition, and it does have a politics and a history. Black nationalism is not monolithic — there's a variety of different versions of black nationalism. In so many slices of the black community, with the escalation of the discourse of whiteness and blackness, racism escalates, both in terms of the life of the mind as well as in practices. We're getting a mentality of closing of ranks. This has happened many, many times in the black community; and it takes a nationalist form in terms of its politics. Black nationalism politics is something that has to be called for what it is, understood symptomatically, and criticized openly. It's a question of, if you're really interested in black freedom, I am too — will your black nationalist view in education, will your black nationalist view in politics deliver the black freedom that you and I are interested in? You're upset with racism in Western scholarship. I am too, and some white folk are too.

As democratic socialists, we have to look at society in a way that cuts across race, gender, region, and nation. For most people in the world, their backs are against the wall. When your back is against the wall, you're looking for weaponry: intellectual and existential weaponry to sustain yourself and your self-confidence and your self-affirmation in conditions that seemingly undermine your sense of possibility; political weaponry to organize, mobilize, to bring your power to bear on the status quo.

If you're Afro-American and you're a victim of the rule of capital, and a European Jewish figure who was born in the Catholic Rhineland and grew up as a Lutheran, by the name of Karl Marx, provides certain analytical tools, then you go there. You can't find too many insightful formulations in Marx about what it is to be black; you don't go to Marx for that. You go to Marx to keep track of the rule of capital, interlocking elites, political, banking, financial, that's one crucial source of your weaponry. You don't care where you get it from, you just want to get people off of your back.

If you want to know what it means to be black, to be African in Western civilization and to deal with issues of identity, with bombardment of degrading images, you go to the blues, you go to literature, you go to Du Bois's analysis of race, you go to Anna Julia Cooper's analysis of race.[1] For what it means to be politically marginalized, you go to a particular tradition that deals with that.

---

[1] *W.E.B. Du Bois* (1868–1963): Historian who studied the lives of blacks in America and leading opponent of racial discrimination. *Anna Julia Cooper* (1858–1964): Educator and civil rights leader who researched slavery.

To gain a universal perspective, the left must have a moral focus on suffering. Once you lose that focus, then you're presupposing a certain level of luxury that is all too common among the professional managerial strata in their debates. Their debates begin to focus on who's going to get what slice of what bureaucratic turf for their bid for the mainstream, for middle-class status. Now, that for me is one slice of the struggle, but it's just a slice. The center of the struggle is a deeper intellectual and political set of issues: understanding the larger historical scope, the post-European age, the struggles of Third World persons as they attempt to deal with their identity, their sense of economic and political victimization. We need to not only understand but also to assist people trying to forge some kinds of more democratic regimes, which is so thoroughly difficult.

Let's not package the debate in static categories that predetermine the conclusion that reinforces polarization — that's the worst thing that could happen. Polarization paralyzes all of us — and we go on our middle-class ways, and the folk we're concerned about continue to go down the drain.

The political challenge is to articulate universality in a way that is not a mere smokescreen for someone else's particularity. We must preserve the possibility of universal connection. That's the fundamental challenge. Let's dig deep enough within our heritage to make that connection to others.

We're not naive, we know that argument and critical exchange are not the major means by which social change takes place in the world. But we recognize it has to have a role, has to have a function. Therefore, we will trash older notions of objectivity, and not act as if one group or community or one nation has a god's-eye view of the world. Instead we will utilize forms of intersubjectivity that facilitate critical exchange even as we recognize that none of us is free of presuppositions and prejudgments. We will put our arguments on the table and allow them to be interrogated and contested. The quest for knowledge without presuppositions, the quest for certainty, the quest for dogmatism and orthodoxy and rigidity is over.

PREPARING FOR DISCUSSION

1. At the beginning of the selection, West contends that the age of Europe and Eurocentrism has been over for almost fifty years. With what events does West identify the beginning and the end of this age? Why do you think that he chooses these particular events as starting and ending points? What evidence does he provide that the age has ended?

2. Despite his high hopes for a multiculturalist age, West is quick to criticize the Afrocentrist perspective of Molefi Kete Asante and others. Why does he believe that Asante's idea of culture needs to be revised? How does he propose to

revise it? After rereading the Asante selection, consider how Asante might respond to West's criticism.

3. In paragraph 7, West calls "Europe" an ideological construct. By this he means that "Europe" was an idea created by a particularly powerful group that wished to establish the cultural dominance of their nations over all others. To what degree does West's definition of Europe deny the geographical reality of what we call "Europe"? Do you suppose he means to suggest that the countries of France, Germany, and Italy have no more in common than do the countries of China, Ecuador, and Saudi Arabia?

4. Early in the selection, West suggests that the idea of universality was a myth or "smokescreen" fostered by Eurocentric thinkers. Later he invites us "to preserve the possibility of [universality]." Given what West has already said about the old universality, why does he believe that a new universality founded upon multiculturalist principles would be any less of a smokescreen?

5. Throughout the selection West adopts the pronoun "we" while addressing his audience. Because the selection was originally delivered as a talk at the Socialist Scholars Conference, we may assume that the first audience was primarily composed of the democratic socialists to whom West refers in paragraph 11. Does this information change your attitude toward this piece? Why do you think that West uses this pronoun? To what degree did you consider yourself to be included in the "we" as you read the piece for a first time?

FROM READING TO WRITING

6. West cites American jazz as one particularly impressive product of what he calls "the cross-fertilization of a variety of different cultures" (paragraph 5) that has occurred throughout world history. In an essay, explore the cross-cultural development of another such product. Which cultures participated in its evolution? How has it continued to evolve through the influence of other cultures?

7. In paragraph 8, West asks, "What do we have in common?" How does he answer this question, if at all? Write an essay in which you attempt to answer this question in light of the selection. To what extent do you believe in our "common humanity"? What examples can you provide for its existence or nonexistence?

THOMAS SOWELL

A World View of Cultural Diversity

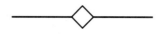

We end this chapter with a global look at cultural diversity, its advantages and its problems. Multiculturalists generally cite pride in one's ethnicity as an important source of self-esteem among minorities. Yet critics warn that the practice of estimating too highly the values of one's own culture, while not considering what other cultures have to offer, can lead only to stagnation. Thinking globally, Thomas Sowell argues not only that some features of one culture may simply be "better" than the analogous features of another culture, but also that without access to another culture's ideas and innovations a culture will not advance. His analysis thus poses interesting problems for self-segregating minority cultures within America.

Sowell, a free-market economist, is considered by many to be the leading black scholar among conservatives. For more than three decades he has voiced his strong opposition to virtually any legislation or court decision directed at eliminating racial discrimination on the controversial grounds that a minority group's economic success is only marginally impeded by racist practices. He likewise rejects any position that paints African Americans as powerless victims who must depend on government help for social and economic advancement. A graduate of Harvard, Columbia, and the University of Chicago, Sowell taught economics at UCLA before joining the Hoover Institute, a conservative think-tank at Stanford, as a senior fellow in 1980. This selection originally appeared in *Society* in 1991.

SELECTED PUBLICATIONS: *Black Education: Myths and Tragedies* (1972); *Affirmative Action: Was It Necessary in Academia?* (1975); *Race and Economics* (1975); *Markets and Minorities* (1981); *The Economics and Politics of Race: An International Perspective* (1983); *Civil Rights: Rhetoric or Reality* (1984); *A Conflict of Visions: Ideological Origins of Political Struggles* (1987); *Race and Culture: A World View* (1994).

Diversity has become one of the most often used words of our time — and a word almost never defined. Diversity is invoked in discussions of everything from employment policy to curriculum reform and from entertainment to politics. Nor is the word merely a description of the long-known fact that the American population is made up of people from many countries, many races, and many cultural backgrounds. All this was well known long before the word "diversity" became an insistent part of our vocabulary, an invocation, an imperative, or a bludgeon in ideological conflicts.

The very motto of the country, *E Pluribus Unum*, recognizes the diversity of the American people. For generations, this diversity has been celebrated, whether in comedies like *Abie's Irish Rose* (the famous play featuring a Jewish boy and an Irish girl) or in patriotic speeches on the Fourth of July. Yet one senses something very different in today's crusades for "diversity" — certainly not a patriotic celebration of America and often a sweeping criticism of the United States, or even a condemnation of Western civilization as a whole.

At the very least, we need to separate the issue of the general importance of cultural diversity — not only in the United States but in the world at large — from the more specific, more parochial, and more ideological agendas that have become associated with this word in recent years. I would like to talk about the worldwide importance of cultural diversity over centuries of human history before returning to the narrower issues of our time.

The entire history of the human race, the rise of man from the caves, has been marked by transfers of cultural advances from one group to another and from one civilization to another. Paper and printing, for example, are today vital parts of Western civilization, but they originated in China centuries before they made their way to Europe. So did the magnetic compass, which made possible the great ages of exploration that put the Western hemisphere in touch with the rest of mankind. Mathematical concepts likewise migrated from one culture to another: trigonometry from ancient Egypt, and the whole numbering system now used throughout the world originated among the Hindus of India, though Europeans called this system Arabic numerals because it was the Arabs who were the intermediaries through which these numbers reached medieval Europe. Indeed, much of the philosophy of ancient Greece first reached Western Europe in Arabic translations, which were then retranslated into Latin or into the vernacular languages of the West Europeans.

Much that became part of the culture of Western civilization originated outside that civilization, often in the Middle East or Asia. The game of chess came from India, gunpowder from China, and various mathematical concepts from the Islamic world, for example. The conquest of Spain by Moslems in the eighth century A.D. made Spain a center for the diffusion into Western Europe of the more advanced knowledge of the Mediterranean world and of the Orient in astronomy, medicine, optics, and geometry.

The later rise of Western Europe to world preeminence in science and technology built upon these foundations, and then the science and technology of European civilization began to spread around the world, not only to European offshoot societies such as the United States or

Australia, but also to non-European cultures, of which Japan is perhaps the most striking example.

The historic sharing of cultural advances, until they became the common inheritance of the human race, implied much more than cultural diversity. It implied that some cultural features were not only different from others but better than others. The very fact that people — all people, whether Europeans, Africans, Asians, or others — have repeatedly chosen to abandon some feature of their own culture in order to replace it with something from another culture implies that the replacement served their purposes more effectively. Arabic numerals are not simply different from Roman numerals; they are better than Roman numerals. This is shown by their replacing Roman numerals in many countries whose own cultures derived from Rome, as well as in other countries whose respective numbering systems were likewise superseded by so-called Arabic numerals.

It is virtually inconceivable today that the distances in astronomy or the complexities of higher mathematics should be expressed in Roman numerals. Merely to express the year of the declaration of American independence as MDCCLXXVI requires more than twice as many Roman numerals as Arabic numerals. Moreover, Roman numerals offer more opportunities for errors, as the same digit may be either added or subtracted, depending on its place in the sequence. Roman numerals are good for numbering kings or Super Bowls, but they cannot match the efficiency of Arabic numerals in most mathematical operations — and that is, after all, why we have numbers at all. Cultural features do not exist merely as badges of identity to which we have some emotional attachment. They exist to meet the necessities and to forward the purposes of human life. When they are surpassed by features of other cultures, they tend to fall by the wayside or to survive only as marginal curiosities, like Roman numerals today.

Not only concepts, information, products, and technologies transfer from one culture to another. The natural produce of the earth does the same. Malaysia is the world's leading grower of rubber trees — but those trees are indigenous to Brazil. Most of the rice grown in Africa today originated in Asia, and its tobacco originated in the Western hemisphere. Even a great wheat-exporting nation like Argentina once imported wheat, which was not an indigenous crop to that country. Cultural diversity, viewed internationally and historically, is not a static picture of differentness but a dynamic picture of competition in which what serves human purposes more effectively survives while what does not tends to decline or disappear.

Manuscript scrolls once preserved the precious records, knowledge, and thought of European or Middle Eastern cultures. But once paper and printing from China became known in these cultures, books were clearly far faster and cheaper to produce and drove scrolls virtually into extinction. Books were not simply different from scrolls; they were better than scrolls. The point that some cultural features are better than others must be insisted on today because so many among the intelligentsia either evade or deny this plain reality. The intelligentsia often use words like "perceptions" and "values" as they argue in effect that it is all a matter of how you choose to look at it.

They may have a point in such things as music, art, and literature from different cultures, but there are many human purposes common to peoples of all cultures. They want to live rather than die, for example. When Europeans first ventured into the arid interior of Australia, they often died of thirst or hunger in a land where the Australian aborigines had no trouble finding food or water. Within that particular setting, at least, the aboriginal culture enabled people to do what both aborigines and Europeans wanted to do — survive. A given culture may not be superior for all things in all settings, much less remain superior over time, but particular cultural features may nevertheless be clearly better for some purposes — not just different.

Why is there any such argument in the first place? Perhaps it is because we are still living in the long, grim shadow of the Nazi Holocaust and are, therefore, understandably reluctant to label anything or anyone "superior" or "inferior." But we do not need to. We need only recognize that particular products, skills, technologies, agricultural crops, or intellectual concepts accomplish particular purposes better than their alternatives. It is not necessary to rank one whole culture over another in all things, much less to claim that they remain in that same ranking throughout history. They do not.

Clearly, cultural leadership in various fields has changed hands many times. China was far in advance of any country in Europe in a large number of fields for at least a thousand years and, as late as the sixteenth century, had the highest standard of living in the world. Equally clearly, China today is one of the poorer nations of the world and is having great difficulty trying to catch up to the technological level of Japan and the West, with no real hope of regaining its former world preeminence in the foreseeable future.

Similar rises and falls of nations and empires have been common over long stretches of human history — for example, the rise and fall of the Roman Empire, the "golden age" of medieval Spain and its decline to the level of one of the poorest nations in Europe today, the centuries-long triumphs of the Ottoman Empire intellectually as well as on the battlefields of Europe and the Middle East, and then its long decline to become known as "the sick man of Europe." Yet, while cultural leadership has changed hands many times, that leadership has been real at given times, and much of what was achieved in the process has contributed enormously to our well-being and opportunities today. Cultural competition is not a zero-sum game. It is what advances the human race.

If nations and civilizations differ in their effectiveness in different   15
fields of endeavor, so do social groups. Here is especially strong resistance to accepting the reality of different levels and kinds of skills, interests, habits, and orientations among different groups of people. One academic writer, for example, said that nineteenth-century Jewish immigrants to the United States were fortunate to arrive just as the garment industry in New York began to develop. I could not help thinking that Hank Aaron was similarly fortunate that he often came to bat just as a home run was due to be hit. It might be possible to believe that these Jewish immigrants just happened to be in the right place at the right time if you restricted yourself to their history in the United States. But, again taking a world view, we find Jews prominent, often predominant, and usually prospering, in the apparel industry in medieval Spain, in the Ottoman Empire, in the Russian Empire, in Argentina, in Australia, and in Brazil. How surprised should we be to find them predominant in the same industry in America?

Other groups have excelled in other special occupations and industries. Indeed, virtually every group excels at something. Germans, for example, have been prominent as pioneers in the piano industry. American piano brands like Steinway and Knabe, not to mention the Wurlitzer organ, are signs of the long prominence of Germans in this industry, where they produced the first pianos in Colonial America. Germans also pioneered in piano-building in Czarist Russia, Australia, France, and England. Chinese immigrants have, at one period of history or another, run more than half the grocery stores in Kingston, Jamaica, and Panama City and conducted more than half of all retail trade in Malaysia, the Philippines, Vietnam, and Cambodia. Other groups have dominated the retail trade in other parts of the world — the Gujaratis from India in East Africa and in Figi or the Lebanese in parts of West Africa, for example.

Nothing has been more common than for particular groups — often a minority — to dominate particular occupations or industries. Seldom do they have any ability to keep out others and certainly not to keep out the majority population. They are simply better at the particular skills required in that occupation or industry. Sometimes we can see why. When Italians have made wine in Italy for centuries, it is hardly surprising that they should become prominent among winemakers in Argentina and in California's Napa Valley. Similarly, when Germans in Germany have been for centuries renowned for their beermaking, how surprised should we be that in Argentina they became as prominent among brewers as Italians among winemakers? How surprised should we be that beermaking in the United States arose where there were concentrations of German immigrants in Milwaukee and St. Louis, for example? Or that the leading beer producers to this day have German names like Anheuser-Busch or Coors, among many other German names?

Just as cultural leadership in a particular field is not permanent for nations or civilizations, neither is it permanent for given racial, ethnic, or religious groups. By the time the Jews were expelled from Spain in 1492, Europe had overtaken the Islamic world in medical science, so that Jewish physicians who sought refuge in the Ottoman Empire found themselves in great demand in that Moslem country. By the early sixteenth century, the sultan of the Ottoman Empire had on his palace medical staff forty-two Jewish physicians and twenty-one Moslem physicians.

With the passage of time, however, the source of the Jews' advantage — their knowledge of Western medicine — eroded as successive generations of Ottoman Jews lost contact with the West and its further progress. Christian minorities within the Ottoman Empire began to replace the Jews, not only in medicine but also in international trade and even in the theater, once dominated by Jews. The difference was that these Christian minorities — notably Greeks and Armenians — maintained their ties in Christian Europe and often sent their sons there to be educated. It was not race or ethnicity as such that was crucial but maintaining contacts with the ongoing progress of Western civilization. By contrast, the Ottoman Jews became a declining people in a declining empire. Many, if not most, were Sephardic Jews from Spain, once the elite of world Jewry. But by the time the state of Israel was formed in the twentieth century, those Sephardic Jews who had settled for centuries in the Islamic world now lagged painfully behind the Ashkenazic Jews of the Western world — notably in income and education. To get some idea what a historic reversal that has been in the relative positions of Sephardic Jews and Ashkenazic Jews, one need only note that Sephardic Jews in colonial America sometimes disinherited their own children for marrying Ashkenazic Jews.

Why do some groups, subgroups, nations, or whole civilizations   20
excel in some particular fields rather than others? All too often, the answer to this question must be: Nobody really knows. It is an unanswered question largely because it is an unasked question. There is an uphill struggle merely to get acceptance of the fact that large differences exist among peoples, not just in specific skills in the narrow sense (computer science, basketball, or brewing beer) but more fundamentally in different interests, orientations, and values that determine which particular skills they seek to develop and with what degree of success. Merely to suggest that these internal cultural factors play a significant role in various economic, educational, or social outcomes is to invite charges of "blaming the victim." It is much more widely acceptable to blame surrounding social conditions or institutional policies.

But if we look at cultural diversity internationally and historically, there is a more basic question of whether blame is the real issue. Surely, no human being should be blamed for the way his culture evolved for centuries before he was born. Blame has nothing to do with it. Another explanation that has had varying amounts of acceptance at different times and places is the biological or genetic theory of differences among peoples. I have argued against this theory in many places but will not take the time to go into these lengthy arguments here. A world view of cultural differences over the centuries undermines the genetic theory as well. Europeans and Chinese, for example, are clearly genetically different. Equally clearly, China was a more advanced civilization than Europe in many ways, scientific, technological, and organizational, for at least a thousand years. Yet over the past few centuries, Europe has moved ahead of China in many of these same ways. If those cultural differences were due to genes, how could these two races have changed positions so radically from one epoch in history to another?

All explanations of differences between groups can be broken down into heredity and environment. Yet a world view of the history of cultural diversity seems, on the surface at least, to deny both. One reason for this is that we have thought of environment too narrowly, as the immediate surrounding circumstances or differing institutional policies toward different groups. Environment in that narrow sense may explain some group differences, but the histories of many groups completely contradict that particular version of environment as an explanation. Let us take just two examples out of many that are available.

Jewish immigrants from Eastern Europe and Italian immigrants from southern Italy began arriving in the United States in large numbers at about the same time in the late nineteenth century, and their large-scale immigration also ended at the same time, when restrictive immigration laws were passed in the 1920s. The two groups arrived here in virtually the same economic condition — namely, destitute. They often lived in the same neighborhoods and their children attended the same schools, sitting side by side in the same classrooms. Their environments, in the narrow sense in which the term is commonly used, were virtually identical. Yet their social histories in the United States have been very different.

Over the generations, both groups rose, but they rose at different rates, through different means, and in a very different mixture of occupations and industries. Even wealthy Jews and wealthy Italians tended to become rich in different sectors of the economy. The California wine industry, for example, is full of Italian names like Mondavi, Gallo, and Rossi, but the only prominent Jewish winemaker, Manischewitz, makes an entirely different kind of wine, and no one would compare Jewish winemakers with Italian winemakers in the United States. When we look at Jews and Italians in the very different environmental setting of Argentina, we see the same general pattern of differences between them. The same is true if we look at the differences between Jews and Italians in Australia, or Canada, or Western Europe.

Jews are not Italians and Italians are not Jews. Anyone familiar with their very different histories over many centuries should not be surprised. Their fate in America was not determined solely by their surrounding social conditions in America or by how they were treated by American society. They were different before they got on the boats to cross the ocean, and those differences crossed the ocean with them.

We can take it a step further. Even Ashkenazic Jews, those originating in Eastern Europe, have had significantly different economic and social histories from those originating in Germanic Central Europe, including Austria as well as Germany itself. These differences have persisted among their descendants not only in New York and Chicago but as far away as Melbourne and Sydney. In Australia, Jews from Eastern Europe have tended to cluster in and around Melbourne, while Germanic Jews have settled in and around Sydney. They even have a saying among themselves that Melbourne is a cold city with warm Jews while Sydney is a warm city with cold Jews.

A second and very different example of persistent cultural differences involves immigrants from Japan. As everyone knows, many Japanese-Americans were interned during the Second World War. What is less well known is that there is and has been an even larger Japanese population in Brazil than in the United States. These Japanese, incidentally, own approximately three-quarters as much land in Brazil as there is in Japan. (The Japanese almost certainly own more agricultural land in Brazil than in Japan.) In any event, very few Japanese in Brazil were interned during the Second World War. Moreover, the Japanese in Brazil were never subjected to the discrimination suffered by Japanese-Americans in the decades before the Second World War.

Yet, during the war, Japanese-Americans overwhelmingly remained loyal to the United States and Japanese-American soldiers won more than their share of medals in combat. But in Brazil, the Japanese were overwhelmingly and even fanatically loyal to Japan. You cannot explain the difference by anything in the environment of the United States or the environment of Brazil. But if you know something about the history of those Japanese who settled in these two countries, you know that they were culturally different in Japan before they ever got on the boats to take them across the Pacific Ocean and they were still different decades later. These two groups of immigrants left Japan during very different periods in the cultural evolution of Japan itself. A modern Japanese scholar has said: "If you want to see Japan of the Meiji era, go to the United States. If you want to see Japan of the Taisho era, go to Brazil." The Meiji era was a more cosmopolitan, pro-American era; the Taisho era was one of fanatical Japanese nationalism.

If the narrow concept of environment fails to explain many profound differences between groups and subgroups; it likewise fails to explain many very large differences in the economic and social performances of nations and civilizations. An eighteenth-century writer in Chile described that country's many natural advantages in climate, soil, and natural resources and then asked in complete bewilderment why it was such a poverty-stricken country. The same question could be asked of many countries today.

Conversely, we could ask why Japan and Switzerland are so prosperous when they are both almost totally lacking in natural resources. Both are rich in what economists call "human capital" — the skills of their people. No doubt there is a long and complicated history behind the different skill levels of different peoples and nations. The point here is that the immediate environment — whether social or geographic — is only part of the story.

Geography may well have a significant role in the history of peoples, but perhaps not simply by presenting them with more or less natural resources. Geography shapes or limits peoples' opportunities for cultural interaction and the mutual development that comes out of this. Small, isolated islands in the sea have seldom been sources of new scientific advances or technological breakthroughs, regardless of where such islands were located and regardless of the race of the people on these islands. There are islands on land as well. Where soil, fertile enough to support human life, exists only in isolated patches, widely separated, there tend to be isolated cultures (often with different languages or dialects) in a culturally fragmented region. Isolated highlands often produce insular cultures, lagging in many ways behind the cultures of the lowlanders of the same race — whether we are talking about medieval Scotland, colonial Ceylon, or the contemporary montagnards of Vietnam.

With geographical environments as with social environments, we are talking about long-run effects, not simply the effects of immediate surroundings. When Scottish highlanders, for example, immigrated to North Carolina in colonial times, they had a very different history from that of Scottish lowlanders who settled in North Carolina. For one thing, the lowlanders spoke English while the highlanders spoke Gaelic on into the nineteenth century. Obviously, speaking only Gaelic in an English-speaking country affects a group's whole economic and social progress.

Geographical conditions vary as radically in terms of how well they facilitate or impede large-scale cultural interactions as they do in their distribution of natural resources. We are not even close to being able to explain how all these geographical influences have operated throughout history. This too is an unanswered question largely because it is an unasked question, and it is an unasked question because many are seeking answers in terms of immediate social environment or are vehemently insistent that they have already found the answer in those terms.

How radically do geographic environments differ, not just in terms of tropical versus arctic climates, but also in the very configuration of the land and how this helps or hinders large-scale interactions among peoples? Consider one statistic: Africa is more than twice the size of Europe, and yet Africa has a shorter coastline than Europe. This seems almost impossible. But the reason is that Europe's coastline is far more convoluted, with many harbors and inlets being formed all around the continent. Much of the coastline of Africa is smooth, which is to say, lacking in the harbors that make large-scale maritime trade possible by sheltering the ships at anchor from the rough waters of the open sea.

Waterways of all sorts have played a major role in the evolution of cultures and nations around the world. Harbors on the sea are not the only waterways. Rivers are also very important. Virtually every major city on earth is located either on a river or a harbor. Whether it is such great harbors as those in Sydney, Singapore, or San Francisco; or London on the Thames, Paris on the Seine, or numerous other European cities on the Danube, waterways have been the lifeblood of urban centers for centuries. Only very recently has man-made, self-powered transportation, like automobiles and airplanes, made it possible to produce an exception to the rule like Los Angeles. (There is a Los Angeles River, but you do not have to be Moses to walk across it in the summertime.) New York has both a long and deep river and a huge sheltered harbor.

None of these geographical features in themselves creates a great city or develops an urban culture. Human beings do that. But geography sets the limits within which people can operate, and in some places it sets those limits much wider than in others. Returning to our comparison of the continents of Europe and Africa, we find that they differ as radically in rivers as they do in harbors. There are entire nations in Africa without a single navigable river — Libya and South Africa, for example.

"Navigable" is the crucial word. Some African rivers are navigable only during the rainy season. Some are navigable only between numerous cataracts and waterfalls. Even the Zaire River, which is longer than any river in North America and carries a larger volume of water, has too many waterfalls too close to the ocean for it to become a major artery of international commerce. Such commerce is facilitated in Europe not only by numerous navigable rivers but also by the fact that no spot on the continent, outside of Russia, is more than 500 miles from the sea. Many places in Africa are more than 500 miles from the sea, including the entire nation of Uganda.

Against this background, how surprised should we be to find that Europe is the most urbanized of all inhabited continents and Africa the least urbanized? Urbanization is not the be-all and end-all of life, but certainly an urban culture is bound to differ substantially from non-urban cultures, and the skills peculiar to an urban culture are far more likely to be found among groups from an urban civilization. Conversely, an interesting history could be written about the failures of urbanized groups in agricultural settlements.

Looking within Africa, the influence of geography seems equally clear. The most famous ancient civilization on the continent arose within a few miles on either side of Africa's longest navigable river, the Nile, and even today the two largest cities on the continent, Cairo and Alexandria, are on that river. The great West African kingdoms in the region served by the Niger River and the long-flourishing East African economy based around the great natural harbor on the island of Zanzibar are further evidences of the role of geography. Again, geography is not all-determining — the economy of Zanzibar has been ruined by government policy in recent decades — but nevertheless, geography is an important long-run influence on the shaping of cultures as well as in narrowly economic terms.

What are the implications of a world view of cultural diversity on the 40 narrower issues being debated under that label in the United States today? Although "diversity" is used in so many different ways in so many different contexts that it seems to mean all things to all people, there are a few themes that appear again and again. One of these broad themes is that diversity implies organized efforts at the preservation of cultural differences, perhaps governmental efforts, perhaps government subsidies to various programs run by the advocates of diversity.

This approach raises questions as to what the purpose of culture is. If what is important about cultures is that they are emotionally symbolic, and if differentness is cherished for the sake of differentness, then this particular version of cultural diversity might make some sense. But cultures exist even in isolated societies where there are no other cultures around — where there is no one else and nothing else from which to be different. Cultures exist to serve the vital, practical requirements of human life — to structure a society so as to perpetuate the species, to pass on the hard-earned knowledge and experience of generations past and centuries past to the young and inexperienced in order to spare the next generation the costly and dangerous process of learning everything all over again from scratch through trial and error — including fatal errors. Cultures exist so that people can know how to get food and put a roof over their head, how to cure the sick, how to cope with the death of loved ones, and how to get along with the living. Cultures are not bumper stickers. They are living, changing ways of doing all the things that have to be done in life.

Every culture discards over time the things that no longer do the job or which do not do the job as well as things borrowed from other cultures. Each individual does this, consciously or not, on a day-to-day basis. Languages take words from other languages, so that Spanish as spoken in Spain includes words taken from Arabic, and Spanish as spoken in Argentina has Italian words taken from the large Italian immigrant population there. People eat Kentucky Fried Chicken in Singapore and stay in Hilton Hotels in Cairo. This is not what some of the advocates of diversity have in mind. They seem to want to preserve cultures in their purity, almost like butterflies preserved in amber. Decisions about change, if any, seem to be regarded as collective decisions, political decisions. But this is not how cultures have arrived where they are. Individuals have decided for themselves how much of the old they wished to retain, how much of the new they found useful in their own lives.

In this way, cultures have enriched each other in all the great civilizations of the world. In this way, great port cities and other crossroads of cultures have become centers of progress all across the planet. No culture has grown great in isolation — but a number of cultures have made historic and even astonishing advances when their isolation was ended, usually by events beyond their control.

Japan was a classic example in the nineteenth century, but a similar story could be told of Scotland in an earlier era, when a country where once even the nobility were illiterate became, within a short time as history is measured, a country that produced world pioneers in field after field: David Hume in philosophy, Adam Smith in economics, Joseph Black in chemistry, Robert Adam in architecture, and James Watt, whose steam engine revolutionized modern industry and transport. In the process, the Scots lost their language but gained world preeminence in many fields. Then a whole society moved to higher standards of living than anyone ever dreamed of in their poverty-stricken past.

There were higher standards in other ways as well. As late as the 45 eighteenth century, it was considered noteworthy that pedestrians in Edinburgh no longer had to be on the alert for sewage being thrown out the windows of people's homes or apartments. The more considerate Scots yelled a warning, but they threw out the sewage anyway. Perhaps it was worth losing a little of the indigenous culture to be rid of that problem. Those who use the term "cultural diversity" to promote a multiplicity of segregated ethnic enclaves are doing an enormous harm to the people in those enclaves. However they live socially, the people in those enclaves are going to have to compete economically for a livelihood. Even if they were not disadvantaged before, they will be very disadvantaged if their competitors from the general population are free to tap the knowledge, skills, and analytical techniques Western civilization has drawn from all the other civilizations of the world, while those in the enclaves are restricted to what exists in the subculture immediately around them.

We need also to recognize that many great thinkers of the past — whether in medicine or philosophy, science or economics — labored not simply to advance whatever particular group they happened to have come from but to advance the human race. Their legacies, whether cures for deadly diseases or dramatic increases in crop yields to fight the scourge of hunger, belong to all people — and all people need to claim that legacy, not seal themselves off in a dead-end of tribalism or in an emotional orgy of cultural vanity.

PREPARING FOR DISCUSSION

1. Articulate as clearly as possible Sowell's definition of "diversity." How does this definition agree or disagree with other definitions of diversity expressed in this chapter? Why does Sowell propose a "world view of cultural diversity" before he returns to consider the problem of diversity in America? How does he finally relate the results of his examination of world history to American society? What possible dangers has the world perspective allowed Sowell to perceive?

2. In paragraph 12, Sowell writes of our reluctance "to label anything or anyone 'superior' or 'inferior'." To what historical circumstances does he attribute this reluctance? By what means does he propose to overcome our hesitation to rank certain features of one culture over analogous features of other cultures?

3. In paragraph 7, Sowell advances the idea that "some cultural features [are] not only different from others but better than others." What is his point in using the word *better* as a descriptive term? Might he have used words like *more useful* or *more practical* in the place of *better* and still have preserved his meaning? Are the moral connotations of the word *better* inappropriate to the essay?

4. Rejecting genetic theories of cultural superiority in certain areas of human endeavor, Sowell proposes a geographically based model of cultural advancement (paragraphs 31–39). In what important ways does Sowell's model differ from Cornel West's "cross-fertilization" model? To what extent might Sowell's model be said to downplay the possibility of reciprocal exchange between different cultures?

5. Generally, Sowell's essay is marked by careful and logical exposition and a rhetorical style that might be called neutral or dispassionate. At certain points in the selection, however, the tone changes. In paragraph 41, for example, he insists that "Cultures are not bumper stickers." Soon thereafter he writes of the potential for American society to degenerate into an "emotional orgy of cultural vanity" (paragraph 46). How would you characterize the tone of these two phrases? How do they differ from the general tone of the essay, and what do they reveal about Sowell's attitude toward his subject matter?

FROM READING TO WRITING

6. Consider Sowell's proposition that a culture advances only by adopting the "better" features of other cultures. Write an essay in which you examine the validity of his proposition using the United States as a test case. Choose and examine in depth an example from American history in which our culture adopted a specific feature from another culture. To what degree did this feature prove to be "better" than the one it replaced? To what degree did it prove to be "worse" than the original?

7. Does Sowell's model work on the individual level as well as the global and national levels? In an essay, consider the degree to which you have adopted "better" ways of performing certain actions from others. What caused you to adopt or not to adopt another's ways? Are you more convinced of the accuracy of Sowell's model after applying it to individuals rather than cultures?

2

The American Dilemma
RACISM · FAIRNESS · OPPORTUNITY

SOME FIFTY YEARS AGO the Swedish economist Gunnar Myrdal published an enormously influential book arguing that America's racial crisis amounted to its most serious national problem. Now a classic, *An American Dilemma* vividly described a society unable to bridge the gap between its officially professed idealism and its daily practice of discrimination and bigotry.

For many political analysts and commentators, both black and white, racism remains exactly what Myrdal argued it was a half-century ago — America's central and defining *dilemma.* In "Race and Racism: Inferiority vs. Equality," Andrew Hacker, a political scientist who has written extensively on the subject of race, examines how enduring racial disparities have resulted in a severely divided society. Hacker asks whites to imagine "how it feels to have an unfavorable — and unfair — identity imposed upon you every waking day." In "Back to Black: Ending Internalized Racism," bell hooks, one of today's most influential cultural critics, exposes the many ways that racism and racial stereotypes can devastate one's self-concept and self-esteem.

Myrdal's *American Dilemma* focused exclusively on African Americans and their heritage of slavery. In "Seeing More than Black and White," however, noted activist Elizabeth Martínez explores racism within a new social context of immigration and a declining white majority. Given the growing complexity of racial categorization, she argues, the "white/Black model of race relations and racism" may be obsolete by the next century.

Although Martínez may be correct, the national debate on racism continues to be framed largely in terms of black and white. And the debate is often contentious, sometimes ugly. One of the biggest flare-ups in recent years was sparked by an 845-page, heavily footnoted book that examined race and intelligence in American life and that was certainly more argued about than actually read. "We are not indifferent to the ways in which this book, wrongly construed, might do harm," the late statistician Richard J. Herrnstein and conservative policy analyst Charles Murray state at the outset of their controversial best-seller, *The Bell Curve.* While a number of critics attacked the book's scientific and statistical validity, Randall Kennedy, a professor at Harvard Law School, pursued a different strategy. In "The Phony War," he examines *The Bell Curve's* success in marketing controversy and capitalizing on the current pessimistic attitude toward race relations in general. At the same time *The Bell Curve* appeared, another book about racial differences was sparking even further controversy — J. Philippe Rushton's *Race, Evolution and Behavior.* In "Race and Crime: An International Dilemma," Rushton, a Canadian professor of psychology, maintains that global statistics indicate significant behavioral differences among the world's three major races. Though Rushton declines to draw policy conclusions from his data, his biogenetic classification of racial differences could reinforce the "pessimistic interpretation" Randall Kennedy fears.

An earlier note of pessimism was struck when President Clinton withdrew his nomination of African American legal theorist Lani Guinier to the position of assistant attorney general for civil rights. In "The Tyranny of the Majority," Guinier explains her notion of alternatives to electoral majorities that would ensure a greater chance of minority representation. Her theme is fairness. President John F. Kennedy liked to say that "life isn't fair." In her essay, Guinier introduces a few simple principles to show how it might be made a little fairer.

Although less pessimistic about race relations in a "post-civil rights era," Glenn C. Loury is no less controversial. In "Black Dignity and the Common Good," the prominent economics professor offers suggestions that challenge the conventional wisdom of both white and black policymakers. "He is clearly," says Randall Kennedy, "the most thoughtful conservative analyst of the race question."

ANDREW HACKER

Race and Racism: Inferiority vs. Equality

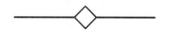

The tremendous successes of the civil rights movement of the 1960s gave rise to the popular belief that the United States was ready to consign three centuries of virulent racism to history. The past two decades of growing racial tension, however, have once again brought into focus a central paradox of American life: While Americans continue to boast of the world's highest standards of justice and equality, racism remains prevalent. In the following selection, Andrew Hacker attempts to define this complex phenomenon and identify its various manifestations including separatism, inequality, and hostility.

Educated at Amherst and Princeton, Hacker is currently professor of political science at Queens College, where he has taught since 1971. His essays and articles have appeared in *Time, Newsweek,* the *Atlantic Monthly, Harper's Magazine,* and the *Nation,* and he is a frequent contributor to the *New York Review of Books.* His major study of racial division, *Two Nations,* the second chapter of which is reprinted here, appeared in 1992. The work takes its title from a remark made by the nineteenth-century English Prime Minister Benjamin Disraeli, who once described the rich and poor as "two nations, between whom there is no intercourse and no sympathy; who are as ignorant of each other's habits, thoughts, and feelings, as if they were dwellers in different zones, or inhabitants of different planets."

SELECTED PUBLICATIONS: *Political Theory: Philosophy, Ideology, Science* (1960); *The End of the American Era* (1970); *Free Enterprise in America* (1977); *U.S.: A Statistical Portrait of the American People* (editor) (1983); *Two Nations: Black and White, Separate, Hostile, Unequal* (1992).

Throughout this nation's history, race has always had a central role. Until recently, however, most notions concerning the races and relations between them either went unquestioned or remained relatively muted. As recently as a generation ago, white Americans in both the South and the North would say that so far as they could see their region had no overpowering racial problems. Most of them really wanted to believe that blacks and whites coexisted quite amiably; separately, to be sure, but that was a matter of mutual choice.

For almost a century after the abolition of slavery, America's black population subsisted under a system of controls. In the South, physical force was blatant and unabashed. The whims of a sheriff, an employer, even the driver of a bus, could hold black lives in thrall. In the North, intimidation and oppression were less explicit but nonetheless real. Fear of the police obviously helped to maintain this submission, for in those days precinct houses were less attentive to legal processes than they claim to be today. An equally effective control lay in the understanding that members of subordinate races did not touch or threaten their betters. This is not to suggest that black Americans were happy with their condition. Many were resentful, if not totally enraged. But given the panoply of power they faced, the most common posture was one of resignation: a minority with barely an avenue of appeal.

Little attention was paid to the conditions under which black Americans lived. It was assumed, for example, that a docile pool would always be available for the arduous labors required by white society. No one thought to ask what domestic servants did after their working hours. Black Americans remained unobtrusive, and apparently uncomplaining, for all intents invisible to white eyes.

These were placid years for white Americans. No serious movements or organized protests arose to upset white sensibilities. No talk of black power was in the air, and only the barest whispers of egalitarian aspirations could be heard. Black Americans knew they were regarded as marginal members of the nation, and realized that white America saw them as an alien appendage.

The real change began during the Second World War, when for the first time black Americans were courted by white society. A shortage of civilian labor forced employers to offer jobs to workers who previously had been excluded. More than a million black women left domestic service never to return. At the outset of the war, blacks were drafted into the armed forces to serve in labor battalions. By its end, they were given the right to fight and die, as many did. Once a society has told men and women that it cannot function without their talents, they will not willingly revert to a subordinate status. Notions of civil rights and racial integrations, of social equality and economic progress, received their impetus in those wartime years. During the decades that followed, they took coherent shape.

In particular, college students in the South decided it was time to end the ignominies inflicted on educated men and women, who could not even order a sandwich at a local lunch counter. Shortly thereafter, ordinary citizens began to demand that most elemental of rights which was still denied to most members of their race: to be allowed to vote for the officials who legislate and tax and exercise power over you.

Most white Americans saw these and related activities as dignified and responsible, and embodying legitimate aims. That black groups eschewed violence also set white minds at ease. Certainly, they felt safe with Martin Luther King, Jr., the most prominent leader in the civil rights movement. Not only was he a minister born into a patrician family, but he had studied and received a doctoral degree at a Northern university. Moreover, he welcomed whites to join in marches and demonstrations, making it a biracial cause.

So until the middle 1960s, there was little talk of a racial crisis or tensions that had grown out of control. Then came the so-called riots in cities like Los Angeles and Newark and Detroit, marked by looting and burning within black neighborhoods. In fact, these were not "race riots," if by that is meant actual confrontations of black and white citizens. The violence never reached downtown business districts or areas where whites lived. However, race became the central issue. The chief response, including gunfire in which many blacks lost their lives, came from white police and national guardsmen. To more than a few observers, the conduct of the police was much more callous and indiscriminate than that of the civilians they had been ordered to control.

After those disturbances, race relations never returned to their former plane. Whites ceased to identify black protests with a civil rights movement led by students and ministers. Rather, they saw a resentful and rebellious multitude, intent on imposing its presence on the rest of the society. Blacks were seen as trying to force themselves into places and positions where they were not wanted or for which they lacked the competence. As the 1970s started, so came a rise in crimes, all too many of them with black perpetrators. By that point, many white Americans felt they had been misused or betrayed. Worsening relations between the races were seen as largely due to the behavior of blacks, who had abused the invitations to equal citizenship white America had been tendering. It is this setting that creates the context of racism.

Something called racism obviously exists. As a complex of ideas and attitudes, which translate into action, it has taken a tragic toll on the lives of all Americans. Unfortunately, the term has been so used and overused that it loses serious meaning. It has served as a rallying cry, a bludgeon, and as a diversion from other issues. But racism is real, an incubus that has haunted this country since Europeans first set foot on the continent. It goes beyond prejudice and discrimination, and even transcends bigotry, largely because it arises from outlooks and assumptions of which we are largely unaware. 10

Racism expresses itself in three distinct but related ways. Of course, this or any trifurcation may seem oversimple, and undoubtedly is. Still, a graphic presentation can expand our understanding of an elusive reality.

Taxicab drivers who refuse to stop for black riders base that decision on the only information they have: the race of the person raising his or her hand. Even if the driver has had some bad experiences, he understands that most black men are law-abiding citizens. At the same time, he knows that some have been known to pull a gun on taxicab drivers. And that "some" is enough to make him wary about every black man. When he drives by a middle-aged black woman without stopping, it is because he thinks she may ask to be taken to a part of the city he would rather not enter. Of course, he has no way of knowing her destination, but he does not want to take the risk. In these and similar cases, his decision not to stop is patently racist, especially since he then proceeds to pick up the first white passenger he sees farther down the block.

Racism has much in common with other "isms." We already have the term "sexism." Other generalizations may apply to height or weight, or age or physical handicaps. "Homophobia" is also an "ism," although it carries connotations of hatred as well. Whether a taxi driver dislikes black people is not really the issue. He may actually feel sorry for the person he left standing in the rain.

In some cases, expressions of racism admit of no exceptions. This was the case with the Nazi ideology, which said that *all* human beings of Jewish origin carried the seeds of depravity. The fact that infants were included in the Holocaust made this conviction clear. (This is not to say that Jews are a race. Still, that Nazis chose to see them that way is itself a fact.)

Racism need not be so rigid or absolute. In fact, few whites insist that   15
the traits they dislike in some black people are to be found in every member of the race. Most are pleased to point to black men and women who are not like "the rest." They may watch black performers regularly on film or television, cheer them at athletic events, and even claim some black people as their friends.

Making — and acting upon — limited impressions is a part of ordinary life. Each day, like the taxicab driver, we base decisions on the one or two facts we gather about people, which may simply be their outward appearance, or their addresses on an application, or how they sound over the telephone. Such presumptions are obviously unfair to the individuals involved. Constraints of time do not always allow us to obtain the fuller information we would like or need.

Racism, we are sometimes told, rests largely on ignorance. If we get to know people better, we will discover that they are quite different from what we have been led to think they are. That is surely so. For example, very few white Americans have ever set foot inside a black family's home. They might be surprised to discover that simply in terms of furniture, appliances, meals, and television-watching, blacks live very much like whites of their own class. While some differences in style can be identified, members of the two races share many common characteristics. Quite obviously, the United States would be a much more harmonious nation if there were fewer racial barriers. Yet even blacks who attain economic and educational parity find that social obstacles remain. How often does one see a party of two couples, one black and one white, on an outing together?

Still, racism is not always based on ignorance. There can be cases where stereotyped judgments contain some elements of truth. While we can agree that taxicab drivers often make decisions on a racist basis, we might grant that in doing so they show a modicum of rationality. Some black men — a higher proportion than among whites — do have intentions that are in fact dangerous. It is one thing for a passenger to refuse to pay a taxi fare; it is another if he holds a loaded gun to the driver's head. And the latter has been a frequent enough occurrence to give many drivers pause. Sad to say, actions that are often unfair can also be reasonable, at least insofar as they are based on sufficient experience to give them a degree of validity.

To reply that taxicab drivers draw on rational odds hardly comforts those subjected to such calculations. Tendencies attributed to common felons get shunted onto surgeons and scholars. Nor does it help to point out that this kind of unfairness is inevitable in a world where we can never come to know each individual in an intimate way. Judgments based on race cut more deeply and cause more harm than other presumptions Americans may make about one another. What every black American knows, and whites should try to imagine, is how it feels to have an unfavorable — and unfair — identity imposed on you every waking day.

In addition to the outlooks and actions of individuals like taxicab drivers, there is also a condition called "institutional racism." The institutions can be colleges and churches, or business firms or governmental bureaus. The Federal Bureau of Investigation and the Los Angeles Police Department, for example, have long had reputations for antipathy toward blacks and other minorities. But not all organizations are so blatant in their biases. Most develop more subtle cultures of their own, which their members usually internalize, often without pause or reflection. Of course, organizational cultures take many forms. But in the United States, an overarching feature is that they tend to be inherently "white." [20]

This is not to say that churches and colleges and corporations actually proclaim a racial preference. All will assert that they welcome parishioners and students and employees of every color, and they hope to increase that diversity. Executives at firms like General Motors and General Electric would be shocked if told that they headed racist firms, as would administrators at Cornell or Columbia. Indeed, the issue barely arises in the minds of their members. So if someone files a lawsuit, the complaint generally comes as a surprise. The organizations reply that they do not discriminate; more than that, most who speak this way truly believe what they say.

Simply stated, most white people prefer not to perceive their nation and its major institutions as "white," and consequently racist. They will say that the United States is a multiracial society, and becomes more so every day. The same strictures, they will add, hold for its major organizations and associations. To claim that the white race holds so preponderant a sway is both untrue and gratuitous.

Black Americans seldom see the reality this way. Black students at Yale University, black members of the Omaha police force, even black passengers on an airline flight, never cease being aware of their white surroundings. When black Americans go to movies, turn on television, or simply scan the comic strips, it seems as if their nation hardly knows or cares that they exist. (They are quite aware of well-known black figures, ranging from Oprah Winfrey to Colin Powell. Still, institutional images are overwhelmingly white.)

American institutions begin with an initial bias against black applicants, since the presumption is that most blacks cannot or will not meet the standards the organization has set. Historically, virtually all of the people associated with Yale University, United Airlines, and the Omaha police force have been white, which has in turn created both the image of these institutions and the way they operate. In this sense, they are "white" organizations, from which it follows that their members are expected to think and act in white ways. This is not as difficult for white people, although some have to make an extra effort if they wish to master class-based aspects of the manner and style. However, for blacks the situation is qualitatively different, since they see themselves as being judged by more coercive criteria, which call on them to deny large parts of themselves.

Black Americans spend much of their lives at a distance from white   25
Americans, in part because they feel more comfortable that way, and partly because their separation has been imposed by white America. This helps to explain why even better-off blacks tend to do less well than whites on tests used by schools and employers. Since blacks of all classes are more likely to be raised in segregated surroundings, they grow up with less exposure to the kinds of reasoning that standardized examinations expect.

From slavery through the present, the nation has never opened its doors sufficiently to give black Americans a chance to become full citizens. White Americans often respond that it rests with blacks to put aside enough of their own culture so they can be absorbed into the dominant stream. Blacks can only shake their heads and reply that they have been doing just that for several centuries, with very little to show for it.

Many black men and women are concluding that they can best be described as African-Americans, considering how much their character and culture owe to their continent of origin. A pride in this heritage and history has helped them survive slavery and subsequent discrimination. Indeed, the nation as a whole has benefited from black Americans who bring to life the rhetoric and rhythms of their ancestral origins.

However, most white Americans interpret the African emphasis in another way. For them, it frequently leads to a more insidious application of racism. As has been reiterated, there persists the belief that members of the black race represent an inferior strain of the human species. In this view, Africans — and Americans who trace their origins to that continent — are seen as languishing at a lower evolutionary level than members of other races.

Of course, this belief is seldom voiced in public. Still, the unhappy fact remains that most white people believe that, compared with other races, persons with African ancestries are more likely to carry primitive traits in their genes. Given this premise — and prejudice — the presumption follows that most individuals of African heritage will lack the intellectual and organizational capacities the modern world requires.

Most whites who call themselves conservatives hold this view, and proclaim it when they are sure of their company. Most liberals and those further to the left deny that present racial disparities are based on genetic inheritance. If they harbor doubts, they keep them to themselves. Their intellectual forebears were not so constrained. Thomas Jefferson offers a case in point.

As the principal author of the Declaration of Independence, he enunciated the new nation's commitment to human equality. Most Americans can recite his phrases from memory:

> We hold these truths to be self-evident: that all men are created equal;
> that they are endowed by their creator with certain unalienable rights;
> that among these are life, liberty, and the pursuit of happiness.

To refer to some truths as self-evident means that all reasonable people should be able to agree on their veracity, without need for further proof or evidence. They are empirical first principles and moral starting points. It is noteworthy that Jefferson set down as the first of these verities the premise "all men are created equal."

There have been endless discussions over what "created equal" could have meant to Jefferson and what it might connote for us today. One thing can be said at the outset: It must refer to more than the possession of equal rights, since those entitlements are listed later and separately in the passage just quoted. Moreover, those who take the egalitarian position are well aware of human differences. No one will deny that some people are taller or gain weight more readily, or can run faster, or have perfect pitch.

However, our current concern is not whether all human beings everywhere are "created equal" in terms of personal potential, but whether this tenet applies to the groups of individuals we have come to call races. Here the terms of the argument can allow for ranges of possible talents *within* racial groups. So what racial equality *does* posit is that within each race there will be a similar distribution of talents, if all members of all races are given a chance to discover and develop those traits. Ideally, then, white Americans and black Americans could be brought to a point where both racial groups would have a virtually identical range of IQ scores. Or, even more ideally, on tests we might devise to gauge more important human qualities.

What is revealing is that while Thomas Jefferson was prepared to affirm an equality among the people to whom the Declaration of Independence applied, he was not so sure about that principle where the slaves of his day were involved. In a letter written fifteen years later, he said:

> Nobody wishes more than I do to see proofs that nature has given to our black brethren talents equal to those of the other colors of men, and that the appearance of a lack of them is owing merely to the degraded condition of their existence in Africa and America.

Can this be the same Jefferson who had earlier affirmed it was "self-evident" that all human beings everywhere are conceived with equal potential to pursue the fullest life? What, we may wonder, led him to make blacks a special case, and now to plead for "proofs" that they had faculties equal to those of other races? We may also speculate about what manner of evidence would have been sufficiently persuasive to Jefferson to undo doubts that have proved so durable. One might think that even in his day at least some blacks had shown sufficient accomplishments to quell his misgivings. As has been noted, racial equality only asks us to assume a comparable range of potentialities within every racial group.

Jeffersonian doubts remain relevant for another reason. Note how much he *wanted* to believe that persons of African origin had capacities equal to those of other races. Why, then, could not Jefferson simply pronounce the inherent equality of blacks also to be a "self-evident" truth? Any deficiencies he might find could be attributed to the oppressive environment of segregation and slavery. That has always been the egalitarian answer. Sadly, even for those who allude to blacks as their "brethren," a desire to believe does not always bring that result. Warring within the minds of Jeffersonians, both in his time and ours, is the hope that blacks are equal — accompanied by the suspicion that they are not.

Not all expressions of racism have been as beset by misgivings as Jefferson's. Since Europeans first embarked on explorations, they have been bemused by the "savages" they encountered in new lands. In almost all cases, these "primitive" peoples were seen as inferior to those who "discovered" them. While they were often described as peaceful and pastoral, as innocent and caring, those were viewed as attributes of children, not fully-formed adults. On the whole, the presumption was that these natives could never attain to a stage where they might emulate European achievements.

Many people still hold views similar to these. Indeed, terms even cruder than "savages" can be heard in private interchanges. But in public discourse, ours is much more a scientific age. So those who believe in the inherent inferiority of certain races feel obliged to allude to research based on experimentation, evidence, and an objective point of view.

One of the most prominent has been William Shockley, a winner of the Nobel Prize, who argued that evidence showed people of African origin to be lower on an evolutionary scale. Another well-known name is Arthur Jensen, a professor of psychology at the University of California. His stated position has been that because black children are genetically inferior, even compensatory programs like Head Start[1] will fail because the native talents are not there.

In the past, this quest was called "eugenics," and it had practical as well as scholarly aims. For it hoped to warn people of supposedly superior strains that they should not mate with their genetic inferiors. The fear was of "mongrelization," a phrase then commonly used, wherein the best human breeds would marry down and produce lesser heirs. Today, such sentiments are seldom stated in so direct a way. Rather than counseling against intermarriage, it will be hinted that even social racial mixing can have deleterious effects. Hence we hear it argued that allowing too many blacks into elite colleges will not only lower intellectual standards, but will undo what those august institutions have sought to achieve.

In rational terms, there is an easy rebuttal to research and reasoning based on racist suppositions. In simplest terms, it is the environmental answer. To begin, while we know that heredity has a role in shaping human beings, this is best considered on an individual level. Within races, through parents or other forebears certain attributes are passed on to successive offspring, although it is not always possible to trace who got what from whom. After all, many permutations and combinations are involved.

Of course, races differ in some outward respects. Each race, taken as a group, carries a pool of genes that gives its members their identifiable color and anatomical structure. But even here there are shades and variations, since very few Americans belong to a "pure" race. (This is particularly true of the growing group of Hispanics.) However, despite more than a century of searching, we have no evidence that any one of those pools of race-based genes has a larger quotient of what we choose to call intelligence or organizational ability or creative capacities.

If more members of some races end up doing better in some spheres, it is because more of them grew up in environments that prepared them for those endeavors. If members of other races had similar rearings, they would display a similar distribution of success. So in terms of potential capacities, our best knowledge is that all races have a comparable range of geniuses and morons and people of average ability. We can test people as much as we please. But there is no way to factor out whether any part of the results reflect "racial" elements in some genetic sense, since we

[1] *Head Start:* A preschool program designed to aid underprivileged children.

would have to adjust for every specific environmental influence as it has affected each individual. (Indeed, even when a white family adopts a black infant, the child knows that she is "black," and that image of herself will affect how she adapts to a "white" environment.)

Of course, remarks such as these will not deflect individuals like Arthur Jensen and William Shockley from sifting through research reports for evidence of racial superiority. Other citizens who are not scientists will settle for deductions of their own or cite accounts that seem to back their suppositions. Indeed, there is reason to believe that most white Americans will share Thomas Jefferson's belief that in terms of evolution and genetics theirs is the most developed race.

At a certain point, the suspicion arises that we are less in the realm of   45
science than of ideology. Scientists, no less than lay people, have political dispositions. And, like the rest of us, the sentiments they hold give shape to what they see. More than that, even Nobel Prize winners can end up seeing not what is actually there, but what they want to see. We are not talking about dishonesty or hypocrisy, but the way human minds — indeed brilliant minds — tend to work.

So it should not be surprising that scientists who stress the role of heredity tend to be politically conservative, while those who emphasize environment veer toward the liberal side of the spectrum. By the same token, lay people select scientific views that support their ideological positions. Even individuals who have never taken a science course feel free to cite some studies as authoritative, if they agree with their findings. Thus racism has always been able to come up with a scientific veneer. This is certainly true today of those who wish to claim that one race or another is by nature inferior. They are fully persuaded that they are citing biology, not displaying bigotry.

Thus the racism blacks face runs deeper than judgments about culture. From the premise of genetic inferiority, there follows the corollary that members of a lesser race should be content to perform tasks unsuited to other strains. This was the rationale for slavery, and it has by no means disappeared. (There are even hints of this in the plea to create more blue-collar jobs for black men.) Nor is the racism applied to blacks found only among persons of European ancestry. Today, inhabitants of every other continent like to think that they have evolved further than those who trace their origins to the region south of the Sahara.

Certainly, compared with other continents, Africa remains most like its primeval self. Even today, white Americans as individuals, and white America's institutions, are unwilling to absorb the people and patrimony of humanity's first continent. This expression of racism goes well beyond personal prejudice and discriminatory institutions. It rests on judgments about culture and civilization, and who dictates the meaning of science and history.

All the observations offered thus far have focused on beliefs and behavior of white Americans. Quite obviously, racism arises in other places
and guises. Most Japanese, for example, feel that they represent the highest evolution of humanity, and have cited Chinese, Koreans, and Americans as their genetic inferiors.

And what about blacks in America; cannot they harbor racist sentiments as well? Some certainly seem to. Leonard Jeffries,[2] a black scholar,
has designated whites as "ice people," labeling them materialistic,
greedy, and inherently driven to domination. By way of contrast, he calls
blacks "sun people," whose chief traits are kindness and caring and communal responsibility. More than that, this scholar has argued, the
melanin that makes for darker pigmentation imparts a mental and moral
superiority to persons who trace their ancestries to Africa. So blacks can
also employ stereotypes that impute inferiority to human beings of another race. Some whites worry about these views, seeing them as mirror
images of white displays of racism, supremacy, and bigotry.

Some blacks reject that symmetry. Thus Coleman Young, the mayor
of Detroit, a predominantly black city, has argued that blacks within the
United States cannot be called racists, for the simple reason that they are
an oppressed people. Racism, he has said, should be attributed only to
those who have the power to cause suffering. What he is suggesting is
that it is insufficient to define racism as a set of ideas that some people
may hold. Racism takes its full form only when it has an impact on the
real world. While most white people may dispute the mayor's reasoning,
he raises an important point. If we care about racism, it is because it scars
people's lives. Individuals who do not have power may hold racist
views, but they seldom cause much harm. (No one cares if homeless
people believe the earth is flat.) The significance of racism lies in the way
it consigns certain human beings to the margins of society, if not painful
lives and early deaths. In the United States, racism takes it highest toll on
blacks. No white person can claim to have suffered in such ways because
of ideas that may be held about them by some black citizens.

Ideas about equality and inferiority and superiority are not simply
figments in people's minds. Such sentiments have an impact on how institutions operate, and opinions tend to be self-fulfilling. If members of a
minority race are believed to be deficient in character or capacities, the
larger society will consign them to subordinate positions.

America has always been the most competitive of societies. It poises
its citizens against one another, with the warning that they must make it

---

[2] *Leonard Jeffries:* African American scholar whose controversial remarks on the role of Jews
in the historical oppression of blacks prompted his removal as chairman of the City College of New York's African American Studies Department.

on their own. Hence the stress on moving past others, driven by a fear of falling behind. No other nation so rates its residents as winners or losers.

If white America orchestrates this arena, it cannot guarantee full security to every member of its own race. Still, while some of its members may fail, there is a limit to how far they can fall. For white America has agreed to provide a consolation prize: No matter to what depths one descends, no white person can ever become black. As James Baldwin has pointed out, white people need the presence of black people as a reminder of what providence has spared them from becoming.

If white people are compelled to compete against one another, they   55
are also urged to believe that any advances blacks may make will be at their expense. Here government and politics reflect a harsh economy. Indeed, this country is less a society, certainly less a community, than any of the countries with which it compares itself. A reason commonly given is that the United States is a large and diverse country. What is less commonly acknowledged is that its culture makes a point of exaggerating differences and exacerbating frictions. This appears most vividly in the stress placed on race.

Competition and whites' fear of failure help to explain the resistance to ensuring opportunities for black Americans, let alone more equitable outcomes. Even allowing for interludes like the New Deal and the Great Society, government is expected to take on obligations only as a late and last resort. Hence the presence in the United States of more violent crime, more of its people in prison, more homeless families and individuals, more children created virtually by accident, more fatal addiction and disease, more dirt and disorder — why prolong the list? — than any other nation deemed industrially advanced and socially civilized.

A society that places so great a premium on "getting ahead" cannot afford to spare much compassion for those who fall behind. If the contest were racially fair, it would at least be true to its own principle of assessing all individuals solely on talent and effort. But keeping black Americans so far behind the starting line means most of the outcomes will be racially foreordained.

PREPARING FOR DISCUSSION

1. Hacker describes "three distinct but related ways" in which racism expresses itself. What are they and how can they be related to one another as Hacker claims? Which of these expressions of racism do you think is most predominant in the United States today? Which one do you think Hacker believes to be the most destructive to social harmony in America?

2. Hacker maintains that most white people "prefer not to perceive their nation and its major institutions as 'white' and consequently racist" (paragraph 22). To what does Hacker attribute this reluctance on the part of many whites to let go

of what he considers to be a misperception? Does Hacker believe that because an institution is "white" it is also racist?

3. Consider Hacker's conclusion that most white conservatives believe that persons of African descent are genetically more inclined to possess "primitive traits" (paragraph 29) than are whites, whereas most liberals reject the idea that "racial disparities" can be traced to genetic factors (paragraph 30). Is this a fair and accurate description of conservative and liberal beliefs? On what grounds does Hacker base his conclusion?

4. Neither scientist that the author mentions in paragraph 39 is a geneticist. William Shockley, an engineer, won his Noble Prize in Physics for his role in the development of the transistor, whereas Arthur Jensen is a psychologist. Do you think that Hacker would be less likely to have dismissed their controversial views on race if these men had received formal training in genetics? If you agree with Hacker that the evaluation of scientific data is often contingent on the political beliefs of the scientist, then what other kinds of scientific "facts" might be thought of as having a political or ideological basis?

5. At the center of Hacker's discussion of race in America (paragraphs 31–36) is an analysis of Jefferson's sense of the word *equal* as it appears in the Declaration of Independence. What does Hacker believe "equal" meant to Jefferson? What do you think the word has come to mean in contemporary America? If the meaning of the word has changed, how do you account for that change?

FROM READING TO WRITING

6. In paragraph 19, Hacker asks whites to imagine "how it feels to have an unfavorable — and unfair — identity imposed upon you every waking day." If you are white, write an essay in which you imagine "how it feels" to be the object of racism. If you are not white and have felt the effects of racism, *describe* what that feels like. Which of the three expressions of racism described by Hacker do you believe to be most harmful? Why?

7. Consider Coleman Young's view that "racism . . . should be attributed only to those who have the power to cause suffering" (paragraph 51). Do you agree or disagree with the proposition that only whites can be considered racists because only they have the power to cause suffering. Write an essay in which you test the validity of the proposition with reference to the current situation of African Americans. In what ways can any group be said to have the power to make others suffer?

Back to Black: Ending Internalized Racism

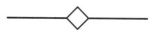

While most accounts of racism in America address discrimination as a phenomenon directed against minorities from without, the number of public discussions about internalized racism continues to grow. Internalized racism may be described as the result of a process by which notions of inferiority directed against minority cultures by a dominant culture take root in the minds of minority individuals. In the 1960s, minority activists found this form of self-hatred difficult to eradicate and even came to see, as bell hooks observes, "self-love as a radical political agenda." In the following selection, hooks reaffirms the need for black self-love in the 1990s.

An important feature of hooks's theoretical work is her unwillingness to divorce issues of race from issues of class and gender. Racism, classism, and sexism, hooks argues, all find their roots in the same notion of domination that has shaped American society. The first step in opposing this hierarchical organization, she believes, is to identify and dispel our own hierarchical ways of thinking. Hooks refers to this important and revolutionary process as "decolonization." Her book *Ain't I a Woman: Black Women and Feminism* was cited by *Publishers Weekly* as one of the "twenty most influential books of the last twenty years." Hooks has taught at Yale and Oberlin College and is currently distinguished professor of English at City College in New York. This selection is taken from her book *Outlaw Culture* (1994).

SELECTED PUBLICATIONS: *Ain't I a Woman: Black Women and Feminism* (1981); *Feminist Theory: From Margin to Center* (1984); *Talking Back: Thinking Feminist, Thinking Black* (1988); *Yearning: Race, Gender, and Cultural Politics* (1990); *Breaking Bread: Insurgent Black Intellectual Life* (with Cornel West) (1991); *Black Looks: Race and Representation* (1992); *Outlaw Culture: Resisting Representations* (1994); *Teaching to Transgress: Education as the Practice of Freedom* (1994).

No social movement to end white supremacy addressed the issue of internalized racism in relation to beauty as intensely as did the Black Power revolution of the sixties. For a time, at least, this movement challenged black folks to examine the psychic impact of white supremacy. Reading Frantz Fanon and Albert Memmi,[1] our leaders began to speak of

---

[1] *Frantz Fanon,* West Indian psychiatrist and social philosopher, and *Albert Memmi,* Tunisian novelist, have written extensively on the question of the liberation of colonial peoples.

colonization and the need to decolonize our minds and imaginations. Exposing the myriad ways white supremacy had assaulted our self-concept and our self-esteem, militant leaders of the black-liberation struggle demanded that black folks see ourselves differently — see self-love as a radical political agenda. That meant establishing a politics of representation which would both critique and integrate ideals of personal beauty and desirability informed by racist standards, and put in place progressive standards, a system of valuation that would embrace a diversity of black looks.

Ironically, as black leaders called into question racist-defined notions of beauty, many white folks expressed awe and wonder that there existed in segregated black life color-caste systems wherein the lighter one's skin the greater one's social value. Their surprise at the way color caste functioned in black life exposed the extent to which they *chose to remain* willfully ignorant of a system that white-supremacist thinking had established and maintained. The construction of color caste hierarchies by white racists in nineteenth-century life is well documented in their history and literature. That contemporary white folks are ignorant of this history reflects the way the dominant culture seeks to erase — and thus deny — this past. This denial allows no space for accountability, for white folks in contemporary culture to know and acknowledge the primary role whites played in the formation of color castes. All black folks, even those who know very little if anything at all about North American history, slavery, and reconstruction, know that racist white folks often treated lighter-skinned black folks better than their darker counterparts, and that this pattern was mirrored in black social relations. But individual black folks who grow to maturity in all-white settings that may have allowed them to remain ignorant of color-caste systems are soon initiated when they have contact with other black people.

Issues of skin color and caste were highlighted by militant black struggle for rights. The slogan "black is beautiful" worked to intervene and alter those racist stereotypes that had always insisted black was ugly, monstrous, undesirable. One of the primary achievements of the Black Power movement was the critique and in some instances the dismantling of color caste hierarchies. This achievement often goes unnoticed and undiscussed, largely because it took place within the psyches of black folks, particularly those of us from working-class or poor backgrounds who did not have access to public forums where we could announce and discuss how we felt. Those black folks who came of age before Black Power faced the implications of color caste either through devaluation or overvaluation. In other words, to be born light meant that one was born with an advantage recognized by everyone. To be born dark was to start life handicapped, with a serious disadvantage. At the onset of the contemporary feminist movement, I had only recently stopped living in a segregated black world and begun life in predominantly white settings. I remember encountering white female insistence that when a child is coming out of the womb one's first concern is to identify its gender, whether male or female; I called attention to the reality that the initial concern for most black parents is skin color, because of the correlation between skin color and success.

Militant black liberation struggle challenged this sensibility. It made it possible for black people to have an ongoing public discourse about the detrimental impact of internalized racism as regards skin color and beauty standards. Darker-skinned blacks, who had historically borne the brunt of devaluation based on color, were recognized as having been wronged by assaultive white supremacist, aesthetic values. New beauty standards were set that sought to value and embrace the different complexions of blackness. Suddenly, the assumption that each individual black person would also seek a lighter partner was called into question. When our militant, charismatic, revolutionary leader Malcolm X chose to marry a darker-skinned woman, he set different standards. These changes had a profound impact on black family life. The needs of children who suffered various forms of discrimination and were psychologically wounded in families or public school systems because they were not the right color could now be addressed. For example, parents of a dark-skinned child who, when misbehaving at school, was called a devil and unjustly punished now had recourse in material written by black psychologists and psychiatrists documenting the detrimental effects of the color-caste system. In all areas of black life the call to see black as beautiful was empowering. Large numbers of black women stopped chemically straightening their hair since there was no longer any stigma attached to wearing one's hair with its natural texture. Those folks who had often stood passively by while observing other black folks being mistreated on the basis of skin color felt for the first time that it was politically appropriate to intervene. I remember when my siblings and I challenged our grandmother, who could pass for white, about the disparaging comments she made about dark-skinned people, including her grandchildren. Even though we were in a small Southern town, we were deeply affected by the call to end color-caste hierarchies. This process of decolonization created powerful changes in the lives of all black people in the United States. It meant that we could now militantly confront and change the devastating psychological consequences of internalized racism.

Even when collective militant black struggle for self-determination 5 began to wane, alternative ways of seeing blackness and defining beauty continued to flourish. These changes diminished as assimilation became the process by which black folks could successfully enter the mainstream. Once again, the fate of black folks rested with white power. If a black person wanted a job and found it easier to get it if she or he did not wear a natural hairstyle, this was perceived by many to be a legitimate reason to change. And of course many black and white folks felt that the gain in civil rights, racial integration, and the lifting of many long-standing racial taboos (for example, the resistance to segregated housing and interracial relationships) meant that militant struggle was no longer needed. Since freedom for black folks had been defined as gaining the rights to enter mainstream society, to assume the values and economic standing of the white privileged classes, it logically followed that it did not take long for interracial interaction in the areas of education and jobs to reinstitutionalize, in less overt ways, a system wherein individual black folks who were most like white folks in the way they looked, talked, and dressed would find it easier to be socially mobile. To some extent, the dangers of assimilation to white standards were obscured by the assumption that our ways of seeing blackness had been fundamentally changed. Aware black activists did not assume that we would ever return to social conditions where black folks would once be grappling with issues of color. While leaders such as Eldridge Cleaver, Malcolm X, George Jackson, and many others repeatedly made the issue of self-love central to black liberation struggle, new activists did not continue the emphasis on decolonization once many rights were gained. Many folks just assumed we had collectively resisted and altered color castes.

Few black activists were vigilant enough to see that concrete rewards for assimilation would undermine subversive oppositional ways of seeing blackness. Yet racial integration meant that many black folks were rejecting the ethic of communalism that had been a crucial survival strategy when racial apartheid was the norm. They were embracing liberal individualism instead. Being free was seen as having the right to satisfy individual desire without accountability to a collective body. Consequently, a black person could not feel that the way one wore one's hair was not political but simply a matter of choice. Seeking to improve class mobility, to make it in the white world, black folks begin to backtrack and assume once again the attitudes and values of internalized racism. Some folks justified their decisions to compromise and assimilate to white aesthetic standards by seeing it as simply "wearing the mask" to get over. This was best typified by those black females who wore straight, white-looking wigs to work covering a natural hairdo. Unfortunately, black acceptance of assimilation meant that a politics of representation affirming white beauty standards was being reestablished as the norm.

Without an organized, ongoing, and collective movement for black self-determination, militant black critical thinkers and activists began to constitute a subculture. A revolutionary militant stance, one that seriously critiqued capitalism and imperialism, was no longer embraced by the black masses. Given these circumstances, the radicalization of a leader such as Martin Luther King, Jr., went unnoticed by most black folks: His passionate critiques of militarism and capitalism were not heard. King was instead remembered primarily for those earlier stages of political work where he supported a bourgeois model of assimilation and social mobility. Those black activists who remained in the public eye did not continue a militant critique and interrogation of white standards of beauty. While radical activists such as Angela Davis had major public forums, continued to wear natural hair, and be black identified, they did not make the ongoing decolonization of our minds and imaginations central to their political agendas. They did not continually call for a focus on black self-love, on ending internalized racism.

Toward the end of the seventies, black folks were far less interested in calling attention to beauty standards. No one interrogated radical activists who began to straighten their hair. Heterosexual black male leaders openly chose their partners and spouses using the standards of the color-caste system. Even during the most militant stages of black power movement, they had never really stopped allowing racist notions of beauty to define female desirability, yet they preached a message of self-love and an end to internalized racism. This hypocrisy also played a major role in creating a framework where color-caste systems could once again become the accepted norm.

The resurgence of interest in black self-determination, as well as of overt white supremacism, created in the eighties a context where attention could be given to the issue of decolonization, of internalized racism. The mass media carried stories about the fact that black children had low self-esteem, that they preferred white images over black ones, that black girls liked white dolls better than black ones. This news was all presented with awe, as though there was no political context for the repudiation and devaluation of blackness. Yet the politics of racial assimilation had always operated as a form of backlash, intended to undermine black self-determination. Not all black people had closed our eyes to this reality. However, we did not have the access to the mass media and public forums that would have allowed us to launch a sustained challenge to internalized racism. Most of us continued to fight against the internalization of white supremacist thinking on whatever fronts we found ourselves. As a professor, I interrogated these issues in classrooms and as a writer in my books.

Nowadays, it is fashionable in some circles to mock the Black Power 10 struggle and see it solely as a failed social movement. It is easy for folks to make light of the slogan "black is beautiful." Yet this mockery does not change the reality that the interrogation of internalized racism embedded in this slogan and the many concrete challenges that took place in all areas of black life did produce radical changes, even though they were undermined by a white-supremacist backlash. Most folks refuse to see the intensity of this backlash, and place responsibility on radical black activists for having too superficial an agenda. The only justifiable critique we can make of the militant black-liberation struggle is its failure to institutionalize sustained strategies of critical resistance. Collectively and individually, we must all assume accountability for this failure.

White-supremacist capitalist patriarchal assaults on movements for black self-determination aimed at ending internalized racism were most effectively launched by the mass media. Institutionalizing a politics of representation which included black images, thus ending years of racial segregation, while reproducing the existing status quo, undermined black self-determination. The affirmation of assimilation as well as of racist white aesthetic standards was the most effective means to undermine efforts to transform internalized racism in the psyches of the black masses. When these racist stereotypes were coupled with a concrete reality where assimilated black folks were the ones receiving greater material reward, the culture was ripe for a resurgence of color-caste hierarchy.

Color-caste hierarchies embrace both the issue of skin color and hair texture. Since lighter-skinned black people are most often genetically connected to intergenerational pairings of both white and black people, they tend to look more like whites. Females who were the offspring of generations of interracial mixing were more likely to have long, straight hair. The exploitative and oppressive nature of color-caste systems in white-supremacist society has always had a gendered component. A mixture of racist and sexist thinking informs the way color-caste hierarchies detrimentally affect the lives of black females differently from black males. Light skin and long, straight hair continue to be traits that define a female as beautiful and desirable in the racist white imagination and in the colonized black mind set. Darker-skinned black females work to develop positive self-esteem in a society that continually devalues their image. To this day, the images of black female bitchiness, evil temper, and treachery continue to be marked by darker skin. This is the stereotype called "Sapphire"; no light skin occupies this devalued position. We see these images continually in the mass media whether they be presented to us in television sitcoms (such as the popular show *Martin*), on cop shows (the criminal black woman is usually dark), and in movies made by black and white directors alike. Spike Lee graphically portrayed the conflict of skin color in his film *School Daze,* not via male characters but by staging a dramatic fight between light-skinned women and their darker counterparts. Merely exploiting the issue, the film is neither critically subversive nor oppositional. And in many theaters black audiences loudly expressed their continued investment in color-caste hierarchies by "dissing" darker-skinned female characters.

Throughout the history of white supremacy in the United States, racist white men have regarded the biracial female as a sexual ideal. In this regard, black men have taken their cues from white men. Stereotypically portrayed as embodying a passionate sensual eroticism as well as a subordinate feminine nature, the biracial black woman has been and remains the standard other black females are measured against. Even when darker-skinned black women are given "play" in films, their characters are usually subordinated to lighter-skinned females who are deemed more desirable. For a time, films that portrayed the biracial black woman as a "tragic mulatto" were passé, but contemporary films such as the powerful drama *One False Move* return this figure to center stage. The impact of militant black-liberation struggle had once called upon white-dominated fashion magazines and black magazines to show diverse images of black female beauty. In more recent times, however, it has been acceptable simply to highlight and valorize the image of the biracial black woman. Black women models such as Naomi Campbell find that they have a greater crossover success if their images are altered by long, straight wigs, weaves, or bonded hair so that they resemble the "wannabes" — folks who affirm the equation of whiteness with beauty by seeking to take on the characteristic look of whiteness. This terrain of "drag" wherein the distinctly black-looking female is made to appear in a constant struggle to transform herself into a white female is a space only a brown-skinned black woman can occupy. Biracially black women already occupied a distinctly different, more valued place within the beauty hierarchy. As in the days of slavery and racial apartheid, white fascination with racial mixing once again determines the standard of valuation, especially when the issue is the valuation of female bodies. A world that can recognize the dark-skinned Michael Jordan as a symbol of black beauty scorns and devalues the beauty of Tracy Chapman. Black male pop icons mock her looks. And while folks comment on the fact that light-skinned and biracial women have become the stars of most movies that depict black folks, no one has organized public forums to talk about the way this mass media focus on color undermines our efforts to decolonize our minds and imaginations. Just as whites now privilege lighter skin in movies and fashion magazines, particularly with female characters, folks with darker skin face a media that subordinates their image. Dark skin is stereotypically coded in the racist, sexist, or colonized imagination as masculine. Hence, a male's power is enhanced by dark looks while a female's dark looks diminish her femininity. Irrespective of people's sexual preferences, the color-caste hierarchy functions to diminish the desirability of darker-skinned females. Being seen as desirable does not simply affect one's ability to attract partners; it enhances class mobility in public arenas, in educational systems, and in the work force.

The tragic consequences of color-caste hierarchy are evident among the very young who are striving to construct positive identity and healthy self-esteem. Black parents testify that black children learn early to devalue dark skin. One black mother in an interracial marriage was shocked when her four-year-old girl expressed the desire that her mom be white like herself and her dad. She had already learned that white was better. She had already learned to negate the blackness in herself. In high

schools all around the United States, darker-skinned black girls must resist the socialization that would have them see themselves as ugly if they
are to construct healthy self-esteem. That means they must resist the efforts of peers to devalue them. This is just one of the tragic implications
of black reinvestment in color-caste hierarchies. Had there never been a
shift in color consciousness among black people, no one would have paid
special attention to the reality that many black children seem to be having as much difficulty learning to love blackness in this racially integrated time of multiculturalism as folks had during periods of intense
racial apartheid. Kathe Sandler's documentary film *A Question of Color*
examines the way black-liberation politics of the sixties challenged color
caste even as she shows recent images of activists who returned to conventional racist-defined notions of beauty. Even though Sandler does not
offer suggestions and strategies for how we can deal with this problem
now, this film is an important intervention because it brings the issue
back into public discourse.

   To describe the problems of color caste we must address it politically   15
as a serious crisis of consciousness if we are not to return to an old model of
class and caste where those blacks who are most privileged will be light-
skinned or biracial, acting as mediators between the white world and a disenfranchised, disadvantaged mass of black folks with dark skin. Right
now there is a new wave of young, well-educated biracial folks who identify as black and who benefit from this identification both socially and
when they enter the work force. Although they realize the implicit racism
when they are valued more by whites than are darker-skinned blacks, the
ethic of liberal individualism sanctions this opportunism. Ironically, they
may be among those who critique color caste even as they accept the perks
that come from the culture's reinvestment in color-caste hierarchies. Until
black folks begin collectively to critique and question the politics of representation that systematically devalues blackness, the devastating effects of
color caste will continue to inflict psychological damage on masses of black
folks. To intervene and transform those politics of representation informed
by colonialism, imperialism, and white supremacy, we have to be willing
to challenge mainstream culture's efforts to "erase racism" by suggesting it
does not really exist. Recognizing the power of mass media images to define social reality, we need lobbyists in the government, as well as organized groups who sponsor boycotts in order to create awareness of these
concerns and to demand change. Progressive nonblack allies in struggle
must join the effort to call attention to internalized racism. Everyone must
break through the wall of denial that would have us believe a hatred of
blackness emerges from troubled individual psyches and acknowledge
that it is systematically taught through processes of socialization in white-
supremacist society. We must acknowledge, too, that black folks who have
internalized white-supremacist attitudes and values are as much agents of
this socialization as their racist nonblack counterparts. Progressive black

leaders and critical thinkers committed to a politics of cultural transformation that would constructively change the lot of the black underclass and thus positively impact the culture as a whole need to make decolonizing our minds and imagination central when we educate for critical consciousness. Learning from the past, we need to remain critically vigilant, willing to interrogate our work as well as our habits of being to ensure that we are not perpetuating internalized racism. Note that more conservative black political agendas, such as the Nation of Islam and certain strands of Afrocentrism, are the only groups who make self-love central, and as a consequence capture the imagination of a mass black public. Revolutionary struggle for black self-determination must become a real part of our lives if we want to counter conservative thinking and offer life-affirming practices to black folks daily wounded by white-supremacist assaults. Those wounds will not heal if left unattended.

PREPARING FOR DISCUSSION

`1. The primary subject of hooks's essay is "internalized racism." Describe this kind of racism and the ways in which it manifests itself according to hooks. What effect did slogans like "black is beautiful" have on traditional racist stereotypes? In what ways did the reaction against stereotypes of this kind affect the correlation between skin color and success?

2. As civil rights for African Americans increased, hooks explains, black militancy began to disappear and to be replaced by an attitude that may be described as "assimilationist." What does hooks see as the dangers of assimilation for black Americans? Why does she link the tendency for African Americans to assimilate with their embracing of "liberal individualism" as a set of cultural values?

3. Hooks contends that assimilation works ultimately "to undermine black self-determination" (paragraph 9). Why does she think it is impossible for African Americans who reject "the ethic of communalism" in favor of individualism to release themselves from the grip of "internalized racism"? Could hooks be said to be limiting the choices of black Americans in their efforts to succeed in a predominantly "white" culture?

4. Throughout the selection, hooks regards "the color-caste hierarchies" as major factors in perpetuating "internalized racism" among African Americans. Do you agree with hooks that skin color and hair texture are directly related to self-esteem among African Americans? Can you think of factors hooks does not mention that might have an even greater effect on black self-esteem?

5. The word *caste* has traditionally referred to any of the hereditary classes into which Indian society had been divided until the twentieth century. Within the caste system the classes were arranged hierarchically, and no member of one caste could associate with a member of another. Movement out of one's caste was impossible. In light of this background, why do you think that hooks has chosen

the word *caste* to describe the hierarchies of skin color and hair texture *within* the black community? How does her use of the word *caste* make the problems she brings to our attention all the more important to address?

FROM READING TO WRITING

6. In a way that transcends the issue of race, hooks maintains that "being seen as desirable does not simply affect one's ability to attract partners; it enhances class mobility in public arenas, in educational systems, and in the work force" (paragraph 13). Write an essay in which you consider the correlation of personal appearance and success from your own perspective. What kinds of difficulties are people who are not "desirable" likely to face in school, in society, or on the job? Do attractive people possess unfair advantages? If so, can anything be done about it?

7. The author notes at several points that the national media are largely responsible for the systematic devaluing of blackness. She refers to several movies and television shows in which this kind of devaluing occurs. Write an essay in which you identify and comment upon the media treatment of African Americans. Can you think of exceptions to hooks's point? To what degree might such depictions be considered intentional or unintentional?

ELIZABETH MARTÍNEZ

Seeing More than Black and White

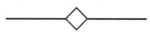

In a public discourse on racism dominated by black and white voices, Latino activists have often found it difficult to be heard. More recently, however, discussions of racism have begun to move beyond the traditional black-white model. In response to the growing number of Latinos — as well as Asian and Pacific Americans — a new concept of racism has begun to emerge. In this version, color ceases to be the key to racial definition and the more complex notion of racial mixture takes center stage. In the following selection originally published in *Z Magazine*, Elizabeth Martínez lays the groundwork for a major reconsideration of racism in America, the main goal of which is greater unity against perceived white oppression.

For more than four decades Elizabeth Martínez has been a major writer, editor, and activist in the Chicano movement. She founded the Mexican-American newspaper *El Grito del Norte* in 1968 and served as its editor until 1973. As an author, Martínez explains, she "tries to write in ways that help people see the world afresh and to understand history in revolutionary dimensions and dream new dreams." In 1982 she ran for governor of California as candidate of the Peace and Freedom party.

SELECTED PUBLICATIONS: *Letters from Mississippi* (editor) (1965); *The Youngest Revolution: A Personal Report on Cuba* (1969); *Viva la Raza! The Struggle of the Mexican-American People* (with Enriqueta Longeaux y Vasquez) (1974); *Four Hundred Fifty Years of Chicano History* (1976); Martínez also publishes frequently in the *Guardian*, the *Nation*, and *Z Magazine*.

U.S. political culture is not only Anglo-dominated but also embraces an exceptionally stubborn national self-centeredness, with no global vision other than relations of domination. The U.S. refuses to see itself as one nation sitting on a continent with 20 others all speaking languages other than English and having the right not to be dominated.

Such arrogant indifference extends to Latinos within the U.S. The mass media complain, "people can't relate to Hispanics" — or Asians, they say. Such arrogant indifference has played an important role in invisibilizing La Raza[1] (except where we become a serious nuisance or a handy scapegoat). It is one reason the U.S. harbors an exclusively white-on-Black concept of racism. It is one barrier to new thinking about racism, so crucial today. There are others.

Good-bye, White Majority

In a society as thoroughly and violently racialized as the United States, white-Black relations have defined racism for centuries. Today the composition and culture of the U.S. are changing rapidly. We need to consider seriously whether we can afford to maintain an exclusively white/Black model of racism when the population will be 32 percent Latino, Asian/Pacific American and Native American — in short, neither Black nor white — by the year 2050. We are challenged to recognize that multi-colored racism is mushrooming, and then strategize how to resist it. We are challenged to move beyond a dualism comprised of two white-supremacist inventions: Blackness and Whiteness.

At stake in those challenges is building a united anti-racist force strong enough to resist contemporary racist strategies of divide-and-conquer. Strong enough, in the long run, to help defeat racism itself. Doesn't an exclusively Black/white model of racism discourage the perception of common interests among people of color and thus impede a solidarity that can challenge white supremacy? Doesn't it encourage the isolation of African Americans from potential allies? Doesn't it

---

[1] *La Raza:* "The Race" — literal translation — term for Hispanic people.

advise all people of color to spend too much energy understanding our lives in relation to whiteness, and thus freeze us in a defensive, often self-destructive mode?

No "Oppression Olympics"

For a Latina to talk about recognizing the multi-colored varieties of racism is not, and should not be, yet another round in the Oppression Olympics. We don't need more competition among different social groupings for that "Most Oppressed" gold. We don't need more comparison of suffering between women and Blacks, the disabled and the gay, Latino teenagers and white seniors, or whatever. We don't need more surveys like the recent, much-publicized Harris Poll showing that different peoples of color are prejudiced toward each other — a poll patently designed to demonstrate that us coloreds are no better than white folk. (The survey never asked people about positive attitudes.)

Rather, we need greater knowledge, understanding, and openness to learning about each other's histories and present needs as a basis for working together. Nothing could seem more urgent in an era when increasing impoverishment encourages a self-imposed separatism among people of color as a desperate attempt at community survival. Nothing could seem more important as we search for new social change strategies in a time of ideological confusion.

My call to rethink concepts of racism in the U.S. today is being sounded elsewhere. Among academics, liberal foundation administrators, and activist-intellectuals, you can hear talk of the need for a new "racial paradigm" or model. But new thinking seems to proceed in fits and starts, as if dogged by a fear of stepping on toes, of feeling threatened, or of losing one's base. With a few notable exceptions, even our progressive scholars of color do not make the leap from perfunctorily saluting a vague multi-culturalism to serious analysis. We seem to have made little progress, if any, since Bob Blauner's 1972 book *Racial Oppression in America*. Recognizing the limits of the white-Black axis, Blauner critiqued White America's ignorance of and indifference to the Chicano/a experience with racism.

Real opposition to new paradigms also exists. There are academics scrambling for one flavor of ethnic studies funds versus another. There are politicians who cultivate distrust of others to keep their own communities loyal. When we hear, for example, of Black/Latino friction, dismay should be quickly followed by investigation. In cities like Los Angeles and New York, it may turn out that political figures scraping for patronage and payola have played a narrow nationalist game, whipping up economic anxiety and generating resentment that sets communities against each other.

So the goal here, in speaking about moving beyond a bi-polar concept of racism, is to build stronger unity against white supremacy. The goal is to see our similarities of experience and needs. If that goal sounds naive, think about the hundreds of organizations formed by grassroots women of different colors coming together in recent years. Their growth is one of today's most energetic motions and it spans all ages. Think about the multicultural environment justice movement. Think about the coalitions to save schools. Small rainbows of our own making are there, to brighten a long road through hellish times.

It is in such practice, through daily struggle together, that we are   10
most likely to find the road to greater solidarity against a common enemy. But we also need a will to find it and ideas about where, including some new theory.

The West Goes East

Until very recently, Latino invisibility — like that of Native Americans and Asian/Pacific Americans — has been close to absolute in U.S. seats of power, major institutions, and the non-Latino public mind. Having lived on both the East and West Coasts for long periods, I feel qualified to pronounce: an especially myopic view of Latinos prevails in the East. This, despite such data as a 24.4 percent Latino population of New York City alone in 1991, or the fact that in 1990 more Puerto Ricans were killed by New York police under suspicious circumstances than any other ethnic group. Latino populations are growing rapidly in many eastern cities and the rural South, yet remain invisible or stigmatized — usually both.

Eastern blinders persist. I've even heard that the need for a new racial paradigm is dismissed in New York as a California hangup. A black Puerto Rican friend in New York, when we talked about experiences of racism common to Black and brown, said, "People here don't see Border Patrol brutality against Mexicans as a form of police repression," despite the fact that the Border Patrol is the largest and most uncontrolled police force in the U.S. It would seem that an old ignorance has combined with new immigrant bashing to sustain divisions today.

While the East (and most of the Midwest) usually remains myopic, the West Coast has barely begun to move away from its own denial. Less than two years ago in San Francisco, a city almost half Latino or Asian/Pacific American, a leading daily newspaper could publish a major series on contemporary racial issues and follow the exclusively Black-white paradigm. Although millions of TV viewers saw massive Latino participation in the April 1992 Los Angeles uprising, which included 18 out of 50 deaths and the majority of arrests, the mass media and most people labeled that event "a Black riot."

If the West Coast has more recognition of those who are neither Black nor white, it is mostly out of fear about the proximate demise of its white majority. A second, closely related reason is the relentless campaign by

California Gov. Pete Wilson to scapegoat immigrants for economic problems and pass racist, unconstitutional laws attacking their health, education, and children's future. Wilson has almost single-handedly made the word "immigrant" mean Mexican or other Latino (and sometimes Asian). Who thinks of all the people coming from the former Soviet Union and other countries? The absolute racism of this has too often been successfully masked by reactionary anti-immigrant groups like FAIR blaming immigrants for the staggering African-American unemployment rate.

Wilson's immigrant bashing is likely to provide a model for other parts of the country. The five states with the highest immigration rates — California, Florida, New York, Illinois, and Texas — all have a governor up for re-election in 1994. Wilson tactics won't appear in every campaign, but some of the five states will surely see intensified awareness and stigmatization of Latinos as well as Asian/Pacific Islanders. 15

As this suggests, what has been a regional issue mostly limited to western states is becoming a national issue. If you thought Latinos were just Messicans down at the border, wake up — they are all over North Carolina, Pennsylvania and 8th Avenue Manhattan now. A qualitative change is taking place. With the broader geographic spread of Latinos and Asian/Pacific Islanders has come a nationalization of racist practices and attitudes that were once regional. The west goes east, we could say.

Like the monster Hydra, racism is growing some ugly new heads. We will have to look at them closely.

The Roots of Racism and Latinos

A bi-polar model of racism — racism as white on Black — has never really been accurate. Looking for the roots of racism in the U.S. we can begin with the genocide against American Indians which made possible the U.S. land base, crucial to white settlement and early capitalist growth. Soon came the massive enslavement of African people which facilitated that growth. As slave labor became economically critical, "blackness" became ideologically critical; it provided the very source of "whiteness" and the heart of racism. Frantz Fanon would write, "colour is the most outward manifestation of race."

If Native Americans had been a crucial labor force during those same centuries, living and working in the white man's sphere, our racist ideology might have evolved differently. "The tawny," as Ben Franklin dubbed them, might have defined the opposite of what he called "the lovely white." But with Indians decimated and survivors moved to distant concentration camps, they became unlikely candidates for this function. Similarly, Mexicans were concentrated in the distant West; elsewhere Anglo fear of them or need for control was rare. They also did not provide the foundation for a definition of whiteness.

Some anti-racist left activists have put forth the idea that only   20
African Americans experience racism as such and that the suffering of
other people of color results from national minority rather than racial oppression. From this viewpoint, the exclusively white/Black model for
racism is correct. Latinos, then, experience exploitation and repression
for reasons of culture and nationality — not for their "race." (It should go
without saying that while racism is an all-too-real social fact, race has no
scientific basis.)

Does the distinction hold? This and other theoretical questions call
for more analysis and more expertise than one article can offer. In the
meantime, let's try out the idea that Latinos do suffer for their nationality
and culture, especially language. They became part of the U.S. through
the 1848–48 war on Mexico and thus a foreign population to be colonized. But as they were reduced to cheap or semi-slave labor, they
quickly came to suffer for their "race" — meaning, as non-whites. In the
Southwest of a super-racialized nation, the broad parallelism of race and
class embraced Mexicans ferociously.

The bridge here might be a definition of racism as "the reduction of
the cultural to the biological," in the words of French scholar Christian
Delacampagne now working in Egypt. Or: "racism exists wherever it is
claimed that a given social status is explained by a given natural characteristic." We know that line: Mexicans are just naturally lazy and have
too many children, so they're poor and exploited.

The discrimination, oppression, and hatred experienced by Native
Americans, Mexicans, Asian/Pacific Islanders, and Arab Americans are
forms of racism. Speaking only of Latinos, we have seen in California and
the Southwest, especially along the border, almost 150 years of relentless
repression which today includes Central Americans among its targets.
That history reveals hundreds of lynchings between 1847 and 1935, the
use of counter-insurgency armed forces beginning with the Texas
Rangers, random torture and murder by Anglo ranchers, forced labor,
rape by border lawmen, and the prevailing Anglo belief that a Mexican
life doesn't equal a dog's in value.

But wait. If color is so key to racial definition, as Fanon and others
say, perhaps people of Mexican background experience racism less than
national minority oppression because they are not dark enough as a
group. For White America, shades of skin color are crucial to defining
worth. The influence of those shades has also been internalized by communities of color. Many Latinos can and often want to pass for whites;
therefore White America may see them as less threatening than darker
sisters and brothers.

Here we confront more of the complexity around us today, with   25
questions like: What about the usually poor, very dark Mexican or Central American of strong Indian or African heritage? (Yes, folks,
200–300,000 Africans were brought to Mexico as slaves, which is far, far

more than the number of Spaniards who came.) And what about the effects of accented speech or foreign name, characteristics that may instantly subvert "passing"?

What about those cases where a Mexican-American is never accepted, no matter how light-skinned, well-dressed, or well-spoken? A Chicano lawyer friend coming home from a professional conference in suit, tie, and briefcase found himself on a bus near San Diego that was suddenly stopped by the Border Patrol. An agent came on board and made a beeline through the all-white rows of passengers direct to my friend. "Your papers." The agent didn't believe José was coming from a U.S. conference and took him off the bus to await proof. José was lucky; too many Chicanos and Mexicans end up killed.

In a land where the national identity is white, having the "wrong" nationality becomes grounds for racist abuse. Who would draw a sharp line between today's national minority oppression, in the form of immigrant-bashing, and racism?

None of this aims to equate the African American and Latino experiences; that isn't necessary even if it were accurate. Many reasons exist for the persistence of the white/Black paradigm of racism; they include numbers, history, and the psychology of whiteness. In particular they include centuries of slave revolts, a Civil War, and an ongoing resistance to racism that cracked this society wide open while the world watched. Nor has the misery imposed on Black people lessened in recent years. New thinking about racism can and should keep this experience at the center.

A Deadly Dualism

The exclusively white/Black concept of race and racism in the U.S. rests on a western, Protestant form of dualism woven into both race and gender relations from earliest times. In the dualist universe there is only black and white. A disdain, indeed fear, of mixture haunts the Yankee soul; there is no room for any kind of multi-faceted identity, any hybridism.

As a people, La Raza combines three sets of roots — indigenous, 30
European, and African — all in widely varying degrees. In short, we represent a profoundly un-American concept: *mestizaje* (pronounced mess-tee-zah-hey), the mixing of peoples and emergence of new peoples. A highly racialized society like this one cannot deal with or allow room for *mestizaje*. It has never learned to do much more than hiss "miscegenation!" Or, like that Alabama high school principal who recently denied the right of a mixed-blood pupil to attend the prom, to say: "your parents made a mistake." Apparently we, all the millions of La Raza, are just that — a mistake.

Mexicans in the U.S. also defy the either-or, dualistic mind in that, on the one hand, we are a colonized people displaced from the ancestral homeland with roots in the present-day U.S. that go back centuries. Those ancestors didn't cross the border; the border crossed them. At the same time many of us have come to the U.S. more recently as "immigrants" seeking work. The complexity of Raza baffles and frustrates most Anglos; they want to put one neat label on us. It baffles many Latinos too, who often end up categorizing themselves racially as "Other" for lack of anything better. For that matter, the term "Latino" which I use here is a monumental simplification; it refers to 20-plus nationalities and a wide range of classes.

But we need to grapple with the complexity, for there is more to come. If anything, this nation will see more *mestizaje* in the future, embracing innumerable ethnic combinations. What will be its effects? Only one thing seems certain: "white" shall cease to be the national identity.

A glimpse at the next century tells us how much we need to look beyond the white/Black model of race relations and racism. White/Black are real poles, central to the history of U.S. racism. We can neither ignore them nor stop there. But our effectiveness in fighting racism depends on seeing the changes taking place, trying to perceive the contours of the future. From the time of the Greeks to the present, racism around the world has had certain commonalities but no permanently fixed character. It is evolving again today, and we'd best labor to read the new faces of this Hydra-headed monster. Remember, for every head that Hydra lost it grew two more.

Sometimes the problem seems so clear. Last year I showed slides of Chicano history to a Oakland high school class with 47 African Americans and three Latino students. The images included lynchings and police beatings of Mexicans and other Latinos, and many years of resistance. At the end one Black student asked, "Seems like we have had a lot of experiences in common — so why can't Blacks and Mexicans get along better?" No answers, but there was the first step: asking the question.

PREPARING FOR DISCUSSION

1. Martínez maintains that racism in America assumes other forms than that of "white on Black." How does she characterize the attitude of the United States toward other North American nations? On what grounds does she argue that this attitude extends to Latinos and other minorities living within our borders?

2. In an effort to define themselves exclusively in relation to whites, Martínez holds, African Americans and other people of color "freeze [themselves] in a defensive, often self-destructive mode" (paragraph 4). What alternative does she propose to fight traditional models of racial identity? What reasons does she provide for the failure of previous alternatives?

3. At several points in the essay, Martínez refers to the "invisibility" of Latinos in America. In paragraph 11, however, she reports that even though the

Latino population continues to grow, they "remain invisible or stigmatized —usually both." Consider the meanings of "invisibility" and "stigmatized." What could it mean to be both "invisible" and "stigmatized"? To what degree do the meanings of these two words oppose each other?

4. Martínez cites, and almost as quickly dismisses, the results of a Harris Poll that concluded that "peoples of color are prejudiced toward each other" (paragraph 5). She maintains that the poll was "patently designed to demonstrate that us coloreds are no better than white folk." Why does she adopt a stereotypical dialect speech to attack the poll's findings? Why does she raise the point that the poll did not take positive attitudes into account? To what degree does this fact compromise the poll's findings?

5. Martínez uses a number of names to describe the ethnic groups to which she refers throughout the selection. Among these names are *Latinos, Hispanics, La Raza,* and *mestizaje.* Do these names refer to the same ethnic group? In other words, are the terms interchangeable? What reasons lie behind Martínez's decision to use one name instead of another at particular points in the essay?

FROM READING TO WRITING

6. A major part of the selection revolves around Martínez's distinction between racism and what she calls "national minority oppression." According to the author, how do the two differ? Write an essay in which you consider whether the distinction is particularly useful or important. Martínez views Latinos as the victims of racism rather than national minority oppression. On what grounds does she establish racism as a major obstacle for Latinos?

7. In paragraph 22, Martínez explores the way in which racist stereotypes are often used to explain the social status of a particular group. Write an essay in which you consider the stereotypes, positive and negative, that have traditionally been ascribed to members of your ethnic group. To what degree do you think that these stereotypes have helped to explain, if not to determine, the social status of your group? To what degree have you been able to free yourself of these stereotypes?

RANDALL KENNEDY

The Phony War

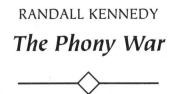

Attacks on both the arguments and the conclusions of *The Bell Curve* have not been limited to its authors' understanding of genetics, their analysis of statistics, or even to the assumptions about race and intelligence that inform the work. For example, legal scholar Randall Kennedy takes a different approach and tries to account for the controversy surrounding the book's publication by appealing to marketplace factors and, even more importantly, the current state of race relations in America. In light of the fact that almost all of the supporting evidence that appears in the book has previously been published elsewhere, Kennedy can only conclude that *The Bell Curve*'s success in creating new controversy depends upon its ability to awaken old pessimistic attitudes about the prospect for racial harmony in our nation.

Educated at Princeton, Kennedy attended Balliol College, Oxford, as a Rhodes scholar. After graduating from Yale Law School, he served from 1983 through 1984 as a law clerk to U.S. Supreme Court Justice Thurgood Marshall. Since 1989 Kennedy has been professor of law at Harvard Law School. He edits the journal *Reconstruction* and has written extensively on racial discrimination and other legal issues affecting blacks in America. The original version of this essay first appeared in the *New Republic* in October 1994, with other articles on *The Bell Curve*.

SELECTED PUBLICATIONS: *Alternative Perspectives on the U.S. Constitution* (1988); Kennedy also publishes frequently in the *Wall Street Journal*, the *New York Times*, *Time*, the *Nation*, and the *Atlantic Monthly*.

Two broad traditions encompass reflection on the prospects in the United States for racial harmony on the basis of racial equality. One is an optimistic tradition. For example, speaking in May 1865, only five months after the Emancipation Proclamation, Frederick Douglass asked whether "the white and colored people of this country can be blended into a common nationality, and enjoy together . . . under the same flag, the inestimable blessings of life, liberty, and the pursuit of happiness, as neighborly citizens of a common country." He answered "most unhesitatingly": "I believe they can." A century later, Martin Luther King, Jr., also spoke optimistically, declaring on one memorable occasion that he had a dream that the descendants of slaves and slaveholders would one day "sit down together at the table of brotherhood," and announcing in another remarkable speech that he had even glimpsed this promised land of racial justice.

A second tradition is pessimistic. Its central theme is that racial equality in America is an impossibility. Thomas Jefferson voiced this perspective when he stated that it is certain that blacks and whites "can never live in a state of equal freedom under the same Government, so insurmountable are the barriers which nature, habit, and opinion have established between them." Alexis de Tocqueville voiced this perspective too, observing in *Democracy in America* that while he did not believe "that the white and black races will ever live in any country upon an equal footing," he anticipated "the difficulty to be still greater in the United States than elsewhere." He predicted that the lingering consequences of slavery would forever poison race relations here. "Slavery recedes," he maintained, "but the prejudice to which it has given birth is immovable."

The pessimistic perspective is more interesting than its counterpart insofar as it has been voiced by a more ideologically diverse set of people. Some of its adherents have been believers in the inferiority of blacks. Others have been black nationalists like Marcus Garvey and Malcolm X who heatedly deny that blacks are by nature inferior but who also believe that whites are incapable of releasing their belief in and commitment to white supremacy. Arguing in favor of black emigration back to Africa, the black nationalist scholar Edward T. Blyden maintained in 1890 that "it ought to be clear to every thinking and impartial mind that there can never occur in this country an equality, social or political, between whites and blacks." Divided over many things, adherents to the pessimistic interpretation of American race relations share a belief that interracial harmony on the basis of racial equality will never be realized.

The Bell Curve and the controversy surrounding it nourish the pessimistic interpretation. First, and most importantly, the book purports to show that whites are, on average, intellectually superior to blacks not only in terms of present accomplishment but also in terms of future capabilities. Jefferson suspected as much. But Murray-Herrnstein now claim to have proven it scientifically with no recourse to the racist superstitions that have discredited previous assertions of white cognitive superiority. The Murray-Herrnstein presentation of this alleged fact will add a mite of legitimacy to the rumor of inferiority that has loudly echoed for generations throughout American culture.

While the alleged fact of white intellectual superiority does not logically lead to any particular policy prescription, belief in this "fact" has historically prompted or facilitated actions of such devastating divisiveness and degradation that it is no wonder that many observers have doubted the possibility of achieving racial equality in America. After all, among the reasons cited for excluding blacks from the witness stand, the jury pool, the voting booth, and all manner of occupations is that, on average, they are simply too unintelligent to be trusted with performing

5

duties that are best regarded as "white man's business." Given the uses to which claims of racial superiority in intelligence have been put, and the vexed status of the claims themselves, one might have supposed that Murray-Herrnstein would be especially rigorous. Already, however, critics have pointed out Murray-Herrnstein's failure to grapple with the complexities that bedevil "race" and "intelligence," their fundamental terms of reference; their complacent acceptance of tainted, unreliable sources; their overlooking of inconvenient facts; their mischaracterizations of those with whom they disagree; and their apparent ignorance of whole bodies of knowledge relevant to their conclusions.

These very deficiencies signal another reason that *The Bell Curve* and the controversy surrounding it lends credence to a pessimistic interpretation of American race relations. For the book's many evident weaknesses raise the question why it attained the prominence it has received. Some of the contributing causes to the unearned, unwarranted recognition accorded to *The Bell Curve* have nothing to do with the current state of race relations. They stem instead from problems in our intellectual culture that often permit, or even promote, the popularizing of poorly executed books. The biggest problem is reflected by the central, organizing metaphor of our intellectual culture: the *marketplace* of ideas. Popularity, sales, marketing, money, advertising — these are the key words of success in the commerce of books. Sometimes excellence and success in commerce overlap as in the scholarly work of Simon Schama (see, e.g., *Citizens: A Chronicle of the French Revolution*) or James M. McPherson (see, e.g., *Battle Cry of Freedom: The Civil War Era*). But it is precisely the rarity of the overlap that makes such examples so salient.

Given that much of our intellectual life is indeed run as a market, it should come as no surprise that an important reason for the *The Bell Curve*'s success is that Murray-Herrnstein (and their supporting cast of public relations consultants, advertisers, and ideological allies) are good at marketing. Knowing that controversiality attracts attention, they invested heavily into making *The Bell Curve* controversial "news." They did so by loudly proclaiming that the book reveals something hidden and taboo. Hence the publisher's dust jacket proudly asserts that *The Bell Curve* "is certain to ignite an explosive controversy." Many editors, reporters, and TV producers are attracted to this sort of talk. They see controversiality as a good in and of itself. And it probably is for those interested only in selling goods in the cultural marketplace. For those interested in the overall health of our culture, however, the fixation on mere controversiality is a pathology in need of treatment. We ought to distinguish between work that is usefully controversial because it opens up novel avenues of thought and work that is controversial merely because it provides an occasion for shouting about preformed views. The Murray-Herrnstein project falls into the latter category.

The creation of controversiality often involves striking a pose of risk-taking. Murray-Herrnstein do this repeatedly. In an essay published in *The New Republic* (after his coauthor's death), Murray claimed that the bigshots with whom they conversed as they researched *The Bell Curve* — "scholars at the top-ranked [of course] universities and think tanks, journalists from the leading [what else?] media, high [not low] public officials, senior [not junior] lawyers, financiers, and corporate executives" — tended to be "scared stiff" about answers to the authors' questions. But Murray-Herrnstein, of course, are not "scared stiff." They fearlessly pursue the Truth no matter where it leads, though interestingly enough it leads unerringly to answers that advance the ideological positions both men have long held. A profile of Murray in *The New York Times Magazine* also shows him cultivating his image as a courageous intellectual. Explaining to the reporter, Jason DeParle, his reasons for writing *The Bell Curve*, Murray is quoted as saying: "Here was a case of stumbling onto a subject that had all the allure of the forbidden. Some of the things we read to do this work, we literally had to hide when we were on planes and trains."

This is an act: the intellectual as Indiana Jones. But the act is a deception. Ensconced at the American Enterprise Institute, feted by *The Wall Street Journal* and *The National Review*, and bankrolled by wealthy supporters of right-wing reaction, Murray has little to fear. His views flatter rather than challenge his supporters. Murray's pose reflects on more than just himself; it reflects as well on his appreciative constituency. He would probably drop this pose if a sufficiently large section of his audience demanded that he quit his unbecoming self-congratulatory applause for his own supposed bravery. But the idea of "intellectual courage" has grown quite popular. As frequently used, the term is misleading or inappropriate. First, the people to whom it is applied typically risk little by taking the positions they articulate. In America, controversiality, even utter outrageousness, pays well. Second, the term is inappropriate inasmuch as it fails to illuminate intellectual quality. It might take "courage" for a would-be astronomer to argue that the sun circles the earth. But his willingness to be contentious should not obscure the utter ignorance and erroneousness of his conclusion.

There is another aspect of the pose of courageousness that warrants   10
comment. Murray-Herrnstein inveigh against the alleged "pariah status of intelligence as a construct and IQ as its measure for the past three decades." Their publisher suggests much the same. According to the dust jacket, the authors "break new ground in exploring the ways that low intelligence . . . lies as the root of many of our social problems" and "demonstrate the truth of another taboo fact: that intelligence levels differ among ethnic groups." This is hype. In fact, over a long period of time, a substantial number of investigators have asserted relationships between intelligence and social differences, including racial differences. These data form the basis of the Murray-Herrnstein speculations. But

they don't design and conduct experiments and otherwise extract primary information. They leave those chores to obscure, moderately paid academics. Murray-Herrnstein synthesize and repackage this material and bring it to a larger, more lucrative market. Their publisher indirectly acknowledges this on the book's jacket copy. Immediately after proclaiming that *The Bell Curve* demonstrates the taboo "fact" that intelligence levels differ among ethnic groups, the publisher writes that while "this finding is already well-known and widely discussed among psychometricians and other scholars," Murray-Herrnstein "open this body of scholarship to the general public." Contrary to the impression they sometimes give, Murray-Herrnstein are not intellectual pioneers; they are popularizers with a knack for sensationalism.

One must look to more than mere marketing, however, to explain *The Bell Curve*'s prominence. One must also look beyond the possibility that the book's visibility is a function of its intellectual merit, for looked at strictly in terms of intellectual craftsmanship, *The Bell Curve* is shoddily constructed. What one must look to are features of our intellectual environment that permit and indeed nurture the success of *The Bell Curve*. The importance of cultural entrepreneurs' hankering for controversiality has already been noted. But to understand what makes the Murray-Herrnstein work a *saleable* controversy requires attention to ugly features of race relations at present. For it is not every controversial utterance that attracts the sort of attention *The Bell Curve* has attracted. Also required are two closely related ingredients that *The Bell Curve* has widely been deemed to have: plausibility and respectability. Much of *The Bell Curve*'s power derives from Murray-Herrnstein's success in tapping into a widespread yearning for explanation and guidance that accepts the claim of cognitive racial inferiority as at least plausible. *The Bell Curve* would not have attracted the attention it has unless the diagnosis it offered was considered to be within the pale of respectable discussion by important arbiters of opinion, e.g., *The New York Times*, *The New Republic*, *Nightline*, etc.

This was best illustrated by the decision of *The New Republic* to print an essay by Charles Murray summarizing the main themes of *The Bell Curve*. Justifying its decision, *The New Republic* wrote that "the notion that there might be resilient ethnic differences in intelligence is not, we believe, an inherently racist belief. It's an empirical hypothesis, which can be examined." The notion that the Holocaust is a lie or greatly exaggerated is also "an empirical hypothesis which can be examined." But one can rest assured that *The New Republic* would have been unwilling to cede any of its pages to Holocaust deniers. It would refuse on several grounds, including the judgment that Holocaust deniers are unworthy of a forum because their claims, like the claim that the earth is flat, has already been decisively refuted. *The New Republic*, however, perceived as open the question of the African American's intellectual inferiority. It is the perceived plausibility of *The Bell Curve*'s racial analysis that prompts arbiters of public opinion to give *The Bell Curve* a hearing. Despite considerable disagreement with it, the notion of black intellectual inferiority is still sufficiently alive to be deemed suitable for serious debate.

The ability of Herrnstein-Murray to reach the highest levels of visibility rests not only on the perceived plausibility of black intellectual inferiority. It rests as well on a willingness by the higher-ups in public opinion management to permit the continued sullying of blacks' racial reputation. Two things in particular contribute to this malign toleration. One is the inability of the black community to discipline effectively those who defame or negligently permit the defamation of African Americans. Notwithstanding all the loose talk about political correctness, it is still largely true that journalists, scholars, and politicians can (and do) show disrespect or even outright antagonism towards blacks without paying much of a price. A second contributing factor also has to do with the convoluted politics of political correctness. Some arbiters of public opinion clearly felt the need to demonstrate publicly that they are not in thrall to PC oversensitivity. To demonstrate independence they joined the pack of journalists whose attention quickly made *The Bell Curve* into a profitable news item.

The Bell Curve controversy nourishes the pessimistic interpretation of American race relations because it elevates to prominence and influence, acclaim and profitability a book whose tone and substance drearily rehashes innuendoes and proposals that should long ago have been consigned to the dustbin of history. At the outset of this century, scholars such as Kelly Miller and W. E. B. Du Bois were forced to write careful refutations of derogatory texts which asserted the racial inferiority of blacks. One assault entitled *The Negro Is a Beast* prompted a response poignantly titled *The Negro Is a Man*. Now, at the close of the century, this struggle continues. It would be a dramatic sign of progress if there existed no felt need to debate Murray-Herrnstein, if one could simply shrug at the *The Bell Curve*'s evident deficiencies, if one did not have to agonize over the dilemma encountered by those who seek, on the one hand, to disinfect this big, sloppy, poisonous book and on the other refrain from honoring it with still more attention. But that is not our present situation. With decisions having already been made to grant *The Bell Curve* tremendous visibility, it must now be debated and refuted and demystified resolutely because its claims, albeit faulty, are nonetheless attractive to influential sectors within American society.

It would be wrong, however, to portray *The Bell Curve* controversy as a reflection of complete stagnation or retrogression in the struggle for racial justice. One of the common deficiencies in recent articulations of the pessimistic interpretation of American race relations is a willful refusal to recognize *dis*continuities as well as continuities in the history of American race relations. The debate surrounding *The Bell Curve*, albeit 15 regrettable in many ways, is nonetheless different from its predecessors. It must be appreciated that Murray-Herrnstein have been met by a quick, vigorous, sustained, and knowledgeable rebuttal. Indeed, the impulse to repudiate *The Bell Curve* is one of the things (among less creditable motivations) that has contributed to the attention it has received. The reaction against *The Bell Curve*, moreover, has not been animated only by liberals or leftists; a significant number of centrists and conservatives have joined in the repudiation as well. While clearly powerful, the cultural-political-social network which loudly and unequivocally champions *The Bell Curve* ethos is by no means ascendant. That is due, in large degree, to effective efforts undertaken by a wide range of people to uproot the racist beliefs, intuitions, and practices that are buried so deeply throughout this culture.

The stigmatization of racism is clearly incomplete. The success of *The Bell Curve* is a dismal testament to that. But the repudiation of *The Bell Curve* and the ongoing dissection of its many failings is also a testament to those strains in American culture which make optimism about the future a sensible alternative.

PREPARING FOR DISCUSSION

1. In his opening paragraphs, Kennedy describes two historical attitudes toward the prospect of racial harmony in the United States. What are these two attitudes and what in particular distinguishes one attitude from the other? Which of these two attitudes does Kennedy believe lies behind the success of *The Bell Curve*? Why?

2. Although the methodological weaknesses of *The Bell Curve* have been widely discussed in the media, the work has nevertheless achieved prominence. Why does Kennedy claim that some of the recognition granted the work has "nothing to do with the current state of race relations" (paragraph 6)? To what aspect of American intellectual culture does Kennedy attribute the book's success?

3. Kennedy claims that while the *New Republic* would never open a debate on whether or not the Holocaust occurred, its editors were willing to publish Murray and Herrnstein's "Race, Genes, and I.Q. — an Apologia" with the editorial explanation that the question of "resilient ethnic differences in intelligence" is still worth debating (paragraph 12). Why does Kennedy believe that the editors of the *New Republic* would *not* publish an article that questioned the historical occurrence of the Holocaust? On what logical grounds does he equate an article refuting that the Holocaust happened with one that purports to demonstrate that intelligence is race-linked?

4. Kennedy traces the controversial reception of *The Bell Curve* to the ability of public relations experts in publishing to generate controversy. On what assumptions about American intellectuals in particular and the reading public in general is Kennedy's scenario based? Do you agree or disagree with these assumptions? If Kennedy's "public relations" thesis is wrong, what other circumstances might account for the prominence of *The Bell Curve*?

5. Kennedy cites "the *marketplace* of ideas" as the "central, organizing metaphor of our intellectual culture" (paragraph 6). Keeping in mind that a metaphor is a way of looking at one thing from the perspective of another — in this case, ideas are viewed as merchandise — how might this particular metaphor alter our traditional notions about the ways that ideas are generated, distributed, and implemented? To the extent that the metaphor suggests that ideas are material goods, what does the metaphor say about the fate of ideas?

FROM READING TO WRITING

6. Of the two historical attitudes toward the prospect of racial harmony in the United States described in the opening paragraphs, with which are you more likely to align yourself? Write an essay in which you describe your own attitude about the future of race relations in our nation. On the basis of what evidence have you arrived at your current attitude?

7. In paragraph 12, Kennedy writes that "the notion of black intellectual inferiority is still sufficiently alive to be deemed suitable for serious debate." Do you agree or disagree with this statement? Write an essay in which you provide evidence from contemporary American culture (other than that of *The Bell Curve*) that supports your position.

J. PHILIPPE RUSHTON

Race and Crime: An International Dilemma

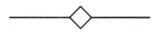

At the same time that the *The Bell Curve* was making the best-seller lists, a process Randall Kennedy describes in the preceding selection, another controversial book dealing with racial differences also appeared, though with far less publicity. Still, book reviewers immediately linked J. Philippe Rushton's *Race, Evolution, and Behavior* (1994) with the Herrnstein and Murray volume. Rushton makes a cameo appearance in *The Bell Curve*, where the authors say, "Controversy unprecedented even for the contentious subject of racial differences has erupted around the work of J. Philippe Rushton." For Rushton, the scientific scrutiny of various types of biological and physiological data demonstrates undeniable differences among what he defines as the three major world races, or "macro-races": Mongoloid, Negroid, and Caucasoid. In the following selection based on his book, Rushton argues that statistical data reliably show that criminal behavior worldwide is highest among blacks and lowest among East Asians, who also outperform the other races on measures of intelligence. Rushton then explains these significant differences within a context of genetics and evolutionary biology.

J. Philippe Rushton is a professor of psychology at the University of Western Ontario in London, Ontario. Unlike Charles Murray, he claims his work is *not* political and maintains "there are no necessary policies that flow from race research." The author of numerous scholarly articles in developmental psychology, Rushton is cited eleven times in *The Bell Curve's* bibliography.

SELECTED PUBLICATIONS: *Altruism, Socialization, and Society* (1980); *Race, Evolution, and Behavior* (1994).

In their magisterial *Crime and Human Nature,* J. Q. Wilson and R. J. Herrnstein noted that the Asian underrepresentation in U.S. crime statistics posed a theoretical problem. The solution proposed by criminologists as early as the 1920s was that the Asian "ghetto" protected members from the disruptive tendencies of the outside society. For blacks, however, the ghetto is said to foster crime.

The overrepresentation of blacks in U.S. crime statistics has existed since the turn of the twentieth century. The census of 1910 showed more blacks than whites in jail, in the north as well as in the south. Official figures from the 1930s through the 1950s showed that the number of blacks arrested for crimes of violence in proportion to the number of whites ranged from 6:1 to 16:1. These statistics have not improved in the interim.

Breaching a long taboo, liberals from Bill Clinton to Jesse Jackson have recently made it respectable to theorize about "black-on-black" crime. Conservative magazines like the *National Review* have also begun to discuss aspects of the race/crime link (see "Blacks . . . and Crime," May 16, 1994; "How to Cut Crime," May 30, 1994). What is yet to be acknowledged, however, is the international generalizability of the race/crime relationship. The matrix found within the United States, with Asians being most law-abiding, Africans least, and Europeans intermediate, is to be observed in other multiracial countries like Britain, Brazil, and Canada. Moreover, the pattern is revealed in China and the Pacific Rim, Europe and the Middle East, and Africa and the Caribbean. Because the "American dilemma" is global in manifestation, explanations must go well beyond U.S. particulars.

I emphasize at the outset that enormous variability exists within each of the populations on many of the traits to be discussed. Because distributions substantially overlap, with average differences amounting to between 4 and 34 percent, it is highly problematic to generalize from a group average to a particular individual. Nonetheless, as I hope to show, significant racial variation exists, not only in crime but also in other traits that predispose to crime, including testosterone, brain size, temperament, and cognitive ability.

The global nature of the racial pattern in crime is shown in data collated from INTERPOL using the 1984 and 1986 yearbooks. After analyzing information on nearly 100 countries, I reported, in the 1990 issue of the *Canadian Journal of Criminology*, that African and Caribbean countries had double the rate of violent crime (an aggregate of murder, rape, and serious assault) than did European countries, and three times more than did countries in the Pacific Rim. Averaging over the three crimes and two time periods, the figures per 100,000 population were, respectively, 142, 74, and 43.

I have corroborated these results using the most recent INTERPOL yearbook (1990). The rates of murder, rape, and serious assault per 100,000 population reported for 23 predominantly African countries, 41 Caucasian countries, and 12 Asian countries were: for murder, 13, 5, and 3; for rape, 17, 6, and 3; and for serious assault, 213, 63, and 27. Summing the crimes gave figures per 100,000, respectively, of 243, 74, and 33. The gradient remained robust over contrasts of racially homogeneous countries in northeast Asia, central Europe, and sub-Saharan Africa, or of racially mixed but predominantly black or white/Amerindian countries in the Caribbean and Central America. In short, a stubborn pattern exists worldwide that requires explanation.

Testosterone and the Family

The breakdown of the black family and the strengths of the Asian family are often used to explain the crime pattern within the United States. Learning to follow rules is thought to depend on family socialization. Since the 1965 Moynihan Report documented the high rates of marital dissolution, frequent heading of families by women, and numerous illegitimate births, the figures cited as evidence for the instability of the black family in America have tripled.

A similarly constituted matrifocal black family exists in the Caribbean with father-absent households, lack of paternal certainty, and separate bookkeeping by spouses. The Caribbean pattern, like the American one, is typically attributed to the long legacy of slavery. However, the slavery hypothesis does not fit data from sub-Saharan Africa. After reviewing long-standing African marriage systems in the 1989 issue of *Ethology and Sociobiology*, anthropologist Patricia Draper of Pennsylvania State University concluded: "coupled with low investment parenting is a mating pattern that permits early sexual activity, loose economic and emotional ties between spouses . . . and in many cases the expectation on the part of both spouses that the marriage will end in divorce or separation, followed by the formation of another union."

The African marriage system may partly depend on traits of temperament. Biological variables such as the sex hormone testosterone are implicated in the tendency toward multiple relationships as well as the tendency to commit crime. One study, published in the 1993 issue of *Criminology* by Alan Booth and D. Wayne Osgood, showed clear evidence of a testosterone-crime link based on an analysis of 4,462 U.S. military personnel. Other studies have linked testosterone to an aggressive and impulsive personality, to a lack of empathy, and to sexual behavior. Testosterone levels explain why young men are disproportionately represented in crime statistics relative to young women, and why younger people are more trouble-prone than older people. Testosterone reliably differentiates the sexes and is known to decline with age.

Ethnic differences exist in average levels of testosterone. Studies show   10
3 to 19 percent more testosterone in black college students and military veterans than in their white counterparts. Studies among the Japanese show a correspondingly lower amount of testosterone than among white Americans. Medical research has focused on cancer of the prostate, one determinant of which is testosterone. Black men have higher rates of prostate cancer than do white men who in turn have higher rates than do Oriental men.

Sex hormones also influence reproductive physiology. Whereas the average woman produces 1 egg every 28 days in the middle of the menstrual cycle, some women have shorter cycles and others produce more than one egg; both events translate into greater fecundity including the birth of dizygotic (two-egg) twins. Black women average shorter menstrual cycles than white women and produce a greater frequency of dizygotic twins. The rate per 1,000 births is less than 4 among east Asians, 8 among whites, and 16 or greater among Africans and African-Americans.

Racial differences exist in sexual behavior, as documented by numerous surveys including those carried out by the World Health Organization. Africans, African-Americans, and blacks living in Britain are more sexually active, at an earlier age, and with more sexual partners than are Europeans and white Americans, who in turn are more sexually active, at an earlier age, and with more sexual partners than are Asians, Asian-Americans, and Asians living in Britain. Differences in sexual activity translate into consequences. Teenage fertility rates around the world show the racial gradient, as does the pattern of sexually transmitted diseases. World Health Organization Technical Reports and other studies examining the worldwide prevalence of AIDS, syphilis, gonorrhea, herpes, and chlamydia typically find low levels in China and Japan and high levels in Africa, with European countries intermediate. This is also the pattern found within the United States.

International data on personality and temperament show that blacks are less restrained and less quiescent than whites and whites are less restrained and less quiescent than Orientals. With infants and young children observer ratings are the main method employed, whereas with adults the use of standardized tests are more frequent. One study in French-language Quebec examined 825 four- to six-year olds from 66 countries rated by 50 teachers. All the children were in preschool French-language immersion classes for immigrant children. Teachers consistently reported better social adjustment and less hostility-aggression from east Asian than from white than from African-Caribbean children. Another study based on twenty-five countries from around the world showed that east Asians were less extraverted and more anxiety-prone than Europeans, who in turn were less outgoing and more restrained than Africans.

Behavior Genetics

Differences between individuals in testosterone and its various metabolites are about 50 percent heritable. More surprising to many are the studies suggesting that criminal tendencies are also heritable. According to American, Danish, and Swedish adoption studies, children who were adopted in infancy were at greater risk for criminal convictions if their biological parents had been convicted than if the adopting parents who raised them had been convicted. In one study of all 14,427 nonfamilial adoptions in Denmark from 1924 to 1947, it was found that siblings and half-siblings adopted separately into different homes were concordant for convictions.

Convergent with this adoption work, twin studies find that identical twins are roughly twice as much alike in their criminal behavior as fraternal twins. In 1986 I reported the results of a study of 576 pairs of adult twins on dispositions to altruism, empathy, nurturance, and aggressiveness, traits which parents are expected to socialize heavily. Yet 50 percent of the variance in both men and women was attributable to genetics. The well-known Minnesota Study of Twins Raised Apart led by Thomas J. Bouchard, Jr., has confirmed the importance of genetic factors to personality traits such as aggressiveness, dominance, and impulsivity. David Rowe at the University of Arizona reviewed much of this literature in his 1994 book *Limits of Family Influence*. He explains how siblings raised together in the same family may differ genetically from each other in delinquency.

Genes code for enzymes, which, under the influence of the environment, lay down tracts in the brains and neurohormonal systems of individuals, thus affecting people's minds and the choices they make about behavioral alternatives. In regard to aggression, for example, people inherit nervous systems that dispose them to anger, irritability, impulsivity, and a lack of conditionability. In general, these factors influence *self-control*, a psychological variable figuring prominently in theories of criminal behavior.

Behavior genetic studies provide information about environmental effects. As described in Rowe's book, the important variables turn out to be within a family, not between families. Factors such as social class, family religion, parental values, and child-rearing styles are not found to have a strong common effect on siblings. Because individual minds channel common environments in separate ways, siblings acquire alternative sets of information. Although siblings resemble each other in their exposure to violent television programs, it is the more aggressive one who identifies with aggressive characters and who views aggressive consequences as positive.

Within-family studies show that intelligence and temperament separate siblings in proneness to delinquency. It is not difficult to imagine how an intellectually less able and temperamentally more impulsive sibling seeks out a social environment different from his or her more able and less impulsive sibling. Within the constraints allowed by the total spectrum of cultural alternatives, people create environments maximally compatible with their genotypes. Genetic similarity explains the tendency for trouble-prone personalities to seek each other out for friendship and marriage.

One objection sometimes made to genetic theories of crime is the finding that crime rates fluctuate with social conditions. Generational changes in crime, however, are expected by genetic theories. As environments become less impeding and more equal, the genetic contribution to individual difference variation necessarily becomes larger. Over the last 50 years, for example, there has been an increase in the genetic contribution to both academic attainment and longevity as harmful environmental effects have been mitigated and more equal opportunities created. Thus, easing social constraints on underlying "at risk" genotypes leads to an increase in criminal behavior.

Intelligence

The role of low cognitive ability in disposing a child to delinquency is established even within the same family where a less able sibling is observed to engage in more deviant behavior than an advantaged sibling. Problem behaviors begin early in life and manifest themselves as an unwillingness or inability to follow family rules. Later, drug abuse, early onset of sexual activity, and more clearly defined illegal acts make up the broad-based syndrome predicted by low intelligence.

Racial differences exist in average IQ-test scores and again the pattern extends well beyond the United States. The global literature on IQ was reviewed by Richard Lynn in the 1991 issue of *Mankind Quarterly*. Caucasoids of North America, Europe, and Australasia generally obtained mean IQs of around 100. Mongoloids from both North America and the Pacific Rim obtained slightly higher means, in the range of 101 to

20

111. Africans from south of the Sahara, African-Americans, and African-Caribbeans (including those living in Britain) obtained mean IQs ranging from 70 to 90.

The question remains of whether test scores are valid measures of group differences in mental ability. Basically, the answer hinges on whether the tests are culture-bound. Doubts linger in many quarters, although a large body of technical work has disposed of this problem among those with psychometric expertise, as shown in the book of surveys by Mark Snyderman and Stanley Rothman. This is because the tests show similar patterns of internal item consistency and predictive validity for all groups, and the same differences are to be found on relatively culture-free tests.

Novel data about speed of decision making show that the racial differences in mental ability are pervasive. Cross-cultural investigations of reaction times have been done on nine- to twelve-year-olds from six countries. In these elementary tasks, children must decide which of several lights is on, or stands out from others, and move a hand to press a button. All children can perform the tasks in less than one second, but more intelligent children, as measured by traditional IQ tests, perform the task faster than do less intelligent children. Richard Lynn found Oriental children from Hong Kong and Japan to be faster in decision time than white children from Britain and Ireland, who were faster than black children from Africa. Arthur Jensen has reported the same three-way pattern in California.

Brain Size

The relation between mental ability and brain size has been established in studies using magnetic resonance imaging, which, *in vivo*, construct three-dimensional pictures of the brain and confirm correlations reported since the turn of the century measuring head perimeter. The brain size/cognitive ability correlations range from about 0.10 to 0.40. Moreover, racial differences are found in brain size. It has often been held that racial differences in brain size, established in the nineteenth century, disappear when corrections are made for body size and other variables such as bias. However, modern studies confirm nineteenth-century findings.

Three main procedures have been used to estimate brain size: (a) weighing wet brains at autopsy; (b) measuring the volume of empty skulls using filler; and (c) measuring external head size and estimating volume. Data from all three sources triangulate on the conclusion that, after statistical corrections are made for body size, east Asians average about 17 cm^3 (1 cubic inch) more cranial capacity than whites who average about 80 cm^3 (5 cubic inches) more than blacks. Ho and colleagues at the Medical College of Wisconsin analyzed brain autopsy data on 1,261 American subjects aged 25 to 80 after excluding obviously damaged brains and reported, in the 1980 issue of *Archives of Pathology and Laboratory Medicine*, that, after controlling for age and body size, white men averaged 100 grams more brain weight than black men, and white women averaged 100 grams more brain weight than black women. With endocranial volume, Beals and colleagues computerized the world database of up to 20,000 crania and published their results in the 1984 issue of *Current Anthropology*. Sex-combined brain cases differed by continental area with populations from Asia averaging 1,415 cm^3, those from Europe averaging 1,362 cm^3, and those from Africa averaging 1,268 cm^3.

Using external head measurements I have found, after corrections are made for body size, that east Asians consistently average a larger brain than do Caucasians or Africans. Three of these studies were published in the journal *Intelligence*. In a 1991 study, from data compiled by the U.S. space agency NASA, military samples from Asia averaged 14 cm^3 more cranial capacity than those from Europe. In a stratified random sample of 6,325 U.S. Army personnel measured in 1988 for fitting helmets, I found that Asian-Americans averaged 36 cm^3 more than European-Americans, who averaged 21 cm^3 more than African-Americans. Most recently, I analyzed data from tens of thousands of men and women aged 25 to 45 collated by the International Labour Office in Geneva and found that Asians averaged 10 cm^3 more than Europeans and 66 cm^3 more than Africans.

Racial differences in brain size and IQ show up early in life. Data from the National Collaborative Perinatal Project on 19,000 black children and 17,000 white children show that black children have a smaller head perimeter at birth and, although they are born shorter in stature and lighter in weight, by age seven "catch-up growth" leads them to be larger in body size than white children, but still smaller in head perimeter. Head perimeter at birth correlated with IQ at age seven in both the black and the white children.

Origins of Race Differences

Racial differences exist at a more profound level than is normally considered. Why do Europeans average so consistently between Africans and Asians in crime, family system, sexual behavior, testosterone level, intelligence, and brain size? It is almost certain that genetics and evolution have a role to play. Transracial adoption studies indicate genetic influence. Studies of Korean and Vietnamese children adopted into white American and white Belgian homes showed that, although as babies many had been hospitalized for malnutrition, they grew to excel in academic ability with IQs ten points higher than their adoptive national norms. By contrast, Sandra Scarr and her colleagues at Minnesota found that at age 17, black and mixed-race children adopted into white middle-class families performed at a lower level than the white siblings with whom they were raised. Adopted white children had an average IQ of 106, an average aptitude based on national norms at the 59th percentile, and a class rank at the 54th percentile; mixed-race children had an average IQ of 99, an aptitude at the 53rd percentile, and a class rank at the 40th percentile; and black children had an average IQ of 89, an aptitude at the 42nd percentile, and a class rank at the 36th percentile.

No known environmental variable can explain the inverse relation across the three races between gamete production (two-egg twinning) and brain size. The only known explanation for this trade-off is life-history theory. A life-history is a genetically organized suite of characters that evolved in a coordinated manner so as to allocate energy to survival, growth, and reproduction. There is, in short, a trade-off between parental effort, including paternal investment, and mating effort, a distinction Patricia Draper referred to as one between "cads" and "dads."

Evolutionary hypotheses have been made for why Asians have the largest brains and the most parenting investment strategy. The currently accepted view of human origins, the "African Eve" theory, posits a beginning in Africa some 200,000 years ago, an exodus through the Middle East with an African/non-African split about 110,000 years ago, and a Caucasoid/Mongoloid split about 40,000 years ago. Evolutionary selection pressures are different in the hot savanna where Africans evolved than in the cold arctic where Asians evolved.

The evidence shows that the further north the populations migrated out of Africa, the more they encountered the cognitively demanding problems of gathering and storing food, gaining shelter, making clothes, and raising children successfully during prolonged winters. The evolutionary sequence fits with and helps to explain how and why the variables cluster. As the original African populations evolved into Caucasoids and Mongoloids, they did so in the direction of larger brains and lower levels of sex hormone, with concomitant reductions in aggression and sexual potency and increases in forward planning and family stability.

Despite the vast body of evidence now accumulating for important genetic and behavioral differences among the three great macro-races, there is much reluctance to accept that the differences in crime are deeply rooted. Perhaps one must sympathize with fears aroused by race research. But all theories of human nature can be used to generate abusive policies. And a rejection of the genetic basis for racial variation in behavior is not only poor scholarship, it may be injurious to unique individuals and to complexly structured societies. Moreover, it should be emphasized that probably no more than about 50 percent of the variance among races is genetic, with the remaining 50 percent due to the environment. Even genetic effects are necessarily mediated by neuroendocrine and psychosocial mechanisms, thus allowing opportunity for benign intervention and the alleviation of suffering.

PREPARING FOR DISCUSSION

1. Rushton's title refers to the famous book on race relations mentioned in the chapter introduction, Gunnar Myrdal's influential *The American Dilemma*. Why does Rushton echo this title? Why is it important to his study that the "American dilemma" is global and that "explanations must go well beyond U.S. particulars"?

2. Rushton accepts the evolutionary theory that human origins began with an "African Eve," some 200,000 years ago. If that is the case, then how, in Rushton's view, did other races evolve and develop different characteristics? In what sense does his explanation depend on environmental factors? In what sense does it depend on genetic factors? What does he mean by "life history theory"?

3. Rushton's title indicates that his essay will be about "race and crime." Yet by crime, he means strictly "violent crime." Do you think his group proportions would be the same if he included all types of criminal behavior: theft, fraud, embezzlement, tax evasion, drunk-driving felonies, violations of public health and safety laws, and so forth? Why do you think he calculates only violent crimes?

4. It is only in his final paragraph that Rushton alludes to the policy implications of his theory. In what ways might his own explanations "be used to generate abusive policies"? What might some of these policies be? If politically abusive policies were implemented as a result of his explanations, would you consider him to be personally responsible for whatever suffering might occur? What implications would your decision have on academic research?

5. An important part of Rushton's explanation depends on his use of "low-investment parenting." He never explicitly defines this social science term. What do you think it means? Why is the concept crucial to Rushton's argument? He also cites an anthropologist who uses a less "scientific" expression — "cads" and "dads." What is meant by that expression?

FROM READING TO WRITING

6. Rushton uses statistical data and psychological research reports to construct his case about racial differences. He never introduces — the way a journalist might — individual anecdotes or his own personal impressions. Using Rushton's data and research, write an essay in which you discuss whether you believe they conform to general public impressions. Do you think, for example, that his racial explanations of crime are confirmed or contradicted by media coverage and popular opinion? Do you think that most people — based on their personal experiences — would find Rushton's conclusions surprising? Why or why not?

7. Rushton concludes his essay by stating that despite "the vast body of evidence now accumulating for important genetic and behavioral differences among the three great macro-races, there is much reluctance to accept that differences in crime are deeply rooted." In an essay, offer some reasons for this reluctance. Rushton mentions the "fears aroused by race research." What is the source of these fears? In your essay consider whether such fears are legitimate or mis-

guided. Do you think the reluctance and fears Rushton mentions are caused by "race research" itself or by the interpretations the research can lead to? Would it, for example, be possible to accept all of Rushton's statistics yet derive from them a totally different explanation? Or, in your opinion, do the data lead to certain conclusions?

LANI GUINIER

The Tyranny of the Majority

$$\diamondsuit$$

In April 1993, President Clinton nominated legal theorist Lani Guinier to the position of assistant attorney general for civil rights. Many politicians and a large segment of the American press immediately responded to the news of Guinier's nomination with charges that her theories were antidemocratic and ultimately divisive. Within a week the president withdrew his nomination on grounds that upon rereading Guinier's writings he found her ideas on social justice to be radically different from his own. At the center of the controversy was Guinier's proposal for electoral reform. The principle of majority rule, she contends, results in the effective silencing of minority interests and leads to a sense of political disenfranchisement among African Americans and other racial groups. Guinier thus proposes a revised electoral system in which the interests of both "winning" and "losing" voters are represented. In the following selection from *The Tyranny of the Majority* (1995), she describes the concept of "cumulative voting" and examines the sociopolitical conditions that, she believes, make such electoral reform necessary.

After graduating from Yale Law School, Guinier was appointed special assistant to Assistant Attorney General Drew S. Days III. From 1981 through 1988 she served as assistant counsel for the NAACP Legal Defense and Educational Fund. Guinier is professor of law at the University of Pennsylvania, where she focuses on legal issues related to race and discrimination.

SELECTED PUBLICATION: *The Tyranny of the Majority: Fundamental Fairness and Representative Democracy* (1995).

I have always wanted to be a civil rights lawyer. This lifelong ambition is based on a deep-seated commitment to democratic fair play — to playing by the rules as long as the rules are fair. When the rules seem unfair, I have worked to change them, not subvert them. When I was eight years old, I was a Brownie. I was especially proud of my uniform, which represented a commitment to good citizenship and good deeds. But one day, when my Brownie group staged a hatmaking contest, I realized that uniforms are only as honorable as the people who wear them. The contest was rigged. The winner was assisted by her milliner mother, who actually made the winning entry in full view of all the participants. At the time, I was too young to be able to change the rules, but I was old enough to resign, which I promptly did.

To me, fair play means that the rules encourage everyone to play. They should reward those who win, but they must be acceptable to those who lose. The central theme of my academic writing is that not all rules lead to elemental fair play. Some even commonplace rules work against it.

The professional milliner competing with amateur Brownies stands as an example of rules that are patently rigged or patently subverted. Yet, sometimes, even when rules are perfectly fair in form, they serve in practice to exclude particular groups from meaningful participation. When they do not encourage everyone to play, or when, over the long haul, they do not make the losers feel as good about the outcomes as the winners, they can seem as unfair as the milliner who makes the winning hat for her daughter.

Sometimes, too, we construct rules that force us to be divided into winners and losers when we might have otherwise joined together. This idea was cogently expressed by my son, Nikolas, when he was four years old, far exceeding the thoughtfulness of his mother when she was an eight-year-old Brownie. While I was writing one of my law journal articles, Nikolas and I had a conversation about voting prompted by a *Sesame Street Magazine* exercise. The magazine pictured six children: four children had raised their hands because they wanted to play tag; two had their hands down because they wanted to play hide-and-seek. The magazine asked its readers to count the number of children whose hands were raised and then decide what game the children would play.

Nikolas quite realistically replied, "They will play both. First they will play tag. Then they will play hide-and-seek." Despite the magazine's "rules," he was right. To children, it is natural to take turns. The winner may get to play first or more often, but even the "loser" gets something. His was a positive-sum solution that many adult rule-makers ignore.

The traditional answer to the magazine's problem would have been a zero-sum solution: "The children — all the children — will play tag, and only tag." As a zero-sum solution, everything is seen in terms of "I win; you lose." The conventional answer relies on winner-take-all majority rule, in which the tag players, as the majority, win the right to decide for all the children what game to play. The hide-and-seek preference becomes irrelevant. The numerically more powerful majority choice simply subsumes minority preferences.

In the conventional case, the majority that rules gains all the power and the minority that loses gets none. For example, two years ago Brother Rice High School in Chicago held two senior proms. It was not planned that way. The prom committee at Brother Rice, a boys' Catholic high school, expected just one prom when it hired a disc jockey, picked a rock band, and selected music for the prom by consulting student preferences. Each senior was asked to list his three favorite songs, and the band would play the songs that appeared most frequently on the lists.

Seems attractively democratic. But Brother Rice is predominantly white, and the prom committee was all white. That's how they got two proms. The black seniors at Brother Rice felt so shut out by the "democratic process" that they organized their own prom. As one black student put it: "For every vote we had, there were eight votes for what they wanted. . . . [W]ith us being in the minority we're always outvoted. It's as if we don't count."

Some embittered white seniors saw things differently. They complained that the black students should have gone along with the majority: "The majority makes a decision. That's the way it works."

In a way, both groups were right. From the white students' perspective, this was ordinary decisionmaking. To the black students, majority rule sent the message: "we don't count" is the "way it works" for minorities. In a racially divided society, majority rule may be perceived as majority tyranny.

That is a large claim, and I do not rest my case for it solely on the actions of the prom committee in one Chicago high school. To expand the range of the argument, I first consider the ideal of majority rule itself, particularly as reflected in the writings of James Madison and other founding members of our Republic. These early democrats explored the relationship between majority rule and democracy. James Madison warned, "If a majority be united by a common interest, the rights of the minority will be insecure." The tyranny of the majority, according to Madison, requires safeguards to protect "one part of the society against the injustice of the other part."

For Madison, majority tyranny represented the great danger to our early constitutional democracy. Although the American revolution was fought against the tyranny of the British monarch, it soon became clear that there was another tyranny to be avoided. The accumulations of all powers in the same hands, Madison warned, "whether of one, a few, or many, and whether hereditary, self-appointed, or elective, may justly be pronounced the very definition of tyranny."

As another colonist suggested in papers published in Philadelphia, "We have been so long habituated to a jealousy of tyranny from monarchy and aristocracy, that we have yet to learn the dangers of it from democracy." Despotism had to be opposed "whether it came from Kings, Lords or the people."

The debate about majority tyranny reflected Madison's concern that the majority may not represent the whole. In a homogeneous society, the interest of the majority would likely be that of the minority also. But in a heterogeneous community, the majority may not represent all competing interests. The majority is likely to be self-interested and ignorant or indifferent to the concerns of the minority. In such case, Madison observed, the assumption that the majority represents the minority is "altogether fictitious."

Yet even a self-interested majority can govern fairly if it cooperates   15
with the minority. One reason for such cooperation is that the self-interested majority values the principle of reciprocity. The self-interested majority worries that the minority may attract defectors from the majority and become the next governing majority. The Golden Rule principle of reciprocity functions to check the tendency of a self-interested majority to act tyrannically.

So the argument for the majority principle connects it with the value of reciprocity: You cooperate when you lose in part because members of the current majority will cooperate when they lose. The conventional case for the fairness of majority rule is that it is not really the rule of a fixed group — The Majority — on all issues; instead it is the rule of shifting majorities, as the losers at one time or on one issue join with others and become part of the governing coalition at another time or on another issue. The result will be a fair system of mutually beneficial cooperation. I call a majority that rules but does not dominate a Madisonian Majority.

The problem of majority tyranny arises, however, when the self-interested majority does not need to worry about defectors. When the majority is fixed and permanent, there are no checks on its ability to be overbearing. A majority that does not worry about defectors is a majority with total power.

In such a case, Madison's concern about majority tyranny arises. In a heterogeneous community, any faction with total power might subject "the minority to the caprice and arbitrary decisions of the majority, who instead of consulting the interest of the whole community collectively, attend sometimes to partial and local advantages."

"What remedy can be found in a republican Government, where the majority must ultimately decide," argued Madison, but to ensure "that no one common interest or passion will be likely to unite a majority of the whole number in an unjust pursuit." The answer was to disaggregate the majority to ensure checks and balances or fluid, rotating interests. The minority needed protection against an overbearing majority, so that "a common sentiment is less likely to be felt, and the requisite concert less likely to be formed, by a majority of the whole."

Political struggles would not be simply a contest between rulers and   20
people; the political struggles would be among the people themselves.
The work of government was not to transcend different interests but to
reconcile them. In an ideal democracy, the people would rule, but the minorities would also be protected against the power of majorities. Again,
where the rules of decisionmaking protect the minority, the Madisonian
Majority rules without dominating.

But if a group is unfairly treated, for example, when it forms a racial
minority, *and* if the problems of unfairness are not cured by conventional
assumptions about majority rule, then what is to be done? The answer is
that we may need an *alternative* to winner-take-all majoritarianism. With
Nikolas's help, I now call the alternative the "principle of taking turns."
In a racially divided society, this principle does better than simple majority rule if it accommodates the values of self-government, fairness, deliberation, compromise, and consensus that lie at the heart of the democratic
ideal.

In my legal writing, I follow the caveat of James Madison and other
early American democrats. I explore decisionmaking rules that might
work in a multi-racial society to ensure that majority rule does not become majority tyranny. I pursue voting systems that might disaggregate
The Majority so that it does not exercise power unfairly or tyrannically. I
aspire to a more cooperative political style of decisionmaking to enable
all of the students at Brother Rice to feel comfortable attending the same
prom. In looking to create Madisonian Majorities, I pursue a positive-
sum, taking-turns solution.

Structuring decisionmaking to allow the minority "a turn" may be
necessary to restore the reciprocity ideal when a fixed majority refuses to
cooperate with the minority. If the fixed majority loses its incentive to follow the Golden Rule principle of shifting majorities, the minority never
gets to take a turn. Giving the minority a turn does not mean the minority gets to rule; what it does mean is that the minority gets to influence
decisionmaking and the majority rules more legitimately.

Instead of automatically rewarding the preferences of the monolithic
majority, a taking-turns approach anticipates that the majority rules, but
is not overbearing. Because those with 51 percent of the votes are not assured 100 percent of the power, the majority cooperates with, or at least
does not tyrannize, the minority.

The sports analogy of "I win; you lose" competition within a political   25
hierarchy makes sense when only one team can win; Nikolas's intuition
that it is often possible to take turns suggests an alternative approach.
Take family decisionmaking, for example. It utilizes a taking-turns approach. When parents sit around the kitchen table deciding on a vacation
destination or activities for a rainy day, often they do not simply rely on a
show of hands, especially if that means that the older children always
prevail or if affinity groups among the children (those who prefer movies

to video games, or those who prefer baseball to playing cards) never get to play their activity of choice. Instead of allowing the majority simply to rule, the parents may propose that everyone take turns, going to the movies one night and playing video games the next. Or as Nikolas proposes, they might do both on a given night.

Taking turns attempts to build consensus while recognizing political or social differences, and it encourages everyone to play. The taking-turns approach gives those with the most support more turns, but it also legitimates the outcome from each individual's perspective, including those whose views are shared only by a minority.

In the end, I do not believe that democracy should encourage rule by the powerful — even a powerful majority. Instead, the ideal of democracy promises a fair discussion among self-defined equals about how to achieve our common aspirations. To redeem that promise, we need to put the idea of taking turns and disaggregating the majority at the center of our conception of representation. Particularly as we move into the twenty-first century as a more highly diversified citizenry, it is essential that we consider the ways in which voting and representational systems succeed or fail at encouraging Madisonian Majorities.

To use Nikolas's terminology, "it is no fair" if a fixed, tyrannical majority excludes or alienates the minority. It is no fair if a fixed, tyrannical majority monopolizes all the power all the time. It is no fair if we engage in the periodic ritual of elections, but only the permanent majority gets to choose who is elected. Where we have tyranny by The Majority, we do not have genuine democracy.

My life's work, with the essential assistance of people like Nikolas, has been to try to find the rules that can best bring us together as a democratic society. Some of my ideas about democratic fair play were grossly mischaracterized in the controversy over my nomination to be Assistant Attorney General for Civil Rights. Trying to find rules to encourage fundamental fairness inevitably raises the question posed by Harvard Professor Randall Kennedy in a summary of this controversy: "What is required to create political institutions that address the needs and aspirations of all Americans, not simply whites, who have long enjoyed racial privilege, but people of color who have long suffered racial exclusion from policymaking forums?" My answer, as Professor Kennedy suggests, varies by situation. But I have a predisposition, reflected in my son's yearning for a positive-sum solution, to seek an integrated body politic in which all perspectives are represented and in which all people work together to find common ground. I advocate empowering voters and their representatives in ways that give even minority voters a chance to influence legislative outcomes.

But those in the majority do not lose; they simply learn to take turns. 30
This is a positive-sum solution that allows all voters to feel that they par-

ticipate meaningfully in the decisionmaking process. This is a positive-sum solution that makes legislative outcomes more legitimate.

I have been roundly, and falsely, criticized for focusing on outcomes. Outcomes are indeed relevant, but *not* because I seek to advance particular ends, such as whether the children play tag or hide-and-seek, or whether the band at Brother Rice plays rock music or rap. Rather, I look to outcomes as *evidence* of whether all the children — or all the high school seniors — feel that their choice is represented and considered. The purpose is not to guarantee "equal legislative outcomes"; equal opportunity to *influence* legislative outcomes regardless of race is more like it.

For these reasons, I sometimes explore alternatives to simple, winner-take-all majority rule. I do not advocate any one procedural rule as a universal panacea for unfairness. Nor do I propose these remedies primarily as judicial solutions. They can be adopted only in the context of litigation after the court first finds a legal violation.

Outside of litigation, I propose these approaches as political solutions if, depending on the local context, they better approximate the goals of democratic fair play. One such decisionmaking alternative is called cumulative voting, which could give all the students at Brother Rice multiple votes and allow them to distribute their votes in any combination of their choice. If each student could vote for ten songs, the students could plump or aggregate their votes to reflect the intensity of their preferences. They could put ten votes on one song; they could put five votes on two songs. If a tenth of the students opted to "cumulate" or plump all their votes for one song, they would be able to select one of every ten or so songs played at the prom. The black seniors could have done this if they chose to, but so could any other cohesive group of sufficient size. In this way, the songs preferred by a majority would be played most often, but the songs the minority enjoyed would also show up on the play list.

Under cumulative voting, voters get the same number of votes as there are seats or options to vote for, and they can then distribute their votes in any combination to reflect their preferences. Like-minded voters can vote as a solid bloc or, instead, form strategic, cross-racial coalitions to gain mutual benefits. This system is emphatically not racially based; it allows voters to organize themselves on whatever basis they wish.

Corporations use this system to ensure representation of minority 35 shareholders on corporate boards of directors. Similarly, some local municipal and county governments have adopted cumulative voting to ensure representation of minority voters. Instead of awarding political power to geographic units called districts, cumulative voting allows voters to cast ballots based on what they think rather than where they live.

Cumulative voting is based on the principle of one person–one vote because each voter gets the same total number of votes. Everyone's preferences are counted equally. It is not a particularly radical idea; thirty states either require or permit corporations to use this election system. Cumulative voting is certainly not antidemocratic because it emphasizes the importance of voter choice in selecting public or social policy. And it is neither liberal nor conservative. Both the Reagan and Bush administrations approved cumulative voting schemes pursuant to the Voting Rights Act to protect the rights of racial- and language-minority voters.

But, as in Chilton County, Alabama, which now uses cumulative voting to elect both the school board and the county commission, any politically cohesive group can vote strategically to win representation. Groups of voters win representation depending on the exclusion threshold, meaning the percentage of votes needed to win one seat or have the band play one song. That threshold can be set case by case, jurisdiction by jurisdiction, based on the size of minority groups that make compelling claims for representation.

Normally the exclusion threshold in a head-to-head contest is 50 percent, which means that only groups that can organize a majority can get elected. But if multiple seats (or multiple songs) are considered simultaneously, the exclusion threshold is considerably reduced. For example, in Chilton County, with seven seats elected simultaneously on each governing body, the threshold of exclusion is now one-eighth. Any group with the solid support of one-eighth the voting population cannot be denied representation. This is because any self-identified minority can plump or cumulate all its votes for one candidate. Again, minorities are not defined solely in racial terms.

As it turned out in Chilton County, both blacks and Republicans benefited from this new system. The school board and commission now each have three white Democrats, three white Republicans, and one black Democrat. Previously, when each seat was decided in a head-to-head contest, the majority not only ruled but monopolized. Only white Democrats were elected at every prior election during this century.

Similarly, if the black and white students at Brother Rice have very different musical taste, cumulative voting permits a positive-sum solution to enable both groups to enjoy one prom. The majority's preferences would be respected in that their songs would be played most often, but the black students could express the intensity of their preferences too. If the black students chose to plump all their votes on a few songs, their minority preferences would be recognized and played. Essentially, cumulative voting structures the band's repertoire to enable the students to take turns. 40

As a solution that permits voters to self-select their identities, cumulative voting also encourages cross-racial coalition building. No one is locked into a minority identity. Nor is anyone necessarily isolated by the identity they choose. Voters can strengthen their influence by forming coalitions to elect more than one representative or to select a range of music more compatible with the entire student body's preferences.

Women too can use cumulative voting to gain greater representation. Indeed, in other countries with similar, alternative voting systems, women are more likely to be represented in the national legislature. For example, in some Western European democracies, the national legislatures have as many as 37 percent female members compared to a little more than 5 percent in our Congress.

There is a final benefit from cumulative voting. It eliminates gerrymandering. By denying protected incumbents safe seats in gerrymandered districts, cumulative voting might encourage more voter participation. With greater interest-based electoral competition, cumulative voting could promote the political turnover sought by advocates of term limits. In this way, cumulative voting serves many of the same ends as periodic elections or rotation in office, a solution that Madison and others advocated as a means of protecting against permanent majority factions.

A different remedial voting tool, one that I have explored more cautiously, is supermajority voting. It modifies winner-take-all majority rule to require that something more than a bare majority of voters must approve or concur before action is taken. As a uniform decisional rule, a supermajority empowers any numerically small but cohesive group of voters. Like cumulative voting, it is race-neutral. Depending on the issue, different members of the voting body can "veto" impending action.

Supermajority remedies give bargaining power to all numerically inferior or less powerful groups, be they black, female, or Republican. Supermajority rules empower the minority Republicans in the Senate who used the Senate filibuster procedure in the spring of 1993 to "veto" the president's proposed economic stimulus package. The same concept of a minority veto yielded the Great Compromise in which small-population states are equally represented in the Senate.

I have never advocated (or imagined) giving an individual member of a legislative body a personal veto. Moreover, I have discussed these kinds of exceptional remedies as the subject of court-imposed solutions only when there has been a violation of the statute and only when they make sense in the context of a particular case. I discuss supermajority rules as a judicial remedy only in cases where the court finds proof of consistent and deeply engrained polarization. It was never my intent that supermajority requirements should be the norm for all legislative bodies, or that simple majority voting would ever in itself constitute a statutory or constitutional violation.

Both the Reagan and Bush administrations took a similar remedial approach to enforcement of the Voting Rights Act. In fact, it was the Reagan administration that *approved* the use of supermajority rules as a remedial measure in places like Mobile, Alabama, where the special five-out-of-seven supermajority threshold is still in place today and is credited with increasing racial harmony in that community.

But — and here I come directly to the claims of my critics — some apparently fear that remedies for extreme voting abuses, remedies like cumulative voting or the Mobile supermajority, constitute "quotas" — racial preferences to ensure minority rule. While cumulative voting, or a supermajority, is quite conventional in many cases and race neutral, to order it as a remedy apparently opens up possibilities of nonmajoritarianism that many seem to find quite threatening.

Indeed, while my nomination was pending, I was called "antidemocratic" for suggesting that majority voting rules may not fairly resolve conflict when the majority and minority are permanently divided. But alternatives to majority voting rules in a racially polarized environment are too easily dismissed by this label. As Chief Justice [Warren] Burger wrote for the Supreme Court, "There is nothing in the language of the Constitution, our history, or our cases that requires that a majority always prevail on every issue." In other words, there is *nothing inherent in democracy that requires majority rule.* It is simply a custom that works efficiently when the majority and minority are fluid, are not monolithic, and are not permanent.

Other democracies frequently employ alternatives to winner-take-all majority voting. Indeed, only five Western democracies, including Britain and the United States, still use single-member-district, winner-take-all systems of representation. Germany, Spain, the Netherlands, and Sweden, among other countries, elect their legislatures under some alternative to winner-take-all majority voting. As the *New Yorker,* in a comment on my nomination, observed, President Clinton was right in calling some of my ideas "difficult to defend," but only because "Americans, by and large, are ignorant of the existence, let alone the details, of electoral systems other than their own."

No one who had done their homework seriously questioned the fundamentally democratic nature of my ideas. Indeed, columnists who attacked my ideas during my nomination ordeal have praised ideas, in a different context, that are remarkably similar to my own. Lally Weymouth wrote, "There can't be democracy in South Africa without a measure of formal protection for minorities." George Will has opined, "The Framers also understood that stable, tyrannical majorities can best be prevented by the multiplication of minority interests, so the majority at any moment will be just a transitory coalition of minorities." In my law journal articles, I expressed exactly the same reservations about unfettered majority rule and about the need sometimes to disaggregate the majority to ensure fair and effective representation for all substantial interests.

The difference is that the minority I used to illustrate my academic point was not, as it was for Lally Weymouth, the white minority in South

Africa. Nor, did I write, as George Will did, about the minority of well-to-do landlords in New York City. I wrote instead about the political exclusion of the black minority in many local county and municipal governing bodies in America.

Yet these same two journalists and many others condemned me as antidemocratic. Apparently, it is not controversial to provide special protections for affluent landlords or minorities in South Africa but it is "divisive," "radical," and "out of the mainstream" to provide similar remedies to black Americans who, after centuries of racial oppression, are still excluded.

Talking about racial bias at home has, for many, become synonymous with advocating revolution. Talking about racial divisions, in itself, has become a violation of the rules of polite society.

We seem to have forgotten that dialogue and intergroup communication are critical to forging consensus. In my case, genuine debate was shut down by techniques of stereotyping and silencing. As Professor Randall Kennedy observes, I was "punished" as the messenger reporting the bad news about our racial situation. I dared to speak when I should have been silent.

My nomination became an unfortunate metaphor for the state of race relations in America. My nomination suggested that as a country, we are in a state of denial about issues of race and racism. The censorship imposed against me points to a denial of serious public debate or discussion about racial fairness and justice in a true democracy. For many politicians and policymakers, the remedy for racism is simply to stop talking about race.

Sentences, words, even phrases separated by paragraphs in my law review articles were served up to demonstrate that I was violating the rules. Because I talked openly about existing racial divisions, I was branded "race obsessed." Because I explored innovative ways to remedy racism, I was branded "antidemocratic." It did not matter that I had suggested race-neutral election rules, such as cumulative voting, as an alternative to remedy racial discrimination. It did not matter that I never advocated quotas. I became the Quota Queen.

The vision behind my by-now-notorious law review articles and my less-well-known professional commitments has always been that of a fair and just society, a society in which even adversely affected parties believe in the system because they believe the process is fair and the process is inclusive. My vision of fairness and justice imagines a full and effective voice for all citizens. I may have failed to locate some of my ideas in the specific factual contexts from which they are derived. But always I have tried to show that democracy in a heterogeneous society is incompatible with rule by a racial monopoly of any color.

I hope that we can learn three positive lessons from my experience. The first lesson is that those who stand for principles may lose in the short run, but they cannot be suppressed in the long run. The second lesson is that public dialogue is critical to represent all perspectives; no one viewpoint should be permitted to monopolize, distort, caricature, or shape public debate. The tyranny of The Majority is just as much a problem of silencing minority viewpoints as it is of excluding minority representatives or preferences. We cannot all talk at once, but that does not mean only one group should get to speak. We can take turns. Third, we need consensus and positive-sum solutions. We need a broad public conversation about issues of racial justice in which we seek win-win solutions to real-life problems. If we include blacks and whites, and women and men, and Republicans and Democrats, and even people with new ideas, we will all be better off.

Most of all, I hope we begin to consider the principle of taking turns   60
as a means to bring us closer to the ideal of democratic fair play. [Supreme Court] Justice Potter Stewart wrote in 1964 that our form of representative self-government reflects "the strongly felt American tradition that the public interest is composed of many diverse interests, [which] . . . in the long run . . . can better be expressed by a medley of component voices than by the majority's monolithic command." In that "strongly felt American tradition," I hope more of us aspire to govern like Madisonian Majorities through "a medley of component voices." In that "strongly felt American tradition," I hope more of us come to reject the "monolithic command" of The fixed Majority.

After all, government is a public experiment. Let us not forget [Supreme Court] Justice Louis Brandeis's advice at the beginning of this century: "If we guide by the light of reason, we must let our minds be bold." At the close of the same century, I hope we rediscover the bold solution to the tyranny of The Majority, which has always been more democracy, not less.

PREPARING FOR DISCUSSION

1. Despite the title of the selection, Guinier believes that it is possible for majorities to rule fairly. What kinds of political circumstances contribute to the fair rule of the majority? What steps, according to Guinier, can a majority take to ensure such fairness? Under what circumstances does a majority become a "majority tyranny"?

2. Most of Guinier's suggestions concerning fairness in government relate to voting and related procedural rules. What modifications in voting procedure does Guinier propose? What specific problems related to minority representation does she hope to remedy through these new practices? On what grounds does she believe her proposed changes will remedy current problems in minority representation?

3. Guinier traces the development of her ideas about "fair play" to her own

experiences as an eight-year-old Brownie and to those of her four-year-old son Nikolas. To what extent is a child's notion of "fair play" liable to differ from an adult's? Does the "taking turns" paradigm seem politically realistic outside the play of children or family life?

4. Guinier frequently appeals to the writings of James Madison in *The Federalist Papers*. She contends rightly that Madison was deeply concerned about the fate of the minority when the majority is fixed and permanent. Yet Madison also considered majority rule "the fundamental principle of free government" (*Federalist* #58) and warned that "all provisions which require more than the majority of any body to its resolutions have a direct tendency to embarrass the operations of the government and an indirect one to subject the sense of the majority to that of the minority" (*Federalist* #75). In other words, Madison worried that a powerful and self-interested minority could not only hinder the workings of government but also subject the majority to the will of a self-interested minority. What elements of Guinier's proposal safeguard American democracy from the dangers posed by Madison? Why does Guinier seem unworried about such a prospect?

5. In paragraph 49, Guinier quotes Chief Justice Warren Burger: "There is nothing in the language of the Constitution, our history, or our cases [on the Supreme Court] that requires that a majority always prevail on every issue." She then rephrases the Burger quotation as "there is nothing inherent in democracy that requires majority rule." In your opinion, has Guinier accurately rephrased Burger's original statement? To what extent does Burger play down Madison's notion of majority rule as "the fundamental principle of free government"? To what extent does Guinier's paraphrase go further than the original?

FROM READING TO WRITING

6. At the beginning of her essay, Guinier retells a story from her childhood that shaped her adult ideas about "fair play." Write an essay in which you recall an incident from your own childhood that affected your own ideas about "fair play" at the time. Does what seemed "fair" then also seem "fair" now? If your views about "fair play" have changed, what subsequent experiences have brought about that change? If they have remained largely intact, what adult experiences have confirmed your childhood notions of "fair play"?

7. Consider Guinier's proposal for "cumulative voting" in light of charges that her proposal is "antidemocratic." Write an essay in which you consider the advantages and disadvantages of "cumulative" voting for certain elections and constituencies. In what ways, if any, does Guinier's proposal represent an improvement over traditional voting procedures? Do you agree with Guinier's critics that her proposal is "antidemocratic"?

GLENN C. LOURY

Black Dignity and the Common Good

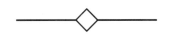

The history of civil rights movements since the 1960s suggests that African American leaders generally embrace the idea that only through protest can blacks attain the legal, social, and economic rights promised to all Americans by the Constitution. By emphasizing the status of African Americans as victims of racism throughout our nation's history, these leaders hope to elicit greater government action on problems ranging from poverty to illiteracy. In recent years, however, voices have begun to emerge within the black community that question the practical and philosophical value of this approach.

One such voice belongs to Glenn C. Loury, who describes himself as a conservative. "We must let go of the past and take responsibility for our future," Loury insists. "No people can be genuinely free so long as they look to others for their deliverance." In the following selection from *One by One from the Inside Out* (1995), he stresses the need for African Americans to redouble their efforts in the name of self-improvement, even as he argues that the eradication of poverty must remain a top priority for the federal government. Loury is university professor and professor of economics at Boston University. He recently testified before the Congressional Subcommittee on Educational and Economic Opportunities on the issue of affirmative action.

SELECTED PUBLICATIONS: *Families, Schools, and Delinquency Prevention* (Edited with James Q. Wilson) (1987); *One by One from the Inside Out: Race and Responsibility in America* (1995); Loury's essays have appeared in the *New York Times*, the *Wall Street Journal*, the *Public Interest*, *Commentary*, and the *New Republic*.

Therefore, since we are surrounded by such a great cloud of witnesses, let us throw off everything that hinders, and the sin that so easily entangles, and let us run with perseverance the race marked out for us.

— HEBREWS 12:1, *NIV*

A "great cloud of witnesses" surrounds us — the spirits of our forebears, whose courage, sacrifices, and faith have made possible the freedoms we enjoy today. These witnesses of course include the great figures of black American political and cultural history, but also the Founding Fathers, who conceived this still maturing democracy of ours, and the humble Americans whose names are not recorded in history books — the simple people who believed in the ideals on which our country was founded even when our political practice strayed far from those ideals, those who made the ultimate sacrifice (at Gettysburg, at Normandy, or in Mississippi) so that we might live as free men and women enjoying equally the rights and responsibilities of citizenship.

For black Americans, this struggle for freedom and equality is the central theme in our historical experience. This struggle, in turn, has played a profound role in shaping the contemporary American social and political conscience. The trauma of slavery, the fratricide of the Civil War, the profound legal ramifications of the Reconstruction amendments, the long dark night of post-Reconstruction retreat from the moral and practical implications of black citizenship, the collective redemption of the civil rights movement — these have worked to make us Americans the people we are. Only the massive westward migration and the still continuing flow of immigrants to our shores rival this history of race relations as factors defining the American character.

Beginning in the mid-1950s and culminating a decade later, the civil rights movement wrought a profound change in American race relations. The civil rights revolution largely succeeded in its effort to eliminate legally enforced second-class citizenship for blacks. The legislation and court rulings to which it led effected sweeping changes in the American institutions of education, employment, and electoral politics. This social transformation represents a remarkable, unparalleled experience, graphically illustrating the virtue and vitality of our free institutions. In barely the span of a generation and with comparatively little violence, a despised and largely disenfranchised minority descendant from chattel slaves used the courts, the legislature, the press, and the rights of petition and assembly of our republic to force a redefinition of its citizenship. One can begin to grasp the magnitude of this accomplishment by comparing it with the turmoil that continues to beset those many nations around the world suffering long-standing conflicts among racial or religious groups.

Yet, despite this success, the hope that the Movement would produce true social and economic equality between the races remains unfulfilled. No compendium of social statistics is needed for us to see the vast disparities in economic advantage that separate the inner-city black poor from the rest of the nation. No profound talents of social observation are required to notice the continuing tension, anger, and fear that shroud our public discourse on matters concerning race. When in 1963, Martin Luther King, Jr., declared his "dream" — that we Americans should one day become a society where a citizen's race would be an irrelevancy, where black and white children would walk hand in hand, where persons would be judged not by the color of their skin but by the content of their character — this seemed to many Americans both a noble and an attainable goal. Today, after his birth has been made an occasion for national celebration, this "dream" that race should become an irrelevancy seems naively utopian; indeed, *this* dream is renounced even by those who now claim his mantle of leadership.

Thus, at the first national celebration of Martin Luther King Day, in 1986, Jesse Jackson decried the widespread focus on King's great speech and stressed instead King's opposition to the Vietnam War — an opposition, be it noted, that King came to only after long agonizing with his conscience and that he always carefully distinguished from the position of the extremists within the antiwar movement. Jackson offered his own interpretation of the 1963 speech: "That so-called 'I have a Dream speech' . . . was not a speech about dreamers and dreaming. It was a speech describing nightmare conditions. . . . Dr. King was not assassinated for dreaming." A few days later, Jackson clarified the meaning of this last comment when, to a national television audience, he stated his belief that King had been killed with the assistance of the FBI and/or the CIA.

Now I mention this not to disparage Reverend Jackson, but merely to indicate the bitterness that continues to characterize race relations in our country. But we must not lose sight of the vision King placed before us; we must not allow the universal truths he championed to be lost amid partisan bickering. It is worth considering at greater length what Martin Luther King actually had to say about his American dream. At the 1961 commencement at Lincoln University he described it thusly:

> One of the first things we notice in this dream is an amazing universalism. It does not say some men [are created equal], but it says all men. It does not say all white men, but it says all men, which includes black men. It does not say all Gentiles, but it says all men, which includes Jews. It does not say all Protestants, but it says all men, which includes Catholics.
>
> And there is another thing we see in this dream that ultimately distinguishes democracy and our form of government from all of the totalitarian regimes that emerge in history. It says that each individual has certain basic rights that are neither conferred by nor derived from the state. To discover where they come from, it is necessary to move back behind the dim mist of eternity, for they are God-given. Very seldom, if ever, in the history of the world has a socio-political document expressed in such profoundly eloquent and unequivocal language the dignity and the worth of the human personality. The American dream reminds us that every man is heir to the legacy of worthiness.

The contrast between this eloquently patriotic statement of King and the partisan carping of many of his successors speaks volumes about how the tone of racial advocacy has changed over the past generation.

Nevertheless, black Americans, and the nation, face a challenge different in character from though perhaps no less severe in degree than that which occasioned the civil rights revolution. It is the challenge of making real for all of our citizens the American dream that, as King aptly put it, "every man is heir to the legacy of worthiness." The bottom stratum of the black community has compelling problems that can no longer be blamed solely on white racism, that will not yield to protest marches or court orders, and that force us to confront fundamental failures in lower-class black urban society. This profound alienation of the ghetto poor from mainstream American life has continued to grow worse in the years since the triumphs of the civil rights movement, even as the success of that movement has provided the basis for an impressive expansion of economic and political power for the black middle class.

The plight of the black lower class reveals an extent of deprivation, a degree of misery, a hopelessness and despair, an alienation that are difficult for most Americans, who do not have direct experience with this social stratum, to comprehend. These conditions pose an enormous challenge to the leadership of our nation and to the black leadership. Yet we seem increasingly unable to conduct a political dialogue out of which a consensus might develop about how to respond to this reality. Two common, partisan themes dominate the current debate: One is to blame it all on racism, to declare that this circumstance proves the continued existence of old-style American racial emnity, only in a more subtle, modernized, and updated form. This is the view of many civil rights activists. From this perspective the tragedy of the urban underclass is a civil rights problem, curable by civil rights methods. Black youth unemployment represents the refusal of employers to hire competent and industrious young men because of their race. Black welfare dependency is the inescapable consequence of the absence of opportunity. Black academic underperformance reflects racial bias in the provision of public education. Black incarceration rates are the result of the bias of the police and judiciary.

The other theme, characterized by the posture of many on the right in our politics, is to blame the conditions of the black lower class on the failures of "Great Society liberals," to chalk the problem up to the follies of big government and big spending, to see it as the legacy of a tragically misconceived welfare state. A key feature of this view is the apparent absence of any felt need to articulate a "policy" on this new race problem. It is as though those shaping the domestic agenda of this government do not see the explicitly racial character of this problem, as if they do not understand the historical experiences that link, symbolically and sociologically, the current urban underclass to our long, painful legacy of racial trauma. Their response has been to promulgate a de facto doctrine of "benign neglect" on the issue of continuing racial inequality. They seem to think that it is enough merely to be right about liberals having been wrong on this question.

These responses feed on each other. The civil rights leaders, repelled 10 by the public vision of conservatives, see more social spending as the only solution to the problem. They characterize every question raised about the cost-effectiveness or appropriateness of a welfare program as evidence of a lack of concern about the black poor; they identify every affirmative action effort, whether aimed at attaining skills training for the ghetto poor or at securing a fat municipal procurement contract for a black millionaire, as necessary and just recompense in light of our history of racial oppression. Conservatives in or out of government, repelled by the public vision of civil rights advocates and convinced that the programs of the past have failed, when addressing racial issues at all talk in formalistic terms about the principle of "color-blind state action." Under President Reagan, federal civil rights officials absurdly claimed that *they* were the true heirs of Martin Luther King's moral legacy, by virtue of their having remained loyal to his "color-blind" ideal — as if King's moral leadership consisted of this and nothing else. Conservative spokesmen pointed to the "trickling down" of the benefits of economic growth as the ultimate solution to these problems; at times they even seemed to court the support of and respond to the influence of segregationist elements; they remained without a positive program of action aimed at narrowing the yawning chasm separating the black poor from the rest of the nation.

There is merit, many would now admit, in the conservative criticism of liberal social policy. It is clear that the Great Society approach to the problems of poor blacks has been inadequate. Intellectually honest persons must now concede that it is not nearly as easy to truly help people as the big spenders would suggest. The proper measure of "caring" ought not to be the size of budget expenditures on poverty programs, if the result is that the recipients remain dependent on such programs. Moreover, many Americans have become concerned about the neutrality toward values and behavior that was so characteristic of the Great Society thrust, the aversion to holding persons responsible for those actions that precipitated their own dependence, the feeling that "society" is to blame for all the misfortune in the world. Characterizing the problem of the ghetto poor as due to white racism is one variant of this argument that "society" has caused the problem. It overlooks the extent to which values and behaviors of inner-city black youths are implicated in the difficulty.

Many Americans, black and white, have also been disgusted with the way in which this dangerous circumstance is exploited for political gain by professional civil rights and poverty advocates. They have watched the minority youth unemployment rate be cited in defense of special admissions programs to elite law schools. They have seen public officials, caught in illegal indiscretions, use the charge of racism as a cover for personal failings of character. They have seen themselves pilloried as "racists" by civil rights lobbyists for taking the opposite side of legitimately arguable policy debates.

Yet none of this excuses (though it may help to explain) the fact that our national government has failed to engage this problem with the seriousness and energy it requires. Ideology has been permitted to stand in the way of formulating practical programs that might begin to chip away at this dangerous problem. The ideological debate has permitted the worthy goals of reducing taxes and limiting growth in the size of government to crowd from the domestic policy agenda the creative reflection that obviously will be needed to formulate a new, non–welfare-oriented approach to this problem.

Ironically, each party to this debate has helped to make viable the otherwise problematic posture of the other. The lack of a positive, high-priority response from a series of Republican administrations to what is now a long-standing, continuously worsening social problem has allowed politically marginal and intellectually moribund elements to retain a credibility and force in our political life far beyond that which their accomplishments would otherwise support. Many observers are reluctant to criticize the civil rights extremists because they do not wish to be identified with a Republican administration's policy on racial matters. Conversely, the shrill, vitriolic, self-serving, and obviously unfair attacks on administration officials by the civil rights lobby have drained their criticism of much of its legitimacy. The "racist" epithet, like the little boy's cry of "wolf," is a charge so often invoked these days that it has lost its historic moral force.

The result of this symbiosis has been to impede the establishment of a political consensus sufficient to support sustained action on the country's most pressing domestic problem. Many whites, chastened by the apparent failures of 1960s-style social engineering but genuinely concerned about the tragedy unfolding in our inner cities, are reluctant to engage this issue. It seems to them a political quagmire in which one is forced to ally oneself with a civil rights establishment no longer able to command broad respect. Many blacks who have begun to doubt the effectiveness of liberal social policy are hindered in expressing an alternative vision by fear of being too closely linked in the public mind with a policy of indifference to racial concerns. We must find a way to rise above this partisan squabbling. A part of our nation is dying. And if we fail to act, that failure will haunt us for generations.

I can personally attest to the difficulties this environment has created. I am an acknowledged critic of the civil rights leadership. I have gladly joined the Republican side on some highly partisan policy debates: on federal enterprise zones, on a youth opportunity wage, on educational vouchers for low-income students, on stimulating ownership among responsible public housing tenants, on requiring work from able-bodied welfare recipients, on dealing sternly with those who violently brutalize their neighbors. I am no enemy of right-to-work laws; I do not despise the institution of private property; I distrust the capacity of public bureaucracies to substitute for the fruit of private initiative. I am, to my own continuing surprise, philosophically more conservative than the vast majority of my academic peers. And I love and believe in this democratic republic.

But I am also a black man, a product of Chicago's South Side, a veteran in spirit of the civil rights revolution. I am a partisan on behalf of the inner-city poor. I agonize at the extraordinary waste of human potential that the despair of ghetto America represents. I cannot help but lament, deeply and personally, how little progress we have made in relieving the suffering that goes on there. It is not enough — far from enough — for me to fault liberals for much that has gone wrong. For me this is not a mere contest of ideologies or competition for electoral votes. And it is because I see this problem as so far from solution, yet so central to my own sense of satisfaction with our public life, that I despair over our government's lack of commitment to its resolution. I believe that such a commitment, coming from the highest levels of our government, without prejudice with respect to the specific methods to be employed in addressing the issue but involving a public acknowledgment of the unacceptability of the current state of affairs, is now required. This is not a call for big spending. Rather, it is a plaintive cry for the need to actively engage this problem, for the elevation of concern for racial inequality to a position of priority on our government's domestic affairs agenda.

In much of my past writing on this subject, I have placed great weight on the importance to blacks of "self-help." Some readers may see my current posture as at variance with those arguments. It is not. I have also written critically of blacks' continued reliance on civil rights–era protest and legal strategies, and of the propagation of affirmative action policies throughout our employment and educational institutions. I have urged blacks to move beyond civil rights. I have spoken of the difference between the "enemy without" — racism — and the "enemy within" the black community — those dysfunctional behaviors of young blacks that perpetuate poverty and dependency. I have spoken of the need for blacks to face squarely the political reality that we now live in the "post–civil rights era"; that claims based on racial justice now carry much less force in American public life than they once did; that it is no longer acceptable to seek benefits for our people in the name of justice while revealing indifference or hostility to the rights of others. Nothing I have said here should be construed as a retraction of these views.

But selling these positions within the black community is made infinitely more difficult when my black critics are able to say: "But your argument plays into the hands of those who are looking for an excuse to abandon the black poor"; and I am unable to contradict them credibly. The deteriorating quality of our public debate about civil rights matters has come to impede the internal realignment of black political strivings that is now so crucial to the interest of the inner-city poor and the political health of the nation. There is a great existential challenge facing black America today: the challenge of taking control of our own future by exerting the requisite moral leadership, making the sacrifices of time and resources, and building the needed institutions so that black social and economic development may be advanced. No matter how windy the debate becomes among white liberals and conservatives as to what should be done in the public sphere, meeting this self-creating challenge ultimately depends on black action. It is to make a mockery of the ideal of freedom to hold that, as free men and women, blacks ought nonetheless to wait passively for white Americans, of whatever political persuasion, to come to the rescue. A people who languish in dependency while the means exist through which we might work toward our own advancement have surrendered our claim to dignity and to the respect of our fellow citizens. If we are to be a truly free people, we must accept responsibility for our fate even when it does not lie wholly in our hands.

But to say this — which is crucial for blacks to consider at this late date — is not to say that there is no public responsibility. It is obvious that in the areas of education, employment training, enforcement of antidiscrimination laws, and provision of minimal subsistence to the impoverished, the government must be involved. Some programs — preschool education for one — cost money, but seem to pay even greater dividends. It is a tragic error that those of us who make the self-help argument in internal dialogue concerning alternative development strategies for black Americans are often construed by the political right as making a public argument for a policy of benign neglect. Expanded self-reliance is but one ingredient in the recipe for black progress, distinguished by the fact that it is essential for black dignity, which in turn is a precondition for true equality of the races in this country.

It makes sense to call for greater self-reliance at this time because some of what needs to be done cannot, in the nature of the case, be undertaken by government. Dealing with behavioral problems; with community values; with the attitudes and beliefs of black youngsters about responsibility, work, family, and schooling are not things government is well suited to do. The teaching of "oughts" properly belongs in the hands of private voluntary associations: churches, families, neighborhood groups. It is also reasonable to ask those blacks who have benefited from the special minority programs, such as the set-asides for black businesses, to contribute to alleviating the suffering of poor blacks, for without the visible ghetto poor, such programs would lack political support. Yet, and obviously, such internal efforts cannot be a panacea for the problems of the inner city. This is truly an American problem; we all have a stake in its alleviation; we all have a responsibility to address it forthrightly.

Thus to begin to make progress on this extremely difficult matter will require enhanced private and public commitment. Yet to the extent that blacks place too much focus on the public responsibility, we place in danger the attainment of true equality for black Americans. By "true equality" I mean more than an approximately equal material provision. Also crucial, I maintain, is equal respect in the eyes of one's fellow citizens. Yet much of the current advocacy of blacks' interests seems inconsistent with achieving equal respect for black Americans. Leaders in the civil rights organizations as well as in the halls of Congress remain wedded to a conception of the black condition and a method of appealing to the rest of the polity which undermine the dignity of our people. Theirs is too much the story of discrimination, repression, hopelessness, and frustration and too little the saga of uplift and the march forward to genuine empowerment whether others cooperate or not. They seek to make blacks into the conscience of America, even if the price is the loss of our souls. They require blacks to present ourselves to American society as permanent victims, incapable of advance without the state-enforced philanthropy of possibly resentful whites. By evoking past suffering and current deprivations experienced by the ghetto poor, some black leaders seek to feed the guilt and, worse, the pity of the white establishment. But I hold that we blacks ought not to allow ourselves to become ever-ready doomsayers, always alert for an opportunity to exploit black suffering by offering it up to more or less sympathetic whites as a justification for incremental monetary transfers. Such a posture seems to evidence a fundamental lack of confidence in the ability of blacks to make it in America, as so many millions of immigrants have done and continue to do. Even if this method were to succeed in gaining the money, it is impossible that true equality of status in American society could lie at the end of such a road.

Much of the current, quite heated, debate over affirmative action reveals a similar lack of confidence in the capabilities of blacks to compete in American society. My concern is with the inconsistency between the broad reliance on quotas by blacks and the attainment of true equality. In one sense the demand for quotas, which many see as the only path to equality for blacks, concedes at the outset the impossibility that blacks could ever be truly equal citizens. For aside from those instances in which hiring goals are ordered by a court subsequent to a finding of illegal discrimination, and with the purpose of providing relief for those discriminated against, the use of differential standards for the hiring of blacks and whites acknowledges the inability of blacks to perform up to the white standard.

So widespread has such a practice become that, especially on the elite levels of employment, all blacks must now deal with the perception that without a quota, they would not have their jobs. All blacks, some of our "leaders" seem proud to say, owe their accomplishments to political pressures for diversity. And the effects of such thinking may be seen in our response to almost every instance of racially differential performance. When blacks cannot pass a high school proficiency test as a condition of obtaining a diploma, throw out the test. When black teachers cannot exhibit skills at the same level as whites, the very idea of testing teachers' skills is attacked. If black athletes less frequently achieve the minimal academic standard set for those participating in intercollegiate sport, then let us promulgate for them a separate, lower standard, even as we accuse of racism those suggesting the need for a standard in the first place. If young black men are arrested more frequently than whites for some criminal offense, then let us proclaim the probability that police are disproportionately concerned about the crimes blacks commit. If black suspension rates are higher than whites' in a given school district, well, let's investigate that district for racist administrative practices. When black students are unable to gain admission at the same rate as whites to the elite public exam school in Boston, let's ask a federal judge to mandate black excellence.

The inescapable truth of the matter is that no judge can mandate excellence. No selection committee can create distinction in black scholars. No amount of circuitous legal maneuvering can obviate the social reality of inner-city black crime or of whites' and blacks' fear of that crime. No degree of double-standard setting can make black students competitive or comfortable in the academically exclusive colleges and universities. No amount of political gerrymandering can create genuine sympathy among whites for the interests and strivings of black people. Yet it is to such maneuvering, such double-standard setting, such gerrymandering that many feel compelled to turn.

Signs of the intellectual exhaustion and increasing political ineffectiveness of this style of leadership are now evident. Yet we cling to this method because of the way in which the claims of blacks were most successfully pressed during the civil rights era. These claims were based, above all else, on the status of blacks as America's historical victims. Maintenance of this claiming status requires constant emphasis on the wrongs of the past and exaggeration of present tribulations. He who leads a group of historical victims, as victims, must never let "them" forget what "they" have done; he must renew the indictment and keep alive the supposed moral asymmetry implicit in the respective positions of victim and victimizer. He is the preeminent architect of what British philosopher G. K. Minogue has called "suffering situations." The circumstance of his group as underdog becomes his most valuable political asset. Such a posture, especially in the political realm, militates against an emphasis on personal responsibility within the group and induces those who have been successful to attribute their accomplishments to fortuitous circumstance, not to their own abilities and character.

The dictates of political advocacy require that personal inadequacies among blacks be attributed to "the system" and that emphasis by black leaders on self-improvement be denounced as irrelevant, self-serving, dishonest. Individual black men and women simply cannot fail on their own, they must be seen as never having had a chance. But where failure at the personal level is impossible, there can also be no personal success. For a black to embrace the Horatio Alger[1] myth, to assert as a guide to *personal* action that "there is opportunity in America," becomes a *politically* repugnant act. For each would-be black Horatio Alger indicts as inadequate or incomplete the deeply entrenched (and quite useful) notion that individual effort can never overcome the inheritance of race. Yet where there can be no black Horatio Algers to celebrate, sustaining an ethos of responsibility that might serve to extract maximal effort from the individual in the face of hardship becomes impossible as well.

James Baldwin spoke to this problem with great insight long ago. In his essay "Everybody's Protest Novel" Baldwin said of the protagonist of Richard Wright's celebrated novel *Native Son*:

> Bigger Thomas stands on a Chicago street corner watching airplanes flown by white men racing against the sun and "Goddamn" he says, the bitterness bubbling up like blood, remembering a million indignities, the terrible, rat-infested house, the humiliation of home-relief, the intense, aimless, ugly bickering, hating it; hatred smoulders through these pages like sulphur fire. All of Bigger's life is controlled, defined by his hatred and his fear. And later, his fear drives him to murder and his hatred to rape; he dies, having come, through this violence, and we are told, for the first time, to a kind of life, having for the first time redeemed his manhood.

But Baldwin rejected this "redemption through rebellion" thesis as untrue to life and unworthy of art. "Bigger's tragedy," he concluded,

> is not that he is cold or black or hungry, not even that he is American, black; but that *he has accepted a theology that denies him life, that he admits the possibility of his being sub-human and feels constrained, therefore, to battle for his humanity according to those brutal criteria bequeathed him at his birth.* But our humanity is our burden, our life; we need not battle for it; we need only to do what is infinitely more difficult — that is, accept it. The failure of the protest novel lies in its rejection of life, the human being, the denial of his beauty, dread, power, in its insistence that it is his categorization alone which is real and which cannot be transcended.

While Baldwin's interest was essentially literary, mine is political. In either case, however, our struggle is against the deadening effect that emanates from the belief that, for the black man, "it is his categorization alone which is real and cannot be transcended." The spheres of politics and culture intersect in this understanding of what the existence of systemic constraint implies for the possibilities of individual personality. For

---

[1] *Horatio Alger:* Nineteenth-century American author credited with originating the "rags-to-riches" myth of success.

too many blacks, dedication to the cause of reform has been allowed to supplant the demand for individual accountability. Race, and the historic crimes associated with it — real crimes! — has become the single lens through which to view social experience. The infinite potential of real human beings has been surrendered on the altar of protest. In this way does the prophecy of failure, evoked by those who take the fact of racism as barring forever blacks' access to the rich possibilities of American life, fulfill itself: "Loyalty to the race" in the struggle to be free of oppression requires the sacrifice of a primary instrument through which genuine freedom might be attained.

Moreover, the fact that there has been in the United States such a tenuous commitment to social provision to the indigent, independent of race, reinforces the ideological trap. Blacks think we must cling to victim status because it provides the only secure basis upon which to press for attention from the rest of the polity to the problems of our most disadvantaged fellows. It is important to distinguish here between the socioeconomic consequences of the claims that are advanced on the basis of the victim status of blacks (such as the pressure for racially preferential treatment) and their symbolic, ideological role. For even though the results of this claiming often accrue to the advantage of better-off blacks and in no way constitute a solution to the problems of the poor, the desperate plight of the poorest makes it unthinkable that whites could ever be let off the hook by blacks relinquishing the historically based claims — that is, by a broad acceptance within the black community of the notion that individual blacks bear personal responsibility for their fate.

The dilemmas of the black underclass pose in stark terms the most pressing, unresolved problem of the social and moral sciences: how to reconcile individual and social responsibility. The problem goes back to Kant.[2] The moral and social paradox of society is this: On the one hand, we are determined and constrained by social, cultural, not to mention biological forces. Yet on the other hand, if society is to work we must believe that and behave as if we do indeed determine our actions. Neither of the pat political formulas for dealing with this paradox is adequate by itself. The mother of a homeless family is not simply a victim of forces acting on her; she is in part responsible for her plight and that of her children. But she is also being acted on by forces — social, economic, cultural, political — larger than herself. She is not an island; she is impacted by an environment; she does not have complete freedom to determine her future. It is callous nonsense to insist that she does, just as it is mindlessness to insist that she can do nothing for herself and her children until "society" reforms. In fact, she is responsible for her condition; but we also must help her — that is *our* responsibility.

Now blacks have in fact been constrained by a history of racism and

---

[2] *Kant:* Influential nineteenth-century German philosopher and ethicist.

30

limited opportunity. Some of these effects continue to manifest themselves into the current day. Yet now that greater opportunity exists, taking advantage of it requires that we accept personal responsibility for our own fate, even though the effects of this past remain with us in part. But emphasis on this personal responsibility of blacks takes the political pressure off those outside the black community, who also have a responsibility, as citizens of this republic, to be actively engaged in trying to change the structures that constrain the black poor in such a way that they can more effectively assume responsibility for themselves and exercise their inherent and morally required capacity to choose. That is, an inherent link exists between these two sides of the "responsibility" coin: between acceptance among blacks of personal responsibility for our actions and acceptance among all Americans of their social responsibilities as citizens.

My point to conservatives should be plain. Rather than simply incanting the "personal responsibility" mantra, we must also be engaged in helping those people who so desperately need our help. We are not relieved of our responsibility to do so by the fact that Ted Kennedy and Jesse Jackson are promoting legislation aimed at helping this same population with which we disagree. Remember King's description of the animating idea of the Declaration of Independence: "*Every* man is heir to the legacy of worthiness." "Those people" languishing in the drug-infested, economically depressed, crime-ridden central cities — those people are *our* people. We must be in relationship with them. The point here transcends politics and policy. The necessity of being engaged with the least among us is a moral necessity. We Americans cannot live up to our self-image as a "city on a hill," a beacon of freedom and hope for all the world, if we fail this test.

My point to blacks should also be plain. We must let go of the past and take responsibility for our future. What may seem to be an unacceptable political risk is also an absolute moral necessity. This is a dilemma from which I believe we blacks can escape only by an act of faith: faith in ourselves, faith in our nation, and ultimately, faith in the God of our forefathers. He has not brought us this far only to abandon us now. As suggested by the citation from the Book of Hebrews with which I began, we are indeed "surrounded by a great cloud of witnesses" — the spirits of our forebears who, under much more difficult and hostile conditions, made it possible for us to enjoy the enormous opportunities we have today. It would be a profound desecration of their memory were we to preach despair to our children when we are in fact so much closer than they were to the cherished goal of full equality. We must believe that our fellow citizens are now truly ready to allow us an equal place in this society. We must believe that we have within ourselves the ability to succeed on a level playing field if we give it our all. We must be prepared to put the past to rest; to forgive if not forget; to retire the outmoded and inhibiting role of the victim.

Embracing the role of the victim has unacceptable costs. It is undigni- 35
fied and demeaning. It leads to a situation where celebration among
blacks of individual success and of the personal traits associated with it
comes to be seen as betrayal of the black poor, because such celebration
undermines the legitimacy of what has proved to be their most valuable
political asset — their supposed helplessness. There is, hidden in this
desperate assertion of victim status by blacks to an increasingly skeptical
white polity, an unfolding tragedy of profound proportions. Black leaders, confronting their people's need and their own impotency, believe
they must continue to portray blacks as "the conscience of the nation."
Yet the price extracted for playing this role, in incompletely fulfilled lives
and unrealized personal potential, amounts to a "loss of our own souls."
As consummate victims we lay ourselves at the feet of our fellows, exhibiting *our* lack of achievement as evidence of *their* failure, hoping to
wring from their sense of conscience what we must assume, by the very
logic of our claim, lies beyond our individual capacities to attain, all the
while bemoaning how limited that sense of conscience seems to be. This
way lies not the "freedom" so long sought by our ancestors but, instead,
a continuing serfdom.

PREPARING FOR DISCUSSION

1. Loury spends the first several paragraphs of his essay reflecting on the
goals, successes, and failures of the civil rights movement of the 1960s. Does
Loury believe the aims of the movement have been fulfilled? In what ways, according to Loury, has "the tone of racial advocacy" in the United States changed
since the 1960s? What does he consider to be the single greatest crisis facing
African Americans today?

2. The author believes that neither of the two most common reasons provided to explain the plight of the black lower classes — racism and the failure of
the welfare state — takes us very far toward solving the problem. What does he
believe the first step toward solving this problem must be? What, specifically, has
prevented our nation from taking this step in the recent past?

3. Loury claims that his "plaintive cry for . . . the elevation of concern for
racial equality to a position of priority" is not "a call for big spending" (paragraph 17). How realistic do you find this claim that increased national attention
to the black lower class need not result in greater spending?

4. In paragraphs 23 and 24, Loury reflects on the psychological repercussions of quotas for black people. What, according to Loury, are the major consequences of these quotas? To what extent does he favor affirmative action
programs? What effect would the reemergence of unfair hiring and admissions
policies have on African Americans' self-esteem? Would the effect likely be more
or less negative than the one potentially produced by the current quotas?

5. The term *responsibility* occurs throughout the selection. What are the "two

sides of the 'responsibility' coin" to which Loury refers in paragraph 32? Does Loury's "coin" analogy suggest that the two types of responsibility are opposed to each other?

FROM READING TO WRITING

6. At several points in the selection, Loury announces that he is both a conservative and a black man, and much of his essay is devoted to resolving what he believes to be a contradiction. Write an essay in which you describe an issue over which your political values and your cultural or ethnic values conflict. Have you, like Loury, been able to arrive at a point of resolution with regard to this conflict? If not, why do you think this conflict cannot be resolved?

7. Consider the notion recalled by Loury in paragraph 27 "that individual effort can never overcome the inheritance of race." Much of Loury's essay, of course, is directed at refuting this notion, and yet, for many others, race becomes *the* determining factor in life. In an essay describe your own attitude toward this notion. Do you believe that individual effort can prevail over entrenched social conditions and prejudices?

3

The New Class Struggle:

POVERTY · POWER · PRESTIGE

ALTHOUGH THE PHRASE "RACE, CLASS, AND GENDER" has become one of the fashionable academic slogans of our time, class rarely enters contemporary political discussion. There are many reasons offered for this. It may be that race and gender studies dominate academic discourse today because people are far more likely to base their identities on these more evident categories than on the more fluid category of class allegiance. Or it may be that Marxism, a system based on class analysis, has fallen into academic and professional disrepute. Or it may be that once individuals reach a certain level of wealth or status — especially individuals who become influential — they no longer feel any connection with those who remain at lower levels. Or it may be, as linguist Noam Chomsky maintains in "The Unmentionable Five-Letter Word," that our national silence about class is simply an indication of the ruling class's success in creating a "picture among the population that we're all one happy family."

What happens when there's a conflict between race and class identity? Does class transcend race, as Chomsky believes? Is racial oppression worse than class oppression? This issue is explored in the following two essays. In "On Being Black and Middle Class," a prominent essayist, Shelby Steele, describes the dilemma of experiencing two identities: "Black though I may be," says Steele, "it is impossible for me to sit in my single-family house with two cars in the driveway and a swing set in the back yard and *not* see the role class has played in my life." In "Cycles of Deprivation and the Ghetto Underclass Debate," William Julius Wilson, another African American scholar and one of the nation's leading public policy experts, examines the importance of class analysis in shaping programs to alleviate inner-city poverty. Wilson takes issue with those who, by studiously avoiding the term *underclass*, "fail to address one of the most important social transformations in recent United States history."

If a new urban underclass represents one end of the American class spectrum, a new "overclass" is at the opposite end. The next two selections examine this emerging privileged class. In "To Have and Have Not," Michael Lind, a senior editor with the *New Republic*, worries about the effect this new, white, highly educated, and relatively invisible elite will have on American democracy. Then, in "The Revolt of the Elites," the late Christopher Lasch, one of our most influential political theorists, warns that these "new professional and managerial elites" have canceled their allegiance to America and feel a greater kinship with their foreign counterparts than with most of their fellow citizens — a situation that spells social and economic disaster for the United States. Criticized by Lasch in the essay, Clinton's Secretary of Labor Robert B. Reich argues in response that, despite America's widening class polarization, he is wholly committed to reviving middle-class opportunity and prosperity and identifies three dominant classes — an underclass, an overclass, and an *anxious* class.

Of the groups Reich identifies, perhaps none is as *anxious* as America's working class. For decades the internationally renowned social scientist Lillian B. Rubin has been studying working-class families from both a psychological and a sociological point of view. In "'People Don't Know Right from Wrong Anymore,'" she finds fragmented, downwardly mobile families who "feel as if they're living on a fault line that threatens to open up and engulf them at any moment."

The gap between blue collar and white collar — or between the working class and the new elite — is daily apparent in social styles, fashions, diet, household possessions, and, as Rubin amply demonstrates, in family values. Though these differences are largely cultural, this widening gap can also have serious economic and political consequences. In "Class Conflict and Environmental Reform," the political activist and best-selling author William Greider analyzes the way social-class differences can stand in the way of important political reform. Though this final selection focuses on class struggle within the environmental movement, Greider reminds us, in a fitting conclusion to this chapter, that class conflict has been a "persistent theme in popular politics throughout American history."

NOAM CHOMSKY

The Unmentionable Five-Letter Word

————◇————

With so much serious attention devoted to issues of race and gender, it is surprising that so little attention has been directed toward a third major cultural issue in this country: class. One way to account for the limited discussion of class differences in the United States might be through an appeal to the view held by many Americans that we live in an essentially *classless* society. Historically, the high degree of social mobility in America made boundaries between one economic group and another seem fluid. Someone born into poverty, for example, might grow rich through ingenuity and hard work. In recent years, however, the potential for upward mobility has greatly decreased, and working wages have fallen. With each year, the economic and ideological gap between rich and poor grows larger as America's wealth becomes increasingly concentrated in the hands of the few.

In the following interview from *The Prosperous Few and the Restless Many,* Noam Chomsky, a professor of linguistics at the Massachusetts Institute of Technology since 1955, offers another account of the uniquely American reluctance to talk about class. He traces this reluctance to conscious efforts by "the ruling classes" to make other Americans believe "that there is no such thing as class." In doing so, they maintain an illusion of social equality that pacifies the rest of the population. Since revolutionizing the study of linguistics in the 1950s, Chomsky has assumed a public role as an outspoken critic of America's foreign and domestic policy. A common theme throughout his writings on politics is that America's historical commitment to human and civil rights, justice, and morality has been increasingly undermined by corporate efforts to maximize profits.

SELECTED PUBLICATIONS: *American Power and the New Mandarins* (1969); *Problems of Knowledge and Freedom* (1971); *Human Rights and American Foreign Policy* (1978); *Some Concepts and Consequences of the Theory of Government and Binding* (1982); *Manufacturing Consent* (with Edward Herman) (1988); *Necessary Illusions: Thought Control in Democratic Society* (1989); *The Prosperous Few and the Restless Many* (1993).

———————

It's a given that ideology and propaganda are phenomena of other cultures. They don't exist in the United States. Class is in the same category. You've called it the "unmentionable five-letter word."

It's kind of interesting the way it works. Statistics about things like quality of life, infant mortality, life expectancy, etc. are usually broken down by race. It always turns out that blacks have horrible statistics as compared with whites.

But an interesting study was done by Vicente Navarro, a professor at Johns Hopkins who works on public health issues. He decided to reanalyze the statistics, separating out the factors of race and class. For example, he looked at white workers and black workers versus white executives and black executives. He discovered that much of the difference between blacks and whites was actually a class difference. If you look at poor white workers and white executives, the gap between them is enormous.

The study was obviously relevant to epidemiology and public health, so he submitted it to the major American medical journals. They all rejected it. He then sent it to the world's leading medical journal, *Lancet,* in Britain. They accepted it right away.

The reason is very clear. In the United States you're not allowed to   5
talk about class differences. In fact, only two groups are allowed to be class-conscious in the United States. One of them is the business community, which is rabidly class-conscious. When you read their literature, it's all full of the danger of the masses and their rising power and how we have to defeat them. It's kind of vulgar, inverted Marxism.

The other group is the high planning sectors of the government. They talk the same way — how we have to worry about the rising aspirations of the common man and the impoverished masses who are seeking to improve standards and harming the business climate.

So they can be class-conscious. They have a job to do. But it's extremely important to make other people, the rest of the population, believe that there is no such thing as class. We're all just equal, we're all Americans, we live in harmony, we all work together, everything is great.

Take, for example, the book *Mandate for Change,* put out by the Progressive Policy Institute, the Clinton think tank. It was a book you could buy at airport newsstands, part of the campaign literature describing the Clinton administration's program. It has a section on "entrepreneurial economics," which is economics that's going to avoid the pitfalls of the right and the left.

It gives up these old-fashioned liberal ideas about entitlement and welfare mothers having a right to feed their children — that's all passé. We're not going to have any more of that stuff. We now have "enterprise economics," in which we improve investment and growth. The only people we want to help are workers and the firms in which they work.

According to this picture, we're all workers. There are firms in which   10
we work. We would like to improve the firms in which we work, like we'd like to improve our kitchens, get a new refrigerator.

There's somebody missing from this story — there are no managers, no bosses, no investors. They don't exist. It's just workers and the firms in which we work. All the administration's interested in is helping us folks out there.

The word *entrepreneurs* shows up once, I think. They're the people who assist the workers and the firms in which they work. The word *profits* also appears once, if I recall. I don't know how that sneaked in — that's another dirty word, like *class*.

Or take the word *jobs*. It's now used to mean *profits*. So when, say, George Bush took off to Japan with Lee Iacocca and the rest of the auto executives, his slogan was "Jobs, jobs, jobs." That's what he was going for.

We know exactly how much George Bush cares about jobs. All you have to do is look at what happened during his presidency, when the number of unemployed and underemployed officially reached about seventeen million or so — a rise of eight million during his term of office.

He was trying to create conditions for exporting jobs overseas. He   15
continued to help out with the undermining of unions and the lowering of real wages. So what does he mean when he and the media shout, "Jobs, jobs, jobs"? It's obvious: "Profits, profits, profits." Figure out a way to increase profits.

The idea is to create a picture among the population that we're all one happy family. We're America, we have a national interest, we're working together. There are us nice workers, the firms in which we work and the government who works for us. We pick them — they're our servants.

And that's all there is in the world — no other conflicts, no other categories of people, no further structure to the system beyond that. Certainly nothing like class. Unless you happen to be in the ruling class, in which case you're very well aware of it.

So then equally exotic issues like class oppression and class warfare occur only in obscure books and on Mars?

Or in the business press and the business literature, where it's written about all the time. It exists there because they have to worry about it.

*You use the term "elite." The political economist and economic historian Samir   20
Amin says it confers too much dignity upon them. He prefers "ruling class." Incidentally, a more recent invention is "the ruling crass."*

The only reason I don't use the word *class* is that the terminology of political discourse is so debased it's hard to find any words at all. That's part of the point — to make it impossible to talk. For one thing, *class* has various associations. As soon as you say the word *class*, everybody falls down dead. They think, "There's some Marxist raving again."

But the other thing is that to do a really serious class analysis, you can't just talk about the ruling class. Are the professors at Harvard part of the ruling class? Are the editors of the *New York Times* part of the ruling class? Are the bureaucrats in the State Department? There are lots of different categories of people. So you can talk vaguely about *the establishment* or *the elites* or the people in *the dominant sectors.*

But I agree, you can't get away from the fact that there are sharp differences in power which in fact are ultimately rooted in the economic system. You can talk about *the masters,* if you like. It's Adam Smith's[1] word, and he's now in fashion. The elite are the masters, and they follow what he called their "vile maxim" — namely, "all for ourselves and nothing for anyone else."

You say that class transcends race, essentially.

It certainly does. For example, the United States *could* become a color-free society. It's possible. I don't think it's going to happen, but it's perfectly possible that it would happen, and it would hardly change the political economy at all. Just as women could pass through the "glass ceiling" and that wouldn't change the political economy at all.

That's one of the reasons that you commonly find the business sector reasonably willing to support efforts to overcome racism and sexism. It doesn't matter that much for them. You lose a little white-male privilege in the executive suite, but that's not all that important as long as the basic institutions of power and domination survive intact.

And you can pay the women less.

Or you can pay them the same amount. Take England. They just went through ten pleasant years with the Iron Lady running things. Even worse than Reaganism.

Lingering in the shadows of the liberal democracies — where there's this pyramid of control and domination, where there's class and race and gender bias — is coercion, force.

That comes from the fact that objective power is concentrated. It lies in various places, like in patriarchy, in race. Crucially it also lies in ownership.

If you think about the way the society generally works, it's pretty much the way the founding fathers said. As John Jay[2] put it, the country should be governed by those who own it, and the owners intend to follow Adam Smith's vile maxim. That's at the core of things. That can remain even if lots of other things change.

On the other hand, it's certainly worth overcoming the other forms of oppression. For people's lives, racism and sexism may be much worse than class oppression. When a kid was lynched in the South, that was worse than being paid low wages. So when we talk about the roots of the system

[1]*Adam Smith:* Eighteenth-century Scottish philosopher considered the father of modern economics.
[2]*John Jay:* Early American statesman from New York.

of oppression, that can't be spelled out simply in terms of suffering. Suffering is an independent dimension, and you want to overcome suffering.

PREPARING FOR DISCUSSION

1. Chomsky alleges that Americans in general "are not allowed to talk about class differences." On what evidence does he make this claim? What particular groups, according to Chomsky, *are* allowed to talk about class? Why are these groups allowed to do so? Do the reasons that these groups are allowed to do so tell us anything about why the rest of America cannot?

2. Although he is hesitant to use the word *class*, Chomsky comes closest to offering a definition of it in paragraph 23. How does he define *class*? Why does he believe that class issues can be understood only through the relation of power to economics? Can you imagine a notion of class difference that rests on something other than the economic system?

3. In paragraphs 25 and 26, Chomsky contends that class transcends race and that the United States could become a "color-free" society but never a class-free one. Why does he hold out this possibility? What does this imply about the way, according to Chomsky, we think about society?

4. At several points during the interview, Chomsky alludes to a model of American life promoted by the government and political organizations like the Progressive Policy Institute. Describe this model. What are its key terms? Do you agree with Chomsky that there is little talk of "bosses" and "profits," while there is much talk of "workers" and "jobs"? How would you describe Chomsky's efforts to characterize government efforts at avoiding issues of class? Do you agree with his characterization?

5. Consider Chomsky's discussion of the way the word *jobs* has come to replace the word *profits* in political discourse. According to Chomsky, how was this transformation achieved? Why is it in the interest of government and business leaders to substitute one word for the other?

FROM READING TO WRITING

6. Test Chomsky's notion that while we rarely mention a class system, we see vestiges of it in every aspect of American life. Write an essay in which you describe the presence or absence of class differences in American institutions. How do these differences, if they exist, manifest themselves? What efforts have been made and by whom in the name of concealing these differences?

7. Even if you disagree with the idea of the existence of a rigid class system in the United States, you could hardly deny that you come from a particular class background (working class, middle class, upper class, etc.). Write an essay in which you explore the political and ethical values of your own class. In what ways has your class background played a greater part in determining who you are than your ethnic or racial background?

SHELBY STEELE

On Being Black and Middle Class

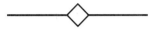

As the next two selections reveal, questions of class and questions of race are often inseparable. One central problem facing analysts of class culture in America is that the values associated with a particular class may at times conflict with the values of a particular racial group. In the following selection, originally published in *Commentary*, January 1988, African American scholar and essayist Shelby Steele describes the "double bind" felt by many middle-class blacks and asks whether he must share their sense of guilt and conflict.

Steele first came to prominence in the late 1980s as the author of a series of essays that questioned whether racism could still be considered a major impediment to the success of African Americans. Steele, a professor of English at San Jose State University, collected several of these essays in *The Content of Our Characters: A New Vision of Race in America* (1990). The book won Steele a National Book Critics Circle Award and the praise of conservatives, white and black, who admired his courage in rejecting the traditional African American position on the effects of racism. He remains an outspoken critic of affirmative action on the grounds that it makes black recipients less confident in their own abilities and leads whites to question black competence at school and in the workplace.

SELECTED PUBLICATIONS: *The Content of Our Characters: A New Vision of Race in America* (1990); Steele's essays have appeared in *Harper's Magazine*, the *American Scholar*, the *Washington Post*, the *New Republic*, and the *New York Times Book Review*.

Not long ago a friend of mine, black like myself, said to me that the term "black middle class" was actually a contradiction in terms. Race, he insisted, blurred class distinctions among blacks. If you were black, you were just black and that was that. When I argued, he let his eyes roll at my naiveté. Then he went on. For us, as black professionals, it was an exercise in self-flattery, a pathetic pretention, to give meaning to such a distinction. Worse, the very idea of class threatened the unity that was vital to the black community as a whole. After all, since when had white America taken note of anything but color when it came to blacks? He then reminded me of an old Malcolm X line that had been popular in the sixties. Question: What is a black man with a Ph.D.? Answer: A nigger.

For many years I had been on my friend's side of this argument. Much of my conscious thinking on the old conundrum of race and class was shaped during my high school and college years in the race-charged sixties, when the fact of my race took on an almost religious significance. Progressively, from the mid-sixties on, more and more aspects of my life found their explanation, their justification, and their motivation in race. My youthful concerns about career, romance, money, values, and even styles of dress became a subject to consultation with various oracular sources of racial wisdom. And these ranged from a figure as ennobling as Martin Luther King, Jr., to the underworld elegance of dress I found in jazz clubs on the South Side of Chicago. Everywhere there were signals, and in those days I considered myself so blessed with clarity and direction that I pitied my white classmates who found more embarrassment than guidance in the face of *their* race. In 1968, inflated by my new power, I took a mischievous delight in calling them culturally disadvantaged.

But now, hearing my friend's comment was like hearing a priest from a church I'd grown disenchanted with. I understood him, but my faith was weak. What had sustained me in the sixties sounded monotonous and off the mark in the eighties. For me, race had lost much of its juju, its singular capacity to conjure meaning. And today, when I honestly look at my life and the lives of many other middle-class blacks I know, I can see that race never fully explained our situation in American society. Black though I may be, it is impossible for me to sit in my single-family house with two cars in the driveway and a swing set in the back yard and *not* see the role class has played in my life. And how can my friend, similarly raised and similarly situated, not see it?

Yet despite my certainty I felt a sharp tug of guilt as I tried to explain myself over my friend's skepticism. He is a man of many comedic facial expressions and, as I spoke, his brow lifted in extreme moral alarm as if I were uttering the unspeakable. His clear implication was that I was being elitist and possibly (dare he suggest?) antiblack — crimes for which there might well be no redemption. He pretended to fear for me. I chuckled along with him, but inwardly I did wonder at myself. Though I never doubted the validity of what I was saying, I felt guilty saying it. Why?

After he left (to retrieve his daughter from a dance lesson) I realized 5 that the trap I felt myself in had a tiresome familiarity and, in a sort of slow-motion epiphany, I began to see its outline. It was like the suddenly sharp vision one has at the end of a burdensome marriage when all the long-repressed incompatibilities come undeniably to light.

What became clear to me is that people like myself, my friend, and middle-class blacks generally are caught in a very specific double bind that keeps two equally powerful elements of our identity at odds with each other. The middle-class values by which we were raised — the work ethic, the importance of education, the value of property ownership, of respectability, of "getting ahead," of stable family life, of initiative, of self-reliance, etc. — are, in themselves, raceless and even assimilationist. They urge us toward participation in the American mainstream, toward integration, toward a strong identification with the society — and toward the entire constellation of qualities that are implied in the word "individualism." These values are almost rules for how to prosper in a democratic, free-enterprise society that admires and rewards individual effort. They tell us to work hard for ourselves and our families and to seek our opportunities whenever they appear, inside or outside the confines of whatever ethnic group we may belong to.

But the particular pattern of racial identification that emerged in the sixties and that still prevails today urges middle-class blacks (and all blacks) in the opposite direction. This pattern asks us to see ourselves as an embattled minority, and it urges an adversarial stance toward the mainstream, an emphasis on ethnic consciousness over individualism. It is organized around an implied separatism.

The opposing thrust of these two parts of our identity results in the double bind of middle-class blacks. There is no forward movement on either plane that does not constitute backward movement on the other. This was the familiar trap I felt myself in while talking with my friend. As I spoke about class, his eyes reminded me that I was betraying race. Clearly, the two indispensable parts of my identity were a threat to each other.

Of course when you think about it, class and race are both similar in some ways and also naturally opposed. They are two forms of collective identity with boundaries that intersect. But whether they clash or peacefully coexist has much to do with how they are defined. Being both black and middle class becomes a double bind when class and race are defined in sharply antagonistic terms, so that one must be repressed to appease the other.

But what is the "substance" of these two identities, and how does each establish itself in an individual's overall identity? It seems to me that when we identify with any collective we are basically identifying with images that tell us what it means to be a member of that collective. Identity is not the same thing as the fact of membership in a collective; it is, rather, a form of self-definition, facilitated by images of what we wish our membership in the collective to mean. In this sense, the images we identify with may reflect the aspirations of the collective more than they reflect reality, and their content can vary with shifts in those aspirations.

But the process of identification is usually dialectical. It is just as necessary to say what we are *not* as it is to say what we are — so that finally identification comes about by embracing a polarity of positive and negative images. To identify as middle class, for example, I must have both positive and negative images of what being middle class entails; then I will know what I should and should not be doing in order to be middle class. The same goes for racial identity.

In the racially turbulent sixties the polarity of images that came to define racial identification was very antagonistic to the polarity that defined middle-class identification. One might say that the positive images of one lined up with the negative images of the other, so that to identify with both required either a contortionist's flexibility or a dangerous splitting of the self. The double bind of the black middle class was in place.

The black middle class has always defined its class identity by means of positive images gleaned from middle- and upper-class white society, and by means of negative images of lower-class blacks. This habit goes back to the institution of slavery itself, when "house" slaves both mimicked the whites they served and held themselves above the "field" slaves. But in the sixties the old bourgeois impulse to dissociate from the lower classes (the "we-they" distinction) backfired when racial identity suddenly called for the celebration of this same black lower class. One of the qualities of a double bind is that one feels it more than sees it, and I distinctly remember the tension and strange sense of dishonesty I felt in those days as I moved back and forth like a bigamist between the demands of class and race.

Though my father was born poor, he achieved middle-class standing through much hard work and sacrifice (one of his favorite words) and by identifying fully with solid middle-class values — mainly hard work, family life, property ownership, and education for his children (all four of whom have advanced degrees). In his mind these were not so much values as laws of nature. People who embodied them made up the positive images in his class polarity. The negative images came largely from the blacks he had left behind because they were "going nowhere."

No one in my family remembers how it happened, but as time went on, the negative images congealed into an imaginary character named Sam, who, from the extensive service we put him to, quickly grew to mythic proportions. In our family lore he was sometimes a trickster, sometimes a boob, but always possessed of a catalogue of sly faults that gave up graphic images of everything we should not be. On sacrifice: "Sam never thinks about tomorrow. He wants it now or he doesn't care about it." On work: "Sam doesn't favor it too much." On children: "Sam likes to have them but not to raise them." On money: "Sam drinks it up and pisses it out." On fidelity: "Sam has to have two or three women." On clothes: "Sam features loud clothes. He likes to see and be seen." And so on. Sam's persona amounted to a negative instruction manual in class identity. 15

I don't think that any of us believed Sam's faults were accurate representations of lower-class black life. He was an instrument of self-definition, not of sociological accuracy. It never occurred to us that he looked very much like the white racist stereotype of blacks, or that he might have been a manifestation of our own racial self-hatred. He simply gave us a counterpoint against which to express our aspirations. If self-hatred was a factor, it was not, for us, a matter of hating lower-class blacks but of hating what we did not want to be.

Still, hate or love aside, it is fundamentally true that my middle-class identity involved a dissociation from images of lower-class black life and a corresponding identification with values and patterns of responsibility that are common to the middle class everywhere. These values sent me a clear message: Be both an individual and a responsible citizen; understand that the quality of your life will approximately reflect the quality of effort you put into it; know that individual responsibility is the basis of freedom and that the limitations imposed by fate (whether fair or unfair) are no excuse for passivity.

Whether I live up to these values or not, I know that my acceptance of them is the result of lifelong conditioning. I know also that I share this conditioning with middle-class people of all races and that I can no more easily be free of it than I can be free of my race. Whether all this got started because the black middle class modeled itself on the white middle class is no longer relevant. For the middle-class black, conditioned by these values from birth, the sense of meaning they provide is as immutable as the color of his skin.

I started the sixties in high school feeling that my class-conditioning was the surest way to overcome racial barriers. My racial identity was pretty much taken for granted. After all, it was obvious to the world that I was black. Yet I ended the sixties in graduate school a little embarrassed by my class background and with an almost desperate need to be "black." The tables had turned. I knew very clearly (though I struggled to repress it) that my aspirations and my sense of how to operate in the world came from my class background, yet "being black" required certain attitudes and stances that made me feel secretly a little duplicitous. The inner compatibility of class and race I had known in 1960 was gone.

For blacks, the decade between 1960 and 1969 saw racial identifica-   20
tion undergo the same sort of transformation that national identity undergoes in times of war. It became more self-conscious, more narrowly focused, more prescribed, less tolerant of opposition. It spawned an implicit party line, which tended to disallow competing forms of identity. Race-as-identity was lifted from the relative slumber it knew in the fifties and pressed into service in a social and political war against oppression. It was redefined along sharp adversarial lines and directed toward the goal of mobilizing the great mass of black Americans in this warlike effort. It was imbued with a strong moral authority, useful for denouncing those who opposed it and for celebrating those who honored it as a positive achievement rather than as a mere birthright.

The form of racial identification that quickly evolved to meet this challenge presented blacks as a racial monolith, a singular people with a common experience of oppression. Differences within the race, no matter how ineradicable, had to be minimized. Class distinctions were one of the first such differences to be sacrificed, since they not only threatened racial unity but also seemed to stand in contradiction to the principle of equality which was the announced goal of the movement for racial progress. The discomfort I felt in 1969, the vague but relentless sense of duplicity, was the result of a historical necessity that put my race and class at odds, that was asking me to cast aside the distinction of my class and identify with a monolithic view of my race.

If the form of this racial identity was the monolith, its substance was victimization. The civil rights movement and the more radical splinter groups of the late sixties were all dedicated to ending racial victimization, and the form of black identity that emerged to facilitate this goal made blackness and victimization virtually synonymous. Since it was our victimization more than any other variable that identified and unified us, moreover, it followed logically that the purest black was the poor black. It was images of him that clustered around the positive pole of the race polarity; all other blacks were, in effect, required to identify with him in order to confirm their own blackness.

Certainly there were more dimensions to the black experience than victimization, but no other had the same capacity to fire the indignation needed for war. So, again out of historical necessity, victimization became the overriding focus of racial identity. But this only deepened the double bind for middle-class blacks like me. When it came to class we were accustomed to defining ourselves against lower-class blacks and identifying with at least the values of middle-class whites; when it came to race we were now being asked to identify with images of lower-class blacks and to see whites, middle class or otherwise, as victimizers. Negative lining up with positive, we were called upon to reject what we had previously embraced and to embrace what we had previously rejected. To put it still more personally, the Sam figure I had been raised to define myself against had now become the "real" black I was expected to identify with.

The fact that the poor black's new status was only passively earned by the condition of his victimization, not by assertive, positive action made little difference. Status was status apart from the means by which it was achieved, and along with it came a certain power — the power to define the terms of access to that status, to say who was black and who was not. If a lower-class black said you were not really "black" — a sellout, an Uncle Tom — the judgment was all the more devastating because it carried the authority of his status. And this judgment soon enough came to be accepted by many whites as well.

In graduate school I was once told by a white professor, "Well, but . . . you're not really black. I mean, you're not disadvantaged." In his mind my lack of victim status disqualified me from the race itself. More recently I was complimented by a black student for speaking reasonably correct English, "proper" English as he put it. "But I don't know if I really want to talk like that," he went on. "Why not?" I asked. "Because then I wouldn't be black no more," he replied without a pause.

To overcome his marginal status, the middle-class black had to identify with a degree of victimization that was beyond his actual experience.
In college (and well beyond) we used to play a game called "nap matching." It was a game of one-upmanship, in which we sat around outdoing
each other with stories of racial victimization, symbolically measured by
the naps of our hair. Most of us were middle class and so had few personal stories to relate, but if we could not match naps with our own bi-
ographies, we would move on to those legendary tales of victimization
that came to us from the public domain.

The single story that sat atop the pinnacle of racial victimization for
us was that of Emmett Till, the Northern black teenager who, on a visit to
the South in 1955, was killed and grotesquely mutilated for supposedly
looking at or whistling at (we were never sure which, though we argued
the point endlessly) a white woman. Oh, how we probed his story, finding in his youth and Northern upbringing the quintessential embodiment
of black innocence, brought down by a white evil so portentous and
apocalyptic, so gnarled and hideous, that it left us with a feeling not far
from awe. By telling his story and others like it, we came to *feel* the im-
mutability of our victimization, its utter indigenousness, as a thing on
this earth like dirt or sand or water.

Of course, these sessions were a ritual of group identification, a
means by which we, as middle-class blacks, could be at one with our
race. But why were we, who had only a moderate experience of victimization (and that offset by opportunities our parents never had), so intent
on assimilating or appropriating an identity that in so many ways contradicted our own? Because, I think, the sense of innocence that is always
entailed in feeling victimized filled us with a corresponding feeling of entitlement, or even license, that helped us endure our vulnerability on a
largely white college campus.

In my junior year in college I rode to a debate tournament with three
white students and our faculty coach, an elderly English professor. The
experience of being the lone black in a group of whites was so familiar to
me that I thought nothing of it as our trip began. But when halfway
through the trip the professor casually turned to me and, in an isn't-the-
world-funny sort of tone, said that he had just refused to rent an apartment in a house he owned to a "very nice" black couple because their
color would "offend" the white couple who lived downstairs. His eyebrows lifted helplessly over his hawkish nose, suggesting that he too, like
me, was a victim of America's racial farce. His look assumed a kind of
comradeship: He and I were above this grimy business of race, though
for expediency we had occasionally to concede the world its madness.

My vulnerability in this situation came not so much from the profes- 30
sor's blindness to his own racism as from his assumption that I would
participate in it, that I would conspire with him against my own race so

that he might remain comfortably blind. Why did he think I would be amenable to this? I can only guess that he assumed my middle-class identity was so complete and all-encompassing that I would see his action as nothing more than a trifling concession to the folkways of our land, that I would in fact applaud his decision not to disturb propriety. Blind to both his own racism and to me — one blindness serving the other — he could not recognize that he was asking me to betray my race in the name of my class.

His blindness made me feel vulnerable because it threatened to expose my own repressed ambivalence. His comment pressured me to choose between my class identification, which had contributed to my being a college student and a member of the debating team, and my desperate desire to be "black." I could have one but not both; I was double-bound.

Because double binds are repressed there is always an element of terror in them: the terror of bringing to the conscious mind the buried duplicity, self-deception, and pretense involved in serving two masters. This terror is the stuff of vulnerability, and since vulnerability is one of the least tolerable of all human feelings, we usually transform it into an emotion that seems to restore the control of which it has robbed us; most often, that emotion is anger. And so, before the professor had even finished his little story, I had become a furnace of rage. The year was 1967, and I had been primed by endless hours of nap-matching to feel, at least consciously, completely at one with the victim-focused black identity. This identity gave me the license, and the impunity, to unleash upon this professor one of those volcanic eruptions of racial indignation familiar to us from the novels of Richard Wright. Like Cross Damon in *Outsider*, who kills in perfectly righteous anger, I tried to annihilate the man. I punished him not according to the measure of his crime but according to the measure of my vulnerability, a measure set by the cumulative tension of years of repressed terror. Soon I saw that terror in *his* face, as he stared hollow-eyed at the road ahead. My white friends in the back seat, knowing no conflict between their own class and race, were astonished that someone they had taken to be so much like themselves could harbor a rage that for all the world looked murderous.

Though my rage was triggered by the professor's comment, it was deepened and sustained by a complex of need, conflict, and repression in myself of which I had been wholly unaware. Out of my racial vulnerability I had developed the strong need of an identity with which to defend myself. The only such identity available was that of me as victim, him as victimizer. Once in the grip of this paradigm, I began to do far more damage to myself than he had done.

Seeing myself as a victim meant that I clung all the harder to my racial identity, which, in turn, meant that I suppressed my class identity. This cut me off from all the resources my class values might have offered me. In those values, for instance, I might have found the means to a more

dispassionate response, the response less of a victim attacked by a victimizer than of an individual offended by a foolish old man. As an individual I might have reported this professor to the college dean. Or I might
have calmly tried to reveal his blindness to him, and possibly won a con-
vert. (The flagrancy of his remark suggested a hidden guilt and even self-
recognition on which I might have capitalized. Doesn't confession
usually signal a willingness to face oneself?) Or I might have simply
chuckled and then let my silence serve as an answer to his provocation.
Would not my composure, in any form it might take, deflect into his own
heart the arrow he'd shot at me?

Instead, my anger, itself the hair-trigger expression of a long-   35
repressed double bind, not only cut me off from the best of my own
resources, it also distorted the nature of my true racial problem. The
righteousness of this anger and the easy catharsis it brought buoyed
the delusion of my victimization and left me as blind as the professor
himself.

As a middle-class black I have often felt myself *contriving* to be
"black." And I have noticed this same contrivance in others — a certain
stretching away from the natural flow of one's life to align oneself with a
victim-focused black identity. Our particular needs are out of sync with
the form of identity available to meet those needs. Middle-class blacks
need to identify racially; it is better to think of ourselves as black and victimized than not black at all; so we contrive (more unconsciously than
consciously) to fit ourselves into an identity that denies our class and fails
to address the true source of our vulnerability.

For me this once meant spending inordinate amounts of time at black
faculty meetings, though these meetings had little to do with my real
racial anxieties or my professional life. I was new to the university, one of
two blacks in an English department of over seventy, and I felt a little isolated and vulnerable, though I did not admit it to myself. But at these
meetings we discussed the problems of black faculty and students within
a framework of victimization. The real vulnerability we felt was covered
over by all the adversarial drama the victim/victimized polarity inspired, and hence went unseen and unassuaged. And this, I think, explains our rather chronic ineffectiveness as a group. Since victimization
was not our primary problem — the university had long ago opened its
doors to us — we had to contrive to make it so, and there is not much energy in contrivance. What I got at these meetings was ultimately an object
lesson in how fruitless struggle can be when it is not grounded in actual
need.

At our black faculty meetings, the old equation of blackness with victimization was ever present — to be black was to be a victim; therefore,
not to be a victim was not to be black. As we contrived to meet the terms
of this formula there was an inevitable distortion of both ourselves and
the larger university. Through the prism of victimization the university

seemed more impenetrable than it actually was, and we more limited in our powers. We fell prey to the victim's myopia, making the university an institution from which we could seek redress but which we could never fully join. And this mind-set often led us to look more for compensations for our supposed victimization than for opportunities we could pursue as individuals.

The discomfort and vulnerability felt by middle-class blacks in the sixties, it could be argued, was a worthwhile price to pay considering the progress achieved during that time of racial confrontation. But what may have been tolerable then is intolerable now. Though changes in American society have made it an anachronism, the monolithic form of racial identification that came out of the sixties is still very much with us. It may be more loosely held, and its power to punish heretics has probably diminished, but it continues to catch middle-class blacks in a double bind, thus impeding not only their own advancement but even, I would contend, that of blacks as a group.

The victim-focused black identity encourages the individual to feel that his advancement depends almost entirely on that of the group. Thus he loses sight not only of his own possibilities but of the inextricable connection between individual effort and individual advancement. This is a profound encumbrance today, when there is more opportunity for blacks than ever before, for it reimposes limitations that can have the same oppressive effect as those the society has only recently begun to remove.

It was the emphasis on mass action in the sixties that made the victim-focused black identity a necessity. But in the eighties and beyond, when racial advancement will come only through a multitude of individual advancements, this form of identity inadvertently adds itself to the forces that hold us back. Hard work, education, individual initiative, stable family life, property ownership — these have always been the means by which ethnic groups have moved ahead in America. Regardless of past or present victimization, these "laws" of advancement apply absolutely to black Americans also. There is no getting around this. What we need is a form of racial identity that energizes the individual by putting him in touch with both his possibilities and his responsibilities.

It has always annoyed me to hear from the mouths of certain arbiters of blackness that middle-class blacks should "reach back" and pull up those blacks less fortunate than they — as though middle-class status were an unearned and essentially passive condition in which one needed a large measure of noblesse oblige to occupy one's time. My own image is of reaching back from a moving train to lift on board those who have no tickets. A noble enough sentiment — but might it not be wiser to show them the entire structure of principles, efforts, and sacrifice that puts one in a position to buy a ticket any time one likes? This, I think, is something members of the black middle class can realistically offer to other blacks. Their example is not only a testament to possibility but also

40

a lesson in method. But they cannot lead by example until they are released from a black identity that regards that example as suspect, that sees them as "marginally" black, indeed that holds *them* back by catching them in a double bind.

To move beyond the victim-focused black identity we must learn to make a difficult but crucial distinction: between actual victimization, which we must resist with every resource, and identification with the victim's status. Until we do this we will continue to wrestle more with ourselves than with the new opportunities which so many paid so dearly to win.

PREPARING FOR DISCUSSION

1. In paragraphs 6 and 7, Steele looks at two sets of what he considers to be the core values of the middle class as well as those of most African Americans. What are these two sets of values and how does Steele characterize the relationship between them? Describe the nature of "the double bind" within which Steele believes most middle-class blacks to be trapped.

2. Much of the selection reflects Steele's own attempt to resolve the conflict he feels between class and race. What evidence does the selection provide to show that the author has achieved some resolution? What evidence does it provide to show that he has not?

3. Though Steele claims that he is caught in the same "double bind" as most middle-class blacks, the selection may nevertheless provide clues as to which group — middle-class Americans or African Americans — Steele most identifies. What can his narration of and subsequent commentary on the incident involving the elderly professor and the student Steele (paragraphs 29–35) tell us about his attitudes about racial identification? Does Steele's emphasis on individual effort and advancement preclude the possibility of identification with other blacks?

4. In paragraph 38, Steele presents "the old equation of blackness with victimization": "to be black was to be a victim; therefore, not to be a victim was not to be black." Does Steele agree with the logic of this equation or with the ideas of racial identity behind it? How does the historical status of African Americans as the victims of white oppressors figure in this equation?

5. Examine the interchange between Steele and a black student in paragraph 25. What reason does the student offer for not wanting to speak "proper" English like his professor? What vestiges of "black English" appear in the student's response? How does the student's use of language relate to his personal identity? How does the professor's?

FROM READING TO WRITING

6. Consider Steele's description of Sam, an imaginary character who embodied for the Steele family most of the negative stereotypical images associated with African Americans (paragraphs 15–16). Perhaps your own family developed an

imaginary character analogous to Sam in an effort at negative "self-definition." Write an essay in which you describe that character — or, if your family did not invent one, do so now on your own. How would you describe your attitude to the character you or your family has created? To what extent are this character's attributes wholly negative?

7. Steele's friend (paragraphs 1–5) maintains a position on race and class that is diametrically opposed to that advanced by Chomsky in the previous selection. Does Steele agree with his friend's position? To what extent does he agree with Chomsky's view that class transcends race? Write an essay in which you attempt to locate Steele's position in relation to the views advanced by his friend and by Chomsky.

WILLIAM JULIUS WILSON

Cycles of Deprivation and the Ghetto Underclass Debate

While Shelby Steele examines the plight of the black middle class in America in the previous selection, African American sociologist William Julius Wilson looks closely at the plight of the black urban underclass. He contends that America's sociologists and urban economists cannot even begin to address the problem of a growing underclass until they fully acknowledge the existence of that class. Only after such acknowledgment occurs, Wilson argues, can liberal sociologists begin their assault on the conservative position that indigenous cultural values are responsible for the predicament faced by the black urban poor rather than economic conditions or faulty federal programs.

Widely regarded as one of America's foremost experts on public policy and race relations, Wilson participated in Clinton's 1992 Economic Conference in Little Rock, Arkansas. A liberal sociologist himself, he has nevertheless come under attack from other liberal social scientists for stressing the importance of economic rather than racial factors in the creation of the black urban underclass. Wilson is the Lucy Flower University Professor of Sociology and Public Policy and the director of the Center for the Study of Urban Inequality at the University of Chicago. He is a MacArthur Prize recipient and a former president of the American Sociological Association. The following selection is excerpted from Wilson's 1987 work *The Truly Disadvantaged*.

SELECTED PUBLICATIONS: *Power, Racism, and Privilege: Race Relations in Theoretical and Sociohistorical Perspectives* (1973); *The Declining Significance of Race: Blacks and Changing American Institutions* (1978); *The Truly Disadvantaged: The Inner City, the Underclass, and Public Policy* (1987); *The Ghetto Underclass: Social Science Perspectives* (editor) (1993).

In the mid-1960s, urban analysts began to speak of a new dimension to the urban crisis in the form of a large subpopulation of low-income families and individuals whose behavior contrasted sharply with the behavior of the general population.[1] Despite a high rate of poverty in ghetto neighborhoods throughout the first half of the twentieth century, rates of inner-city joblessness, teenage pregnancies, out-of-wedlock births, female-headed families, welfare dependency, and serious crime were significantly lower than in later years and did not reach catastrophic proportions until the mid-1970s.

These increasing rates of social dislocation signified changes in the social organization of inner-city areas. Blacks in Harlem and in other ghetto neighborhoods did not hesitate to sleep in parks, on fire escapes, and on rooftops during hot summer nights in the 1940s and 1950s, and whites frequently visited inner-city taverns and nightclubs.[2] There was crime, to be sure, but it had not reached the point where people were fearful of walking the streets at night, despite the overwhelming poverty in the area. There was joblessness, but it was nowhere near the proportions of unemployment and labor-force nonparticipation that have gripped ghetto communities since 1970. There were single-parent families, but they were a small minority of all black families and tended to be incorporated within extended family networks and to be headed not by unwed teenagers and young adult women but by middle-aged women who usually were widowed, separated, or divorced. There were welfare recipients, but only a very small percentage of the families could be said to be welfare-dependent. In short, unlike the present period, inner-city communities prior to 1960 exhibited the features of social organization — including a sense of community, positive neighborhood identification, and explicit norms and sanctions against aberrant behavior.[3]

Although liberal urban analysts in the mid-1960s hardly provided a definitive explanation of changes in the social organization of inner-city neighborhoods, they forcefully and candidly discussed the rise of social dislocations among the ghetto underclass. "The symptoms of lower-class society affect the dark ghettos of America — low aspirations, poor education, family instability, illegitimacy, unemployment, crime, drug addiction, and alcoholism, frequent illness and early death," stated Kenneth B. Clark, liberal author of a 1965 study of the black ghetto. "But because Negroes begin with the primary affliction of inferior racial status, the burdens of despair and hatred are more pervasive."[4] In raising important issues about the experiences of inequality, liberal scholars in the 1960s sensitively examined the cumulative effects of racial isolation and chronic subordination on life and behavior in the inner city. Whether the focus was on the social or the psychological dimensions of the ghetto, facts of inner-city life "that are usually forgotten or ignored in polite discussions" were vividly described and systematically analyzed.[5]

Indeed, what was both unique and important about these earlier studies was that discussions of the experiences of inequality were closely tied to discussions of the structure of inequality in an attempt to explain how the economic and social situations into which so many disadvantaged blacks are born produce modes of adaptation and create norms and patterns of behavior that take the form of a "self-perpetuating pathology."[6] Nonetheless, much of the evidence from which their conclusions were drawn was impressionistic — based mainly on data collected in ethnographic or urban field research that did not capture long-term trends.[7] Indeed, the only study that provided at least an abstract sense of how the problem had changed down through the years was the Moynihan report on the Negro family, which presented decennial census statistics on changing family structure by race.[8]

However, the controversy surrounding the Moynihan report had the effect of curtailing serious research on minority problems in the inner city for over a decade, as liberal scholars shied away from researching behavior construed as unflattering or stigmatizing to particular racial minorities. Thus, when liberal scholars returned to study these problems in the early 1980s, they were dumbfounded by the magnitude of the changes that had taken place and expressed little optimism about finding an adequate explanation. Indeed, it had become quite clear that there was little consensus on the description of the problem, the explanations advanced, or the policy recommendations proposed. There was even little agreement on a definition of the term *underclass*. From the perspective of liberal social scientists, policymakers, and others, the picture seemed more confused than ever.

However, if liberals lack a clear view of the recent social changes in the inner city, the perspective among informed conservatives has crystallized around a set of arguments that have received increasing public attention. Indeed, the debate over the problems of the ghetto underclass has been dominated in recent years by conservative spokespersons as the views of liberals have gradually become more diffuse and ambiguous. Liberals have traditionally emphasized how the plight of disadvantaged groups can be related to the problems of the broader society, including problems of discrimination and social-class subordination. They have also emphasized the need for progressive social change, particularly through governmental programs, to open the opportunity structure. Conservatives, in contrast, have traditionally stressed the importance of different group values and competitive resources in accounting for the experiences of the disadvantaged; if reference is made to the larger society, it is in terms of the assumed adverse effects of various government programs on individual or group behavior and initiative.

In emphasizing this distinction, I do not want to convey the idea that serious research or discussion of the ghetto underclass is subordinated to ideological concerns. However, despite pious claims about objectivity in social research, it is true that values influence not only our selection of problems for investigation but also our interpretation of empirical data. And although there are no logical rules of discovery that would invalidate an explanation simply because it was influenced by a particular value premise or ideology, it is true that attempts to arrive at a satisfactory explanation may be impeded by ideological blinders or views restricted by value premises. The solution to this problem is not to try to divest social investigators of their values but to encourage a free and open discussion of the issues among people with different value premises in order that new questions can be raised, existing interpretations challenged, and new research stimulated.

I believe that the demise of the liberal perspective on the ghetto underclass has made the intellectual discourse on this topic too one-sided. It has made it more difficult to achieve the above objective and has ultimately made it less likely that our understanding of inner-city social dislocations will be enhanced. With this in mind I should like to explain, in the ensuing discussion, why the liberal perspective on the ghetto underclass has receded into the background and why the conservative perspective enjoys wide and increasing currency. I should then like to suggest how the liberal perspective might be refocused to challenge the now-dominant conservative views on the ghetto underclass and, more important, to provide a more balanced intellectual discussion of why the problems in the inner city sharply increased when they did and in the way that they did.

The Declining Influence of the Liberal Perspective
on the Ghetto Underclass

The liberal perspective on the ghetto underclass has become less persuasive and convincing in public discourse principally because many of those who represent traditional liberal views on social issues have been reluctant to discuss openly or, in some instances, even to acknowledge the sharp increase in social pathologies in ghetto communities. This is seen in the four principal ways in which liberals have recently addressed the subject. In describing these four approaches I want it to be clear that some liberals may not be associated with any one of them, some with only one, and others with more than one. But I believe that these approaches represent the typical, recent liberal reactions to the ghetto underclass phenomenon and that they collectively provide a striking contrast to the crystallized, candid, and forceful liberal perspective of the mid-1960s. Let me elaborate.

One approach is to avoid describing any behavior that might be con- 10 strued as unflattering or stigmatizing to ghetto residents, either because of a fear of providing fuel for racist arguments or because of a concern of being charged with "racism" or with "blaming the victim." Indeed, one of the consequences of the heated controversy over the Moynihan report on the Negro family is that liberal social scientists, social workers, jour- nalists, policymakers, and civil rights leaders have been, until very re- cently, reluctant to make any reference to race at all when discussing issues such as the increase of violent crime, teenage pregnancy, and out- of-wedlock births. The more liberals have avoided writing about or re- searching these problems, the more conservatives have rushed headlong to fill the void with popular explanations of inner-city social dislocations that much of the public finds exceedingly compelling.

A second liberal approach to the subject of underclass and urban so- cial problems is to refuse even to use terms such as *underclass*. As one spokesman put it: "'Underclass' is a destructive and misleading label that lumps together different people who have different problems. And that it is the latest of a series of popular labels (such as the 'lumpen prole- tariat,' 'undeserving poor,' and the 'culture of poverty') that focuses on individual characteristics and thereby stigmatizes the poor for their poverty."[9] However, the real problem is not the term *underclass* or some similar designation but the fact that the term has received more system- atic treatment from conservatives, who tend to focus almost exclusively on individual characteristics, than from liberals, who would more likely relate these characteristics to the broader problems of society. While some liberals debate whether terms such as *underclass* should even be used, conservatives have made great use of them in developing popular arguments about life and behavior in the inner city.[10]

Regardless of which term is used, one cannot deny that there is a het- erogeneous grouping of inner-city families and individuals whose behav- ior contrasts sharply with that of mainstream America. The real challenge is not only to explain why this is so, but also to explain why the behavior patterns in the inner city today differ so markedly from those of only three or four decades ago. To obscure these differences by eschewing the term *underclass*, or some other term that could be helpful in describing changes in ghetto behavior, norms, and aspirations, in favor of more neu- tral designations such as *lower class* or *working class* is to fail to address one of the most important social transformations in recent United States history.

Indeed, the liberal argument to reject the term *underclass* reflects the lack of historical perspective on urban social problems. We often are not aware of or lose sight of the fact that the sharp increase in inner-city dislo- cations has occurred in only the last several years. Although a term such as *lumpen proletariat* or *underclass* might have been quite appropriate in Karl Marx's description of life and behavior in the slums of nineteenth-century England, it is not very appropriate in descriptions of life and behavior in America's large urban ghettos prior to the mid-twentieth century. Indeed, in the 1940s, 1950s, and as late as the 1960s such communities featured a vertical integration of different segments of the urban black population. Lower-class, working-class, and middle-class black families all lived more or less in the same communities (albeit in different neighborhoods), sent their children to the same schools, availed themselves of the same recreational facilities, and shopped at the same stores. Whereas today's black middle-class professionals no longer tend to live in ghetto neighborhoods and have moved increasingly into mainstream occupations outside the black community, the black middle-class professionals of the 1940s and 1950s (doctors, teachers, lawyers, social workers, ministers) lived in higher-income neighborhoods of the ghetto and serviced the black community. Accompanying the black middle-class exodus has been a growing movement of stable working-class blacks from ghetto neighborhoods to higher-income neighborhoods in other parts of the city and to the suburbs. In the earlier years, the black middle and working classes were confined by restrictive covenants to communities also inhabited by the lower class; their very presence provided stability to inner-city neighborhoods and reinforced and perpetuated mainstream patterns of norms and behavior.[11]

This is not the situation in the 1990s. Today's ghetto neighborhoods are populated almost exclusively by the most disadvantaged segments of the black urban community, that heterogeneous grouping of families and individuals who are outside the mainstream of the American occupational system. Included in this group are individuals who lack training and skills and either experience long-term unemployment or are not members of the labor force, individuals who are engaged in street crime and other forms of aberrant behavior, and families that experience long-term spells of poverty and/or welfare dependency. These are the populations to which I refer when I speak of the *underclass*. I use this term to depict a reality not captured in the more standard designation *lower class*.

In my conception, the term *underclass* suggests that changes have taken place in ghetto neighborhoods, and the groups that have been left behind are collectively different from those that lived in these neighborhoods in earlier years. It is true that long-term welfare families and street criminals are distinct groups, but they live and interact in the same depressed community and they are part of the population that has, with the exodus of the more stable working- and middle-class segments, become increasingly isolated socially from mainstream patterns and norms of behavior. It is also true that certain groups are stigmatized by the label *underclass*, just as some people who live in depressed central-city communities are stigmatized by the term *ghetto* or *inner city*, but it would be far worse to obscure the profound changes in the class structure and social behavior of ghetto neighborhoods by avoiding the use of the term *underclass*. Indeed, the real challenge is to describe and explain these developments accurately so that liberal policymakers can appropriately address them. And it is difficult for me to see how this can be accomplished by rejecting a term that aids in the description of ghetto social transformations.

A third liberal approach to the subject of problems in the inner city and the ghetto underclass is to emphasize or embrace selective evidence that denies the very existence of an urban underclass. We have seen this approach in two principal ways. First, in the aftermath of the controversy over Daniel Patrick Moynihan's unflattering depiction of the black family, a number of liberals, particularly black liberals, began in the late 1960s and early1970s to emphasize the positive aspects of the black experience.[12] Thus earlier arguments, which asserted that some aspects of ghetto life were pathological,[13] were rejected and replaced with those that accented the strengths of the black community. Arguments extolling the strengths and virtues of black families replaced those that described the breakup of black families. In fact, aspects of ghetto behavior described as pathological in the studies of the mid-1960s were reinterpreted or redefined as functional because, it was argued, blacks were demonstrating their ability to survive and even flourish in an economically depressed and racist environment. Ghetto families were portrayed as resilient and capable of adapting creatively to an oppressive society. These revisionist arguments purporting to "liberate" the social sciences from the influence of racism helped shift the focus of social scientists away from discussions of the consequences of racial isolation and economic class subordination to discussions of black achievement. Since the focus was solely on black achievement, little attention was paid to internal differences within the black community. Moreover, since the problems were defined in racial terms, very little discussion was devoted either to problems created by economic shifts and their impact on the poor black community or to the need for economic reform. In short, such arguments effectively diverted attention from the appropriate solutions to the dreadful economic condition of poor blacks and made it difficult for blacks to see, in the words of one perceptive observer, "how their fate is inextricably tied up with the structure of the American economy."[14]

More recently, in response to arguments by conservatives that a growing number of inner-city residents get locked into a culture of poverty and a culture of welfare, some liberals have been quick to cite research indicating that only a small proportion of Americans in poverty and on welfare are persistently poor and persistently on welfare. The problem of long-term poverty and welfare dependency began to receive detailed and systematic empirical attention when it became possible to track the actual experiences of the poor and those who receive welfare with adequate longitudinal data provided by the Michigan Panel Study of Income Dynamics (PSID). A series of initial studies based on the PSID revealed that only a very small percentage of those in poverty and on welfare were long-term cases. For example, one study found that only 3 percent of the population was poor throughout a ten-year time span;[15] another study reported that only 2.2 percent of the population was poor eight of the ten years (1968–78) covered in the research.[16] These studies have been widely cited and have been said to provide powerful evidence against the notion of an underclass.[17]

However, more recent studies based on the PSID data seriously challenge interpretations based on these findings.[18] Specifically, these studies revealed that the previous PSID research on spells of poverty and welfare dependency observed over a fixed time frame — say, eight or ten years — underestimated the length of spells because some individuals who appear to have short spells of poverty or welfare receipt are actually beginning or ending long spells. To correct for this problem, the more recent studies first identified spells of poverty and welfare receipt, then calculated exit probabilities by year to estimate the duration of spells. With this revised methodology it was found that, although most people who become poor during some point in their lives experience poverty for only one or two years, a substantial subpopulation remains in poverty for a very long time. Indeed, these long-term poor constitute about 60 percent of those in poverty at any given point in time and are in a poverty spell that will last eight or more years. Furthermore, families headed by women are likely to have longer spells of poverty — at a given point in time, the average child who became poor when the family makeup changed from married-couple to female-headed is in the midst of a poverty spell lasting almost twelve years. It was reported that "some 20 percent of poverty spells of children begin with birth. When they do, they tend to last ten years. The average poor black child today appears to be in the midst of a poverty spell which will last for almost two decades."[19] Similar findings were reported on spells of welfare receipt. Long-term welfare mothers tend to belong to racial minorities, were never married, and are high school dropouts.

Thus, despite the findings and interpretations of earlier PSID reports on long-term poverty and welfare dependency, there is still a firm basis for accepting the argument that a ghetto underclass has emerged and exhibits the problems of long-term poverty and welfare dependency. Accordingly, liberal attempts to deny the existence of an underclass on the basis of the earlier optimistic Michigan panel studies now seem especially questionable.

Finally, a fourth liberal approach to the subject of the ghetto underclass and urban social problems is to acknowledge the rise in inner-city social dislocations while emphasizing racism as the explanation of these changes. There are two basic themes associated with this thesis. The more popular theme is that the cycle of pathology characterizing the ghetto can only be comprehended in terms of racial oppression and that "the racial dehumanization Americans permit is a symptom of the deep-seated, systematic and most dangerous social disease of racism."[20] In response to this argument, I should like to emphasize that no serious student of American race relations can deny the relationship between the disproportionate concentration of blacks in impoverished urban ghettos and historic racial subjugation in American society. But to suggest that the recent rise of social dislocations among the ghetto underclass is due mainly to contemporary racism, which in this context refers to the "conscious refusal of whites to accept blacks as equal human beings and their willful, systematic effort to deny blacks equal opportunity,"[21] is to ignore a set of complex issues that are difficult to explain with a race-specific thesis. More specifically, it is not readily apparent how the deepening economic class divisions between the haves and have-nots in the black community can be accounted for when this thesis is invoked,[22] especially when it is argued that this same racism is directed with equal force across class boundaries in the black community.[23] Nor is it apparent how racism can result in a more rapid social and economic deterioration in the inner city in the post–civil rights period than in the period that immediately preceded the notable civil rights victories. To put the question more pointedly, even if racism continues to be a factor in the social and economic progress of some blacks, can it be used to explain the sharp increase in inner-city social dislocations since 1970? Unfortunately, no one who supports the contemporary racism thesis has provided adequate or convincing answers to this question.

The problem is that the proponents of the contemporary racism thesis fail to distinguish between the past and the present effects of racism on the lives of different segments of the black population. This is unfortunate because once the effects of historic racism are recognized it becomes easier to assess the importance of current racism in relation to nonracial factors such as economic-class position and modern economic trends. Moreover, once this distinction is made it clears the way for appropriate policy recommendations. Policy programs based on the premise that the recent rise of social dislocations, such as joblessness, in the inner city is due to current racism will be significantly different from policy programs based on the premise that the growth of these problems is due more to nonracial factors.

However, some liberals know that "racism is too easy an explanation" because, in the words of Michael Harrington, it implies "that the social and economic disorganization faced by black Americans was the result of the psychological state of mind of white America, a kind of deliberate — and racist — ill will." Harrington goes on to acknowledge that such racism exists and has to be vigorously fought, but he emphasizes that "it is a relatively simple part of the problem. For there is an economic structure of racism that will persist even if every white who hates blacks goes through a total conversion." In this more complex version, racism is seen not as a state of mind but as "an occupational hierarchy rooted in history and institutionalized in the labor market."[24] Also, it is argued that this economic structure of racism will become even more oppressive in the future because massive economic trends in the economy — the technological revolution, the internationalization of capital, and the world division of labor — will have an adverse effect in areas where blacks have made the most significant gains.

The problem with this argument is not the association between economic shifts and the deteriorating economic position of some blacks, which I believe is true and should be emphasized, but that this whole question is discussed in terms of an "economic structure of racism." In other words, complex problems in the American and worldwide economies that ostensibly have little or nothing to do with race, problems that fall heavily on much of the black population but require solutions that confront the broader issues of economic organization, are not made more understandable by associating them directly or indirectly with racism. Indeed, because this term has been used so indiscriminately, has so many different definitions, and is often relied on to cover up lack of information or knowledge of complex issues, it frequently weakens rather than enhances arguments concerning race. Indiscriminate use of this term in any analysis of contemporary racial problems immediately signals that the arguments typify worn-out themes and make conservative writers more interesting in comparison because they seem, on the surface at least, to have some fresh ideas.

Thus, instead of talking vaguely about an economic structure of racism, it would be less ambiguous and more effective to state simply that a racial division of labor has been created due to decades, even centuries, of discrimination and prejudice; and that because those in the low-wage sector of the economy are more adversely affected by impersonal economic shifts in advanced industrial society, the racial division of labor is reinforced. One does not have to "trot out" the concept of racism to demonstrate, for example, that blacks have been severely hurt by deindustrialization because of their heavy concentration in the automobile, rubber, steel, and other smokestack industries.[25]

In sum, the liberal perspective on the ghetto underclass and inner-city social dislocations is less persuasive and influential in public discourse today because many of those who represent the traditional liberal views on social issues have failed to address straightforwardly the rise of social pathologies in the ghetto. As I have attempted to show, some liberals completely avoid any discussion of these problems, some eschew terms such as *underclass,* and others embrace selective evidence that denies the very existence of an underclass and behavior associated with the underclass or rely on the convenient term *racism* to account for the sharp rise in the rates of social dislocation in the inner city. The combined effect of these tendencies is to render liberal arguments ineffective and to enhance conservative arguments on the underclass, even though the conservative thesis is plagued with serious problems of interpretation and analysis. It is to the conservative perspective that I now turn.

The Increasing Influence of the Conservative Perspective on the Underclass

If the most forceful and influential arguments on the ghetto underclass in the 1960s were put forth by liberals, conservative arguments have moved to the forefront in the 1990s, even though they have undergone only slight modification since the 1960s. Indeed, many students of social behavior recognize that the conservative thesis represents little more than the application of the late Oscar Lewis's culture-of-poverty arguments to the ghetto underclass.[26] Relying on participant observation and life-history data to analyze Latin American poverty, Lewis described the culture of poverty as "both an adaptation and a reaction of the poor to their marginal position in a class stratified, highly individuated, capitalistic society."[27] However, he also noted that once the culture of poverty comes into existence, "it tends to perpetuate itself from generation to generation because of its effect on the children. By the time slum children are age six or seven," argued Lewis, "they have usually absorbed the basic values and attitudes of their subculture and are not psychologically geared to take full advantage of changing conditions or increased opportunities which may occur in their life-time."[28]

Although Lewis was careful to point out that basic structural changes in society may alter some of the cultural characteristics of the poor, conservative students of inner-city poverty who have built on his thesis have focused almost exclusively on the interconnection between cultural traditions, family history, and individual character. For example, they have argued that a ghetto family that has had a history of welfare dependency will tend to bear offspring who lack ambition, a work ethic, and a sense of self-reliance.[29] Some even suggest that ghetto underclass individuals have to be rehabilitated culturally before they can advance in society.[30]

In the 1960s, before the civil rights revolution ran its course and before the Great Society programs began to wind down, such arguments were successfully beaten back by forceful liberal critics who blamed society for the plight of the ghetto underclass and who called for progressive social reforms to improve their economic and social chances in life. There was considerable optimism and confidence among liberals in the latter half of the 1960s not only because they felt they understood the problems of the inner city, but also because they believed they had the potential solution in the form of Great Society and civil rights programs. Conservative students of urban poverty worked in an intimidating atmosphere, and those who dared to write or speak out on the subject received the full brunt of the liberal onslaught.[31]

Arguments that associated ghetto-specific behavior (i.e., behavior that departs from mainstream patterns) with ingrained cultural characteristics (that whole array of norms, values, orientations, and aspirations) received the most attention from liberal critics in the 1960s. These critics contended that ghetto-specific behavior is largely due to segregation, limited opportunities, and external obstacles against advancement — which were determined by different historical circumstances. They further argued that even if one were able to demonstrate a direct relationship between ghetto-specific behavior and values or other cultural traits, this would be only the first step in a proper social analysis. Analysis of the historical and social roots of these cultural differences represents the succeeding and, indeed, more fundamental step.[32]

In short, liberal scholars in the 1960s argued that cultural values do not ultimately determine behavior or success. Rather, cultural values emerge from specific social circumstances and life chances and reflect one's class and racial position. Thus, if underclass blacks have limited aspirations or fail to plan for the future, it is not ultimately the product of different cultural norms but the consequence of restricted opportunities, a bleak future, and feelings of resignation resulting from bitter personal experiences. Accordingly, behavior described as socially pathological and associated with the ghetto underclass should be analyzed not as a cultural aberration but as a symptom of class and racial inequality.[33] As economic and social opportunities change, new behavioral solutions originate and develop into patterns, later to be complemented and upheld by norms. If new situations appear, both the patterns of behavior and the norms eventually undergo change. "Some behavioral norms are more persistent than others," wrote Herbert Gans in 1968, "but over the long run, all of the norms and aspirations by which people live are nonpersistent: They rise and fall with changes in situations."[34]

In the 1960s liberals effectively used this thesis not only to challenge the conservative arguments about culture and underclass behavior but also to explain why ghetto communities were so different from mainstream communities. The assertions about the relationship between culture and social structure were rendered plausible by evidence reported and interpreted in a series of urban field studies in the later 1960s.[35] On the other hand, conservative assertions about underclass life and behavior were weakened because of a lack of direct evidence and because they seemed to be circular in the sense that cultural values were inferred from the behavior of the underclass to be explained, and then these values were used as the explanation of the behavior.[36]

Thus, by the end of the 1960s, the most forceful and persuasive arguments on the ghetto underclass had been provided by liberals, not conservatives. A few years later, just the opposite would be true, even though the conservative thesis of the interplay between cultural tradition, family biography, and individual character remains largely unchanged. To understand this development, it is important to note the unsettling effect of the heated controversy over the Moynihan report on those who represent traditional liberal views.

As I mentioned previously, liberals became increasingly reluctant to research, write about, or publicly discuss inner-city social dislocations following the virulent attacks against Moynihan. Indeed, by 1970 it was clear to any sensitive observer that if there was to be research on the ghetto underclass that would not be subjected to ideological criticism, it would be research conducted by minority scholars on the strengths, not the weaknesses, of inner-city families and communities.[37] Studies of ghetto social pathologies, even those organized in terms of traditional liberal theories, were no longer welcomed in some circles. Thus, after 1970, for a period of several years, the deteriorating social and economic conditions of the ghetto underclass were not addressed by the liberal community as scholars backed away from research on the topic, policymakers were silent, and civil rights leaders were preoccupied with the affirmative action agenda of the black middle class.

By 1980, however, the problems of inner-city social dislocations had reached such catastrophic proportions that liberals were forced to readdress the question of the ghetto underclass, but this time their reactions were confused and defensive. The extraordinary rise in inner-city social dislocations following the passage of the most sweeping antidiscrimination and antipoverty legislation in the nation's history could not be explained by the 1960 explanations of ghetto-specific behavior. Moreover, because liberals had ignored these problems throughout most of the 1970s, they had no alternative explanations to advance and were therefore ill prepared to confront a new and forceful challenge from conservative thinkers. The result was a diffuse and confused reaction typified by the four responses to the subject that I discussed above.

The new conservative challenge does not represent a change in the basic premise of the interplay among cultural tradition, family biography, and individual character; rather, it builds on this premise with the argument that the growth of liberal social policies has exacerbated, not alleviated, ghetto-specific cultural tendencies and problems of inner-city social dislocations. Widely read neoconservative books such as *Thinking about Crime, Wealth and Poverty, Civil Rights: Rhetoric or Reality,* and *Losing Ground* present a range of arguments on the negative effects of liberal social policy on the behavior and values of the ghetto underclass.[38] Thus liberal changes in the criminal justice system are said to have decreased the sanctions against aberrant behavior and thereby contributed to the rise of serious inner-city crime since 1965; affirmative action pressures are linked with the deteriorating plight of the underclass because, while they increase the demand for highly qualified minority members, they decrease the demand for the less qualified due to the cost, particularly at times of discharge and promotion; and the Great Society and other social welfare programs have been self-defeating because they have made people less self-reliant, promoted joblessness, and contributed to the rise of out-of-wedlock births and female-headed families. Thus, unlike their liberal counterparts, conservatives have attempted to explain the sharp rise in the rates of social dislocation among the ghetto underclass, and their arguments, which strike many as new and refreshing, have dominated public discourse on this subject for the last several years. But there are signs that this is beginning to change. There are signs of a liberal revival. And the spark for this revival, I believe, is Charles Murray's provocative book, *Losing Ground.*

Probably no work has done more to promote the view that federal programs are harmful to the poor. As reported in a recent *New York Times* editorial, "This year's budget-cutter bible seems to be 'Losing Ground,' Charles Murray's book appraising social policy in the last 30 years. The Reagan budget . . . is likely to propose deep reductions in education, child nutrition and housing assistance, and elimination of programs like the Job Corps, revenue sharing and urban development grants. In agency after agency, officials cite the Murray book as a philosophical base for these proposals, for it concludes that social-welfare programs, far from relieving poverty, increase it and should be stopped."[39] Indeed, *Losing Ground* not only attributes increasing poverty to programs such as those of the Great Society, it also explains increasing rates of joblessness, crime, out-of-wedlock births, female-headed families, and welfare dependency, especially among the ghetto underclass, in terms of such programs as well. Murray argues that recent changes in social policy have effectively changed the rewards and penalties that govern human behavior.

Losing Ground initially drew rave reviews in a variety of newspapers and periodicals, partly because Murray seemed to have marshaled an impressive array of statistics to support his arguments. But following that, critics from liberal quarters awakened and responded with powerful criticisms that have devastated the central core of Murray's thesis.[40] For example, whereas Murray maintains that the availability of food stamps and increases in Aid for Families with Dependent Children (AFDC) payments have had a negative effect on poor black family formation and work incentives, liberal critics have appropriately pointed out that the real value of these two combined programs increased only from 1960 to 1972; after that time, their real value declined sharply because states neglected to adjust AFDC benefit levels to inflation, yet "there were no reversals in the trends of either family composition or work effort."[41] Moreover, in 1975, Congress enacted the Earned Income Tax Credit, which further expanded the advantages of working, for the poor. Thus, if welfare incentives lead to black joblessness and family dissolution as Murray argues, "these trends should have reversed themselves in the

1970s, when the relative advantage of work over welfare increased sharply."[42] They did not, of course; black joblessness, female-headed families, and illegitimacy soared during the 1970s.

Whereas Murray contends that despite substantial increases in spending on social programs, from 1968 to 1980 the poverty rate failed to drop — thus indicating that these programs were not successful — liberal critics argue that Murray "neglects the key facts that contradict his message," namely, that the unemployment rate in 1980 was twice that of 1968.[43] When unemployment increases, poverty also rises. What Murray fails to consider, they argue, is that many people slipped into poverty because of the economic downturn and were lifted out by the broadening of benefits. According to Robert Greenstein, director of the Center on Budget and Policy Priorities in Washington, D.C., "The two trends roughly balanced each other and the poverty rate remained about the same" from 1968 to 1980.[44]

Murray, on the other hand, maintains that the slowing of the economy had nothing at all to do with the failure of the poverty rate to decline in the 1970s. He argues that the economy, according to the Gross National Product (GNP), grew more in the 1970s than in the 1950s, when the poverty rate dropped. Liberal critics have responded with the argument that, although growth in the GNP does create jobs, in the 1970s the growth was insufficient to handle the "unusually large numbers of women and young people (from the baby boom generation) who were entering the job market," resulting in an increase in unemployment. Moreover, real wages, which had risen steadily in the 1950s and 1960s, stopped growing in the 1970s. Greenstein states that "when unemployment rises and real wages fall, poverty increases — and low income groups (especially black males) are affected the most." Thus, liberal critics maintain that far from being unimportant, the economy was the major cause of the failure of poverty to decline in the 1970s. If it had not been for the benefit programs that Murray attacks, the poverty rate would have risen further still.[45]

Murray's book has indeed "lit a fire" under liberals; if these and other responses are any indication, we could be seeing the beginnings of a major revival in the liberal approach to the ghetto underclass phenomenon. But the responses are still largely in reaction to what conservative thinkers are saying. In conclusion I should like to suggest how the liberal perspective might be refocused to provide the kind of intellectual and social policy leadership needed to balance the public discourse on the ghetto underclass.

Conclusion: Toward a Refocused Liberal Perspective

If the liberal perspective on the ghetto underclass is to regain the influence it has lost since the 1960s, it will be necessary to do more than simply react to what conservative scholars and policymakers are saying.

Liberals will also have to propose thoughtful explanations of the rise in inner-city social dislocations. Such explanations should emphasize the dynamic interplay between ghetto-specific cultural characteristics and social and economic opportunities. This would necessitate taking into account the effects not only of changes in American economic organization but also of demographic changes and changes in the laws and policies of the government as well. In this connection, the relationships between joblessness and family structure, joblessness and other social dislocations (crime, teenage pregnancy, welfare dependency, etc.), and joblessness and social orientation among different age groups would receive special attention.

However, thoughtful explanations of the recent rise in the problems of the underclass depend on careful empirical research. It is not sufficient to rely solely on census data and other secondary sources. Liberals will have to augment such information with empirical data on the ghetto underclass experience and on conditions in the broader society that have shaped and continue to shape that experience. This calls for a number of different research strategies ranging from survey to ethnographic to historical.

But first, liberals will have to change the way they have tended to approach this subject in recent years. They can no longer afford to be timid in addressing these problems, to debate whether or not concepts such as the *underclass* should even be used, to look for data to deny the very existence of an underclass, or, finally, to rely heavily on the easy explanation of racism.

These are my suggestions for refocusing the liberal perspective. It will not be easy and there is a lot of work to be done. But such an effort is needed if we are to provide a more balanced public discourse on the problems of the ghetto underclass.

Notes

1. Kenneth B. Clark, *Dark Ghetto: Dilemmas of Social Power* (New York: Harper and Row, 1965); Lee Rainwater, "Crucible of Identity: The Negro Lower-Class Family," *Daedalus* 95 (Winter 1966): 176–216; Daniel P. Moynihan, *The Negro Family: The Case for National Action* (Washington, D.C.: Office of Policy Planning and Research, U.S. Department of Labor, 1965); and idem, "Employment, Income and the Ordeal of the Negro Family," in *The Negro American*, ed. Talcott Parsons and Kenneth B. Clark (Boston: Beacon Press, 1965), pp. 134–59.
2. David L. Lewis, *When Harlem Was in Vogue* (New York: Alfred A. Knopf, 1981); Clark, *Dark Ghetto*; and Thomas Sowell, *Civil Rights: Rhetoric or Reality?* (New York: William Morrow, 1984).
3. See St. Clair Drake and Horace R. Cayton, *Black Metropolis: A Study of Negro Life in a Northern City*, vol. 2 (New York: Harper and Row, 1945).
4. Clark, *Dark Ghetto*, p. 27.
5. Rainwater, "Crucible of Identity," p. 173.
6. Clark, *Dark Ghetto*, p. 81.
7. See, e.g., Roger D. Abrahams, *Deep Down in the Jungle* (Hatboro, Pa.: Folklore Associ-

ates, 1964); Clark, *Dark Ghetto*; Rainwater, "Crucible of Identity"; and Elliot Liebow, *Tally's Corner: A Study of Negro Streetcorner Men* (Boston: Little, Brown, 1967).

8. Moynihan, *Negro Family.*
9. Richard McGahey, "Poverty's Voguish Stigma," *New York Times*, March 12, 1982, p. 29. Also see, Michael B. Katz, *In the Shadow of the Poorhouse: A Social History of Welfare in America* (New York: Basic Books, 1986), esp. pp. 274–75.
10. For a discussion of recent conservative analyses of the underclass, see Ken Auletta, *The Underclass* (New York: Random House, 1982).
11. Drake and Cayton, *Black Metropolis.*
12. Moynihan, *Negro Family.* See, e.g., Joyce Ladner, ed., *The Death of White Sociology* (New York: Random House, 1973); Robert B. Hill, *The Strength of Black Families* (New York: Emerson Hall, 1972); Nathan Hare, "The Challenge of a Black Scholar," *Black Scholar* 1 (1969): 58–63; Abdul Hakim Ibn Alkalimat [Gerald McWorter], "The Ideology of Black Social Science," *Black Scholar* 1 (1969): 28–35; and Robert Staples, "The Myth of the Black Matriarchy," *Black Scholar* 2 (1970): 9–16.
13. Clark, *Dark Ghetto*; E. Franklin Frazier, *The Negro Family in the United States* (Chicago: University of Chicago Press, 1939); Moynihan, *Negro Family*; Rainwater, "Crucible of Identity."
14. Orlando Patterson, *Ethnic Chauvinism: The Reactionary Impulse* (New York: Stein and Day, 1977), p. 155. Also see Martin Kilson, "Black Social Classes and Intergenerational Poverty," *Public Interest* 64 (Summer 1981): 58–78.
15. Martha S. Hill, "Some Dynamic Aspects of Poverty," in *Five Thousand American Families: Patterns of Economic Progress*, ed. M. S. Hill, D. H. Hill, and J. N. Morgan, vol. 19 (Ann Arbor: Institute for Social Research, University of Michigan Press, 1981).
16. Mary Corcoran and Greg J. Duncan, "Demographic Aspects of the Underclass," paper presented at the Annual Meeting of the Population Association of America, Pittsburgh, Pa., 1983.
17. See, e.g., Katz, *Shadow of the Poorhouse.*
18. Mary Jo Bane and David T. Ellwood, "Slipping into and out of Poverty: The Dynamics of Spells," working paper no. 1199, National Bureau of Economic Research, Cambridge, Mass., 1983; idem, *The Dynamics of Dependence: The Routes to Self-Sufficiency* (Washington, D.C.: U.S. Department of Health and Human Services, 1983).
19. Bane and Ellwood, "Slipping into and out of Poverty," p. 36.
20. Kenneth B. Clark, "The Role of Race," *New York Times Magazine*, October 5, 1980, p. 109.
21. Carl Gershman, "Carl Gershman Responds," *New York Times Magazine*, October 5, 1980, p. 33.
22. See William Julius Wilson, *The Declining Significance of Race: Blacks and Changing American Institutions*, 2d ed. (Chicago: University of Chicago Press, 1980).
23. See, e.g., Clark, "Role of Race"; Alphonoso Pinkney, *The Myth of Black Progress* (Boston: Cambridge University Press, 1984); and Charles V. Willie, "The Inclining Significance of Race," *Society* 15 (July/August 1978): 10, 12–15.
24. Michael Harrington, *The New American Poverty* (New York: Holt, Rinehart and Winston, 1984), p. 140.
25. Barry Bluestone and Bennett Harrison, *The Deindustrialization of America: Plant Closings, Community Abandonment, and the Dismantling of Basic Industry* (New York: Basic Books, 1982).
26. Oscar Lewis, "The Culture of Poverty," in *On Understanding Poverty: Perspectives from the Social Sciences*, ed. Daniel Patrick Moynihan (New York: Basic Books, 1968), p. 187–200. Also see idem, *Five Families: Mexican Case Studies in the Culture of Poverty* (New York: Basic Books, 1959); idem, *The Children of Sanchez* (New York: Random House, 1961); and idem, *La Vida: A Puerto Rican Family in the Culture of Poverty — San Juan and New York* (New York: Random House, 1966).
27. Lewis, "Culture of Poverty," p. 188.
28. Ibid.

29. For a good discussion of these points, see Auletta, *Underclass,* esp. chap. 2.

30. See, e.g., Edward Banfield, *The Unheavenly City,* 2d ed. (Boston: Little, Brown, 1970).

31. For examples of the tone of the more popular and ideological liberal critiques, see Charles A. Valentine, *Culture and Poverty: Critique and Counter Proposals* (Chicago: University of Chicago Press, 1968); and William Ryan, *Blaming the Victim* (New York: Random House, 1971).

32. See Herbert J. Gans, "Culture and Class in the Study of Poverty: An Approach to Anti-Poverty Research," in Moynihan, *On Understanding Poverty,* pp. 201–8; Lee Rainwater, "The Problem of Lower-Class Culture and Poverty-War Strategy," in Moynihan, *Understanding Poverty,* pp. 229–59; Hylan Lewis, "Culture, Class and the Behavior of Low-Income Families," paper prepared for Conference on Views of Lower-Class Culture, New York, N.Y., June 1963; and Stephen Steinberg, *The Ethnic Myth: Race, Ethnicity and Class in America* (New York: Atheneum, 1981). Steinberg's analysis is a succinct restatement of points made by liberal critics in the 1960s.

33. Gans, "Culture and Class"; Rainwater, "Problem of Lower-Class Culture"; Lewis, "Culture, Class and the Behavior of Low-Income Families"; and Steinberg, *Ethnic Myth.*

34. Gans, "Culture and Class," p. 211.

35. See, e.g., Clark, *Dark Ghetto;* Liebow, *Tally's Corner;* Ulf Hannerz, *Soulside: Inquiries into Ghetto Culture and Community* (New York: Columbia University Press, 1969); and Lee Rainwater, *Behind Ghetto Walls: Black Families in a Federal Slum* (Chicago: Aldine, 1970).

36. For a discussion of this point, see Stanley Lieberson, *A Piece of the Pie: Black and White Immigrants since 1880* (Berkeley: University of California Press, 1980), chap. 1.

37. For a discussion of this point see William Julius Wilson, "Reflections on the Insiders and Outsiders Controversy," in *Black Sociologists,* ed. James E. Blackwell and Morris Janowitz (Chicago: University of Chicago Press, 1972).

38. James Q. Wilson, *Thinking about Crime* (New York: Basic Books, 1975); George Gilder, *Wealth and Poverty* (New York: Basic Books, 1981); Sowell, *Civil Rights;* Charles Murray, *Losing Ground: American Social Policy, 1950–1980* (New York: Basic Books, 1984).

39. "Losing More Ground," *New York Times,* February 3, 1985, p. 22.

40. See, e.g., Robert Greenstein, "Losing Faith in 'Losing Ground,'" *New Republic,* March 25, 1985, pp. 12–17; Robert Kuttner, "A Flawed Case for Scrapping What's Left of the Great Society," *Washington Post Book World,* December 17, 1984, pp. 34–35; David Ellwood and Lawrence Summers, "Poverty in America: Is Welfare the Answer or the Problem?" paper presented at a conference on Poverty and Policy: Retrospect and Prospects, Williamsburg, Va., December 6, 1984; Christopher Jencks, "How Poor Are the Poor?" *New York Review of Books,* May 9, 1985, pp. 41–49; and Sheldon Danziger and Peter Gottschalk, "Social Programs — a Partial Solution to, But Not a Cause of Poverty: An Alternative to Charles Murray's View," *Challenge Magazine,* May/June 1985.

41. Danziger and Gottschalk, "Social Programs," p. 36.

42. Greenstein, "Losing Faith," p. 14.

43. Ibid.; Danziger and Gottschalk, "Social Programs"; and Jencks, "How Poor Are the Poor?"

44. Greenstein, "Losing Faith," p. 14.

45. Ibid., p. 15; Danziger and Gottschalk, "Social Programs"; Kuttner, "Flawed Case"; Jencks, "How Poor Are the Poor?"; and Ellwood and Summers, "Poverty in America."

PREPARING FOR DISCUSSION

1. At the beginning of the selection, Wilson briefly discusses the rapid deterioration of social conditions in poor urban neighborhoods. What features, according to Wilson, characterize social organization? To what factors does he

attribute the decline of such organization among the urban poor? In what ways does the emergence of the term *underclass* constitute a response to the sharp changes in urban society witnessed by Wilson and other sociologists?

2. Wilson notes a decline in the influence of the liberal perspective on urban poverty over the last two decades. How does he characterize the liberal perspective? What were the methodological strengths and weaknesses of the liberal approach? Why has the conservative perspective dominated public discussion about the urban poor in recent years? What, according to Wilson, can liberals do to reestablish leadership in public policy?

3. Wilson describes the conservative perspective on the causes of urban poverty as one based on "the interconnection between cultural traditions, family history, and individual character" (paragraph 27). Alternately, he describes the liberal perspective as one rooted in the notion that "cultural values emerge from specific social circumstances and life chances and reflect one's class and racial position" (paragraph 30). Which of these perspectives most resembles Wilson's? Does he succeed in proving that the conservative thesis does not account for the new urban poverty?

4. Wilson tends to reject "a race-specific thesis" that traces the cause of urban black poverty to contemporary racism. He argues that such a thesis would not explain "the deepening economic class divisions between the haves and the have-nots in the black community," since most blacks have been subject to racism regardless of class (paragraph 20). Do you agree with Wilson that "racism is too easy an explanation" for the rapid decline in social organization in the ghetto? Can it be argued that while racism is directed at all blacks, the urban poor are less prepared to respond to its effects?

5. After defining "underclass" in paragraph 14, Wilson argues that the avoidance of the term by some liberal social scientists "obscure[s] the profound changes in the class structure and social behavior of ghetto neighborhoods" (paragraph 15). Do you agree with Wilson that the use or avoidance of a single term will determine how realistically people look at the issue of urban poverty? How important is terminology in this debate?

FROM READING TO WRITING

6. Wilson sets out in detail both liberal and conservative views of declining social conditions among the urban black poor. Write an essay in which you describe your own sense of the causes of this growing problem. Which ideological view does your position most resemble? To what extent is your view on the causes of poverty consistent with other political views you hold?

7. In paragraphs 23 and 24, Wilson argues that inner-city residents are confronted by problems of economic organization that "are not made more understandable by associating them directly or indirectly with racism." Write an essay on whether or not you believe that urban black poverty is one of these problems. Do you agree or disagree with Wilson that this problem can be discussed productively without reference to racial conflict in America?

MICHAEL LIND

To Have and Have Not

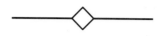

Throughout American history, the notion of a permanent ruling class has been viewed as antithetical to the ideal of a democratic society. Yet today there is growing and legitimate concern that a "relatively new and still evolving political and social oligarchy" is gradually solidifying into the most powerful minority in the country. The members of this new "overclass" consist not only of political and business leaders, but of media executives, college professors, labor leaders, lawyers, journalists, and Foreign Service officers as well. These well-educated professionals, with their dependents, constitute about 20 percent of the population, and while they lack a collective political purpose, their common economic agenda has been felt by the rest of the American public for several years. In the following selection — an essay that appeared in *Harper's Magazine* in 1995 — Michael Lind takes a closer look at the new American elites and points out that their most powerful tool in the successful accumulation of wealth and power has been their relative invisibility.

While Lind has been a neoconservative for most of his career as a writer and editor, he recently began to distance himself from the Right partly in response to the ascendancy of fundamentalist Christian groups and their values within the Republican party. A former executive editor of the conservative journal the *National Interest*, Lind served for a time as a senior editor at the traditionally liberal *Harper's Magazine* before joining the staff of the *New Republic*.

SELECTED PUBLICATIONS: *The Next American Nation: The New Nationalism and the Fourth American Revolution* (1995); Lind's essays have appeared in the *New Republic*, the *New York Review of Books*, *Harper's Magazine*, the *Atlantic*, the *New Yorker*, the *New York Times Book Review*, the *Washington Post*, *Foreign Affairs*, and the *National Interest*.

Judging by the headlines that have been leading the news for the last several years, public debate in the United States at the end of the twentieth century has become a war of words among the disaffected minorities that so often appear on the never-ending talk show jointly hosted by Oprah, Larry King, Jenny Jones, and the McLaughlin Group. Conservatives at war with liberals; Christian fundamentalists at odds with liberal Jews; blacks at war with whites; whites at war with Hispanic immigrants; men at war with women; heterosexuals at war with homosexuals; and the young at war with the old. A guide to the multiple conflicts in progress would resemble the Personals pages in the *Village Voice*, with "versus" or "contra" substituted for "seeking" (Pro-Sex Classicists versus Anti-Sex Modernists).

The noise is deceptive. Off-camera, beyond the blazing lights, past the ropy tangle of black cords and down the hall, in the corner offices (on Capitol Hill as well as at General Electric, the Walt Disney Company, and CBS News), people in expensive suits quietly continue to go about the work of shifting the center of gravity of wealth and power in the United States from the discounted many to the privileged few. While public attention has been diverted to controversies as inflammatory as they are trivial — Should the Constitution be amended to ban flag-burning? Should dirty pictures be allowed on the Internet? — the American elites that subsidize and staff both the Republican and Democratic parties have steadfastly waged a generation-long class war against the middle and working classes. Now and then the television cameras catch a glimpse of what is going on, as they did last year during the NAFTA [North American Free Trade Agreement] and GATT [General Agreement on Trade and Tariffs] debates, when a Democratic president and a bipartisan majority in Congress collaborated in the sacrifice of American labor to the interests of American corporations and foreign capital. More recently, with a candor rare among politicians, House Speaker Newt Gingrich argued against raising the minimum wage in the United States — on the grounds that a higher minimum wage would handicap American workers in their competition with workers *in Mexico.*

The camera, however, quickly returns to the set and the shouting audience, while assistant producers hold up placards with the theme for the day: the Contract with America, the New Covenant, Affirmative Action, Moral Renewal. It's against the rules to talk about a rapacious American oligarchy, and the suggestion that the small group of people with most of the money and power in the United States just *might* be responsible to some degree for what has been happening to the country over the last twenty years invariably invites the news media to expressions of wrath and denial. Whenever a politician proposes to speak for the many — whether he is on the left (Jerry Brown), right (Patrick Buchanan), or center (Ross Perot) — the Op-Ed pages in the nation's better newspapers (the *Washington Post*, the *New York Times*, the *Wall Street Journal*) issue stern warnings of "demagogy." Yes, the pundits admit, economic and social inequality have been growing in the United States, with alarming results, but the ruling and possessing class cannot be blamed, because, well, there is no ruling and possessing class.

The American oligarchy spares no pains in promoting the belief that it does not exist, but the success of its disappearing act depends on equally strenuous efforts on the part of an American public anxious to believe in egalitarian fictions and unwilling to see what is hidden in plain sight. Anybody choosing to see the oligarchy in its native habitat need do nothing else but walk down the street of any big city to an office tower housing a major bank, a corporate headquarters or law firm, or a national television station. Enter the building and the multiracial diversity of the street vanishes as abruptly as the sound of the traffic. Step off the elevator at the top of the tower and apart from the clerical and maintenance staff hardly anybody is nonwhite. The contrast between the street and the tower is the contrast between the grass roots and the national headquarters, the field office and the home office. No matter what your starting point, the closer you come to the centers of American politics and society, the more everyone begins to look the same. Though corporate executives, shop stewards, and graduate-student lecturers could not be more different, the people who run big business bear a remarkable resemblance to the people who run big labor, who in turn might be mistaken for the people in charge of the media and the universities. *They are the same people*. They differ in their opinions — and in almost no other way. Almost exclusively white, disproportionately mainline Protestant or Jewish, most of the members of the American elites went to one of a dozen Ivy League colleges or top state universities. Not only do they have advanced professional or graduate degrees — J.D.'s, M.B.A.'s, Ph.D.'s, M.D.'s — but usually at least one of their parents (and sometimes both) has advanced professional or graduate degrees. They dress the same. They talk the same. They walk the same. They have the same body language, the same gestures. They eat the same food, drink the same drinks, and play the same sports. They read the same publications. They . . . but I should say *we*. As a second-generation professional with an Ivy League diploma, having worked for liberal Democrats and conservative Republicans, business lobbyists and pro-labor intellectuals, among professors and journalists and lawyers and Foreign Service officers, I am a card-carrying member of the overclass. So, in all likelihood, reader, are you.

Amounting, with their dependents, to about 20 percent of the population,[1] this relatively new and still evolving political and social oligarchy is not identified with any particular region of the country. Homogeneous and nomadic, the overclass is the first truly national upper class in American history. In a managerial capitalist society like our own, the essential distinction is not between the "bourgeoisie" (the factory owners) and the "proletariat" (the factory workers) but between the credentialed minority (making a living from fees or wages supplemented by stock options) and the salaried majority. The salaried class — at-will employees, lacking a four-year college education, paid by the hour, who can be fired at any

5

---

[1] Defined as individuals with professional or graduate education (which is roughly correlated with high income), and without counting dependents, the members of the overclass account for no more than 5 percent of the U.S. population. (Lind's note)

time — constitutes the real "middle class," accounting, as it does, for three-quarters of the population.

The white overclass, then, properly perceived, is neither a middle class nor a high bourgeoisie but a sort of guild oligarchy, like those that ran early modern Italian and Dutch city-states. Our later-day oligarchs (lawyers, bankers, publishers, anchorpersons) are the contemporary equivalents of the plump and goateed syndics, haloed by starched collars, who gaze smugly back at us through honey veils of impasto from the paintings of Rembrandt and Hals. The precedent for our class war can't be found in the slapstick melee pitting thick-necked proles against top-hatted, umbrella-wielding bourgeois that enlivens Sergei Eisentein's *Ten Days That Shook the World*. We should think, instead, of the civic discord between great guilds and lesser guilds — the bankers and merchants versus the artisans — that troubled cities like Florence and Milan in the Renaissance, and that resembled the struggle over universal health care between the insurance lobby and the AFL-CIO.

At least the syndics of Amsterdam and the Venetian families in the Golden Book did not add insult to injury by insisting that they were not "elites." The most remarkable thing about our own American oligarchy is the pretense that it doesn't constitute anything as definite as a social class. We prefer to assign good fortune to our individual merit, saying that we owe our perches in the upper percentiles of income and education not to our connections but solely to our own I.Q., virtue, brio, genius, *sprezzatura*, chutzpah, gumption. Had we been switched at birth by accident, had we grown up in a ghetto or barrio or trailer park, we would have arrived at our offices at ABC News or the Republican National Committee or the ACLU in more or less the same amount of time. The absence of black and Hispanic Americans in our schools and our offices and our clubs can only be explained, we tell ourselves, not by *our* extrinsic advantages but by *their* intrinsic defects. Compared with us (and perhaps with middle-class East Asian immigrants), most blacks and Hispanics must be disproportionately lazy, even (if Charles Murray and the late Richard Herrnstein are to be believed) disproportionately retarded. What other explanation for their failure to rise can there be? America, after all, is a classless society.

Or rather a two-class society. The belated acknowledgment of an "underclass" as a distinct group represents the only exception to the polite fiction that everyone in the United States, from a garage mechanic to a rich attorney (particularly the rich attorney), belongs to the "middle class." Over the past decade the ghetto poor have been the topic of conversation at more candlelight-and-wine dinner parties than I can recall, but without looking at the program or the wine list it is impossible to tell whether one is among nominal liberals or nominal conservatives. The same kind of people in the same kind of suits go on about "the blacks" as though a minority within a 12 percent minority were taking over the country, as if Washington were Pretoria and New York a suburb of Johannesburg. Not only do the comfortable members of the overclass single out the weakest and least influential of their fellow citizens as the cause of all their sorrows but they routinely, and preposterously, treat the genuine pathologies of the ghetto — high levels of violence and illegitimacy — as the major problems facing a country with uncontrollable trade and fiscal deficits, a low savings rate, an obsolete military strategy, an anachronistic and corrupt electoral system, the worst system of primary education in the First World, and the bulk of its population facing long-term economic decline.

To be sure, upper classes in other societies have often fretted, sometimes to the point of panic, about the lower orders, and in Japan, as in Britain and France (to an even greater degree than in the United States), the people in charge tend to go to the same schools, not a dozen but one or two. But in those countries people at least acknowledge the existence of an upper stratum, and the public-school old-boy network or the *énarquate* retains some tradition of responsibility for the less fortunate, some sense of noblesse oblige based on self-preservation if not on superior morality. (As Disraeli observed in 1848, "The palace is not safe when the cottage is not happy.") Among all the industrial democracies, only in the United States do the members of the oligarchy absolve themselves with the comforting notion that their class does not exist. Willing to pursue collective economic interests but lacking any sense of a political commonwealth, the American overclass at the end of the twentieth century takes as its own what Adam Smith identified as "the vile maxim of the masters of mankind. . . . All for ourselves, and nothing for other people." The sentiment is heartfelt and bipartisan.

During the past generation, the prerogatives of our new oligarchy 10
have been magnified by a political system in which the power of money to buy TV time has become a good deal more important than the power of labor unions or party bosses to mobilize voters. Supported by the news media, which it largely owns, the oligarchy has waged its war of attrition against the wage-earning majority on several fronts: regressive taxation, the expatriation of industry, and mass immigration. Regressive taxes like the Social Security payroll tax and state sales taxes shift much of the tax burden from the rich to middle-income Americans. After the Reagan-era tax reforms, 75 percent of the American people owed more taxes than they would have owed had the 1977 tax laws been left untouched; only the wealthiest 5 percent of the public received any significant benefit from the tax cuts. Continuing the program, Newt Gingrich's Republicans are sponsoring yet another windfall for the wealthy. Under the tax-cut legislation passed by the House, which Gingrich called the "crown jewel" of the Contract with America, individuals earning $350,000 a year would

receive a tax reduction of $13,000, while families making $30,000 a year would get only 50 cents a day. (Some crown. Some jewel.)[2]

Owing in large part to the bipartisan preference for regressive over progressive taxation, and despite the cries of anguish from Senator Phil Gramm and the editorial writers employed by the *Wall Street Journal*, the United States now stands second to last among the major industrialized countries in the rate of taxation on income — and dead last in terms of economic equality. The replacement of progressive income taxation by a flat tax, along with the adoption of national sales taxes (reforms favored by many conservative Democrats as well as Republicans), would further shift the national tax burden from the credentialed minority to the wage-earning majority. Average Americans have not only been taxed *instead* of the rich; they have been taxed to *repay* the rich. Borrowing, which accounted for only 5.3 percent of federal spending in the 1960s, increased to 29.9 percent in the 1990s. Interest payments on the debt (which last year amounted to $203 billion) represent a transfer of wealth from ordinary American taxpayers to rich Americans and foreigners without precedent in history.

On the second front of the class war, corporate elites continue to use the imperatives of global free trade as a means of driving down American wages and nullifying the social contract implicit in both the New Deal and the Great Society. U.S. corporations now lead the world in the race to low-wage countries with cheap and politically repressed labor forces. Concentrated in "export-processing zones" in Third World countries, and usually not integrated into the local economy, much of the transnational investment brings together foreign capital and technology with inexpensive and docile labor to manufacture consumer electronics, shoes, luggage, or toys. The export-processing zone is nothing new; it used to be called the plantation. In the nineteenth and early twentieth centuries, plantations owned by American, British, and European investors produced raw materials and agriculture for export; modern technology now permits factory work to be done in the same countries. The banana republic is being replaced by the sweatshop republic as national, middle-class capitalism gives way to global plantation capitalism.

Many advocates of free trade claim that higher productivity growth in the United States will offset any downward pressure on wages caused by the global sweatshop economy, but the appealing theory falls victim to an unpleasant fact. Productivity *has* been going up in America, without resulting wage gains for American workers. Between 1977 and 1992, the average productivity of American workers increased by more than 30 percent, while the average real wage *fell* by 13 percent. The logic is

[2] In the version of the Contract with America legislation first passed by the House, two-thirds of the spending cuts would come from programs for low-income families, while roughly half the money from the cuts would go to the wealthiest 10 percent of American households. Fully one-fifth of the savings would go to the wealthiest 1 percent of families. (Lind's note)

inescapable. No matter how much productivity increases, wages will fall if there is an abundance of workers competing for a scarcity of jobs — an abundance of the sort created by the globalization of the labor pool for U.S.-based corporations.[3]

Even skilled production often can be done more cheaply elsewhere. Software research and design is now being done by local computer specialists in India, in Russia, and in Poland. Since 1979, the real wages of high school dropouts have declined by 20 percent, while the incomes of workers with more than four years of college have risen by 8 percent. There are two ways to interpret the better performance of professionals relative to other workers in the new, internationalized economy. The most common explanation (the one preferred by the overclass and its publicists in the major news media) is that the world economy, in some vague way, rewards expertise and high-tech skills — though if this were so, one would expect multilingual physicists to be growing spectacularly rich rather than bond traders, corporate vice presidents, and partners in large law firms, whose skills have little or nothing to do with high technology. A more plausible explanation is that professionals in the United States benefit from a vigorously enforced form of protectionism based on credentials and licensing. A corporation can hire an Indian computer programmer to do the work of an American computer programmer for a fraction of the wage, but it cannot hire an Indian lawyer to try a case in the United States. Permit legal briefs to be written in India and submitted to American courts by fax from Indian lawyers, and legal fees in the United States would quickly plummet, the skill, education, and productivity of American lawyers notwithstanding.

Not all nonprofessional jobs can be expatriated to Mexico or 15 Malaysia, and a great many low-skilled services — from truck driving to nursing and sales and restaurant work — still must be performed in America. Accordingly, on a third front of the class war, the American gentry support a generous immigration policy. Enlarging the low-skill labor pool in the United States has the same effect as enlarging the labor pool through the expatriation of American-owned industry. From the point of view of members of the white overclass, of course, this is good news — if mass immigration ended tomorrow, they would probably have to pay higher wages, fees, and tips. In the 1980s, during the "Massachusetts Miracle," the state's unemployment rate fell to half the national average, 2.2 percent. As a result of a tight labor market, wages for workers at McDonald's rose to more than $7 an hour. So unfortunate a development prompted a study from the Twentieth Century Fund in which

---

[3] According to Common Cause, the leading first-time contributor to the Republican National Committee since the 1994 congressional elections, Fruit of the Loom, gave $100,000 to the RNC in February 1995, three days before the House Ways and Means trade subcommittee held hearings on a bill to ease quotas on low-wage Caribbean countries in which the corporation has commercial ventures. The subcommittee approved the measure. (Lind's note)

author Thomas Muller took note of the awful consequences: "In many areas of the Northeast, a scarcity of clerks in the late 1980s caused a noticeable deterioration in service.... This is not an argument that long lines or *flip behavior by salespeople* will fundamentally affect America's well-being, but they do constitute an irritant that can diminish the quality of our life [emphasis added]." In a seller's market for labor, it seems, there is a danger that the help will get uppity.

"As the number of working mothers increases," Muller wrote, "such [household] help, once considered a luxury, is becoming more and more a necessity. Were it not for recent immigrants, nannies, maids, and gardeners would be a vanishing breed ... " Although the vast majority of Americans still do not consider the employment of "nannies, maids, or gardeners" to be a necessity rather than a luxury, the 1 percent of the population that employs live-in servants (c.f., the recent difficulties of Zoe Baird, Kimba Wood, and Arianna Huffington) cannot enjoy an appropriate degree of comfort without a supporting cast of deferential helots. Our own overclass Americans are as dependent on Latina maids as were the members of the nineteenth-century Northeastern establishment on Irish "Bridgets" and the antebellum Southern planters on house slaves. (In this connection, J. P. Morgan's definition of the leisure class, which he saw as the bulwark of civilization, is instructive: "All those who can afford to hire a maid.")

The *Wall Street Journal*, ever mindful of the short-run interests of the overclass, has called for an amendment to the U.S. Constitution consisting of five words: "There shall be open borders." If the United States and Mexican labor markets were merged (together with the capital markets already integrated by NAFTA), then American investment would flow south to take advantage of cheap labor, and tens of millions of Mexican workers would migrate north to better-paying jobs, until wages stabilized somewhere above the contemporary Mexican level (between $4 and $5 a day) but below the current American minimum wage of $4.25 an hour. The numbers of the white overclass would remain fixed, while the pool of cheap labor expanded, and Muller's dream of heaven would come true: Every American who is not a maid or gardener might be able to afford one.

Although the inequalities of income in the United States are now greater than at any time since the 1930s, and although numerous observers have remarked on the fact and cited abundant statistics in support of their observations, the response of the American overclass has been to blame everybody but its nonexistent self — to blame the ghetto, or the schools, or the liberal news media, or the loss of family values. In a characteristic argument that appeared in early April on the Op-Ed page of the *Washington Post* ("Raising the Minimum Wage Isn't the Answer"), James K. Glassman dismissed the idea that public policy can help the majority of workers whose real wages continue to fall: "[T]he ultimate answer lies with workers themselves. . . . Government can help a bit through tax breaks for education, but ultimately the cure for low working wages may be nothing more mysterious than high personal diligence."

In any other democracy, an enraged citizenry probably would have rebelled by now against a national elite that weakens unions, slashes wages and benefits, pits workers against low-wage foreign and immigrant competition — and then informs its victims that the chief source of their economic problems is a lack of "high personal diligence." But for whom could an enraged citizen vote? The American overclass manages to protect itself from popular insurgencies, not only through its ownership of the news media but also by its financial control of elections and its use of affirmative-action patronage.

Of the three defenses, the uniquely corrupt American system of funding elections is by far the most important, which is no doubt why campaign finance reform was left out of the Contract with America. The real two-party system in the United States consists not of the Democrats and the Republicans but of the party of voters and the party of donors. The donor party is extraordinarily small. Roughly 10 percent of the American people make political contributions, most of them in minimal amounts. The number of large political donors is even smaller. Citizen Action, an independent consumer group, found that in the 1989–90 election cycle only 179,677 individual donors gave contributions equal to or greater than $200 to a federal candidate: "Thirty-four percent of the money spent by federal candidates was directly contributed by no more than one-tenth of one percent of the voting age population." One may reasonably doubt that this one-tenth of one percent is representative of the electorate or the population at large.

We were taught in civics classes that the United States is a "pluralistic" democracy in which Madisonian "factions" balance one another, ensuring that no single minority or economic interest will prevail. We were lied to. Labor does not balance big business; consumer groups do not balance big business; *nobody* balances big business anymore. Contrary to conservative claims that liberal and left-wing "special interests" dominate Congress, PAC funds come, overwhelmingly, from business. Citizens vote occasionally; dollars vote continually.[4] During the first two months of this year, "soft money" contributions, chiefly from industry, flowed into the coffers of the Republican National Committee at the rate of $123,121 per day, and during the recently ended two-year congressional campaign cycle, then Majority Leader Richard A. Gephardt (D., Mo.) accumulated PAC money in the amount of $1,001,400,

20

---

[4] *PAC (Political Action Committee)*: Organizations that exert influence over elected officials through campaign contributions. (Lind's note)

while Speaker Newt Gingrich (R., Ga.) received $763,220. As recently as last April, President Clinton appeared at a $50,000-a-couple fund-raiser at Steven Spielberg's home in Hollywood. Because the same economic oligarchy subsidizes almost all of our politicians, our political fights are as inconsequential as TV wrestling.

Armed with the political advantage secured by the purchase of congressmen, senators, and presidents, the overclass shores up its defense against genuinely representative democracy (i.e., a popular coalition uniting middle-class and working-class Americans of all races and regions) by adopting a strategy of divide and rule expressed in the language of multiculturalism. The dynamics of a divided society similar to our own were noted in 1947 by Gunnar Myrdal: "In a society where there are broad social classes and, in addition, more minute distinctions and splits in the lower strata, *the lower class groups will to a great extent take care of keeping each other subdued,* thus relieving to that extent the higher classes of this otherwise painful task necessary to the monopolization of its power and advantages." Centuries before today's multiculturalists adopted the slogan "Celebrate diversity," William Smith, a slave trader, explained his reasons for celebrating diversity among the exploited:

> As for the languages of *Gambia*, they are so many and so different, that the Natives, on either side of the River, cannot understand each other; which, if rightly consider'd, is no small Happiness to the *Europeans* who go thither to trade for slaves. . . . [T]he safest Way is to trade with the different Nations, on either side of the River, and having some of every Sort on board, there will be no more Likelihood of their succeeding in a Plot than of finishing the Tower of Babel.

Unified along the lines of economic interest, the wealthy American minority hold the fragmented majority at bay by pitting blacks against whites in zero-sum struggles for government patronage and by bribing potential black and Hispanic leaders, who might otherwise propose something other than rhetorical rebellion, with the gifts of affirmative action. The policy was promoted by Richard Nixon, who, as much as any American politician, deserves to be acknowledged as the father of racial preferences.

"What most militants want," Nixon explained in 1968, using the language of gangsterism to support his proposal for minority contracting preferences, "is not separation, but to be included in . . . to have a share of the wealth, and a piece of the action." Racial-preference policies give middle-class and wealthy blacks and Hispanics "a share of the wealth and a piece of the action." The ritual that symbolizes civil-rights "progress" in today's oligarchic America is the "integration" of an all-white country club, which invariably means admitting one of the wealthiest black citizens who can be found in the local community. Similarly, in the matter of presidential Cabinet posts, diversity means appointing rich professionals educated in the Ivy League who happen to belong to different races and sexes.

The Ivy League, in its turn, rigs its admissions policies to disproportionately benefit well-off black and Hispanic Americans (at Harvard, for example, 70 percent of black undergraduates are the children of parents in managerial or professional fields, while at Cornell twice as many minority students, in some years, come from the suburbs as from the cities). In order not to lose accreditation, most colleges and universities try to have approximately as many black students as there are black Americans in the general population, around 12 percent. These goals and timetables can be met only by drastically lowering admissions standards for black students, who for obvious historical reasons are far less academically prepared than many of their white competitors.[5]

"To get past racism, we must here take account of race," McGeorge Bundy, the former aide to Presidents Kennedy and Johnson, declared magisterially in "The Issue before the Court: Who Gets Ahead in America?", an article in the *Atlantic Monthly* that appeared in November 1977 during the formative period of affirmative action in college admissions. Bundy could afford to be generous in redistributing opportunities from middle-class whites to middle-class blacks and Hispanics because so many members of his class are safely insulated from the effects of racial preference by the largest affirmative-action program in the United States: legacy preference.[6]

Legacies, or children of alumni, are three times more likely to be accepted to Harvard than other high school graduates with the same (sometimes better) scores (at Harvard, the dean of admissions reads legacy applications — but not those of non-legacies). Children of Yale graduates are two and a half times more likely than non-alumni kin to be admitted to Yale. According to a former Princeton dean of admissions, legacies at "one Ivy League university" had average SAT scores of 1,280,

---

[5] In 1989 a black high school graduate in California with the minimum high school GPA had a 70 percent chance of being accepted to Berkeley, while a white high school student with the same score had only a 9 percent chance of admission. Between 1985 and 1990, the average LSAT score for white students admitted to the University of Texas Law School was in the ninety-second percentile as compared with the fifty-fifth percentile for black students. This enormous gap gives the lie to the argument that affirmative action affects only marginally qualified whites — the "margin" in this case is thirty-seven percentile points. (Lind's note)

[6] Bundy was born into a rich Boston Brahmin family. On his mother's side, he was kin to the influential Lowells. His father, Harvey H. Bundy, a partner in the elite Boston law firm of Choate, Hall and Stewart, succeeded John Foster Dulles as board chairman of the Carnegie Endowment for International Peace. After attending Groton and Yale, McGeorge Bundy became dean of Harvard College. His older brother William, married Dean Acheson's daughter; his sister Katherine was related by marriage to Jacqueline Onassis and Louis Auchincloss. (Lind's note)

compared with the average of 1,350 out of a possible 1,600 for the total freshman class.[7]

As the number of black and Hispanic students at selective universities and partners in prestigious law firms is artificially maintained, the average wages of black and Hispanic workers, along with those of white workers, continue to stagnate or decline. The tokenism embodied in racial preference and multiculturalism is thus about as threatening to the American elite as an avant-garde sculpture in the lobby of a bank.

Meanwhile, behind the Potemkin Village facade of contemporary America, with its five separate-but-equal official races and its racially authentic folk art, the American oligarchy goes busily about the work of constructing its own enclave society, an America-within-America, linked to the international economy and detached from the destiny of the native middle class. What Lewis Lapham has called "the new feudalism" reverses the trend of the past thousand years toward the government's provision of basic public goods like policing, public roads and transport networks, and public schools. In the United States — to a degree unmatched in any other industrial democracy — these public goods are once again becoming private luxuries, accessible only to the affluent few. Federal spending declined in the 1980s for services like law enforcement and government (by 42 percent), for education and training (by 40 percent), and for the transportation infrastructure (by 32 percent); and most of the growth in government spending in recent decades has taken the form of non-means-tested entitlements, like Social Security and Medicare, that benefit middle- and upper-income Americans.

If the notion of a neo-feudal United States seems far-fetched, consider the "feudal" elements of modern America. Increasing numbers of affluent white Americans have been withdrawing into gated suburbs, many of them indistinguishable from private cities, whose community associations provide not only security but trash collection, street cleaning, and utilities. The inhabitants have sought permission from local governments to block off public streets with gates and other barriers to traffic (a California appeals court recently ruled that seven metal gates installed by the Los Angeles suburb of Whitley Heights represented an illegal "return to feudal times" — but only *after* their installation had been approved by the Los Angeles City Council). Some of the richer residents within the walls seek not only permission to barricade themselves but exemption from taxes — on the argument that taxes for public municipal

30

---

[7] The late Christopher Lasch, in *The Revolt of the Elites and the Betrayal of Democracy* (W. W. Norton, 1995), describes "the professional and managerial class" as a "meritocracy" or "an aristocracy of talent." However, the fact that the white overclass, by means of legacy preference, has rigged higher education in its favor proves that it is afraid of genuine meritocracy. (Lind's note)

services on top of the fees they pay their private community associations constitute "double taxation."

Because the affluent would rather hire mercenary forces than pay for police, the number of private security guards in the United States now exceeds the number of publicly employed policemen. To help those who cannot afford to rent police officers, the right is trying to make it easier to carry concealed weapons at the mall, in the office, and on the subway; holsters and body armor may once again become fashion accessories. A chorus of conservative voices proposes the replacement of public schools with taxpayer-subsidized vouchers to private schools, and the idea of replacing the national highway system with private toll roads is not a fantasy confined to dystopian science fiction. More than ten states now have projects for such roads, which would allow the happy few to drive their expensive cars on state-of-the-art, computer-enhanced highways while ordinary Americans fume in traffic on crumbling public streets.

The new American urban architecture reflects the same evolution of American society from republicanism to feudalism. Downtown office complexes begin to resemble medieval castles — collections of towers connected by skyways and sealed off from the growing horde of the unemployable poor. The celebrated architect Frank Gehry specializes in what cultural critic Mike Davis calls "carceral" architecture — for example, "stealth houses" for the wealthy, hiding their opulent interiors from thieves behind plain gray walls. Gehry's 1984 Goldwyn Branch Library in Hollywood (inspired by the same architect's fortified U.S. Chancellery in Damascus, a building bristling with ten-foot steel stakes and stylized sentry boxes) prompted Davis to describe it as "probably the most menacing library ever built, a bizarre hybrid of a drydocked dreadnaught and a cavalry fort."

The dream of withdrawal probably explains the enthusiasm in overclass circles for the "virtual corporation," a dematerialized entity consisting solely of a small management team temporarily contracting out work, here to Mexicans and South Koreans, there to Hungarians and Czechs, in the manner of the nabobs who lived it up in eighteenth-century London on their rents from Caribbean plantations run on their behalf by thuggish overseers. This is the vision expressed by the television commercials for IBM and the American Express Card and the magazine advertisements for new computers and fax machines that show a middle-aged executive communicating with his office from a beach resort or a corporate lawyer tucking in her child via a videophone in a busy airport. Virtual capitalism thus meets the virtual family in the utopia of American overclass: Dad will bask in the Caribbean sun sketching out marketing designs on his laptop computer while Mom keeps an eye on Baby, via satellite, as she flies from New York to Frankfurt to Tokyo. Off-camera, never seen, is the Latina maid who actually changes Baby's diapers, and, in this or that Third World shantytown of tin roofs and open sewers, the employees, or rather the independent contractors, of Dad's or Mom's virtual corporation, workers as likely as not without benefits, without insurance, without civil rights, without a voice in their governments, laboring to make products they can never afford to buy.

Some American executives have begun to follow the factories to Fortunate Isles. The *Wall Street Journal* and *Fortune* recently portrayed, with considerable sympathy, a number of rich American expatriates, among them the heirs to the Dart container and Campbell's soup fortunes, who have renounced their U.S. citizenship and begun new lives in more humane societies, like the Turks and Caicos Islands and Belize. Senator Phil Gramm last spring denounced a proposal to tax these expatriates as a measure reminiscent of "Nazi Germany," apparently secure in the belief that the old American republican ideal of civic obligation is nothing but totalitarianism in disguise. No doubt, when the overclass revolution is completed, persecuted tycoons will no longer be driven out of their hostile homeland. In *America libre,* it will no longer be necessary to move to Jamaica to be able to afford maids and chauffeurs on a lawyer's salary, or to relocate production to Honduras in order to pay the working classes no more than a few cents an hour (House Majority Leader Dick Armey favors abolishing the minimum wage). North America shall come to resemble Columbus's mistaken perception of it as simply one more Caribbean island populated by dusky masses born to be servants. The United States, which the eighteenth-century American elite sought to refashion as a new Roman Republic, and which the nineteenth-century American patriciate conceived of as a new and greater Britain, shall be renovated by the new white overclass as a New Honduras or a New Belize.

Until that blessed day, the bipartisan white overclass, secure behind urban fronts and suburban walls, as well as the metaphorical moats of legacy preference, expensive schooling, and an impregnable interest rate, has neither reason nor incentive to moderate its ruthless pursuit of its own short-term concerns. In a more homogeneous society, the growing concentration of power and wealth in the hands of a privileged minority might be expected to produce a strong reaction on the part of the majority. In present-day America, however, no such reaction is likely to take place. Although heavily outnumbered, the unified few rest secure in the knowledge that any insurgency will almost certainly dissipate in quarrels among the fragmented many rather than in open rebellion; during the 1992 Los Angeles riots, black, Hispanic, and white rioters turned on Korean middlemen rather than march on Beverly Hills. The belligerent guests on the never-ending talk show, urged on by the screaming audience, will continue to enact allegorical conflicts, while, off-camera and upstairs, the discreet members of the class that does not exist ponder the choice of marble or mahogany for the walls of the executive suite from which they command.

35

PREPARING FOR DISCUSSION

1. Throughout the selection Lind maintains that the ruling class in America is largely invisible. To what factors does he attribute the failure of most Americans to recognize the existence of a ruling class? To what factors does he attribute the success of the American elites in remaining invisible?

2. In paragraphs 18–28, Lind describes how the American ruling class protects itself from popular revolt. What does he cite as the three primary ways that the elites protect themselves? Which of these methods does he hold to be the most important?

3. Lind holds that the multicultural movement is viewed favorably by the elites because it fuels hostilities between minority and lower-class populations. On what assumptions about multiculturalist values does he base his analysis? In what ways might his argument be viewed as a cynical critique of multiculturalism? How would you describe his notion that affirmative action programs are little more than ways of buying off minorities?

4. In describing the new American elites, Lind admits that even though they share similar economic goals, they seem to lack a common political purpose. Does this lack of agreement about political goals among the elites make it more or less difficult to view them as a distinct class? In your own definition of class, what role do shared political and cultural views play?

5. In paragraph 4, Lind maintains that corporate heads resemble labor leaders, who in turn resemble media executives and university presidents. In fact, Lind insists that *"[t]hey are the same people."* What does Lind mean by this remark? Are we to take the remark literally? If we do not take it literally, how are we meant to take it?

FROM READING TO WRITING

6. In paragraph 33, Lind notes the growing number of commercials that envision the elitist utopia he has been describing. Write an essay in which you describe one such commercial on television or radio. To what type of person is the commercial meant to appeal? What kinds of images does it present to the viewer and what do these images suggest about the particular product or service being advertised?

7. Lind has offered only one version of elitism in America. In your own life you have probably encountered elitism in its various forms. Write an essay in which you describe one such encounter. How did you respond to elitism at the time of the encounter? Is elitism necessarily something we respond to negatively? How did the encounter affect you?

CHRISTOPHER LASCH

The Revolt of the Elites

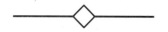

While Michael Lind is interested primarily in establishing the existence of an elite "overclass," Christopher Lasch goes one step further in the following selection and cynically asks, "What is 'American' about the new elites?" He questions their allegiance to this country and laments the absence of any sign of public-spiritedness among their ranks. Their "revolt," Lasch contends, signals the end of a long era of "noblesse oblige" during which the American upper classes felt an obligation to lighten the financial burden of the lower classes through philanthropy and public works. The new elites, according to the author, feel no such obligation as they pursue their own selfishly narrow social and economic goals with little or no interference from the government.

Educated at Harvard and Columbia, Lasch was one of the foremost critics of what he called "the culture of narcissism." In his 1977 bestseller of the same name, he offered a deeply pessimistic account of the decline of morality in the age of consumer capitalism. For this work, he received an American Book Award. At the time of his death in 1994, Lasch was Watson Professor of History at the University of Rochester and a contributing editor to the politically moderate Catholic journal *New Oxford Review*. This selection originally appeared in *Harper's Magazine* in 1994 and was adapted from *The Revolt of the Elites*, published the following year.

SELECTED PUBLICATIONS: *The Agony of the American Left* (1969); *Haven in a Heartless World: The Family Besieged* (1977); *The Culture of Narcissism: American Life in an Age of Diminishing Expectations* (1978); *The Minimal Self: Psychic Survival in Troubled Times* (1984); *The True and Only Heaven: Progress and Its Critics* (1992); *The Revolt of the Elites and the Betrayal of Democracy* (1995).

When José Ortega y Gasset published *The Revolt of the Masses* in 1930, he could not have foreseen a time when it would be more appropriate to speak of a revolt of the elites. Writing in the era of the Bolshevik revolution and the rise of fascism, in the aftermath of a cataclysmic war that had torn Europe apart, Ortega attributed the crisis of Western culture to the "political domination of the masses." In our time, however, the chief threat seems to come not from the masses but from those at the top of the social hierarchy, the elites who control the international flow of money and information, preside over philanthropic foundations and institutions of higher learning, manage the instruments of cultural production, and thus set the terms of public debate. Members of the elite have lost faith in the values, or what remains of them, of the West. For many people, the very term "Western civilization" now calls to mind an organized system of domination designed to enforce conformity to bourgeois values and to keep the victims of patriarchal oppression — women, children, homosexuals, people of color — in a permanent state of subjection. In a remarkable turn of events that confounds our expectations about the course of history, something that Ortega never dreamed of has occurred — the revolt of the elites.

From Ortega's point of view, one that was widely shared at the time, the value of cultural elites lay in their willingness to assume responsibility for the exacting standards without which civilization is impossible. They lived in the service of demanding ideals. "Nobility," Ortega wrote, "is defined by the demands it makes on us — by obligations, not by rights." The mass man, on the other hand, had no use for obligations and no understanding of what they implied, "no feeling for [the] great historical duties." Instead, he asserted the "rights of the commonplace." At once resentful and self-satisfied, he rejected "everything that is excellent, individual, qualified, and select." Lacking any comprehension of the fragility of civilization or the tragic character of history, he was concerned only with his own well-being and looked forward to a future of "limitless possibilities" and "complete freedom." His many failings included a "lack of romance in his dealings with women." Erotic love, a demanding ideal in its own right had no attraction for him. His attitude toward the body was severely practical: he made a cult of physical fitness and submitted to hygienic regimens that promised to keep it in good repair and to extend its longevity. Above all, however, it was the "deadly hatred of all that is not itself" that characterized the mass mind, as Ortega described it. Incapable of wonder or respect, the mass man was the "spoiled child of human history." The mass man, according to Ortega, took for granted the benefits conferred by civilization and demanded them "peremptorily, as if they were natural rights." Though he enjoyed advantages brought about by the general "rise of the historic level," he felt no obligation either to his progenitors or to his progeny. His "incredible ignorance of history" made it possible for him to think of the present moment as far superior to the civilizations of the past and to forget, moreover, that contemporary civilization was itself the product of centuries of historical development, not the unique achievement of an age that had discovered the secret of progress by turning its back on the past.

All the habits of mind that Ortega attributed to the masses are now, I submit, more characteristic of the upper levels of society than of the lower or middle levels. It can hardly be said that ordinary people today look forward to a world of "limitless possibility." Any sense that the masses are riding the wave of history has long since departed. The radical movements that disturbed the peace of the twentieth century have failed one by one, and no successors have appeared on the horizon. The industrial working class, once the mainstay of the socialist movement, has become a pitiful remnant of itself. The hope that "new social movements" would take its place in the struggle against capitalism, which briefly sustained the left in the late Seventies and early Eighties, has come to nothing. Not only do the new social movements — feminism, gay rights, welfare rights, agitation against racial discrimination — have nothing in common; their only coherent demand aims at inclusion in the dominant structures rather than at a revolutionary transformation of social relations.

The masses today have lost interest in revolution. Indeed, their political instincts are demonstrably more conservative than those of their self-appointed spokesmen and would-be liberators. It is the working and lower middle classes, after all, who favor limits on abortion, cling to the two-parent family as a source of stability in a turbulent world, resist experiments with "alternative lifestyles," and harbor deep reservations about affirmative action and other ventures in large-scale social engineering. Today, it is the masses, not the elites, who possess the highly developed sense of limits that Ortega identified with civilization. Members of the working and lower middle classes understand, as their betters do not, that there are inherent limits on human control over the course of social development, over nature and the body, over the tragic elements in human life and history. While young professionals subject themselves to an arduous schedule of physical exercise and dietary controls designed to keep death at bay — to maintain themselves in a state of permanent youthfulness, eternally attractive and remarriageable — ordinary people, on the other hand, accept the body's decay as something against which it is more or less useless to struggle. Upper-middle-class liberals have mounted a crusade to sanitize American society — to create a "smoke-free environment," to censor everything from pornography to "hate speech," and at the same time, incongruously, to extend the range of personal choice in matters where most people feel the need for solid moral guidelines.

When confronted with resistance to these initiatives, members of today's elite betray the venomous hatred that lies not far beneath the smiling face of upper-middle-class benevolence. They find it hard to understand why their hygienic conception of life fails to command universal enthusiasm. In the United States, "Middle America" — a term that has both geographical and social implications — has come to symbolize everything that stands in the way of progress: "family values," mindless patriotism, religious fundamentalism, racism, homophobia, retrograde views of women. Middle Americans, as they appear to the makers of educated opinion, are hopelessly dowdy, unfashionable, and provincial. They are at once absurd and vaguely menacing — not because they wish to overthrow the old order but precisely because their defense of it appears so deeply irrational that it expresses itself, at the higher reaches of its intensity, in fanatical religiosity, in a repressive sexuality that occasionally erupts into violence against women and gays, and in a patriotism that supports imperialist wars and a national ethic of aggressive masculinity. Simultaneously arrogant and insecure, the new elites regard the masses with mingled scorn and apprehension.

The revolt of the elites against older conceptions of prudence and constraint is occurring at a time when the general course of history no longer favors the leveling of social distinctions but runs more and more in the direction of a two-class society in which the favored few monopolize the advantages of money, education, and power. It is undeniable, of course, that the comforts of modern life are still distributed far more widely than they were before the Industrial Revolution. It was this democratization of comfort that Ortega had in mind when he spoke of the "rise of the historic level." Like many others, Ortega was struck by the unheard-of abundance generated by the modern division of labor, by the transformation of luxuries into necessities, and by the popularization of standards of comfort and convenience formerly confined to the rich. These facts — the material fruits of modernization — are not in question. In our time, however, the democratization of abundance — the expectation that each generation would enjoy a standard of living beyond the reach of its predecessors — has given way to a reversal in which age-old inequalities are beginning to reestablish themselves, sometimes at a frightening rate, sometimes so gradually as to escape notice.

People in the upper 20 percent of the income structure now control half the country's wealth. In the last twenty years, only they have experienced a net gain in family income. In the brief years of the Reagan Administration alone, their share of the national income rose from 41.5 percent to 44 percent. The middle class, generously defined as those with incomes ranging from $15,000 to $50,000 a year, declined from 61 percent of the population in 1970 to 52 percent in 1985. These figures convey only a partial, imperfect impression of momentous changes that have taken place in a remarkably short period of time. The steady growth of unemployment, now expanded to include white-collar workers, is more revealing. So is the growth of the "contingent labor force." The number of part-time jobs has doubled since 1980 and now amounts to a quarter of all available jobs. No doubt this massive growth of part-time employment helps to explain why the number of workers covered by retirement plans, which rose from 22 percent to 45 percent between 1950 and 1980, slipped back to 42.6 percent by 1986. It also helps to explain the decline in union membership and the steady erosion of union influence. All these developments, in turn, reflect the loss of manufacturing jobs and the shift to an economy increasingly based on information and services.

The upper middle class, the heart of the new professional and managerial elites, is defined, apart from its rapidly rising income, not so much by its ideology as by a way of life that distinguishes it, more and more unmistakably, from the rest of the population. This way of life is glamorous, gaudy, sometimes indecently lavish. The prosperity enjoyed by the professional and managerial classes, which make up most of the upper 20 percent of the income structure, derives in large part from the emerging marital pattern inelegantly known as "assortative mating" — the tendency of men to marry women who can be relied on to bring in income more or less equivalent to their own. Doctors used to marry nurses; lawyers and executives, their secretaries. Now upper-middle-class men tend to marry women of their own class, business or professional associates with lucrative careers of their own. "What if the $60,000 lawyer marries another $60,000 lawyer," Mickey Kaus asks in his book *The End of Equality*, "and the $20,000 clerk marries a $20,000 clerk? Then the difference between their incomes suddenly becomes the difference between $120,000 and $40,000"; and "although the trend is still masked in the income statistics by the low average wages of women," Kaus adds, "it's obvious to practically everyone, even the experts, that something like this is in fact happening." It is unnecessary to seek further for an explanation of feminism's appeal to the professional and managerial class.

How should this new social elite be described? Their investment in education and information, as opposed to property, distinguishes them from the rich bourgeoisie, the ascendancy of which characterized an earlier stage of capitalism, and from the old proprietary class — the middle class, in the strict sense of the term — that once made up the bulk of the population. These groups constitute a "new class" only in the sense that their livelihood rests not so much on the ownership of property as on the manipulation of information and professional expertise. They embrace too wide a variety of occupations — brokers, bankers, real-estate promoters and developers, engineers, consultants of all kinds, systems analysts, scientists, doctors, publicists, publishers, editors, advertising executives, art directors, moviemakers, entertainers, journalists, television producers and directors, artists, writers, university professors — to be described as a "new class" or a "new ruling class." Furthermore, they lack a common political outlook.

In Secretary of Labor Robert Reich, the new American elite has found its philosopher. Reich's category of "symbolic analysts" in his book *The Work of Nations* serves as a clumsy but useful, empirical, and rather unpretentious description of the new elite. These are people, as Reich describes them, who live in a world of abstract concepts and symbols, ranging from stock-market quotations to the visual images produced by Hollywood and Madison Avenue, and who specialize in the interpretation and deployment of symbolic information. Reich contrasts them with the two other principal categories of labor — "routine producers," who

perform repetitive tasks and exercise little control over the design of production, and "inperson servers," whose work also consists of the routine,
for the most part, but "must be provided person-to-person" and therefore cannot be "sold worldwide." If we allow for the highly schematic
and necessarily imprecise character of these categories, they correspond
closely enough to everyday observation to give us a fairly accurate impression not only of the occupational structure but of the class structure
of American society today. The "symbolic analysts" are clearly rising in
wealth and status while the other categories, which make up 80 percent
of the population, are declining.

Reich's portrait of the "symbolic analysts" is extravagantly flattering.
In his eyes, they represent the best and brightest in American life. Educated at "elite private schools" and "high-quality suburban public
schools, where they are tracked through advanced courses," they enjoy
every advantage their doting parents can provide.

> Their teachers and professors are attentive to their academic needs.
> They have access to state-of-the-art science laboratories, interactive com-
> puters and video systems in the classroom, language laboratories, and
> high-tech school libraries. Their classes are relatively small; their peers
> are intellectually stimulating. Their parents take them to museums and
> cultural events, expose them to foreign travel, and give them music
> lessons. At home are educational books, educational toys, educational
> videotapes, microscopes, telescopes, and personal computers replete
> with the latest educational software.

These privileged young people acquire advanced degrees at the "best
[universities] in the world," the superiority of which is proved by their
ability to attract foreign students in great numbers. In this cosmopolitan
atmosphere, they overcome the provincial folkways that impede creative
thought, according to Reich. "Skeptical, curious, and creative," they become problem solvers par excellence, equal to any challenge. Unlike
those who engage in mind-numbing routines, they love their work,
which engages them in lifelong learning and endless experimentation.

Old-fashioned intellectuals tend to work by themselves and to be
jealous and possessive about their ideas. By contrast, the new brain
workers — producers of high-quality "insights" in a variety of fields
ranging from marketing and finance to art and entertainment — operate
best in teams. Their "capacity to collaborate" promotes "system thinking" — the ability to see problems in their totality, to absorb the fruits of
collective experimentation, and to "discern larger causes, consequences,
and relationships." Since their work depends so heavily on "networking," they settle in "specialized geographic pockets" populated by people
like themselves. These privileged communities — Cambridge, Silicon
Valley, Hollywood — become "wondrously resilient" centers of artistic,
technical, and promotional enterprise. These new workers represent the

epitome of intellectual achievement, in Reich's admiring view, and of the good life conceived as the exchange of "insights," "information," and professional gossip.

The geographical concentration of knowledge producers, once it reaches a critical mass, incidentally provides a market for the growing class of "inperson servers" who cater to their needs. "It is no accident," says Reich,

> that Hollywood is home to a conspicuously large number of voice coaches, fencing trainers, dancing instructors, performers' agents, and suppliers of photographic, acoustic and lighting equipment. Also found in close proximity are restaurants with precisely the right ambience favored by producers wooing directors and directors wooing screenwriters, and everyone in Hollywood wooing everyone else.

Universal admission to the class of "creative" people would best meet Reich's ideal of a democratic society, but since this goal is clearly unattainable, the next best thing, presumably, is a society composed of "symbolic analysts" and their hangers-on. The latter are themselves consumed with dreams of stardom but are content, in the meantime, to live in the shadow of the stars, waiting to be discovered. They are symbiotically united with their betters in the continuous search for marketable talent that can be compared, as Reich's imagery makes clear, only to the rites of courtship. One might add the more jaundiced observation that the circles of power — finance, government, art, entertainment — overlap and become increasingly interchangeable.

Though Reich turns to Hollywood for a particularly compelling example of the "wondrously resilient" communities that spring up wherever there is a concentration of "creative" people, his description of the new kind of elite community fits the nation's capital as well. Washington becomes a parody of Tinseltown; executives take to the airwaves, creating overnight the semblance of political movements; movie stars become political pundits, even presidents; reality and the simulation of reality become more and more difficult to distinguish. Ross Perot launches his presidential campaign from *Larry King Live*. Hollywood stars take a prominent part in the Clinton campaign and flock to Clinton's inaugural, investing it with the glamour of a Hollywood opening. TV anchormen and interviewers become celebrities; celebrities in the world of entertainment take on the role of social critics. The boxer Mike Tyson issues a three-page open letter from the Indiana prison where he is serving a six-year term for rape condemning the President's "crucifixion" of Lani Guinier. The star-struck Rhodes scholar Robert Reich, prophet of the new world of "abstraction, system thinking, experimentation, and collaboration," joins the Clinton Administration in the incongruous capacity of secretary of labor — administrator, in other words, of the one category of employment ("routine production") that has no future at all (according to his own account) in a society composed of "symbolic analysts" and "in-person servers." Only in a world in which words and images bear ever less resemblance to the things they appear to describe would it be possible for a man like Reich to refer to himself, without irony, as secretary of labor or to write so glowingly of a society governed by "the best and the brightest." (The last time the best and the brightest got control of the country, they dragged it into a protracted, demoralizing war in Southeast Asia, from which the country still has not fully recovered.)

The arrogance of the elite, in its revolt against civilizing limits, should not be confused with the pride, characteristic of aristocratic classes, that rests on the inheritance of an ancient lineage and on the obligation to defend its honor. Neither valor and chivalry nor the code of courtly, romantic love, with which these values are closely associated, has any place in the worldview of the best and the brightest. A meritocracy has no more use for chivalry and valor than a hereditary aristocracy has for brains. Although hereditary advantages play an important part in the attainment of professional or managerial status, the new class has to maintain the fiction that its power rests on intelligence alone. Hence it has little sense of ancestral gratitude or of an obligation to live up to responsibilities inherited from the past. It thinks of itself as a self-made elite owing its privileges exclusively to its own efforts. Even the concept of a republic of letters, which might be expected to appeal to elites with such a large stake in higher education, is almost entirely absent from their frame of reference.

Meritocratic elites find it difficult to imagine a community, even a community of the intellect, that reaches into both the past and the future and is constituted by an awareness of intergenerational obligation. The "zones" and "networks" admired by Reich bear little resemblance to communities in any traditional sense of the term. Populated by transients, they lack the continuity that derives from a sense of place and from standards of conduct self-consciously cultivated and handed down from generation to generation. The "community" of the best and the brightest is a community of contemporaries, in the double sense that its members think of themselves as agelessly youthful and that the mark of this youthfulness is precisely their ability to stay on top of the latest trends.

The identification and promotion of "the best and the brightest" is the meritocratic ideal. Meritocracy, however, is a parody of democracy. It offers opportunities for advancement, in theory at least, to anyone with the talent to seize them; but "opportunities to rise," as R. H. Tawney pointed out in *Equality*, "are no substitute for a general diffusion of the means of civilization," of the "dignity and culture" that are needed by all "whether they rise or not." Social mobility does not undermine the influence of elites; if anything, it helps to solidify their influence by supporting the illusion that it rests solely on merit. Furthering upward mobility merely strengthens the likelihood that elites will exercise power irresponsibly, precisely because they recognize so few obligations to their predecessors or to the communities they profess to lead. Their lack of gratitude disqualifies meritocratic elites from the burden of leadership, and, in any case, they are less interested in leadership than in escaping from the common lot — the very definition of meritocratic success.

The inner logic of meritocracy has seldom been more rigorously exposed than in the British writer Michael Young's dystopian novel, *The Rise of the Meritocracy, 1870–2033* (1959), a work written in the tradition of Tawney, G. D. H. Cole, George Orwell, E. P. Thompson, and Raymond Williams.[1] Young's narrator, a historian writing in the fourth decade of the twenty-first century, approvingly chronicles the "fundamental change" of the century and a half beginning around 1870 — the redistribution of intelligence "between the classes." "By imperceptible degrees an aristocracy of birth has turned into an aristocracy of talent." Thanks to industry's adoption of intelligence testing, the abandonment of the principle of seniority, and the growing influence of the school at the expense of the family, "the talented have been given the opportunity to rise to the level which accords with their capacities, and the lower classes consequently reserved for those who are also lower in ability." In Young's world, a doctrinaire belief in equality collapsed in the face of the practical advantages of an educational system that "no longer required the clever to mingle with the stupid."

Young's imaginative projection sheds a great deal of light on trends in the United States, where a seemingly democratic system of elite recruitment leads to results that are far from democratic — segregation of social classes, contempt for manual labor, collapse of the common schools, loss of a common culture. As Young describes it, meritocracy has the effect of making elites more secure than ever in their privileges (which can now be seen as the appropriate reward of diligence and brainpower) while nullifying working-class opposition. "The best way to defeat opposition," Young's historian observes, "is . . . appropriating and educating the best children of the lower classes while they are still young." Liberals and conservatives alike ignore the real objection to meritocracy — that it drains talent away from the lower classes and thus deprives them of effective leadership — and content themselves with dubious arguments to the effect that education does not live up to its promise of fostering social mobility. If it did, they seem to imply, no one would presumably have any reason to complain. Those who are left behind, knowing that "they have had every chance," cannot legitimately complain about their lot. "For the first time in human history the inferior

20

[1] *R. H. Tawney, G. D. H. Cole, George Orwell, E. P. Thompson, and Raymond Williams:* Twentieth-century British authors known for their analyses of social and economic injustice.

man has no ready buttress for his self-regard." It should not surprise us, then, that meritocracy also generates an obsessive concern with "self-esteem." The new therapies (sometimes known collectively as the recovery movement) seek to counter the oppressive sense of failure in those who fail to climb the educational ladder even while they leave intact the existing structure of elite recruitment — the acquisition of educational credentials.

An aristocracy of talent is superficially an attractive ideal, which appears to distinguish democracies from societies based on hereditary privilege. Meritocracy, however, turns out to be a contradiction in terms: The talented retain many of the vices of aristocracy without its virtues. Their snobbery lacks any acknowledgment of reciprocal obligations between the favored few and the multitude. Although they are full of "compassion" for the poor, they cannot be said to subscribe to a theory of noblesse oblige, which would imply a willingness to make a direct and personal contribution to the public good. Obligation, like everything else, has been depersonalized; exercised through the agency of the state, the burden of supporting it falls not on the professional and managerial class but, disproportionately, on the lower middle and working classes. The policies advanced by new-class liberals on behalf of the downtrodden and oppressed — racial integration of the public schools, for example — require sacrifices from the ethnic minorities who share the inner cities with the poor, seldom from the suburban liberals who design and support those policies.

To an alarming extent, the privileged classes — by an expansive definition, the top 20 percent — have made themselves independent not only of crumbling industrial cities but of public services in general. They send their children to private schools, insure themselves against medical emergencies by enrolling in company-supported plans, and hire private security guards to protect themselves against the mounting violence. It is not just that they see no point in paying for public services they no longer use; many of them have ceased to think of themselves as Americans in any important sense, implicated in America's destiny for better or worse. Their ties to an international culture of work and leisure — of business, entertainment, information, and "information retrieval" — make many members of the elite deeply indifferent to the prospect of national decline.

The market in which the new elites operate is now international in scope. Their fortunes are tied to enterprises that operate across national boundaries. They are more concerned with the smooth functioning of the system as a whole than with any of its parts. Their loyalties — if the term is not itself anachronistic in this context — are international rather than regional, national, or local. They have more in common with their counterparts in Brussels or Hong Kong than with the masses of Americans not yet plugged in to the network of global communications.

In the borderless global economy, money has lost its links to nation- 25 ality. David Rieff, who spent several months in Los Angeles collecting material for his book *Los Angeles: Capital of the Third World*, reports that "at least two or three times a week . . . I could depend on hearing someone say that the future 'belonged' to the Pacific Rim." The movement of money and population across national borders has transformed the "whole idea of place," according to Rieff. The privileged classes in Los Angeles feel more kinship with their counterparts in Japan, Singapore, and Korea than with most of their own countrymen.

The changing class structure of the United States mirrors changes that are taking place all over the industrial world. In Europe, referenda on unification have revealed a deep and widening gap between the political classes and the more humble members of society, who fear that the European Economic Community will be dominated by bureaucrats and technicians devoid of any feelings of national identity or allegiance. Even in Japan, the very model of successful industrialization in the last two or three decades, public-opinion polls conducted in 1987 revealed a growing belief that the country could no longer be described as middle-class, ordinary people having failed to share in the vast fortunes accumulated in real estate, finance, and manufacturing.

Outside of the industrial democracies, with their increasing social polarization, the global disparity between wealth and poverty has become so glaring that it is hardly necessary to review the evidence of growing inequality. In Latin America, Africa, and large parts of Asia, the sheer growth in numbers, together with the displacement of rural populations by the commercialization of agriculture, has subjected civic life to unprecedented strains. Vast urban agglomerations — they can scarcely be called cities — have taken shape, overflowing with poverty, wretchedness, disease, and despair. Paul Kennedy projects twenty of these "megacities" by 2025, each with a population of 11 million or more. Mexico City will already have more than 24 million inhabitants by the year 2000; São Paulo, more than 23 million; Calcutta, 16 million; Bombay, 15.5 million. As the collapse of civic life in these swollen cities continues, not only the poor but also the middle classes will experience conditions unimaginable a few years ago. Middle-class standards of living can be expected to decline throughout what is all too hopefully referred to as the developing world. In a country like Peru, once a prosperous nation with reasonable prospects of evolving parliamentary institutions, the middle class for all practical purposes has ceased to exist.

A middle class, as Walter Russell Mead reminds us in his study of the declining American empire, *Mortal Splendor*, "does not appear out of thin air." Its power and numbers "depend on the overall wealth of the domestic economy"; and in countries, accordingly, where "wealth is concentrated in the hands of a tiny oligarchy and the rest of the population is desperately poor, the middle class can grow to only a limited extent. . . . [It] never escapes its primary role as a servant class to the oligarchy." Unfortunately, this description now applies to a growing list of nations that have prematurely reached the limits of economic development, countries in which a rising "share of their own national product goes to foreign investors or creditors." Such a fate may well await even industrial nations like the United States.

The world of the late twentieth century thus presents a curious spectacle. On the one hand it is now united, through the agency of the market, as it never was before. Capital and labor flow freely across political boundaries that seem increasingly artificial and unenforceable. Popular culture follows in their wake. On the other hand, tribal loyalties have seldom been so aggressively promoted. Religious and ethnic warfare breaks out in one country after another: in India and Sri Lanka, in large parts of Africa, in the former Soviet Union and the former Yugoslavia.

It is the weakening of the nation-state that underlies both these developments — the movement toward unification and the seemingly contradictory movement toward fragmentation. The state can no longer contain ethnic conflicts; nor can it contain the forces leading to globalization. Ideologically, nationalism comes under attack from both sides: from advocates of ethnic and racial particularism and also from those who argue that the only hope of peace lies in the internationalization of everything from weights and measures to the artistic imagination.

Fears that the international language of money will speak more loudly than local dialects inspire the reassertion of ethnic particularism in Europe, while the decline of the nation-state weakens the only authority capable of holding ethnic rivalries in check. The revival of tribalism, in turn, reinforces a reactive cosmopolitanism among elites. Curiously enough, it is Robert Reich, notwithstanding his admiration for the new elite of "symbolic analysts," who provides one of the most penetrating accounts of the "darker side of cosmopolitanism." Without national attachments, he reminds us, people have little inclination to make sacrifices or to accept responsibility for their actions. "We learn to feel responsible for others because we share with them a common history . . . a common culture . . . a common fate." The denationalization of business enterprise tends to produce a class of cosmopolitans who see themselves as "world citizens, but without accepting . . . any of the obligations that citizenship in a polity normally implies." But the cosmopolitanism of the favored few, because it uniformed by the practice of citizenship, turns out to be a higher form of parochialism. Instead of supporting public services, the new elites put their money into the improvement of their own self-enclosed enclaves. They gladly pay for private and suburban schools, private police, and private systems of garbage collection; but they have managed to relieve themselves, to a remarkable extent, of the obligation to contribute to the national treasury. Their acknowledgment of civic obligations does not extend beyond their own immediate neighborhoods. The "secession of the symbolic analysts," as Reich calls it, provides us with a particularly striking instance of the revolt of elites against the constraints of time and place.

The decline of nations is closely linked to the global decline of the middle class. It is the crisis of the middle class, and not simply the growing chasm between wealth and poverty, that needs to be emphasized in a sober analysis of our prospects. Ever since the sixteenth and seventeenth centuries, the fortunes of the nation-state have been bound up with those of the trading and manufacturing classes. The founders of modern nations, whether they were exponents of royal privilege like Louis XIV or republicans like Washington and Lafayette, turned to this class for support in their struggle against the feudal nobility. A large part of the appeal of nationalism lay in the state's ability to establish a common market within its boundaries, to enforce a uniform system of justice, and to extend citizenship both to petty proprietors and to rich merchants, alike excluded from power under the old regime. The middle class understandably became the most patriotic, not to say jingoistic and militaristic element in society. But the unattractive features of middle-class nationalism should not obscure its positive contributions in the form of a highly developed sense of place and a respect for historical continuity — hallmarks of the middle-class sensibility that can be appreciated more fully now that middle-class culture is everywhere in retreat. Whatever its faults, middle-class nationalism provided a common ground, common standards, a common frame of reference without which society dissolves into nothing more than contending factions, as the founding fathers of America understood so well. The revolt of the masses that Ortega feared is no longer a plausible threat. But the revolt of the elites against time-honored traditions of locality, obligation, and restraint may yet unleash a war of all against all.

A Response to Christopher Lasch

ROBERT REICH

Class Anxieties

Much of what the late Christopher Lasch wrote in his long and distinguished career I agreed with entirely, and even when I could not agree I admired his honesty, insight, and fervor. The world of ideas will be dimmer without him. Ordinarily, it would be an honor to have my own work discussed in his final book, excerpted as his final essay, "The Revolt of the Elites." But, to my dismay, Lasch's interpretation of my work is severely at odds with my intent. The essay cites my book *The Work of Nations* and dubs me the "philosopher" of "the new American elite." It suggests that I approve of, even celebrate, the withdrawal of the country's best educated and most successful from the American commonwealth. Yet my actual goal is precisely the opposite.

Although I am reluctant to challenge an eminent thinker who cannot respond, I am even more reluctant to let stand the impression his essay might leave about my diagnosis and prescription. Simply put, what I term "the secession of the successful," and what Lasch calls "the revolt of the elites," presents a mortal threat to the American way of life. In the final line of his essay, Lasch writes that "the revolt of the elites against time-honored traditions of locality, obligation, and restraint may yet unleash a war of all against all." Exactly. As labor secretary, I have warned that America's middle class is splintering into three new groups: an *underclass* largely trapped in center cities, increasingly isolated from the core economy; an *overclass* of those who are positioned to ride profitably the waves of change; and, in between, the largest group, an *anxious class*, most of whom hold a job but are justifiably uneasy about their own standing and fearful for their children's future.

What divides these three fragments of the old middle class is the quality of their formal education and their capacity and opportunity to learn throughout their working life. Skills have always been relevant to earnings, of course. But skills have never been as important as they are today. They now determine where the fundamental fault line runs through the American workforce. Lasch perceives the importance of this fault line but, I submit, misreads some of its contours and misgauges the average worker's odds of crossing this divide.

It is undeniable that, by whatever measure (income, unemployment risk, pension benefits, or health insurance), the workforce has become starkly separated over the last two decades. Well-educated workers have generally improved their lot while less well-educated workers have suffered a precipitous drop in living standard. Lasch justifiably laments one of the consequences of this divide: the increasing physical separation of Americans. The overclass has moved to elite suburbs — occasionally into their own gated communities or residential compounds policed by their own security force. The underclass finds itself quarantined in surroundings that are often unspeakably bleak and violent. And the anxious class is trapped, too, not only by houses and apartments that are often too small for growing families but also by the frenzy of effort it takes to preserve their standing now that many families need two or three paychecks to deliver the standard of living one job used to supply.

In other words, even as America's economic tide continues to rise, it no longer lifts us all. This core argument animates *The Work of Nations* and reinforces its conclusion that our country's greatest challenge is "to improve the living standards of the majority of Americans . . . who are losing ground in the global economy." I came to Washington precisely to advance that goal, making all the more painful Lasch's suggestion that as secretary of labor I am content merely to preside over "the one category of employment ('routine production') that has no future at all." The premise that there is "no future" for the majority of America's workers is repellent and, fortunately, at odds with the facts. The economy that is now emerging is not simply a shrinkage or re-sorting of the old economy but, rather, a fundamental re-formation rich with new opportunities and new paths into the middle class.

When nations are wise and lucky — as America has been for most of its history — an implicit social compact knits together business success, rising living standards, and inclusive politics. But the erosion of the old middle class poses a threat to the bargain that has paid off so well for so many American citizens and American companies.

In order to revive America's sense of shared destiny, we need to restore the connections between the two defining national traditions of free enterprise and middle-class prosperity. We need to renew the compact among American businesses, American government, and American working men and women. Individuals must face the realities of the new economy, and ensure that they and their children have the basic intellectual tools to prosper in it. Business must invest in its workers, both because a skilled and flexible workforce is the key source of competitive advantage and because the widening gaps in our society clearly imperil business as well. And government must clear away the obstacles that clutter the path to opportunity.

This administration is engaged in resolving the problems Lasch so eloquently details in his essay. Were Lasch still with us, he might argue that the centrifugal forces that are pulling America apart call for still more radical remedies. That may be. But I hope he would also agree that the goal is within our grasp, that it is possible to build a new middle class and a new ladder into it for the underclass. Redoubling our energies in pursuit of this goal and reaffirming that no task is more essential to our future are fitting practical monuments to Lasch's memory.

ROBERT REICH *is currently the United States secretary of labor. His response to Lasch appeared in the form of a letter to* Harper's *Magazine in February 1995.*

PREPARING FOR DISCUSSION

1. While Lasch's essay and the essay by Lind that preceded it both concern the "secession of the elites," each author construes the term *elite* in a slightly different manner. What is the primary definition of *elite* for each author? To what degree does the rapidly rising incomes of the upper fifth of American society participate in Lasch's definition? What are the primary values of the new elites as compared with those of an older generation of elites?

2. The author traces the rise of a new cosmopolitan elite to the decline of middle-class American values. What are these values and why, according to Lasch, does the elites' rejection of or revolt against them weaken this new class's allegiance to America? In what social and cultural phenomena does Lasch find evidence of this elitist withdrawal from the American mainstream?

3. Consider Lasch's critique of meritocracy. One aspect of Thomas Jefferson's thinking about the new democracy he had helped to found was that a "natural aristocracy" based upon individual talent or meritocracy would come to replace an older aristocracy based on heredity and wealth. Given that Jefferson held meritocracy to be an important component of democracy, on what grounds can Lasch hold that meritocracy is antidemocratic? What does he mean when he calls "meritocracy a parody of democracy" (paragraph 19)?

4. Lasch notes that historically the upper-class values of leadership and ancestral obligation or noblesse oblige prompted the old elites to assume much of the responsibility and financial burden for social services that now fall to the middle and working classes (paragraph 22). Thus, while the author acknowledges the need for the endurance of middle-class values, he also notes the disappearance of old elitist values. In your view, is Lasch's essay an exercise in nostalgia, or is it a plan for rescuing democratic principles?

5. In paragraph 4, Lasch makes a distinction between "members of the working and lower middle classes" and "their betters." To what social group does Lasch's use of the term *betters* refer? Why does he use this particular term to refer to this group? Does *betters* have any moral overtones?

FROM READING TO WRITING

6. Lasch notes the efforts of the new elites to "sanitize American society" (paragraph 4). Write an essay in which you consider one of the efforts that Lasch notes or identify one on your own. Why has this effort been made? Are you sympathetic to the effort in question? If so, do your reasons for supporting such an effort differ from or correspond with those which Lasch attributes to the "new elites"?

7. Consider Reich's reply to Lasch's essay. Write an essay in which you attempt to characterize the attitudes of both Lasch and Reich to the possibility of a newly emergent middle class. Which of the two attitudes do you find more realistic and why? How might the tone of Reich's reply have differed if he were not writing as the U.S. secretary of labor?

LILLIAN B. RUBIN

"People Don't Know Right from Wrong Anymore": Working-Class Families in the 1990s

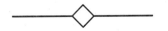

The social, cultural, and ethical values of America's working class are seldom touched upon by social scientists and economists increasingly preoccupied with the long-term effects of joblessness and falling wages. Yet by ascertaining what these values are and how they have changed over the last two decades, we might be able to understand why so many members of the working class now feel like outsiders in their own society. As social psychologist Lillian B. Rubin explains in the following selection, "It's as if their beliefs and values have no place in the institutional world they inhabit, not in the schools their children attend, not on the television shows they watch, not in the films they see, not in the music they hear, not in the laws their government promulgates."

Nearly twenty years after her pioneering study of working-class families, *Worlds of Pain*, Rubin finds that the sense of crisis within these families has only deepened. This growing sense of despair in the face of changing cultural norms, the author implies, does not bode well for America's future social stability. Rubin received her doctorate in psychology from the University of California at Berkeley. She lives in San Francisco, where she is a practicing psychotherapist and senior research fellow at the Institute for the Study of Social Change. This selection originally appeared in *Tikkun* in 1994.

SELECTED PUBLICATIONS: *Busing and Backlash: White against White in an Urban School District* (1972); *Worlds of Pain: Life in the Working Class* (1976); *Intimate Strangers: Men and Women Together* (1983); *Erotic Wars: What Happened to the Sexual Revolution?* (1990); *Families on the Fault Line: America's Working Class Speaks about the Family, the Economy, Race, and Ethnicity* (1994).

"I can't believe what kids do today!" exclaims Marguerite Jenkins, a white forty-year-old divorcee whose seventeen-year-old daughter, Candy, had just had an abortion.

I last met Marguerite more than twenty years ago when I interviewed her for *Worlds of Pain*. The slim, pretty young woman who welcomed me into her home then is gone now, replaced by an older, heavier version who bears the visible marks of life's difficulties. As I listen to her angry words about her daughter, the memory of our last meeting moves from the recesses of my mind into awareness. At age twenty, Marguerite already had two children under three; Candy wouldn't come into the world for another three years. Her firstborn son had been conceived when she was still in high school. But abortion wasn't an option then. So a few months after she discovered she was pregnant, she left school and married Larry Jenkins, the nineteen-year-old father of the child she was carrying. By the time I met her she was a distraught and overburdened young mother, worrying because her husband had just lost yet another job, fearful that her dream of living happily ever after was crumbling.

I remember the story Marguerite told of finding out she was pregnant — her terror; her anger at her father, who wanted to throw her out of the house; at her mother, who didn't protect her from her father's rage; her bitterness because they were more concerned about what others would think than about the predicament she found herself in. Hearing Marguerite now, I can understand her concern for her daughter, her fear that Candy will repeat her mistakes. But given her own experience, I wonder about her outrage, her seeming lack of compassion for Candy and for what she might be feeling. So I say, "I'm a little surprised to hear you talk so angrily, since you got pregnant when you were about her age."

She looks somewhat abashed at the reminder, shifts uncomfortably in her chair, then says, "C'mon, you know it's different now. Sure, I got caught, too, but we got married. *We had to get married; we didn't have a choice.*"

"We had to get married" — words spoken by 44 percent of the   5
couples I interviewed two decades ago. But what does "had to" mean? These marriages weren't coerced, at least not by any obvious outside agent. There were no old-style shotgun weddings, no self-righteous fathers avenging the violation of their daughters' virtue by forcing their errant lovers into saying their vows. The compulsion was internal, part of the moral culture of the community in which they lived. It was simply what one did.

Sometimes the young couple married regretfully; often one partner, usually the man, was ambivalent. It didn't really matter; they did what was expected. If you "got caught," you got married; that was the rule, understood by all. As one of the men I interviewed then put it: "If you knocked up a girl, you married her; that was it. You just did it, that's all. End of story."

But in fact, it was only the beginning of the story. Seven years and three children after Marguerite and Larry Jenkins did what their parents and their community expected of them, he walked out. Young, unskilled, and seething at being tied down by responsibilities he was unable to meet, Larry floated from one dead-end job to another, at each one acting out his resentment until he got fired or quit. Marguerite, frightened for her children, furious with disappointment, and exhausted from their constant battles, finally gave him an ultimatum: Shape up or get out! To her surprise, he stormed out of the house and came back only to claim his belongings a few days later. "I said it, but I didn't really think he'd do it. I figured I'd finally scare him into being more responsible," she explains as she reviews those years.

With no family to help her and three small children whose father couldn't or wouldn't support them, Marguerite had no choice: She spent the next five years on the welfare rolls. "I was so ashamed to go down to the welfare office. I can't explain how bad I felt; I wasn't raised that way. My parents, they had their problems, but my father was a hard worker. He didn't make much, but we got by without charity.

"I used to think welfare people were freeloaders, you know, like they were lazy bums. Then it happened to me and I kept thinking: *I can't believe it! How did this happen to me? I'm not like that.*" She looks away, trying to contain the tears that well up as the memory of those hard times washes over her.

"Marrying Larry, that whole thing, it was a giant mistake right from   10
the beginning. You get married with this dream that everything's going to be wonderful, but it never works out that way, does it? How could it? We were babies, and there we were trying to be grown-ups. We had two kids by the time I was nineteen and he was, I don't know, maybe not even twenty-one yet. I wasn't ready to be a wife and a mother, and he sure wasn't ready to be a decent husband and father."

The Jenkinses' story is a common one among the families I met twenty years ago. Two young people thrust into a marriage by the lack of acceptable moral or social alternatives, only to divorce a few years later. Since they married so young, sometimes even before they finished high school, the women had little opportunity to develop any marketable skills, certainly none that would enable them to support their children and pay for child care while they worked. Of the thirty-two *Worlds of Pain* families I was able to locate, eighteen (56 percent) had been divorced. All but one of the men had remarried by the time I met them again. The lone exception had separated from his wife a few months earlier and was already involved with a woman in what he took to be a serious relationship.

For the women it was different: Only eleven had remarried; the rest had been single for five years or more. All of them talked about the economic devastation divorce wrought in their families. Well over half needed some form of public assistance during the years when they were divorced. Some were on the welfare rolls; others got by with food stamp supplements alone. For the women who haven't remarried, life continues to be economically unstable at best.

If their own young marriages so often were, as Marguerite Jenkins says, "a giant mistake right from the beginning," why aren't such women more supportive of their daughters' choices? Indeed, why aren't they pleased that the young women they raised have so many more options available to them? I ask the question: "Given what's happened in your own life, I wonder why you're not glad that Candy could make other choices?"

"Don't get me wrong, I think it's okay to have an abortion; I'm — what do they call it? — oh yeah, for choice," explains Marguerite. "I mean, I don't think people should run around having abortions just like that, but nobody's got a right to tell somebody what to do about being pregnant or not. God knows, I don't want her to do what I did. It's just that . . ." She stops, searching for the right words, and after a moment or two, continues, still uncertain. "I don't know exactly how to say it. Look, I was scared to death when I found out I was pregnant, and so was Larry. These kids, they're not even bothered now."

It's this sense that their children see the world so differently that's so   15
hard for working-class parents. For it seems to say that now, along with the economic dislocation they suffer, even their children are out of their reach, that they can no longer count on shared values to hold their families together. It doesn't help either that no matter where they look, they don't see a reflection of themselves. If they look up, they see a life-style and values they abhor, the same ones that, they believe, are corrupting their children. If they shift their gaze downward, they see the poor, the homeless, the helpless — the denizens of the dangerous underclass whose moral degeneracy has, in the working-class view, led to their fall. It's as if their beliefs and values have no place in the institutional world they inhabit, not in the schools their children attend, not on the television shows they watch, not in the films they see, not in the music they hear, not in the laws their government promulgates.

It's true that this isn't a problem only for working-class families. Middle-class parents also worry about the changing cultural norms; they also fret endlessly about "what kids do today." Indeed, generational conflict over changing values and life-styles is common to all families, with parents generally holding onto the old ways and children pulling for the new ones. But it's also true that the issues that create conflict in families differ quite sharply by class.

Middle-class parents long ago accepted the norms, values, and behavior that have only recently filtered down into the working class — the open expression of premarital sex, for example, or living together without benefit of clergy. Partly perhaps these changes came earlier and with less upheaval in middle-class families because it was their children who initiated the struggle for change. But there are other reasons as well. High among them is the fact that middle-class parents are likely to be more educated than those in the working class. And it's widely under-

stood that a college education tends to broaden perspectives and liberalize attitudes about the kind of life-style and value changes we have seen
in the last few decades.

Since most working-class parents haven't been exposed to the array
of ideas found in a college classroom, they tend to be more tradition
bound. "You get used to doing things one way and then you think it's the
right way," says thirty-six-year-old Jane Dawson, a white mother of two
teenagers. Without the expanded horizons that higher education affords,
the old way often becomes the only way. "If it was good enough for us,
it's fine for my kids," proclaims her husband, Bill.

But the cultural changes that have swept the land during these past
decades will not be stayed by parental nostalgia, fear, or authority. The
young people in this study agree that their values about such issues as
sexual behavior, marriage, and gender roles are radically different from
those their parents hold. And they're pained by the family conflicts these
differences stir. But they also insist that they're not the thoughtless, hedo-
nistic lot of their parents' imaginations. "My mom thinks I think getting
pregnant is no big deal, but she doesn't understand," says Candy Jenkins, her blue eyes turning stormy with anger when we talk about this a
few days after my meeting with her mother. "Just because I didn't carry
on like some kind of a crazy person, she thinks I didn't care. But it's not
true; I did care. I was scared to death when I found out."

"I was scared to death when I found out" — the same words spoken   20
decades apart by a mother and her daughter. Both shared the fear of their
parents' response. "I thought my father would kill me," says Marguerite.
"I was afraid my mother would murder me," shudders Candy. Beyond
that, however, the words have entirely different meanings for each of
them.

For Marguerite, getting pregnant was a problem; not to have gotten
married would have been a catastrophe. For her, therefore, the critical
question was: *Will he marry me?* "I was terrified. What if Larry reneged
and wouldn't marry me? What would I do?"

For Candy, however, the pregnancy could be taken care of; marriage
loomed like a calamity. "The one thing I knew was I didn't want to get
married and have a baby. I was really scared my mom would try to make
me. She kept going on about how ashamed she was, and what was she
going to tell grandma, and all like that. But she didn't push me about getting married. I mean, she talked about it, but she knew it was a bum idea,
too. Look at what happened to her."

For Marguerite, shame was a big issue, not just the memory of her
own shame, but the fact that it wasn't one of her daughter's preoccupations. "I just can't get over it," Marguerite remarks, shaking her head in
bewilderment. "I wanted to die because I was so ashamed. I felt like I'd
never be able to hold my head up again. Now these kids, it's like it's

nothing to them; they've got no shame. I'll bet half the school knows she was pregnant. They probably compare notes about their damn abortions," she concludes with disgust.

Shame and guilt — the emotions that give evidence of the effectiveness of our social norms, that reassure us that the moral culture has been internalized, that there will be a price for its violation. If our young suffer, if they're tormented by shame, haunted by guilt, we can at least be assured that they share our values about good and evil, right and wrong. Without that, the gap between us seems disturbingly wide and the future frighteningly uncertain.

But to cast the issue in these terms — that is, either we suffer shame and guilt or we don't — misses the point. It's not true that our children don't experience these feelings. But what evokes them is not fixed in eternity. Rather, it changes with time, each historical moment delivering up its own variation of a culture's norms and values, each one defining its transgressions and eliciting shame and guilt for their violation.

For Marguerite's mother, divorce would have been unthinkable, a humiliating and guilt-ridden scandal, a painful public admission of failure and inadequacy. By the time Marguerite was divorced, it was a sad but commonplace event, certainly nothing to hide in shame about. For Marguerite, her pregnancy was a shameful confession that she had, in the language of the day, "gone all the way" — an act, once it became known, that threatened to cast her out of respectable society and to label her a "slut." For Candy, there was a mix of feelings, some of them no doubt the same as her mother felt decades earlier — regret, fear, sadness, confusion, anger at herself for taking sexual chances when she knew better. But not shame — not because she's a less moral person than her mother but because she grew up in a sexual culture that gives permission for a level of sexual freedom unknown to her mother's generation.

"As long as two people love each other, there's nothing wrong with making love," declares Tory, the white sixteen-year-old daughter of the Bowen family. "I don't understand why it's only supposed to be okay if you're married. I mean, why is getting married such a big deal?"

This, perhaps, is one of the most important changes underlying the permissiveness about sex. If getting married is no longer "such a big deal," why wait for marriage to explore one's sexuality? If sexual relations outside marriage are acceptable once people have been divorced, then why not before they get married? Repeatedly, the young people I met raised these and other questions as we discussed the changing norms around marriage and sex.

The sexual revolution, which changed the rules about the expression of female sexuality; the gender revolution, with its demand for the reordering of traditional roles and relationships; the divorce revolution, which fractured the social contract about marriage and commitment; the shifts in the economy, which forced increasing numbers of married women into the labor force — all these have come together to create a profoundly different consciousness about marriage and its role divisions for young people today.

Twenty years ago it was marriage that occupied the dreams of a working-class high-school girl. Among the *Worlds of Pain* families, the women were, on average, eighteen when they married; the men, twenty. Two decades later, none of the families I reinterviewed has a son who married at twenty or younger, and just one has a daughter who was only eighteen when she married. The others either married considerably later or are still single — some at twenty-four and twenty-five — something that almost never happened by choice twenty years ago.

The national statistics tell the same story. In 1970, the average age at which women married for the first time was 20.6 years; for men, it was 22.5. Two decades later it had jumped to 24.2 for women, 26.2 for men. Today 18.8 percent of women and 29.4 percent of men are still unmarried when they reach thirty, compared with 6.2 percent and 9.4 percent, respectively, twenty years ago.

Women in particular are much more ambivalent about hearing wedding bells than they were a couple of generations ago, aware that the changes they have undergone, the kind of marital partnerships they now long for, are rarely matched by the men who are their prospective mates. Therefore, they talk of wanting to explore the options available, to live life more fully and openly before taking on the responsibilities of marriage and parenthood.

But delaying the trip to the altar isn't a rejection of marriage and the commitment it entails. Rather, it's a dream deferred, part of a changing culture, which itself has developed in response to shifting social realities. For the culture of a nation, a group, or a tribe is a living thing, stretching, changing, expanding, or contracting as new needs arise and old ones die, as the exigencies of living in one era give way to new ones in the next. So, for example, now that great advances in medical technology have lengthened the life span beyond anything earlier generations ever dreamed of, the age when people marry moves upward.

When people died at fifty and large families were the norm, there was a good chance at least one parent would never live to see the children into adulthood. Therefore, it made no sense to wait until twenty-five or thirty before starting a family. Now, when, on the average, women live to nearly eighty and men to a little over seventy, we can marry and bear children very much later, safe in the knowledge that we'll be around to raise and nurture them as long as they need us. The forty-year-old first-time father today worries about whether he'll be able to play football with his son at twelve, not whether he'll be alive when the boy becomes a man.

I don't mean that we think consciously about the impact of our longer life. It's the kind of knowledge that generally remains out of awareness but that, nevertheless, profoundly influences our life decisions. For a social change of this magnitude, one that gives us so many more years of life, also adds stages to the life course that were unknown before. Adolescence is extended, adulthood becomes another stage in our continuing growth and development, and old age appears on the scene as a part of life that requires planning and attention — changes and additions that have social, cultural, and psychological repercussions.

The same is true for the culture of marriage. When life ended at fifty, people didn't feel deprived if their relationships weren't intimate or companionable enough. They were too busy earning a living, raising their children, and hoping they'd survive long enough to see them grown. Now, when wives and husbands know they have decades of active life ahead of them after shepherding their children into adulthood, the emotional quality of the marital relationship takes on fresh importance. *What will we talk about after the children are gone?* becomes a crucial question when people expect to live thirty or forty years beyond that marker event. And marriage takes on a different and more complex character as a whole new set of needs comes to the fore.

Although class, race, and ethnicity all affect marriage patterns, only among African-Americans do the marital statistics tell a significantly different story. In 1991 just over 41 percent of Black Americans were married, compared to nearly 62 percent among whites and Hispanics. Thirty-five percent of Blacks have never been married, while for whites the comparable figure is 20 percent. And Black brides and grooms are, on the average, two years older than their white counterparts when they walk down the aisle for the first time.

For as long as I can remember, I've heard these differences explained as an artifact of culture — an explanation that suggests that Blacks value marriage less or that their moral code is less lofty than the one by which other Americans live. It's an easy explanation, one that allows us to look away from unpalatable social realities and their effect on the most personal decisions of our lives. If culture is the culprit, then it's people who need fixing, not society. But, in fact, beneath these cold statistics lies a story of immeasurable human suffering and loneliness.

This is not to say that culture plays no part in the marriage patterns of African-Americans. Their history of slavery and the prejudice and discrimination they have suffered since then undoubtedly have left their mark in the shape of subcultural variations that affect beliefs and attitudes about marriage. Obviously, too, the cultural fallout from past experience can take on a life of its own and linger into the present long after the immediate provocations are gone. But in this case, it's the social and economic realities of life in the Black community today, not the adversity and suffering of the past, that control the difference in marriage rates between Blacks and Americans of other ethnic and racial groups.

The official unemployment rate for adult Black men, for example, is   40 roughly 15 percent, compared with 6.8 percent for white men. And it's common knowledge that more than twice that number never make it to the Labor Department's unemployment statistics. At the same time, Black men in the prime marriageable ages of twenty-five to thirty who are lucky enough to have jobs earn nearly one-third less than whites: $14,333 compared with $20,153. With unemployment so high and underemployment virtually epidemic, it's hard to imagine how either women or men could make serious plans for marriage. A man who can barely support himself isn't likely to look forward to taking on the responsibilities of a wife and children. Nor is a woman apt to see him as a great marriage prospect. Add to these economic realities the fact that roughly one in eighty young black men is a victim of violent death and that half the inmates of our state prisons are Black men, and we have a picture of a community with an acute shortage of marriageable men.

These are the social conditions out of which the marriage patterns of the African-American community have grown. To speak of culture and its effect on the timing and sequencing of the various life stages, including when or if we marry, without knowing the particular life circumstances of a people misses the crucial connection between the emergence of cultural forms and the structure of social life. In the African-American community, eligible women far outnumber marriageable men — the major reason that fewer people are able to make the trip to the altar and also why those who marry do so substantially later than men and women in other ethnic and racial groups.

For a Black woman, then, finding a man with whom to share her life presents a far more daunting challenge than for others of the same class and age — a source of concern to both parents and daughters in the African-American families I met. "I worry that my daughter's never going to find a good man," Regina Peterson, a forty-year-old Black cashier says, shaking her head sadly. "It's not like when I was coming up; there were still some good men around then, like her father. He's a good man; he always took care of his family, even when it was hard. But today, whew, I don't know what these young girls will do. It's a real problem."

Regina's husband, Sherman, echoes her worries and adds angrily. "The young men today, they're nothing but bums. I don't want no daughter of mine taking up with the likes of them."

When I meet Althea, the Petersons' eighteen-year-old daughter, she talks solemnly about the difficulties the dearth of marriageable men raise for Black women, then exclaims hotly: "It's crazy; it makes me so mad. The papers and the TV keep saying about how Black girls are always having babies without being married. But who are we supposed to marry, tell me, huh? It's not like there's some great guys around here, sitting around just waiting for us. Most of the guys around here, they're hanging on the corner talking big talk, but they're never going to amount to anything. When I see those white people on the TV telling us we should get married, I just want to tell them to shut up because they don't know what they're talking about. What Black girl wouldn't want to be married instead of raising her kids alone?"

I wonder, as I listen to her, what this young woman who's headed for the middle class will do when her time comes. So I ask: "What about you? Will you have children alone if you don't find someone to marry?"

She sits quietly for a moment, her chin resting on her closed fist, her brow furrowed in an expression of sober concentration, then says, "I can't say what I'll do. Right now I know I have to get educated if I want to make something of myself. When I finish college and have a good job, then I'll see. I know I want children some day; not now, but someday. And I'd like to be married like my parents; I know it's better for kids that way. But what if I can't find someone to marry? Then I don't know for sure, but I think I probably would have kids on my own. It's better than not having any, isn't it?" she concludes rhetorically.

With the changed economy, the fantasies about marriage that once separated white women from their Black counterparts have faded. Like their Black sisters, few white working-class girls or young women now harbor the illusion that they'll be stay-at-home moms. Since it's harder to convince themselves that they're working just to mark time until real life begins with the man of their dreams, work becomes a more central part of their life plan.

Twenty-year-old Nancy Krementz, a white clerk in a New York insurance company who lives with her family, talks about her expectations: "If I'm going to have to work after I get married anyway, I might as well wait. This way I get to do things I wouldn't be able to if I was married and had kids. This job I've got is okay, but I really want to work myself up a little. I figure if I'm going to have to work, I want to do something more interesting. So I'm taking some night courses on the computer now, and maybe I can get one of the better jobs in the company. I don't know, sometimes I even think maybe I'll go to college. I couldn't do that if I was married, could I?"

The men also have no plans to rush into marriage. "I'm not going to get married for a long time," says Nancy's nineteen-year-old brother, Michael. "It's not like it used to be when my father was growing up. People expected to get married right away out of school. But not now. I'm going to have some fun before I get married, you know, meet a lot of girls, travel around, things like that."

For the men, such dreams aren't new, even if they were rarely fulfilled. But the women's talk about work, about travel, about wanting to live on their own for a while — all options that few young working-class women dared dream of in my earlier study — represents a dramatic shift from the past. "Sure, I want to get married some day, but I'm not ready to settle down — not for a long time yet," says Claire Stansell, a white nineteen-year-old office worker. "There's too many other things I want to do, like traveling and seeing different things. You know," she says, her eyes opening wide, "the first time I was ever on an airplane was last year after I graduated high school and got a job."

The changing marriage patterns have had a profound affect on the lives of working-class families. Among the families I interviewed two decades ago, it was unthinkable for an unmarried daughter to live outside the family home. From father's house to husband's, that was the expectation, the accepted way of life for a young working-class woman then. Even sons generally were expected to live at home until they married, partly because their earnings were important to the family economy but also because it was the way of the world in which they lived. Now, both daughters and sons are eager to leave the parental roof as quickly as they can afford it.

But how does this fit with all the stories we hear about adult children who don't want to leave home these days because it's easier, cheaper, and more comfortable to live with their parents? Once again, class tells. Middle-class adolescents have long expected to leave home at eighteen, when they go off to college. For them, therefore, there may be some novelty in coming back into the family household as adults, essentially able to live their lives as they please.

For the grown children of working-class families, however, it isn't living at home that's new; it's the cultural changes over the last two decades that have made it possible to think about leaving. For them, this has been a liberation — a liberation the failing economy has stripped from them and about which they're unhappy and resentful.

But the culture of class isn't the whole answer. Class culture is, after all, bred in the economics of class. And it's in their different economic situations that particular attitudes about living at home are born, as this chance conversation I had with the twenty-four-year-old son of an upper middle-class white professional family shows so clearly: "I moved back into the old homestead because it's more comfortable than anything I can afford," he explained easily. "My old room's still there; the food and service is great; and it doesn't cost anything. I've got plenty of privacy; nobody pays any attention to my comings and goings. So why not? This way I get to live the life I'm used to, which I can't afford on my own. I can travel when I want and do what I want. Instead of wasting the money I make on the exorbitant rents you have to pay in this city, I put it into living a decent life. I guess it's got its down side, but the up side outweighs it by a lot so far."

He spoke so easily about freedom and privacy that I found myself wondering: *Would this be equally true for the daughters in these families? Would parents be as easy about a daughter's privacy, about her comings and goings, about where she might be spending the night, or with whom she might be sharing her bed?* Although there are no good studies to answer these questions, the significantly smaller proportion of women aged twenty-five to thirty-four who live under the parental roof — 32 percent of single men, 20 percent of women — suggests that far fewer women than men voluntarily make this choice.

This digression aside, my conversation with my young friend was illuminating, since it raised so sharply the difference class makes for young adults who live at home. As Katherine Newman, an anthropologist writing about the declining fortunes of the middle class, puts it, "It is precisely among the more affluent of America's families that the drop in a young person's standard of living is most acutely apparent when they move out on their own. Hence it comes as little surprise to discover that children living in households with annual incomes above $50,000 are more likely to remain at home with their parents than those in households less well heeled."

For the working-class young, living at home is a necessity, not a choice. And necessity rarely makes good bedfellows or housemates. Like the adult children of middle-class families, the young people I met also "get to live the life" they're used to. But it's not a life they covet. For there's not much of an "up side" to outweigh the down in a house that was already too small to permit privacy when they were children, a house whose walls seem even more confining in adulthood. Nor does living at home allow them the freedom to travel or the chance to do what they want — the very things that make living with mom and dad an attractive alternative for the children of the middle class.

In working-class families, where it's a stretch to pay the bills each month, there's no free ride for adult children who live under the parental roof. Instead, a substantial portion of their income goes to paying their way. Socially, too, living at home confines their lives much more closely than if they were out of the house. For unlike the culturally liberal middle-class parents of the young man above, most working-class parents continue to try to keep a tight rein on their children and to insist on a code of moral behavior that more closely matches their own.

In *Worlds of Pain* I argued that the authoritarian child-rearing style so often found in working-class families stems in part from the fact that parents see around them so many young people whose lives are touched by the pain and delinquency that so often accompanies a life of poverty. Therefore, these parents live in fear for their children's future — fear that they'll lose control, that the children will wind up on the streets or, worse yet, in jail.

But the need for the kind of iron control working-class parents so 60 often exhibit has another, more psychological dimension, as well. For only if their children behave properly by their standards, only if they look and act in ways that reflect honor on the family, can these parents begin to relax about their status in the world, can they be assured that they will be distinguished from those below. This is their ticket to respectability — the neat, well-dressed, well-behaved, respectful child; the child who can be worn as a badge, the public certification of the family's social position.

Since neither the internal needs nor the external conditions change when children reach adulthood, working-class parents continue to try to control their adult children's behavior so long as they live under the parental roof. "It's my house; he'll do what I say," is a favorite saying of fathers in these households. Obviously, it doesn't work that way much of the time. But this doesn't keep them from trying — an effort that makes for plenty of intergenerational conflict.

It was no surprise, therefore, that — whether male or female — every one of the working-class young adults I interviewed was itching to find a way out of the parental home. "As soon as I got a job and saved some money, me and my two friends found this apartment," explains Emily Petrousso, a white nineteen-year-old who shares a tiny one-bedroom apartment with two roommates.

"How did your parents feel about your moving out?"

She makes a face, wrinkling her nose, and says with a shrug, "My mom's okay; I think she understands. But my father, he's something else; like, he's living in another century. He still thinks it's terrible that I don't live in his house and get his permission to go out on a date. Both of them worry about the neighborhood I live in; like, they're afraid it's not safe and stuff like that. But it's okay now. It was a big deal at first, but they got used to it. And anyhow they knew they couldn't stop me."

"They knew they couldn't stop me" — a sentence her parents wouldn't have dared to speak at her age and precisely the source of parental concern. "You got no control over kids anymore!" storms Emily's father, George, a second-generation Greek-American. "What the hell's a kid like that doing out there living by herself? We got room here; nobody gets in her way. If my sister would've even *thought* about something like that, my father would've killed her. I'm just glad he's not alive to see what kids do today. It's not right; I tell my wife that all the time. But even she don't listen; she just sticks up for her."   65

His wife, Nicole, whose role in the family has always been to soothe and smooth the relationships between father and children, tells it this way: "He thinks I stick up for Emily; I don't know, maybe I do, but it's only because he gets so crazy sometimes, and I'm afraid if he keeps going at her like that, she'll stop coming around." She pauses, thinks for a moment, then continues with a sigh, "So I keep telling him she's a good girl, but everything's different now. You can't compare what we were like. I mean, I didn't even *think* about the things she talks about doing, like going on some kind of a trip by myself or with a girlfriend. *Who thought about things like that?* I don't know; what do you say to kids today about anything. It's so different now."

"Is it just different, or do you also think it's worse?" I ask Nicole.

She looks surprised at the question, then after a moment leans forward in her chair and lowers her voice as if to confide a guilty secret: "You know, I ask myself that question, but I don't hear anybody else wondering about it like I do. So then I think maybe there's something wrong with me. Everybody's always talking about how bad things are, you know, how the kids do such terrible things, and all that. But sometimes I sit here thinking I don't know if it's so bad; it's such a different world. I mean, some things are worse, sure, but maybe not everything. I mean, was it so good in our days?

"In a way I'm kind of glad she doesn't live here now. This way I don't have to see what she's doing all the time. I know she does things I wouldn't like; she doesn't tell me, but I know. My husband, he knows, too, I guess. It's why he's so angry at her all the time." She sighs, "Me? I worry a lot because I don't know how it'll end." She pauses as she hears her words and laughs. "That's it, you don't know the end of the story, so you worry."

"You don't know the end of the story, so you worry." This is precisely the issue. But it's not just the end of the moral story that's in question, it's the economic future that's also unknown. True, working-class parents have always worried about economic hard times for themselves and their children. But until the recent turmoil in the economy, they could also dream about a better future. It's this new reality that has turned up the emotional register around the cultural changes. At the very moment that the economy has let them down, the moral structure on which they've built their lives has been shaken by a jolting, jarring upheaval that has shifted the ground on which they stand. If the old values are gone, what's to separate them from those below? What's to protect their children from falling into the abyss?

Is it any wonder that these families feel as if they're living on a fault line that threatens to open up and engulf them at any moment? Both economically and culturally they're caught in a whirlwind of change that leaves them feeling helplessly out of control. As they struggle with the shifting cultural norms — with the gap between the ideal statements of the culture in which they came to adulthood and the one into which their children are growing today — nothing seems to make sense anymore. Even those who inveigh most forcefully against the new morality and proclaim most angrily that "people don't know right from wrong anymore" are no longer so sure about what they really believe. Consequently, they respond to my questions about any number of the moral issues that vex them with unequivocal answers about right and wrong — only to retreat into uncertainty and ambivalence in the next sentence. They yearn for a past when, it seems to them, moral absolutes reigned, yet they're confused and uncertain about which of yesterday's moral strictures they want to impose on themselves and their children today.

It isn't that they're unaware that the absolutes didn't govern so absolutely, that what people said and what they did were often at odds. But the unambiguous rules seemed at least to promise a level of stability and a consensus that's missing now, not just in families but in the nation at large. The very clarity they seek eludes them, however, as they're forced by circumstances to make choices in their own families that fly in the face of their stated beliefs.

People who worry about the high divorce rate and insist on the sanctity of the family bond suddenly become less certain when marital misery hits home. Asked whether they would want their own child to stay in an obviously bad marriage — one where a spouse is abusive, an alcoholic, or a drug user, for example — the answer is an emphatic no, a response that's delivered especially forcefully by women who themselves have done so.

Women who say they believe mothers belong at home with their children leave to go to work every day. It's an economic necessity, they explain. But listen to them for a while and they'll soon admit that there's much about being in the world of work that they enjoy—and that they wouldn't give it up easily.

People who shudder at the idea of homosexuality take a deep breath   75
and another look when a son or daughter comes out of the closet. They may weep bitter tears when they hear the news; they may deny the reality of what they've heard; they may rail against God; they may blame themselves. But in most families, acceptance eventually comes. Asked how it's possible, given their earlier fears, feelings, and hostilities, they have many answers. "I see that he's happier now." "Her partner's such a nice person." "I didn't really understand about it before." "It's his choice; what can I do?" But the bottom line is: "This is my child!"

Parents who disapprove strongly of premarital sex also wish their children wouldn't marry as young as they themselves did. But they know, too, that their daughters are unlikely to remain celibate into their twenties. I say "daughters" because, despite the changing norms around female sexuality, a son's sexual activity is taken for granted, a daughter's is still a problem for most working-class parents. Asked to choose between an early marriage for a girl and premarital sex, most parents — especially mothers — opt for sex, consoling themselves with the hope that their daughters will wait until "they're old enough." What this means varies, of course, but the most common response is, "at least until they're eighteen."

People who don't approve of abortion will also tell you that they wouldn't want their sons and daughters to "have to marry." Forced to make a choice between a teenage marriage, an adoption, and an abortion, they agonize; they suffer; they equivocate. But when the last word is in, most come down on the side of abortion.

Tales from the abortion battlefront suggest that this is not uncommon, even among people who are antiabortion activists. During the 1992 presidential election, Vice President Dan Quayle, an ardent and outspoken foe of abortion, was asked what he'd do if his teenage daughter became pregnant. The politician retreated; the father stepped forward. "I hope that I never have to deal with it," he replied. "But obviously I would counsel her and talk to her and support her on whatever decision she made." Incredulous, the interviewer pressed on: "If the decision was abortion you'd support her?" The vice president stood firm: "I'd support my daughter."

A few days later, President Bush, also a staunch opponent of abortion, was asked what he'd do if one of his granddaughters told him she was considering an abortion. He'd try to talk her out of it, he said, but would support her decision. "So in the end the decision would be hers?" the interviewer asked. "Well, who else's — who else's could it be?" said this president, who has spoken out frequently and forcefully against allowing other women to make that choice.

Even more interesting than what these politicians-turned-father-and-grandfather said is what they *didn't* say. Neither ruled out the question as absurd, a product of some wild fantasy, of the fevered imagination of the media in an election year. Neither said: *My teenage daughter sexually active? Impossible! My granddaughter pregnant and unmarried? Never!* Nor did anyone else, not even Marilyn Quayle, who disagreed with her husband and insisted that she'd force her daughter to carry the child to term. 80

This ambivalence, this simultaneous holding of two seemingly contradictory sets of beliefs shouldn't surprise us. Changing cultures mean stormy times. The interaction between new norms and values and the people who must live them out is never tranquil and easy. The old consciousness doesn't go quietly into the night. Instead, it fusses and fumes, drags its feet, goads us with reminders of its existence, and foments an internal struggle that leaves us anxious and bewildered, wondering what we believe, how we feel.

It's not uncommon to find ourselves doing new things, even wanting to do them, while at the same time feeling uneasy about them. Many of the women who were in the forefront of the sexual revolution, for example, were surprised at the internal conflict their new behaviors stirred. Observing this contest between the old and the new, some researchers concluded that the sexual constraints of the past were "natural," that women couldn't or didn't want to shed them. But those pundits misread the data. Partly they misunderstood what they saw because their vision was blurred by their deeply internalized traditional beliefs about the nature of female sexuality. But it was also because they didn't appreciate the messiness inherent in the process of cultural change, didn't understand that the internalization and integration of new cultural mores often lags well behind behavioral changes.

Indeed, the internal resistance to new ways of being generally has nothing to do with whether we can or want to change. Psychologists see this all the time — people who come into psychotherapy wanting to change, yet, when faced with the possibility, they retreat in fear. We call it "resistance," but in fact it's a normal human response. The old ways worked, perhaps imperfectly, perhaps with more pain than was necessary, but we accommodated and survived. Psychologically, therefore, it's hard to give them up even when we know there's a better way.

In our struggle to make sense of our rapidly changing world, to define rules for living that meet today's needs, old values are forced into a confrontation with the new realities of family and social life. The result is the emergence of values that are different — different and not always as firm and clear as we'd like them to be. Therefore, we become edgy and confused, wanting to reach back to the past, to a time when everything seemed more certain. But it's well to remember what historians of the family have been telling us for some time now: The golden age of the family for which we yearn with such intensity never really existed. Instead, families have always been a "haven in a heartless world" and a breeding ground for pain, sorrow, disappointment, and discontent. Everyone who has ever lived in a family knows both sides. But our longing for what seems from this distance to be the simplicity and certainty of earlier times has blinded us to this complex reality of family life.

Yes, there are real problems in the family today, problems as large or larger than any we have ever known. Yes, we live in what one family scholar has called an "embattled paradise." Yes, the changing cultural norms often leave parents and children without a blueprint for caring and responsible social and personal behavior. These are issues that deserve our serious attention and our considered thought. But the transformation of family life will not be reversed with endless discussions about the state of our moral culture. Instead, they serve to turn our attention away from the central problems families face today — problems wrought at least in part by a government and an economy that long ago stopped working for all but the most privileged.

85

PREPARING FOR DISCUSSION

1. Rubin's essay attempts to account for a generational split between working-class parents and their children, which is greater than the split in other classes. What primary reasons does she offer for that split? Why, according to Rubin, does it threaten to grow even larger? Why are middle-class parents better equipped to deal with their children's values no matter how different they may be from their own?

2. Rubin maintains that shame and guilt are important signs that a person has successfully internalized the values of his or her culture. She also notices that what might have caused shame in the mother does not cause shame in the daughter. Why, according to Rubin, are parents and children likely to feel shame and

guilt for different reasons? Does the difference necessarily indicate a disappearance of these feelings in working-class youth?

3. Rubin maintains that "delaying the trip to the altar isn't a rejection of marriage and the commitment it entails" (paragraph 33). Rather, she describes marriage as "a dream deferred" in response to changing cultural and social conditions, including rising life expectancy and higher expectations for the quality of the marital relationship itself. Consider your own opinion about the best age at which to get married. To what extent have the class reasons that Rubin supplies for deferring marriage entered into your considerations? Are there important factors that she excludes? What are they?

4. The author attributes the low marriage rate among black Americans to larger social problems rather than cultural values. Consider the statistics Rubin provides to support this view (paragraph 40). She compares unemployment rates and the average salaries for black and white men. How might these results differ if she focused only on unemployment rates and salaries for *working-class* black and white men? If the differential for working-class blacks and whites were less than that for all black men and all white men, would you be more or less inclined to accept Rubin's social explanation for lower marriage rates among blacks?

5. In paragraphs 4 and 5, Rubin quotes Marguerite Jenkins — "We had to get married" — and then asks what "had to" could mean in this context. She then explains that Marguerite was not coerced into marriage by an angry parent but that the compulsion to marry came from Marguerite's internalizing of the moral culture in which she lived. If Marguerite had used the words "wanted to" or "chose to" or "were destined to" instead of "had to," how might Rubin's interpretation of her words have changed? Are the words "had to" the only words Marguerite could have used to convey her values regarding marriage?

FROM READING TO WRITING

6. Rubin discusses why parents and children are liable to have very different moral and cultural values. Write an essay in which you consider the extent to which your values differ from those of your parents. Choose one particular value that you and your parents do not share and trace the historical and cultural causes for the difference. Do you find Rubin's explanation of the difference valid? What other reasons can you provide for the difference? Is class a factor in these differences?

7. In a few years, most of you will have the choice whether to leave home for good or not. Write an essay in which you reflect upon your upcoming decision to leave or to stay at home. What factors will play a major role in making your decision? To what degree are those factors related to class background?

WILLIAM GREIDER

Class Conflict and Environmental Reform

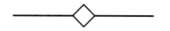

This chapter ends by considering the current role played by class differences in the American political process. In recent years, class tensions have emerged that threaten to block collective political action across class lines. The clash between working-class and middle-class social aims have made cooperation between the two economic groups increasingly difficult. Without such cooperation, however, the majority of Americans will lack the means to combat proposed measures designed to benefit the wealthy minority. In the following selection, William Greider takes a closer look at the class conflicts that divide the environmental movement and prevent it from accomplishing major legislative reform in Washington.

Greider, a former assistant managing editor of the *Washington Post,* has been a journalist since graduating from Princeton in 1956. An important critic of "Reaganomics," the first Reagan administration's plan to lower income taxes while raising defense spending, Greider questioned the decisions of the major economic policymakers of the early 1980s and also predicted the severe recession, runaway deficit, and inequitable distribution of wealth that followed. His most recent book, *Who Will Tell the People?* (1992), from which this selection is excerpted, examines the decay of the American political process.

SELECTED PUBLICATIONS: *Secrets of the Temple: How the Federal Reserve Runs the Country* (1987); *Who Will Tell the People? The Betrayal of American Democracy* (1992); Greider also publishes frequently in *Rolling Stone.*

Citizens remain weak because their inherited ideas of how to do politics allow them to evade the class conflicts within their own ranks. The environmental movement, though its broad values are almost universally shared by the public, is unable to mobilize its potential impact because it cannot resolve its own differences.

The movement is splintered into many different pieces, including different social classes that do not even talk to one another, much less try to work out a common political agenda. On one end are Ivy League lawyers, urbane and well educated and completely comfortable in the inner circles of government. On the other end are the thousands of homegrown neighborhood activists, utterly skeptical of government and engaged in "rude and crude" politics at the factory gates.

A few years ago, Lois Marie Gibbs of the Citizen's Clearinghouse for

Hazardous Wastes tried to build some bridges across this social chasm. She organized a series of roundtable discussions and invited thirty or so community activists from the grassroots to meet with Washington-based lawyers and lobbyists from the so-called Big Ten, the leading national environmental organizations.

"It was hilarious," Gibbs said. "People from the grassroots were at one end of the room, drinking Budweiser and smoking, while the environmentalists were at the other end of the room eating yogurt. We wanted to talk about victim compensation. They wanted to talk about ten parts per billion benzene and scientific uncertainty. A couple of times, it was almost war.

"We were hoping that, by seeing these local folks, the people from the Big Ten would be more apt to support the grassroots position, but it didn't work that way. They went right on with the status quo position. The Big Ten approach is to ask: What can we support to achieve a legislative victory? Our approach is to ask: What is morally correct? We can't support something in order to win if we think it is morally wrong." 5

Most of the citizens drawn into grassroots environmental activism are unusual; they come from the social ranks that are least active politically, people who are poor or who are familiarly described as "working class." On the whole, these "middle Americans," as sociologist Herbert J. Gans called them, are the most disaffected and culturally inclined to practice "political avoidance." They are wary of elections and formal politics and even large civic organizations, cynical about government at all levels. Instead of political activism, Gans noted, they normally concentrate their energies on nurturing and defending their own small, private spaces — family or church or immediate neighborhood.[1]

On the other hand, most of the citizens who lead the major environmental organizations are the offspring of the affluent managerial class, people who feel at ease in the higher realms of politics and skilled at the rationalistic policy analysis. Many are idealistic professionals, committed to large intellectual conceptions of the environmental problem but not personally confronted by the risks of poisonous industrial pollution.

These class distinctions were playfully delineated by *Outside* magazine when it published a consumer's guide to the environmental movement. Citizen's Clearinghouse: "Typical member: quit the church choir to organize toxic dump protest." Natural Resources Defense Council: "Typical member: Andover '63, Yale '67, Harvard Law '70, Pentagon anti-war marches '68, '69, '70." Environmental Defense Fund: "Typical member: lawyer with a green conscience and a red Miata." Conservation Foundation: "As connected as they come and is quite friendly with many less-than-pure corporations like Exxon and Chevron."[2]

The environmental movement is a complicated spectrum of tastes and aspirations, ranging from the aesthetics of bird watchers to the radicalized politics of angry mothers. All share a generalized commitment to the environmental ethic, but have very different conceptions of what that means and how to accomplish their goals. These differences are rooted in their economic classes. An environmentalist who graduated from an Ivy League law school is more likely to believe in the gradual perfectability of the legal system, the need to legislate and litigate.

However, if one lives on the "wrong side of the tracks," downwind   10
from toxic industrial fumes, these activities look pointless and even threatening. The idea of passing more laws seems a futile diversion. There are already plenty of laws. The problem is political power. "It's not illegal to build an incinerator and it's not illegal to poison people," Lois Gibbs said. "Poor people know that they need to organize and fight to win."[3]

The corrosive consequence of this underlying conflict is lost political power — a popular cause that is unable to realize its full strength because it cannot reconcile its own internal differences. "It does hurt us," Gibbs agreed, "because we don't have any people lobbying on the Hill, while the Big Ten lobby could turn out the people — if they were connected to the grassroots. But they don't have the constituency we have. They don't want to dirty their hands, dealing with these people from the grassroots."

Some leaders in the major environmental organizations recognize the same dilemma. Richard Ayres, chairman of the Clean Air Coalition formed by the Big Ten groups, sees Washington-based lobbyists like himself trapped between the grassroots demands for fundamental change and a political system that will not even consider them. The Big Ten works for incremental victories and, when even those are watered down by Washington politics, the grassroots activists become even more disenchanted. Young people sign up for Greenpeace, not the Audubon Society.

"If the central government won't respond to a situation, it drives the moderates out," Ayres said. "People far from Washington are saying we ought to be doing recycling and changes in the production processes that will prevent pollution. But we're caught in the middle, having to say: 'We can't do that. Congress won't touch it.'"

Major organizations in Washington cannot easily align with the fervor of the grassroots environmentalists: This would threaten their own standing within the political establishment. When a GE lobbyist wanted to cut a deal on CFCs in the new clean-air legislation, he phoned a lobbyist from the NRDC to see if his organization would go along with the compromise. That's real power—having a putative veto on insider negotiations — but it is usually quite limited. The Big Ten groups have such influence only so long as they adhere to the constricted terms of the Washington regulatory debate.

"If I represent an industry, I can always get into the argument in the   15
Executive Branch or Congress by nature of the fact that I have money," Curtis Moore, former Republican counsel for the Senate environmental

affairs committee, explained. "But if you're an environmental group, you can't get into the argument unless they want to let you in. And they're not going to let you in if they think you're crazy, if you don't think in the same terms they do. So you have to sound reasonable or you won't even get in the room. And you don't find many people in the major environmental groups who are willing to be seen as unreasonable."

Moore's point is crucial to understanding the compromised performance of citizen politics. The admission ticket to the debate is: "You have to sound reasonable." The broad ranks of citizens whose own views have become "radicalized" by experience, as Lois Gibbs put it, will always sound "unreasonable" to the governing elites. They not only won't get a seat at the table, but may conclude that the Big Ten environmentalists are in collusion too, bargaining settlements with government and business behind closed doors.

Grassroots leaders, for instance, attacked the League of Women Voters for accepting grants from Dow Chemical and Waste Management to finance educational projects on hazardous wastes. The LWV [League of Women Voters] in New England sponsored a series of conferences at which environmentalists and business representatives discussed their differences on key policy issues, but community-based leaders were not invited. "We were told that grassroots people are too ignorant or too hysterical to be able to participate meaningfully," Lois Gibbs complained.[4]

The grassroots suspicion of collusion between big-name environmentalists and industrial polluters is not entirely imaginary. When the CEO of Waste Management wanted to lobby EPA Administrator Reilly in 1989 to block state-enacted restrictions on hazardous wastes, he arranged a breakfast meeting through a mutual friend — the president of the National Wildlife Federation. The industry lobbyists warned Reilly that a "balkanization" was being fostered in many states by the grassroots agitation for tougher restrictions and the federal agency must "make its presence felt." Reilly, himself the former president of the Conservation Foundation, obliged.[5]

Class conflict is, of course, a persistent theme in popular politics throughout American history. Differences of culture and class have always set citizens against one another, separating the people who, in theory, ought to be allies. Racial antagonism remains the most divisive barrier between people, white and black, who have common interests. Differences of region and religion are now much less influential than in earlier eras, but the differences of income and economic perspective are greater now than they were a generation ago. The inability of people to confront and overcome the class biases that divide them is one of the oldest failures of American democracy.

Eras of popular reform usually fail to produce genuine change, political scientist Samuel P. Huntington has argued, because they nearly always embody unnatural marriages of conflicting class interests. "Middle upper strata [of citizens] may have an ideological commitment to political reform, but they also have an economic interest in not permitting reform to alter significantly the existing distribution of income and wealth," Huntington wrote. "The poorer classes, on the other hand, may have an interest in substantial economic change, but they lack the ideological motivation to make that change a reality and, indeed, they are mobilized for political action by appeals to values which guarantee that major economic change will not become a reality."[6]

Citizens from the lower economic ranks seek to preserve the independence of their own community institutions and are skeptical of grand causes that intrude, especially if these seem to be controlled from above. Middle-class reformers, on the other hand, are willing to use governmental power on behalf of good-government reforms, but not in ways that will change power relationships in the economic order. "Upper-class and upper-middle-class hypocrisy combines with lower-class cynicism to perpetuate the status quo," Huntington concluded.

This bleak view wrongly presumes an endless stalemate for democratic possibilities, but it does accurately describe the present reality, both in the environmental movement and in many other public-spirited reform campaigns. Middle-class reformers, whether they are environmentalists or consumer advocates, tend to focus on perfecting the processes of government, not changing the underlying arrangements of power. Grassroots advocates have the advantage of being able to see the underlying power realities more clearly and are therefore willing to confront power directly. But they are handicapped by their own lack of access to the debate — and their "unreasonable" attitudes.

The other great obstacle within the environmental movement has been the inability to reconcile bedrock tensions between its moral claims and economic self-interest. The civil rights movement could finesse this conflict because of the unifying fact of race. The environmental movement has mostly tried to smother it with righteousness. Everyone wants to advance the environmental ethic, of course, but the underlying conflict is about jobs and profit and economic growth versus environmental protection. This is not a question the mainline organizations have wished to face directly, nor have many of the grassroots advocates.

Penny Newman, a community activist who led the fight against the notorious Stringfellow acid pits in Riverside, California, observed: "Too often the only time community-based environmentalists meet the workers is when we are protesting against corporate practices and the workers are bused into public hearings to advance the company's agenda — so that the company can orchestrate the conflict between workers and the community."

In the Los Angeles basin, for instance, enforcement of the increasingly stringent air-pollution standards needed to free that city of its terrible smog will directly threaten scores of furniture-making factories that release highly toxic fumes in the air — and also employ seventy thousand workers, most of them Mexican-Americans. The companies, especially smaller firms that cannot afford new emissions-control systems, threaten to close down and move their production to Mexico. Some of the upper-class environmentalists regard this as an acceptable solution since, after all, many of the furniture workers were themselves migrants from Mexico. Send them all back to Mexico — the jobs and the people.

Again, low-wage workers wind up paying the price for everyone else's well-being. Groups like the Labor/Community Strategy Center in Los Angeles are trying to mobilize an alternative approach that speaks for both the low-income communities and their workers — that represents both their environmental complaints and their economic interests.

"Industry begins the battle with a captive army of workers whose livelihoods are in some way dependent upon the production of toxics and who are predisposed to believe company claims that environmentalists are well-to-do, anti-working-class crybabies," wrote Eric Mann, director of the Los Angeles Strategy Center. "Workers may argue in turn that if life is reduced to a battle between one self-interested force (the environmentalists) attempting to take their jobs versus another self-interested force (corporate management) attempting to 'save' their jobs, then they have no other self-interested option but to side with corporate power."[7]

Community organizers in many places are trying to break out of this self-defeating conflict by synthesizing the community's overall concerns — the right to protection from industrial poisons and the requirements for promoting stable economic prosperity. This approach entails a much more complicated politics, of course, but it has the virtue of facing the buried conflicts more honestly.

An environmental politics grounded in the perspectives of communities would undoubtedly lead to different kinds of public policies — transitional assistance to threatened workers or small businesses, for instance, or government-sponsored centers for treating hazardous wastes in a serious manner. It would encourage people to ask the larger strategic questions about the production processes themselves. It would assume from the start, as grassroots activists say, that the poisonous stuff should not be dumped in anybody's backyard.

If any of the major environmental groups were to realign their own politics with these positive energies emanating from the grassroots, they would necessarily have to rethink their own policy priorities and methods — and listen respectfully to what these people from the communities are trying to say. Inevitably, this would put at risk the environmentalists' good standing as "reasonable" participants in Washington politics. But they would also discover a source of new political strength — the power that comes from real people.

Notes

1. The contours of "political avoidance" are described by Herbert J. Gans, *Middle American Individualism,* The Free Press, 1988.
2. *Outside* magazine, September 1990. The magazine's lowest regard — "Milquetoast" — was for the National Wildlife Federation and the Nature Conservancy.
3. Lois Gibbs's remark on poor people is from Ana Radelat, "Avenging Angel," *Public Citizen,* September 1990.
4. The community leaders were invited to subsequent conferences at the behest of Tufts University, a cosponsor, according to a letter from Lois Gibbs to Nancy Newman, league president, October 21, 1986.
5. Grassroots activists dubbed the private meeting between Reilly, Waste Management's Dean Buntrock and Jay Hair, president of the Wildlife Federation, "Reillygate." Details are from the EPA investigative record into charges that Reilly's meeting was in violation of agency rules. The administrator was cleared and the controversy never achieved visibility in the national press but was covered aggressively by some local newspapers where citizen groups are aroused on toxic-waste issues. See the *Winston-Salem Journal,* April 21, 1989.
6. Samuel P. Huntington was among the academics who originally expressed alarm at the upsurge of citizen politics, fearing that reformers were immobilizing government. In the 1970s, he described these challenges as "an excess of democracy" but moderated his views subsequently when it became clear that neither government nor business interests were in danger of losing their power. Samuel P. Huntington, *American Politics: The Promise of Disharmony,* Harvard University Press, 1981.
7. My account of class conflicts in the environmental movement has been enriched by Eric Mann, "Environmentalism in the Corporate Climate," and Robert Gottlieb, "Earth Day Revisited," both in *Tikkun,* March 1990. Penny Newman was quoted in Mann's essay.

PREPARING FOR DISCUSSION

1. Throughout the selection, Greider argues that citizens from different social and economic backgrounds can rarely work together for the same cause. What reason does he offer for this lack of cooperation? How are these differences reflected in the relative success or failure of the cause?

2. Though Greider initially seems to take a neutral position with regard to the different socioeconomic groups working within the environmental movement, he gradually shifts his political sympathies to one of these groups. With which group does he eventually side? Where in the selection can you find evidence for his preference? On what grounds does he side with one group over the other?

3. Greider assumes that the "grassroots" movement he describes and the environmentalist lobby in Washington are working for the same cause. Yet he also notes that the grassroots position is often more interested in obtaining compensation for victims of environmental pollution than in passing new "clean-air" legislation. Is Greider wrong in assuming that the two groups are working for the same cause? In what kinds of issues is each group generally interested? How much do these sets of issues overlap?

4. In paragraph 23, Greider establishes an opposition between economic

growth and environmental protection. This opposition is often exploited by conservative politicians who warn voters that a vote for stricter environmental measures might deprive them of their jobs in the future. Do you believe this opposition exists with respect to most environmental issues? For example, does the protection of an endangered species always result in the reduction of industrial productivity?

5. In paragraph 16, Greider observes that "the admission ticket to the [environmental] debate is: 'You have to sound reasonable.'" What does Greider mean by "reasonable" in this context? To what degree does a person's ability to "sound reasonable" mean that the same person is making a "reasonable" argument? Does Greider suggest that working-class environmentalists merely need to change the way they "sound," rather than their positions?

FROM READING TO WRITING

6. Greider describes two sets of class values at odds within the environmental movement. With which set of values do you tend to identify more? Write an essay in which you explain your position with reference to your own social and economic background. If you agree more with the values of the group whose class differs from your own, what reasons can you offer for your crossing class lines?

7. While this selection focuses primarily on the environmental movement, the class conflict described by its author occurs within other social movements. Write an essay in which you describe class conflict and the cause of it in another major movement. What are the values and goals of each group in the movement? To what extent are these antithetical to one another?

4

The Gender Debate
ROLES · RIGHTS · REACTION

ALTHOUGH GENDER DEBATES HAVE INTENSIFIED in recent years, the connection between gender and politics is hardly new. Back in the 1930s the prominent British writer Rebecca West would claim in her monumental book on Yugoslavia that "idiocy is the female defect," whereas the male defect is "lunacy." Playing on the Greek and Latin roots of those terms, she maintained that women are too "intent on their private lives" (*idiocy* comes from the Greek root meaning "private person"), while men are "so obsessed by public affairs that they see the world as by moonlight" (*lunacy* derives from the Latin term for moon). In such ways were gender differences politically polarized even prior to World War II and the contemporary women's movement.

Today we are so accustomed to hearing that men and women perceive the world in different ways that the topic has become a staple of television talk shows and newspaper columns. More important, it has become a central issue of feminist politics, as the award-winning poet and cultural critic Katha Pollitt points out in "Feminism at the Crossroads." Pollitt examines the two dominant types of feminism attracting adherents today: "difference feminism," which concentrates on women's special status based on their differences from men, and "equality feminism," which concentrates on the ways men and women are alike.

Difference feminism or equality feminism? This debate so often comes down to another, perhaps more fundamental question: Are gender differences biologically innate or socially conditioned? In "Gender," the well-known social theorist and policy expert James Q. Wilson examines this perenially daunting issue by reviewing new research that he believes strongly tips the balance toward the side of innate differences.

West, perhaps wisely, did not speculate on whether women's preoccupation with private life and men's obsession with public affairs is a result of innate or social factors. Yet her observation of over a half-century ago bears directly on two recent essays that examine the relationship of gender and language. Why do male voices dominate cultural and political opinion, wonders feminist social critic Naomi Wolf in "Are Opinions Male?" Is it because men are less afraid to express themselves publicly? Then Deborah Tannen, a linguistics professor and best-selling author, offers evidence that presumably supports West's observation. In "Put Down that Paper and Talk to Me!," Tannen explores the reasons behind a common gender stereotype: the wife who tries to talk to a husband who is hiding behind a newspaper.

In this instance, the powerful newspaper image may also suggest that the media in general are more attuned to male interests than female. In "Blame It on Feminism," the Pulitzer Prize–winning journalist Susan Faludi explores this possibility, arguing that the media have so inflated the limited successes of the women's movement that it in turn has stimulated an angry backlash of antifeminism. Contemporary feminism is also challenged by a reluctance of many women to identify themselves as feminists even when they politically support feminist goals. In "Feminism's Identity Crisis," the lawyer and public policy expert Wendy Kaminer analyzes the internal conflicts within the women's movement and suggests that these cannot simply be explained by a backlash caused by media misrepresentations.

KATHA POLLITT

Feminism at the Crossroads

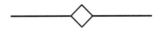

The relatively new field of gender studies has brought about an unprecedented reexamination of differences between the sexes. Most people
would acknowledge that genuine physical differences, hormonal and
anatomical, exist between men and women. Yet until quite recently, very
little time and effort were devoted to understanding how such physiological factors affect our social roles, or, alternatively, whether biology plays
any part at all in shaping our social identities as women or men. Growing
interest in such questions is a direct result of the women's movement that
began in the 1960s and has occupied a major place on the stage of American politics and society ever since. Accordingly, this chapter begins with
poet and cultural critic Katha Pollitt's reflections on the two major currents of ideas about gender and their consequences for the future of the
feminist movement in America.

Pollitt has written on many aspects of gender and feminism, including date rape, surrogate motherhood, fetal rights, the Anita Hill controversy, and breast implants. "The only child of two progressives," she
was highly active in the antiwar movement of the late 1960s as an undergraduate at Radcliffe. After receiving an MFA in writing from Columbia, she began to publish the poems that would culminate in
Antarctic Traveler, winner of the National Book Critics Circle poetry
prize in 1982. This selection originally appeared in *Dissent* in 1994 and
was adapted from a talk Pollitt had given in 1993.

SELECTED PUBLICATIONS: *Reasonable Creatures: Essays on Women and
Feminism* (1994); Pollitt also publishes frequently in the *Nation* and
Mother Jones.

Feminism, like Broadway, the novel, and God, has been declared dead
many times. Indeed, unlike those other items, it has been declared dead
almost since its birth — by which I mean its modern rebirth in the 1960s.
Feminism has also, as Susan Faludi demonstrated so cleverly in *Backlash,*
been blamed for making women miserable, for causing everything from
infertility — see? you waited too long to get pregnant because you were
hell-bent on a fancy career and didn't settle for that nice boy next door
twenty years ago, and now look — to poverty and divorce, which in this
version of life is always initiated by men. And if that line doesn't work,
there are always children, as in: feminism is all right for *women,* but what
about the kids, foisted off on day-care centers run by child molesters and

239

deprived of paternal authority by divorce, which in this version of life is always initiated by women.

So it's with great pleasure and some relief that I observe that we are not gathered here tonight to debate whether feminism is actively bad or just irrelevant, but to discuss its future direction. "Feminism at the Crossroads" — that sounds dramatic, doesn't it, full of promise, or is it threat? — of challenge at any rate, opportunities to be seized or missed, of signposts that if rightly read will send women onto the broad main highway of civic life and personal happiness but if misread or wrongly chosen will send them down some ill-lit alley, or even up the proverbial garden path. I will quarrel a bit with that metaphor later, but first I'd like to observe that a crossroads is a much more exciting place to be than a graveyard, so clearly we are making progress!

What are the street signs on the feminist crossroads? Women today are enjoying a lively debate on a number of issues, although perhaps "enjoying" is not the *mot juste* here, given how acrimonious these debates can become. There's a debate around sexuality issues, which tends to be played out over pornography. And there's a debate about gender roles in marriage, which is expressed around issues of, say, the "mommy track" at work, whereby women would trade professional advancement for a schedule that would make it easier for them to fulfill a modified version of traditional domestic roles at home: you'll notice that nobody calls it the "parent track." There's a debate about work itself: should women enter the male-dominated professions on terms already laid down, or change them? Or fight for the upward valuation of the traditional female jobs? Grade-school teacher or college professor? Nurse or doctor? Fight for the right of women soldiers to enter combat, or fight the military itself?

What all these debates have in common is that they tend to divide into two broad camps: In one fall those who would shore up and protect some notion of women as different from men — whether by nature, nurture, or more or less immutable social function — who, because of that difference, need special protections in order not to be disadvantaged by a male-dominant social order. And in the other, we find those who see gender as a more fluid social construction, with the sexes sharing a broad range of traits and ways of life, and who see their feminist task as opening every social possibility/opportunity to women. To oversimplify greatly, one can pose the question as, which do women need, more freedom or more protection? More respect for individual variations among women or more respect for traditional feminine traits and roles?

But if one street sign reads freedom and another protection, we can see that there are problems with our crossroads metaphor. In the first place, if standing at the crossroads means having to choose a direction, it will immediately become apparent that American feminism has been divided over which path to take for over a century. Although I'm sure

Andrea Dworkin would take issue with me here, I see important continuities between the antipornography movement and, say, the Women's Christian Temperance Union (WCTU): both use powerful Puritan energies already present in American society in order to mount a challenge to male domestic irresponsibility and violence: men will be tamed by being deprived of their evil pleasures (rather than: women will be empowered by confronting inequality head-on); both mistake a symbol for a cause; both share a certain sense of women as pure and nonsexual and better than men: Frances Willard, the head of the WCTU, even espoused the ideal of marriage without sex entirely. And today's pro-sex feminists can trace their lineage back to Frances Wright, Victoria Woodhull, the Utopian feminists of the Oneida community, and other early nineteenth-century social experiments. Similarly, the debate over whether women need more protection or more equality at work has a long history, with surprising people lining up on both sides of the issue: Eleanor Roosevelt, for example, opposed the Equal Rights Amendment because she believed it would expose women to increased exploitation in the workplace, and supported so-called protective legislation that limited the hours of working women.

A second problem with our crossroads metaphor is that it assumes that, along the special/equal or protection/freedom divide women will line up on one side or the other. As Ann Snitow suggested in "Pages from a Gender Diary" (*Dissent*, Spring 1989) this is a misleading picture, which better fits hardened crusaders of the movement than it does most women. It may be true that at some deep philosophical level there is a contradiction between wanting more sexual freedom and wanting less pornography, or wanting to see women's experience reflected across the academic board and wanting independent women's studies departments, or wanting to break down the gender-segregated workforce and wanting comparable worth for the historically underpaid jobs in which women predominate. But at the practical level of lived daily life, one finds surprisingly few women who feel compelled to take a hard and consistent line. In her interesting book, *Feminism without Illusions*, Elizabeth Fox-Genovese argues that there is a contradiction between the individualism at the heart of the modern American women's movement and the demands it also makes, or ought to make, for more collective responsibility for the disadvantaged. But many women, including myself, don't see it as an either/or situation. Last year, to give an example from my own work, I wrote an article attacking the wing of feminism I called "difference feminism," that is, the notion that women are more or less immutably different from men in ways that have important moral consequences. For example, that women are kinder, gentler, more harmonious, and less competitive than men. I argued that the different social styles of the two sexes are more apparent than real and do not, in any case, translate into moral and political differences in the public realm, and that it was a great mistake to base claims to political power on, for example, the supposed superior altruism and honesty of female politicians. I still think I was right, despite the suspicious fact that of all the essays I've written for the *Nation*, this was the one that got the most favorable comment from men. But the fact is, many women have no trouble at all believing simultaneously that women are morally superior to men and that they are also equal to men. In the same way, women can both admire Hillary Rodham Clinton because she is a smart, powerful working mother, and live with the unfortunate fact that her current political position was achieved through marriage.

A very good example of how close the two different strains of feminism can be is the response to Anita Hill. Now there's certainly a way to read Hill's charges that fits in with protectionist, women-are-better feminism: as many pointed out at the time of the Thomas hearings, not every woman would be disgusted, bowled over, and physically upset by off-color remarks of the sort she claimed Thomas made to her — plenty of women, indeed, have been known to make such remarks themselves. Her ten-year silence also fits a certain vision of women as unable to defend themselves, thus needing lots of extra help from the law and the state. But the political effect of Hill's testimony could not have been more activist: women, the lesson was, must win political power in order for their concerns to be addressed.

It should not, perhaps, surprise us that in daily life, and in the political realm as well, feminists, and many women who resist the label too, should find themselves traveling all roads at once rather than marching firmly down one path or the other. This reflects women's real condition: most women work *and* have children; are married *and* know that marriage these days may well not be for life. Women who have abortions also have babies; women who resent men's interest in pornography *also* have forced Harlequin romances to include semi-explicit sex scenes. They want to have sexual adventures *and* not to be raped or abused. To be both women *and* human beings. It's not so surprising, then, that we find women who consider themselves to be feminists shifting back and forth between these two camps. And historically, indeed, both have achieved some success.

On the whole, however, I would say that feminism's best hope lies with equality, because although equality has the defect of sometimes seeming rather counter-intuitive — why legally treat pregnancy like an illness when we all know very well it *isn't* an illness — it has the great advantage of being open-ended. Protectionist or difference feminism says, in effect: this is what women are like, this is the kind of life they lead, so let's shape social policy and the law to acknowledge and reflect it. For example, the "mommy track" says, look, we all know women do most of the child care and most of the housework, so let's make it easier for them to get through the double day of paid employment and domestic responsibilities. In the short run, this might even genuinely help women — but it also assumes that gender roles in the family aren't going to change, even though they are rapidly doing so, even as we speak, and throws its weight behind keeping those roles the same. Protectionist policies of the past have a way of outdating themselves. When the Soviet Union, in its early days, instituted a policy whereby women could take off from work while they had their menstrual periods, that probably seemed the height of compassion, common sense, and enlightened social policy. But what it really did was ensure that women would do all the domestic labor — after all, they had those days off, free for the asking — and enshrine in law ideas about menstruation that seem fairly fantastic today.

If I had to predict which road feminism will take, I would have to say   10
that the material conditions for protectionist or "difference" feminism seem to be steadily eroding. Fewer and fewer women can afford to make stay-at-home motherhood the basis for a full identity; you will notice that stay-at-home childless wifehood, once also a common lifestyle, is no longer even discussed as a rational choice. Families are small and not very stable; that seems likely to remain the case, even if the family-values crowd succeeds in making abortion harder to achieve or divorce more difficult to obtain. In the workplace, gender barriers are slowly breaking down: that women are naturally more caring than men may suit the self-image of nurses and social workers, but doesn't really do much for, say, bartenders and marines. Little by little, the genders are converging: they are educated more alike and raised more alike than ever before, and out of economic necessity as much as anything else, their roles within marriage are converging too. Consider the recent census report that 20 percent of fathers care for children while their wives are working.

The idea that men and women are radically different species of being, which not so long ago struck so many as an indisputable fact of nature, is more and more coming to be revealed as a historical construct, connected to the rise of the bourgeois industrial household, a social form whose end we are living through. In that sense, then, protectionist or difference feminism is at bottom a nostalgic project, which I think today appeals to women at least partly because it seems to protect them against new and uncertain social forms and understandings — the sexually predatory behavior, for example, of many male college students, which in previous situations was directed toward women of inferior social class rather than those of their own. The truth is, though, that it can't protect them, it can only make them feel better for a little while, like praying in a foxhole.

So perhaps the real way feminism will resolve its indecisiveness at the crossroads is that it will continue to debate and hesitate and try both roads at once until one day it sees that in fact the crossroads has disappeared. And then, of course, being feminists, we'll all congratulate ourselves over how right we were to choose what was, in fact, the only possible path — equality, which will at that point be understood to mean not women being the same as men, but both sexes sharing a more or less common life.

PREPARING FOR DISCUSSION

1. Pollitt identifies two main currents of thought about gender. What are they? With which of these two currents does she associate the war on pornography being led by such feminist thinkers as Andrea Dworkin (see p. 390) and Catharine A. MacKinnon? With which of the two currents does Pollitt identify?

2. In paragraph 9, Pollitt points to the "open-endedness" of "equality" feminism as one of its advantages. Why is this an advantage? Does Pollitt make a successful distinction between "equality" and "sameness" either directly or indirectly anywhere in the selection?

3. In paragraph 6, Pollitt connects women's special status and protection with their equal status and freedom. Why does she align her categories this way? Can you think of instances in which protection is a necessary condition of freedom, rather than its opposite?

4. While she acknowledges that the crossroads metaphor of her title has many disadvantages, Pollitt nevertheless refuses to abandon it. What are the problems with the metaphor and how does she attempt to resolve them? Does she resolve these problems successfully or does the metaphor break down?

5. In paragraph 10, Pollitt mentions "the family-values crowd" as working hard to make abortion less accessible and divorce less easily obtainable. Why does Pollitt use this phrase to describe this group? Would she also use the phrase "the pro-choice crowd" or "the feminist crowd"? Why or why not?

FROM READING TO WRITING

6. Consider your own views regarding "difference" and "equality" feminism as Pollitt describes them. Which of the two sets of ideas about women in relation to men do you tend to identify with the most? Write an essay in which you set forth the reasons for your identification with one of the two views. What personal experiences or observations have led you to accept one view over the other?

7. Though Pollitt believes that the future of feminism lies with the movement for greater equality, she acknowledges that women are likely to remain the victims of violent behavior by men. Write an essay in which you consider whether greater equality will result in more or less violence against women. Does greater equality tend to place women in more potentially menacing situations? Or does it ensure greater interaction and understanding between men and women so that violence is less likely to occur?

JAMES Q. WILSON

Gender

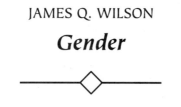

Katha Pollitt's arguments for "equality" feminism in the last selection assume that innate differences between men and women are either unimportant or virtually nonexistent. On the basis of this assumption, we would expect to find that male and female children raised in exactly the same fashion would express similar social traits upon reaching adolescence and adulthood. Several recent studies, however, suggest that important innate differences do exist between women and men. In the following selection, neoconservative scholar James Q. Wilson cites a number of these studies and attempts to explain gender difference by pointing to a corresponding difference in innate sociability between male and female children.

After receiving his doctorate at the University of Chicago, Wilson taught at Harvard for many years before becoming James Collins Professor of Management at UCLA. He established his reputation as a leading social theorist on urban problems through a series of major studies on the social and biological factors behind criminal behavior. While Wilson generally stresses the role of the family in reinforcing behaviors that can predispose a person toward crime, he also believes that genetic factors are at work in shaping the criminal mind. In addition to having acted as a consultant to the Drug Enforcement Agency, he has also served as a member of the U.S. Attorney General's Task Force on Violent Crime. Wilson's 1993 book, *The Moral Sense,* from which this selection is taken, was named a *New York Times* Notable Book of the Year.

SELECTED PUBLICATIONS: *Thinking about Crime* (1975); *Crime and Human Nature* (with Richard J. Herrnstein) (1985); *Bureaucracy: What Government Agencies Do and Why They Do It* (1989); *The Moral Sense* (1993).

Nature has played a cruel trick on humankind. It has made males essential for reproduction but next to useless for nurturance. Yet if the child is to do more than survive — if it is to grow up in an orderly and safe environment and be part of an elaborate and useful culture — it must be part of a community. For such a complex social organization to develop, men must be induced to provide resources and act cooperatively, if for no other reason than to prevent their quarrelsomeness from leading to a war of all against all. Living in a community requires of them sympathy, prudence, and above all, commitment.

245

Unfortunately, when men are born they are on average much less amenable to socialization than women. Compared to their sisters, men are born neurologically less advanced: they are four to six weeks less well developed and thus, correspondingly, more in need of care.[1] They are more likely to be hyperactive, autistic, color-blind, left-handed, and prone to learning disorders.[2] If they are born prematurely with a very low birth weight, boys will suffer more harm and display more conduct problems than premature girls.[3] Boys can't even sing as well; males are less likely to sing in tune than females.[4] If the mother used alcohol or drugs, a male infant is more likely to be adversely affected than a female one.[5] If raised in a discordant or broken family, boys suffer more adverse consequences than do girls.[6]

Men are more aggressive than women. Though child-rearing practices may intensify or moderate this difference, the difference will persist and almost surely rests on biological factors. In every known society, men are more likely than women to play roughly, drive recklessly, fight physically, and assault ruthlessly, and these differences appear early in life.[7] Some people with a romanticized notion of primitive cultures imagine that before men were corrupted by civilization they lived in harmony with one another, but this was scarcely the case. One review of the archaeological evidence suggests that in the state of nature, about one-quarter of all the human males died in fights, a rate of violent death that is about the same as the anthropologist Napoleon Chagnon found to be true among Yąnomamö men now living in the Amazon basin.[8]

The neurochemical basis of the greater aggressiveness of human males is not well understood, but a growing body of evidence implicates hormones (such as testosterone), enzymes (such as monoamine oxidase), and neurotransmitters (such as serotonin).* As they grow up, men are much more likely than women to cause trouble in school, to be alcoholics or drug addicts, and to commit crimes.[9] Though some aspects of the human personality change as people grow up, aggression in males is least likely to change, at least through adolescence.[10]

It is not hard to explain why women care for their infants; without   5 the female breast the child would perish. If there ever existed women who lacked the inclination to nourish their offspring, those offspring would have died. To the extent that that inclination is genetic, nature would have selected for women who cared for their children. But men

*Males, especially younger ones, have significantly higher levels of testosterone and lower levels of platelet monoamine oxidase than do women or older males, conditions that are heritable and associated with higher levels of impulsivity and aggressiveness (Eysenck, 1990; Bridge et al., 1985; Olweus et al., 1988). Some accidents of nature such as the fetal androgenization of female infants and pseudohermaphroditism among male infants, provide data showing that biological endowment is at least as important as child rearing in explaining gender differences in many forms of behavior, including aggression (Imperato-McGinley et al., 1979; Earhardt and Baker, 1974). [Wilson's note]

have been less important for the survival of the child. Though it would have been helpful had they gathered food while the mothers nursed, females living where fruits, nuts, and vegetables were naturally available could often collect enough food to meet at least their minimal requirements. Among many primates this continues to be the case. That men are not essential for infant care under all circumstances is suggested by the fact that today, and possibly for many millennia, men are less likely than women to invest in child care, and despite that reluctance the human race has survived.

No woman needs to be reminded of the fact that men are less likely than women to get up when the baby cries, feed it, or fret over its moods and needs. Infidelity is more common among men than women.[11] (Men also have more premarital sexual intercourse and with a greater variety of partners than do women.)[12] Single-parent households, a large, growing, and worrisome feature of modern life, are, in the vast majority of cases, female-headed households. In this regard the human male is very much like most other male primates. Among most mammals, the male contributes little to offspring development beyond his sperm and, in some cases, defense against rivals and predators. Since human infants require a long period of care after birth, a central problem for women living anywhere but in the most nurturant environments is to find ways of inducing the male to supply the resources necessary to make this care possible.

Because resources are scarce, it is to the mother's advantage if the father will supply her and her alone. In this regard mankind does not manage to do as well as many species of birds. Monogamous pair bonding is common to quail and uncommon to mankind. Among human societies monogamy is the rule in only a minority of cases (roughly 17 percent); polygyny — that is, one husband taking more than one wife — is far more common.[13] And even in monogamous societies, infidelity is widespread. By contrast, polyandry — that is, a wife taking more than one husband — is vanishingly rare. (Of course, even in polygynous societies, most men will invest in child care to some degree.) The high rates of divorce and separation with which we are all too familiar provide ample evidence that humans have not yet figured out how to solve a problem that quail and wolves have solved without reading a single book.

It seems clear that Mother Nature would much prefer to produce only girls, because she does such a poor job of producing boys. Her preferences are quite clear in this regard: all fetuses begin as females; only in the third month of gestation does masculinization begin. And when it does begin, it sometimes is a process prone to error, leading to all manner of deficiencies and abnormalities. Not only do men have a shorter life expectancy than women, a fact that might be explained by their more violent tendencies, but the higher mortality rate appears almost from the beginning: male fetuses are more likely than female ones to die in utero, and male infants have a higher death rate than female infants.* Having invented the male, Mother Nature doesn't quite know what to do with him. It is as if she had suddenly realized, too late, what every student of biology now knows: asexual reproduction is far more efficient than sexual reproduction. But now we are stuck with men who are likely to be both troublesome and vulnerable.

At one time the traits that we judge to be troublesome may have been useful and those that we take to be vulnerabilities may have been irrelevancies. When prehistoric man hunted for wild animals, aggressiveness and even hyperactivity were adaptive. Even after he had settled into sedentary communities, aggression and physical activity were useful if, as was often the case, his communities were threatened by enemies. That he might be color-blind, have a speech defect, or be dyslexic was of little importance. Evolution has selected for traits in males that have aided them in hunting and in competition with other males for access to females, but at the price of reduced longevity.[14]

Even though evolution has equipped men with traits that make them   10
good hunters but not necessarily good fathers, most men who father children will aid in their care. In this respect, the human male is more like a bird, wolf, or butterfly than he is like many other primates.[15] Most male baboons do not invest much in caring for their offspring; male humans invest substantially. As a consequence, family life among humans is not only possible but even commonplace.

Why? Why should a man, who can in a few moments conceive a fetus that will grow in the mother's belly and be dependent on the mother for food for many months after its birth, stick around to care for it? And why should he even forsake other women, along with the sexual opportunities they can offer, to cling to the mother alone? If the principle of evolution is reproductive fitness — that is, selection for creatures that maximize the number of genes they reproduce in the next generation — then evolution ought to select for the genes of those males who produce the largest number of offspring. That would mean selecting for the most promiscuous males, and under those circumstances, family life would be next to impossible.

Sexual Selection

The chief answer to this puzzle is female choice. Females who nurture their young for extended periods will, on the average, prefer to mate with males who are likely to aid in that nurture for a long period of time.

---

*McMillen, 1979; Trivers, 1985:306. The higher death rate of males is probably a consequence, at every age, of the presence of the male sex hormone. Castrated male cats live much longer than intact ones, and not simply because they fight less (Hamilton, Hamilton, and Mestler, 1985). Among humans, eunuchs outlive intact males (Hamilton and Mestler, 1969). [Wilson's note]

In species that do not require extended infant care, the female will pair with the male that makes the most impressive display of size, strength, plumage, coloration, or territorial defense.* In these cases the female is selecting mates whose vigor creates the best prospects for the survival of offspring even when the female alone must provide the care after birth. Selection for these traits, however, does not make possible an elaborate social life. But in other species, and notably among humans, females will select mates that seem not only vigorous but inclined to make long-term investments in child care.

Just why the human female, unlike many primate females, should have begun to select for dependability is unclear. But having done so, males biologically disposed to share in nurturance began to have a reproductive advantage.† The result of female choice is evident in what we observe in males today. Despite the difficulty in socializing young ones, adult males usually respond warmly to infants. Many if not most men find fathering, and not just inseminating, to be a rewarding activity; they respond instinctively and with compassion to the sight, sounds, and touch of their offspring.[16]

Though as a group men invest far more heavily in child care than do, for example, male rhesus monkeys, individual men vary greatly in this disposition. As a result, the choice of mate made by (or for) women will be based on a careful evaluation of the suitability of various men. When the choice is left to the women, it typically occurs after a long period of courtship in which men are tested in various ways for loyalty and affection; sometimes sexual favors are granted or withheld on the basis of evidence that the man will be a good father — that is, will be dependable, caring, and monogamous. When the choice is made by the bride's family, much the same evaluation occurs, though with less emphasis on affection and more on reputation, wealth, status, and other signs of both having a

---

*The female choice model has been suggested by Mark Ridley (1978) as an explanation for paternal care among various animal species, but he was frank to admit that there was not much evidence for it among the lower life forms. More recently Robert Trivers has supplied some additional evidence, as among female African weaverbirds who, before bonding, inspect the elaborate nests built by males, rejecting those who build poorly and selecting those who build well (Trivers, 1985:249–56; 1972:171–72). [Wilson's note]

†I am aware that some forms of male investment in child care may result, not from females having selected nurturant males, but from males wishing to maximize the number and fecundity of their offspring. In the latter case, the male is managing a tradeoff between impregnating as many females as possible and helping ensure the survival of the results of those impregnations. Time devoted to survival is time taken away from impregnation. For many nonhuman males, and possibly for some human ones, there is an optimal strategy that produces the maximum number of surviving offspring. I am indebted to Robert Boyd for pointing this out to me. In my view, the kind of human male investment that we now see, and have seen through most of recorded history, reflects a disposition to nurture one's kind, however small the number, and not to maximize the total number of offspring. [Wilson's note]

capacity for support and being embedded in a network of social obligations that will guarantee support (but perhaps not fidelity).

Courtship is a way of testing commitment. If the woman is sexually easy, the value of the test will be lessened, as the man will have less of an incentive to produce evidence of commitment in order to acquire sexual access. If the man is deceitful, he may be able to fool a woman into thinking that commitment is assured when in fact it is not. Since individuals differ in these respects, the process is imperfect. Its imperfection has supplied the themes of thousands of years of songs, plays, and stories that give expression to the continuing differences between the sexes.

The songs and stories portray women who want commitment coping with men who want action. In modern times the signal of commitment is romantic love: if the man is sensitive to the woman's feelings and caring of her needs and responses, his expression of those feelings is taken to be a sign of an enduring emotional investment. But romance can be feigned or be a short-lived prelude to sex. Love is the currency; women hope it is an asset that will be invested, but men may treat it merely as the price of consumption. Female choice — in Darwin's terms, sexual selection — has shaped the evolutionary development of men, but without making men like women. As a result, one would expect the moral development of men and women to differ.

Gender and Culture

Some of that difference will be shaped by the way in which a society's culture and economic system makes certain traits more adaptive than others. Mary Maxwell West and Melvin J. Konner illustrate this by sketching the differences in styles of fathering in five nonindustrial cultures.[17] Hunter-gatherers, such as the !Kung San bushmen of Africa, and fishermen, such as the Lesu of Melanesia, can feed themselves without constant labor and do not depend on possessing capital stocks (such as cattle) that must be defended against rival tribes. Women supply some of the food by their own foraging or gardening. Neither finding food supplies nor protecting land or cattle are full-time preoccupations, freeing men to spend time with their families. Family life in these places tends to be monogamous, and the men are deeply involved in child care. They often hold and fondle their children, who are indulged by both parents.

By contrast, the Bedouins of the Arabian desert raise cattle, and the Thonga in South Africa practice both farming and herding. They have both cattle and land to protect, as well as the cash income that those stocks generate. Fighting is commonplace, both within the group and among rival groups. In this warrior culture, fierceness and bravery are highly valued, leading to a strong emphasis on male authority and heavy discipline. Men remain aloof from their children and often mistreat their wives. Subsistence living based on scarce capital assets, it would appear, reduces male involvement in child care and rewards male aggressiveness.*

This explanation of the warrior culture also appears in Robert Edgerton's comparison of four East African tribes, the members of which were divided between areas where the economy rested on either farming or herding. Both groups had capital stocks to protect, but the pastoralists were most at risk from raids by rival tribes endeavoring to steal their cattle. Accordingly, the pastoralists were more militaristic, more given to direct expressions of aggression, and more inclined to respect central authority than were the farmers, who tended instead to secrecy, caution, indirect action, mutual suspicion, and jealousy. Such evidence as Edgerton gathered on male dominance and aloofness showed that both traits were clearly stronger among the pastoralists than among the farmers. In one tribe, the Kamba of Kenya, the antagonism between men and women was especially acute. A male Kamba herder stressed the need to show that men were "always superior" to women and that he was entitled to "come and go as he pleases" and to buy, sell, and beat his wife. The women described their husbands as "never affectionate" and not involved in rearing children. Though the women professed to accept this as a natural state of affairs, many revealed a smoldering antagonism that they expressed indirectly by means of witchcraft directed against the men.[18]

Modern society presents an especially complex challenge to the task [20] of socializing males. Industrialization and the division of labor improve the standard of living while moving production out of the household. As the standard of living rises, improvements in diet reduce the age at which women can conceive and thus the age at which they first give birth. Contraception separates sexuality from procreation. The father's role in child care is reduced because he spends more time away from home. For most men aggression is no longer adaptive, because capital stocks are now conserved and managed by bureaucratic processes that require conformity and technical competence more than boldness and physical prowess. But while they are no longer adaptive, aggressive impulses are still present. The rise of large cities weakens kinship controls on such aggression, brings groups with different standards of conduct into close contact, and multiplies opportunities for violent exchanges.

These circumstances require of society that it invent and enforce rules to regulate aggression among men and to ensure that they care for the children they beget and the wives they take. Legal codes take on great importance but are rarely sufficient. In Anglo-Saxon countries, the control of male behavior since the eighteenth century (at least) has required

---

*In the fifth case, the villagers of Sondup'o in Korea practice large-scale, intensive agriculture, and father-child relations are intermediate between the harshness of the Thonga-Bedouin and the warmth of the !Kung-Lesu. [Wilson's note]

the preachings of the church, the discipline of the factory, and the super-vision of the temperance society.

During the nineteenth century, these informal methods of control reached their greatest strength; we in the United States and Great Britain refer to these teachings as "Victorian morality." As applied to male be-havior, that morality was, in essence, the code of the gentleman. The in-vention of the "gentleman" constituted the emergence of a society-wide definition of proper behavior to replace the premodern definitions en-forced by kinship groupings and the feudal definitions enforced by the aristocracy.

The requirements of gentlemanly behavior included everything from table manners and the obligation to play games fairly to one's responsi-bilities toward ladies and one's duty to country. So successful were these moral exhortations and codes of gentility that, so far as we can tell, both alcohol abuse and crime rates declined in England and America during a period — the second half of the nineteenth century — characterized by rapid urbanization, massive immigration, and the beginnings of industri-alization. Though not without its oft-remarked hypocrisies and its heavy reliance on a double standard governing male and female conduct, the code of the gentleman was the most successful extralegal mechanism ever invented for adapting male behavior to the requirements of modern life.[19]

In those places where the moral code was weak, the legal system im-potent, and bureaucratic structures absent, the warrior culture often emerged. If large numbers of unmarried young men were thrown to-gether outside of the control mechanisms of the conventional economic system, they would reduce their investment in family life or child care in favor of using their physical prowess to acquire and defend free-floating forms of wealth.

One example is the discovery of gold in remote areas. There were two American gold rushes in the mid-nineteenth century, the famous one in California and a lesser-known one in Appalachia. The former attracted single males whose life, devoted to acquisition and defense in an area be-yond the reach of the law, came close to the Hobbesian state of nature: solitary, poor, nasty, brutish, and short. Sixteen thousand people died in the California mining camps, victims of disease, murder, and insanity.[20] Such family life as existed was male-dominated, with little paternal in-vestment in child care. The Appalachia gold rush, by contrast, attracted Cornish miners who arrived with their families and soon became part of well-organized mining companies. Owing, it would seem, to the com-bined effect of familial bonds and bureaucratic constraints, the North Carolina gold rush produced relatively little violence.*

---

*Glass, 1984. I am indebted to Professor David Courtwright of the University of North Florida for calling my attention to the gold rush literature. [Wilson's note]

Marauding male gangs have excited fear for as long as man has lived in cities. From time to time we forget that young men in groups are always a potential challenge to social order, and so we are surprised when they appear in places that we think of as tranquil and civilized. We are astonished to learn of football gangs tearing apart trains, pubs, and athletic grounds in stately, sedate England. England? Supposedly, people there are utterly civil, with violent crime scarcely a problem and daily life moving in the orderly, class-ridden, but polite tempos of *Masterpiece Theatre.* What terrible thing — poverty? alienation? despair? — could produce football riots in England?

This idealized view of England can only be sustained if one forgets that in every society, a certain small fraction of young males will have an inordinate taste for violence and a low degree of self-control. What is striking about England and other civilized places is not that there are young thugs, but that in some places they organize themselves into gangs. England, contrary to popular belief, has a rate of burglary and robbery not much different from that in the United States.[21] But whereas American gangs are found chiefly among the inner-city poor and are territorially based, British gangs are found chiefly among football (in American terminology, soccer) supporters and are not territorial. They go to every game, traveling by bus, rail, or plane, trashing these conveyances along the way and spoiling for a good fight. Bill Burford's horrifying account of these gangs — or "firms," as they call themselves — does not depict unemployed, disenfranchised youth searching for meaning; it depicts young men of the sort always found overrepresented among the criminal classes — thrill seekers with a predisposition to alcoholism and violence, young toughs who *enjoy the fight.*[22] What is surprising is not that they exist but that they manage to sustain a modicum of organization, with captains and lieutenants, and that the physical conditions of British athletic grounds (or in American terms, stadiums) contribute to their sense of being a caged minority. That these gangs are intensely patriotic, singing "Rule Britannia" while destroying property and assaulting women, is not at all surprising; men in groups define sharply, however implausibly, the boundaries within which someone is either in or out.

Lionel Tiger's well-known book *Men in Groups* suggests the evolutionary origins and social functions of such behavior: it derives from the need for males to hunt, defend, and attack.[23] Much of the history of civilization can be thought of as an effort to adapt these male dispositions to contemporary needs by restricting aggression or channeling it into appropriate channels. That adaptation has often required extraordinary measures, such as hunting rituals, rites of passage, athletic contests, military discipline, guild apprenticeships, or industrial authority. (By contrast, one almost never reads of equivalent rituals, authority systems, or fraternal rules employed to socialize women, in part because they have often been confined to a subordinate status and in part because the realities of childbirth and child care provide an automatic process of socialization.) Modern society, with its rapid technological change, intense division of labor, and ambiguous allocation of social roles, frequently leaves some men out, with their aggressive predispositions either uncontrolled or undirected. Gangs are one result.

Matters get worse when the gangs can earn profits from illegal alcohol and drug distribution systems. Prohibiting the sale of certain commodities provides economic opportunities in which young males have a comparative advantage, and this in turn leads to the emergence of a warrior culture that underinvests in family life. Economic activity is separated from family maintenance and organized around capital that can be seized by predation. In these warrior societies, today as in the past, status among males is largely determined by physical combat and sexual conquest. Women can no longer control male behavior by requiring monogamous commitment in exchange for sexual access. Moreover, since women can, through contraception or abortion, control their reproductive rate, what once was a moral obligation gives way to a utilitarian calculation. The obligation was: "She is going to have a kid, and so I must marry her." The utilitarian calculation is: "If she wants to have the kid when she doesn't have to, then raising it is her problem."As a result, the children are raised apart from their fathers.

Among male animals generally, and perhaps among male humans as well, the more a male engages in promiscuous sexuality and intraspecies fighting, the less he invests in caring for his offspring. But the reverse is also true: the less he invests in caring for offspring, the more he is disposed to compete, violently if need be, with others for sexual access to a large number of women.[24] A culture that does not succeed in inducing its males to care for their offspring not only produces children that lack adequate care but also creates an environment that rewards predatory sexuality.

Gender and Family

Although men and women come together out of natural attraction, it is not clear why a household — that is, an enduring and cohesive family — should be the result. If the household is, as Aristotle put it, "the partnership constituted by nature for [the needs of] daily life,"[25] what is there in nature that produces not simply sex but partnership? We know why men and women come together, but what keeps them together? Unless we can explain that, we cannot explain the social unit that forms human character. Moral life begins not with sexual congress but with emotional commitment — the formation and maintenance of the family.

The needs of the woman may lead her to try to select males who will invest in child care, but this preference is not strong enough to produce families unless it is powerfully reinforced by cultural expectations and social sanctions. As Lionel Tiger and Robin Fox have argued, the chief function of human kinship systems is to "protect the mother-infant bond from the relative fragility and volatility of the male-female bond."[26] The weakening of the family in many Western societies is familiar evidence that these kinship systems and their cultural and legal supports are far more fragile than one would have guessed even forty years ago.

So fragile, indeed, that one can now say that the conditions of child rearing have changed fundamentally for many youngsters. In the 1950s, the typical American child lived in a two-parent family with a stay-at-home mother, a working father, and several siblings. By the 1990s, the typical child spent at least some time (among black children, most of the time) with a single mother and had only one sibling.[27] The public believes that the consequences of this have been harmful, and the scholarly evidence bears them out. Compared with children who are raised by their biological father and mother, those raised by mothers, black or white, who have never married are more likely to be poor, to acquire less schooling, to be expelled or suspended from school, to experience emotional or behavioral problems, to display antisocial behavior, to have trouble getting along with their peers, and to start their own single-parent families. These unhappy outcomes afflict both girls and boys, but they have a more adverse effect on boys.[28]

The better-off the parent, the less likely it is that the child will have to live in a one-parent household. But one should not infer from this that the problem of single-parent children can be solved simply by raising parental incomes. Consider black children. At every income level, they are more likely to live with a single parent than are white children at those income levels.[29] And for all children, there was a sharp decline in their prospects of having a two-parent family during the very period — the 1960s and 1970s — when family incomes were rising.

This is not a peculiarly American phenomenon. David Popenoe, a sociologist, has studied families in Sweden, where he found a similar increase in single-parent households. By 1980, 18 percent of all Swedish households with children had but one parent (the figure in the United States for that year was 21.5 percent, though by 1984 it had become 26 percent).[30] There remain industrial societies in which the overwhelming majority of children grow up in families with fathers — Japan, New Zealand, and Switzerland are three of them. But these three countries may be standing (for how long?) against a powerful tide that has been running in the opposite direction.

The consequences of mother-only families for the socialization of the male child seem bleak. I say "seem" because it is not easy to prove that a single-parent family, independently of other factors, produces undersocialized males. One reason is that mother-only households often suffer from so many problems, such as poverty, that isolating the effect of parenting on children is difficult. Another is that women who bear children without marrying may differ temperamentally from those who do marry. And finally, mother-child relations occupy a much more prominent place in academic studies than do father-child relations in part because "mothers are the main moral socializers of children of both sexes" in virtually every culture.[31]

The main, but not the only socializers. In one of the few studies to follow similarly situated children over many years and observe the relationship between their behavior and the role of their fathers, Sheppard Kellam and his co-workers studied several hundred poor, black first-graders living in a depressed neighborhood near the University of Chicago. Each lived in one of eighty-six different family types, depending on how many and what kinds of adults were present. Of the 1,391 families, about one-third had a mother as the only adult present; another third consisted of a mother and a father. Only a tiny fraction was headed by a father with no mother present. The remainder was made up of various combinations of mothers, grandparents, uncles, aunts, adult brothers and sisters, and various unrelated adults. By the time the children entered the third grade, those who lived with their mothers alone were the worst off in terms of their socialization.[32] After ten years, the boys who had grown up in mother-only families (which by then made up about half the total) reported more delinquencies, regardless of family income, than those who had grown up in families with multiple adults, especially a father.[33] Comparable findings have come from studies in Detroit.[34] The most common and most plausible interpretation of these studies is that the presence of a decent father helps a male child learn to control aggression; his absence impedes it.[35]

Not only does it appear that two-parent families do a better job of developing the moral senses of male children, but they also seem to have a beneficial effect on the husbands themselves. Of all of the institutions through which men may pass — schools, factories, the military — marriage has the largest effect. For every race and at every age, married males live longer than unmarried ones, having lower rates of homicide, suicide, accidents, and mental illness. Crime rates are lower for married than unmarried males and incomes are higher. Drug dealers are less likely to be married than young males who are not dealers.[36] Infant mortality rates are higher for unmarried than for married women, whether black or white, and these differences cannot be explained by differences in income or availability of medical care.[37]

Though some of these differences can be explained by female selectivity in choosing mates, I doubt that all can. Marriage not only involves screening people for their capacity for self-control, but it also provides inducements — the need to support a mate, care for a child, and maintain a home — that increase that capacity.

When the mother in a mother-only family is also a teenager, or at least a teenager living in urban America, the consequences for the child

40

are even grimmer. The most authoritative survey of what we know about the offspring of adolescent mothers concluded that the children suffer increasingly serious cognitive deficits and display a greater degree of hyperactivity, hostility, and poorly controlled aggression than is true of children born to older mothers of the same race, and this is especially true of the boys.[38]

Gender, Temperament, and Moral Senses

These findings support the view that males and females differ in temperament, especially with respect to aggression, that boys are harder to socialize than girls, and that female choice does not guarantee the selection of dependable mates. Given these differences in temperament, socialization, and reproductive success, one should not be surprised to find evidence that men and women differ in their moral orientation.*

An awareness of these differences has led many people in the past (and some today) to argue that morality is more natural to women than to men and to justify differences in the roles and rights of the two sexes by the claim that women, being purer, finer, and more emotional than men, are properly confined to the home, where their more delicate sensibilities fit them for rearing children and sustaining a refuge from the cruelties and competition of the outside world.† The argument is not only self-serving (for males), it is also incorrect. Both males and females learn moral behavior in the family; were that not the case, human communities would be impossible. Neither sex is "more" or "less" moral than the other. But they do seem to differ.

Early childhood experiences interacting with innate temperamental differences may create a disposition to give greater emphasis to one or the other of the several moral senses. One person may be more inclined to emphasize justice, fairness, and duty, another to stress sympathy, care, and helping. If Harvard's Carol Gilligan and her colleagues are correct, the former emphasis is more characteristic of men, the latter of women.[39] For example, when people are asked to describe moral dilemmas that they have faced or that they encounter in Aesop's fables, boys overwhelmingly do so in terms of justice (honoring contracts, making a fair

---

*I am acutely aware of the risks I run in writing of gender differences. On no topic is it easier to produce misunderstandings or arouse resentments. To some, any talk of differences implies a claim about rights. It does not. People can be equal without being the same. [Wilson's note]

†Of course, there have been some cultures in which the seclusion of women in the home or harem was justified on the grounds that they are *less* moral than men because they are by nature lascivious, seductive, and wanton. In the extreme case, women were portrayed as witches or succubi. It is noteworthy that in medieval Europe the most common charge against witches was that they killed babies, a most unwomanly thing to do (Cohn, 1975:100). [Wilson's note]

division, or respecting rights) while girls are more likely to do so in terms of care (helping people in need, resolving conflict). It must be stressed that these are differences in what people say about a story, not in what they will do in a real-life situation or even how they will react to a real-life dilemma. Yet they are consistent with many obvious facts of life. Women are more likely than men to dislike violence in motion pictures, less likely to enjoy sports that emphasize violence, and far less likely to commit crimes of violence. This is exactly what one would expect of people who say that they keenly experience the pain and sympathize with the plight of others.*

A clearer test of gender differences comes from the many experiments conducted to see how people will divide rewards after performing some task. Brenda Major and Kay Deaux summarize these findings this way: under every experimental condition, women take less of the reward for themselves than do men, and they do so regardless of whether the partners with whom they are sharing are male or female. This does not mean that women are less greedy than men, but rather that they seem to apply somewhat different principles to the allocation process.

When a woman has performed better than her partner in some common task, she tends to split the reward equally; when a man has performed better than his partner, he divides the reward equitably (that is, in proportion to the value of each person's contributions). Men also give more to female partners than they do to male ones, whereas women do not allow the sex of their partner to influence their allocation decisions. [45]

These findings hold true under one important condition: the participants expect to have further interactions with their partners. When they don't — when they perform a task with somebody they never expect to meet again — men and women allocate rewards in the same way. It is the prospect of future involvement that leads women to reduce the share they give themselves even when they are entitled to more.[40] The clear im-

---

*The Gilligan argument has not gone unopposed. For example, one review of male-female differences in empathy concluded that, while there were large differences between men and women in *self-reported* empathy, the evidence of differences in empathic *behavior* was inconclusive (Eisenberg and Lennon, 1983). A review of some fifty studies that attempt to describe the stage of moral reasoning that a person has achieved concluded that there was little evidence of a "sex bias" in the test: that is, men and women were about equally likely to be found at a given stage (Walker, 1984, 1986; for a rejoinder, see Baumrind, 1986). The difficulty with this conclusion is that these tests, based on Lawrence Kohlberg's theory of moral development, only describe the stage a person has reached based on that person's verbal reaction to some hypothetical moral dilemmas. No one has clearly shown, so far as I can tell, that how people respond to real moral issues, and especially how they behave in actual moral quandaries, can be predicted from their reaction to these fictional stories, especially since Kohlberg kept changing the way in which these reactions were to be scored. If there are no differences in empathic behavior, it is hard to explain why prisons are filled with male inmates. If there are no differences in empathic feelings, it is hard to understand why men and women spend so much time saying that they don't understand each other. [Wilson's note]

plication is that women assign a higher value to ongoing relationships than do men. Brenda Major is not quite certain how to explain this difference and suggests that it probably has a variety of causes. But it is striking how consistent this is with the Gilligan theory (Major published her work before Gilligan's appeared).

When Jean Piaget observed boys and girls at play, he noticed that boys were more concerned with rules, and girls with relationships. When a dispute arose, the boys were more likely to argue about the rules and search for fair procedures for applying them, while the girls were more inclined to manage conflict by making exceptions to the rules or ignoring them entirely. Piaget suggested that girls regarded a rule as "good as long as the game repaid it."[41] Many years later Janet Lever came to the same conclusion after observing fifth-grade children playing at school. Compared to the girls' games, the boys' games were more competitive, more complex, involved more players, often split close friends between different teams, and lasted longer.[42] The greater length reflected both the complexity of the game and the fact that disputes over what constituted fair play were resolved by boys through the application of rules or the decision to repeat the play. Girls, by contrast, were more likely to play short, simple, turn-taking games and to react to disputes by ending the game. To the girls, maintaining their relationships was more important than continuing the game.[43] Judy Dunn, watching young children at home, was struck by the fact that as early as two years of age, girls conversed more about their feelings than did boys. Similarly, the aggressiveness of males is more often expressed by direct physical confrontation, whereas the aggressive impulses of females more often takes the form of organized social ostracism.[44]

Though some students of child development suggest that individuals move through various stages of moral reasoning, with the highest stage being the one at which the individual applies universal principles of justice to moral dilemmas,[45] this claim, in my view, assigns too much importance to how a person formulates justifications for his moral inclinations and too little to the inclinations themselves. (I also am a bit suspicious of any theory that says that the highest moral stage is one in which people talk like college professors.) Ranking moral stages from low to high does not capture the reality of many moral problems, which often involve choosing which of several moral sentiments ought to govern one's action. For these reasons, the theory that men and women differ in the kinds of moral sentiments they emphasize cannot be tested by measuring what stage each gender is in; much less can the worth of a man's moral sentiments be compared with that of a woman's by noting where each stands in the presumed hierarchy of moral stages. To say that the two sexes differ is not the same thing as saying that morality defined as justice and fairness is superior to morality defined as benevolence and caring. Everyone applies various combinations of principles and feelings to the management of moral problems. Sometimes principle and feeling coincide, and so no difficulty arises; indeed, in these circumstances we act reflexively, without having engaged in moral reasoning at all. Sometimes they diverge; and then, if we are calm and self-aware, we struggle to reconcile the competing dispositions.[46]

It is difficult to say exactly how these gender differences, to the extent that they exist, emerge. Nature and nurture interact in ways that are complex and hard to disentangle. Boys are more aggressive than girls (nature at work), but over many millennia their aggressiveness has been moderated by female selection of mates (nature modified by human choices that affect reproductive success) and continues to be moderated or exacerbated by child-rearing practices (nurture) that reflect both infant temperament (nature) and parental attitudes (nurture).

Gender and Social Roles

However complex the origin of the more fundamental gender differences, they are remarkably resistant to planned change. The most impressive demonstration of that resistance — impressive both because of the quality of the research and the initial suppositions of the author — comes from the studies by Melford E. and Audrey Spiro of a kibbutz, one of the Israeli collective farms.[47] When the Spiros first studied it in 1951, the kibbutz was already thirty years old; when they returned in 1975, it had been in existence for nearly sixty years. It represented, thus, a mature example of a bold experiment: to achieve on a farm a wholly egalitarian society based on collective ownership, cooperative enterprise, a classless society, and the group rearing of children in an atmosphere that accorded no significance to differences in gender. Within a week after birth, infants were brought to a communal nursery; at one year of age, they moved into a Toddlers' House; at five years of age, they entered kindergarten; and so on through grammar school and high school, living always with other children and never with their parents, except for brief daily visits. Although there were slight differences in dress, in general male and female children were treated in exactly the same way: they dressed together, bathed together, played together, and slept together; they were given the same toys and the same chores. Though men and women married and lived together, the family as a parent-child unit and sex-differentiated roles within the family were abolished, not only in the assignment of rights, duties, and opportunities, but even in dress. Communal facilities — the kitchen, laundry, dining room, nursery, and school — were to be staffed without regard to gender, and women, who wore pants, avoided cosmetics, and retained their maiden names, were encouraged to work the fields alongside the men.

The communal nursery was successful in discouraging clear sex-role identifications among the children. In their fantasy play, boys rarely assumed adult male roles, some boys chose to wear ribbons and dresses during their games, and boys and girls played together and not in same-sex groups.[48] But from the first some gender differences in behavior appeared despite efforts to discourage them. Just as in conventional families, boys played more strenuous games than girls.* Boys were more likely to pretend they were driving machines and girls more likely to play with dolls and baby buggies; girls engaged in more artistic games and boys in more mechanical ones. As they got older, the formal sexual equality of life continued: boys and girls lived together, took showers together, and could indulge their sexual curiosity without adult interference or guidance. But the signs of sexual identification continued to appear. At parties girls spontaneously sang, danced, and initiated activity; boys increasingly sat on the sidelines and watched. Girls began assisting the nurses, boys the farmers. Teachers began to remark that the girls were socially more sensitive, the boys more egotistical.[49]

As they entered high school, the behavior of the kibbutz adolescents was still different in many ways from that of conventional teenagers. In the kibbutz there was virtually no dating and no intense or morbid curiosity about sex. But evidence of shame and embarrassment had begun to appear. The girls protested against taking showers with boys, began undressing in the dark, and took to wearing nightclothes in bed, all to avoid male eyes. Teachers reported that the girls kept themselves and their living areas cleaner than did the boys, whereas the boys were more aggressive in classroom discussions. The physics class attracted boys, the psychology class girls.[50]

But the biggest changes occurred among the adults who had been born and raised on the kibbutz. The family reasserted itself: sabra women sought renewed contact with their children, though not at the expense of abandoning collective education; the children's living quarters were increasingly staffed by women; and sabra men began to do most of the major agricultural jobs and to dominate the leadership roles and discussion in the communal meetings.[51] Women returned to feminine styles in clothing and opened a beauty parlor. This is not to say that there was now sexual inequality in the kibbutz, only that there was sexual diversity — in roles, preferences, styles, and modes of thought — within a structure of legal and formal equality.

The link between Gilligan's studies of gender differences in moral dispositions and the Spiros' observations of gender differences in roles may be this: the moral role played by women in the kibbutz tended to be

---

*Felton Earls (1987) observed that three-year-old boys, even when playing with girls in the same sandbox, were more likely to pretend that they were riding, flying, colliding, breaking, or plowing, while the girls were more inclined to pretend they were mothering or caretaking. Similar patterns have been observed by Jack and Jeanne Block (1980), Marjorie Honzik (1951), and Evelyn Goodenough (1957). These authors, without explaining why, ascribed these differences entirely to socialization. [Wilson's note]

expressive while those played by men tended to be instrumental.* When conflict arose in the children's houses, the girls tended to handle it by supplying assistance, sharing, and cooperation, while the boys more often relied on initiating activities, applying rules, or issuing directives. Predictably, the most aggressive children were boys. Both boys and girls would attempt to control the aggression, but only the girls would console the victims of it.[52]

It is hard to imagine that a free society will ever make a more deter-   55
mined effort to eliminate gender differences in social roles than did the Israeli kibbutzim. It is also hard to imagine that such an effort would be studied by anyone more sympathetic to its goals than Melford and Audrey Spiro. As the former put it in 1979:

> As a cultural determinist, my aim in studying personality development in Kiryat Yedidim [the pseudonym of the kibbutz] was to observe the influence of culture on human nature or, more accurately, to discover how a new culture produces a new human nature. In 1975 I found (against my own intentions) that I was observing the influence of human nature on culture.[53]

The effect on the author's thinking was, as he put it, a "kind of Copernican revolution." His conclusions are supported by another large-scale study of a kibbutz, this done by Lionel Tiger and Joseph Shepher.[54] These findings help explain the absence of matriarchal societies. Despite recurring claims to the contrary, some by scholars as distinguished as Lewis Henry Morgan[55] and by polemicists as skilled as Friederich Engels,[56] no credible historical evidence has been adduced to show that a society ruled by women has ever existed. Joan Bamberger, a feminist scholar, has shown that the case for matriarchy has rested on two errors: confounding myth with history (as with the myths of the Amazon women) and confusing matrilineal descent (the inheritance through the female line of property and family name) with matriarchal authority (the enduring rule of women over men).[†]

This argument about matriarchy is a bit misplaced, for it proceeds on the assumption that the only authority that counts is that which is wielded publicly and officially or is embodied in offices and rules. Everyday experience should remind us of the countless ways in which men and women alike wield influence without controlling offices. Peggy

---

*The distinction between instrumental and expressive roles has been made by many scholars, principally Talcott Parsons (1951:79–88). [Wilson's note]

†Bamberger (1974) goes on to argue that many of these myths, far from being celebrations of female authority, were in fact condemnations of it. The leitmotif was that of powerful women who abused their power through moral failures — for example, by incest — and as a consequence were stripped of their authority. Edward Westermarck, in his monumental history of marriage, long ago showed that male rule was quite compatible with matrilineal descent (1926:15–23). [Wilson's note]

Reeves Sanday, an anthropologist, has explored in great detail the many and subtle ways in which women exercise informal power, especially in those cultures in which human survival is not threatened by invasion or deprivation. Without the prospect of war or want, a culture tends to evolve a well-understood sexual division of labor, which often leads to the creation of spheres of relatively autonomous action for females and males alike.[57]

That matriarchy has never existed says nothing, of course, about the moral worth or legal rights of men or women. But viewed in light of the evidence from the kibbutzim, it does suggest that the explanation of male domination of political structures may involve more than merely male oppression. While the greater physical strength of men has no doubt been an important factor in maintaining male authority, especially in preindustrial societies, and while cultural conventions no doubt continue to sustain many aspects of male advantage, the differing orientations of men and women of the sort suggested by Gilligan and Spiro may also help account for this pattern.

I offer this conjecture: The innately greater aggressiveness of males reflects not only a combative nature but the legacy of selection for domination. That tendency may be moderated or exaggerated by parental training. As young boys begin to take pleasure in childhood games, they discover through spontaneous interaction that some principle for controlling aggression and allocating roles must be maintained if the game, and thus its pleasures, are to continue. When each person is, in varying degrees, asserting a desire to dominate, only two principles for moderating conflict are available: the authority of the most powerful or skillful participant, or the authority of norms that allocate roles either equally (for example, taking turns) or equitably (for example, awarding positions in the game on the basis of skill or effort). Whichever principle of authority is accepted, each tends toward the creation of rule-based systems organized around roles, claims, and rights. Prolonged experience in rule-based systems, whether they rest on the authority of a dominant figure or on the legitimacy of the rules themselves, contributes to acquiring both a moral orientation that emphasizes justice or fairness and a hierarchical orientation toward the management of conflict and the organization of common undertakings. To borrow the phrase of Louis Dumont, males tend to become *homo hierarchicus*.[58]

By contrast, to the extent that young girls are innately disposed to avoid physical aggression or, as a result of natural selection, partake of a nurturant (protomaternal?) predisposition (and of course individual girls, like individual boys, will differ greatly in these inclinations), they will find that their childhood will generate fewer competing demands for domination requiring rule-based management. Their play, as Piaget, Lever, and others have observed, will be less in need of, and less receptive to, formal principles of authority; the maintenance of personal

60

relationships will take precedence over the allocation of rights and roles. Through prolonged involvement in play where sustaining relationships is more important than managing dominance, girls tend to acquire both a moral orientation that emphasizes caring and harmony and a nonhierarchical orientation toward the organization of common undertakings. Insofar as power relationships are hierarchical (as they almost always are), women will tend to be excluded, or, if included, confined (in part by fiat and in part by choice) to less authoritative roles.

Deborah Tannen finds abundant evidence of these differences in social orientation in the everyday language of men and women, especially in the ways in which the two sexes seem to misunderstand each other (the title of her best-selling book was *You Just Don't Understand*).[59] Men speak in order to report, women to establish rapport; men give directions, women make suggestions; male discourse suggests that independence is important, female discourse that intimacy is crucial. Men are more likely to make decisions "on the merits," women to feel that consultation is as important as decisiveness. When an emotional problem arises, men are inclined to suggest a solution, women to extend sympathy, often by describing similar difficulties of their own. The complaints men and women make about each other's behavior are so well known as scarcely to bear repeating; many grow out of these linguistic — actually, personality — differences: "He is so aloof," "She is so moody"; "He doesn't listen," "She is insecure"; "He never talks to me," "She never stops talking."

Tannen's sociolinguistic analysis, taken together with Gilligan's and Major's psychological inquiries, suggests how gender may affect at least two of the moral senses. Take the sense of fairness: It is a human sentiment, common to both sexes. But fairness, as we have seen, requires a judgment about proportionality: if people ought to get what they deserve or reciprocate what they receive, then the person evaluating the situation must decide how equal or unequal are the contributions of each party. If a person greatly values intimacy, community, and mutual esteem, then that person will tend to evaluate the inputs — the work, effort, time, or manner — of each party in the group equally. Several scholars have noted that in girls' play groups there is a stress on connection and similarity, reflecting a fear of rejection.[60] From one perspective this appears to be simply an adolescent preoccupation with popularity and conformity, but seen more deeply it reveals an egalitarian ethos that is maintained by striving to see all inputs to some common endeavor as relatively equal, so that the allocation of rewards will also be roughly the same.

Boys also value popularity and certainly are in some sense conformists, but their relationships are substantially more competitive — in athletic achievements, material acquisition, and displays of masculine toughness. Like most male primates, boys participate from an early age in dominance hierarchies. This means that when contributions to joint activities are assessed, males will emphasize the differences in inputs to a greater degree than will females. It does not mean that one gender is more or less fair in its outlook than the other, only that the specific application of the norm of fairness or reciprocity will reflect a different assessment of inputs. To oversimplify, men will be more likely to value equity, women equality.

A parallel difference in emphasis can be imagined with respect to sympathy. One can respond to the plight of another by expressions of care or by offers of solutions. In the first instance, empathy is the goal ("let's share our feelings"), in the latter it is simply a motive ("I can help you fix that"). Women may be more likely to take the first view: when an acquaintance suffers a reversal, sympathy requires that one display one's feelings and thereby draw tighter the bonds of friendship. Men may be more likely to take the latter: the adversity of a friend is an occasion to supply help but not, except within narrow limits, emotion. Help is "what friends are for"; emotion, extravagantly displayed, is simply and wrongly a loss of self-control that helps neither and embarrasses both. These differences may mean not that one sex has a greater or lesser capacity for sympathy (though they may mean that), but that people, equally affected by the plight of another, may choose to make either an expressive or an instrumental reaction to it.

Culture versus Gender

These observations about gender differences in moral sentiments are based on evidence that is fragmentary, in some cases controversial, and limited to Western sources. Despite these shortcomings, I advance them because they are consistent with my experiences. But my experiences are, of course, rather parochial. I was reminded of this when Grace Goodell, an anthropologist who has devoted years to studying the cultures of the industrialized nations of the Pacific Rim, suggested to me that in some respects the moral thinking of successful East Asian businessmen seems to resemble that of eleven-year-old Western girls.[61]

For example, East Asian businessmen often manage their commercial relationships with one another in ways that are designed to maintain those relationships more than to assert legal claims, just as Western girls manage their games in ways that keep the game going even at some cost to the rules. In the Asian business world, anyone who emphasizes contractual obligations, legal rights, or formal rules is guilty of a grave breach of etiquette. These executives are competitive, often fiercely so, but the competition is constrained by a moral sense that neither party should embarrass the other, even at some cost in money. Fairness, abstractly conceived, is less important than comity.

These dispositions may grow out of the interaction between temperamental endowments and child-rearing practices of the sort already mentioned, practices that (at least in Japan) stress emotional interdependency

65

and control behavior by the threat of social isolation. Self-control, sincerity, and collective decision making are greatly esteemed.[62] Preschool education continues this emphasis. When teachers, parents, and child-development specialists in China, Japan, and the United States were asked to state the most important things that children ought to learn in preschool, the first choice in Japan was sympathy and a concern for others, followed by cooperation. In the United States, the most common response was self-reliance (followed by cooperation); sympathy was rarely mentioned.[63] But in the Japanese preschool, exactly the same gender differences in behavior were observed as one would see in an American preschool or an Israeli kibbutz: the boys acted like warriors, the girls like healers and peacemakers.[64] How gender differences, which seem universal, interact with culture to affect moral sentiments is a subject about which almost everything remains to be learned.

Whether the gender differences in moral sentiments that Gilligan observes in the United States will be found in East Asian (or other) cultures remains to be seen. But the problem of male socialization is, I think, the same everywhere; cultures differ not in whether they must cope with it, but how and with what success.

Notes

1. Rossi, 1987:68; Durden-Smith and DeSimone, 1983; Hoyenga and Hoyenga, 1979.
2. Eibl-Eibesfeldt, 1989:271–72.
3. Breslau, Klein, and Allen, 1988.
4. Rossi, 1987:68.
5. Earls, 1987.
6. Hoffman, 1981:364.
7. Maccoby and Jacklin, 1974, 1980; Hyde, 1986.
8. Symons, 1979:144–46; Edgerton, 1992:204; Chagnon, 1968.
9. Wilson and Herrnstein, 1985: ch. 4.
10. Olweus, 1979, 1984a, 1984b.
11. Symons, 1979:214; Lawson and Samson, 1988.
12. Symons, 1979:213–15.
13. Murdock and White, 1969.
14. Trivers, 1985:311.
15. Ibid., 239.
16. Lynn, 1974; Rypma, 1976; Berman, 1980; Katz and Konner, 1981; Lancaster and Lancaster, 1983.
17. West and Konner, 1976; Katz and Konner, 1981.
18. Edgerton, 1971:273–76, 289–91.
19. Wilson, 1991: ch. 3.
20. Helper, 1855; Courtwright, 1991.
21. Farrington and Langan, 1992.
22. Burford, 1992.
23. Tiger, 1970.
24. Symons, 1979:23.
25. Aristotle, *Politics*, 1252a29, 1252b13.
26. Tiger and Fox, 1971:71; see also Tiger and Shepher, 1975:279.

27. Sawhill, 1992.
28. Ibid., and Dawson, 1991.
29. Farley and Allen, 1987.
30. Popenoe, 1988:174.
31. Hoffman, 1981:372.
32. Kellam, Ensminger, and Turner, 1977.
33. Ensminger, Kellam, and Rubin, 1983.
34. Hoffman, 1971.
35. Hoffman, 1981:365.
36. Kraus and Lilienfeld, 1959; Gove, 1973; Rand, 1987; Reuter, 1990.
37. Eberstadt, 1991.
38. Brooks-Gunn and Furstenberg, 1986.
39. Gilligan, 1982; Lyons, 1983; Gilligan and Wiggins, 1987; Gilligan, Ward, and Taylor, 1988; Johnston, 1985.
40. Major and Deaux, 1982; Major and Adams, 1983.
41. Piaget, 1932:83.
42. Lever, 1976, 1978.
43. Gilligan, 1982:10.
44. Cairns and Cairns, 1985.
45. Kohlberg, 1981.
46. Cf. Kagan, 1984:124.
47. Spiro and Spiro, 1975, 1979.
48. Spiro and Spiro, 1975:240–44.
49. Ibid., 280–82.
50. Spiro and Spiro, 1975:329–36.
51. Ibid., 350–51, 469–71; Spiro and Spiro, 1979:15–25.
52. Spiro and Spiro, 1979:92–94.
53. Ibid., 106.
54. Tiger and Shepher, 1975, esp. 262–63. See also Spiro and Spiro, 1975.
55. Morgan, 1877.
56. Engels, 1884.
57. Sanday, 1981, esp. ch. 6.
58. Dumont, 1970.
59. Tannen, 1990; Maltz and Borker, 1982; Goodwin and Goodwin, 1987.
60. Tannen, 1990: 217–18; Goodwin and Goodwin, 1987.
61. Grace Goodell, private communication.
62. Wagatsuma and De Vos, 1984:148–51, 230–33.
63. Tobin, Wu, and Davidson, 1989:190.
64. Ibid., 34.

PREPARING FOR DISCUSSION

1. Wilson makes the simple statement in paragraph 3 that "Men are more aggressive than women." How does he account for male aggressiveness historically? He also writes that while aggressive impulses still exist in modern society, they are no longer "adaptive." What social conditions have made aggression non-adaptive and what accounts for the persistence of some aggressive behavior?

2. Consider Wilson's reflections on the possibility of a matriarchal society (paragraphs 56–58). Why does he take issue with those who have maintained the

historical existence of such societies? What gender-based considerations, according to Wilson, make the existence of such societies virtually impossible? How would you describe the difference between the expressive and instrumental functions ascribed to males and females, respectively, throughout the selection?

3. Wilson notes that male children raised without a responsible adult male presence in the home will be more aggressive and suffer from lack of "socialization" (paragraph 37). Yet he has also noted previously that women are far less aggressive than men. Do these observations contradict each other? What factors other than the absence of a male parent might account for the lower degree of socialization found among boys raised by single women?

4. Wilson takes time to analyze the phenomenon of male gangs. To what gender-based factors does he attribute the existence of male gangs? How might the growing number of violent female gangs in our cities constitute a challenge to Wilson's account? How could he explain the existence of such "girl gangs" without abandoning his original theory?

5. In the first paragraph, Wilson writes that "if the child is to do more than survive — if it is to grow up in an orderly and safe environment and be part of an elaborate and useful culture — it must be part of a community." Recalling that Wilson suggests that males in our culture have generally played a lesser role in rearing children than females, what do you make of his use of the pronoun *it* to refer to a child? Do you think it likely that a woman writer would use the same pronoun in referring to a child? Why or why not?

FROM READING TO WRITING

6. Does it make any difference whether we regard gender difference as biologically innate or socially constructed? Write an essay in which you consider this question carefully, framing your answer in current social, economic, political, or cultural attitudes.

7. According to Wilson, gender affects one's sense of fairness. Male children are more likely to emphasize rules, while female children are more likely to emphasize sympathy and helping. Does Wilson's sense of gender-based notions of fairness adequately describe your own childhood experience? Can you offer an alternative scheme for describing children's attitudes about fairness?

NAOMI WOLF

Are Opinions Male?

◇

In this and the next selection, we take a closer look at the way gender differences express themselves through language, both written and spoken. Here feminist social critic and journalist Naomi Wolf surveys American newspapers and magazines to illustrate the great discrepancy in the number of male and female voices appearing on the op-ed pages and in weekly columns across the country. In response to her findings, Wolf is forced to ask whether the way in which women are socialized makes them less likely to air their opinions in public.

Wolf came to national prominence in 1991 with the publication of her first book, *The Beauty Myth*. While doing graduate work in literature as a Rhodes scholar at Oxford, she grew increasingly disturbed by the presence in literature and in life of an unrealistic standard of beauty that she believed was imposed on women in Western societies. She wrote *The Beauty Myth* to illustrate how this Western obsession with beauty "is, in fact, the last way men can defend themselves against women claiming power." This selection originally appeared in the *New Republic*.

SELECTED PUBLICATIONS: *The Beauty Myth: How Images of Beauty Are Used against Women* (1991); *Fire with Fire: The New Female Power and How It Will Change the Twenty-First Century* (1993); Wolf also publishes frequently in the *Wall Street Journal*, the *New Republic, Glamour, Ms.,* and *Esquire*.

What is that vast silent wavelength out on the opinion superhighway? It is the sound of women not talking.

Despite women's recent strides into public life, the national forums of debate — op-ed pages, political magazines, public affairs talk shows, newspaper columns — remain strikingly immune to the general agitation for female access. The agora of opinion is largely a men's club.

A simple count of the elite media bears out the charge. In 1992, the putative Year of the Woman, *Crossfire* presented 55 female guests, compared with 440 male guests. Of the print media, the most elite forums are the worst offenders: according to a survey conducted by Women, Men, and Media, during a one-month period in 1992, 13 percent of the op-ed pieces published in the *Washington Post* were written by women; 16 percent of the articles on the *New York Times* op-ed page were by women. Over the course of the year, the *New Republic* averaged 14

269

percent female contributors; *Harper's*, less than 20 percent; the *Nation*, 23 percent; the *Atlantic Monthly*, 33 percent. The *National Interest* ran the remarkable ratio of 80 male bylines to 1 female. The *Washington Monthly* ran 33 women to 108 men; *National Review*, 51 female bylines to 505 male (and 12 of those female bylines belonged to one columnist, Florence King). Talk radio, an influential forum for airing populist grievances, counts 50 female hosts in its national association's roster that totals 900. Eric Alterman's book about opinion-makers, *Sound and Fury*, chronicles female pundits only in passing.

What is going on here? Is there an unconscious — or conscious — editorial bias against women's opinions? Or are opinions themselves somehow gendered male — does female socialization conspire against many women's ability or desire to generate a strong public voice?

The answer to the first question is an unhesitant yes: on the nuts-and-bolts level of feminist analysis, women are being left out of the opinion mix because of passive but institutionalized discrimination on the part of editors and producers. General-interest magazines, newspapers, and electronic forums tend to view public affairs as if they can be clothed exclusively in gray flannel suits, and rely on an insular Rolodex of white men.

In self-defense some male (and female) public opinion editors point to the allegedly "personal" way in which women tend to write about politics and express their public opinions. Women are accused of writing too much about their "feelings" and their "bodies" — as if such subjects were by nature ill-suited to respectable public discussion. And yes, this charge has some merit. But a double standard is at work here. Men, too, write about their feelings and bodies, but that discussion is perceived as being central and public. Though masculinists lay claim to passionless "objectivity," "logic," and "universality" as being the hallmarks of male debate, a glance shows how spurious is their position. What, after all, was the gays-in-the-military debate except a touch-feely all-night boys-only slumber party, in which Dad — in the form of Sam Nunn[1] — came downstairs to have a bull session with earnest youths lying on bunk beds? What were the snuggled-up military boys asked about but their feelings — feelings about being ogled, objectified, harassed; fears of seduction and even rape? Had it been young women interviewed in their dorm rooms about their fears of men, the whole exercise, cloaked in the sententious language of "national preparedness," would have been dismissed as a radical-feminist fiesta of victim-consciousness, encouraging oversensitive flowers to see sexual predators under every bed.

Indeed, the nationalism of German skinheads, the high melodrama of the World Cup, and the recent convulsion of Japan-bashing — all of

[1] *Sam Nunn:* U.S. Senator from Georgia and one of Congress's most outspoken supporters of the ban on homosexuals in the military.

these are, on one level, complex sociopolitical developments; on another, they are a continuing global C.R.[2] session on vulnerability and self-esteem conducted primarily by men about men. One could read the Western canon itself as a record of men's deep feelings of alternating hope and self-doubt — whether it recounts Dick Diver[3] destroying himself because his wife is wealthier than he, or King Lear raging on a heath at the humiliation of being stripped of his world.

So women and men often actually theorize about parallel experiences, but the author's maleness will elevate the language as being importantly public, while the author's femaleness stigmatizes it as being worthlessly private. Women writing about the stresses and failures of maternity, for instance, are deviating onto the literary mommy track, but when men write about the stresses and failures of paternity, they are analyzing "the plight of inner-city youths," "cultural breakdown," or "child abuse hysteria." A woman recounting her own experience of systematic oppression is writing a "confessional"; but when a man writes intensely personal, confessional prose — whether it is Rousseau in his *Confessions*[4] or Bob Packwood in his diaries — he is engaged in pioneering enlightenment, or, even in William Safire's terms, acting as "a Pepysian diarist . . . [who] has kept voluminous notes on life as a lightning rod."[5]

Of course, many women write about issues unmarked by gender, from city council elections to computer chips. But when women talk about politics, culture, science, and the law in relation to female experience — i.e., rape statutes, fertility drugs, misogyny in film, or abortion rights — they are perceived as talking about their feelings and bodies. Whereas when men talk about their feelings and bodies — i.e., free speech in relation to their interest in pornography, gun ownership in relation to their fear of criminal assault, the drive for prostate cancer research in relation to their fears of impotence, new sexual harassment guidelines in relation to their irritation at having their desire intercepted in the workplace — they are read as if they are talking about politics, culture, science, and the law.

Thus, much of what passes for rational public debate is an exchange of subjective *male* impressions about *masculine* sensibilities and the *male* body — an exchange that appears "lucid" and "public" because men arrogate the qualities of transparency and generalization when discussing male emotions and the experiences of male flesh, but assign to women the qualities of opacity and particularity when they discuss their own.

10

---

[2] *C.R.:* Consciousness-raising.

[3] *Dick Diver:* Protagonist in F. Scott Fitzgerald's 1934 novel *Tender Is the Night.*

[4] Confessions: The major autobiographical work by the French writer and philosopher Jean-Jaques Rousseau (1712–78).

[5] *William Safire:* Language columnist for the *New York Times,* he is referring to Samuel Pepys (1633–1703), an Englishman famous for his *Diary,* kept from 1660 to 1669.

The lack of media oxygen for women writers of opinion can strangle voice, putting them into an impossible double bind. Many women also write from a personal vantage point alone because they feel it is one realm over which they can claim authority. As Jodie Allen, an editor at the *Washington Post,* puts it, "When they sit down to write, they think, why should anyone listen to me? At least if I take it from the 'women's' point of view, they can't deny I'm a woman. It becomes a self-fulfilling prophecy." With the "public/male, private/female" split so schematized, many other women writers of opinion must assume "the female perspective," as if shouldering a heroic but cumbersome burden. They are forced, by the relative paucity of female pundits at the highest levels, to speak "for women" rather than simply hashing out the issues in a solitary way.

This extreme is represented sometimes by an Anna Quindlen, whose "maternal punditry" beats a lonely drum on the guy terrain of the *Times* op-ed page. The meager allocation of space for female pundits at the highest levels, what Quindlen calls "a quota of one," does indeed force the few visible women writers of opinion who take a feminist stance into becoming stoic producers of that viewpoint, counted upon to generate a splash of sass and color, a provocative readerly-writerly tussle, in the gray expanses of male perspectives and prose. Editors seem to treat these few female pundits as cans in six-packs marked, for instance, "Lyrical African American Women Novelists"; "Spunky White Female Columnists with Kids"; or, perhaps, the reliable category, "Feminists (Knee-Jerk to Loony)." As Quindlen once remarked, a newspaper editor explained that he could not syndicate her column because "we already run Ellen Goodman." Popular discourse treats such writers as sound bite producers when it needs someone to say "multiculturalism is good" or "rape is bad."

So the few "pundits of identity" achieve, in the minds of those who decide what ideas inhabit the op-ed pages and who should argue with whom about what, a hard-won commerce in the perspectives inflected by gender, or by gender and race. But few can hope to take for granted the sweet oxygen that any writer needs in order to flourish: space to speak for no one but oneself.

The other extreme of the female public voice is perhaps represented by a Jeane Kirkpatrick: a voice so Olympian, so neck-up and uninflected by the experiences of the female body, that the subtle message received by young female writers is: to enter public voice, one must abide by the no-uterus rule. This voice gives a publication the benefit of a woman's name on the title page, without the mess and disruption of women's issues entering that precious space. This is the message absorbed by the legions of young women I meet. Though many writers are avidly trying to seek it out, we still lack the space and encouragement to range from the personal to the political, from identity to universality, with the ease and un-self-consciousness assumed by men.

So women are left out, or included under conditions of constraint. 15 But do we leave ourselves out of the public forum as well? When I have asked editors at the *New Republic,* the *Washington Post, Harper's,* and the *New York Times* op-ed page about the gender imbalance in their forums, this is the overwhelming message. Women simply do not submit articles in the same numbers that men do. And this is accurate: during one randomly selected month at the *New Republic* (February 1992), 8 women submitted unsolicited manuscripts, versus 15 men; during another month (October 1993), the ratio was 8 women to 55 men. According to Toby Harshaw, staff member of the *New York Times* op-ed page, in the morning mail of November 8, of about 150 unsolicited manuscripts, the ratio of men to women was 10 to 1.

Why is this? Some editors argue that one reason for the imbalance is that women have not yet reached the highest echelons of public life: "Our biggest groups that submit are think tanks, lawyers, universities, and government officials," says Harshaw. And the overwhelming majority of pieces from these groups, he notes, are by men. Yet while that argument has some validity, it cannot account for the extent of the imbalance: at the middle ranks of the law and the academy, women are reaching parity with men. What makes many women reluctant to write and submit opinion journalism, compared with men?

There is, I think, a set of deeply conditioned, internal inhibitions that work in concert with the manifest external discrimination to keep fewer women willing to submit opinion pieces, and to slug it out in public arenas. The problem is not, of course, that women can't write. They write, one can argue, with more facility than men do: women have dominated the novel — at least in its popular form — since its birth; and, if anything, social enculturation encourages girls to be more literary than most boys. No, the problem is that the traits required by writing opinion journalism or appearing on adversarial public affairs shows are often in conflict with what are deemed "appropriate" female speech patterns and behavior.

Dr. Deborah Tannen, the Georgetown University linguist, asserted that women and men often speak in different ways — women seek intimacy and consensus, she claims, while men seek status and independence. She notes that boys are raised to see boy-to-boy conflict as a way to express bonding, while girls are raised to avoid conflict in their play and enforce consensus. Psychologists Jean Baker Miller and Carol Gilligan suggest that women are more "relational" and men more "autonomous."

I don't agree with Miller or Gilligan that these tendencies are due to any primal psychic development; but women are surely encouraged to show such traits by virtue of social conditioning. And the act of writing an opinion piece — or appearing on *Crossfire* — calls for skills that are autonomous, contrarian, and independent (not to say bloody-minded).

Writing opinion journalism is a cranky, self-satisfied, and in traditionally feminine terms, extremely rude way to behave in public. The momentum to thrash out an opinion piece often begins with the conviction that others are wrong and that oneself is right, or that others are not saying the one thing that must be said. One is not *listening;* one is not set on enhancing others' well-being; one is certainly not demonstrating a "fusion of identity and intimacy," which pursuit Gilligan claims motivates women.

Unfortunately, you can't write strong, assertive prose if you are too   20
anxious about preserving consensus; you can't have a vigorous debate if you are paralyzed with concern about wounding the sensitivities of your opposite number. Writing a bold declarative sentence that claims that the world is this way and not that, or that President Clinton should do X and is a fool to do Y, demands the assumption of a solitary, even arrogant, stance. In Gilliganesque "different voice" terms, it is lonely and emotionally unrewarding; it is, according to such theories, almost by definition an engagement in "masculine" values and patterns of speech.

Without a countervailing encouragement into speech, the social pressure on women to exhibit "connection" and suppress "autonomy" can inhibit many women's public assertiveness. Tannen describes English Professor Thomas Fox's observations of male and female freshman students' different approaches to writing analytical papers. He looked at a Ms. M. and a Mr. H. "In her speaking as well as her writing [to be read by the class]," Tannen reports, "Ms. M. held back what she knew, appearing uninformed and uninterested, because she feared offending her classmates. Mr. H. spoke with authority and apparent confidence because he was eager to persuade his peers. She did not worry about persuading; he did not worry about offending." But in Ms. M.'s papers that were to be read only by the professor — her "private" writing — Ms. M. was clear, forceful, and direct. In this anecdote we see, essentially, that of the two, Mr. H., at seventeen, is being socialized to write opinion journalism and shout down interruptions on *The McLaughlin Group;* whereas Ms. M. is being socialized to write celebrity puff pieces in *Entertainment Weekly.*

Many women are raised to care — or to feel guilty if they don't care — about wounding the feelings of others. And yet, to write most purely out of herself, a writer must somehow kill off the inhibiting influence of the need for "connection." The woman writer of opinion must delve into what early feminists called "the solitude of self." When Camille Paglia claims that women have not produced great artists for the same reasons that they have not produced a Jack the Ripper, she touches, perhaps inadvertently, upon a real creative problem for women: fidelity to nothing but one's own voice can in fact depend upon a kind of radical solipsism, an ecstatic, highly unfeminine disregard for the importance of others if their well-being obtrudes upon the emergence of that transcendent vision.

Virginia Woolf returned often in her diaries to this theme, to the need to be impervious both to criticism and approval: "I look upon disregard or abuse as part of my bargain," Woolf wrote. "I'm to write what I like and they're to say what they like." Woolf's opinion of unsuccessful women's novels says volumes about the social disincentives many women face in writing damn-the-torpedoes opinion pieces: "It was the flaw in the center that had rotted them. [The novelist] had altered her values in deference to the opinions of others." And yet the world conspires against us, and within us, to have us do just that.

This internal dilemma is compounded by an external convention: even for the many women who are willing and eager to express strong opinions, conventions about how women are permitted to speak in print or on TV hem them in. The authoritative female voice asserting judgments about the real world is an unseemly voice. The globalizing tone that the conventions of opinion journalism or TV debate require involves an assumption of authority that women are actively dissuaded from claiming. A female writer of opinion at the *Post* concurs: "Op-ed language is the language of a certain level of abstraction; this is a language more often used by more men because more men are expert at it — you have to learn that language." As Professor Rhonda Garelick, who teaches French literary theory at the University of Colorado, put it to me, "It is just now becoming true for me that I can make 'sweeping' statements. But even as I make them, I am aware that it is an unusual verbal structure for me because I'm a woman. And I am always pleasurably surprised when they are accepted. The effect is good, but it is certainly something I am trained not to do by a lifetime of being a woman. I always opted for carefulness, precision, detail in what I said or wrote — but to take that leap [and write]: I must mean this large thing — that is disconcerting. And that's what opinion journalism is."

Since the authoritative voice can be so disconcerting for many women to use, women writers often have turned to fiction to give safe cover to their longing to express their political points of view: *Jane Eyre* conceals a passionate outburst about feminism; *Uncle Tom's Cabin* sugarcoats an antislavery polemic. As Emily Dickinson warned, "Tell all the truth but tell it slant." A prominent feminist muckraker keeps on her refrigerator the motto, "Tell the truth and run." 25

We know as women that the act of "taking a position" in a sweeping way — "standing one's ground" above one's own byline, asserting one's view about the world of fact rather than fantasy — is a dangerous one, an act that will be met with punishment. When I have interviewed college women about their fears of leadership and public voice, they often use metaphors of punitive violence when describing their anxiety about expressing opinions in public: "having it blow up in my face"; "I'll be torn apart"; "ripped to shreds"; "they'll shoot me down."

Punishment — is that not too strong a word? This is the end of the twentieth century, after all; women no longer need to write under pseudonyms to conceal the force of their opinions. Yet when we look at what happens when women "take a stand," the common female fear of punishment for expressing an opinion suggests no phantom anxiety. A woman who enters public debate is indeed likely to be punished. A complex set of rules ensures it. Some involve ad feminam attacks: the absurd attacks on Chelsea Clinton's appearance that flitted across the public stage in the last year or so were in fact attacks on her mother, a message to all women contemplating entering public life that their children can be held hostage in retribution.

Others involve chivalry: when a woman tries to argue with men — as Rodham Clinton did in presenting her views on health care — the debate can be neatly sidestepped by labeling her "charming" and "disarming." These terms ensure that she cannot be seen to fight and win by virtue of her wits, for her potential adversaries preemptively "disarm" themselves — yield their weapons — and let themselves be "charmed" — go into a trance of delight that, presumably, mere reason cannot penetrate. Rodham Clinton's experience eerily reevokes the debate-evasive reaction that Virginia Woolf anticipated after she finished the immensely (if elegantly) confrontational essay that became *A Room of One's Own:* "I forecast, then, that I shall get no criticism, except of the evasive, jocular kind . . . that the press will be kind and talk of its charm and sprightliness; Also I shall be attacked for a feminist and hinted at for a Sapphist. . . . I am afraid it will not be taken seriously."

Still others involve stigmatizing the woman's anger: if the female antagonist is less than universally admired (or doesn't happen to be married to the president), she is called "shrill," as Geraldine Ferraro was when she debated George Bush ("rhymes with rich").[6] Female radio personalities have told me that when they ask male guests tough questions, their listeners call in and tell them to stop being rude to the men. It was front-page news when, in a speech, President Clinton lost his temper at the press — something that a cool-headed leader is rightly expected not to do; but it was front-page news when his wife directed anger at the insurance industry — something that a leader in her position should do if she is to serve her constituency well.

I do not believe that the "different voice" concerns lie deep in   30
women; granted permission to do so without punishment, as many women as men would write blustery, cantankerous prose and flock to the delights of public argument. Women do not lack the desire or ability to fight hard or write fiercely; we lack a behavioral paradigm that makes doing so acceptable.

When a woman does engage in public debate, she is often torn in

[6] Here Wolf refers to the 1984 vice presidential debate.

two. She may be anguished by her own sense that her strong voice is in a state of conflict with her longing for approval and her discomfort with conflict. I feel this role conflict often myself: in a recent book, I argued hard with a certain writer's ideas; when I subsequently met her and liked her, I wanted to beg forgiveness — even though my views of her work had not changed. I feel a kind of terror when I am critical in public and experience a kind of nausea when I am attacked. The knowledge that another person and I publicly disagree makes me feel that I have left something unresolved, raw in the world; even if I "win" — especially if I win — I also lose, because I am guilty, in traditionally feminine terms, of a failure to create harmony and consensus; this bruise to identity manifests at the level of my sense of femininity.

Now I know that this anxiety is unhelpful, even retrograde; and it is directly at odds with my even stronger wish to enjoy the fray without this grief. But there it is. And if I, with my strong feminist upbringing, feel this sense of two drives in a state of absolute conflict when I enter public debate, I doubt that I can be alone. If a woman thinks of herself as someone who is warm and kind in private life, how can she also be a critic in public life, an agonist? This sense of role conflict can feel to many as if it is built in to women's participation in public life.

Women also lack any paradigm for expressing dissent with other women in a way that is perceived as a sign of respect. Men have rituals for expressing conflict as a form of honor, even of friendship; British male parliamentarians are famous for braying at one another and then joking over the urinal. But women lack any such social patterns. If a woman engages in hard debate with another woman, she is a "spoiler" or a "mudslinger," as Liz Holtzman was accused of being when she attacked Ferraro in the 1992 Senate race; the fact that Senator Nancy Kassebaum *disagreed* with Senator Patty Murray about what to do with the Packwood investigation made news.[7] Woman-to-woman argument is seen, even by women, as a breakdown of precious consensus, or a cat-fight, or a "betrayal of sisterhood" — a situation that can force women in public to suppress their legitimate differences of opinion; whereas man-to-man argument is understood as being the stuff of democracy.

Why is all this "subjective," "emotional" stuff a fit subject for the pages of a policy journal? Because the psychic disincentives for women to argue in public, or to write strong opinionated journalism, have profound implications for the health of democracy, Woolf wrote, "The effect of discouragement upon the mind of the artist should be measured." These psychological and social barriers to women's opinionated public speech to make it literally not worth it, in many women's minds, to run for office, contradict an adversary, or take a controversial public stance. If many women feel ridicule and hostility more acutely than men do, if

[7] *Robert Packwood:* U.S. Senator from Oregon who resigned in 1995 after being reprimanded by the House Ethics Committee on charges of sexual misconduct.

they are uncomfortable with isolation, then ridicule, hostility, and the threat of isolation can be — and are — standard weapons in the arsenal used to scare women away from public life.

In essence, certain kinds of forceful speech and interchange are de-   35 fined as male and prohibited to women, as a subtle but immensely effective means to maintain the world of opinion and policymaking as an all-male preserve. And then, in a vicious circle, many women preemptively internalize the barriers, which keeps them wary of storming their way into the marketplace of opinions.

The response to this state of affairs has to be a complex one. To begin with, editors and producers must root out their own often unwitting bias. They are welching on their commitment to inform citizens of a real range of views, leaving half the population ill-prepared to pursue their interests within the democratic process. They are also shortchanging us as a nation, for their unacknowledged warp in perspective leaves "women's issues" and female talking heads, no matter how pressing the topic nor how perspicacious the voices, to languish in the journalistic harem of women's magazines, crowded in among celebrity pets and the latest news on the French manicure. Because of this omission of "women's perspectives" and hard facts about women, we endure wildly off-the-mark debate and create faulty policy in a vacuum of information.

Further gender polarization is not the answer. Just as we are learning to integrate "male" and "female" perspectives about sexual harassment as we seek a newer, fairer social contract in the workplace, we must integrate "male" and "female" views and patterns of expression as we renegotiate the contract about what it is appropriate to say, and how it is appropriate to say it, in the forums of opinion.

The last solution to this dilemma, for all of us who are women still ambivalent about waging opinion, is internal: the only way forward is through. We must realize that public debate may starve the receptors for love and approval, but that it stimulates the synapses of self-respect. Let us shed the lingering sense that authority is something that others — male others — bestow upon us; whenever we are inclined to mumble invective into our coffee, let us flood the airwaves instead. Let's steal a right that has heretofore been defined as masculine: the right to be in love with the sound of one's own voice.

PREPARING FOR DISCUSSION

1. Consider the kinds of information Wolf uses to make her point about the discrepancy in the number of male and female voices in the media. Do you find her evidence convincing?

2. Wolf contends that women are less likely to express their opinions than

men. Does she believe that women are innately less opinionated than men or that women have been trained not to voice opinions as assertively? Do you agree with her?

3. It would be interesting to test Wolf's theory of male dominance in other types of print media. What would she have found, for example, if she had looked at imaginative literature rather than journalism? Examine some of your library's literary journals or magazines. Does Wolf's theory hold up in areas of writing other than journalism? What aspects of her essay, if any, support her attempt to extend her theory to other kinds of writing, such as poetry and fiction?

4. In paragraph 24, Wolf notes that most women are hesitant to make "'sweeping' statements" about cultural and sociopolitical positions. How prone is Wolf herself to sweeping statements in this selection? Do you think that she would consider her own view that male voices dominate the media as a sweeping statement? If not, how would she characterize it?

5. In paragraph 17, Wolf writes that the editorial establishment does not allow women "to slug it out in public arenas." What does Wolf's choice of phrase suggest about her view of public discourse? Do you think that her use of such idioms is largely conscious or unconscious?

FROM READING TO WRITING

6. Select several columns written by women and men from local and national newspapers. After reading the columns carefully, write an essay in which you compare those written by women with those written by men. Do the columns reflect the male and female argumentative styles and methods that Wolf observes in her essay? If not, how could Wolf's thesis be changed to account for similarities as well as differences?

7. If Wolf's theory about women's hesitation to voice their opinions is true, we should see evidence of such behaviors in the classroom. In an essay, describe the ways women and men express themselves in class. Can your findings be reconciled with Wolf's theory? Under what classroom conditions do you think Wolf's theory is likely to hold? Under what classroom conditions do you think it is not likely to hold?

DEBORAH TANNEN

"Put Down that Paper and Talk to Me!":
Rapport-talk and Report-talk

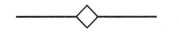

A popular motif from American newspaper and magazine cartoons serves as the basis for linguist Deborah Tannen's title. A husband and wife sit at the breakfast table. The husband silently reads the morning news, holding the paper before him like a shield, while his wife tries in vain to capture his attention. The scene's popularity, Tannen suggests, is a measure of its accuracy in describing gender relations in this country. It not only reflects the failure of women and men to communicate, but also the failure of women and men to understand each other's conversational styles and needs. In the following selection, Tannen attempts to get at the root of these failures and offers some keys to greater verbal understanding between the sexes.

Since receiving her Ph.D. in linguistics from the University of California at Berkeley, Tannen has become the leading American theorist on the ways in which men and women communicate. Her theories have made her a widely sought-after speaker at universities and a frequent guest on such news programs as *CBS News, ABC World News Tonight,* and National Public Radio's *All Things Considered.* Tannen is university professor at Georgetown University, where she is a member of the Linguistics Department. The selection reprinted here originally appeared in her 1990 book *You Just Don't Understand: Women and Men in Conversation,* which remained on the *New York Times* best-seller list for three years.

SELECTED PUBLICATIONS: *Conversational Style: Analyzing Talk among Friends* (1984); *That's Not What I Meant!: How Conversational Style Makes or Breaks Your Relations with Others* (1986); *You Just Don't Understand: Women and Men in Conversation* (1990); *Gender and Conversational Interaction* (1993); *Gender and Discourse* (1994); *Talking from 9 to 5* (1994).

I was sitting in a suburban living room, speaking to a women's group that had invited men to join them for the occasion of my talk about communication between women and men. During the discussion, one man was particularly talkative, full of lengthy comments and explanations. When I made the observation that women often complain that their husbands don't talk to them enough, this man volunteered that he heartily agreed. He gestured toward his wife, who had sat silently beside him on the couch throughout the evening, and said, "She's the talker in our family."

Everyone in the room burst into laughter. The man looked puzzled and hurt. "It's true," he explained. "When I come home from work, I usually have nothing to say, but she never runs out. If it weren't for her, we'd spend the whole evening in silence." Another woman expressed a similar paradox about her husband: "When we go out, he's the life of the party. If I happen to be in another room, I can always hear his voice above the others. But when we're home, he doesn't have that much to say. I do most of the talking."

Who talks more, women or men? According to the stereotype, women talk too much. Linguist Jennifer Coates notes some proverbs:

> A woman's tongue wags like a lamb's tail.
> Foxes are all tail and women are all tongue.
> The North Sea will sooner be found wanting in water than a woman be
> at a loss for a word.

Throughout history, women have been punished for talking too much or in the wrong way. Linguist Connie Eble lists a variety of physical punishments used in Colonial America: Women were strapped to ducking stools and held underwater until they nearly drowned, put into the stocks with signs pinned to them, gagged, and silenced by a cleft stick applied to their tongues.

Though such institutionalized corporal punishments have given way to informal, often psychological ones, modern stereotypes are not much different from those expressed in the old proverbs. Women are believed to talk too much. Yet study after study finds that it is men who talk more — at meetings, in mixed-group discussions, and in classrooms where girls or young women sit next to boys or young men. For example, communications researchers Barbara and Gene Eakins tape-recorded and studied seven university faculty meetings. They found that, with one exception, men spoke more often and, without exception, spoke for a longer time. The men's turns ranged from 10.66 to 17.07 seconds, while the women's turns ranged from 3 to 10 seconds. In other words, the women's longest turns were still shorter than the men's shortest turns.

When a public lecture is followed by questions from the floor, or a 5 talk show host opens the phones, the first voice to be heard asking a question is almost always a man's. And when they ask questions or offer comments from the audience, men tend to talk longer. Linguist Marjorie Swacker recorded question-and-answer sessions at academic conferences. Women were highly visible as speakers at the conferences studied; they presented 40.7 percent of the papers at the conferences studied and made up 42 percent of the audiences. But when it came to volunteering and being called on to ask questions, women contributed only 27.4 percent. Furthermore, the women's questions, on the average, took less than half as much time as the men's. (The mean was 23.1 seconds for women, 52.7 for men.) This happened, Swacker shows, because men (but not women) tended to preface their questions with statements, ask more than one question, and follow up the speaker's answer with another question or comment.

I have observed this pattern at my own lectures, which concern issues of direct relevance to women. Regardless of the proportion of women and men in the audience, men almost invariably ask the first question, more questions, and longer questions. In these situations, women often feel that men are talking too much. I recall one discussion period following a lecture I gave to a group assembled in a bookstore. The group was composed mostly of women, but most of the discussion was being conducted by men in the audience. At one point, a man sitting in the middle was talking at such great length that several women in the front rows began shifting in their seats and rolling their eyes at me. Ironically, what he was going on about was how frustrated he feels when he has to listen to women going on and on about topics he finds boring and unimportant.

Rapport-talk and Report-talk

Who talks more, then, women or men? The seemingly contradictory evidence is reconciled by the difference between what I call *public* and *private speaking*. More men feel comfortable doing "public speaking," while more women feel comfortable doing "private" speaking. Another way of capturing these differences is by using the terms *report-talk* and *rapport-talk*.

For most women, the language of conversation is primarily a language of rapport: a way of establishing connections and negotiating relationships. Emphasis is placed on displaying similarities and matching experiences. From childhood, girls criticize peers who try to stand out or appear better than others. People feel their closest connections at home, or in settings where they *feel* at home — with one or a few people they feel close to and comfortable with — in other words, during private speaking. But even the most public situations can be approached like private speaking.

For most men, talk is primarily a means to preserve independence and negotiate and maintain status in a hierarchical social order. This is done by exhibiting knowledge and skill, and by holding center stage through verbal performance such as story-telling, joking, or imparting information. From childhood, men learn to use talking as a way to get and keep attention. So they are more comfortable speaking in larger groups made up of people they know less well — in the broadest sense, "public speaking." But even the most private situations can be approached like public speaking, more like giving a report than establishing rapport.

Private Speaking: The Wordy Woman and the Mute Man

What is the source of the stereotype that women talk a lot? Dale Spender   10
suggests that most people feel instinctively (if not consciously) that
women, like children, should be seen and not heard, so any amount of
talk from them seems like too much. Studies have shown that if women
and men talk equally in a group, people think the women talked more.
So there is truth to Spender's view. But another explanation is that men
think women talk a lot because they hear women talking in situations
where men would not: on the telephone; or in social situations with
friends, when they are not discussing topics that men find inherently interesting; or, like the couple at the women's group, at home alone — in
other words, in private speaking.

Home is the setting for an American icon that features the silent man
and the talkative woman. And this icon, which grows out of the different
goals and habits I have been describing, explains why the complaint
most often voiced by women about the men with whom they are intimate
is "He doesn't talk to me" — and the second most frequent is "He doesn't
listen to me."

A woman who wrote to Ann Landers is typical:

> My husband never speaks to me when he comes home from work.
> When I ask, "How did everything go today?" he says, "Rough . . ." or
> "It's a jungle out there." (We live in Jersey and he works in New York
> City.)
>
> It's a different story when we have guests or go visiting. Paul is the
> gabbiest guy in the crowd — a real spellbinder. He comes up with the
> most interesting stories. People hang on every word. I think to myself,
> "Why doesn't he ever tell *me* these things?"
>
> This has been going on for 38 years. Paul started to go quiet on me
> after 10 years of marriage. I could never figure out why. Can you solve
> the mystery?
>
> — The Invisible Woman

Ann Landers suggests that the husband may not want to talk because he
is tired when he comes home from work. Yet women who work come
home tired too, and they are nonetheless eager to tell their partners or
friends everything that happened to them during the day and what these
fleeting, daily dramas made them think and feel.

Sources as lofty as studies conducted by psychologists, as down to
earth as letters written to advice columnists, and as sophisticated as
movies and plays come up with the same insight: Men's silence at home
is a disappointment to women. Again and again, women complain, "He
seems to have everything to say to everyone else, and nothing to say
to me."

The film *Divorce American Style* opens with a conversation in which
Debbie Reynolds is claiming that she and Dick Van Dyke don't commu-

nicate, and he is protesting that he tells her everything that's on his mind. The doorbell interrupts their quarrel, and husband and wife compose themselves before opening the door to greet their guests with cheerful smiles.

Behind closed doors, many couples are having conversations like   15 this. Like the character played by Debbie Reynolds, women feel men don't communicate. Like the husband played by Dick Van Dyke, men feel wrongly accused. How can she be convinced that he doesn't tell her anything, while he is equally convinced he tells her everything that's on his mind? How can women and men have such different ideas about the same conversations?

When something goes wrong, people look around for a source to blame: either the person they are trying to communicate with ("You're demanding, stubborn, self-centered") or the group that the other person belongs to ("All women are demanding"; "All men are self-centered"). Some generous-minded people blame the relationship ("We just can't communicate"). But underneath, or overlaid on these types of blame cast outward, most people believe that something is wrong with them.

If individual people or particular relationships were to blame, there wouldn't be so many different people having the same problems. The real problem is conversational style. Women and men have different ways of talking. Even with the best intentions, trying to settle the problem through talk can only make things worse if it is ways of talking that are causing trouble in the first place.

Best Friends

Once again, the seeds of women's and men's styles are sown in the ways they learn to use language while growing up. In our culture, most people, but especially women, look to their closest relationships as havens in a hostile world. The center of a little girl's social life is her best friend. Girls' friendships are made and maintained by telling secrets. For grown women too, the essence of friendship is talk, telling each other what they're thinking and feeling, and what happened that day: who was at the bus stop, who called, what they said, how that made them feel. When asked who their best friends are, most women name other women they talk to regularly. When asked the same question, most men will say it's their wives. After that, many men name other men with whom they do things such as play tennis or baseball (but never just sit and talk) or a chum from high school whom they haven't spoken to in a year.

When Debbie Reynolds complained that Dick Van Dyke didn't tell her anything, and he protested that he did, both were right. She felt he didn't tell her anything because he didn't tell her the fleeting thoughts and feelings he experienced throughout the day — the kind of talk she would have with her best friend. He didn't tell her these things because to him they didn't seem like anything to tell. He told her anything that seemed important — anything he would tell his friends.

Men and women often have very different ideas of what's important — and at what point "important" topics should be raised. A woman told me, with lingering incredulity, of a conversation with her boyfriend. Knowing he had seen his friend Oliver, she asked, "What's new with Oliver?" He replied, "Nothing." But later in the conversation it came out that Oliver and his girlfriend had decided to get married. "That's nothing?" the woman gasped in frustration and disbelief.

For men, "Nothing" may be a ritual response at the start of a conversation. A college woman missed her brother but rarely called him because she found it difficult to get talk going. A typical conversation began with her asking, "What's up with you?" and his replying, "Nothing." Hearing his "Nothing" as meaning "There is nothing personal I want to talk about," she supplied talk by filling him in on her news and eventually hung up in frustration. But when she thought back, she remembered that later in the conversation he had mumbled, "Christie and I got into another fight." This came so late and so low that she didn't pick up on it. And he was probably equally frustrated that she didn't.

Many men honestly do not know what women want, and women honestly do not know why men find what they want so hard to comprehend and deliver.

"Talk to Me!"

Women's dissatisfaction with men's silence at home is captured in the stock cartoon setting of a breakfast table at which a husband and wife are sitting: He's reading a newspaper; she's glaring at the back of the newspaper. In a Dagwood strip, Blondie complains, "Every morning all he sees is the newspaper! I'll bet you don't even know I'm here!" Dagwood reassures her, "Of course I know you're here. You're my wonderful wife and I love you very much." With this, he unseeingly pats the paw of the family dog, which the wife has put in her place before leaving the room. The cartoon strip shows that Blondie is justified in feeling like the woman who wrote to Ann Landers: invisible.

Another cartoon shows a husband opening a newspaper and asking his wife, "Is there anything you would like to say to me before I begin reading the newspaper?" The reader knows that there isn't — but that as soon as he begins reading the paper, she will think of something. The cartoon highlights the difference in what women and men think talk is for: To him, talk is for information. So when his wife interrupts his reading, it must be to inform him of something that he needs to know. This being the case, she might as well tell him what she thinks he needs to know before he starts reading. But to her, talk is for interaction. Telling things is a way to show involvement, and listening is a way to show interest and caring. It is not an odd coincidence that she always thinks of things to tell him when he is reading. She feels the need for verbal interaction most keenly when he is (unaccountably, from her point of view) buried in the newspaper instead of talking to her.

Yet another cartoon shows a wedding cake that has, on top, in place of the plastic statues of bride and groom in tuxedo and gown, a breakfast scene in which an unshaven husband reads a newspaper across the table from his disgruntled wife. The cartoon reflects the enormous gulf between the romantic expectations of marriage represented by the plastic couple in traditional wedding costume, and the often disappointing reality represented by the two sides of the newspaper at the breakfast table — the front, which he is reading, and the back, at which she is glaring.

These cartoons, and many others on the same theme, are funny because people recognize their own experience in them. What's not funny is that many women are deeply hurt when men don't talk to them at home, and many men are deeply frustrated by feeling they have disappointed their partners, without understanding how they failed or how else they could have behaved.

Some men are further frustrated because, as one put it, "When in the world am I supposed to read the morning paper?" If many women are incredulous that many men do not exchange personal information with their friends, this man is incredulous that many women do not bother to read the morning paper. To him, reading the paper is an essential part of his morning ritual, and his whole day is awry if he doesn't get to read it. In his words, reading the newspaper in the morning is as important to him as putting on makeup in the morning is to many women he knows. Yet many women, he observed, either don't subscribe to a paper or don't read it until they get home in the evening. "I find this very puzzling," he said. "I can't tell you how often I have picked up a woman's morning newspaper from her front door in the evening and handed it to her when she opened the door for me."

To this man (and I am sure many others), a woman who objects to his reading the morning paper is trying to keep him from doing something essential and harmless. It's a violation of his independence — his freedom of action. But when a woman who expects her partner to talk to her is disappointed that he doesn't, she perceives his behavior as a failure of intimacy: He's keeping things from her; he's lost interest in her; he's pulling away. A woman I will call Rebecca, who is generally quite happily married, told me that this is the one source of serious dissatisfaction with her husband, Stuart. Her term for his taciturnity is *stinginess of spirit.* She tells him what she is thinking, and he listens silently. She asks him what he is thinking, and he takes a long time to answer, "I don't know." In frustration she challenges, "Is there nothing on your mind?"

For Rebecca, who is accustomed to expressing her fleeting thoughts and opinions as they come to her, *saying* nothing means *thinking* nothing. But Stuart does not assume that his passing thoughts are worthy of utterance. He is not in the habit of uttering his fleeting ruminations, so just as Rebecca "naturally" speaks her thoughts, he "naturally" dismisses his as soon as they occur to him. Speaking them would give them more weight and significance than he feels they merit. All her life she has had practice in verbalizing her thoughts and feelings in private conversations with people she is close to; all his life he has had practice in dismissing his and keeping them to himself.

What to Do with Doubts

In the above example, Rebecca was not talking about any particular kind   30
of thoughts or feelings, just whatever Stuart might have had in mind. But the matter of giving voice to thoughts and feelings becomes particularly significant in the case of negative feelings or doubts about a relationship. This difference was highlighted for me when a fifty-year-old divorced man told me about his experiences in forming new relationships with women. On this matter, he was clear: "I do not value my fleeting thoughts, and I do not value the fleeting thoughts of others." He felt that the relationship he was currently in had been endangered, even permanently weakened, by the woman's practice of tossing out her passing thoughts, because, early in their courtship, many of her thoughts were fears about their relationship. Not surprisingly, since they did not yet know each other well, she worried about whether she could trust him, whether their relationship would destroy her independence, whether this relationship was really right for her. He felt she should have kept these fears and doubts to herself and waited to see how things turned out.

As it happens, things turned out well. The woman decided that the relationship was right for her, she could trust him, and she did not have to give up her independence. But he felt, at the time that he told me of this, that he had still not recovered from the wear and tear of coping with her earlier doubts. As he put it, he was still dizzy from having been bounced around like a yo-yo tied to the string of her stream of consciousness.

In contrast, this man admitted, he himself goes to the other extreme: He never expresses his fears and misgivings about their relationship at all. If he's unhappy but doesn't say anything about it, his unhappiness expresses itself in a kind of distancing coldness. This response is just what women fear most, and just the reason they prefer to express dissatisfactions and doubts — as an antidote to the isolation and distance that would result from keeping them to themselves.

The different perspectives on expressing or concealing dissatisfactions and doubts may reflect a difference in men's and women's awareness of the power of their words to affect others. In repeatedly telling him what she feared about their relationship, this woman spoke as though she assumed he was invulnerable and could not be hurt by what she said; perhaps she was underestimating the power of her words to affect him. For his part, when he refrains from expressing negative thoughts or feelings, he seems to be overestimating the power of his words to hurt her, when, ironically, she is more likely to be hurt by his silence than his words.

These women and men are talking in ways they learned as children and reinforced as young adults and then adults, in their same-gender friendships. For girls, talk is the glue that holds relationships together. Boys' relationships are held together primarily by activities: doing things together, or talking about activities such as sports or, later, politics. The forums in which men are most inclined to talk are those in which they feel the need to impress, in situations where their status is in question.

Making Adjustments

Such impasses will perhaps never be settled to the complete satisfaction of both parties, but understanding the differing views can help detoxify the situation, and both can make adjustments. Realizing that men and women have different assumptions about the place of talk in relationships, a woman can observe a man's desire to read the morning paper at the breakfast table without interpreting it as a rejection of her or a failure of their relationship. And a man can understand a woman's desire for talk without interpreting it as an unreasonable demand or a manipulative attempt to prevent him from doing what he wants to do.

A woman who had heard my interpretations of these differences between women and men told me how these insights helped her. Early in a promising relationship, a man spent the night at her apartment. It was a weeknight, and they both had to go to work the next day, so she was delighted when he made the rash and romantic suggestion that they have breakfast together and report late for work. She happily prepared breakfast, looking forward to the scene shaped in her mind: They would sit facing each other across her small table, look into each other's eyes, and say how much they liked each other and how happy they were about their growing friendship. It was against the backdrop of this heady expectation that she confronted an entirely different scene: As she placed on the table an array of lovingly prepared eggs, toast, and coffee, the man sat across her small table — and opened the newspaper in front of his face. If suggesting they have breakfast together had seemed like an invitation to get closer, in her view (or obstructing her view) the newspaper was now erected as a paper-thin but nonetheless impenetrable barrier between them.

Had she known nothing of the gender differences I discuss, she would simply have felt hurt and dismissed this man as yet another

35

clunker. She would have concluded that, having enjoyed the night with her, he was now availing himself of her further services as a short-order cook. Instead, she realized that, unlike her, he did not feel the need for talk to reinforce their intimacy. The companionability of her presence was all he needed, and that did not mean that he didn't cherish her presence. By the same token, had he understood the essential role played by talk in women's definition of intimacy, he could have put off reading the paper — and avoided putting her off.

The Comfort of Home

For everyone, home is a place to be offstage. But the comfort of home can have opposite and incompatible meanings for women and men. For many men, the comfort of home means freedom from having to prove themselves and impress through verbal display. At last, they are in a situation where talk is not required. They are free to remain silent. But for women, home is a place where they are free to talk, and where they feel the greatest need for talk, with those they are closest to. For them, the comfort of home means the freedom to talk without worrying about how their talk will be judged.

This view emerged in a study by linguist Alice Greenwood of the conversations that took place among her three preadolescent children and their friends. Her daughters and son gave different reasons for their preferences in dinner guests. Her daughter Stacy said she would not want to invite people she didn't know well because then she would have to be "polite and quiet" and put on good manners. Greenwood's other daughter, Denise, said she liked to have her friend Meryl over because she could act crazy with Meryl and didn't have to worry about her manners, as she would with certain other friends who "would go around talking to people probably." But Denise's twin brother, Dennis, said nothing about having to watch his manners or worry about how others would judge his behavior. He simply said that he liked to have over friends with whom he could joke and laugh a lot. The girls' comments show that for them being close means being able to talk freely. And being with relative strangers means having to watch what they say and do. This insight holds a clue to the riddle of who talks more, women or men.

Public Speaking: The Talkative Man and the Silent Woman

So far I have been discussing the private scenes in which many men are silent and many women are talkative. But there are other scenes in which the roles are reversed. Returning to Rebecca and Stuart, we saw that when they are home alone, Rebecca's thoughts find their way into words effortlessly, whereas Stuart finds he can't come up with anything to say. The reverse happens when they are in other situations. For example, at a

40

meeting of the neighborhood council or the parents' association at their children's school, it is Stuart who stands up and speaks. In that situation, it is Rebecca who is silent, her tongue tied by an acute awareness of all the negative reactions people could have to what she might say, all the mistakes she might make in trying to express her ideas. If she musters her courage and prepares to say something, she needs time to formulate it and then waits to be recognized by the chair. She cannot just jump up and start talking the way Stuart and some other men can.

Eleanor Smeal, president of the Fund for the Feminist Majority, was a guest on a call-in radio talk show, discussing abortion. No subject could be of more direct concern to women, yet during the hour-long show, all the callers except two were men. Diane Rehm, host of a radio talk show, expresses puzzlement that although the audience for her show is evenly split between women and men, 90 percent of the callers to the show are men. I am convinced that the reason is not that women are uninterested in the subjects discussed on the show. I would wager that women listeners are bringing up the subjects they heard on *The Diane Rehm Show* to their friends and family over lunch, tea, and dinner. But fewer of them call in because to do so would be putting themselves on display, claiming public attention for what they have to say, catapulting themselves onto center stage.

I myself have been the guest on innumerable radio and television talk shows. Perhaps I am unusual in being completely at ease in this mode of display. But perhaps I am not unusual at all, because, although I am comfortable in the role of invited expert, I have never called in to a talk show I was listening to, although I have often had ideas to contribute. When I am the guest, my position of authority is granted before I begin to speak. Were I to call in, I would be claiming that right on my own. I would have to establish my credibility by explaining who I am, which might seem self-aggrandizing, or not explain who I am and risk having my comments ignored or not valued. For similar reasons, though I am comfortable lecturing to groups numbering in the thousands, I rarely ask questions following another lecturer's talk, unless I know both the subject and the group very well.

My own experience and that of talk show hosts seems to hold a clue to the difference in women's and men's attitudes toward talk: Many men are more comfortable than most women in using talk to claim attention. And this difference lies at the heart of the distinction between report-talk and rapport-talk.

Report-talk in Private

Report-talk, or what I am calling public speaking, does not arise only in the literally public situation of formal speeches delivered to a listening audience. The more people there are in a conversation, the less well you know them, and the more status differences among them, the more a conversation is *like* public speaking or report-talk. The fewer the people, the more intimately you know them, and the more equal their status, the more it is like private speaking or rapport-talk. Furthermore, women feel a situation is more "public" — in the sense that they have to be on good behavior — if there are men present, except perhaps for family members. Yet even in families, the mother and children may feel their home to be "backstage" when Father is not home, "onstage" when he is: Many children are instructed to be on good behavior when Daddy is home. This may be because he is not home often, or because Mother — or Father — doesn't want the children to disturb him when he is.

The difference between public and private speaking also explains the   45
stereotype that women don't tell jokes. Although some women are great raconteurs who can keep a group spellbound by recounting jokes and funny stories, there are fewer such personalities among women than among men. Many women who do tell jokes to large groups of people come from ethnic backgrounds in which verbal performance is highly valued. For example, many of the great women stand-up comics, such as Fanny Brice and Joan Rivers, come from Jewish backgrounds.

Although it's not true that women don't tell jokes, it is true that many women are less likely than men to tell jokes in large groups, especially groups including men. So it's not surprising that men get the impression that women never tell jokes at all. Folklorist Carol Mitchell studied joke telling on a college campus. She found that men told most of their jokes to other men, but they also told many jokes to mixed groups and to women. Women, however, told most of their jokes to other women, fewer to men, and very few to groups that included men as well as women. Men preferred and were more likely to tell jokes when they had an audience: at least two, often four or more. Women preferred a small audience of one or two, rarely more than three. Unlike men, they were reluctant to tell jokes in front of people they didn't know well. Many women flatly refused to tell jokes they knew if there were four or more in the group, promising to tell them later in private. Men never refused the invitation to tell jokes.

All of Mitchell's results fit in with the picture I have been drawing of public and private speaking. In a situation in which there are more people in the audience, more men, or more strangers, joke telling, like any other form of verbal performance, requires speakers to claim center stage and prove their abilities. These are the situations in which many women are reluctant to talk. In a situation that is more private, because the audience is small, familiar, and perceived to be members of a community (for example, other women), they are more likely to talk.

The idea that telling jokes is a kind of self-display does not imply that it is selfish or self-centered. The situation of joke telling illustrates that status and connection entail each other. Entertaining others is a way of establishing connections with them, and telling jokes can be a kind of gift giving, where the joke is a gift that brings pleasure to receivers. The key issue is asymmetry: One person is the teller and the others are the audience. If these roles are later exchanged — for example, if the joke telling becomes a round in which one person after another takes the role of teller — then there is symmetry on the broad scale, if not in the individual act. However, if women habitually take the role of appreciative audience and never take the role of joke teller, the asymmetry of the individual joke telling is diffused through the larger interaction as well. This is a hazard for women. A hazard for men is that continually telling jokes can be distancing. This is the effect felt by a man who complained that when he talks to his father on the phone, all his father does is tell him jokes. An extreme instance of a similar phenomenon is the class clown, who, according to teachers, is nearly always a boy.

Rapport-talk in Public

Just as conversations that take place at home among friends can be like public speaking, even a public address can be like private speaking: for example, by giving a lecture full of personal examples and stories.

At the executive committee of a fledgling professional organization, the outgoing president, Fran, suggested that the organization adopt the policy of having presidents deliver a presidential address. To explain and support her proposal, she told a personal anecdote: Her cousin was the president of a more established professional organization at the time that Fran held the same position in this one. Fran's mother had been talking to her cousin's mother on the telephone. Her cousin's mother told Fran's mother that her daughter was preparing her presidential address, and she asked when Fran's presidential address was scheduled to be. Fran was embarrassed to admit to her mother that she was not giving one. This made her wonder whether the organization's professional identity might not be enhanced if it emulated the more established organizations.

Several men on the committee were embarrassed by Fran's reference to her personal situation and were not convinced by her argument. It seemed to them not only irrelevant but unseemly to talk about her mother's telephone conversations at an executive committee meeting. Fran had approached the meeting — a relatively public context — as an extension of the private kind. Many women's tendency to use personal experience and examples, rather than abstract argumentation, can be understood from the perspective of their orientation to language as it is used in private speaking.

A study by Celia Roberts and Tom Jupp of a faculty meeting at a secondary school in England found that the women's arguments did not carry weight with their male colleagues because they tended to use their own experience as evidence, or argue about the effect of policy on individual students. The men at the meeting argued from a completely different perspective, making categorical statements about right and wrong.

The same distinction is found in discussions at home. A man told me that he felt critical of what he perceived as his wife's lack of logic. For example, he recalled a conversation in which he had mentioned an article he had read in *The New York Times* claiming that today's college students are not as idealistic as students were in the 1960s. He was inclined to accept this claim. His wife questioned it, supporting her argument with the observation that her niece and her niece's friends were very idealistic indeed. He was incredulous and scornful of her faulty reasoning; it was obvious to him that a single personal example is neither evidence nor argumentation — it's just anecdote. It did not occur to him that he was dealing with a different logical system, rather than a lack of logic.

The logic this woman was employing was making sense of the world as a more private endeavor — observing and integrating her personal experience and drawing connections to the experiences of others. The logic the husband took for granted was a more public endeavor — more like gathering information, conducting a survey, or devising arguments by rules of formal logic as one might in doing research.

Another man complained about what he and his friends call women's "shifting sands" approach to discussion. These men feel that whereas they try to pursue an argument logically, step by step, until it is settled, women continually change course in midstream. He pointed to the short excerpt from *Divorce American Style* quoted above as a case in point. It seemed to him that when Debbie Reynolds said, "I can't argue now. I have to take the French bread out of the oven," she was evading the argument because she had made an accusation — "All you do is criticize" — that she could not support.

This man also offered an example from his own experience. His girlfriend had told him of a problem she had because her boss wanted her to do one thing and she wanted to do another. Taking the boss's view for the sake of argumentation, he pointed out a negative consequence that would result if she did what she wanted. She countered that the same negative consequence would result if she did what the boss wanted. He complained that she was shifting over to the other field of battle — what would happen if she followed her boss's will — before they had made headway with the first — what would happen if she followed her own.

Speaking for the Team

A final puzzle on the matter of public and private speaking is suggested by the experience I related at the opening of this chapter, in which a women's group I addressed had invited men to participate, and a talkative man had referred to his silent wife as "the talker in our family." Following their laughter, other women in the group commented that this woman was not usually silent. When their meetings consisted of women only, she did her share of talking. Why, then, was she silent on this occasion?

One possibility is that my presence transformed the private-speaking group into a public-speaking event. Another transformation was that there were men in the group. In a sense, most women feel they are "backstage" when there are no men around. When men are present women are "onstage," insofar as they feel they must watch their behavior more. Another possibility is that it was not the presence of men in general that affected this woman's behavior, but the presence of *her husband.* One interpretation is that she was somehow cowed, or silenced, by her husband's presence. But another is that she felt they were a team. Since he was talking a lot, the team would be taking up too much time if she spoke too. She also may have felt that because he was representing their team, she didn't have to, much as many women let their husbands drive if they are in the car, but do the driving themselves if their husbands are not there.

Obviously, not every woman becomes silent when her husband joins a group; after all, there were many women in the group who talked a lot, and many had brought spouses. But several other couples told me of similar experiences. For example, when one couple took evening classes together, he was always an active participant in class discussion, while she said very little. But one semester they had decided to take different classes, and then she found that she was a talkative member of the class she attended alone.

Such a development can be viewed in two different ways. If talking in a group is a good thing — a privilege and a pleasure — then the silent woman will be seen as deprived of her right to speak, deprived of her voice. But the pleasures of report-talk are not universally admired. There are many who do not wish to speak in a group. In this view, a woman who feels she has no need to speak because her husband is doing it for her might feel privileged, just as a woman who does not like to drive might feel lucky that she doesn't have to when her husband is there — and a man who does not like to drive might feel unlucky that he has to, like it or not.

Avoiding Mutual Blame

The difference between public and private speaking, or report-talk and rapport-talk, can be understood in terms of status and connection. It is not surprising that women are most comfortable talking when they feel safe and close, among friends and equals, whereas men feel comfortable talking when there is a need to establish and maintain their status in a group. But the situation is complex, because status and connection are bought with the same currency. What seems like a bid for status could be intended as a display of closeness, and what seems like distancing may have been intended to avoid the appearance of pulling rank. Hurtful and unjustified misinterpretations can be avoided by understanding the conversational styles of the other gender.

When men do all the talking at meetings, many women — including researchers — see them as "dominating" the meeting, intentionally preventing women from participating, publicly flexing their higher-status muscles. But the *result* that men do most of the talking does not necessarily mean that men *intend* to prevent women from speaking. Those who readily speak up assume that others are as free as they are to take the floor. In this sense, men's speaking out freely can be seen as evidence that they assume women are at the same level of status: "We are all equals," the metamessage of their behavior could be, "competing for the floor." If this is indeed the intention (and I believe it often, though not always, is), a woman can recognize women's lack of participation at meetings and take measures to redress the imbalance, without blaming men for intentionally locking them out.

The culprit, then, is not an individual man or even men's styles alone, but the difference between women's and men's styles. If that is the case, then both can make adjustments. A woman can push herself to speak up without being invited, or begin to speak without waiting for what seems a polite pause. But the adjustment should not be one-sided. A man can learn that a woman who is not accustomed to speaking up in groups is *not* as free as he is to do so. Someone who is waiting for a nice long pause before asking her question does not find the stage set for her appearance, as do those who are not awaiting a pause, the moment after (or before) another speaker stops talking. Someone who expects to be invited to speak ("You haven't said much, Millie. What do you think?") is not accustomed to leaping in and claiming the floor for herself. As in so many areas, being admitted as an equal is not in itself assurance of equal opportunity, if one is not accustomed to playing the game in the way it is being played. Being admitted to a dance does not ensure the participation of someone who has learned to dance to a different rhythm.

PREPARING FOR DISCUSSION

1. Tannen begins her essay with an attempt to dispel a popular stereotype about women. What is that stereotype and to what source does Tannen attribute it? Does she succeed in exploding it entirely? If not, under what conditions does the stereotype tend to be accurate?

2. Tannen makes a useful and important distinction between what she calls "rapport-talk" and "report-talk." Which gender does she believe is more likely to talk in the interest of establishing connections between people? Which gender does she believe is more likely to speak in the interest of imparting information to

other people? In what type of environment, according to Tannen, are we likely to find "rapport-talk" as the predominant mode of exchange? In what type of environment are we more likely to find "report-talk" as the predominant mode?

3. Throughout the selection, Tannen reports on a number of studies carried out by both women and men. In one instance, a female scientist recounts the differing responses of her own son and daughter to a particular situation — inviting friends to dinner (paragraph 39). Given Tannen's thesis that gender affects the way that each sex responds to the world, how can the social behavior of men and women be studied objectively by either men or women? For instance, even forgetting the parental relationship involved, would you consider the study mentioned above to be gender-blind?

4. Tannen's method of arguing her points depends heavily on anecdotes. Moreover, she contends that women tend to argue more from the basis of private experience than men who, in general, appeal to objective evidence (paragraph 51). Consider Tannen's statement that women possess a "different logical system [from men], rather than a lack of logic." Do you agree with her that women's arguments tend to be logical in ways *different* from those made by men? Can you describe that different logic? What dangers attend a view of the world that depends on subjective experience?

5. Tannen often resorts to theatrical metaphors when describing the social and conversational behaviors of men and women. Locate several of these metaphors. Why do you think Tannen has chosen to use them? Do they help her to describe the behaviors in which she is interested? What other kinds of metaphors might have served her purposes as well?

FROM READING TO WRITING

6. Tannen's work, in this selection and in her books, involves the intensive study of conversational styles. How would you describe your own conversational style? Write an essay in which you reflect upon that style. In particular, you might consider what kinds of things you tend to reveal or conceal about yourself. Do you tend to say just what's on your mind, or do you wait to choose exactly the right words before speaking? Do you think that the way you speak is determined largely by your gender?

7. Like Naomi Wolf in the previous selection, Tannen prefers to think that the different ways women and men act and speak depend upon the different social roles to which each sex has been traditionally assigned. Write an essay in which you argue for or against this view of gender.

SUSAN FALUDI

Blame It on Feminism

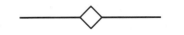

Has the feminist movement of the last quarter century really led to major changes in women's status or have the movement's modest gains been so magnified by the national media as to invite an angry and damaging response from conservatives hostile to feminist ideals? Journalist and author Susan Faludi garners evidence for such a backlash and tries to account for its growing momentum as a reaction to the feminist victories of the last few decades.

Faludi's plans to write her controversial first book *Backlash: The Undeclared War against American Women*, from which this selection is taken, began to take shape after reading about a nationally publicized 1986 study concluding that college-educated career women in their thirties were likely to remain unmarried. Faludi and other reporters questioned the study's conclusions on the grounds that the research methods used in gathering information were flawed, but the national media ignored the journalists' findings and let the study stand unchallenged. *Backlash* thus began as a record of the way that the American media help to promulgate myths about women's lives and status. After graduating Harvard, where she served as managing editor of the *Harvard Crimson*, Faludi worked for several major newspapers including the *New York Times* and the *Atlanta Journal-Constitution*. As a reporter for the San Francisco bureau of the *Wall Street Journal*, Faludi won a Pulitzer Prize for explanatory journalism in 1991.

SELECTED PUBLICATIONS: *Backlash: The Undeclared War against American Women* (1991); Faludi's articles have appeared in *Esquire, Newsweek,* the *New York Times, Ms.,* and *Mother Jones.*

To be a woman in America at the close of the twentieth century — what good fortune. That's what we keep hearing, anyway. The barricades have fallen, politicians assure us. Women have "made it," Madison Avenue cheers. Women's fight for equality has "largely been won," *Time* magazine announces. Enroll at any university, join any law firm, apply for credit at any bank. Women have so many opportunities now, corporate leaders say, that they don't really need opportunity policies. Women are so equal now, lawmakers say, that they no longer need an Equal Rights Amendment. Women have "so much," former president Ronald Reagan says, that the White House no longer needs to appoint them to high office. Even American Express ads are saluting a woman's right to charge it. At last, women have received their full citizenship papers.

And yet . . .

Behind this celebration of the American woman's victory, behind the news, cheerfully and endlessly repeated, that the struggle for women's rights is won, another message flashes: you may be free and equal now, but you have never been more miserable.

This bulletin of despair is posted everywhere — at the newsstand, on the TV set, at the movies, in advertisements and doctors' offices and academic journals. Professional women are suffering "burnout" and succumbing to an "infertility epidemic." Single women are grieving from a "man shortage." The *New York Times* reports: childless women are "depressed and confused" and their ranks are swelling. *Newsweek* says: unwed women are "hysterical" and crumbling under a "profound crisis of confidence." The health-advice manuals inform: high-powered career women are stricken with unprecedented outbreaks of "stress-induced disorders," hair loss, bad nerves, alcoholism, and even heart attacks. The psychology books advise: independent women's loneliness represents "a major mental-health problem today." Even founding feminist Betty Friedan has been spreading the word: she warns that women now suffer from "new problems that have no name."

How can American women be in so much trouble at the same time   5
that they are supposed to be so blessed? If women got what they asked for, what could possibly be the matter now?

The prevailing wisdom of the past decade has supported one, and only one, answer to this riddle: it must be all that equality that's causing all that pain. Women are unhappy precisely because they are free. Women are enslaved by their own liberation. They have grabbed at the gold ring of independence, only to miss the one ring that really matters. They have gained control of their fertility, only to destroy it. They have pursued their own professional dreams — and lost out on romance, the greatest female adventure. "Our generation was the human sacrifice" to the women's movement, writer Elizabeth Mehren contends in a *Time* cover story. Baby-boom women, like her, she says, have been duped by feminism: "We believed the rhetoric." In *Newsweek*, writer Kay Ebeling dubs feminism the "Great Experiment That Failed" and asserts, "Women in my generation, its perpetrators, are the casualties."

In the eighties, publications from the *New York Times* to *Vanity Fair* to *The Nation* have issued a steady stream of indictments against the women's movement, with such headlines as "When Feminism Failed" or "The Awful Truth about Women's Lib." They hold the campaign for women's equality responsible for nearly every woe besetting women, from depression to meager savings accounts, from teenage suicides to eating disorders to bad complexions. The *Today* show says women's liberation is to blame for bag ladies. A guest columnist in the *Baltimore Sun* even proposes that feminists produced the rise in slasher movies. By making the "violence" of abortion more acceptable, the author reasons, women's-rights activists made it all right to show graphic murders on screen.

At the same time, other outlets of popular culture have been forging the same connection: in Hollywood films, of which *Fatal Attraction* is only the most famous, emancipated women with condominiums of their own slink wild-eyed between bare walls, paying for their liberty with an empty bed, a barren womb. "My biological clock is ticking so loud it keeps me awake at night," Sally Field cries in the film *Surrender*, as, in an all-too-common transformation in the cinema of the eighties, an actress who once played scrappy working heroines is now showcased groveling for a groom. In prime-time television shows, from *thirtysomething* to *Family Man*, single, professional, and feminist women are humiliated, turned into harpies, or hit by nervous breakdowns; the wise ones recant their independent ways by the closing sequence. In popular novels, from Gail Parent's *A Sign of the Eighties* to Stephen King's *Misery*, unwed women shrink to sniveling spinsters or inflate the fire-breathing she-devils; renouncing all aspirations but marriage, they beg for wedding bands from strangers or swing axes at reluctant bachelors. Even Erica Jong's high-flying independent heroine literally crashes by the end of the decade, as the author supplants *Fear of Flying*'s saucy Isadora Wing, an exuberant symbol of female sexual emancipation in the seventies, with an embittered careerist-turned-recovering-"codependent" in *Any Woman's Blues* — a book that is intended, as the narrator bluntly states, "to demonstrate what a dead end the so-called sexual revolution had become and how desperate so-called free women were in the last few years of our decadent epoch."

Popular psychology manuals peddle the same diagnosis for contemporary female distress. "Feminism, having promised her a stronger sense of her own identity, has given her little more than an identity *crisis*," the best-selling advice manual *Being a Woman* asserts. The authors of the era's self-help classic, *Smart Women/Foolish Choices*, proclaim that women's distress was "an unfortunate consequence of feminism" because "it created a myth among women that the apex of self-realization could be achieved only through autonomy, independence, and career."

In the Reagan and Bush years, government officials have needed no 10 prompting to endorse this thesis. Reagan spokeswoman Faith Ryan Whittlesey declared feminism a "straitjacket" for women, in one of the White House's only policy speeches on the status of the American female population — entitled "Radical Feminism in Retreat." The U.S. attorney general's Commission on Pornography even proposed that women's professional advancement might be responsible for rising rape rates: with more women in college and at work now, the commission members reasoned in their report, women just have more opportunities to be raped.

Legal scholars have railed against the "equality trap." Sociologists have claimed that "feminist-inspired" legislative reforms have stripped women of special "protections." Economists have argued that well-paid working women have created a "less stable American family." And demographers, with greatest fanfare, have legitimated the prevailing wisdom with so-called neutral data on sex ratios and fertility trends; they say they actually have the numbers to prove that equality doesn't mix with marriage and motherhood.

Finally, some "liberated" women themselves have joined the lamentations. In *The Cost of Loving: Women and the New Fear of Intimacy*, Megan Marshall, a Harvard-pedigreed writer, asserts that the feminist "Myth of Independence" has turned her generation into unloved and unhappy fast-trackers, "dehumanized" by careers and "uncertain of their gender identity." Other diaries of mad Superwomen charge that "the hard-core feminist viewpoint," as one of them puts it, has relegated educated executive achievers to solitary nights of frozen dinners and closet drinking. The triumph of equality, they report, has merely given women hives, stomach cramps, eye "twitching" disorders, even comas.

But what "equality" are all these authorities talking about?

If American women are so equal, why do they represent two-thirds of all poor adults? Why are more than 70 percent of full-time working women making less than twenty-five thousand dollars a year, nearly double the number of men at that level? Why are they still far more likely than men to live in poor housing, and twice as likely to draw no pension? If women "have it all," then why don't they have the most basic requirements to achieve equality in the work force: unlike that of virtually all other industrialized nations, the U.S. government still has no family-leave and child-care programs.

If women are so "free," why are their reproductive freedoms in   15
greater jeopardy today than a decade earlier? Why, in their own homes, do they still shoulder 70 percent of the household duties—while the only major change in the last fifteen years is that now men *think* they do more around the house? In thirty states, it is still generally legal for husbands to rape their wives; and only ten states have laws mandating arrest for domestic violence — even though battering is the leading cause of injury to women (greater than rapes, muggings, and auto accidents combined).

The word may be that women have been "liberated," but women themselves seem to feel otherwise. Repeatedly in national surveys, majorities of women say they are still far from equality. In poll after poll in the decade, overwhelming majorities of women said they need equal pay and equal job opportunities, they need an Equal Rights Amendment, they need the right to an abortion without government interference, they need a federal law guaranteeing maternity leave, they need decent child-care services. They have none of these. So how exactly have women "won" the war for women's rights?

Seen against this background, the much ballyhooed claim that feminism is responsible for making women miserable becomes absurd — and irrelevant. The afflictions ascribed to feminism, from "the man shortage" to "the infertility epidemic" to "female burnout" to "toxic day care," have had their origins not in the actual conditions of women's lives but rather in a closed system that starts and ends in the media, popular culture, and advertising — an endless feedback loop that perpetuates and exaggerates its own false images of womanhood. And women don't see feminism as their enemy, either. In fact, in national surveys, 75 to 95 percent of women credit the feminist campaign with *improving* their lives, and a similar proportion say that the women's movement should keep pushing for change.

If the many ponderers of the Woman Question really wanted to know what is troubling the American female population, they might have asked their subjects. In public-opinion surveys, women consistently rank their own *inequality*, at work and at home, among their most urgent concerns. Over and over, women complain to pollsters of a lack of economic, not marital, opportunities; they protest that working men, not working women, fail to spend time in the nursery and the kitchen. It is justice for their gender, not wedding rings and bassinets, that women believe to be in desperately short supply.

As the last decade ran its course, the monitors that serve to track slippage in women's status have been working overtime. Government and private surveys are showing that women's already vast representation in the lowliest occupations is rising, their tiny presence in higher-paying trade and craft jobs stalled or backsliding, their minuscule representation in upper management posts stagnant or falling, and their pay dropping in the very occupations where they have made the most "progress."

In national politics, the already small numbers of women in both   20
elective posts and political appointments fell during the eighties. In private life, the average amount that a divorced man paid in child support fell by about 25 percent from the late seventies to the mid-eighties (to a mere $140 a month). And government records chronicled a spectacular rise in sexual violence against women. Reported rapes more than doubled from the early seventies — at nearly twice the rate of all other violent crimes and four times the overall crime rate in the United States.

The truth is that the last decade has seen a powerful counterassault on women's rights, a backlash, an attempt to retract the handful of small and hard-won victories that the feminist movement did manage to win for women. This counterassault is largely insidious: in a kind of pop-culture version of the big lie, it stands the truth boldly on its head and proclaims that the very steps that have elevated women's position have actually led to their downfall.

The backlash is at once sophisticated and banal, deceptively "progressive" and proudly backward. It deploys both the "new" findings of "scientific research" and the dime-store moralism of yesteryear; it turns into media sound bites both the glib pronouncements of pop-psych trend-watchers and the frenzied rhetoric of New Right preachers. The backlash has succeeded in framing virtually the whole issue of women's rights in its own language. Just as Reaganism shifted political discourse far to the right and demonized liberalism, so the backlash convinced the public that women's "liberation" was the true contemporary American scourge — the source of an endless laundry list of personal, social, and economic problems.

But what has made women unhappy in the last decade is not their "equality" — which they don't yet have — but the rising pressure to halt, and even reverse, women's quest for that equality. The "man shortage" and the "infertility epidemic" are not the price of liberation; in fact, they do not even exist. But these chimeras are part of a relentless whittling-down process — much of it amounting to outright propaganda — that has served to stir women's private anxieties and break their political wills. Identifying feminism as women's enemy only furthers the ends of a backlash against women's equality by simultaneously deflecting attention from the backlash's central role and recruiting women to attack their own cause.

Some social observers may well ask whether the current pressures on women actually constitute a backlash — or just a continuation of American society's long-standing resistance to women's equal rights. Certainly hostility to female independence has always been with us. But if fear and loathing of feminism is a sort of perpetual viral condition in our culture, it is not always in an acute stage; its symptoms subside and resurface periodically. And it is these episodes of resurgence, such as the one we face now, that can accurately be termed "backlashes" to women's advancement. If we trace these occurrences in American history, we find such flare-ups are hardly random; they have always been triggered by the perception — accurate or not — that women are making great strides. These outbreaks are backlashes because they have always arisen in reaction to women's "progress," caused not simply by a bedrock of misogyny but by the specific efforts of contemporary women to improve their status, efforts that have been interpreted time and again by men — especially men grappling with real threats to their economic and social well-being on other fronts — as spelling their own masculine doom.

The most recent round of backlash first surfaced in the late seventies   25
on the fringes, among the evangelical Right. By the early eighties, the fundamentalist ideology had shouldered its way into the White House. By the mid-eighties, as resistance to women's rights acquired political and social acceptability, it passed into the popular culture. And in every case, the timing coincided with signs that women were believed to be on the verge of a breakthrough.

Just when the women's quest for equal rights seemed closest to achieving its objectives, the backlash struck it down. Just when a "gender gap" at the voting booth surfaced in 1980, and women in politics began to talk of capitalizing on it, the Republican party elevated Ronald Reagan and both political parties began to shunt women's rights off their platforms. Just when support for feminism and the Equal Rights Amendment reached a record high in 1981, the amendment was defeated the following year. Just when women were starting to mobilize against battering and sexual assaults, the federal government cut funding for battered-woman's programs, defeated bills to fund shelters, and shut down its Office of Domestic Violence — only two years after opening it in 1979. Just when record numbers of younger women were supporting feminist goals in the mid-eighties (more of them, in fact, than older women) and a majority of all women were calling themselves feminists, the media declared the advent of a younger "postfeminist generation" that supposedly reviled the women's movement. Just when women racked up their largest percentage ever supporting the right to abortion, the U.S. Supreme Court moved toward reconsidering it.

In other words, the antifeminist backlash has been set off not by women's achievement of full equality but by the increased possibility that they might win it. It is preemptive strike that stops women long before they reach the finish line. "A backlash may be an indication that women really have had an effect," feminist psychiatrist Dr. Jean Baker Miller has written, "but backlashes occur when advances have been small, before changes are sufficient to help many people. . . . It is almost as if the leaders of backlashes use the fear of change as a threat before major change has occurred." In the last decade, some women did make substantial advances before the backlash hit, but millions of others were left behind, stranded. Some women now enjoy the right to legal abortion — but not the forty-four million women, from the indigent to the military worker, who depend on the federal government for their medical care. Some women can now walk into high-paying professional careers — but not the millions still in the typing pools or behind the department-store sales counters. (Contrary to popular myth about the "have-it-all" baby-boom women, the largest percentage of women in this generation remain in office support roles.)

As the backlash has gathered force, it has cut off the few from the many — and the few women who have advanced seek to prove, as a social survival tactic, that they aren't so interested in advancement after all. Some of them parade their defection from the women's movement, while their working-class peers founder and cling to the splintered remains of the feminist cause. While a very few affluent and celebrity women who are showcased in news stories boast about going home to "bake bread," the many working-class women appeal for their economic rights — flocking to unions in record numbers, striking on their own for pay equity, and establishing their own fledgling groups for working-women's rights. In 1986, while 41 percent of upper-income women were claiming in the Gallup poll that they were not feminists, only 26 percent of low-income women were making the same claim.

Women's advances and retreats are generally described in military terms: battles won, battles lost, points and territory gained and surrendered. The metaphor of combat is not without its merits in this context, and, clearly, the same sort of martial accounting and vocabulary is already surfacing here. But by imagining the conflict as two battalions neatly arrayed on either side of the line, we miss the entangled nature, the locked embrace, of a "war" between women and the male culture they inhabit. We miss the reactive nature of a backlash, which, by definition, can exist only in response to another force.

In times when feminism is at a low ebb, women assume the reactive role — privately and, most often, covertly struggling to assert themselves against the dominant cultural tide. But when feminism itself becomes the tide, the opposition doesn't simply go along with the reversal: it digs in its heels, brandishes its fists, builds walls and dams. And its resistance creates countercurrents and treacherous undertows.

The force and furor of the backlash churn beneath the surface, largely invisible to the public eye. On occasion in the last decade, they have burst into view. We have seen New Right politicians condemn women's independence, antiabortion protesters firebomb women's clinics, fundamentalist preachers damn feminists as "whores." Other signs of the backlash's wrath, by their sheer brutality, can push their way into public consciousness for a time — the sharp increase in rape, for example, or the rise in pornography that depicts extreme violence against women.

More subtle indicators in popular culture may receive momentary, and often bemused, media notice, then quickly slip from social awareness: a report, for instance, that the image of women on prime-time TV shows has suddenly degenerated. A survey of mystery fiction finding the number of tortured and mutilated female characters mysteriously multiplying. The puzzling news that, as one commentator put it, "so many hit songs have the B word [bitch] to refer to women that some rap music seems to be veering toward rape music." The ascendancy of violently misogynist comics like Andrew Dice Clay, who calls women "pigs" and "sluts," or radio hosts like Rush Limbaugh, whose broadsides against "femi-Nazi" feminists helped make his syndicated program the most popular radio talk show in the nation. Or word that, in 1987, the American Women in Radio and Television couldn't award its annual prize to ads that feature women positively: it could find no ad that qualified.

These phenomena are all related, but that doesn't mean they are somehow coordinated. The backlash is not a conspiracy, with a council dispatching agents from some central control room, nor are the people who serve its ends often aware of their role; some even consider themselves feminists. For the most part, its workings are encoded and internalized, diffuse and chameleonic. Not all of the manifestations of the backlash are of equal weight or significance, either; some are mere ephemera thrown up by a culture machine that is always scrounging for a "fresh" angle. Taken as a whole, however, these codes and cajolings, these whispers and threats and myths, move overwhelmingly in one direction: they try to push women back into their "acceptable" roles — whether as Daddy's girl or fluttery romantic, active nester or passive love object.

Although the backlash is not an organized movement, that doesn't make it any less destructive. In fact, the lack of orchestration, the absence of a single string-puller, only makes it harder to see — and perhaps more effective. A backlash against women's rights succeeds to a degree that it appears *not* to be political, that it appears not to be a struggle at all. It is most powerful when it goes private, when it lodges inside a woman's mind and turns her vision inward, until she imagines the pressure is all in her head, until she begins to enforce the backlash, too — on herself.

In the last decade, the backlash has moved through the culture's se- 35 cret chambers, traveling through passageways of flattery and fear. Along the way, it has adopted disguises: a mask of mild derision or the painted face of deep "concern." Its lips profess pity for any woman who won't fit the mold, while it tries to clamp the mold around her ears. It pursues a divide-and-conquer strategy: single versus married women, working women versus homemakers, middle versus working class. It manipulates a system of rewards and punishments, elevating women who follow its rules, isolating those who don't. The backlash remarkets old myths about women as new facts and ignores all appeals to reason. Cornered, it denies its own existence, points an accusatory finger at feminism, and burrows deeper underground.

Backlash happens to be the title of a 1947 Hollywood movie in which a man frames his wife for a murder he's committed. The backlash against women's rights works in much the same way: its rhetoric charges feminists with all the crimes it perpetrates. The backlash line blames the women's movement for the "feminization of poverty" — while the backlash's own instigators in Washington have pushed through the budget cuts that have helped impoverish millions of women, have fought pay-equity proposals, and undermined equal-opportunity laws. The backlash line claims the women's movement cares nothing for children's rights — while its own representatives in the capital and state legislatures have blocked one bill after another to improve child care, slashed billions of dollars in aid for children, and relaxed state licensing standards for day-care centers. The backlash line accuses the women's movement of creating a generation of unhappy single and childless women — but its purveyors in the media are the ones guilty of making single and childless women feel like circus freaks.

To blame feminism for women's "lesser life" is to miss its point entirely, which is to win women a wider range of experience. Feminism remains a pretty simple concept, despite repeated — and enormously effective — efforts to dress it up in greasepaint and turn its proponents into gargoyles. As Rebecca West wrote sardonically in 1913, "I myself have never been able to find out precisely what feminism is: I only know that people call me a feminist whenever I express sentiments that differentiate me from a doormat."

The meaning of the word "feminism" has not really changed since it first appeared in a book review in *The Athenaeum* on April 27, 1895, describing a woman who "has in her the capacity of fighting her way back to independence." It is the basic proposition that, as Nora put it in Ibsen's *A Doll's House* a century ago, "Before everything else I'm a human being." It is the simply worded sign hoisted by a little girl in the 1970 Women's Strike for Equality: "I AM NOT A BARBIE DOLL." Feminism asks the world to recognize at long last that women aren't decorative ornaments, worthy vessels, members of a "special-interest group." They are half (in fact, now more than half) of the national population, and just as deserving of rights and opportunities, just as capable of participating in the world's events, as the other half. Feminism's agenda is basic: it asks that women not be forced to "choose" between public justice and private happiness. It asks that women be free to define themselves — instead of having their identity defined for them, time and again, by their culture and their men.

The fact that these are still such incendiary notions should tell us that American women have a way to go before they enter the promised land of equality.

PREPARING FOR DISCUSSION

1. Faludi points to a number of social and cultural phenomena as indicators of continued gender discrimination. On what particular phenomena does she focus? What phenomena does she cite to prove that the women's equality movement has made few real gains? Why does she think that even these gains are in danger of being lost?

2. Faludi seems unwilling to blame the feminist backlash she describes on misogyny alone. What other factors does she hold responsible for the backlash? To what extent does she hold women responsible for it?

3. Faludi holds that most of the "afflictions ascribed to feminism" have their source in the misrepresentation of women by the media and advertising. Consider the examples she cites in support of her thesis. To what degree does her thesis depend upon the very cultural institutions she attacks?

4. Consider Faludi's account of the "spectacular" rise in sexual violence against women in comparison to other sorts of violent crime. In what ways might

a distinction between actual and reported incidents (assuming that there are always more actual crimes committed than those reported) change the portrait of violence against women offered by the author? If Faludi learned that only the number of reported crimes has risen substantially, while the rise of actual sex crimes against women remained proportionate to the rise of other kinds of violent crime, do you think that she would consider this information a victory for feminism rather than a setback?

5. In paragraph 4, Faludi preserves the original phrasing of a number of newspaper and magazine articles concerning women's physical and emotional health. Why has she chosen to reprint the original words with quotation marks rather than paraphrasing them? How would you describe the words and phrases in quotes? Where else in the selection does she employ this method? Why?

FROM READING TO WRITING

6. Because Faludi argues that many of the problems attributed to feminism are the consequence of the media's misrepresentation of women, you might want to test her thesis. Examine a current movie, television show, or commercial that considers women's lives and issues either directly or indirectly. Write an essay in which you consider whether the women presented resemble women you know. In your opinion, are the media images of women more or less realistic than media images of men?

7. How has feminism influenced your own life and the lives of those around you? Write an essay in which you consider whether that influence has been largely positive, negative, or mixed. You might want to include some personal experiences in your essay. On the basis of those experiences, how would you characterize the current state of feminism?

WENDY KAMINER

Feminism's Identity Crisis

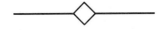

A recent poll of American women shows that they are more willing to say they support the feminist agenda than to call themselves feminists. Most feminist theorists dismiss these results, maintaining that feminism has always had to deal with an image problem created by a media largely hostile to feminist ideas and attitudes. Is it possible, however, that the phenomenon points to some deeper conflict within the women's movement itself? Or that women are more uncertain than before about feminist ideals, especially those concerning private life? Lawyer and social critic Wendy Kaminer, troubled by the poll's results and other signs of disaffection with the women's movement, entertains these possibilities and tries to offer some reasons that the feminist label just will not stick to most women.

A graduate of Smith College and Boston University Law School, Kaminer practiced law as a staff attorney in the New York Legal Aid Society and the New City Mayor's Office before embarking on her writing career. In addition to serving as a contributing editor for the *Atlantic Monthly* (where this selection first appeared in 1993), she has been a public policy fellow at Radcliffe College since 1987. Kaminer was the recipient of a 1993 Guggenheim fellowship for her most recent book, *It's All the Rage: Crime and Culture.*

SELECTED PUBLICATIONS: *A Fearful Freedom: Women's Flight from Equality* (1990); *I'm Dysfunctional, You're Dysfunctional: The Recovery Movement and Other Self-Help Fashions* (1992); *It's All the Rage: Crime and Culture* (1995); Kaminer also publishes frequently in the *New York Times* and *Mirabella.*

My favorite political moment of the 1960s was a Black Panther rally in a quadrangle of Smith College on a luxuriant spring day. Ramboesque in berets and ammunition belts, several young black males exhorted hundreds of young white females to contribute money to Bobby Seale's defense fund. I stood at the back of the crowd watching yarn ties on blonde ponytails bobbing up and down while the daughters of CEOs nodded in agreement with the Panthers' attack on the ruling class.

It was all so girlish — or boyish, depending on your point of view. Whatever revolution was fomenting posed no apparent threat to gender roles. Still, women who were not particularly sensitive to chauvinism in the counterculture or the typical fraternity planned to attend graduate or professional school and pursue careers that would have been practically unthinkable for them ten years earlier. Feminism was altering their lives as much as draft avoidance was altering the lives of their male counterparts.

Today, three decades of feminism and one Year of the Woman later, a majority of American women agree that feminism has altered their lives for the better. In general, polls conducted over the past three years indicate strong majority support for feminist ideals. But the same polls suggest that a majority of women hesitate to associate themselves with the movement. As Karlyn Keene, a resident fellow at the American Enterprise Institute, has observed, more than three quarters of American women support efforts to "strengthen and change women's status in society," yet only a minority, a third at most, identify themselves as feminists.

Many feminists take comfort in these polls, inferring substantial public support for economic and political equality, and dismissing women's wariness of the feminist label as a mere image problem (attributed to unfair media portrayals of feminists as a strident minority of frustrated women). But the polls may also adumbrate unarticulated ambivalence about feminist ideals, particularly with respect to private life. If widespread support for some measure of equality reflects the way women see, or wish to see, society, their unwillingness to identify with feminism reflects the way they see themselves, or wish to be seen by others.

To the extent that it challenges discrimination and the political exclusion of women, feminism is relatively easy for many women to embrace. It appeals to fundamental notions of fairness; it suggests that social structures must change but that individuals, particularly women, may remain the same. For many women, feminism is simply a matter of mommy-tracking, making sure that institutions accommodate women's familial roles, which are presumed to be essentially immutable. But to the extent that feminism questions those roles and the underlying assumptions about sexuality, it requires profound individual change as well, posing an unsettling challenge that well-adjusted people instinctively avoid. Why question norms of sex and character to which you've more or less successfully adapted?

Of course, the social and individual changes demanded by feminism are not exactly divisible. Of course, the expansion of women's professional roles and political power affects women's personality development. Still, many people manage to separate who they are in the workplace from who they are in bed, which is why feminism generates so much cognitive dissonance. As it addresses and internalizes this dissonance and women's anxiety about the label "feminism," as it embarks on a "third wave," the feminist movement today may suffer less from a mere image problem than from a major identity crisis.

It's difficult, of course, to generalize about how millions of American women imagine feminism and what role it plays in their lives. All one can say with certitude is that different women define and relate to feminism differently. The rest — much of this essay — is speculation, informed by conversations with editors of women's magazines (among the most reliable speculators about what women want), polling data, and ten years of experience studying feminist issues.

Resistance to the Label

Robin Morgan, the editor in chief of *Ms.*, and Ellen Levine, the editor in chief of *Redbook*, two veterans of women's magazines and feminism, offer different views of feminism's appeal, each of which seems true, in the context of their different constituencies. Morgan sees a resurgent feminist movement and points to the formation of new feminist groups on campus and intensified grass-roots activity by women addressing a range of issues, from domestic violence to economic revitalization. Ellen Levine, however, believes that for the middle-class family women who read *Redbook* (the average reader is a thirty-nine-year-old wage-earning mother), feminism is "a non-issue." She says, "They don't think about it; they don't talk about it." They may not even be familiar with the feminist term of art "glass ceiling," which feminists believe has passed into the vernacular. And they seem not to be particularly interested in politics. The surest way not to sell *Redbook* is to put a woman politician on the cover: the January, 1993, issue of *Good Housekeeping*, with Hillary Clinton on the cover, did poorly at the newsstands, according to Levine.

Editors at more upscale magazines — *Mirabella, Harper's Bazaar,* and *Glamour* — are more upbeat about their readers' interest in feminism, or at least their identification with feminist perspectives. Gay Bryant, *Mirabella's* editor in chief, says, "We assume our readers are feminists with a small 'f.' We think of them as strong, independent, smart women; we think of them as pro-woman, although not all of them would define themselves as feminists politically." Betsy Carter, the executive editor of *Harper's Bazaar,* suggests that feminism has been assimilated into the culture of the magazine: "Feminism is a word that has been so absorbed in our consciousness that I don't isolate it. Asking me if I believe in feminism is like asking me if I believe in integration." Carter says, however, that women tend to be interested in the same stories that interest men: "Except for subjects like fly-fishing, it's hard to label something a man's story or a woman's story." In fact, she adds, "it seems almost obsolete to talk about women's magazines." Carter, a former editor at *Esquire,* recalls that *Esquire's* readership was 40 percent female, which indicated to her that "women weren't getting what they needed from the women's magazines."

Ruth Whitney, the editor in chief of *Glamour,* might disagree. She   10
points out that *Glamour* runs monthly editorials with a decidedly "feminist" voice that infuses the magazine. *Glamour* readers may or may not call themselves feminists, she says, but "I would call *Glamour* a mainstream feminist magazine, in its editorials, features, fashions, and consumerism." *Glamour* is also a pro-choice magazine; as Whitney stresses, it has long published pro-choice articles — more than any other mainstream women's magazine, according to her. And it is a magazine for which women seem to constitute the norm: "We use the pronoun 'she' when referring to a doctor, lawyer, whomever, and that does not go unnoticed by our readers."

Some women will dispute one underlying implication of Betsy Carter's remarks — that feminism involves assimilation, the merger of male and female spheres of interest. Some will dispute any claims to feminism by any magazine that features fashion. But whether *Ms.* readers would call *Harper's Bazaar, Mirabella,* and *Glamour* feminist magazines, or magazines with feminist perspectives, their readers apparently do, if Betsy Carter, Gay Bryant, and Ruth Whitney know their audiences.

Perhaps the confident feminist self-image of these up-scale magazines, as distinct from the cautious exploration of women's issues in the middle-class *Redbook,* confirms a canard about feminism — that it is the province of upper-income urban professional women. But *Ms.* is neither up-scale nor fashionable, and it's much too earnest to be sophisticated. Feminism — or, at least, support for feminist ideals — is not simply a matter of class, or even race.

Susan McHenry, a senior editor at *Working Woman* and the former executive editor of *Emerge,* a new magazine for middle-class African-Americans, senses in African-American women readers "universal embrace of women's rights and the notion that the women's movement has been helpful." Embrace of the women's movement, however, is equivocal. "If you start talking about the women's movement, you hear a lot about what we believe and what white women believe."

For many black women, devoting time and energy to feminist causes or feminist groups may simply not be a priority. Black women "feel both racism and sexism," McHenry believes, but they consider the fight for racial justice their primary responsibility and assume that white women will pay primary attention to gender issues. Leslie Adamson, the executive secretary to the president of Radcliffe College, offers a different explanation. She doesn't, in fact, "feel" sexism and racism equally: "Sex discrimination makes me indignant. Racial discrimination makes me enraged." Adamson is sympathetic to feminism and says that she has always "had a feminist mind." Still, she does not feel particularly oppressed as a woman. "I can remember only two instances of sex discrimination in my life," she says. "Once when I was in the sixth grade and wanted to take shop and they made me take home economics; once when I visited my husband's relatives in Trinidad and they wouldn't let me talk about politics. Racism has always affected me on a regular basis." Cynthia Bell, the communications director for Greater Southeast Healthcare System, in Washington, D.C., offers a similar observation: "It wasn't until I graduated from college that I encountered sexual discrimination. I remember racial discrimination from the time I remember being myself."

Black women who share feminist ideals but associate feminism with white women sometimes prefer to talk about "womanism," a term endorsed by such diverse characters as Alice Walker (who is credited with coining it) and William Safire. Susan McHenry prefers to avoid using the term "women's movement" and talks instead about "women moving." She identifies with women "who are getting things done, regardless of what they call themselves." But unease with the term "feminism" has been a persistent concern in the feminist movement, whether the unease is attributed to racial divisions or to residual resistance to feminist ideals.

It is, in fact, a complicated historical phenomenon that reflects feminism's successes as well as its failures.

"The Less Tainted Half"

That feminism has the power to expand women's aspirations and improve their lives without enlisting them as card-carrying feminists is a tribute to its strength as a social movement. Feminism is not dependent on ideological purity (indeed, it has always been a mixture of conflicting ideologies) or any formal organizational structure. In the nineteenth century feminism drew upon countless unaffiliated voluntary associations of women devoted to social reform or self-improvement. Late-twentieth-century feminism has similarly drawn upon consciousness-raising groups, professional associations, community-action groups, and the increased work-force participation of middle-class women, wrought partly by economic forces and a revolution in birth control. Throughout its 150-year history feminism has insinuated itself into the culture as women have sought to improve their status and increase their participation in the world outside the home. If women are moving in a generally feminist direction — toward greater rights and a fairer apportionment of social responsibilities — does it matter what they call themselves?

In the nineteenth century many, maybe most, women who took part in the feminist movement saw themselves as paragons of femininity. The great historic irony of feminism is that the supposed feminine virtues that justified keeping women at home — sexual purity, compassion, and a talent for nurturance — eventually justified their release from the home as well. Women were "the less tainted half of the race," Frances Willard, the president of the National Woman's Christian Temperance Union, declared, and thus were the moral guardians of society.

But in the long run, identifying feminism with femininity offered women limited liberation. The feminine weaknesses that were presumed to accompany feminine virtues justified the two-tier labor force that kept women out of executive positions and political office and out of arduous, high-paying manual-labor jobs (although women were never considered too weak to scrub floors). By using femininity as their passport to the public sphere, women came to be typecast in traditional feminine roles that they are still playing and arguing about today. Are women naturally better suited to parenting than men? Are men naturally better suited to waging war? Are women naturally more cooperative and compassionate, more emotive and less analytic, than men?

A great many American women (and men) still seem to answer these questions in the affirmative, as evidenced by public resistance to drafting women and the private reluctance of women to assign, and men to assume, equal responsibility for child care. Feminism, however, is popularly deemed to represent an opposing belief that men and women are equally capable of raising children and equally capable of waging war. Thus feminism represents, in the popular view, a rejection of femininity.

Feminists have long fought for day-care and family-leave programs, but they still tend to be blamed for the work-family conundrum. Thirty-nine percent of women recently surveyed by *Redbook* said that feminism had made it "harder" for women to balance work and family life. Thirty-two percent said that feminism made "no difference" to women's balancing act. This may reflect a failure of feminists to make child care an absolutely clear priority. It may also reflect the association of feminism with upper-income women like Zoë Baird,[1] who can solve their child-care problems with relative ease. But, as Zoë Baird discovered, Americans are still ambivalent about women's roles within and outside the home.

Feminism and the careerism it entails are commonly regarded as a zero-sum game not just for women and men but for women and children as well, Ellen Levine believes: wage-earning mothers still tend to feel guilty about not being with their children and worry that "the more women get ahead professionally, the more children will fall back." Their guilt does not seem to be assuaged by any number of studies showing that the children of wage-earning mothers fare as well as the children of full-time homemakers, Levine adds. It seems to dissipate only as children grow up and prosper.

Feminists who dismiss these worries as backlash risk trivializing the inevitable stresses confronting wage-earning mothers (even those with decent day care). Feminists who respond to these worries by suggesting that husbands should be more like wives and mothers are likely to be considered blind or hostile to presumptively natural sex differences that are still believed to underlie traditional gender roles.

To the extent that it advocates a revolution in gender roles, feminism also comes as a reproach to women who lived out the tradition, especially those who lived it out unhappily. Robin Morgan says, "A woman who's been unhappily married for forty years and complains constantly to her friends, saying, 'I've got to get out of this,' might stand up on a talk show and say feminism is destroying the family."

The Wages of Equality

Ambivalence about equality sometimes seems to plague the feminist movement almost as much today as it did ten years ago, when it defeated the Equal Rights Amendment. Worth noting is that in the legal arena feminism has met with less success than the civil rights movement. The power of the civil rights movement in the 1960s was the power to

---

[1] *Zoë Baird:* President Clinton's nominee for attorney general who was disqualified for hiring illegal aliens for child care.

demonstrate the gap between American ideals of racial equality and the American reality for African-Americans. We've never had the same professed belief in sexual equality: federal equal-employment law has always treated racial discrimination more severely than sex discrimination, and so has the Supreme Court. The Court has not extended to women the same constitutional protection it has extended to racial minorities, because a majority of justices have never rejected the notion that some degree of sex discrimination is only natural.

The widespread belief in equality demonstrated by polls is a belief in equality up to a point — the point where women are drafted and men change diapers. After thirty years of the contemporary women's movement, equal-rights feminism is still considered essentially abnormal. Ellen Levine notes that middle-class family women sometimes associate feminism with lesbianism, which has yet to gain middle-class respectability. Homophobia is not entirely respectable either, however, so it may not be expressed directly in polls or conversations; but it has always been a subtext of popular resistance to feminism. Feminists have alternately been accused of hating men and of wanting to be just like them.

There's some evidence that the fear of feminism as a threat to female sexuality may be lessening: 77 percent of women recently surveyed by *Redbook* answered "yes" to the question "Can a woman be both feminine and a feminist?" But they were answering a question in the abstract. When women talk about why they don't identify with feminists, they often talk about not wanting to lose their femininity. To the extent that an underlying belief in feminine virtues limits women to feminine roles, as it did a hundred years ago, this rejection of the feminist label is a rejection of full equality. In the long run, it matters what women call themselves.

Or does it? Ironically, many self-proclaimed feminists today express some of the same ambivalence about changing gender roles as the "I'm not a feminist, but . . ." women (" . . . but I believe in equal opportunity or family leave or reproductive choice"). The popular image of feminism as a more or less unified quest for androgynous equality, promoted by the feminists' nemesis Camille Paglia, is at least ten years out of date.

The Comforts of Gilliganism

Central to the dominant strain of feminism today is the belief, articulated by the psychologist Carol Gilligan, that women share a different voice and different moral sensibilities. Gilligan's work — notably *In a Different Voice* (1982) — has been effectively attacked by other feminist scholars, but criticisms of it have not been widely disseminated, and it has passed with ease into the vernacular. In a modern-day version of Victorian True Womanhood, feminists and also some anti-feminists pay tribute to women's superior nurturing and relational skills and their general "ethic of caring." Sometimes feminists add parenthetically that differences between men and women may well be attributable to culture, not nature. But the qualification is moot. Believers in gender difference tend not to focus on changing the cultural environment to free men and women from stereotypes, as equal-rights feminists did twenty years ago; instead they celebrate the feminine virtues.

It was probably inevitable that the female solidarity at the base of the feminist movement would foster female chauvinism. All men are jerks, I might agree on occasion, over a bottle of wine. But that's an attitude, not an analysis, and only a small minority of separatist feminists turn it into an ideology. Gilliganism addresses the anxiety that is provoked by that attitude — the anxiety about compromising their sexuality which many feminists share with nonfeminists.

Much as they dislike admitting it, feminists generally harbor or have   30 harbored categorical anger toward men. Some would say that such anger is simply an initial stage in the development of a feminist consciousness, but it is also an organizing tool and a fact of life for many women who believe they live in a sexist world. And whether or not it is laced with anger, feminism demands fundamental changes in relations between the sexes and the willingness of feminists to feel like unnatural women and be treated as such. For heterosexual women, feminism can come at a cost. Carol Gilligan's work valorizing women's separate emotional sphere helped make it possible for feminists to be angry at men and challenge their hegemony without feeling unwomanly. Nancy Rosenblum, a professor of political science at Brown University, says that Gilliganism resolved the conflict for women between feminism and femininity by "de-eroticizing it." Different-voice ideology locates female sexuality in maternity, as did Victorian visions of the angel in the house. In its simplest form, the idealization of motherhood reduces popular feminism to the notion that women are nicer than men.

Women are also widely presumed to be less warlike than men. "Women bring love; that's our role," one woman explained at a feminist rally against the Gulf War which I attended; it seemed less like a rally than a revival meeting. Women shared their need "to connect" and "do relational work." They recalled Jane Addams,[2] the women's peace movement between the two world wars, and the Ban the Bomb marches of thirty years ago. They suggested that pacifism was as natural to women as childbirth, and were barely disconcerted by the presence of women soldiers in the Gulf. Military women were likely to be considered self-hating or male-identified or the hapless victims of a racist, classist economy, not self-determined women with minds and voices all their own. The war was generally regarded as an allegory of male supremacy; the patriarch Bush was the moral equivalent of the patriarch Saddam

---

[2] *Jane Addams:* (1860-1935) Urban reformer, suffragist, and founder of Hull House, a home for many of Chicago's poor.

Hussein. If only men would listen to women, peace, like a chador, would enfold us.

In part, the trouble with True Womanhood is its tendency to substitute sentimentality for thought. Constance Buchanan, an associate dean of the Harvard Divinity School, observes that feminists who believe women will exercise authority differently often haven't done the hard work of figuring out how they will exercise authority at all. "Many feminists have an almost magical vision of institutional change," Buchanan says. "They've focused on gaining access but haven't considered the scale and complexity of modern institutions, which will not necessarily change simply by virtue of their presence."

Feminists who claim that women will "make a difference" do, in fact, often argue their case simply by pointing to the occasional female manager who works by consensus, paying little attention to hierarchy and much attention to her employees' feelings — assuming that such women more accurately represent their sex than women who favor unilateral decision-making and tend not to nurture employees. In other words, different-voice feminists often assume their conclusions: the many women whose characters and behavior contradict traditional models of gender difference (Margaret Thatcher is the most frequently cited example) are invariably dismissed as male-identified.

From Marilyn to Hillary

Confronted with the challenge of rationalizing the accommodating profound differences among women, in both character and ideology, feminism has never been a tranquil movement, or a cheerfully anarchic one. It has always been plagued by bitter civil wars over conflicting ideas about sexuality and gender which lead to conflicting visions of law and social policy. If men and women are naturally and consistently different in terms of character, temperament, and moral sensibility, then the law should treat them differently, as it has through most of our history, with labor legislation that protects women, for example, or with laws preferring women in custody disputes: special protection for women, not equal rights, becomes a feminist goal. (Many feminists basically agree with Marilyn Quayle's assertion that women don't want to be liberated from their essential natures.) But if men and women do not conform to masculine and feminine character models, if sex is not a reliable predictor of behavior, then justice requires a sex-neutral approach to law which accommodates different people's different characters and experiences (the approach championed by Ruth Bader Ginsburg twenty years ago).

In academia this has been dubbed the "sameness-difference" debate, though no one on either side is suggesting that men and women are the same. Advocates of laws protecting women suggest that men and women tend to differ from each other in predictable ways, in accord with gender stereotypes. Equal-rights advocates suggest that men and women differ unpredictably and that women differ from one another unpredictably.

It's fair to say that both sides in this debate are operating in the absence of conclusive scientific evidence confirming or denying the existence of biologically based, characterological sex differences. But this is a debate less about science than about law. Even if we could compromise, and agree that sex and gender roles reflect a mixture of natural and cultural programming, we'd still have to figure out not only what is feasible for men and women but also what is just. If there are natural inequities between the sexes, it is hardly the business of law to codify them.

In the 1980s this debate about sex and law became a cottage industry for feminist academics, especially post-modernists who could take both sides in the debate, in celebration of paradox and multiculturalism. On one side, essentialism — a belief in natural, immutable sex differences — is anathema to postmodernists, for whom sexuality itself, along with gender, is a "social construct." Sensitivity to race- and class-based differences among women also militates against a belief in a monolithic feminine culture: from a postmodern perspective, there is no such category as "woman." Taken to its logical conclusion, this emphasis on the fragmentation of the body politic makes postmodern feminism an oxymoron: feminism and virtually all our laws against sex discrimination reflect the presumption that women do in fact constitute a political category. On the other side, to the extent that postmodernism includes multiculturalism, it endorses tribalism, or identity politics, which for some feminists entails a strong belief in "women's ways." Thus the theoretical rejection of essentialism is matched by an attitudinal embrace of it.

Outside academia, debates about sex and justice are sometimes equally confused and confusing, given the political and ideological challenges of affirmative-action programs and the conflicting demands on women with both career aspirations and commitments to family life. Feminists often have to weigh the short-term benefits of protecting wage-earning mothers (by mommy-tracking, for example) against the long-term costs of a dual labor market. Sometimes ideological clarity is lost in complicated strategy debates. Sometimes ideological conflicts are put aside when feminists share a transcendent social goal, such as suffrage or reproductive choice. And sometimes one ideological strain of feminism dominates another. In the 1970s equal-rights feminism was ascendent. The 1980s saw a revival of protectionism.

Equal-rights feminism couldn't last. It was profoundly disruptive for women as well as men. By questioning long-cherished notions about sex, it posed unsettling questions about selfhood. It challenged men and women to shape their own identities without resort to stereotypes. It posed particular existential challenges to women who were accustomed to knowing themselves through the web of familial relations. As

Elizabeth Cady Stanton observed more than a hundred years ago, equal-rights feminism challenges women to acknowledge that they are isolated individuals as well. Stressing that like "every human soul" women "must make the voyage of life alone," Stanton, the mother of seven and a political organizer who spent most of her life in crowds, exhorted women to recognize the "solitude of self."

This emphasis on individual autonomy didn't just scare many   40
women; it struck them as selfish — as it might be if it were unaccompanied by an ongoing commitment to family and community. Twenty years ago feminists made the mistake of denigrating homemaking and volunteer work. It's hard to imagine how else they might have made their case. Still, the feminist attack on volunteering was simplistic and ill-informed. Feminists might have paid attention to the historical experiences of middle-class African-American women combining paid work, volunteering, and family life. They might have paid attention to the critical role played by the volunteer tradition in the nineteenth-century feminist movement. Women's sense of their maternal responsibilities at home and in the wider world was at the core of their shared social conscience, which feminists ignored at their peril. Feminism will not succeed with American women, as Constance Buchanan notes, until it offers them a vision that reconciles the assertion of equal rights with the assumption of social responsibilities.

That's the vision Hillary Clinton is striving to embody, as a family woman and a feminist, an advocate of civil rights and a preacher of a caring and sharing politics of meaning. I wish her luck: the difficulty she encountered during the campaign persuading people that she has a maternal side reflects the strong popular presumption that a commitment to equality is incompatible with a willingness to nurture.

We should know better. In fact millions of American women working outside the home are exercising rights and assuming responsibilities — for better or worse, that's one of the legacies of feminism. Women who sought equal rights in the 1970s have not abandoned their families, like Meryl Streep in *Kramer vs. Kramer*, as anti-feminists predicted they would. Instead they have overworked themselves, acting as breadwinners and primary caretakers, too. Given the absence of social and institutional support — family leave and day care — it's not surprising that women would turn for sustenance to traditional notions of sex difference. The belief that they were naturally better suited to child care than men would relieve them of considerable anger toward their husbands. As Victorian women invoked maternal virtue to justify their participation in the public sphere, so contemporary American women have used it to console themselves for the undue burdens they continue to bear in the private one.

Notions of immutable sex differences explained a range of social inequities — the plight of displaced homemakers, the persistence of sexual violence, the problems of women working double shifts within and outside the home. The general failure of hard-won legal rights to ensure social justice (which plagued civil rights activists as well as feminists) might have been considered a failure of government — to enforce civil rights laws and make them matter or to provide social services. It might have been considered a failure of community — our collective failure to care for one another. Instead it was roundly condemned as a failure of feminism, because it provided convenient proof of what many men and women have always believed — that biology is destiny after all. Equal-rights feminism fell out of favor, even among feminists, because it made people terribly uncomfortable and because legal rights were not accompanied by a fair division of familial and communal responsibilities.

Feminism Succumbs to Femininity

The feminist drive for equal rights was supposed to have been revitalized last year, and it's true that women were politically activated and made significant political gains. It's clear that women are moving, but in what direction? What is the women's movement all about?

Vying for power today are poststructural feminists (dominant in academia in recent years), political feminists (office-holders and lobbyists), different-voice feminists, separatist feminists (a small minority), pacifist feminists, lesbian feminists, careerist feminists, liberal feminists (who tend also to be political feminists), anti-porn feminists, eco-feminists, and womanists. These are not, of course, mutually exclusive categories, and this is hardly an exhaustive list. New Age feminists and goddess worshippers widen the array of alternative truths. And the newest category of feminism, personal-development feminism, led nominally by Gloria Steinem, puts a popular feminist spin on deadeningly familiar messages about recovering from addiction and abuse, liberating one's inner child, and restoring one's self-esteem.

The marriage of feminism and the phenomenally popular recovery movement is arguably the most disturbing (and potentially influential) development in the feminist movement today. It's based partly on a shared concern about child abuse, nominally a left-wing analogue to right-wing anxiety about the family. There's an emerging alliance of anti-pornography and anti-violence feminists with therapists who diagnose and treat child abuse, including "ritual abuse" and "Satanism" (often said to be linked to pornography). Feminism is at risk of being implicated in the unsavory business of hypnotizing suspected victims of abuse to help them "retrieve" their buried childhood memories. Gloria Steinem has blithely praised the important work of therapists in this field without even a nod to the potential for, well, abuse when unhappy, suggestible people who are angry at their parents are exposed to suggestive hypnotic techniques designed to uncover their histories of victimization.

But the involvement of some feminists in the memory-retrieval

45

industry is only one manifestation of a broader ideological threat posed to feminism by the recovery movement. Recovery, with its absurdly broad definitions of addiction and abuse, encourages people to feel fragile and helpless. Parental insensitivity is classed as child abuse, along with parental violence, because all suffering is said to be equal (meaning entirely subjective); but that's appropriate only if all people are so terribly weak that a cross word inevitably has the destructive force of a blow. Put very simply, women need a feminist movement that makes them feel strong.

Enlisting people in a struggle for liberation without exaggerating the ways in which they're oppressed is a challenge for any civil rights movement. It's a particularly daunting one for feminists, who are still arguing among themselves about whether women are oppressed more by nature or by culture. For some feminists, strengthening women is a matter of alerting them to their natural vulnerabilities.

There has always been a strain of feminism that presents women as frail and naturally victimized. As it was a hundred years ago, feminist victimism is today most clearly expressed in sexuality debates — about pornography, prostitution, rape, and sexual harassment. Today sexual violence is a unifying focal point for women who do and women who do not call themselves feminists: 84 percent of women surveyed by *Redbook* considered "fighting violence against women" to be "very important." (Eighty-two percent rated workplace equality and 54 percent rated abortion rights as very important.) Given this pervasive, overriding concern about violence and our persistent failure to address it effectively, victimism is likely to become an important organizing tool for feminism in the 1990s.

Feminist discussions of sexual offenses often share with the recovery   50
movement the notion that, again, there are no objective measures of suffering: all suffering is said to be equal, in the apparent belief that all women are weak. Wage-earning women testify to being "disabled" by sexist remarks in the workplace. College women testify to the trauma of being fondled by their dates. The term "date rape," like the term "addiction," no longer has much literal, objective meaning. It tends to be used figuratively, as a metaphor signifying that all heterosexual encounters are inherently abusive of women. The belief that in a male-dominated culture that has "normalized" rape, "yes" can never really mean "yes" has been popularized by the anti-pornography feminists Andrea Dworkin and Catharine MacKinnon. (Dworkin devoted an entire book to the contention that intercourse is essentially a euphemism for rape.) But only five years ago Dworkin and MacKinnon were leaders of a feminist fringe. Today, owing partly to the excesses of multiculturalism and the exaltation of victimization, they're leaders in the feminist mainstream.

Why is feminism helping to make women feel so vulnerable? Why do some young women on Ivy League campuses, among the most privileged people on the globe, feel oppressed? Why does feminist victimology seem so much more pervasive among middle- and upper-class whites than among lower-income women, and girls, of color? Questions like these need to be aired by feminists. But in some feminist circles it is heresy to suggest that there are degrees of suffering and oppression, which need to be kept in perspective. It is heresy to suggest that being raped by your date may not be as traumatic or terrifying as being raped by a stranger who breaks into your bedroom in the middle of the night. It is heresy to suggest that a woman who has to listen to her colleagues tell stupid sexist jokes has a lesser grievance than a woman who is physically accosted by her supervisor. It is heresy, in general, to question the testimony of self-proclaimed victims of date rape or harassment, as it is heresy in a twelve-step group to question claims of abuse. All claims of suffering are sacred and presumed to be absolutely true. It is a primary article of faith among many feminists that women don't lie about rape, ever; they lack the dishonesty gene. Some may call this feminism, but it looks more like femininity to me.

Blind faith in women's pervasive victimization also looks a little like religion. "Contemporary feminism is a new kind of religion," Camille Paglia complains, overstating her case with panache. But if her metaphor begs to be qualified, it offers a nugget of truth. Feminists choose among competing denominations with varying degrees of passion, and belief; what is gospel to one feminist is a working hypothesis to another. Still, like every other ideology and "ism" — from feudalism to capitalism to communism to Freudianism — feminism is for some a revelation. Insights into the dynamics of sexual violence are turned into a metaphysic. Like people in recovery who see addiction lurking in all our desires, innumerable feminists see men's oppression of women in all our personal and social relations. Sometimes the pristine earnestness of this theology is unrelenting. Feminism lacks a sense of black humor.

Of course, the emerging orthodoxy about victimization does not infect all or even most feminist sexuality debates. Of course, many feminists harbor heretical thoughts about lesser forms of sexual misconduct. But few want to be vilified for trivializing sexual violence and collaborating in the abuse of women.

The Enemy Within

The example of Camille Paglia is instructive. She is generally considered by feminists to be practically pro-rape, because she has offered this advice to young women: don't get drunk at fraternity parties, don't accompany boys to their rooms, realize that sexual freedom entails sexual risks, and take some responsibility for your behavior. As Paglia says, this might once have been called common sense (it's what some of our mothers told us); today it's called blaming the victim.

Paglia is right: It ought to be possible to condemn date rape without   55
glorifying the notion that women are helpless to avoid it. But not everyone can risk dissent. A prominent feminist journalist who expressed misgivings to me about the iconization of Anita Hill chooses not to be
identified. Yet Anita Hill is a questionable candidate for feminist saint-
hood, because she was, after all, working for Clarence Thomas voluntarily, apparently assisting him in what feminists and other civil rights
activists have condemned as the deliberate nonenforcement of federal
equal-employment laws. Was she too hapless to know better? Feminists
are not supposed to ask.

It is, however, not simply undue caution or peer pressure that
squelches dissent among feminists. Many are genuinely ambivalent
about choosing sides in sexuality debates. It is facile, in the context of the
AIDS epidemic, to dismiss concern about date rape as "hysteria." And it
takes hubris (not an unmitigated fault) to suggest that some claims of victimization are exaggerated, when many are true. The victimization of
women as a class by discriminatory laws and customs, and a collective
failure to take sexual violence seriously, are historical reality. Even today
women are being assaulted and killed by their husbands and boyfriends
with terrifying regularity. When some feminists overdramatize minor
acts of sexual misconduct or dogmatically insist that we must always believe the woman, it is sometimes hard to blame them, given the historical
presumption that women lie about rape routinely, that wife abuse is a
marital squabble, that date rape and marital rape are not real rape, and
that sexual harassment is cute.

Feminists need critics like Paglia who are not afraid to be injudicious.
Paglia's critiques of feminism are, however, flawed by her limited knowledge of feminist theory. She doesn't even realize what she has in common with feminists she disdains — notably Carol Gilligan and the
attorney and anti-pornography activist Catharine MacKinnon. Both
Paglia and MacKinnon suggest that sexual relations are inextricably
bound up with power relations; both promote a vision of male sexuality
as naturally violent and cruel. But while Paglia celebrates sexual danger,
MacKinnon wants to legislate even the thought of it away. Both Paglia
and Gilligan offer idealized notions of femininity. But Gilligan celebrates
gender stereotypes while Paglia celebrates sex archetypes. Paglia also
offers a refreshingly tough, erotic vision of female sexuality to counteract
the pious maternalism of *In a Different Voice*.

To the extent that there's debate between Paglia and the feminist
movement, it's not a particularly thoughtful one, partly because it's occurring at second hand, in the media. There are thoughtful feminist debates being conducted in academia, but they're not widely heard. Paglia
is highly critical of feminist academics who don't publish in the mainstream; but people have a right to choose their venues, and besides, access to the mainstream press is not easily won. Still, their relative

isolation is a problem for feminist scholars who want to influence public policy. To reach a general audience they have to depend on journalists to draw upon and sometimes appropriate their work.

In the end feminism, like other social movements, is dependent on the vagaries of the marketplace. It's not that women perceive feminism just the way *Time* and *Newsweek* present it to them. They have direct access only to the kind and quantity of feminist speech deemed marketable. Today the concept of a feminist movement is considered to have commercial viability once again. The challenge now is to make public debates about feminist issues as informed as they are intense.

It's not surprising that we haven't achieved equality; we haven't even defined it. Nearly thirty years after the onset of the modern feminist movement, we still have no consensus on what nature dictates to men and women and demands of law. Does equality mean extending special employment rights to pregnant women, or limiting the Sixth Amendment rights of men standing trial for rape, or suspending the First Amendment rights of men who read pornography? [More than] thirty years after the passage of landmark federal civil rights laws, we still have no consensus on the relationship of individual rights to social justice. But, feminists might wonder, why did rights fall out of favor with progressives just as women were in danger of acquiring them? 60

The most effective backlash against feminism almost always comes from within, as women either despair of achieving equality or retreat from its demands. The confident political resurgence of women today will have to withstand a resurgent belief in women's vulnerabilities. Listening to the sexuality debates, I worry that women feel so wounded. Looking at feminism, I wonder at the public face of femininity.

PREPARING FOR DISCUSSION

1. The author notes that American women are generally hesitant to call themselves feminists. How does Kaminer account for this hesitation? Why does she reject feminist efforts to locate the source of the problem in the media's representation of women? What particular features of contemporary feminist thought does she believe most trouble American women?

2. Kaminer cites anti-pornography theorist Andrea Dworkin (whose work also appears in this book) and Catharine MacKinnon "as two mainstream feminist leaders who only a few years ago would have been regarded as members of the feminist fringe." How does Kaminer account for their movement into the mainstream? Why has the victimization of women become such a pervasive theme in contemporary feminist discourse and what are its effects, according to Kaminer, on American women? What evidence does she provide for a feminist stand against the victimization theme?

3. Kaminer relies heavily on the editors of a number of major women's

magazines to speculate about the role of feminism in American women's lives. How does she arrive at the conclusion that these editors are "among the most reliable speculators about what women want"? Why might these editors *not* be the best people to consult to determine the role of feminism in the lives of ordinary American women?

4. While arguing that women who have sought equal rights have not abandoned their families, Kaminer cites the character played by Meryl Streep in the movie *Kramer vs. Kramer* as a negative stereotype (paragraph 42). Why do you think she uses this example? Do you think that her appeal to examples from Hollywood movies is a convincing way of making her point?

5. Consider *Glamour* editor Ruth Whitney's remark: "We use the pronoun 'she' when referring to a doctor, lawyer, whomever, and that does not go unnoticed by our readers" (paragraph 10). To what extent do you think that the use of "she" instead of "he" as the standard pronoun when the gender of a person is not otherwise indicated makes a significant difference in the way we view gender roles? Do you think that Whitney would have been as willing to use the pronoun "she" if the words "criminal" or "dictator" had been substituted for "doctor" and "lawyer"?

FROM READING TO WRITING

6. Katha Pollitt's essay, which appears earlier in this chapter, stresses that the dominant feminist attitude at the moment is one that views women as different from men only in the way they are socialized. Yet Kaminer writes that "the dominant strain of feminism is the belief . . . that women share a different voice and different moral sensibilities." Write an essay in which you consider whether either of these two "dominant" views is more prevalent within your social group. Be sure to supply examples that indicate a range of attitudes in your community.

7. To what degree are you willing as either a woman or a man to call yourself a feminist or pro-feminist? Write an essay in which you establish your reasons for identifying or sympathizing with the feminist movement, or, alternatively, for rejecting feminist ideals and attitudes. Remember to be clear about what particular features of feminism you are accepting or rejecting in making a decision. If you agree with certain feminist values but reject the label "feminist," how do you account for your rejection?

5

The Politics of Sexuality

IDENTITY · BIGOTRY · VIOLENCE

IN CURRENT POLITICAL DISCUSSION, sexuality covers a broad range of issues: sexual identity and orientation, homophobia and the extension of civil rights to gay men and lesbians, as well as abuse and violence resulting from the sexual dominance of men over women. Though some of these issues spill over into other political areas (e.g., gender, family values, multiculturalism) they are grouped together in this chapter. In fact, all of these issues are introduced in the opening selection, "A New Politics of Sexuality." In this essay the poet and activist June Jordan eloquently describes the political territory covered by our current sexual conflicts: "I believe the Politics of Sexuality is the most ancient and probably the most profound arena for human conflict." Sexual oppression, she argues, is "deeper and more pervasive than any other oppression, than any other bitterly contested domain." She outlines the different ways "in which some of us seek to dictate to others of us what we should do, what we should desire, and what we should dream about, and how we should behave ourselves, generally, on the planet."

Once an unmentionable topic, sexual preferences are now often at the forefront of public discussion. Speaking as a homosexual, Andrew Sullivan, the editor of the influential *New Republic*, argues that the "cultural categories and social departments into which we once successfully consigned sexuality — departments that helped us avoid the anger and honesty with which we are now confronted — have begun to collapse." In "The Politics of Homosexuality," after examining four popular political stances toward homosexuality and demonstrating why each is badly flawed, Sullivan proposes a new, largely nonconfrontational, position. His style of argument is echoed by one of the nation's most politically visible proponents of gay and lesbian rights, Massachusetts Democratic Congressman Barney Frank. In "Fighting Gay and Lesbian Discrimination," Frank proposes a set of "realistic" political tactics for dealing with gay and lesbian discrimination.

Far more outspoken and confrontational in political style is Camille Paglia. A lesbian and libertarian, Paglia continues to address what she calls "the modern sex wars" in her controversial books, essays, and lectures. In "Sex Crime: Rape," she reminds Americans that sexuality is a deep biological and psychic force — one of the most powerful human drives. As such, sexuality cannot be conveniently regulated and legislated to suit the narrow ideological positions of various interest groups, whether feminist, gay, or fundamentalist. Though she considers herself a true feminist (in the "liberated" sense of the 1960s), Paglia has been especially critical of today's feminists for their puritanical response to natural forces and their "Betty Crocker" view of reality.

Two central issues of the "modern sex wars" — violence against women and gay liberation — are brought together in Jean Bethke Elshtain's "The Politics of Displacement." A noted political theorist, Elshtain is deeply critical of the way the famous feminist slogan "the personal is political" has fueled such ideological issues as women's victimization and sexual orientation. The real victim today, Elshtain concludes, may not be feminism or gay liberation but democratic civic life.

The popular conservative commentator and radio personality Rush Limbaugh also takes issue with the "personal is political" maxim. In "To Ogle Or Not to Ogle" Limbaugh reviews what he believes are ludicrously exaggerated examples of harassment. Like many libertarians, Limbaugh disapproves of extending the role of government into private affairs. Resenting the "politicization of social relationships," Limbaugh is especially bothered by the fact that "so many people think the government should intervene to solve" such questions.

Yet for many pro-feminists there is no way around the "politicization" of relationships, especially when those relationships are grounded in male dominance. For radical feminist and political activist Andrea Dworkin, abuse and violence are not aberrations of heterosexual relationships — they are an inseparable part of such relationships. In fact, sexual abuse and violence are so much a part of male-female relationships that most women are no longer conscious of their victimization. When men or women, therefore, speak of letting these relationships remain "natural," Dworkin has a response: "The natural relation of the sexes means that women are made to be used the way men use us now, in a world of civil, social, and economic inequality based on sex; a world in which women have limited rights, no physical integrity, and no real self-determination."

The reality of the world Dworkin sees does not, of course, go unquestioned. As with many significant social issues, a large part of the debate over abuse and violence involves statistics. Do we or do we not live in a world in which violence against women is quantifiably pervasive? And whose statistical data do we believe? Is Super Bowl Sunday *really* the scariest day of the year for women? In "Noble Lies," the ethics philosopher Christina Hoff Sommers takes a hard look at how feminist advocacy groups distort and sensationalize statistics to persuade us that in today's America violence against women has reached epidemic proportions.

JUNE JORDAN

A New Politics of Sexuality

Until quite recently, the discourse on sexuality in America had been severely limited by the fact that those who dominated the discourse
tended to be straight and male. By virtue of their second-class status in
American society, homosexuals and women seldom made contributions
to the conversation. The gay liberation and women's movements of the
last several decades, however, have irreversably altered this discourse.
New voices constantly emerge to challenge received ideas about human
sexuality and its social ramifications. In this selection, poet and educator
June Jordan appeals for greater understanding between groups traditionally oppressed on account of their gender or sexual orientation even
as she urges a fresh and highly politicized view of sexuality to help foster that understanding.

An internationally acclaimed poet as well as a writer on politics,
Jordan is currently a professor of African American studies and
women's studies at the University of California at Berkeley. She has previously taught at the City College of New York, the State University of
New York at Stony Brook, Sarah Lawrence College, and Yale. She is a
regular political columnist for the *Progressive*, in which this selection
originally appeared in 1991, and is on the board of directors for the Center for Constitutional Rights.

SELECTED PUBLICATIONS: *Civil Wars* (1981); *On Call: New Political
Essays, 1981–1985* (1986); *Moving Towards Home: Political Essays* (1989);
Technical Difficulties: African-American Notes on the State of the Union (1992).

A s a young worried mother, I remember turning to Dr. Benjamin
Spock's *Common Sense Book of Baby and Child Care* just about as often as I'd
pick up the telephone. He was God. I was ignorant but striving to be
good: a good Mother. And so it was there, in that best-seller pocketbook
of do's and don't's, that I came upon this doozie of a guideline: Do not
wear miniskirts or other provocative clothing because that will upset
your child, especially if your child happens to be a boy. If you give your
offspring "cause" to think of you as a sexual being, he will, at the least,
become disturbed; you will derail the equilibrium of his notions about
your possible identity and meaning in the world.

It had never occurred to me that anyone, especially my son, might
look upon me as an asexual being. I had never supposed that "asexual"
was some kind of positive designation I should, so to speak, lust after. I

was pretty surprised by Dr. Spock. However, I was also, by habit, a creature of obedience. For a couple of weeks I actually experimented with lusterless colors and dowdy tops and bottoms, self-consciously hoping thereby to prove myself as a lusterless and dowdy and, therefore, excellent female parent.

Years would have to pass before I could recognize the familiar, by then, absurdity of a man setting himself up as the expert on a subject that presupposed women as the primary objects for his patriarchal discourse — on motherhood, no less! Years passed before I came to perceive the perversity of dominant power assumed by men, and the perversity of self-determinating power ceded to men by women.

A lot of years went by before I understood the dynamics of what anyone could summarize as the Politics of Sexuality.

I believe the Politics of Sexuality is the most ancient and probably the   5
most profound arena for human conflict. Increasingly, it seems clear to me that deeper and more pervasive than any other oppression, than any other bitterly contested human domain, is the oppression of sexuality, the exploitation of the human domain of sexuality for power.

When I say sexuality, I mean gender: I mean male subjugation of human beings because they are female. When I say sexuality I mean heterosexual institutionalization of rights and privileges denied to homosexual men and women. When I say sexuality I mean gay or lesbian contempt for bisexual modes of human relationship.

The Politics of Sexuality therefore subsumes all of the different ways in which some of us seek to dictate to others of us what we should do, what we should desire, what we should dream about, and how we should behave ourselves, generally, on the planet. From China to Iran, from Nigeria to Czechoslovakia, from Chile to California, the politics of sexuality — enforced by traditions of state-sanctioned violence plus religion and the law — reduces to male domination of women, heterosexist tyranny, and, among those of us who are in any case deemed despicable or deviant by the powerful, we find intolerance for those who choose a different, a more complicated — for example, an interracial or bisexual — mode of rebellion and freedom.

We must move out from the shadows of our collective subjugation — as people of color/as women/as gay/as lesbian/as bisexual human beings.

I can voice my ideas without hesitation or fear because I am speaking, finally, about myself. I am black and I am female and I am a mother and I am bisexual and I am a nationalist and I am an antinationalist. And I mean to be fully and freely all that I am!

Conversely, I do not accept that any white or black or Chinese   10
men — I do not accept that, for instance, Dr. Spock — should presume to tell me, or any other woman, how to mother a child. He has no right. He

is not a mother. My child is not his child. And, likewise, I do not accept that anyone — any woman or any man who is not inextricably part of the subject he or she dares to address — should attempt to tell any of us, the objects of her or his presumptuous discourse, what we should do or what we should not do.

Recently, I have come upon gratuitous and appalling pseudoliberal pronouncements on sexuality. Too often, these utterances fall out of the mouths of men and women who first disclaim any sentiment remotely related to homophobia, but who then proceed to issue outrageous opinions like the following:

- That it is blasphemous to compare the oppression of gay, lesbian, or bisexual people to the oppression, say, of black people, or of the Palestinians.

- That the bottom line about gay or lesbian or bisexual identity is that you can conceal it whenever necessary and, so, therefore, why don't you do just that? Why don't you keep your deviant sexuality in the closet and let the rest of us — we who suffer oppression for reasons of our ineradicable and always visible components of our personhood such as race or gender — get on with our more necessary, our more beleaguered struggle to survive?

Well, number one: I believe I have worked as hard as I could, and then harder than that, on behalf of equality and justice — for African Americans, for the Palestinian people, and for people of color everywhere.

And, no, I do not believe it is blasphemous to compare oppressions of sexuality to oppressions of race and ethnicity: Freedom is indivisible or it is nothing at all besides sloganeering and temporary, short-sighted, and short-lived advancement for a few. Freedom is indivisible, and either we are working for freedom or you are working for the sake of your self-interests and I am working for mine.

If you can finally go to the bathroom, wherever you find one, if you can finally order a cup of coffee and drink it wherever coffee is available, but you cannot follow your heart — you cannot respect the response of your own honest body in the world — then how much of what kind of freedom does any one of us possess?

Or, conversely, if your heart and your honest body can be controlled by the state, or controlled by community taboo, are you not then, and in that case, no more than a slave ruled by outside force?

What tyranny could exceed a tyranny that dictates to the human heart, and that attempts to dictate the public career of an honest human body?

Freedom is indivisible; the Politics of Sexuality is not some optional "special-interest" concern for serious, progressive folk.

And, on another level, let me assure you: If every single gay or lesbian or bisexual man or woman active on the Left of American politics decided to stay home, there would be *no* Left left.

One of the things I want to propose is that we act on that reality: that we insistently demand reciprocal respect and concern from those who cheerfully depend upon our brains and our energies for their, and our, effective impact on the political landscape.

Last spring, at Berkeley, some students asked me to speak at a rally against racism. And I did. There were 400 or 500 people massed on Sproul Plaza, standing together against that evil. And, on the next day, on that same Plaza, there was a rally for bisexual and gay and lesbian rights, and students asked me to speak at that rally. And I did. There were fewer than seventy-five people stranded, pitiful, on that public space. And I said then what I say today: That was disgraceful! There should have been just one rally. One rally: Freedom is indivisible.

As for the second, nefarious pronouncement on sexuality that now enjoys mass-media currency: the idiot notion of keeping yourself in the closet — that is very much the same thing as the suggestion that black folks and Asian Americans and Mexican Americans should assimilate and become as "white" as possible — in our walk/talk/music/food/ values — or else. Or else? Or else we should, deservedly, perish.

Sure enough, we have plenty of exposure to white everything so why would we opt to remain our African/Asian/Mexican selves? The answer is that suicide is absolute, and if you think you will survive by hiding who you really are, you are sadly misled: There is no such thing as partial or intermittent suicide. You can only survive if you — who you really are — do survive.

Likewise, we who are not men and we who are not heterosexist — we, sure enough, have plenty of exposure to male-dominated/hetero-sexist this and that.

But a struggle to survive cannot lead to suicide: Suicide is the opposite of survival. And so we must not conceal/assimilate/integrate into the would-be dominant culture and political system that despises us. Our survival requires that we alter our environment so that we can live and so that we can hold each other's hands and so that we can kiss each other on the streets, and in the daylight of our existence, without terror and without violence and sometimes fatal reactions from the busybodies of America.

Finally, I need to speak on bisexuality. I do believe that the analogy is interracial or multiracial identity. I do believe that the analogy for bisexuality is a multicultural, multi-ethnic, multiracial world view. Bisexuality follows from such a perspective and leads to it, as well.

Just as there are many men and women in the United States whose parents have given them more than one racial, more than one ethnic identity and cultural heritage to honor; and just as these men and women must deny no given part of themselves except at the risk of self-deception and the insanities that must issue from that; and just as these men and women embody the principle of equality among races and ethnic

20

25

communities; and just as these men and women falter and anguish and choose and then falter again and then anguish and then choose yet again how they will honor the irreducible complexity of their God-given human being — even so, there are many men and women, especially young men and women, who seek to embrace the complexity of their total, always-changing social and political circumstance.

They seek to embrace our increasing global complexity on the basis of the heart and on the basis of an honest human body. Not according to ideology. Not according to group pressure. Not according to anybody's concept of "correct."

This is a New Politics of Sexuality. And even as I despair of identity politics — because identity is given and principles of justice/equality/ freedom cut across given gender and given racial definitions of being, and because I will call you my brother, I will call you my sister, on the basis of what you *do* for justice, what you *do* for equality, what you *do* for freedom and *not* on the basis of who you are, even so I look with admiration and respect upon the new, bisexual politics of sexuality.

This emerging movement politicizes the so-called middle ground: Bisexuality invalidates either/or formulation, either/or analysis. Bisexuality means I am free and I am as likely to want and to love a woman as I am likely to want and to love a man, and what about that? Isn't that what freedom implies?

If you are free, you are not predictable and you are not controllable. 30 To my mind, that is the keenly positive, politicizing significance of bisexual affirmation: To insist upon complexity, to insist upon the validity of all of the components of social/sexual complexity, to insist upon the equal validity of all of the components of social/sexual complexity.

This seems to me a unifying, 1990s mandate for revolutionary Americans planning to make it into the twenty-first century on the basis of the heart, on the basis of an honest human body, consecrated to every struggle for justice, every struggle for equality, every struggle for freedom.

PREPARING FOR DISCUSSION

1. Jordan begins her essay with a personal anecdote about her dependence on Dr. Benjamin Spock's *Common Sense Book of Baby and Child Care*. Why does she choose to relate this story? Why does she now consider it "absurd" for a male doctor "to [set] himself up" as an authority on motherhood?

2. Define as precisely as you can the New Politics of Sexuality espoused by Jordan in the essay. How does it differ from the "Old" Politics of Sexuality and who stands to benefit most by its appearance? What is the role or status of heterosexual white males within this new politics?

3. In paragraph 10, Jordan asserts that no one who does not belong to a particular group should venture to address issues involving that group. For instance, she believes that Dr. Spock has no business offering women advice on how to raise their children. In the next paragraph, she relates that she has worked hard for the Palestinian people of the Middle East. In what ways, if any, has she violated her own principle? On what grounds can she claim fellowship with Palestinians?

4. In paragraph 18, Jordan suggests that white heterosexual males do not form part of the Left. On what grounds does she exclude these men from the Left? Does she provide any evidence to support her claim? What does her generalization assume about straight white men in America?

5. In paragraph 22, the author uses the word *suicide* in place of words like *concealment, assimilation,* and *integration.* Why does she do this? What is she saying about any effort to deemphasize ethnic, gender, or sexual differences between oneself and another individual? Why does she choose the word *survival* as the alternative to *suicide?* What other words might she be using *survival* in place of?

FROM READING TO WRITING

6. Jordan draws an analogy between bisexuality and multiculturalism (paragraph 25). Write an essay in which you consider the ground on which Jordan constructs her analogy. Is her analogy valid? You might want to review the first chapter on diversity to discover whether Jordan's sense of multicultural values is similar to any you find there.

7. After considering the many ways in which Jordan defines sexuality, write an essay that sets out in a clear and concise manner your own definition of sexuality. Do your own views correspond with Jordan's? If not, how do you differ from her in your basic assumptions about human beings and freedom?

ANDREW SULLIVAN

The Politics of Homosexuality

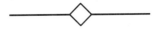

In his first month of office, President Bill Clinton learned just how dangerous a political issue homosexuality could be when he attempted to introduce reforms in the military's policy on gay recruits. He had not anticipated so violent a reaction to the reforms, especially in a country that in recent years had been making slow but genuine progress in civil rights for gay men and lesbians. Behind President Clinton's miscalculation was a misunderstanding, shared by most straight Americans, of the politics of homosexuality. In the following selection, which first appeared in the *New Republic* in 1993, English political journalist and editor Andrew Sullivan explains why none of the four dominant views of homosexuality offers a workable solution to gay-straight relations in America.

Educated at Oxford, Sullivan came to the United States on a Harkness fellowship to study politics at Harvard. Shortly after completing his doctorate in 1990, he was named editor of the *New Republic*, where he had previously served as associate editor from 1987 to 1989. Since 1992, he has also been the primary analyst of American politics for the *London Sunday Times*, Britain's largest-selling nontabloid Sunday newspaper. A leading exponent of gay marriage and of the end to the military ban on homosexuals, Sullivan seems confident in his ability to reconcile his neo-conservative politics with his status as a gay man.

SELECTED PUBLICATIONS: *Virtually Normal: An Argument About Homosexuality* (1995). Sullivan's articles appear frequently in the *London Sunday Times*, the *New York Times*, the *Wall Street Journal*, *Esquire*, and the *Public Interest*.

Over the last four years I have been sent letters from strangers caught in doomed, desperate marriages because of repressed homosexuality and witnessed several thousand virtually naked, muscle-bound men dance for hours in the middle of New York City, in the middle of the day. I have lain down on top of a dying friend to restrain his hundred-pound body as it violently shook with the death-throes of AIDS and listened to soldiers equate the existence of homosexuals in the military with the dissolution of the meaning of the United States. I have openly discussed my sexuality on a television talk show and sat on the porch of an apartment building in downtown D.C. with an arm around a male friend and watched as a dozen cars in a half hour slowed to hurl abuse. I have seen mass advertising explicitly cater to an openly gay audience and watched my own father break down and weep at the declaration of his son's sexuality.

These different experiences of homosexuality are not new, of course. But that they can now be experienced within one life (and that you are now reading about them) *is* new. The cultural categories and social departments into which we once successfully consigned sexuality — departments that helped us avoid the anger and honesty with which we are now confronted — have begun to collapse. Where once there were patterns of discreet and discrete behavior to follow, there is now only an unnerving confusion of roles and identities. Where once there was only the unmentionable, there are now only the unavoidable: gays, "queers," homosexuals, closet cases, bisexuals, the "out" and the "in," paraded for every heterosexual to see. As the straight world has been confronted with this, it has found itself reaching for a response: embarrassment, tolerance, fear, violence, oversensitivity, recognition. When Sam Nunn conducts hearings, he knows there is no common discourse in which he can now speak, that even the words he uses will betray worlds of conflicting experience and anxieties. Yet speak he must. In place of the silence that once encased the lives of homosexuals, there is now a loud argument. And there is no easy going back.

This fracturing of discourse is more than a cultural problem; it is a political problem. Without at least some common ground, no effective compromise to the homosexual question will be possible. Matters may be resolved, as they have been in the case of abortion, by a stand-off in the forces of cultural war. But unless we begin to discuss this subject with a degree of restraint and reason, the visceral unpleasantness that exploded earlier this year will dog the question of homosexuality for a long time to come, intensifying the anxieties that politics is supposed to relieve.[1]

There are as many politics of homosexuality as there are words for it, and not all of them contain reason. And it is harder perhaps in this passionate area than in any other to separate a wish from an argument, a desire from a denial. Nevertheless, without such an effort, no true politics of sexuality can emerge. And besides, there are some discernible patterns, some sketches of political theory that have begun to emerge with clarity. I will discuss here only four, but four that encompass a reasonable span of possible arguments. Each has a separate analysis of sexuality and a distinct solution to the problem of gay-straight relations. Perhaps no person belongs in any single category; and they are by no means exclusive of one another. What follows is a brief description of each: why each is riven by internal and external conflict; and why none, finally, works.

The first I'll call, for the sake of argument, the conservative politics of   5
sexuality. Its view of homosexuality is as dark as it is popular as it is unfashionable. It informs much of the opposition to allowing openly gay men and women to serve in the military and can be heard in living rooms, churches, bars, and computer bulletin boards across America. It is found in most of the families in which homosexuals grow up and critically frames many homosexuals' view of their own identity. Its fundamental assertion is that homosexuality as such does not properly exist. Homosexual behavior is aberrant activity, either on the part of heterosexuals intent on subverting traditional society or by people who are prey to psychological, emotional, or sexual dysfunction.

For adherents to the conservative politics of sexuality, therefore, the homosexual question concerns everyone. It cannot be dismissed merely

[1] Here Sullivan refers to the public uproar over suggestions by President Clinton that gay men and lesbians be allowed to serve openly in the military.

as an affliction of the individual but is rather one that afflicts society at large. Since society depends on the rearing of a healthy future generation, the existence of homosexuals is a grave problem. People who would otherwise be living productive and socially beneficial lives are diverted by homosexuality into unhappiness and sterility, and they may seek, in their bleak attempts at solace, to persuade others to join them. Two gerundives cling to this view of homosexuals: practicing and proselytizing. And both are habitually uttered with a mixture of pity and disgust.

The politics that springs out of this view of homosexuality has two essential parts: with the depraved, it must punish; with the sick, it must cure. There are, of course, degrees to which these two activities can be promoted. The recent practice in modern liberal democracies of imprisoning homosexuals or subjecting them to psychological or physiological "cures" is a good deal less repressive than the camps for homosexuals in Castro's Cuba, the spasmodic attempt at annihilation in Nazi Germany or the brutality of modern Islamic states. And the sporadic entrapment of gay men in public restrooms or parks is a good deal less repressive than the systematic hunting down and discharging of homosexuals that we require of our armed forces. But the differences are matters of degree rather than of kind; and the essential characteristic of the conservative politics of homosexuality is that it pursues the logic of repression. Not for conservatives the hypocrisy of those who tolerate homosexuality in private and abhor it in public. They seek rather to grapple with the issue directly and to sustain the carapace of public condemnation and legal sanction that can keep the dark presence of homosexuality at bay.

This is not a distant politics. In twenty-four states sodomy is still illegal, and the constitutionality of these statutes was recently upheld by the Supreme Court. Much of the Republican Party supports this politics with varying degrees of sympathy for the victims of the affliction. The [party's 1992] Houston convention was replete with jokes by speaker Patrick Buchanan that implicitly affirmed this view. Banners held aloft by delegates asserted "Family Rights For Ever, Gay Rights Never," implying a direct trade-off between tolerating homosexuals and maintaining the traditional family.

In its crudest and most politically dismissible forms, this politics invokes biblical revelation to make its civic claims. But in its subtler form, it draws strength from the natural law tradition, which, for all its failings, is a resilient pillar of Western thought. Following a Thomist[2] argument, conservatives argue that the natural function of sexuality is clearly procreative; and that all expressions of it outside procreation destroy human beings' potential for full and healthy development. Homosexuality — far

---

[2] *Thomist:* Reference to philosopher St. Thomas Aquinas's (1225?–1274) notion of "natural law."

from being natural — is clearly a perversion of, or turning away from, the legitimate and healthy growth of the human person.

Perhaps the least helpful element in the current debate is the asser- 10 tion that this politics is simply bigotry. It isn't. Many bigots may, of course, support it, and by bigots I mean those whose "visceral recoil" from homosexuals (to quote Buchanan) expresses itself in thuggery and name-calling. But there are some who don't support anti-gay violence and who sincerely believe discouragement of homosexuality by law and "curing" homosexuals is in the best interest of everybody.

Nevertheless, this politics suffers from an increasingly acute internal contradiction and an irresistible external development. It is damaged, first, by the growing evidence that homosexuality does in fact exist as an identifiable and involuntary characteristic of some people, and that these people do not as a matter of course suffer from moral or psychological dysfunction; that it is, in other words, as close to "natural" as any human condition can be. New data about the possible genetic origins of homo- sexuality are only one part of this development. By far the most impor- tant element is the testimony of countless homosexuals. The number who say their orientation is a choice make up only a tiny minority; and the candor of those who say it isn't is overwhelming. To be sure, it is in the interests of gay people to affirm their lack of choice over the matter; but the consensus among homosexuals, the resilience of lesbian and gay minori- ties in the face of deep social disapproval and even a plague, suggests that homosexuality, whatever one would like to think, simply is not often chosen. A fundamental claim of natural law is that its truths are self- evident: across continents and centuries, homosexuality is a self-evident fact of life.

How large this population is does not matter. One percent or 10 per- cent: as long as a small but persistent part of the population is involuntar- ily gay, then the entire conservative politics of homosexuality rests on an unstable footing. It becomes simply a politics of denial or repression. Faced with a sizable and inextinguishable part of society, it can only pre- tend that it does not exist, or needn't be addressed, or can somehow be dismissed. This politics is less coherent than even the politics that op- posed civil rights for blacks thirty years ago, because at least that had some answer to the question of the role of blacks in society, however sub- ordinate. Today's conservatives have no role for homosexuals; they want them somehow to disappear, an option that was once illusory and is now impossible.

Some conservatives and conservative institutions have recognized this. They've even begun to use the term "homosexual," implicitly ac- cepting the existence of a constitutive characteristic. Some have avoided it by the innovative term "homosexualist," but most cannot do so with- out a wry grin on their faces. The more serious opponents of equality for homosexuals finesse the problem by restricting their objections to "radical homosexuals," but the distinction doesn't help. They are still forced to confront the problem of *un*radical homosexuals, people whose sexuality is, presumably, constitutive. To make matters worse, the Roman Catholic Church — the firmest religious proponent of the conservative politics of homosexuality — has explicitly conceded the point. It declared in 1975 that homosexuality is indeed involuntary for many. In the recent Universal Catechism, the Church goes even further. Homosexuality is described as a "condition" of a "not negligible" number of people who "do not choose" their sexuality and deserve to be treated with "respect, compassion and sensitivity." More critically, because of homosexuality's involuntary nature, it cannot of itself be morally culpable (although homosexual *acts* still are). The doctrine is thus no longer "hate the sin but love the sinner"; it's "hate the sin but accept the condition," a position unique in Catholic theology, and one that has already begun to creak under the strain of its own tortuousness.

But the loss of intellectual solidity isn't the only problem for the conservative politics of homosexuality. In a liberal polity, it has lost a good deal of its political coherence as well. When many people in a liberal society insist upon their validity as citizens and human beings, repression becomes a harder and harder task. It offends against fundamental notions of decency and civility to treat them as simple criminals or patients. To hunt them down, imprison them for private acts, subject government workers to surveillance and dismissal for reasons related to their deepest sense of personal identity becomes a policy not simply cruel but politically impossible in a civil order. For American society to return to the social norms around the question of homosexuality of a generation ago would require a renewed act of repression that not even many zealots could contemplate. What generations of inherited shame could not do, what AIDS could not accomplish, what the most decisive swing toward conservatism in the 1980s could not muster, must somehow be accomplished in the next few years. It simply cannot be done.

So even Patrick Buchanan is reduced to joke-telling; senators to professions of ignorance; military leaders to rationalizations of sheer discomfort. For those whose politics are a mere extension of religious faith, such impossibilism is part of the attraction (and spiritually, if not politically, defensible). But for conservatives who seek to act as citizens in a secular, civil order, the dilemma is terminal. An unremittingly hostile stance toward homosexuals runs the risk of sectarianism. At some point, not reached yet but fast approaching, their politics could become so estranged from the society in which it operates that it could cease to operate as a politics altogether.

The second politics of homosexuality shares with the first a conviction that homosexuality as an inherent and natural condition does not exist. Homosexuality, in this politics, is a cultural construction, a binary social conceit (along with heterosexuality) forced upon the sexually amorphous (all of us). This politics attempts to resist this oppressive construct, subverting it and subverting the society that allows it to fester. Where the first politics takes as its starting point the Thomist faith in nature, the second springs from the Nietzschean desire to surpass all natural necessities, to attack the construct of "nature" itself. Thus the pursuit of a homosexual existence is but one strategy of many to enlarge the possibility for human liberation.

Call this the radical politics of homosexuality. For the radicals, like the conservatives, homosexuality is definitely a choice: the choice to be a "queer," the choice to subvert oppressive institutions, the choice to be an activist. And it is a politics that, insofar as it finds its way from academic discourse into gay activism (and it does so fitfully), exercises a peculiar fascination for the adherents of the first politics. At times, indeed, both seem to exist in a bond of mutual contempt and admiration. That both prefer to use the word "queer," the one in private, the other in irony, is only one of many resemblances. They both react with disdain to those studies that seem to reflect a genetic source for homosexuality; and they both favor, to some extent or other, the process of outing, because for both it is the flushing out of deviant behavior: for conservatives, of the morally impure, for radicals, of the politically incorrect. For conservatives, radical "queers" provide a frisson of cultural apocalypse and a steady stream of funding dollars. For radicals, the religious right can be tapped as an unreflective and easy justification for virtually any political impulse whatsoever.

Insofar as this radical politics is synonymous with a subcultural experience, it has stretched the limits of homosexual identity and expanded the cultural space in which some homosexuals can live. In the late 1980s the tactics of groups like Act-Up and Queer Nation did not merely shock and anger, but took the logic of shame-abandonment to a thrilling conclusion. To exist within their sudden energy was to be caught in a liberating rite of passage, which, when it did not transgress into political puritanism, exploded many of the cozy assumptions of closeted homosexual and liberal heterosexual alike.

This politics is as open-ended as the conservative politics is closed-minded. It seeks an end to all restrictions on homosexuality, but also the subversion of heterosexual norms, as taught in schools or the media. By virtue of its intellectual origins, it affirms a close connection with every other minority group, whose cultural subversion of white, heterosexual, male norms is just as vital. It sees its crusades — now for an AIDS czar, now against the Catholic Church's abortion stance, now for the Rainbow Curriculum, now against the military ban — as a unified whole of protest, glorifying in its indiscriminateness as in its universality.

But like the conservative politics of homosexuality, which also 20

provides a protective ghetto of liberation for its disciples, the radical politics of homosexuality now finds itself in an acute state of crisis. Its problem is twofold: its conception of homosexuality is so amorphous and
indistinguishable from other minority concerns that it is doomed to be
ultimately unfocused; and its relationship with the views of most homosexuals — let alone heterosexuals — is so tenuous that at moments of
truth (like the military ban) it strains to have a viable politics at all.

The trouble with gay radicalism, in short, is the problem with subversive politics as a whole. It tends to subvert itself. Act-Up, for example,
an AIDS group that began in the late 1980s as an activist group dedicated
to finding a cure and better treatment for people with AIDS, soon found itself awash in a cacophony of internal division. Its belief that sexuality
was only one of many oppressive constructions meant that it was constantly tempted to broaden its reach, to solve a whole range of gender
and ethnic grievances. Similarly, each organizing committee in each state
of [a May 1993] march on Washington was required to have a 50 percent
"minority" composition. Even *Utah.* Although this universalist tempta-
tion was not always given in to, it exercised an enervating and dissipat-
ing effect on gay radicalism's political punch.

More important, the notion of sexuality as cultural subversion dis-
tanced it from the vast majority of gay people who not only accept the
natural origin of their sexual orientation, but wish to be integrated into
society as it is. For most gay people — the closet cases and barflies, the
construction workers and investment bankers, the computer program-
mers and parents — a "queer" identity is precisely what they want to
avoid. In this way, the radical politics of homosexuality, like the conservative politics of homosexuality, is caught in a political trap. The more it
purifies its own belief about sexuality, the less able it is to engage the
broader world as a whole. The more it acts upon its convictions, the less
able it is to engage in politics at all.

For the "queer" fundamentalists, like the religious fundamentalists,
this is no problem. Politics for both groups is essentially an exercise in
theater and rhetoric, in which dialogue with one's opponent is an admission of defeat. It is no accident that Act-Up was founded by a play-
wright, since its politics was essentially theatrical: a fantastic display of
rhetorical pique and visual brilliance. It became a national media hit, but
eventually its lines became familiar and the audience's attention wa-
vered. New shows have taken its place and will continue to do so: but
they will always be constrained by their essential nature, which is performance, not persuasion.

The limits of this strategy can be seen in the politics of the military
ban. Logically, there is no reason for radicals to support the ending of the
ban: it means acceptance of presumably one of the most repressive institutions in American society. And, to be sure, no radical arguments have
been made to end the ban. But in the last few months, "queers" have

been appearing on television proclaiming that gay people are just like anybody else and defending the right of gay Midwestern Republicans to serve their country. In the pinch, "queer" politics was forced to abandon its theoretical essence if it was to advance its purported aims: the advancement of gay equality. The military ban illustrated the dilemma perfectly. As soon as radicalism was required actually to engage America, its politics disintegrated.

Similarly, "queer" radicalism's doctrine of cultural subversion and separatism has the effect of alienating those very gay Americans most in need of support and help: the young and teenagers. Separatism is even less of an option for gays than for any other minority, since each generation is literally umbilically connected to the majority. The young are permanently in the hands of the other. By erecting a politics on a doctrine of separation and difference from the majority, "queer" politics ironically broke off dialogue with the heterosexual families whose cooperation is needed in every generation, if gay children are to be accorded a modicum of dignity and hope.

There's an argument, of course, that radicalism's politics is essentially instrumental; that by stretching the limits of what is acceptable it opens up space for more moderate types to negotiate; that, without Act-Up and Queer Nation, no progress would have been made at all. But this both insults the theoretical integrity of the radical position (they surely do not see themselves as mere adjuncts to liberals) and underestimates the scope of the gay revolution that has been quietly taking place in America. Far more subversive than media-grabbing demonstrations on the evening news has been the slow effect of individual, private Americans becoming more open about their sexuality. The emergence of role models, the development of professional organizations and student groups, the growing influence of openly gay people in the media, and the extraordinary impact of AIDS on families and friends have dwarfed radicalism's impact on the national consciousness. Likewise, the greatest public debate about homosexuality yet — the military debate — took place not because radicals besieged the Pentagon, but because of the ordinary and once-anonymous Americans within the military who simply refused to acquiesce in their own humiliation any longer. Their courage was illustrated not in taking to the streets in rage but in facing their families and colleagues with integrity.

And this presents the deepest problem for radicalism. As the closet slowly collapses, as gay people enter the mainstream, as suburban homosexuals and Republican homosexuals emerge blinking into the daylight, as the gay ghettos of the inner cities are diluted by the gay enclaves of the suburbs, the whole notion of a separate and homogeneous "queer" identity will become harder to defend. Far from redefining gay identity, "queer" radicalism may actually have to define itself in opposition to it. This is implicit in the punitive practice of "outing" and in the increasingly anti-gay politics of some "queer" radicals. But if "queer" politics is to survive, it will either have to be proved right about America's inherent hostility to gay people or become more insistent in its separatism. It will have to intensify its hatred of straights or its contempt for gays. Either path is likely to be as culturally creative as it is politically sterile.

Between these two cultural poles, an appealing alternative presents itself. You can hear it in the tone if not the substance of civilized columnists and embarrassed legislators, who are united most strongly by the desire that this awkward subject simply go away. It is the moderate politics of homosexuality. Unlike the conservatives and radicals, the moderates do believe that a small number of people are inherently homosexual, but they also believe that another group is susceptible to persuasion in that direction and should be dissuaded. These people do not want persecution of homosexuals, but they do not want overt approval either. They are most antsy when it comes to questions of the education of children but feel acute discomfort in supporting the likes of Patrick Buchanan and Pat Robertson.

Thus their politics has all the nuance and all the disingenuousness of classically conservative politics. They are not intolerant, but they oppose the presence of openly gay teachers in school; they have gay friends but hope their child isn't homosexual; they are in favor of ending the military ban but would seek to do so either by reimposing the closet (ending discrimination in return for gay people never mentioning their sexuality) or by finding some other kind of solution, such as simply ending the witch hunts. If they support sodomy laws *(pour décourager les autres)*,[3] they prefer to see them unenforced. In either case, they do not regard the matter as very important. They are ambivalent about domestic partnership legislation but are offended by gay marriage. Above all, they prefer that the subject of homosexuality be discussed with delicacy and restraint, and are only likely to complain to their gay friends if they insist upon "bringing the subject up" too often.

This position too has a certain coherence. It insists that politics is a   30
matter of custom as well as principle and that, in the words of Nunn, caution on the matter of sexuality is not so much a matter of prejudice as of prudence. It places a premium on discouraging the sexually ambivalent from resolving their ambiguity freely in the direction of homosexuality, because, society being as it is, such a life is more onerous than a heterosexual one. It sometimes exchanges this argument for the more honest one: that it wishes to promote procreation and the healthy rearing of the next generation and so wishes to create a cultural climate that promotes heterosexuality.

---

[3] pour décourager les autres: "To discourage others" (French).

But this politics too has become somewhat unstable, if not as un-stable as the first two. And this instability stems from an internal prob-lem and a related external one. Being privately tolerant and publicly disapproving exacts something of a psychological cost on those who maintain it. In theory, it is not the same as hypocrisy; in practice, it comes perilously close. As the question of homosexuality refuses to disappear from public debate, explicit positions have to be taken. What once could be shrouded in discretion now has to be argued in public. For those who privately do not believe that homosexuality is inherently evil or always chosen, it has become increasingly difficult to pretend otherwise in pub-lic. Silence is an option — and numberless politicians are now availing themselves of it — but increasingly a decision will have to be made. Are you in favor of or against allowing openly gay women and men to con-tinue serving their country? Do you favor or oppose gay marriage? Do you support the idea of gay civil rights laws? Once these questions are asked, the gentle ambiguity of the moderates must be flushed out; they have to be forced either into the conservative camp or into formulating a new politics that does not depend on a code of discourse that is fast be-coming defunct.

They cannot even rely upon their gay friends anymore. What ulti-mately sustained this politics was the complicity of the gay elites in it: their willingness to stay silent when a gay joke was made in their pres-ence, their deference to the euphemisms — roommate, friend, compan-ion — that denoted their lovers, husbands, and wives, their support of the heterosexual assumptions of polite society. Now that complicity, if not vanished, has come under strain. There are fewer and fewer J. Edgar Hoovers and Roy Cohns,[4] and the thousands of discreet gay executives and journalists, businessmen and politicians who long deferred to their sexual betters in matters of etiquette. AIDS rendered their balancing act finally absurd. Many people — gay and straight — were forced to have the public courage of their private convictions. They had to confront the fact that their delicacy was a way of disguising shame; that their silence was a means of hiding from themselves their intolerance. This is not an easy process; indeed, it can be a terrifying one for both gay and straight people alike. But there comes a point after which omissions become com-missions; and that point, if not here yet, is coming. When it arrives, the moderate politics of homosexuality will be essentially over.

The politics that is the most durable in our current attempt to deal with the homosexual question is the contemporary liberal politics of ho-mosexuality. Like the moderates, the liberals accept that homosexuality

---

[4] *J. Edgar Hoover*, longtime director of the FBI, and *Roy Cohn*, a prominent American lawyer, were both alleged to be homosexuals.

exists, that it is involuntary for a proportion of society, that for a few more it is an option and that it need not be discouraged. Viewing the issue primarily through the prism of the civil rights movement, the liberals seek to extend to homosexuals the same protections they have granted to other minorities. The prime instrument for this is the regulation of private activities by heterosexuals, primarily in employment and housing; to guarantee non-discrimination against homosexuals.

Sometimes this strategy is echoed in the rhetoric of Edward Kennedy, who, in the hearings on the military gay ban, linked the gay rights agenda with the work of such disparate characters as John Kennedy, Cesar Chavez, and Martin Luther King, Jr. In other places, it is reflected in the fact that sexual orientation is simply added to the end of a list of minority conditions, in formulaic civil rights legislation. And this strategy makes a certain sense. Homosexuals are clearly subject to private discrimination in the same way as many other minorities; and linking the causes helps defuse some of the trauma that the subject of homosexuality raises. Liberalism properly restricts itself to law — not culture — in addressing social problems; and by describing all homosexuals as a monolithic minority, it is able to avoid the complexities of the gay world as a whole, just as blanket civil rights legislation draws a veil over the varieties of black America by casting the question entirely in terms of non-black attitudes.

But this strategy is based on two assumptions: that sexuality is equivalent to race in terms of discrimination, and that the full equality of homosexuals can be accomplished by designating gay people as victims. Both are extremely dubious. And the consequence of these errors is to mistarget the good that liberals are trying to do.

Consider the first. Two truths (at least) profoundly alter the way the process of discrimination takes place against homosexuals and against racial minorities and distinguish the history of racial discrimination in this country from the history of homophobia. Race is always visible; sexuality can be hidden. Race is in no way behavioral; sexuality, though distinct from sexual activity, is profoundly linked to a settled pattern of behavior.

For lesbians and gay men, the option of self-concealment has always existed and still exists, an option that means that in a profound way, discrimination against them is linked to their own involvement, even acquiescence. Unlike blacks three decades ago, gay men and lesbians suffer no discernible communal economic deprivation and already operate at the highest levels of society: in boardrooms, governments, the media, the military, the law, and industry. They may have advanced so far because they have not disclosed their sexuality, but their sexuality as such has not been an immediate cause for their disadvantage. In many cases, their sexuality is known, but it is disclosed at such a carefully calibrated level that it never actually works against them. At lower levels of society, the same pattern continues. As in the military, gay people are not uniformly discriminated against; *openly* gay people are.

Moreover, unlike blacks or other racial minorities, gay people are not subject to inherited patterns of discrimination. When generation after generation is discriminated against, a cumulative effect of deprivation may take place, where the gradual miseration of a particular ethnic group may intensify with the years. A child born into a family subject to decades of accumulated poverty is clearly affected by a past history of discrimination in terms of his or her race. But homosexuality occurs randomly anew with every generation. No sociological pattern can be deduced from it. Each generation gets a completely fresh start in terms of the socioeconomic conditions inherited from the family unit.

This is not to say that the psychological toll of homosexuality is less problematic than that of race, but that it is different: in some ways better; in others, worse. Because the stigma is geared toward behavior, the level of shame and collapse of self-esteem may be more intractable. To reach puberty and find oneself falling in love with members of one's own sex is to experience a mixture of self-discovery and self-disgust that never leaves a human consciousness. If the stigma is attached not simply to an obviously random characteristic, such as skin pigmentation, but to the deepest desires of the human heart, then it can eat away at a person's sense of his own dignity with peculiar ferocity. When a young person confronts her sexuality, she is also completely alone. A young heterosexual black or Latino girl invariably has an existing network of people like her to interpret, support, and explain the emotions she feels when confronting racial prejudice for the first time. But a gay child generally has no one. The very people she would most naturally turn to — the family — may be the very people she is most ashamed in front of.

The stigma attached to sexuality is also different from that attached to race because it attacks the very heart of what makes a human being human: her ability to love and be loved. Even the most vicious persecution of racial minorities allowed, in many cases, for the integrity of the marital bond or the emotional core of a human being. When it did not, when Nazism split husbands from wives, children from parents, when apartheid or slavery broke up familial bonds, it was clear that a particularly noxious form of repression was taking place. But the stigma attached to homosexuality *begins* with such a repression. It forbids, at a child's earliest stage of development, the possibility of the highest form of human happiness. It starts with emotional terror and ends with mild social disapproval. It's no accident that, later in life, when many gay people learn to reconnect the bonds of love and sex, they seek to do so in private, even protected from the knowledge of their family.

This unique combination of superficial privilege, acquiescence in

40

repression and psychological pain is a human mix no politics can easily tackle. But it is the mix liberalism must address if it is to reach its goal of using politics to ease human suffering. The internal inconsistency of this politics is that by relying on the regulation of private activity, it misses its essential target — and may even make matters worse. In theory, a human rights statute sounds like an ideal solution, a way for straights to express their concern and homosexuals to legitimate their identity. But in practice, it misses the point. It might grant workers a greater sense of security were they to come out in the office; and it might, by the publicity it generates, allow for greater tolerance and approval of homosexuality generally. But the real terror of coming out is deeper than economic security, and is not resolved by it; it is related to emotional and interpersonal dignity. However effective or comprehensive anti-discrimination laws are, they cannot reach far enough to tackle this issue; it is one that can only be addressed person by person, life by life, heart by heart.

For these reasons, such legislation rarely touches the people most in need of it: those who live in communities where disapproval of homosexuality is so intense that the real obstacles to advancement remain impervious to legal remedy. And even in major urban areas, it can be largely irrelevant. (On average some 1 to 2 percent of anti-discrimination cases have to do with sexual orientation; in Wisconsin, which has had such a law in force for more than a decade and is the largest case study, the figure is 1.1 percent.) As with other civil rights legislation, those least in need of it may take fullest advantage: the most litigious and articulate homosexuals, who would likely brave the harsh winds of homophobia in any case.

Anti-discrimination laws scratch the privileged surface, while avoiding the problematic depths. Like too many drugs for AIDS, they treat the symptoms of the homosexual problem without being anything like a cure; they may buy some time, and it is a cruel doctor who, in the face of human need, would refuse them. But they have about as much chance of tackling the deep roots of the gay-straight relationship as AZT has of curing AIDS. They want to substitute for the traumatic and difficult act of coming out the more formal and procedural act of legislation. But law cannot do the work of life. Even culture cannot do the work of life. Only life can do the work of life.

As the experience in Colorado[5] and elsewhere shows, this strategy of using law to change private behavior also gives a fatal opening to the conservative politics of homosexuality. Civil rights laws essentially dictate the behavior of heterosexuals, in curtailing their ability to discriminate. They can, with justification, be portrayed as being an infringement of individual liberties. If the purpose of the liberal politics is to ensure the

---

[5] Here the author refers to a piece of antigay legislation drafted, voted on, and defeated in Colorado in the early 1990s.

equality of homosexuals and their integration into society, it has thus achieved something quite peculiar. It has provided fuel for those who want to argue that homosexuals are actually seeking the infringement of heterosexuals' rights and the imposition of their values onto others. Much of this is propaganda, of course, and is fueled by fear and bigotry. But it works because it contains a germ of truth. Before most homosexuals have even come out of the closet, they are demanding concessions from the majority, including a clear curtailment of economic and social liberties, in order to ensure protections few of them will even avail themselves of. It is no wonder there is opposition, or that it seems to be growing. Nine states now have propositions to respond to what they see as the "special rights" onslaught.

In the process, the liberal politics of homosexuality has also reframed   45 the position of gays in relation to straights. It has defined them in a permanent supplicant status, seeing gay freedom as dependent on straight enlightenment, achievable only by changing the behavior of heterosexuals. The valuable political insight of radicalism is that this is a fatal step. It could enshrine forever the notion that gay people are a vulnerable group in need of protection. By legislating homosexuals as victims, it sets up a psychological dynamic of supplication that too often only perpetuates cycles of inadequacy and self-doubt. Like blacks before them, gay people may grasp at what seems to be an escape from the prison of self-hatred, only to find it is another prison of patronized victimology. By seeking salvation in the hands of others, they may actually entrench in law and in their minds the notion that their equality is dependent on the goodwill of their betters. It isn't. This may have made a good deal of sense in the case of American blacks, with a clear and overwhelming history of accumulated discrimination and a social ghetto that seemed impossible to breach. But for gay people — already prosperous, independent, and on the brink of real integration — that lesson should surely now be learned. To place our self-esteem in the benevolent hands of contemporary liberalism is more than a mistake. It is a historic error.

If there were no alternative to today's liberal politics of homosexuality, it should perhaps be embraced by default. But there is an alternative politics that is imaginable, which once too was called liberal. It begins with the view that for a small minority of people, homosexuality is an involuntary condition that can neither be denied nor permanently repressed. It adheres to an understanding that there is a limit to what politics can achieve in such an area, and trains its focus not on the behavior of private heterosexual citizens but on the actions of the public and allegedly neutral state. While it eschews the use of law to legislate culture, it strongly believes that law can affect culture indirectly. Its goal would be full civil equality for those who, through no fault of their own, happen to be homosexual; and would not deny homosexuals, as the other four politics do, their existence, integrity, dignity, or distinctness. It would attempt neither to patronize nor to exclude.

This liberal politics affirms a simple and limited criterion: that all *public* (as opposed to private) discrimination against homosexuals be ended and that every right and responsibility that heterosexuals enjoy by virtue of the state be extended to those who grow up different. And that is all. No cures or re-educations; no wrenching civil litigation; no political imposition of tolerance; merely a political attempt to enshrine formal civil equality, in the hope that eventually, the private sphere will reflect this public civility. For these reasons, it is the only politics that actually tackles the core *political* problem of homosexuality and perhaps the only one that fully respects liberalism's public-private distinction. For these reasons, it has also the least chance of being adopted by gays and straights alike.

But is it impossible? By sheer circumstance, this politics has just been given its biggest boost since the beginning of the debate over the homosexual question. The military ban is by far the most egregious example of proactive government discrimination in this country. By conceding, as the military has done, the excellent service that many gay and lesbian soldiers have given to their country, the military has helped shatter a thousand stereotypes about their nature and competence. By focusing on the mere admission of homosexuality, the ban has purified the debate into a matter of the public enforcement of homophobia. Unlike anti-discrimination law, the campaign against the ban does not ask any private citizens to hire or fire anyone of whom they do not approve; it merely asks public servants to behave the same way with avowed homosexuals as with closeted ones.

Because of its timing, because of the way in which it has intersected with the coming of age of gay politics, the military debate has a chance of transforming the issue for good. Its real political power — and the real source of the resistance to it — comes from its symbolism. The acceptance of gay people at the heart of the state, at the core of the notion of patriotism, is anathema to those who wish to consign homosexuals to the margins of society. It offends conservatives by the simplicity of its demands, and radicals by the traditionalism of the gay people involved; it dismays moderates, who are forced publicly to discuss this issue for the first time; and it disorients liberals, who find it hard to fit the cause simply into the rubric of minority politics. For instead of seeking access, as other minorities have done, gays in the military are simply demanding recognition. They start not from the premise of suppliance, but of success, of proven ability and prowess in battle, of exemplary conduct and ability. This is a new kind of minority politics. It is less a matter of complaint than of pride; less about subversion than about the desire to contribute equally.

The military ban also forces our society to deal with the real issues at   50
stake in dealing with homosexuals. The country has been forced to dis-

cuss sleeping arrangements, fears of sexual intimidation, the fraught emotional relations between gays and straights, the violent reaction to homosexuality among many young males, the hypocrisy involved in much condemnation of gays, and the possible psychological and emotional syndromes that make homosexuals allegedly unfit for service. Like a family engaged in the first, angry steps toward dealing with a gay member, the country has been forced to debate a subject honestly — even calmly — in a way it never has before. This is a clear and enormous gain. Whatever the result of this process, it cannot be undone.

But the critical measure necessary for full gay equality is something deeper and more emotional perhaps than even the military. It is equal access to marriage. As with the military, this is a question of formal public discrimination. If the military ban deals with the heart of what it is to be a citizen, the marriage ban deals with the core of what it is to be a member of civil society. Marriage is not simply a private contract; it is a social and public recognition of a private commitment. As such it is the highest public recognition of our personal integrity. Denying it to gay people is the most public affront possible to their civil equality.

This issue may be the hardest for many heterosexuals to accept. Even those tolerant of homosexuals may find this institution so wedded to the notion of heterosexual commitment that to extend it would be to undo its very essence. And there may be religious reasons for resisting this that require far greater discussion than I can give them here. But *civilly* and *emotionally*, the case is compelling. The heterosexuality of marriage is civilly intrinsic only if it is understood to be inherently procreative; and that definition has long been abandoned in civil society. In contemporary America, marriage has become a way in which the state recognizes an emotional and economic commitment of two people to each other for life. No law requires children to consummate it. And within that definition, there is no civil way it can logically be denied homosexuals, except as a pure gesture of public disapproval. (I leave aside here the thorny issue of adoption rights, which I support in full. They are not the same as the right to marriage and can be legislated, or not, separately.)

In the same way, emotionally, marriage is characterized by a kind of commitment that is rare even among heterosexuals. Extending it to homosexuals need not dilute the special nature of that commitment, unless it is understood that gay people, by their very nature, are incapable of it. History and experience suggest the opposite. It is not necessary to prove that gay people are more or less able to form long-term relationships than straights for it to be clear that, at least, *some* are. Giving these people a right to affirm their commitment doesn't reduce the incentive for heterosexuals to do the same, and even provides a social incentive for lesbians and gay men to adopt socially beneficial relationships.

But for gay people, it would mean far more than simple civil equality. The vast majority of us — gay and straight — are brought up to understand that the apex of emotional life is found in the marital bond. It may not be something we achieve, or even ultimately desire, but its very existence premises the core of our emotional development. It is the architectonic institution that frames our emotional life. The marriages of others are a moment for celebration and self-affirmation; they are the way in which our families and friends reinforce us as human beings. Our parents consider our emotional lives to be more important than our professional ones, because they care about us at our core, not at our periphery. And it is not hard to see why the marriage of an offspring is often regarded as the high point of any parent's life.

Gay people always know this essential affirmation will be denied   55
them. Thus their relationships are given no anchor, no endpoint, no way of integrating them fully into the network of family and friends that makes someone a full member of civil society. Even when those relationships become essentially the same — or even stronger — than straight relationships, they are never accorded the dignity of actual equality. Husbands remain "friends"; wives remain "partners." The very language sends a powerful signal of fault, a silent assumption of internal disorder or insufficiency. The euphemisms — and the brave attempt to pretend that gay people don't need marriage — do not successfully conceal the true emotional cost and psychological damage that this signal exacts. No true progress in the potential happiness of gay teenagers or in the stability of gay adults or in the full integration of gay and straight life is possible, or even imaginable, without it.

These two measures — simple, direct, requiring no change in heterosexual behavior and no sacrifice from heterosexuals — represent a politics that tackles the heart of homophobia while leaving homophobes their freedom. It allows homosexuals to define their own future and their own identity and does not place it in the hands of the other. It makes a clear, public statement of equality, while leaving all the inequalities of emotion and passion to the private sphere, where they belong. It does not legislate private tolerance, it declares public equality. It banishes the paradigm of victimology and replaces it with one of integrity. It requires one further step, of course, which is to say the continuing effort for honesty on the part of homosexuals themselves. This is not easily summed up in the crude phrase "coming out"; but it finds expression in the myriad ways in which gay men and lesbians talk, engage, explain, confront, and seek out the other. Politics cannot substitute for this; heterosexuals cannot provide it. And, while it is not in some sense fair that homosexuals have to initiate the dialogue, it is a fact of life. Silence, if it does not equal death, equals the living equivalent.

It is not the least of the ironies of this politics that its objectives are in some sense not political at all. The family is prior to the liberal state; the military is coincident with it. Heterosexuals would not conceive of such rights as things to be won, but as things that predate modern political discussion. But it says something about the unique status of homosexuals in our society that we now have to be political in order to be prepolitical. Our battle is not for political victory but for personal integrity. Just as many of us had to leave our families in order to join them again, so now as citizens, we have to embrace politics, if only ultimately to be free of it. Our lives may have begun in simplicity, but they have not ended there. Our dream, perhaps, is that they might.

A Comment on Discrimination

BARNEY FRANK
Fighting Gay and Lesbian Discrimination

Elected officials have discovered two important political facts: (1) there is more support for fair treatment for gay men and lesbians than many politicians believed in 1980 and (2) equally importantly, there is much less bigotry against homosexuals in our society than almost all politicians believed in 1980.

The first of these phenomena has been more frequently chronicled. During the eighties, gay men and lesbians organized themselves politically at the local and national level. This effort drew particular strength from the outrage and concern over society's response — or lack thereof — to AIDS. Helping this organizational drive were the increasing numbers of gay men and lesbians who were talking candidly about their sexual orientation to relatives, friends, co-workers, and in some cases casual acquaintances or perfect strangers. All of this activity meant that politicians — who are generally in very good touch with their districts — became much more aware than they had been not only of the presence of gay and lesbian constituents but of their concerns. It meant also that the friends, relatives, and others to whom people have come out offered a second layer of support. No organization has had more impact in its lobbying and educational work against antihomosexual policies than Parents and Friends of Lesbians and Gays. Few politicians want to argue with a father asserting his right to love his daughter as much as anyone else in America.

Less talked about but equally important, most politicians are finding that there is less prejudice in America based on sexual orientation than we had thought. The evidence I offer for this proposition comes from the conversations I have had with politicians who had opposed legislation harmful to gays nervously. They were convinced they were right on the merits, but they worried about the political storm. Members of Congress have suffered far less at the polls on this issue than they anticipated they would. This does not mean that no one lost votes; and obviously those most vulnerable to defeat if they alienated even a small number of anti-gay obsessives probably avoided the problem by voting against the antidiscrimination position. It does mean that there are many fewer voters prepared to make crusades against homosexuals a significant factor in their voting behavior than we had thought.

This, I think, is part of a larger social phenomenon in which race and sexual orientation are mirror opposites. Officially — legally and philosophically — America considers itself a nation opposed to racism. In fact, racism continues to be a serious problem in our society, and thus in our politics. The reverse is true with homosexuality. We have no national policies opposing discrimination against gays and lesbians. On the contrary, a presidential order banning gay men and lesbians from serving in the armed forces — a clear example of official bigotry — is still in effect. But as more and more gay men and lesbians make their sexual orientation clear, prejudice in our day-to-day lives, while still present, is diminishing. In short, I believe that America is both more racist and less homophobic in fact than it is in theory.

The major difference in my judgment is that the white majority feels far more threatened by nonwhites than the straight majority feels threatened by gay men and lesbians. People are far likelier to disapprove of homosexuality in the abstract than they are to disapprove of people being of a different race; but they are much more prone to fear racial minorities than to worry about harm coming to them from those who don't share their sexual orientation.

This conclusion has some significant consequences for liberals when thinking about how best to reestablish our acceptability to the national electorate.

Most importantly, this argument confirms the point that the liberals must become more credible as opponents of crime if we are to win the political battle over civil rights. And if we succeed in persuading the swing voters that we share the strong feelings they have on the crime issue, we need not retreat at all from the specifics of our positions against racial discrimination.

Also, the political realities of race and gender orientation make clear that integration rather than separatism is the best strategy for achieving policies that fight discrimination. Among activists in all three groups — feminists, African-Americans, and gay men and lesbians — there is a tension between those who focus on dismantling barriers to participation in mainstream American society and those eager to make radical changes in our society. This disagreement is ideological more than political. Most of those who push for wholesale change genuinely dislike significant aspects of American life and would pursue their agenda no matter what their race or sexual orientation.

To them political debate goes beyond specific issues to the merits of America's political and social life and the best ways to restructure it. They contend that, given the nature of American society, only a radical assault on mainstream values led by women, African-Americans, lesbians, and gay men — or some combination of these overlapping categories — will have any effect. Most of these people claim that integrating their groups into American society is not only an unworthy moral goal but an unattainable political one. The discriminatory aspects of white, male mainstream American society are so deeply entrenched, they argue, that only a significant rearrangement of American social patterns can weaken them.

The question then becomes, which tactics have been most successful in fighting discrimination — those of confrontation or those of integration? Unlike the broad argument on the merits of American life, we can resolve this question empirically by looking at the histories of various antidiscrimination movements since the 1960s. To me the evidence is clear: the more a group assails the American mainstream in general, the more angrily it denounces it values and belittles its way of life, the less likely that group will succeed politically. This does not mean that extreme incivility in the short term will not produce results. The racial violence in the cities in the sixties may well have produced some short-term gains, and student dissenters frequently won concessions on specific points from university administrators and, less frequently, from local officials. But over the long term, all of us on the liberal side have paid a price for these gains in the loss of mainstream support for not only the specific movements involved but for those identified with them politically.

Not that civil disobedience, militancy, and unwillingness to compromise on some matters of deep principle are always politically unwise. But in my experience they are unwise when they are resorted to out of a sense of frustration and not out of a rational analysis of their potential political effect. I wish that today's activists in various movements understood better that Mohandas Gandhi and Martin Luther King were not only devoutly committed to the principles of fairness and equality but also very clever political actors who thought long, hard, and well about the impact their demonstrations might or might not have.

There is one enduring rule to be learned from this analysis: opposition to discrimination on the ground that, because of their suffering, victims have become more capable of showing those who aren't victims of discrimination how to lead a better moral life is about as counterproductive as political activity can get. Unfortunately, the tendency to make this argument is present among all of the groups discussed here, in varying degree; even more unfortunately, this attitude gets a sympathetic response from liberal political leaders. Nothing does more damage to the cause of antidiscrimination efforts than for liberal politicians to make our arguments for fairness part of an attack on the basic moral content of American society.

The consequence of indulging these arguments is to weaken us politically, particularly in national elections, without in any way strengthening the antidiscrimination cause. Indeed, precisely because this does weaken us politically, it leaves us less useful in the fight against whatever discrimination exists.

In summary, the best thing we can do to advance the fight against discrimination and to wage a successful national campaign on this issue is to make clear that we oppose bigotry as a sign of our commitment to American ideals, not as the forerunner of an all-out assault on how Americans live. Those of us who believe that America is good and just but capable of being better and fairer have a decided political advantage over those who view our society as a mean and selfish one in need of radical surgery. We err — and we lose elections — in sacrificing that advantage because we think the angriest people on our left insist that we do so.

Massachusetts Democrat BARNEY FRANK *is now serving his eighth term in the U.S. House of Representatives. The selection printed here is excerpted from his book* Speaking Frankly *(1992).*

PREPARING FOR DISCUSSION

1. Sullivan maintains that the conservative and radical positions on homosexuality are much closer to each other than they might appear initially. On what grounds does he establish a similarity between the two views? Why does he think that both views will ultimately tend to exclude their adherents from the current discourse on gay-straight relations?

2. Consider Sullivan's characterization of moderate attitudes toward homosexuality. What inconsistencies does he believe such attitudes are plagued by? How is a moderate likely to feel about the presence of openly gay men and women in the military? Why does Sullivan believe that they are more likely than not to hesitate in offering a position on this matter?

3. Sullivan does not agree with the first liberal position he describes: that from a legislative standpoint, gay men and lesbians might properly be regarded as just another minority group. One distinction he attempts to make between sexuality and race is that while "race is in no way behavioral; sexuality . . . is profoundly linked to a settled pattern of behavior" (paragraph 36). Consider recent arguments about race, including those in the second chapter of this book. Would you agree with Sullivan that race cannot be linked to behavior? Or, alternatively, that sexual orientation is always linked to specific behaviors?

4. In paragraphs 45–56, Sullivan notes that the goal of the second brand of liberal politics he proposes "would be full civil equality for those who, *through no fault of their own, happen to be homosexual*" (emphasis added). While the phrases Sullivan uses toward the end of his sentence do not imply a denial of the existence of homosexuality, they could nevertheless be taken to sound somewhat apologetic. Are such phrases consistent with the second liberal attitude toward homosexuality espoused by the author? What does his use of these phrases communicate about his own attitude?

5. The author notes that the language used to describe mutually committed homosexual couples — "friends" and "partners" — reflects the sense of "disorder" and "insufficiency" that accompanies the attitudes of even tolerant heterosexuals toward gay and lesbian relationships. What alternatives does Sullivan offer for these terms? Do his terms seem more or less appropriate to you than the terms they are supposed to replace?

FROM READING TO WRITING

6. After reviewing Sullivan's classification of the prevailing attitudes toward gays in America, write an essay in which you consider which, if any, of these views you have most fully identified with in the past or develop your own view. Has Sullivan's essay encouraged you to change that view or confirmed it? To what extent do you agree with the final option offered by the author?

7. Sullivan rejects the notion that marriage presumes procreation and child-rearing. In an essay, consider the merits and inconsistencies of each position. Do you agree with Sullivan that marriage signifies lasting emotional and economic commitment only? Even if the law does not require that marriages produce children, do you think that marriage evolved historically for reasons *other* than procreation and child-rearing?

CAMILLE PAGLIA

Sex Crime: Rape

One triumph of feminism in the 1980s was its success in persuading American women that rape was not a sex crime but an act of violence against women. A decade later, literary critic and self-proclaimed "reactionary feminist" Camille Paglia charges the women's movement with gross negligence in educating a generation of middle-class, college-educated women who are now unprepared for the sexual risks they take when they come into contact with men.

In the early 1990s, the little-known literary critic came to national prominence when she unleashed an all-out attack on some of the most inviolable tenets of modern feminism. She not only accused feminists of suppressing some of the most basic truths about human sexuality, but she also assailed the feminist establishment's views on date rape, pornography, and sexual education. At the heart of her approach lies the assumption that sex crimes are the result of neither misogyny nor the patriarchal structures within American society. Rather, they are the direct product of human biological forces that largely resist containment by social defenses. Having previously taught literature at Bennington, Wesleyan, and Yale, Paglia is currently professor of humanities at the University of the Arts in Philadelphia. Her controversial best-seller, *Sexual Personae: Art and Decadence from Nefertiti to Emily Dickinson,* was nominated for a National Book Critics Circle Award in 1991. This selection first appeared in her 1994 book, *Vamps and Tramps: New Essays.*

SELECTED PUBLICATIONS: *Sexual Personae: Art and Decadence from Nefertiti to Emily Dickinson* (1990); *Sex, Art, and American Culture: Essays* (1992); *Vamps and Tramps: New Essays* (1994).

The area where contemporary feminism has suffered the most self-inflicted damage is rape. What began as a useful sensitization of police officers, prosecutors, and judges to the claims of authentic rape victims turned into a hallucinatory overextension of the definition of rape to cover every unpleasant or embarrassing sexual encounter. Rape became the crime of crimes, overshadowing all the wars, massacres, and disasters of world history. The feminist obsession with rape as a symbol of male-female relations is irrational and delusional. From the perspective of the future, this period in America will look like a reign of mass psychosis, like that of the Salem witch trials.

Rape cannot be understood in isolation from general criminology, which most feminists have not bothered to study. Psychopathology was an early interest of mine, partly because of my own aggressive and deviant impulses as a tomboy in the Fifties. Two comprehensive, analytic, and nonjudgmental books I acquired as a teenager gave me the intellectual framework for my later approaches to abnormal behavior: Richard von Krafft-Ebing's *Psychopathia Sexualis* (1886) and Emile Durkheim's *Suicide* (1897). In college and graduate school, I gathered the material on rape, homosexuality, and other controversial themes that appears in *Sexual Personae*. By the time Susan Brownmiller's *Against Our Will* appeared in 1975, I knew enough to find its interpretative framework seriously inadequate. That book is one of many well-meaning feminist examples of the limitation of white middle-class assumptions in understanding extreme emotional states or acts.

The philistinism of feminist discourse on rape in the Eighties and Nineties has been astonishing. My generation was well-educated in the Sixties in major literary texts that have since been marginalized by blundering women's studies: our sense of criminality and the mystery of motivation came principally from [Fyodor] Dostoyevsky's *Crime and Punishment*, [Albert] Camus's *The Stranger*, and [Jean] Genet's *The Maids*. There was also [Edgar Allan] Poe's "The Tell-Tale Heart" and "The Cask of Amontillado," as well as eerie films like Fritz Lang's *M*, Alfred Hitchcock's *Psycho*, and Richard Fleischer's *Compulsion* (on the Leopold and Loeb case).[1] The shrill feminist melodrama of male oppressor/female victim came straight out of nickelodeon strips of mustache-twirling villains and squealing maidens tied to train tracks. Those who revere and live with great art recognize Clytemnestra, Medea, Lady Macbeth, and Hedda Gabler — conspirators and death-dealers of implacable will — as equally the forebears of modern woman.

Rape should more economically be defined as either stranger rape or the forcible intrusion of sex into a nonsexual context, such as a professional situation. However, even the latter is excusable if a sexual overture is welcomed, as can be the case in both gay and straight life. There *is* such a thing as seduction, and it needs encouragement rather than discouragement in our puritanical Anglo-American world. The fantastic fetishism of rape by mainstream and anti-porn feminists has in the end trivialized rape, impugned women's credibility, and reduced the sympathy we should feel for legitimate victims of violent sexual assault.

What I call Betty Crocker feminism — a naively optimistic Polyannaish or Panglossian view of reality — is behind much of this. Even the most morbid of the rape ranters have a childlike faith in the perfectibility of the universe, which they see as blighted solely by nasty men. They simplistically project outward onto a mythical "patriarchy" their own inner

5

---

[1] Leopold and Loeb were tried and convicted of murdering a Chicago schoolboy in the 1920s.

conflicts and moral ambiguities. In *Sexual Personae*, I critiqued the sunny Rousseauism[2] running through the last two hundred years of liberal thinking and offered the dark tradition of [the Marquis de] Sade, Darwin, Nietzsche, and Freud as more truthful about human perversity. It is more accurate to see primitive egotism and animality ever-simmering behind social controls — cruel energies contained and redirected for the greater good — than to predicate purity and innocence ravaged by corrupt society. Nor does the Foucault[3] view of numb, shapeless sensoriums tyrannically impinged on by faceless systems of language-based power make any more sense, in view of daily news reports of concretely applied and concretely suffered random beatings, mutilations, murders, arson, massacres, and ethnic exterminations around the world.

Rape will not be understood until we revive the old concept of the barbaric, the uncivilized. The grotesque cliché "patriarchy" must go, or rather be returned to its proper original application to periods like Republican Rome or Victorian England. What feminists call patriarchy is simply *civilization*, an abstract system designed by men but augmented and now co-owned by women. Like a great temple, civilization is a gender-neutral structure that all should respect. Feminists who prate of patriarchy are self-exiled in grass huts.

Ideas of civilization and barbarism have become unfashionable because of their political misuse in the nineteenth century. The West has neither a monopoly on civilization nor the right or obligation to impose its culture on others. Nor, as *Sexual Personae* argues, are any of us as individuals ever completely civilized. However, it is equally wrong to dismiss all progressive theories of history, which is not just scattered bits of data upon which we impose wishful narratives. Societies do in fact evolve in economic and political complexity.

Even though we no longer wish to call one society "higher" or "more advanced" than another, it is unwise to equate tribal experience, with its regimentation by tradition and its suppression of the individual by the group, with life under industrial capitalism, which has produced liberalism and feminism. Law and order, which protect women, children, and the ill and elderly, are a function of hierarchy, another of the big bad words of feminism. Law and order were achieved only a century ago in the American West, which still lives in our national mythology. Disintegration into banditry is always near at hand, as was shown in 1989 in the notorious case of the Central Park woman jogger — a savage attack significantly called "wilding" by its schoolboy perpetrators. Sex crime means back to nature.

[2] *Rousseauism:* A reference to French social philosopher Jean-Jacques Rousseau (1712–1778), who argued that human beings would be basically good if left untouched by modern society.

[3] *Foucault:* French historian and cultural thinker Michel Foucault (1926–1984).

When feminism rejected Freud twenty-five years ago, it edited out of its mental life the barbarities of the homicidal Oedipal psychodrama, which the annals of crime show is more than a metaphor. The irony is that Freud's master paradigm of "family romance," which structures our adult relationships in love and at work, has a special appropriateness to the current feminist debate. Too much of the date-rape and sexual harassment crisis claimed by white middle-class women is caused partly by their own mixed signals, which I have observed with increasing distress as a teacher for over two decades.

The predominant fact of modern sexual history is not patriarchy but 10 the collapse of the old extended family into the nuclear family, an isolated unit that, in its present form, is claustrophobic and psychologically unstable. The nuclear family can work only in a pioneer situation, where the punishing physicality of farmwork keeps everyone occupied and spent from dawn to dusk. The middle-class nuclear family, where the parents are white-collar professionals who do brainwork, is seething with frustrations and tensions. Words are charged, and real authority lies elsewhere, in bosses on the job. Marooned in the suburbs or in barricaded urban apartments, upwardly mobile families are frantically overscheduled and geographically transient, with few ties to neighbors and little sustained contact with relatives.

Two parents alone cannot transmit all the wisdom of life to a child. Clan elders — grandparents, great-grandparents, aunts, uncles, cousins — performed this function once. Today, poor inner-city or rural children are more likely to benefit from the old extended family or from the surrogate family of long-trusted neighbors, since working-class people are less likely to make repeated moves for job promotions. The urban child sees the harshness of the street; the rural child witnesses the frightening operations of nature. Both have contact with an eternal reality denied the suburban middle-class child, who is cushioned from risk and fear and who is expected to conform to a code of genteel good manners and repressed body language that has changed startlingly little since the Victorian era.

The sex education of white middle-class girls is clearly deficient, since it produces young women unable to foresee trouble or to survive sexual misadventure or even raunchy language without crying to authority figures for help. A sense of privilege and entitlement, as well as ignorance of the dangers of life, has been institutionalized by American academe, with its summer-resort, give-the-paying-customers-what-they-want mentality. Europe has thus far been relatively impervious to the date-rape hysteria, since its tortured political history makes sugary social fantasies of the American kind less possible. Fun-and-fabulous teenage dating is not high on the list of priorities for nations which, in the lifetime of half their population, had firsthand knowledge of war, devastation, and economic collapse. The media-fueled disproportion and distortion of the date-rape debate are partially attributable to American arrogance and parochialism.

White middle-class girls at the elite colleges and universities seem to want the world handed to them on a platter. They have been sheltered, coddled, and flattered. Having taught at a wide variety of institutions over my ill-starred career, I have observed that working-class or lower-middle-class girls, who are from financially struggling families and who must take a patchwork of menial off-campus jobs to stay in school, are usually the least hospitable to feminist rhetoric. They see life as it is and have fewer illusions about sex. It is affluent, upper-middle-class students who most spout the party line — as if the grisly hyperemotionalism of feminist jargon satisfies their hunger for meaningful experience outside their eventless upbringing. In the absence of war, invent one.

The real turmoil is going on inside the nuclear family, which, with its caged quarters and cheerful ethic of "togetherness," must generate invisible barriers to the threat of incest. Here is the real source of the epidemic eating disorders, blamed by incompetent feminist analysts on the media. Anorexia, for example, remains primarily a white middle-class phenomenon. The daughter stops her disturbing sexual maturation by stripping off her female contours, the hormone-triggered fleshiness of breasts, hips, and buttocks. She wants to remain a child, when her innocent erotic stratagems had no consequence. Again and again, among students as well as the date-rape heroines canonized on television talk shows, I have seen the flagrant hair-tossing and eye-batting mannerisms of Daddy's little girl, who since childhood has used flirtation and seductiveness to win attention within the family.

Provocation and denial are built into the circuitry of the white middle-class girl, with her depressing flatness of sexual imagination, her strange combination of "low self-esteem" with hectoring moral superiority in groups, inflamed by feminist rhetoric. The eating disorders are symptomatic not of external forces or media conspiracies but of a major breakdown in the female sex role. In the Anglo-American world, the successful woman is now defined in exclusively professional terms. The role of mother, still central in Latin and Asian cultures, has been devalued. Feminism should be about options. I myself have no talent for motherhood and have sought only a career. But I recognize that no role may be more important than bearing and raising children and that most men, whatever their contributions to the child's later development, are not and will never be proficient at infant care.

Over the past forty years, there has been an increasingly long postponement of marriage and childbirth by middle-class women. For example, my parents married at twenty-one in 1946, a year before I was born. Today, it would be unheard-of for a girl at an elite school to marry at that age. Maternity is considered an accident, a misfortune, the vulgar prerogative of misguided working-class teenagers. If a Yale sophomore were to drop out of school to marry, she would be treated as a traitor to her class, "throwing away" her expensive education, "wasting" her life. In the Sixties, by contrast, it was considered a radical gesture for a girl to disappoint her parents' expectations by leaving college and running off with her ragged hippie boyfriend to bake bread and have babies in a commune.

Modern society is now structured so as to put a crippling impediment between women's physical development and their career ambitions. Feminist ideology began by claiming to give women freedom, enlightenment, and self-determination, but it has ended by alienating professional women from their own bodies. Every signal from the body — like the sudden quiet inwardness and psychological reorientation of girls at puberty, when they mysteriously recede in classroom assertiveness — is automatically interpreted in terms of social oppression. Teachers are supposedly "discouraging" the girls; adjusting your behavior to attract a mate is dismissed as a voluntary or legitimate choice. Girls are taught the mechanics of reproduction and sexual intercourse as clinically as if they were learning to operate a car or computer. The repressed, sanitized style of the WASP managerial class now governs public discussion of sex. Anything dark or ambiguous is blamed on "ignorance," "superstition," or "lack of education."

It was after my tumultuous lecture at Brown University in March 1992 that I saw this process of cultural repression most clearly. Taking questions at the reception, I sat with an African-American security guard as several hundred students seethed around me. Those who doubt the existence of political correctness have never seen the ruthless Red Guards in action, as I have done on campus after campus. For twenty years, meaningful debate of controversial issues of sex or race was silenced by overt or covert intimidation.

As I watched a half-dozen pampered, white middle-class girls, their smooth, plump cheeks contorted with rage, shriek at me about rape, I had two thoughts. First, America is failing its young women; these are infantile personalities, emotionally and intellectually undeveloped. Second, it's not rape they're screaming about. Rape is simply a symbol of the horrors and mysteries of the body, which their education never deals with or even acknowledges. It was a Blakean epiphany: I suddenly saw the fear and despair of the lost, stripped of old beliefs but with nothing solid to replace them. Feminism had constructed a spectral sexual hell that these girls inhabited; it was their entire cultural world, a godless new religion of fury and fanaticism. Two months later, as I sat in London, discoursing at length with poised, literate, witty Cambridge University women of the same age as those at Brown, I became even more indignant at the travesty of Ivy League education.

Women are not in control of their bodies; nature is. Ancient mythol- 20
ogy, with its sinister archetypes of vampire and Gorgon, is more accurate
than feminism about the power and terror of female sexuality. Science is
far from untangling women's intricate hormonal system, which is daunt-
ingly intertwined with the emotions. Women live with unpredictability.
Reproduction remains a monumental challenge to our understanding.
The Eleusinian Mysteries,[4] with their secret, torch-lit night rituals, represented woman's grandeur on the scale that she deserves. We must return
to pagan truths.

The elite schools, defining women students only as "future leaders,"
masters of the social realm, limit and stunt them. The mission of feminism is to seek the full political and legal equality of women with men.
There should be no impediments to women's social advance. But it is the
first lesson of Buddhism, Hinduism, and Judeo-Christianity that we are
much greater than our social selves. I envision two spheres: one is social,
the other sexual and emotional. Perhaps one-third of each sphere over-
laps the other; this is the area where feminism has correctly said, "The
personal is political." But there is vastly more to the human story. Man
has traditionally ruled the social sphere; feminism tells him to move over
and share his power. But woman rules the sexual and emotional sphere,
and there she has no rival. Victim ideology, a caricature of social history,
blocks women from recognition of their dominance in the deepest, most
important realm.

Ambitious young women today are taught to ignore or suppress every
natural instinct, if it conflicts with the feminist agenda imposed on them.
All literary and artistic works, no matter how great, that document the ambivalence of female sexuality they are trained to dismiss as "misogynous."
In other words, their minds are being programmed to secede from their
bodies — exactly the opposite of what the Sixties sexual and cultural revolution was all about. There is a huge gap between feminist rhetoric and
women's actual sex lives, where feminism is of little help except with a certain stratum of deferential, malleable, white middle-class men. In contrast,
Hollywood actresses, used to expressing emotional truths, are always
reappearing after pregnancy to proclaim, "I'm not important. My child is
important." The most recent was Kelly McGillis, who said, "Motherhood
has changed me. I'm not as ambitious as I used to be." It is nature, not patriarchal society, that puts motherhood and career on a collision course.

My first inkling of the psychological maelstrom suffered by this generation of female students came in 1980, when I returned to New Haven
after eight years away (at my first job at Bennington, which ended with a
bang). Yale College had admitted its first women in 1969, while I was
a graduate student. Returning to the Cross Campus Library, brand-
new when I left, I was horrified to find the stalls of the women's toilets

---

[4] *Eleusinian Mysteries:* Ancient Greek religious rites.

covered with bizarre, ranting graffiti. There was little humor or bawdiness; the principal imagery was of nausea, disgust, and self-loathing. "Something is going wrong with feminism," I said to friends at the time. The Yale graffiti seemed demented, psychotic, like those one would expect to find at New York's Port Authority Bus Terminal. When Brown girls created a national furor in 1990 by posting names of alleged rapists in the toilets, the media completely missed the real story: why were squalid toilets now the forum for self-expression by supposed future leaders? These sewer spaces, converted to pagan vomitoria, offer women students their sole campus rendezvous with their own physiology.

The strident rape discourse is a hysterical eruption from the deepest levels of American bourgeois life. Early in this phase of feminism, it was still possible to say, "Taste your menstrual blood" — that is, reclaim your physicality. Today, with the callow new brand of yuppie feminist with her simpering, prom-queen manner, we have regressed to the Fifties era of cashmere sweaters and pearls. The blood and guts of women's reproductive cycle are light-years beyond the reach of these dollhouse moppets. White middle-class feminists of every age have shown themselves spectacularly unable to confront the grossness of their own physiological processes. The passages in *Sexual Personae* vividly depicting that humid, labyrinthine reality have made them flee like Victorian spinsters shrieking at a mouse.

Until the bloody barbarousness of procreation is fully absorbed,   25
without the abstract jargon and genteel euphemisms that now dominate gender studies, rape will not be understood. By defining rape in exclusively social terms — as an attack by the powerful against the powerless — feminism has missed the point. It is woman, as mistress of birth, who has the real power. As my colleague Jack DeWitt likes to say, "Any woman is more powerful than any man."

Rape is an act of desperation, a confession of envy and exclusion. All men — even, I have written, Jesus himself — began as flecks of tissue inside a woman's womb. Every boy must stagger out of the shadow of a mother goddess, whom he never fully escapes. Because of my history of wavering gender and sexual orientation, I feel I have a special insight into these matters: I see with the eyes of the rapist. Hence I realize how dangerously misleading the feminist rape discourse is. Rape is a breaking and entering; but so is the bloody act of defloration. Sex is inherently problematic.

Women have it. Men want it. What is *it?* The secret of life, symbolized in heroic sagas by the golden fleece sought by Jason, or by the Gorgon's head brandished as a sexual trophy by Cellini's Perseus. The rapist is sickened by the conflict between his humiliating neediness and his masculine rage for autonomy. He feels suffocated by woman and yet entranced and allured by her. He is betrayed into dependency by his own impulses, the leaping urges of the body. Stalking women like prey returns him to prehistoric freedom, when the wiliest, swiftest, and strongest survived. Rape-murder is a primitive theft of energy, a cannibalistic drinking of life force.

When toddlers or schoolgirls are kidnapped, brutally assaulted, and killed, the world is rightly horrified and sickened. But why are we surprised? Heinous acts of profanation and degradation fill the annals of history and great literature — Neoptolemus' slaughter of Priam at the altar, Herod's massacre of the innocents, the immurement and bestial death of Dante's Ugolino. Until recently, most societies had a clear idea of what constitutes "uncivilized" or "ungodly" behavior and punished it accordingly. Today, in contrast, there is a tendency to redefine the victimizer as himself a victim — of a broken home or abusive parents — and then, ironically, to broaden criminality to areas of consensual activities where women are equally responsible for their behavior. When feminist discourse is unable to discriminate the drunken fraternity brother from the homicidal maniac, women are in trouble.

Rape-murder comes from the brutish region of pure animal appetite. Feminist confidence that the whole human race can be "reeducated" to totally eliminate the possibility of rape is pure folly. Even if, very optimistically, 80 percent of all men could be reprogrammed, 20 percent would remain, toward whom women would still have to remain vigilant. Even if 99 percent were neutralized — absurdly unlikely — that would leave 1 percent, against whom women's level of self-defense would need to be just as high as against 90 percent. Wave after wave of boys hit puberty every year. Do feminists, with their multicultural pretensions, really envision a massive export of white bourgeois good manners all around the world? Speak of imperialism! When Balthasar, one of the Magi, advises Ben-Hur to leave vengeance to God, the sheik murmurs, "Balthasar is a good man. But until all men are like him, we must keep our swords bright."

The dishonesty and speciousness of the feminist rape analysis are demonstrated by its failure to explore, or even mention, man-on-man sex crimes. If rape were really just a process of political intimidation of women by men, why do men rape and kill other males? The deceptively demure persona of the soft-spoken, homosexual serial-murderer Jeffrey Dahmer, like that of handsome, charming Ted Bundy, should warn everyone that we still live in a sexual jungle. Nothing in feminist ideology addresses the grim truth that beauty itself may be an incitement to destroy, that there is a frenzy of primitive pleasure in torturing captives or smashing things. I learned from art about the willful violation of innocence. When babies, nuns, or grandmothers are raped, it can be understood only in terms of what pagan antiquity called "pollution," a sullying of the sacred. Feminist overstress on power differentials gets us nowhere; it cannot explain spasmodic bursts of slashing criminal lust.

The problem with America's current preoccupation with child abuse is that cultural taboos automatically eroticize what is forbidden. Marking off zones of purity increases their desirability and ensures their profanation. Children are not that innocent, and we must put an end to Anglo-American hypocrisy on this question. Children, sanctified by Victorian Romanticism, are quite capable of perverse and horrific fantasy, without adult suggestion. A century after Freud proposed his theory of infantile sexuality, most parents (outside of Malibu or Tribeca) still cannot intellectually accept it — partly because doing so would activate the incest taboo. The enormous publicity about child abuse has certainly increased safety awareness, but I doubt it has lowered the crime rate. Snatching a perfect child from under the noses of society's guardians has become the ultimate subversive act of the outlaw. Such criminality, I maintained in *Sexual Personae*, is the product not of a bad environment but of the opposite, a failure of social conditioning. Serial rape-murderers, cool, logical, and precise, are not "insane" and deserve to be executed, not as deterrence but as justice for the survivors.

Far from being inhuman or "monstrous," sex crime is a ritual enactment of natural aggressions latent in all sexuality, which is primarily mating behavior and has only recently been redefined in recreational terms. The best survey I have yet seen of the clashing psychodynamics of eroticism is Edmund Spenser's *The Faerie Queene* (1590), which remains amazingly applicable today, four hundred years after it was written. Spenser sees the fine gradations of sexual behavior, from chivalrous courtship to duplicitous seduction and loutish brigandage. Studying the poem in depth in the Seventies, I identified what I called its "rape cycle." Like a specter stalking a college mixer, Spenser acutely describes the tantalizing sexual vulnerability of passive feminity and the militant warriorship of mature, self-reliant womanhood. Naiveté evokes its own destruction. This is not "blaming the victim"; it is saying victimhood cannot become a vocation.

Until feminism permits the return of the ancient identification of woman and nature in its full disturbing power, rape will remain an engima. Rape is an invasion of territory, a despoilment of virgin ground. The radically different sexual geography of men's and women's bodies has led to feminist inability to understand male psychology. "She made me do it": this strange assertion by rapists expresses man's sense of subservience to woman's sexual allure. The rapist feels enslaved, insignificant: women seem enclosed, impervious. From the outside, female sexuality glows like the full moon. The stormy complexity of the rapist's inner life has been obscured by the therapeutic jargon he is soon speaking in prison, once he has been brainwashed by the social-welfare workers. Until women grasp the blood-sport aspect of rape, they will be unable to protect themselves.

Films of the mating behavior of most other species — a staple of public television in America — demonstrate that the female *chooses*. Males pursue, show off, brawl, scuffle, and make general fools of themselves for love. A major failing of most feminist ideology is its dumb, ungenerous stereotyping of men as tyrants and abusers, when in fact — as I know full well, from my own mortifying lesbian experience — men are tormented by women's flirtatiousness and hemming and hawing, their manipulations and changeableness, their humiliating rejections. Cock teasing is a universal reality. It is part of women's merciless testing and cold-eyed comparison shopping for potential mates. Men will do anything to win the favor of women. Women literally *size up* men — "What can you show me?" — in bed and out. If middle-class feminists think they conduct their love lives perfectly rationally, without any instinctual influences from biology, they are imbeciles.

Following the sexual revolution of the Sixties, dating has become a 35 form of Russian roulette. Some girls have traditional religious values and mean to remain virgin until marriage. Others are leery of AIDS, unsure of what they want, but can be convinced. For others, anything goes: they'll jump into bed on the first date. What's a guy to do? Surely, for the good of the human species, we want to keep men virile and vigorous. They should feel free to seek sex and to persuade reluctant women. As a libertarian, I believe that we have absolute right to our own body and that no one may lay a hand on us without our consent. But consent may be nonverbal, expressed by language or behavior — such as going to a stranger's apartment on the first date, which I think should correctly be interpreted as consent to sex. "Verbal coercion" is a ridiculous concept: I agree with Ovid that every trick of rhetoric should be used in the slippery art of love.

Sexual personae are the key to this new age of uncertainty. I follow the gay male model in defining every date as a potential sexual encounter. Given that the rules are in flux, the issue of sexual availability must be negotiated, implicitly or explicitly, from the first moment on. Women must take responsibility for their share in this exchange, which means they must scrupulously critique their own mannerisms and clothing choices and not allow themselves to drift willy-nilly into compromising situations. As a teacher, I have seen time and again a certain kind of American middle-class girl who projects winsome malleability, a soft, unfocused, help-me-please persona that, in adult life, is a recipe for disaster. These are the ones who end up with the string of abusive boyfriends or in sticky situations with overfamiliar male authority figures who call them "honey."

Deconstruction of the bourgeois code of "niceness" is a priority here. My generation tried it but seems mostly to have failed. Second, white girls need a crash course in common sense. You get back what you put out. Or as I say about girls wearing Madonna's harlot outfits, if you advertise, you'd better be ready to sell! Suburban girls don't realize that they were raised in an artificially pacified zone and that the world at large, including the college campus, is a far riskier place. I call my feminism "streetwise" or "street-smart" feminism. Women from working-class families usually agree with my view of the foolhardiness of feminist rhetoric, which encourages girls to throbbingly proclaim, "We can dress just as we want and go anywhere we want at any time!" This is true only to the point that women are willing to remain in a state of wary alertness and to fight their own fights. Men are in danger too. In America, one sees overprotected white girls bopping obliviously down the city street, lost in their headphones, or jogging conspicuously and bouncingly braless, a sight guaranteed to invite unwanted attention.

It is tremendously difficult to convince feminist professional women of the existence of unconscious or subliminal erotic communication. As my friend Bruce Benderson says, their middle-class world has "no subtext." Women of the Sixties had far bolder and more salacious imaginations. The career system into which women have definitively won entry over and past twenty-five years seems to have rigidified their thinking. Stalinist literalism has become the norm. Shocked disbelief greets suggestions that many women may take pleasure in rape fantasies, established long ago by Nancy Friday in her pioneering 1973 study, *My Secret Garden,* and dramatized today in the staggering mass-market popularity of Harlequin Romances, where heroines are overwhelmed by passionate, impetuous men. My warning description of the buffoonish "fun element" and "mad infectious delirium" of gang rape particularly infuriated many middle-class feminists, even though the point is easily proved by movies like *Two Women, The Virgin Spring, A Clockwork Orange, Deliverance, Death Wish,* or *North Dallas Forty.* That men can satisfy their desires on an inert or unconscious object seems intolerable to such women, though it is a fact of life, palatable or not. Male sexual functioning does not depend on female response. And the illicit is always highly charged.

All crimes of sex or mutilation contain pagan paradigms, hidden ritual symbolism we must learn to read. Pious rubrics like "Violence against Women" — the stentorian title of a 1993 Congressional bill — are too simplistic. Surges of instinctual power are going on beneath the surface of every human exchange. Having sex with a woman is an earned action and honorific for young men, who lack an internal rite of passage like menstruation and who must therefore create an adult sexual identity for themselves in ways that women do not. Sex crime is revenge against women as an abstract class for wounds already suffered by men as a class — the wound of birth and its consequent galling dependencies. Until we widen the lens to take in nature, women will not know what is happening or how to control it. Victimization is a dead end. Better to meditate instead on the great pagan archetypes of the mother, with her terrible duality of creation and destruction. Women must accept their own ambivalence in order to wield their birthright of dominion over men.

PREPARING FOR DISCUSSION

1. Paglia thinks that feminists must be very careful about the way they define rape if they mean not to trivialize sex crime. What is Paglia's own definition of rape? Why is it significant that she chooses to classify rape as a sex crime rather than an act of violence against women?

2. Paglia seems to single out schools like Yale and Brown for special condemnation. Why does she choose these "elite schools" as starting points for her attack on current trends of sex education for young women? What disturbs her most about the content of this education?

3. A common theme of Paglia's is that women hold more power than men because they rule the sexual and emotional spheres. Most important, writes Paglia, "it is woman, as mistress of birth, who has the real power." Could such a view ultimately limit women socially and politically rather than liberate them? Is it fair to say that sexual and emotional power (which Paglia grants women) is more "real" than political and social power (which she grants men)?

4. In addressing the question of date rape, Paglia writes that going to "a stranger's apartment on the first date . . . should be correctly interpreted as consent to sex" (paragraph 35). Do you agree with most feminists, who would typically label such a view "blaming the victim"? Can nonverbal signals be reliable signs of consent?

5. Paglia argues against the feminist use of "patriarchy" in place of "civilization." What do you think feminists mean by "patriarchy"? Do they intend to use it as a substitute for "civilization" as a whole or just particular aspects of it? Do you think that Paglia is correct in classifying "civilization" as a gender-neutral word?

FROM READING TO WRITING

6. Paglia argues that women must think more clearly about the nature of animal biology if they are to understand rape. Write an essay in which you examine whether rape may better be understood from the standpoint of biology, as Paglia insists, or from the standpoint of social practice and conditioning.

7. According to Paglia, the media have been instrumental in perpetuating misconceptions about rape in general and date rape in particular. Recall some recent movies or television shows in which such rapes were committed. Compare these portrayals with the ways that rape and rape-related issues are presented by the news media. Write an essay on your findings and account for any differences you observe between news media and popular culture presentations of the issue.

JEAN BETHKE ELSHTAIN

The Politics of Displacement

———◇———

The current popularity of television talk shows on which families reveal their dysfunctionality or gay men and lesbians state their sexual orientation to a nationwide audience indicates more than anything else a breakdown of the traditional boundary between public and private life in America. In this selection, political scientist and ethicist Jean Bethke Elshtain adds a new phrase to the American political vocabulary: the politics of displacement. Briefly, the politics of displacement describes a social condition in which private concerns (like family life or sexual orientation) routinely become public issues. Elshtain questions the wisdom of feminists and gay persons who would invite greater scrutiny from fellow citizens and the federal government in the name of greater security against violence and discrimination.

Educated at Wisconsin, Colorado, and Brandeis, Elshtain is widely considered a leading voice within the communitarian movement, which stresses politically engaged citizenship over individualism and group identity. In the early 1980s, she was a member of the Institute of Advanced Study at Princeton. Having served for several years as Centennial Professor of Political Science at Vanderbilt University, Elshtain is now the Laura Spelman Rockefeller Professor of Ethics at the University of Chicago.

SELECTED PUBLICATIONS: *Public Man, Private Woman: Women in Social and Political Thought* (1981); *Women and War* (1987); *Power Trips and Other Journeys: Essays in Feminism as Civil Discourse* (1991); *Democracy on Trial* (1993).

———

Have we democratic citizens become more fearful than hopeful? Let me remind you of a few of our most paralyzing collective fears: the next generation's way of life will not be better than that of previous generations; America's position in the world will falter; communities will continue to disintegrate; families will continue to collapse; the center simply will not hold. Fearful, we retreat or participate in the politics of resentment — finding somebody or some group to blame for all our ills: foreigners without, enemies within. If the great Roman republican citizen Cicero lamented that "we have lost the res publica," I bemoan the loss of something similar, the public citizen, and I embrace, as an alternative, a new social covenant in which we reach out once more to our fellow citizens from a stance of goodwill and work to defuse our discontents, so we might forge working alliances across various groups. Then and only then, I suggest, can we reclaim the great name *citizen*. For *citizen* is the name we give to our public identities and actions in a democratic society.

But wait, some readers will surely proclaim, do we not daily see frenetic activity, as people take to the streets and the airwaves demanding recognition for who and what they are? Is there not already a great deal of active participation — lobbying, meeting, marching, debating? Is this not citizenship of the robust sort?

I must demur and hope that I will be successful, in what follows, in explaining the distinction between what I tag the *politics of displacement* and authentic democratic possibilities. Roughly put, the politics of displacement involves two trajectories. In the first, everything private — from one's sexual practices to blaming one's parents for one's lack of "self-esteem" — becomes grist for the public mill. In the second, everything public — from the grounds on which politicians are judged to health policies to gun regulations — is privatized and played out in a psychodrama on a grand scale, that is, we fret as much about a politician's sexual life as about his foreign policy; or we favor insured health care only if it pays for our own guaranteed comfort, described as medical needs or even aesthetic wants, and oppose it if it does not; or we see in firearm regulation only an assault, no doubt limited and imperfect, on our identity as gun-toting vigilantes, rather than as a way to try to control slaughter in our streets without eroding the rights of hunters and others.

The complete collapse of a distinction between public and private is anathema to democratic thinking, which holds that the differences between public and private identities, commitments, and activities are of vital importance. Historically, it has been the antidemocrats who have insisted that political life must be cut from one piece of cloth; they have demanded overweening and unified loyalty to the monarch or the state, unclouded by other passions, commitments, and interests. Something similar is going on as politics gets displaced in the ways I will reveal, beginning with a reminder of what democrats are talking about when they evoke the terms *public* and *private*.

Public and Private

Public and *private* are terms of ordinary discourse, always defined and understood in relation to each other. One definition of *private* is "not open to the public," and the common definition of *public* is "of or pertaining to the whole, done or made in behalf of the community as a whole." In part, these contrasts derive from the Latin word for public, *pubes*, which refers to the age of maturity, when signs of puberty begin to appear; then and only then does the child enter, or become qualified for, public things. Similarly, *publicus* is that which belongs to, or pertains to, "the public," the people. But there is another meaning of public: open to scrutiny; and of private: what is not subjected to the persistent gaze of publicity. This barrier to full revelation is necessary, or so defenders of constitutional democracy have long insisted, to preserve the possibility of different sorts of relationships — both the mother *and* the citizen, the friend *and* the official, and so on.

Minimally, a *political* perspective requires us to differentiate the activity we call "politics" from other activities and relationships. If all conceptual boundaries are blurred and all distinctions between public and private eliminated, no politics can exist, by definition. By *politics*, I refer to that which is, in principle, held in common and what is, in principle, open to public scrutiny and judgment. If I am correct that politics of displacement is a growing phenomenon, operating on the level of elite opinion and popular culture alike, especially in America, it bears deep implications for how we will think about and conduct politics in the years ahead. In our boredom and our despair, we take to the airwaves and the streets to proclaim the awful and ugly truth about a spouse, a friend, a lover, a parent, a child, or a despised enemy or group. And this ugly phenomenon, this eruption of *publicity* and the substitute of publicity for that which is authentically either private or public, is now America's leading growth industry.

A politics of displacement is a dynamic that connects and interweaves public and private imperatives in a way that is dangerous to the integrity of both. It is more likely for a politics of displacement to take hold when certain conditions prevail. First, established public and private, secular and religious institutions and rules are in flux, and people have a sense that the center does not hold. Second, there are no clearly established public institutions to focus dissent and concern. Third, and finally, private values, exigencies, and identities come to take precedence in all things, including public involvement as a citizen.[1]

This, clearly, is the world we are now in. But note that *private* here does not refer to our need to preserve certain relationships and institutions but rather to that diminished universe of one: me and my fleeting angers, resentments, sentiments, and impulses. A recent important study, based on group discussions with involved citizens, found that people depend on "little-noticed meeting places — places of worship, libraries, community halls — where they can interact with others, offer their own thinking and become committed to, and sometimes engaged in, the solution [to a political question or problem]. These places are becoming fewer, the researchers said."[2] The fewer such civic sites, the more likely is a politics of displacement.

A displaced politics features a world of triumphalist I's, "a population of monads . . . , simple, irreducible entities, each defined by a unique point of view," in the words of political theorist Sheldon Wolin.[3] To the extent that there is a "we" in this world if I's, it is that of the discrete group with whom the I identifies. For example, in current debates over multiculturalism, some argue that if one is an African American, one must "think black" and identify exclusively with one's racial group or designation. Similarly, a white person "thinks white" and cannot do otherwise. For persons thus identified, the category of "citizen" is a matter of indifference at best, contempt at worst. Increasingly, we come to see ourselves exclusively along racial or gender or sexual-preference lines. If this is who I am, why should I care about the citizen? That is for dupes who actually believed their high school civics teacher.

To the extent that a politics of displacement pertains, all is defined as   10
"political" and watered down to the lowest common denominator. Thus, everything I "want" gets defined politically as a "right." Thus, for example, my desire, now a right, to have easy access to a pornography channel on cable television is conflated with my right to be safe from arrest or torture for my political views. Civil rights are trivialized in this process. Political ideals and private desires are blurred or collapsed. By extension, of course, there is no such thing as an authentically private sphere. Intimate life is pervaded with politics; private identity becomes a recommendation for, or authentication of, one's political stance. It follows that my rage quotient goes through the roof in political contestation, because to argue against my subjective pronouncements is also to unhinge my private identity. This is muddled thinking, of course, but it seems to be where we are — to our own peril and that of our civic descendants.

Take, for example, the 1970s feminist slogan "The personal is political." On the one hand, this was an exciting and transformative move, compelling men and women to attend to the undeniable fact that certain political interests were often hidden behind a gloss of professed concern for the sanctity of the private realm. Feminists argued that political and ethical values were often trivialized by being privatized, as a whole range of questions regarding women, children, and families was sealed off as irrelevant to political discussion and debate. Children's health, for example, was the private concern of parents, especially mothers. But what if there is asbestos in the insulation of the local school building, and it is well known that asbestos causes health problems? Surely, here, the threat to health is a public one, involving all children who attend that school and their families. To politicize and to challenge the notion of separate spheres — the male public world and the female private world — in this way was a vital and important civic possibility. Feminists who were committed to ideals of civility and civic culture recognized that there are many ways to carve up the universe of debate in social and political life.

But from the beginning, there were problems embedded in the assertion that the personal is political *tout court*. In its give-no-quarter form in radical feminist argument, any distinction between the personal and political was disdained. Note that the claim was not that the personal and political are interrelated in ways previously hidden by male-dominated political ideology and practice, or that the personal and political might be analogous to each other along certain axes of power and privilege. Rather, there was a collapse of one into the other: The personal *is* political. Nothing personal was exempt from political definition, direction, and manipulation — not sexual intimacy, not love, not parenting. The total collapse of public and private as central distinctions in an enduring democratic drama followed, at least in theory. The private sphere fell under a thoroughgoing politicized definition. Everything was grist for a voracious publicity mill; nothing was exempt, there was nowhere to hide. This situation got nasty fast. For example, I have been involved in these debates long enough to recall the time when women who married and bore children became the target of all sorts of polemical assaults in feminist argumentation. They were "collabos," women who collaborated with the male "enemy," women who had been turned into "mutilated, muted, moronized . . . docile tokens mouthing male texts" — not a generous image, to say the least, but one made possible by defining male-female relationships as *essentially* those of a victimizer to a victim.[4]

But more serious than the problem of rhetorical excess is the one that puts democracy continuously on trial: If there are no distinctions between public and private, personal and political, it follows that there can be no differentiated activity or set of institutions that are genuinely political, the purview of citizens and the bases of order, legitimacy, and purpose in a democratic community. As columnist and writer Christopher Hitchens, himself a person of the Left, wrote: "I remember feeling an uneasy premonition when, in the period of defeat and demoralization that followed the 1960s, it was decided that the Left could be revived with the assertion that 'the personal is political.' The consequences of that rather dubious claim are now all around us, except that personality has deposed politics altogether."[5] If genuine politics ceases to exist, what rushes in to take its place is pervasive force, coercion, and manipulation: power of the crassest sort suffusing the entire social landscape, from its lowest to its loftiest points. If you live in a world of pervasive fear and anxiety, a world this sort of rhetoric helps to construct, you become ripe — or the story of Western political thought warns us — for antidemocratic solutions. If the problem is totalistic, so must the solution be. This goes against the grain of the democratic temperament, one always aware that no single perspective, no single political platform or slogan, can speak the whole truth about our situation.

There are few alternatives in such a world: One is either victim or victimizer, oppressed or oppressor, abject or triumphant. Politics as a particular sphere of human activity disappears in this yearning for a totalistic solution to all human woes, this world of refined and competing resentments. The possibility that certain vital relationships are possible *only* because they take place beyond the full glare of public scrutiny and preserve others against scrutiny (snooping by roaming Nosy Parkers, as my British friends call them) is simply forsworn. Do I exaggerate? Perhaps. But let us take a closer look. I hope to convince you that my concerns and criticisms are warranted from a democratic point of view. We have long been familiar with the terrible invasion of private life and speech characteristic of twentieth-century totalitarian societies. People in such situations learn to censor themselves or, growing careless, may find that conversation around a kitchen table or in the bedroom with one's spouse becomes the public property of the police or, worse, of the entire society.

In a 1984 interview with Philip Roth, the Czech novelist Milan Kundera noted a "magic border" between "intimate life and public life . . . that can't be crossed with impunity," for any "man who was the same in both public and intimate life would be a monster." Says Kundera: 15

> He would be without spontaneity in his private life and without responsibility in his public life. For example, privately to you I can say of a friend who's done something stupid, that he's an idiot, that his ears ought to be cut off, that he should be hung upside down and a mouse stuffed in his mouth. But if the same statement were broadcast over the radio spoken in a serious tone — and we all prefer to make such jokes in a serious tone — it would be indefensible.[6]

Kundera went on to recall the tragedy of a friend, a writer named Jan Prochazka, whose intimate "kitchen table" talks were recorded by the state police in pre-1989 Czechoslovakia and assembled into a "program" that was broadcast on state radio: "He finds himself in a state of complete humiliation: the secret eye observes him even when he kisses his wife in the bedroom or stands in front of the toilet bowl. Such a man can only die" — as Prochazka did, humiliated by his ordeal. According to Kundera, *intimate life* — a creation of European civilization "during the last 400 years," understood as "one's personal secret, as something valuable, inviolable, the basis of one's originality" — is now in jeopardy everywhere, not just in statist societies with a secret police apparatus.

Are his fears well placed? Consider two examples drawn from contemporary American society, both of which flow from the collapse of the personal into the political and therefore exemplify the politics of displacement. Of course, there are no precise parallels in a democratic society to the terror Kundera so poignantly described. But we have our own "soft" versions of an utter disregard for public and private distinctions.

The Ideology of Women's Victimization

For my first example, let me zero in on battered women and take up various solutions to the problem proposed by some analysts and activists that display and deepen a politics of displacement, turning, as they do, on the erosion of any public-private distinction. The first assertion usually made, one that all fair-minded persons will surely endorse, is that domestic violence is not just a private affair; we must all be concerned when a fellow citizen is assaulted, degraded, and denied dignity. But if you are working from a perspective that erodes *any* distinction between public and private and you find this assertion nothing more than bourgeois hypocrisy, your proposed solutions start to take on many features of antidemocratic totalism.

The standard totalist case works like this: We must, as part of an interim strategy, expand the arrest powers of the police and promote the jurisprudential conviction that women are a special legal category requiring unique protection.[7] Precious little attention is paid to the fact that enhancing police and juridical prerogatives to intervene may lead to the abuse of society's least powerful, such as poor blacks and Hispanics, should they be deemed the most menacing members of a generic male threat. When this potential danger is acknowledged, it is usually seen as a chance worth taking. Mandated counseling, even behavioral conditioning of violent or "potentially violent" men, coupled with compulsory punishment and no appeal, are common parts of the panoply of interim proposals that have been made; the potential abuses inherent in extending the therapeutic powers of the state as part of its policing function are commonly ignored. Indeed, the history of the so-called social hygiene movements of the late-nineteenth and early-twentieth centuries in the United States and Canada tells us as much. In those movements, "women's sexuality" was policed and restricted to certain standards of class and ethnicity. The dangerous impulsive threat of black men, the crafty wiles of Italian seducers, and the opium-inflamed manipulations of Chinese "white slavers" fed the moral panic and calls for, among other things, restrictions on immigration and harsh treatment of black men — who were accused of such infractions as "reckless eyeballing."

These programs and their contemporary analogues rely heavily on   20
the state's policing powers, which, in other contexts, are trounced as being part of the patriarchal order. But that is only the beginning in totalist scenarios that locate the *solution* to the problem of violence once and for all in a "total restructuring of society that is feminist, antiracist, and socialist," in the words of one advocate.[8] It is unclear whether such a society would be democratic or whether, indeed, there would be any politics worthy of the name at all. Remember the Marxist dream that one glorious day politics will come to an end, absorbed into administration in the classless society? Presumably in this radical feminist version of an ideal future, some sort of powerful state must be on hand to plan everything and to redistribute, given the commitment to socialism, but this is not spelled out.

Most important, in this new society as imagined by radical activist and writer Susan Schechter, family life would be open for *community scrutiny* because the family would be part of and accountable to the community. Community-based institutions could hear complaints and dispense justice, and community networks could hold individuals accountable for their behavior and offer protection to women. If a *false separation* did not exist between the family and the community, women might lose their sense of isolation and gain a sense of entitlement to a violence-free life.[9]

But what about the repressive potential of the all-powerful "community institutions" and the policing state here envisaged? The author of this plan for eviscerating any public-private distinction goes no further in specifying how this robust communitarian world — a future perfect gemeinschaft — is to be generated out of what she portrays as our current battlefield.

Because Schechter assumes that "total restructuring" will produce a moral consensus, all dissidents having been banished, silenced, punished, or reeducated, she skirts problems of coercion and control that are otherwise implicit in her scheme for hearing complaints and dispensing justice with no provisions for the accused to be defended or his accusers cross-examined, and certainly no presumption of innocence until proven guilty. With every aspect of life opened up for inspection and, in her words, scrutiny, Schechter prescribes a world that democrats must find singularly unattractive.[10]

Even in old-fashioned traditional communities of the sort I grew up in, a rural Colorado village of 185, there was room for backsliders, town drunks, loners, dreamers, and harmless eccentrics. Why do these prophets of totally restructured worlds "beyond compromise" not tell us what will happen to such folks in their brave new societies? Not every social misfit is a violent abuser. In the society of scrutiny, total accountability, and instant justice, the social space for difference, dissent, refusal, and indifference is squeezed out. This is where matters stand unless or until advocates who share this theoretical orientation tell us how the future community of scrutiny will preserve any freedom worthy of the name. I doubt that those who make such proposals have really considered the implications of their arguments for democratic civil life. For example, contained within the paean to intrusive communities in a reconstructed future is the unequivocal claim that "who women choose as emotional and sexual partners cannot be open for public scrutiny" — an embrace of the public-private distinction and the possibility for concealment wholly at odds with the plans for a society in which "family life will be open to community scrutiny."[11]

There seem to be a few loose threads dangling here. A more democratic way of tending to these matters is to begin by giving individuals wide berth in ordering their private lives as they see fit. The public's interest becomes legitimate when there is a pattern of physical harm that is persistent, not haphazard — when one family member is beaten or bruised or injured by another. No democratic society can permit such assaults to persist. We have devised ways — imperfect, to be sure — of dealing with such situations that preserve our simultaneous commitment to protection for those who are harmed and due process for those who are accused. What seems to be lacking in too many cases is rigorous enforcement of extant statutes and bringing the full force of the law to bear against violent offenders. In part through the efforts of feminist organizers, the issue of battered women is now widely accepted as a public, not merely a private, concern. This is as it should be, but it is quite different from arguing that everything that goes on inside a family ought to be subject to public scrutiny.

Such conjecture leads to another related concern: the notion that women are society's prototypical victims. There are, of course, real victims in the world, and among their number are all too many women. But an ideology of victimhood diverts attention from concrete and specific instances of female victimization in favor of pushing a relentless worldview structured around the victim-victimizer dichotomy. The aim is to promote what can only be called moral panic, as women are routinely portrayed as helpless and demeaned. Note that the language of victimization describes women in passive terms. Jettisoning all the complexities of real victimization, it recasts women as helpless prey to male lust and assault. According to this, *all* women are assaulted, though some may not yet recognize it; all are harmed, one way or another. The ideology of victimization fuels women's fear and, paradoxically, disempowers them; it does not enable them to see themselves as citizens with both rights and responsibilities.

Eight years ago, I researched the issue of women as victims of crime. I learned that, on the best available evidence, the assertion that women are the *principal* victims of violent crime is false: The most vulnerable body to inhabit in America today, as it was when I conducted my research, is that of a young black male. As well, on the best available evidence, violence against women is *not* on a precipitous upsurge compared with other crimes. Yet popular perception, fueled by the victimization narrative, holds otherwise. As a result, women are more likely to *think* of themselves as crime victims: They have assumed an ideology of victimization that is startlingly out of proportion to the actual threat. The perception of "women as victims" goes beyond a deeply rooted belief that violence against women is skyrocketing; it holds that women are special targets of crime in general and of violent crime in particular. Yet the figures on this score have been remarkably consistent over the past decade: Most perpetrators of violent crimes are young males; most victims of violent crimes are males similar in age and race to the perpetrators. And, as I already indicated, African American youths are the most threatened of all.

The fear-of-crime syndrome has a debilitating effect on behavior, as women internalize a distorted perception of themselves. For example, in 1991, half of the 250 American movies made for television depicted women undergoing abuse of one kind or another. This could give television viewers the impression that women have a 50 percent chance each week of being victims of a violent crime. Often such trashy programs are given a feminist gloss, but by portraying women in peril in the home, the workplace, and the street, they ill serve women or any feminism worthy of the name. Women are shown either as trembling wrecks or as fierce avengers with scant regard for what is usually called due process.

Identity Politics: Gay Liberation or Civic Equality?

My second example of the politics of displacement is drawn from the intense arena of so-called identity politics. Remember that a central characteristic of the politics of displacement is that private identity takes precedence over public ends or purposes; indeed, one's private identity becomes who and what one is *in public,* and public life is about confirming that identity. The citizen gives way before the aggrieved member of a self-defined or contained group. Because the group is aggrieved — the word of choice in most polemics is *enraged* — the civility inherent in those rule-governed activities that allow a pluralist society to persist falters. This assault on civility flows from an embrace of what might be called a politicized ontology — that is, persons are to be judged not by what they do or say but by what they *are.* What you are is what your racial or sexual identity dictates. Your identity becomes the sole ground of politics, the sole determinant of political good and evil. Those who disagree with my "politics," then, are the enemies of my identity.

For my example of identity politics, I turn to the important controversies generated by the gay liberation movement. Gay liberation, in its displaced version, stands in contrast to an equal rights agenda, including a demand for dignity and recognition based on an inclusive democratic strategy. I have participated in this latter effort myself, chairing a task force that established the Committee on the Status of Lesbians and Gays for the American Political Science Association. The task force's statement of principles emphasized collegiality and dignity and the insistence that anyone hired to join an academic department should be invited to participate fully in the life of that department, without regard to sexual orientation. Bad behavior is bad behavior, no matter who commits it, and only behavior, not identity, should be criticized. "Hitting on" students is gauche and unacceptable, whether the lech in question is gay or straight.

But mark this: From the beginning of the movement for gay liberation, there was tension in the claim that gays, labeled an "oppressed class" by radical theorists, were forced to call on the very society that was oppressing them not only to protect their rights but to legitimate what became known as a "homosexual ethos" or a "gay lifestyle." The argument that gays are oppressed, then, results in two different claims: either that society has no business scrutinizing the private sexual preferences of anybody, including gays; or that government *must* intrude in the area of private identity because gays, like women, require a unique sort of public protection and "validation," in today's lexicon.[12] The politics of democratic civility and equity holds that *all* citizens, including gays, have a right, as individuals, to be protected from intrusion or harassment and to be free from discrimination in such areas as employment and housing. They also have a right to create their own forms of "public space" within which to express and to reveal their particular concerns and to argue in behalf of policies they support. This I take as a given when a public-private distinction of a certain sort is cherished and upheld. This distinction is an ongoing imperative in a democratic constitutional system; ignoring or violating it is not only an illegality but an assault on the constitutive political ethic of a democratic society.

But no one has a *civil* right, as a gay, a disciple of an exotic religion, or a political dissident, to full public sanction of his or her activities, values, beliefs, or habits. To be publicly legitimated, or "validated," in one's activities, beliefs, or habits may be a political aim — indeed, it is the overriding aim of the politics of displacement — but it is hardly a civil right. Paradoxically, in his quest to attain sanction for the *full* range of who he is, the cross-dresser or sadomasochist, the variations are nigh endless, puts his life on full display. He opens himself up to *publicity* in ways that others are bound to find quite uncivil, in part because a certain barrier — the political philosopher Hannah Arendt would have called it the boundary of shame — is harshly breached.

I readily concede that "shame" has few defenders as we near the end of the twentieth century in the West. But I hope you will hear me out. If, as I have argued, and many of my betters before me, notably Tocqueville, have insisted, democracy is about not only constitutions, rules, public accountability, and deliberation but also everyday life, habits, and dispositions, then it makes some sense to think about shame and shamelessness. Shame — or its felt experience as it surrounds our body's functions, passions, and desires — requires veils of civility that conceal some activities and aspects of ourselves even as we boldly and routinely display and reveal others when we take part in public activities for all to see. When one's intimate life is put on display on television or the streets or in other public spaces, one not only invites but actively seeks the exploitation of one's body to a variety of ends not fully under one's control. For one has then withdrawn the body's intimacy from interpersonal relations and exposed it to an unknown audience. Thus one may become an occasion for scandal or abuse or even violence toward others through one's relentless self-exposure. Flaunting one's most intimate self, making a public thing of oneself, is central to the politics of displacement, no matter who undertakes it — gay or straight; arguing for a position, winning approval, or inviting dissent as a citizen is something quite different.

Shame is central to safeguarding the freedom of the body: small wonder, then, that so many philosophers, theologians, and political theorists have found in shame, or the need for privacy and concealment, a vital and powerful feature of our human condition that we would overturn at our peril. This is not to embrace duplicity and disguise; rather, it means holding on to the concealment necessary for a rich personal life and human dignity. We emerge from our very particular, private sites into the exposure of a public existence where we can come to know and thus work to attain what is at once self-revelatory and central to human solidarity and fellowship — what is in common. There have been times in our century — terrible times — when this notion has come home to people in the most brutal way. Dietrich Bonhoeffer, the great German theologian and martyr to the anti-Nazi cause, wrote that shame is not "good in itself" and that to argue that way is "moralistic, puritanical, totally unbiblical." Rather, shame gives "reluctant witness to its own fallen state." From this division, this recognition of our incompleteness, the human being "does not show himself in its nakedness."[13] Indeed, we can go public only from a stance of rectitude that permits us to respect others as we cannot if we are driven by a longing for the innocence of the Garden, a yearning to restore a lost unity. Hence Bonhoeffer's condemnation of the ideologue, the one who sees himself justified in his own idea, through his very shamelessness. The ideologue looks into the mirror of the self and declares it good: he is a child of light; the others are the minions of darkness. We breach the boundary of shame at our risk, Bonhoeffer suggests, for what gets unleashed may in the end destroy much more than it saves or preserves.

How does all this bear on our current politics of displacement? The thread of the arguments I am tying together begins with the recognition that in Western democracies governed by notions of rights and the rule of law, the politically and culturally different have traditionally embraced certain principles of civility as their best and most enduring guarantee that government will not try to coerce them to concur with, or conform to, the majority. If I go about my business respectful of the fact that you, too, must go about yours, we need not share or even understand each other's beliefs, rituals, and values completely. But we do understand that we share a civil world — that we are, for better or for worse, "in it together."

Militant liberationists, in contrast to civil-society activists, seek official, mandated protection and approval of their private identities and behavior. These claims against society require public remedies. To this end, some go so far as to endorse wrenching disclosures and invasions of the privacy of others, called "outing" — whereby those who prefer not to go public with their homosexual orientation are forced "into the open" by others who publish their names in newspapers, post their pictures on telephone posts, or broadcast their names at rallies. Such an activity may well have the practical result of strengthening the ethos of a society of scrutiny: Nothing is exempt, if not from one's "enemies," then, ironically, even tragically, from one's ostensible friends and allies. As a result, the demand for public validation of sexual preferences, by ignoring the distinction between the personal and the political, threatens to erode authentic civil rights, including the right to privacy. Recently, important homosexual writers and analysts have opened up this debate and invited all of us, whatever our sexual orientation, to participate.[14]

What follows from these brave forays into civil society is often lively disputation from those who do not share one's orientation and heated denunciation from the totalists who do. This should not surprise us. For those who push a strong version of identity politics, any politics that does not revolve around their identities is of no interest to them. There is no broader identification with a common good beyond that of the group of which one is a member. Hence the argument made during the Vietnam War by an identity-politics activist that gays "do not get validated by our participation in anti-war marches" becomes understandable because in those marches one made common cause with other citizens who found the war abhorrent. If politics is reducible to the "eruption of radical feelings," something as seemingly "ordinary" as protest against an unjust war lacks radical panache.[15] Personal authenticity becomes the test of political credibility. One can cure one's personal ills only through political rebellion based on sexual identity. The demands that issue from such a politics of displacement go far beyond the quest for civic freedom and for what Greek democrats called *isonomia*, or equality: Nothing less than personal happiness and sexual gratification are claimed as *political* rights. And one cannot even reach the stage of *disagreement*. Philosopher James L. Nash aired his frustration on this score, recounting a failed attempt at a "gay/straight dialogue":

> In one of the first programs, I began to stake out what I hoped would be common ground, a "staging area" for further exploration, by asking if the other panelists accepted the value of fidelity in sexual intimacy, no matter what the orientation of partners. My lesbian conversation partner declared that she regarded sexual fidelity as an alien value which heterosexuals, especially male heterosexuals, were unjustly and oppressively seeking to impose on her. Moreover, she argued that by holding sexual promiscuity to be somehow morally inferior to fidelity, I was adopting a position which was tantamount to homophobia. Naturally I resisted her presupposition that gay people are more promiscuous than straight folk, and that therefore my position entailed an antigay prejudice. She disagreed. End of conversation.[16]

Both homosexuals and heterosexuals have altogether too many "end of conversation" weapons in our armamentaria today. The victim is civic life in the here and now and, over time, a polity worthy of being called democratic.

Notes

1. I first articulated my concern about the politics of displacement in my book *Public Man, Private Woman: Women in Social and Political Thought* (Princeton, N.J.: Princeton University Press, 1981).
2. Mike Feinsilber, "General Public 'Knows' What Should Be Done," *Los Angeles Times,* November 10, 1993, p. A-16.
3. Sheldon Wolin, "Democracy, Difference and Re-Cognition," *Political Theory* 21, no. 3 (1993): 468.
4. The quotes are drawn from Mary Daly, never one to shrink from vicious alliteration. For a full discussion and longer citations, see the chapter on feminism — radical, liberal, Marxist, and psychoanalytic — in *Public Man, Private Woman.*
5. Christopher Hitchens, "The New Complainers," *Dissent* (Fall 1993): 560–64.
6. Milan Kundera, "In Defense of Intimacy," an interview with Philip Roth, *The Village Voice,* June 26, 1984, p. 42.
7. There is something of a paradox here, of course, for egalitarian feminists who respect some public-private distinction challenge the whole concept of "protection" and the ideology behind it. Radical feminists, at least to certain ends and purposes, endorse a sweeping affirmation of the notion. My reference point in this discussion is one of the standard feminist works on the subject of battered women, Susan Schechter's *Women and Male Violence: The Visions and Struggles of the Battered Women's Movement* (Boston: South End Press, 1982). The subtitle alone — "visions and struggles" — locates the reader as one who is either with or against the project, either struggling for or blocking the way to a new world.
8. Ibid., p. 238.
9. Ibid., p. 239. Emphasis added.
10. For my complete riposte to the argument, written in the heat of battle, see "Politics and the Battered Woman," *Dissent* (Winter 1985): 55–61. Recently, scholars have begun to challenge the inflated figures used by advocates. See Warren Farrell, "Spouse Abuse: A Two-Way Street," *USA Today,* June 29, 1994, p. 15A.
11. Schechter, *Women and Male Violence,* p. 271.
12. A full version of my critical examination of gay liberationist ideology is available in my piece "The Paradox of Gay Liberation," *Salmagundi* (Fall 1982–Winter 1983): 250–80.
13. Dietrich Bonhoeffer, *Creation and Fall* (New York: Collier Books, 1959), p. 79.
14. See, for example, Bruce Bawer, *A Place at the Table* (New York: Poseidon Books, 1993).
15. I here draw on militant liberationist texts discussed and cited at greater length in "The Paradox of Gay Liberation." One unanswered question, of course, is why the eruption of "feelings" must inevitably cut one's own way.
16. James L. Nash, "On the Air: No Room for Dialogue," *Commonweal,* January 28, 1994, pp. 8–9.

PREPARING FOR DISCUSSION

1. Elshtain's essay begins with a rather abstract discussion about the blurring of the distinction between private and public spheres, which she labels "the politics of displacement." How are the discussions of battered women and gay

liberation that follow linked to the opening section? Why does Elshtain believe that all three discussions are bound together by the notion of civility?

2. Elshtain notices a profound contradiction in the arguments of those people who, while they argue against the existence of the patriarchy, nevertheless demand that the state's policing powers be increased to fight domestic violence. Describe the contradiction. On what grounds does Elshtain hold that within a "radical feminist version of an ideal future, some sort of powerful state must be on hand to plan everything" (paragraph 20)?

3. In paragraph 28, Elshtain notes that half of the movies made for television feature the abuse of women in one form or another. Does it follow logically from this statistic that women viewers could come away with the impression that they have a 50 percent chance each week of being abused in some way? What kinds of inferences can or cannot be made on the basis of the initial statement?

4. On the issue of gay liberation, Elshtain acknowledges the right of homosexuals to be free from discrimination and harassment. Yet she does not believe that gay people have a right to what she calls "validation" or "full public sanction" of homosexual practices and values that define who the gay person *is*. She then cites cross-dressing and sadomasochism as two of those practices. Does she mean to imply that these practices are typical of homosexuals? Why do you think she chooses these particular practices to make her case?

5. Consider Elshtain's use of the word *dialogue* near the end of the selection (paragraph 37). What sense of the word does she have in mind? How might she describe the relation between "dialogue" and the democratic process? Why do current trends in both homosexual and heterosexual communities threaten an "end of conversation" between the two groups?

FROM READING TO WRITING

6. Elshtain spends much of her essay insisting on the separation of public and private spheres. Where would you draw a line between the two? In an essay, consider an issue from family life other than battered women that is widely held to be a public issue. In your opinion, is the issue a public one open to legal strictures or must it remain private? On what grounds do you make your decision?

7. Elshtain maintains that one result of the politics of displacement is that people "are to be judged not by what they do or say but by what they *are*" (paragraph 29). In an essay, consider the extent to which you agree with Elshtain that your sexual identity determines who you are. If you reject "identity politics" as Elshtain describes it, what factors do determine your political stance?

RUSH H. LIMBAUGH

To Ogle or Not to Ogle

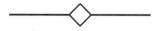

The Clarence Thomas confirmation hearings of 1991 ignited a national debate over what constitutes sexual harassment. To many, Anita Hill's testimony marked a turning point in the way Americans thought about appropriate behavior between men and women in school and at work. To others, the testimony was the sign that feminism had finally gone too far; now, even looking at a woman the wrong way might be classified as a form of sexual harassment. Conservative political commentator and radio talk-show host Rush Limbaugh confronts the issue head on in the following excerpt from his 1992 best-seller *The Way Things Ought to Be.* He denies the existence of a sex war and argues that both sexes simply need a better understanding of the "natural" differences between men and women.

After dropping out of college, Limbaugh pursued a rocky career in radio through the 1970s and early 1980s until he began hosting his own controversial talk-show, first in Sacramento and then in New York City. Currently, *The Rush Limbaugh Show* is heard on more than 600 radio stations, while his television show remains one of the most popular late-night offerings since it first aired in 1992. His first book sold over two million copies in hardcover, while his second made publishing history with a first printing of two million copies.

SELECTED PUBLICATIONS: *The Way Things Ought to Be* (1992); *See, I Told You So* (1993); *The Limbaugh Letter* (a monthly newsletter).

Here are some reports from the sexual harassment battlefront. Read these carefully. Some are humorous, but they make a point about how far this issue has poisoned relations between the sexes. Sexual harassment is a legitimate issue, but its exploitation by feminists who seek to advance their political agenda has resulted in total confusion and chaos. What are we men supposed to be anymore? How are we supposed to act?

• In 1991 the Canadian subsidiary of Sears was attacked by feminists for selling boxer shorts, that, during daylight or bright light, said NO, NO, NO all over them. But when the lights went out, or when darkness descended, the NO, NO, NO magically and wonderfully became YES, YES, YES through the use of fluorescent paint. The feminists became hysterical and claimed that this encouraged date rape. Sears caved and pulled the shorts off its shelves. I'll tell you, folks, this is crazy. Absurd. Rape? Now think:

By the time a man sees those boxer shorts, the question of NO or YES has no doubt been settled. I'd say consent is manifest in this situation, wouldn't you? If not, what rapist would be stopped by the word NO plastered all over the shorts?

• A recent study by three management professors found that men who work in a predominantly male workplace are more loyal and more likely to stay on the job than if they work with a lot of women. Men are more comfortable around other men at the workplace, especially with the constant threat of lawsuits. If that cloud was lifted, I think there would be a lot less tension at the workplace. Men can no longer enjoy themselves or tell jokes with a lot of women around, because anything they say within the earshot of women can be construed as sexual harassment. Many men say they feel they can't even be friendly in the office now because you never know when a woman, for whatever reason, will accuse you of sexual harassment. You don't believe me? Well, Claudia Weathers of the NOW Legal Defense Fund says that sexual "harassment can be almost anything that the employee finds offensive." Sorry, but that is not a beautiful thing. It is wacky and bizarre, not to mention preposterous. One cannot write open-ended laws like that. Allison Weatherfield, a crony of Ms. Weathers at the NOW gang, says a man can ask a woman out only once and then very carefully. If she says no, he should never ask her out again. And these women think they are representing the mainstream? It's getting to the point where a man who naturally expresses any interest in a woman whatsoever can be accused of lecherous behavior. My friends, if this isn't men vs. women, at least as far as these freak feminists are concerned, then what is it? I, for one, have had it with this creeping philosophy which says that men, in their natural state, are all rapists, molesters, and reprobates. That's what these dimwits really believe and I resent it.

• Almost any kind of attention paid to women can now run afoul of the New Fascists. Consider the case of Richard Hummel, a University of Toronto professor. Last year, he was banned from a campus swimming pool and ordered to take sensitivity counseling. What had he done? "They" said he was ogling female swimmers. One woman said he had "leered" at her through his swim mask and used his flippers to catch up with her in the pool. Another stated he regularly swam to the bottom of the pool and ogled women swimming above him near the surface. He was found to have violated the university's harassment regulations. So, just *looking* is harassment? Good grief, that's what men are supposed to do. That's how the old ball gets rolling. Heck, most can't help it. It's built in, biologically, from the factory. Blame it on a defect in the womb. You know something else? They wouldn't have minded one bit if it were Warren Beatty ogling them. They would have probably shoved each other out of the way so he could get a better angle.

Well, a petition was posted in the men's locker room defending Mr. Hummel. It stated: "Looking, by any name, in itself does not constitute sexual harassment in the free environment of recreational activity." If Professor Hummel can be found guilty of harassing women by merely looking at them, what will be next?

• Helen Gurley Brown, the editor of *Cosmopolitan* magazine, wrote an op-ed piece for *The Wall Street Journal* at the height of the Anita Hill frenzy. She made some very valid points about how sexual harassment must be clearly defined for there to be a legal problem. Otherwise, a lot of creative energy at the office would be stifled. She described a game called Scuttle, which was played at a radio station she had worked at forty-odd years ago. The object of the game was to chase a woman, catch her, and pull her panties off. Brown claimed the game was enjoyed by all concerned. Folks, it's obvious that times have changed. The only time I see panties being thrown around at radio stations is when some long-haired, maggot-infested FM-type rock star shows up to mumble his way through an interview. But I believe Helen Gurley Brown when she says it happened. Feminists were outraged that she would tell that story. She was unrepentant, though.

• Have you heard of Mrithi, the gorilla? He was the star of the movie *Gorillas in the Mist,* and he used to live in Rwanda. He doesn't live there anymore because he died, the victim of a bloody civil war in Rwanda. I learned of Mrithi's sudden and shocking death one afternoon near the conclusion of my show. An assistant stormed into the studio with the bulletin: Mrithi was dead. It was not a beautiful thing. It was a sad thing. I read further and came across a quote attributed to a woman named McKeenen, who was involved with some animal defense fund. Choking back tears, she had said, "He was the first gorilla who ever touched me." The first gorilla who ever touched her? Again: the first gorilla who ever touched her! Be still my beating heart. All we men have to do today is *look* at a woman the wrong way and we find ourselves accused of sexual harassment, lechery, and molestation. Yet, here is this woman sobbing because she was never again going to be *touched by a gorilla?* This settles it for me. I'm going to dress as a gorilla from now on at every Halloween party I attend.

I Know Sexual Harassment When I See It

One of the assertions made in the Anita Hill fiasco was that only women are truly qualified to recognize sexual harassment. Men don't understand what it is. This, of course, is more stupidity. It is based on the fallacious premise that you must experience something in order to be qualified to understand and comment on it. I resent that very much. I'm a decent person, and I think a decent person knows when there is sexual harassment.

If I had a sister or a wife and I saw her being harassed, I would know it. I would try to stop it.

But men are now being told they have to shut up and have harassment defined for them by someone else with an ax to grind. I'm convinced that there are women today who simply want to punish men for being themselves. If someone asks a woman out to dinner after work and uses the word *baby*, that can now be construed as sexual harassment. I don't condone groping or sidling up to someone, but a joke or the raising of an eyebrow at work is in another league.

Even feminists are divided on the issue of sexual harassment. Camille Paglia, a self-described "renegade feminist," is a professor at the University of the Arts in Philadelphia. She says that harassment of women is one of the risks women have to take into account when they have any dealings with men. She believes women's studies programs that attack men are "junk" and are destroying a whole generation of women. As for the William Kennedy Smith rape trial, she felt that if a woman drinks with a man until 3:00 A.M. and then goes home with him, she should realize the risks she is taking. I don't agree with all of Paglia's conclusions, but she proves that there is no monolithic view of sexual harassment, even in the feminist community.

Private Clubs

Sexual harassment has become such a vague, all-encompassing term that we now see feminists who have invaded previously all-male preserves complaining about the behavior they see there. They charge harassment. This shows the need for both sexes to have some private space to themselves that is free from contact with the other sex. Before feminism infested American life, there were clear rules between the sexes. Men had to honor and respect women. Now that women are forcing themselves into locker rooms and private clubs, they are finding out what men are really like. Men use crude language among themselves all the time. They act grossly sometimes. Yet, women who want to invade these male preserves turn around and demand that this kind of normal male behavior stop. They can't have it both ways.

And they have no sense of humor about any of this. One of my fabulous routines from the Rush to Excellence concerts concerns a San Francisco men's club which lost its battle to exclude women from membership. The courts ruled that they had to admit women on the basis that businesswomen were being unfairly denied opportunities to do business. This is specious. If some businessman wanted to discuss a deal with a woman, all he had to do was invite her to lunch or dinner with him. How much business did women think they were going to get as a result of forcing their way in? Anyway, after one year, the female members demanded their own exercise room. They were probably tired of being ogled by a bunch of slobbering men while they pumped iron and rode LifeCycles clad in leotards and spandex. The men agreed and, with grace and humanity, offered to install the first three exercise machines in the women's new workout room. The ladies were thrilled.

When they arrived on that first exciting day they found, to their stunned amazement, a washing machine, an ironing board, and a vacuum cleaner. Heh, heh, heh.

Well. When I guested on the CBS *Morning News*, this wonderful segment from my *Rush to Excellence II* video was aired to promote my upcoming interview. Paula Zahn said to her co-host, Harry Smith, "If he says that on this show, he won't get out of this studio alive. Who thinks that is funny?"

Sexual Differences

Harassment really can be in the eye of the beholder. There are those who will tell you there are no basic, natural differences in the ways that men and women look at a given situation. Baloney. Evidence of these differences is all around us. Examples of such are called in to my show every day.

An acquaintance of mine from Sacramento, Fred Hayward, has an organization called Men's Rights, Inc. Fred opposes discrimination against men in the media. Every year he gave out awards that showed media items that men could take offense at if they chose to view them the same way that feminists view everything in the media.

One year the award went to a jeans commercial. The ad showed a man and woman wearing jeans and walking through what looked like New York's Central Park. What was unusual was that she had her hand full of his butt. Now, Fred became mad as hell at this and told me about it. Imagine if the roles had been reversed, and the man had been shown with his hand on *her* butt. You would have heard such feminist carping that the ad would have been taken off the air.

I told Fred to calm down. You see, I said, you're missing the point. The difference is that every man looking at that ad wishes he were in it. Every man in the world would like to have a gorgeous woman like that coming on to him. Especially today, when women are supposed to be aggressive and taking things into their own hands — so to speak — men would view that prospect with pleasure. But women would understandably find an ad with a man holding a woman's rear threatening. Most women would find that too forward an act. Most men wouldn't. Just another one of those natural differences that feminists find offensive and bothersome — because, try as they might, they know they will never be able to change it.

Earlier this year, another example came up on my show. I had a bad sore throat and my voice was somewhat weak. This woman called and said she had the *perfect* cure. I said, "Hmm, what is it?" She said: "A throat massage. With my tongue." I was stunned and incredulous, totally taken aback. But — and this is the important thing — I was not offended. I laughed and told her I found her idea intriguing. (I had never tried it.) "Is your tongue long enough to do that?" I asked. "Oh, yes," she said. "No problem whatsoever." I confess, I liked that exchange. I was smiling and all the people watching the show were in tears. It was a hoot.

Well, I got a prof note (electronic mail) on my computer from a guy   20
who asked me to imagine how much outrage there would have been if a female talk show host had been told that by a male caller. The guy was right. Think about it. There would have been hysterical accusations of sexism, vulgarity, and obscenity. Shouts of "It's Daryl Gates's[1] fault" would have echoed through the streets of America. Someone would have called the ACLU, the NAACP, Interpol, the EEOC, the NAB, *A Current Affair*, the NOW gang, and any other agency to which they could complain. A massive search by land and air would be launched to find this beast, this rat, and bring him to justice. Anita Hill would make a speech offering solutions to the crisis. Emergency aid would be allocated by Congress to counsel the poor hostette on dealing with such terror.

Yet, my good friends, I didn't feel at all sexually harassed by the call. I liked it. It just proves how men and women instinctively and naturally look at events differently. And this is nothing new. It's always been this way. It's a beautiful thing.

I'd like to say to any women who have read this chapter and been offended or outraged that I apologize. It was not the purpose of the chapter to offend. Anyone, without any talent at all, can do that. I have simply tried to be as honest as I can be about my feelings on this sensitive and touchy subject. Yes, it is a tender subject, too, and I have been tender and gentle in discussing it. I want people to get along with one another, without making a legal case out of everything. I deeply resent the politicization of social relationships. It bothers me to no end, especially when so many people think the government should intervene to solve these things.

Let me leave you with a thought that most honestly summarizes my sentiments: I love the women's movement . . . especially when I am walking behind it.

PREPARING FOR DISCUSSION

1. The author objects to one of the arguments that came out of the Anita Hill allegations that "only women are truly qualified to recognize sexual harassment" (paragraph 8). On what ground does Limbaugh disagree with this formulation?

---

[1] *Daryl Gates:* Los Angeles police commissioner during the Rodney King police beating affair of the early 1990s.

Do you agree or disagree with the notion that "someone must experience something in order to understand and comment on it"?

2. Limbaugh cites Camille Paglia's views on the William Kennedy Smith rape trial (Paglia's essay on rape as a sex crime is included earlier in this chapter). Why does Limbaugh include the feminist's view in his essay? Would he agree with Paglia that women must accept the risk of harassment whenever they deal with men?

3. At several points in the selection, Limbaugh relates jokes and stories at the expense of women. Consider the "exercise equipment" story as well as the gag line with which the selection ends. Limbaugh claims that he believes sexual harassment to be a "legitimate issue." Does the presence of such jokes within his examination of the issue support his claim? How are the jokes meant to function? What effect do they have on his argument?

4. Limbaugh argues that most men are biologically programmed to "look" at women. Does this argument in and of itself excuse behavior that many women find offensive? Can you think of other biological instincts that most human beings possess? Under what circumstances do we act on those instincts in civil society? Under what kinds of circumstances might we try to repress them?

5. Limbaugh begins the selection with "Here are some reports from the sexual harassment battlefront." Why does he use this war metaphor at the start of the selection? What does it imply about the relationship between men and women? Is Limbaugh alone in using military metaphors to talk about sexual politics?

FROM READING TO WRITING

6. Examine Limbaugh's analysis of the advertisement that places the woman in a sexually assertive posture toward the man. Find some other ads in which this situation occurs. Write an essay in which you analyze the ads and determine whether they tend to confirm or to disprove Limbaugh's analysis. Do you think that most men would find these ads nonthreatening?

7. Limbaugh writes that he "deeply resent[s] the politicization of social relationships." Write an essay in which you consider the extent to which social relationships between men and women are affected by their increasing political nature. Have your own relationships with the opposite sex been politicized in recent years? Is there behavior you no longer engage in or values you no longer hold as a result of this politicization?

ANDREA DWORKIN

Violence against Women:
It Breaks the Heart, Also the Bones

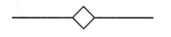

In the past, feminists have generally spoken out against prostitution and pornography on the grounds that such practices amount to little more than forms of slavery for women. Recently, however, even traditional heterosexual arrangements like marriage and consensual sex between a man and a woman have come under attack as forms that perpetuate violence against women. Radical feminist, author, and lecturer Andrea Dworkin worries that most women are not even aware of the fact that they have been victims of violence at the hands of men.

After graduating from Bennington, Dworkin lived in Europe for several years during which time she survived an abusive marriage and began her career as a writer focusing on physical violence against women. By the late 1970s, she was back in the United States, where she continued her writing and helped to organize the first Take Back the Night March to protest violence against women, including prostitution and pornography. Always a controversial and powerful voice within the women's movement, Dworkin, in recent years, has even shocked other feminists with her radical position that in most Western societies sex can only be regarded as a punishment for being a woman. With legal theorist Catharine MacKinnon, Dworkin has coauthored an ordinance that defines pornography as a civil rights violation against women. This selection is from her collected writings, *Letters from a War Zone* (1988).

SELECTED PUBLICATIONS: *Women Hating* (1974); *Pornography: Men Possessing Women* (1981); *Intercourse* (1987); *Pornography and Civil Rights: A New Day for Women's Equality* (with Catharine A. MacKinnon) (1988); *Letters from a War Zone: Writings 1976–1987* (1988).

What breaks the heart about violence against women is that people, including women, do not know it when they see it, when they do it or collaborate in it, when they experience it — even as victims of it. What breaks the spirit of those fighting for women's rights is that one can never take for granted a realization that a woman is an actual human being who, when hurt, is hurt.

The hurting of women is so basic to the sexual pleasure of men, to the social and sexual dominance that men exercise over women, to the economic degradation imposed on women by men, that women are simply considered those creatures made by God or biology for what would be abuse if it were done to men (human beings); but it is being done to women, so it is not abuse; it is instead simply what women are for.

The natural relation of the sexes means that women are made to be used the way men use us now, in a world of civil, social, and economic inequality based on sex; a world in which women have limited rights, no physical integrity, and no real self-determination. This condition of inequity is even good for us, because we are different from men. When men are deprived of social equality, they are hurt in their rights to self-respect and freedom. Inequality actually causes women to thrive, and provides the best environment for sexual pleasure and personal fulfillment.

This nature of ours has entirely to do with sex: sex is our natural function, and our lives are supposed to be predetermined by this natural use to which our bodies are put for reproduction or for pleasure, depending on the ideology of the person making the claim. Our nature is such that we crave the cruelties men so generously provide. We like pain, especially in sex. We make men hurt us. We especially like to be forced to have sex while refusing to have it; our refusal encourages men to use physical force, violence, and humiliation against us, which is why we refuse in the first place. As our hormones secretly surge and our genes smirk in self-satisfied delight, we say no, intending through refusal to provoke an antagonism sufficiently destructive to satisfy us when finally it is vented on us in sex. We are hungry for a certain vulgar brutality, which is lucky for us, since we get so much of it. In marriage, being beaten is proof to us that we are loved. Evidence is cited of obscure villages in remote places where, if a man does not beat his wife, she feels unloved, since no woman at hand seems to find it proof at all. (In those obscure villages, no doubt the women of New York and Dublin are cited to the same end.) We particularly enjoy being sold on street corners (does bad weather increase our fun?). We entice our fathers to rape us, because even little girls are born women. In technologically advanced societies, we eschew becoming brain surgeons for the delight of finding photographers who will shoot our genitals: camera or gun, we don't mind.

One thing should be clear, but apparently it is not: if this were indeed   5
our nature, we would be living in paradise.

If pain, humiliation, and physical injury made us happy, we would be ecstatic.

If being sold on street corners were a good time, women would jam street corners the way men jam football matches.

If forced sex were what we craved, even we would be satisfied already.

If being dominated by men made us happy we would smile all the time.

Women resist male domination because we do not like it.   10

Political women resist male domination through overt, rude, unmistakable rebellion. They are called unnatural, because they do not have a nature that delights in being debased.

Apolitical women resist male domination through a host of bitter subversions, ranging from the famous headache to the clinical depression epidemic among women to suicide to prescription-drug tranquilization to taking it out on the children; sometimes a battered wife kills her husband. Apolitical women are also called unnatural, the charge hurled at them as nasty or sullen or embittered individuals, since that is how they fight back. They too are not made happy by being hurt or dominated.

In fact, a natural woman is hard to find. We are domesticated, tamed, made compliant on the surface, through male force, not through nature. We sometimes *do* what men say we *are*, either because we believe them or because we hope to placate them. We sometimes try to become what men say we should be, because men have power over our lives.

Male domination is a system of social institutions, sexual practices, economic relations, and emotional devastations. At the same time, it is something men do to women through commonplace behaviors. It is not abstract or magical; and any woman's life illustrates the ways in which male dominance is used on real women by real men. Underlying the big social realities of male dominance are the flesh-and-blood realities of rape, battery, prostitution, and incest, as well as being used in banal, demeaning ways in sex, as domestics, to have children *for* men. We are treated as if we are worthless in how we are talked to, looked at, in common social interchanges. The acts of violence and the acts of insult are justified by the nature we are presumed to have: an inferior nature, specially marked by its compulsive need for force in sex. The inferiority of women is best described as an immovable, barely comprehensible stupidity. Getting hurt is what we want.

Women do not simply endure having this peculiar nature. We cele-   15
brate it by actively seeking to be dominated and hurt, that is, fulfilled. Men only respond; we provoke. A man is going about his business, bothering no one, when a woman calls attention to herself — by walking down the street, for instance. The man, intending no harm, tries to please the woman by doing to her whatever her language and behavior suggest she does not want. As he inflicts this kindness on her, strictly through solicitude for her real desire, indicated by her resistance and repugnance, he is only responding to what has been her purpose from the beginning: she has wanted his attention so that he would do whatever she is appearing to resist. He knows what she wants because he knows what she is.

In the world of male domination, there are no individual women who are unique persons. There is only a generic *she*, frequently called *cunt* so that what defines the genus is clear. She is the hole between her legs. Her nature justifies whatever men need to do to make that hole accessible to them on their terms. She is valued insofar as men value entry into her. For the rest, she is decorative or does housework.

Feminists think that many of the so-called normal uses of women under male domination are abuses of women. This is because feminists think that women are human beings. This means that when a woman is hurt, she is hurt, not fulfilled. When she is forced, she is forced, not fulfilled. When she is humiliated, she is humiliated, not fulfilled. Inequality wrongs her. Pain hurts her. Exploitation robs her of her rights over herself. Broken bones and bruises are physical injuries, not grandiose romantic gestures. Feminism is an esoteric and nasty politic, practiced only by unnatural women who do not like being hurt at all.

If women are human beings, as feminists suspect, then crimes of violence against women are human rights violations that occur on a massive, almost unimaginable scale. These crimes are committed most frequently in private, in intimacy; but they are committed all the time, every day and every night, all over the world, by normal men. Unbending, powerful social institutions, including church and state, cloak these crimes in a protective legitimacy, so that, for instance, forced sex in marriage is a legally secured right of marriage for the man, socially acceptable, commonplace, unremarkable. Battery, incest, forced pregnancy, prostitution, and rape originate in this same sanctioned ownership of men over women. That ownership is both collective and class-based (men as a class own women as a class) and it is particular, private, individual, one human being (male) having rights over sexual and reproductive chattel (female).

In practice, a man can rape his wife or daughter, beat his wife or daughter, or prostitute his wife or daughter, with virtually no state interference, except in exceptional circumstances (for instance, if the victim dies). The state in fact actively supports male dominance achieved through or expressed in violence. Marriage, for example, is a legal license to rape: it is a state-backed entitlement to fuck a woman without regard for her will or integrity; and a child finds herself in the same feudal relationship to her father because of his state-backed power as head-of-the-household.

Sometimes, laws prohibit acts of violence against women. Battery is illegal, but no police will interfere; husbands are rarely arrested for beating their wives, even though an experimental program in Minneapolis showed that immediate arrest and real convictions with real jail sentences had a serious impact on stopping battery. It ended the legal impunity of the batterer, and it also introduced, frequently for the first time, 20 the idea that it was not natural or right for husbands to hit their wives — it introduced the idea to the husband.[1]

Rape is illegal. A man is not supposed to be able to rape anyone but his own wife with impunity. But rape is widespread, rarely even reported to the police (one in ten or eleven rapes are reported in the United States), more rarely prosecuted, and convictions are unusual and unlikely. This is because juries view the woman as responsible for the sex act, no matter how abusive it is. The woman's sexual history is explored to convict her of being wanton: any sexual experience is used to show that her nature is responsible for what happened to her, not the man who did it.

The right to rape as a male right of dominance is never the issue in rape cases. Historically, rape was considered a crime against the man to whom the woman belonged as chattel: her husband or her father. In her husband's house, she was private property. In her father's house, she was a virgin to be sold as such to a husband. Rape was rather like stealing a car and smashing it into a tree. The value of the property is hurt. If the woman was already damaged goods — not private enough as property before the rapist got hold of her — or if she consented (a corpse could meet the legal standard for consent in a rape case) — then the putative rapist was not responsible for her low value and he would not be convicted of rape. The woman as a separate human being with rights over her own body does not exist under traditional rape laws. That is why feminists want rape laws changed: so that rape is a crime against the woman raped, not her keeper. The difficulty in accomplishing this is unpleasantly simple: the injuries of rape to a human being are self-evident; but the injuries of rape to a woman are not injuries at all — they are sexual events that she probably liked, even initiated, no matter how badly she is hurt, women being what women are.

In trying to understand violence against women, one must consistently look at how laws work, not at what they say, to see whether they in fact further violence against women, regulate it (for instance, by establishing some conditions under which violence is condoned and others under which it is discouraged), or stop it. Under male domination, law virtually always furthers or regulates violence against women by keeping women subordinate to men, allowing or encouraging violence against at least some women all the time, and holding women responsible for the violence done to us with its doctrinal insistence that we actually provoke violence and get sexual pleasure from it.

---

[1] In Seattle, a judge ordered the police force to enforce laws against "domestic violence," i.e. wife-battery. As a result, police began arresting any woman who fought back or resisted marital rape. One woman was arrested because she had scratched her husband's face when he tried to force sex on her. The police claim they have no choice: if they must enforce these laws that they do not want to enforce, they must enforce them against any spouse who commits any act of violence. This is one example of how the legal system works to make reforms meaningless and women's rights ludicrous. [Dworkin's note]

The feminist fight against violence against women is also necessarily a fight against male law: because the way the law really works — in rape, battery, prostitution, and incest — women are its victims.

The state, then, keeps women available to men for abuse — that is one of its functions. The dominance of men over women through violence is not an unfortunate series of accidents or mistakes but is instead state policy, backed by police power.

For conceptual clarity, I am going to divide the crimes of violence against women into two categories: simple crimes, which include rape, battery, incest, torture, and murder; and complex crimes, which include sexual harassment, prostitution, and pornography. These acts are the primary violent abuses of women in the West. In other societies, other acts may have the same mainstream cultural significance — for instance, clitoridectomy or infibulation or dowry burnings.

The simple crimes are acts of violation that are relatively easy to comprehend as discrete events once the violation is made known. The act is usually committed in privacy or in secret, but if a victim tells about it, one can see what happened, how, when, where, for how long, by whom, to whom, even why. Even though these acts are committed so frequently that they are commonplace, they are usually committed in private, done to women as individuals. Each time a rape happens, it happens to a particular woman, a particular child. There is no sense of public contagion: rape is not experienced as spreading through the community like cholera. There is also no sense of public enjoyment of the crime, public complicity, public enthusiasm.

In complex crimes, there is contagion. The community knows that there is a public dimension to the abuse, that there is mass complicity, mass involvement. The crimes are in the public air, they happen outside the privacy of the home, they happen to many nameless, faceless women, who are moving through public space: many men are doing these things to many women, all at once, not in private at all. There is a sense of "everyone does it — so what?" with many of the elements that distinguish sexual harassment; prostitution and pornography are widely taken to be things men need and things men use — lots of men, most men.

The violence itself in a complex crime is a convoluted mass of violations involving many kinds of sexual abuse; it is hard to pull them apart. There is a machine-like quality to the abuse, as if women's bodies were on an assembly line, getting processed, getting used: getting drilled, getting screwed, getting hammered, getting checked over, poked, passed on.

The complex crimes are done to the already disappeared: the women are anonymous; they have no personal histories that matter and no personal qualities that can change the course of events. Sexual harassment, for instance, makes women vagabonds in the labor market: cheap labor, immediately replaceable, moving out of low paid job after low paid job. Prostitution and pornography erase all personality.

In complex crimes, there is ongoing intimidation and intricate coercion that exists on many levels. There is a profit motive as well as a pleasure/power motive: big business, one way or another, stands behind the abuser. The simple crimes are most often done in secret, but the complex crimes have real social visibility. Sexual harassment happens in a society of fellow workers; prostitutes have a social presence on the streets; the point of pornography is that it is on view.

All the simple and complex crimes of violence are also acts of sex. Under male domination, there is no phenomenological division between sex and violence. Every crime of violence committed against a woman is sexual: sex is central to the targeting of the victim, the way in which she is hurt, why she is hurt, the sense of entitlement the man has to do what he wants to her, the satisfaction the act gives him, the social support for the exploitation or injury. The social support can be mainstream or subterranean, fully sanctioned by the system or implicit in how it works.

In most crimes of violence against women, a sex act involving penetration of the woman, not always vaginally, not always with a penis, is intrinsic to the violence or the reason for it. In some crimes of violence, for instance, battery, while rape is part of the long-term configuration of the abuse, sex is more frequently exhausted, brutalized compliance; it occurs as if in the eye of the hurricane — after the last beating and to try to forestall the next one. Sometimes the beating is the sexual event for the man.

When feminists say *rape is violence, not sex,* we mean to say that from our perspective as victims of forced sex, we do not get sexual pleasure from rape; contrary to the rapist's view, the pornographer's view, and the law's view, rape is not a good time for us. This is a valiant effort at cross-cultural communication, but it is only half the story: because for men, rape and sex are not different species of event. Domination is sexual for most men, and rape, battery, incest, use of prostitutes and pornography, and sexual harassment are modes of domination imbued with sexual meaning. Domination is power over others and also hostility toward and dehumanization of the powerless. The domination of men over women is both expressed and achieved through sex *as men experience sex,* not as women wish it would be. This means that we have to recognize that sex and violence are fused for men into dominance; and that not only is violence sexual[2] but also sex is consistently used to assert dominance.

This is a desperate and tragic reality. Those closest to us — those in-   35

---

[2] New experimental research in the United States shows that films showing extreme and horrific violence against women that are not sexually explicit sexually stimulated nearly a third of the men who watched them. The films are called "splatter" films. They are made from the point of view of the killer as he stalks a female victim. She ends up splattered. The researchers told me that they could not construct a film scenario of violence against women that did not sexually stimulate a significant percentage of male viewers. [Dworkin's note]

side us — cannot separate sex and violence, because for them they are not separate: the fusion of sex and violence is the dominance that gives them pleasure. Our lives are held hostage to this pleasure they want. Rape, battery, incest, torture, murder, sexual harassment, prostitution, and pornography are acts of real violence against us enjoyed by our husbands, fathers, sons, brothers, lovers, teachers, and friends. They call these acts by different names when they do them.

Pornography especially shows how dominance and abuse are pleasure and entertainment. In the United States, pornography saturates the environment, private and public. In Ireland, access to it is more restricted at this time; and yet, videos showing the torture of women, allowable under Irish censorship laws because video is not covered, have reached an avid population of male consumers. No time to develop an appetite for the violence was required. Normal men, having rights of sexual dominance, took to torture videos like ducks to water. Pornography is central to male dominance, even when access to it is limited, because every form of sexual abuse is implicated in it and it is implicated in every form of sexual abuse; and it is apprehended by men as pure pleasure.

In the United States, perhaps three-quarters of the women in pornography are incest victims. Women are recruited through being raped and beaten. Forced sex is filmed; so is torture, gang rape, battery; and the films are used (as blackmail, sexual humiliation, and threat) to keep new women in prostitution. Once seasoned,[3] prostitutes are used in films as their pimps determine. Rapes of women who are not prostitutes, not runaway children, not on the streets to stay, are filmed and sold on the commercial pornography market. Pornography has actually introduced a profit motive into rape. Women in pornography are penetrated by animals and objects. Women are urinated on and defecated on. All of these things are done to real women in pornography; then the pornography is used so that these acts are committed against other real women.

The worthlessness of women as human beings is entirely clear when it is understood that pornography is a form of mass entertainment, in the United States now grossing an estimated eight billion dollars a year. Men, the primary consumers of pornography, are entertained by these acts of sexual abuse.

The lives of women are circumscribed by the terrorism of pornography, because it is the distilled yet entirely trivialized terror of rape, battery, incest, torture, and murder — women are objects, not human, assaulted and hurt, used in sex, because men want and like sexual dominance. Pornography is the prostitution of the women in it, and it is a metaphysical

---

[3] "Seasoning" is the process of making a woman or a girl into a compliant prostitute. It usually involves raping her, having her gang-raped, drugging her, beating her, repeated and purposeful humiliation. It often involves filming these acts, showing her the film (making her watch herself), and threatening to send the pictures to her family or school. [Dworkin's note]

definition of all women as whores by nature; so it is also the terror of being born to be used, traded, and sold. The substance of this terror — its details, its ambiance — is the pleasure, is the entertainment, for the men who watch. It is hard to imagine how much they hate us.

It is also difficult to understand how absolutely, resolutely indiffer-   40
ent to our rights they are. Yet these men who like to see us being used or hurt are not indifferent to rights as such: they guard their own. They claim, for instance, that in being entertained by pornography they are exercising rights of theirs, especially rights of expression or speech. How is it possible that in watching rape — or, frankly, in watching female genitals, women's legs splayed — they are exercising rights of speech? It must be that our pain is what they want to say. Perhaps our genitals are words they use. Incomprehensible as it may be to us, their enjoyment in our abuse is articulated as a civil liberty of theirs. The logic of the argument is that if their rights to pornography (to possession, exploitation, and abuse of us) are abrogated, they will be unable to say what they want to say. They must have "freedom of speech."

Also, the sexual exploitation of women is held to be "sexual liberation." The uses of women in pornography are considered "liberating." What is done to us is called "sexual freedom."

Our abuse has become a standard of freedom — the meaning of freedom — the requisite for freedom — throughout much of the Western world.

Being hurt, being threatened with physical injury as a condition of life, being systematically exploited, has profoundly disturbing effects on people. They get numb; they despair; they are often ignoble, becoming indifferent to the suffering of others in their same situation. People are also known to fight oppression and to hate cruelties they are forced to endure; but women are supposed to enjoy being hurt, being used, being made inferior. The remedies historically used by oppressed peoples to fight domination and terror are not supposed to be available to women: because what is done to us is supposed to be appropriate to what we are — *women*. God, nature, and men concur.

But sometimes we dissent. We see the violence done to us as violence, not love, not romance, not inevitable and natural, not our fate, not to be endured and suffered through, not what we are for because of what we are.

Feminists call this often painful process of learning to see with our   45
own eyes *consciousness-raising*. We discard the eyes of men, which had become our eyes. We break the isolation that violence creates; we find out from each other how much we are treated the same, how much we have in common in how we are used, the acts of insult and injury committed against us because we are women.

Consciousness means that we have developed an acute awareness of both our suffering and our humanity: what happens to us and what we have a right to. We know we are human and so the suffering (inferior status, exploitation, sexual abuse) is an intolerable series of violations that must be stopped. Experiencing suffering as such — instead of becoming numb — forces us to act human: to resist oppression, to demand fairness, to create new social arrangements that include us as human. When humans rebel against suffering, the heroes of history, known and unknown, are born.

So even though women are expected to enjoy being used and being hurt, women resist; women fight back; women organize; women are brave; women go up against male power and stop it in its tracks; women fight institutions of male dominance and weaken them; women create social and political conflict, so that male power is challenged and hurt; women retaliate against rapists and batterers and pimps; women infiltrate male systems of power; women change laws to benefit women and increase our rights; women provide secret refuge for battered women and above-ground advocacy for rape victims and abortions for pregnant women who need help; women create work and wealth for other women to subvert the economic hold men have over women; sometimes women kill; women sit-in and picket and commit civil disobedience to destroy pornographers and militarists; women sue to stop sex discrimination; women claim more and more public space to change the configurations of public power; feminists keep refining the targets, so that we attack male power where it is most vulnerable and where we can best amass collective strength in our respective countries; feminists go at male power where it is most dangerous, so heavy on top that it must topple over if we push hard enough; feminists keep thinking, writing, talking, organizing, marching, demonstrating, with militance and patience and a rebelliousness that burns. The fight is hard and ugly and deadly serious. Sometimes women are killed. Often, women are hurt. Vengeance against women is real, physical, economic, psychological: swift and cruel. Still: women resist, women fight back, women want to win.

What we want to win is called freedom or justice when those being systematically hurt are not women. We call it equality, because our enemies are family. No violent reform will work for us, no blood coup followed by another regime of illegitimate power: because our enemy is family; and we cannot simply wipe him out and kill him dead.

The burden is very great. Because the enemy is family, and because he is so cruel and so arrogant and so intimate and so close, because he smiles when we hurt and pays money to be entertained by our abuse, we know we have to go to the roots of violence, the roots of domination, the roots of why power gives pleasure and how hierarchy creates exploitation. We know we have to level social hierarchies. We know we have to destroy the pleasure and possibility of sexual domination. We know we have to raise ourselves up and pull men down, not tenderly. We know we have to end the violence against us by ending the rights of men over us. There is no friendly domination, no self-respecting submission.

Violence against women hurts the heart, also the bones. Feminists are 50 unnatural women who do not like being hurt at all.

PREPARING FOR DISCUSSION

1. Dworkin worries that most women do not know violence when they see it or even when they experience it as victims. Why does she believe that this situation has evolved? What role have men played in reducing women's abilities to distinguish violent acts from other forms of behavior?

2. Dworkin devotes several paragraphs to marriage and its disadvantages for women. How does she define marriage from a legal and social perspective? What do the different definitions have in common? Would you conclude from this discussion that Dworkin is thoroughly opposed to the institution of marriage in all of its forms?

3. Dworkin offers many definitions of rape. Locate them within the selection. After reading these definitions, would you say that she identifies all sexual acts between a man and a woman as rape? In classifying so wide a range of acts as rape, does Dworkin inadvertently trivialize the idea of rape?

4. Dworkin argues that men feel they have a right to pornography as a result of the constitutional protections of expression. Hoping to show that the argument against censorship is illogical, she writes that "if their rights to pornography are abrogated, they will be unable to say what they want to say." Does she succeed in proving the argument against censorship illogical? Does the right to free expression apply to the viewers of pornography — Dworkin focuses on these — or to the people who make pornography?

5. Beginning in paragraph 3, Dworkin adopts the first-person plural pronoun "we" and continues to use it for several more paragraphs. Why does Dworkin use this pronoun? Is the "we" meant to reflect the actual views of real women?

FROM READING TO WRITING

6. In the last paragraphs of the selection, Dworkin repeats the phrase "enemy is family" several times. What does she mean by this phrase? Write an essay in which you consider the implications of her phrase. Do you agree with the terms she uses to describe male family members, teachers, friends, boyfriends, and so forth?

7. Beginning in paragraph 18, Dworkin describes marriage as the sanctioned ownership of women by men. Consider other modern views of marriage and then your own ideas about what marriage is. Write an essay in which you agree or disagree with the particular sense of marriage Dworkin supplies. How does Dworkin's sense of marriage compare with your own?

CHRISTINA HOFF SOMMERS

Noble Lies

In book 3 of Plato's *Republic,* Socrates introduces the concept of the
"noble lie" as a way to excuse rulers who tell their people falsehoods for
the general good of the state. In the following selection, philosopher
Christina Hoff Sommers wonders if feminists have not already told so
many "noble lies" that the integrity of the women's movement is now in
question. In her words, "even the best-intentioned 'noble lie' ultimately
discredits the finest cause." She especially worries that feminists routinely misuse statistics and distort the findings of scholarly studies to
present a more disturbing and therefore more compelling picture of
male violence against women in America. In trying to ascertain why
gender feminism attempts to present such a disparaging view of men,
Sommers arrives at another disturbing conclusion: that "gender feminists" will stop at nothing to persuade other women that there exists an
all-out war between the sexes. Ultimately, she suggests, women must
ask themselves how the propagation of lies helps in any way to relieve
the actual suffering of women.

Sommers received her doctorate from Brandeis and has been associate professor of philosophy at Clark University since 1980. She is the editor of two textbooks on ethics. This selection is from her 1994 book, *Who
Stole Feminism?*

SELECTED PUBLICATIONS: *Who Stole Feminism? How Women Have Be-
trayed Women* (1994); Sommers also publishes in the *New Republic,* the
Wall Street Journal, the *American Scholar,* and the *New England Journal of
Medicine.*

---

*Pity, wrath, heroism filled them, but the power of putting two and two together
was annihilated.*

— E. M. FORSTER, *A Passage to India*

Statistics and studies on such provocative subjects as eating disorders,
rape, battery, and wage differentials are used to underscore the plight of
women in the oppressive gender system and to help recruit adherents to
the gender feminist cause. But if the figures are not true, they almost never
serve the interests of the victimized women they concern. Anorexia is
a disease; blaming men does nothing to help cure it. Battery and rape
are crimes that shatter lives; those who suffer must be cared for, and those
who cause their suffering must be kept from doing further harm. But in all

401

we do to help, the most loyal ally is truth. Truth brought to public light re-cruits the best of us to work for change. On the other hand, even the best-intentioned "noble lie" ultimately discredits the finest cause.

Gender feminist ideology holds that physical menace toward women is the norm. The cause of battered women has been a handy bandwagon for this creed. Gloria Steinem's portrait of male-female intimacy under patriarchy is typical: "Patriarchy *requires* violence or the subliminal threat of violence in order to maintain itself. . . . The most dangerous situation for a woman is not an unknown man in the street, or even the enemy in wartime, but a husband or lover in the isolation of their own home."[1] Steinem's description of the dangers women face in their own home is reminiscent of the Super Bowl hoax of January 1993.[2]

Some days before that Super Bowl, American women were alerted that a sharp increase in battering was to be expected on the day of the game. The implications were sensational, but purportedly there were re-liable studies. In the current climate, the story had a certain ring of plau-sibility, and it quickly spread. Here is the chronology.

Thursday, January 28

A news conference was called in Pasadena, California, the site of the forthcoming Super Bowl game, by a coalition of women's groups. At the news conference reporters were informed that significant anecdotal evi-dence suggested that Super Bowl Sunday is "the biggest day of the year for violence against women."[3] Prior to the conference, there had been re-ports of increases as high as 40 percent in calls for help from victims that day. At the conference, Sheila Kuehl of the California Women's Law Cen-ter cited a study done at Virginia's Old Dominion University three years before, saying that it found that police reports of beatings and hospital admissions in northern Virginia rose 40 percent after games won by the Redskins during the 1988–89 season. The presence of Linda Mitchell at the conference, a representative of a media "watchdog" group called Fairness and Accuracy in Reporting (FAIR), lent credibility to the cause.

At about this time a very large media mailing was sent by Dobisky Associates, warning at-risk women, "Don't remain at home with him during the game." The idea that sports fans are prone to attack wives or girlfriends on that climactic day persuaded many men as well: Robert Lipsyte of the *New York Times* would soon be referring to the "Abuse Bowl."[4]

5

Friday, January 29

Lenore Walker, a Denver psychologist and author of *The Battered Woman*, appeared on "Good Morning America" claiming to have compiled a ten-year record showing a sharp increase in violent incidents against women on Super Bowl Sundays. Here, again, a representative from FAIR, Laura Flanders, was present to lend credibility to the cause.

Saturday, January 30

A story in the *Boston Globe* written by Lynda Gorov reported that women's shelters and hotlines are "flooded with more calls from victims [on Super Bowl Sunday] than on any other day of the year." Gorov cited "one study of women's shelters out West" that "showed a 40 percent climb in calls, a pattern advocates said is repeated nationwide, including in Massachusetts."[5]

Ms. Gorov asked specialists in domestic violence to explain the phenomenon. Many felt that everything about the Super Bowl is calculated to give men the idea that women are there for their use and abuse. "More than one advocate mentioned provocatively dressed cheerleaders at the game may reinforce abusers' perceptions that women are intended to serve men," she wrote. According to Nancy Isaac, an expert on domestic violence at the Harvard School of Public Health, men see the violence as their right: "It's: 'I'm supposed to be king of my castle, it's supposed to be my day, and if you don't have dinner ready on time, you're going to get it.'"

Other newspapers joined in. Robert Lipsyte described the connection between the tension generated by the big game and the violence it causes: "Someone shut up that kid or someone's going to get pounded."[6] Michael Collier of the *Oakland Tribune* wrote that the Super Bowl causes "boyfriends, husbands and fathers" to "explode like mad linemen, leaving girlfriends, wives and children beaten."[7] Journalists and television commentators all over the country sounded the alarm. CBS and the Associated Press called Super Bowl Sunday a "day of dread," and just before the game, NBC broadcast a public service spot reminding men that domestic violence is a crime.

In this roiling sea of media credulity was a lone island of professional integrity. Ken Ringle, a *Washington Post* staff writer, took the time to call around to check on the sources of the story.[8] When Ringle asked Janet Katz, professor of sociology and criminal justice at Old Dominion and one of the principal authors of the study cited by Ms. Kuehl at the Thursday press conference, about the connection between violence and football games, she said: "That's not what we found at all." Instead, she told Ringle, they had found that an increase in emergency room admissions "was not associated with the occurrence of football games in general."[9]

Ringle then called Charles Patrick Ewing, a professor at the University of Buffalo, whom Dobisky Associates had quoted as saying, "Super Bowl Sunday is one day in the year when hot lines, shelters and other agencies that work with battered women get the most reports and complaints of domestic violence." "I never said that," Ewing told Ringle. When told about Ewing's denial, Frank Dobisky corrected himself, saying that the quote should have read *"one of the days* of the year." But that explanation either makes the claim incoherent, since only one day can have "the most" battery complaints, or trivializes it, since *any* day (including April Fool's Day) could now be said to be the day of heightened brutality.

Ringle checked with Lynda Gorov, the *Boston Globe* reporter. Gorov told him she had never seen the study she cited but had been told of it by FAIR. Ms. Mitchell of FAIR told Ringle that the authority for the 40 percent figure was Lenore Walker. Walker's office, in turn, referred calls on the subject to Michael Lindsey, a Denver psychologist and an authority on battered women.

Pressed by Ringle, Lindsey admitted he could find no basis for the report. "I haven't been any more successful than you in tracking down any of this," he said. "You think maybe we have one of these myth things here?" Later, other reporters got to Ms. Walker, pressing her to detail her findings. "We don't use them for public consumption," she explained, "we use them to guide us in advocacy projects."[10]

It would have been more honest for the feminists who initiated the campaign to admit that there was no scientific basis for saying that football fans are more brutal to women than are chess players or Democrats; nor was there any hard data for the claim that there was a significant rise in domestic violence on Super Bowl Sunday.

Ringle's unraveling of the "myth thing" was published on the front page of the *Washington Post* on January 31. On February 2, *Boston Globe* staff writer Bob Hohler published what amounted to a retraction of Ms. Gorov's story. Hohler had done some more digging and had gotten FAIR's Steven Rendall to back off from the organization's earlier support of the claim. "It should not have gone out in FAIR materials," said Rendall.

Hohler got another set of interviews, this time with psychologists who told him that they had their doubts about the story from the very beginning. One expert, Joan Stiles, public education coordinator for the Massachusetts Coalition of Battered Women's Service Groups, told the *Globe* that the Super Bowl story "sensationalized and trivialized" the battering problem, and damaged the cause's credibility. Lundy Bancroft, a training director for a Cambridge-based counseling program for men who batter, said, "I disbelieved the 40 percent thing from the moment I heard it." Bancroft also suggested that the campaign to pressure NBC to air the domestic-violence spot "unfairly stigmatized" football fans. "There is no stereotypical batterer," he said. As Michael Lindsey commented to Ken Ringle, "When people make crazy statements like this, the credibility of the whole cause can go right out the window."

According to Ringle, Linda Mitchell from FAIR would later acknowledge that she was aware during the original news conference that Ms.

Kuehl was misrepresenting the Old Dominion study. Ringle asked her whether she did not feel obligated to challenge her colleague. "I wouldn't do that in front of the media," Mitchell said. "She has a right to report it as she wants." (FAIR would later take issue with Ringle's interpretation of Mitchell's remarks.)

Hohler's investigations fully supported the conclusions Ringle had reached. Ringle wrote: "Despite their dramatic claims, none of the activists appears to have any evidence that a link actually exists between football and wife-beating. Yet the concept has gained such credence that their campaign has rolled on anyway, unabated."[11]

Of the shelters and hot lines monitored on the Sunday of the twenty-seventh Super Bowl, some reported variations in the number of calls for help that day, and others did not. In Buffalo, whose team (and fans) had suffered a crushing defeat, there were no unusual increases.

Not surprisingly, Ringle's story generated a flurry of media activity. FAIR sent a letter to the *Washington Post* attacking the piece, claiming that it contained errors and quotes taken out of context. A subsequent column in the *Washington Post* mentioned that FAIR was unhappy with Ringle's reporting, but the paper otherwise supported the gist of his piece. And then there was more. The *American Journalism Review* did its own investigation of Ringle's reporting. Its conclusion was both that Ringle was correct in reporting that there was no solid data to support the 40 percent figure but that Ringle had twisted and used quotes selectively to support his thesis. Ringle's response? He stands by his story.[12]

Despite Ringle's exposé and the ensuing media attention, the Super Bowl Sunday "statistic" will be with us for a while, doing its divisive work. In the book *How to Make the World a Better Place for Women in Five Minutes a Day*, a comment under the heading "Did You Know?" informs readers that "Super Bowl Sunday is the most violent day of the year, with the highest reported number of domestic battering cases."[13] How a belief in that misandrist canard can make the world a better place for women is not explained.

How many women in the United States are brutalized by the men in their lives? Here is a cross section of the various answers:

> During the 9-year period, intimates committed 5.6 million violent victimizations against women, an annual average of 626,000. (U.S. Department of Justice, 1991)[14]

> Approximately 1.8 million women a year are physically assaulted by their husbands or boyfriends. *(Behind Closed Doors: Violence in the American Family)*[15]

> In the past year, 3 million women have been battered. (Senator Joseph Biden, 1991)[16]

> Total domestic violence, reported and unreported, affects as many as 4 million women a year. (Senator Biden's staff report, 1992)[17]

An estimated three to four million women are brutally beaten each year in the U.S. *(Feminist Dictionary)*[18]

Nearly 6 million wives will be abused by their husbands in any one year. *(Time* magazine, September 5, 1983)

More than 50 percent of all women will experience some form of violence from their spouses during marriage. More than one-third are battered repeatedly every year. (National Coalition against Domestic Violence)[19]

The estimates of the number of women beaten per second vary:

A woman is beaten every eighteen seconds. (Gail Dines, 1992)[20]

An American woman is beaten by her husband or boyfriend every 15 seconds. *(New York Times,* April 23, 1993)

Every twelve seconds, a woman in the United States is beaten by her husband or lover. *(Mirabella,* November 1993)[21]

A gong [will be] sounded every ten seconds for a woman being battered in the United States. ("The Clothesline Project," Johns Hopkins University)[22]

In the United States, every 7.4 seconds a woman is beaten by her husband. *(Annals of Emergency Medicine,* June 1989)

6.5 million women annually are assaulted by their partners . . . one every five seconds. (BrotherPeace, 1993)[23]

Sometimes the same source will give the figure both in millions of women and in seconds — without acknowledging that the two are inconsistent. Since there are 31,536,000 seconds in a year, the fifteen-second rate would amount to 2.1 million assaults. Three to four million would mean one every 7.9 or 10.5 seconds. This mistake is common:

According to the National Coalition against Domestic Violence, 3 million to 4 million women are battered every year in the U.S., one every 15 seconds. (Mary McGrory, *Washington Post,* October 20, 1987)

Domestic violence affects an estimated 4 to 5 million women a year. Every 15 seconds, an American woman is abused by her partner. *(Christian Science Monitor,* October 12, 1990)

There are 3 million to 4 million women beaten by husbands or lovers every year; that's one every 15 seconds. *(Chicago Tribune,* February 10, 1992)

Richard J. Gelles and Murray A. Straus are academic social scientists (from the University of Rhode Island and the University of New Hampshire, respectively) who have been studying domestic violence for more than twenty-five years. Their research is among the most respected and frequently cited by other social scientists, by police, by the FBI, and by the personnel in domestic violence agencies.

For a long time, Gelles and Straus were highly regarded by feminist activists for the pioneer work they had done in this once-neglected area. But they fell out of favor in the late 1970s because their findings were not informed by the "battery is caused by patriarchy" thesis. The fact that they were men was also held against them.

Gelles and Straus do find high levels of violence in many American families; but in both of their national surveys they found that women were just as likely to engage in it as men. They also found that siblings are the most violent of all.[24] They distinguish between minor violence, such as throwing objects, pushing, shoving, and slapping (no injuries, no serious intimidation), and severe violence, such as kicking, hitting or trying to hit with an object, hitting with fist, beating up, and threatening with gun or knife — actions that have a high probability of leading to injury or are accompanied by the serious threat of injury. The vast majority of family disputes involve minor violence rather than severe violence. In their 1985 Second National Family Violence Survey, sponsored by the National Institute of Mental Health, they found that 16 percent of couples were violent — the "Saturday Night Brawlers" (with the wife just as likely as the husband to slap, grab, shove, or throw things). In 3 to 4 percent of couples, there was at least one act of severe violence by the husband against the wife. But in their surveys they also found that "women assault their partners at about the same rate as men assault their partners. This applies to both minor and severe assaults."[25]

Gelles and Straus are careful to say that women are *far more likely* to be injured and to need medical care. But overall, the percentage of women who are injured seriously enough to need medical care is still relatively small compared with the inflated claims of the gender feminists and the politicians — fewer than 1 percent.[26] Murray Straus estimates that approximately 100,000 women per year are victims of the severe kinds of violence shown in the TV film *The Burning Bed.* That is a shockingly high number of victims, but it is far short of Senator Biden's claim, derived from feminist advocacy studies, that more than three or four million women are victims of "horrifying" violence.

Straus and Gelles have made other discoveries not appreciated by gender feminists. Among them is the finding that because of changing demographics and improved public awareness, there was a significant *decrease* in wife battery between 1975 and 1985.[27] Moreover, though they once reported that battery increased during pregnancy, they now say they were mistaken: "Data from the 1985 Second National Family Violence Survey indicate that the previously reported association between pregnancy and husband-to-wife violence is spurious, and is an artifact of the effect of another variable, age."[28]

Gelles and Straus consider domestic violence to be a serious national problem. They have for years been advocates for social, medical, and legal intervention to help battered women. All the same, according to their studies, more than 84 percent of families are not violent, and among the 16 percent who are, nearly half the violence (though not half the injuries) is perpetrated by women.

Journalists, activists, and even gender feminists make extensive use of Gelles and Straus's research. Some researchers manipulate their data to get shocking figures on abuse. If you overlook the researchers' distinction between minor and severe violence, if you never mention that women do just as much of the shoving, grabbing, pushing, and slapping, you arrive at very high figures for battery: three million, four million, six million, depending on how slack you are in what you count as battery.

The National Coalition against Domestic Violence gives shocking figures on abuse in their fundraising brochure: "More than 50 percent of all women will experience some form of violence from their spouses during marriage. More than one-third are battered repeatedly every year." We get the impression that one-third of all married women (18 million) are repeatedly being battered. Where did the coalition get these figures? Either they relied on their own special gender feminist sources or they creatively interpreted the FBI's, Department of Justice's, or Gelles and Straus's studies to suit their purposes. The latter is what the Commonwealth Fund, a New York State philanthropy concerned with public health, did in their Women's Health Survey.

In July 1993, the Commonwealth Fund released the results of a telephone survey of 2,500 women, designed and carried out by Louis Harris and Associates. The Commonwealth and Harris investigators took their questions directly from the Gelles and Straus survey and got the following results:

I would like you to tell me whether, in the past twelve months, your spouse or partner ever:

		YES	NO
1.	Insulted you or swore at you	34%	66%
2.	Stomped out of the room or house or yard	34	66
3.	Threatened to hit you or throw something at you	5	95
4.	Threw or smashed or hit or kicked something	11	89
5.	Threw something at you	3	97
6.	Pushed, grabbed, shoved, or slapped you	5	95
7.	Kicked, bit, or hit you with a fist or some other object	2	98
8.	Beat you up	0	100
9.	Choked you	0	99
10.	Threatened you with a knife or gun	0	100
11.	Used a knife or gun	0	100

Using these findings, and based on the assumption that there are approximately 55 million women married or living with someone as a couple, the Harris/Commonwealth survey concluded that as many as four million women a year were victims of physical assaults, and 20.7 million were verbally or emotionally abused by their partners.[29]

Newspapers around the country, including the *Wall Street Journal*, the *Washington Post*, the *Detroit News*, and the *San Francisco Chronicle*,[30] carried the bleak tidings that 37 percent of married women are emotionally abused and 3.9 million are physically assaulted every year.

No one mentioned that all the survey questions were taken from the   35
questionnaire that Gelles and Straus had used in their 1975 and 1985 Family Violence Surveys with very different results. Interpreted as Gelles and Straus interpret the data, the survey actually showed that domestic violence was still *decreasing*. The survey had found that 2–3 percent of the respondents had suffered what Gelles and Straus classify as "severe violence."

But the most interesting finding of all, and one entirely overlooked by the press, for it did not harmonize with the notes of alarm in the Harris/Commonwealth press releases, was the response the poll received to questions 8 through 11, about the most severe forms of violence. Gelles and Straus had estimated that these things happen to fewer than 1 percent of women. According to the survey sample, the percentage of women who had these experiences was virtually *zero:* all respondents answered "no" to all the questions on severe violence.[31] This finding does not, of course, mean that no one was brutally attacked. But it does suggest that severe violence is relatively rare.[32]

So where did the four million figure for physical assault come from? And the twenty million for psychological abuse? Clearly the interpreters of the Harris/Commonwealth poll data were operating with a much wider conception of "abuse" than Gelles and Straus. Looking at the "survey instrument," we find that they had indeed opened the door wide to the alarmist conclusions they disseminated. For some of the answers that Gelles and Straus counted as minor and not indicative of abuse, the Harris/Commonwealth people took seriously. For example, the questionnaire asked "whether in the past 12 months your partner ever: 1) insulted you or swore at you; or 2) stomped out of the room or house or yard." Thirty-four percent of women answered "yes" to these questions, and all were classified as victims of "emotional and verbal abuse." Had men been included, one wonders whether they would not have proved to be equally "abused."

To arrive at the figure of four million for *physical* abuse, the survey used the simple expedient of ignoring the distinction between minor and severe violent acts, counting all acts of violence as acts of abuse. Five percent of the women they spoke to said they had been "pushed, grabbed, shoved, or slapped"; they were all classified as victims of domestic violence and added in to get a projection of four million victims nationwide. No effort was made to find out if the aggression was mutual or whether it was physically harmful or seriously intimidating. If a couple has a fight, and she stomps out of the room (or yard), and he grabs her arm, this would count as a violent physical assault on her.[33]

If the survey's *data* can be trusted and we interpret them in the careful and reasonable way that Gelles and Straus recommend, then we may learn that the worst kinds of abuse may be abating. That is still nothing to celebrate. If up to 3 percent of American women who are married or living with partners are at risk of serious abuse, that would amount to 1.6 million women. If the higher figures Gelles and Straus found are right (3–4 percent), then the number of women at risk is 2.2 million. Both numbers are tragically large and speak of an urgent need for prevention and for shelters and other help for the victims.

But how does this help the gender feminist in her misandrist campaign? She needs to find that a large proportion of men are batterers; a meager 3 or 4 percent will not serve her purpose. As for journalists and the newscasters, their interests too often lie in giving a sensational rather than an accurate picture of gender violence, and they tend to credit the advocacy sources. Better four million or five than one or two. Evidently, *Time* magazine felt six was even better. And all the better, too, if the media's readers and viewers get the impression that the inflated figures refer not to slaps, shoves, or pushes but to brutal, terrifying, life-threatening assaults.

Gender feminists are committed to the doctrine that the vast majority of batterers or rapists are not fringe characters but men whom society regards as normal — sports fans, former fraternity brothers, pillars of the community. For these "normal" men, women are not so much persons as "objects." In the gender feminist view, once a woman is "objectified" and therefore no longer human, battering her is simply the next logical step.

Just how "normal" are men who batter? Are they ordinary husbands? These are legitimate questions, but the road to reasonable answers is all too often blocked by feminist dogmas. By setting aside the feminist roadblocks, we can discern some important truths.

Are the batterers really just your average Joe? If the state of Massachusetts is typical — *the large majority of batterers are criminals.* Andrew Klein, chief probation officer in Quincy Court, Quincy, Massachusetts, studied repeat batterers for the Ford Foundation. In his final report he said, "When Massachusetts computerized its civil restraining order files in 1992, linking them with the state's criminal offender record data base, it found that almost 80 percent of the first 8,500 male subjects of restraining orders had prior criminal records in the state."[34]

Many of the batterers' records were for offenses like drunk driving and drugs, but almost half had prior histories of violence against male

40

and female victims. Klein continues: "In other words, these men were generally violent, *assaulting other males as well as female intimates*. The average number of prior crimes against persons complaints was 4.5" (my emphasis).[35]

The gender feminist believes that the average man is a potential batterer because that is how men are "socialized" in the patriarchy. But ideology aside, there are indications that those who batter are *not* average. Talk of a generalized misogyny may be preventing us from seeing and facing the particular effect on women and men of the large criminal element in our society.

Massachusetts may not be typical. Still, the Massachusetts batterers' profile suggests it is not helpful to think of battery exclusively in terms of misogyny, patriarchy, or gender bias. We need to understand why the number of sociopaths in our society, especially violent male sociopaths, is so high.

My prediction is that Mr. Klein's important findings will be ignored. What use is it to gender warriors like Marilyn French and Gloria Steinem to show that violent *criminals* tend to abuse their wives and girlfriends and other males as well? Their primary concern is to persuade the public that the so-called normal man is a morally defective human being who gets off on hurting women.

There are other important studies that could help shed light on battering and could ultimately help many victims who are ignored because their batterers do not fit the gender feminist stereotype.[36] It turns out that lesbians may be battering each other at the same rate as heterosexuals. Several books and articles document the problem of violence among lesbians.[37] Professor Claire Renzetti, a professor of sociology at St. Joseph's University in Philadelphia, has studied the problem of lesbian violence and summarized the findings in *Violent Betrayal: Partner Abuse in Lesbian Relationships:*

> It appears that violence in lesbian relationships occurs at about the same frequency as violence in heterosexual relationships. The abuse may . . . [range] from verbal threats and insults to stabbings and shootings. Indeed, batterers display a terrifying ingenuity in their selection of abusive tactics, frequently tailoring the abuse to the specific vulnerabilities of their partners.[38]

Once again, it appears that battery may have very little to do with patriarchy or gender bias. Where noncriminals are involved, battery seems to be a pathology of intimacy, as frequent among gays as among straight people.

Battery and rape research is the very stuff of gender feminist advocacy. Researchers who try to pursue their investigations in a nonpolitical way are often subject to attack by the advocates. Murray Straus reports that he and some of his co-workers "became the object of bitter scholarly and personal attacks, including threats and attempts at intimidation."[39] In the late seventies and early eighties his scholarly presentations were sometimes obstructed by booing, shouting, or picketing. When he was being considered for offices in scientific societies, he was labeled an antifeminist.

In the November 1993 issue of *Mirabella*, Richard Gelles and Murray Straus were accused of using "sexist 'reasoning'" and of producing works of "pop 'scholarship.'" The article offers no evidence for these judgments.[40] In 1992 a rumor was circulated that Murray Straus had beaten his wife and sexually harassed his students. Straus fought back as best he could and in one instance was able to elicit a written apology from a domestic violence activist.

Richard Gelles claims that whenever male researchers question exaggerated findings on domestic battery, it is never long before rumors begin circulating that he is himself a batterer. For female skeptics, however, the situation appears to be equally intimidating. When Suzanne K. Steinmetz, a co-investigator in the First National Family Violence Survey, was being considered for promotion, the feminists launched a letter-writing campaign urging that it be denied. She also received calls threatening her and her family, and there was a bomb threat at a conference where she spoke. As long as researchers are thus intimidated, we will probably remain in the dark about the true dimension of a problem that affects the lives of millions of American women.

Another factor limiting the prospects for sound research in this area is the absence of a rigorous system of review. In most fields, when a well-known study is flawed, critics can make a name for themselves by showing up its defects. This process keeps researchers honest. However, in today's environment for feminist research, the higher your figures for abuse, the more likely you'll reap rewards, regardless of your methodology. You'll be mentioned in feminist encyclopedias, dictionaries, "fact sheets," and textbooks. Your research will be widely publicized; Ellen Goodman, Anna Quindlen, and Judy Mann will put you in their columns. Fashion magazines will reproduce your charts and graphs. You may be quoted by Pat Schroeder, Joseph Biden, and surgeons general from both parties. Senator Kennedy's office will call. You should expect to be invited to give expert testimony before Congress. As for would-be critics, they're in for grief.

Notes

1. Gloria Steinem, *Revolution from Within: A Book of Self-Esteem* (Boston: Little, Brown, 1992), pp. 259–61.
2. A brief account of the hoax is also to be found in the preface to *Who Stole Feminism?*
3. Ken Ringle, "Wife-Beating Claims Called Out of Bounds," *Washington Post*, January 31, 1993, p. A1.

4. Reported in Jean Cobb, "A Super Bowl — Battered Women Link?" *American Journalism Review,* May 1993, p. 35.

5. *Boston Globe,* January 30, 1993, p. 13.

6. Quoted in "Football's Day of Dread," *Wall Street Journal,* February 5, 1993, p. A10.

7. Ibid.

8. Ringle, "Wife-Beating Claims."

9. Ibid.

10. Bob Hohler, "Super Bowl Gaffe," *Boston Globe,* February 2, 1993, p. 17.

11. Ringle, "Wife-Beating Claims."

12. Joann Byrd, "Violence at Home," *Washington Post,* February 28, 1993; op ed, p. C6; Jean Cobb, "A Super Bowl — Battered Women Link?" *American Journalism Review,* May 1993, pp. 33–38.

13. Donna Jackson, *How to Make the World a Better Place for Women in Five Minutes a Day* (New York: Hyperion, 1992), p. 62. Ms. Jackson is editor-at-large for *New Woman* magazine.

14. "Female Victims of Violent Crime," by Caroline Wolf Harlow (Washington, D.C.: U.S. Department of Justice, 1991), p. 1.

15. Murray Straus, Richard Gelles, and Suzanne Steinmetz, *Behind Closed Doors: Violence in the American Family* (New York: Anchor Books, 1980).

16. *Congressional Quarterly Almanac,* 1991, p. 294.

17. Senator Joseph Biden, chairman, Senate Judiciary Committee, *Violence against Women: A Week in the Life of America* (U.S. Government Printing Office, 1992), p. 3.

18. Cheris Kramarae and Paula A. Treichler, eds., *A Feminist Dictionary* (London: Pandora Press, 1985), p. 66.

19. Fundraising brochure sent out by the National Coalition against Domestic Violence, Washington, D.C., 1993. The headline of the brochure is "Every 15 Seconds a Woman is Battered in This Country." That would add up to a total of 2.1 million incidents.

20. Poster, University of Massachusetts, Amherst, advertising lecture appearance of Gail Dines, October 13, 1992: "Images of Violence against Women."

21. Marilyn French also gives this figure, "In the United States, a man beats a woman every twelve seconds," *The War against Women* (New York: Simon & Schuster, 1992), p. 187.

22. The Clothesline Project is a traveling exhibit on domestic violence. It was on display at Johns Hopkins University on October 22, 1993. They did sound a gong at ten-second intervals from 10:00 A.M. to 5:00 P.M.

23. BrotherPeace is a men's antiviolence group in St. Cloud, Minnesota. The figures are from their fact sheet, called "Statistics for Men."

24. Gelles and Straus found that two-thirds of teenagers physically attack a sister or brother at least once in the course of a year, and in more than one-third of these cases, the attack involves severe forms of violence such as kicking, punching, biting, choking, and attacking with knives and guns. "These incredible rates of intrafamily violence by teenagers make the high rates of violence by their parents seem modest by comparison," in Richard Gelles and Murray Straus, *Physical Violence in American Families* (New Brunswick, N.J.: Transaction Publishers, 1990), p. 107.

25. Ibid., p. 162.

26. Ibid., chap. 5.

27. The population is aging. Men and women marry at a later age and have fewer children. Such changes might explain a drop in the percentage of women who are abused. See Gelles and Straus, *Intimate Violence: The Causes and Consequences of Abuse in the American Family* (New York: Touchstone, 1989), pp. 111 and 112.

28. Gelles and Straus, *Physical Violence in American Families,* p. 285.

29. Commonwealth Fund, survey of women's health (New York: Commonwealth Fund, July 14, 1993), p. 8.

30. Ibid. Clippings from newspapers around the country are included in the survey results.

31. This is consistent with Gelles and Straus's figure of less than 1 percent for pathological

abuse. The Commonwealth sample had a margin of error of 2 percent either way. There could be other explanations: as Gelles and Straus say, the women who are most brutally and dangerously abused would probably be afraid to talk about it. But if there are several million out there, surely the Harris poll would have found at least one.

32. Incidentally, rape crisis feminist researchers like Diana Russell, author of *Rape in Marriage* (Bloomington: Indiana University Press, 1990), have declared an epidemic of marital rape. But when the Harris poll asked, "In the past year, did your partner ever try to, or force you to, have sexual relations by using physical force, or not?" 100 percent of the more than 2,500 respondents said "not." Here again one may be sure that marital rape is out there, but this poll suggests it's rarer than Russell says. Using Russell as their source, the feminist compendium "WAC Stats: The Facts about Women" (New York: Women's Action Coalition, 1993) says that "more than one in every seven women who have ever been married have been raped in marriage" (p. 49).

33. Bias reappears in another Harris/Commonwealth finding that 40 percent of American women are severely depressed. As it happened, Harris and Associates had appointed Lois Hoeffler, a gender feminist advocate, as principal investigator in charge of the survey of women's health. For an account of her views and her participation in a poll that resulted in sensational and depressing conclusions, see chapter 11 of *Who Stole Feminism?*

34. Andrew Klein, "Spousal/Partner Assault: A Protocol for the Sentencing and Supervision of Offenders" (Qunicy, Mass.: Quincy Court, 1993), p. 5.

35. Ibid., p. 7.

36. See, for example, Kerry Lobel, ed., *Naming the Violence: Speaking Out about Lesbian Violence* (Seattle, Wash.: Seal Press, 1986).

37. Claire Renzetti, *Violent Betrayal: Partner Abuse in Lesbian Relationships* (Newbury Park, Calif.: Sage Press, 1992). Claudia Card, "Lesbian Battering," in the American Philosophical Association's *Newsletter on Feminism and Philosophy*, November 1988, p. 3.

38. Renzetti, *Violent Betrayal*, p. 115.

39. Gelles and Straus, in *Physical Violence in American Families*, p. 11.

40. *Mirabella*, November 1993, p. 78. In its June 1993 issue, *Mirabella* did its own SLOP survey on women's health and found that 31 percent of their respondents were beaten by their husbands or boyfriends. Eighteen percent were beaten by more than one person. The survey was cosponsored by the Center for Women's Policy Studies.

PREPARING FOR DISCUSSION

1. In the first part of her essay, Sommers recounts the "Super Bowl hoax of January 1993." What point does she wish to illustrate about the "gender feminism's" use of statistics and studies? Does the fact that the story about the rise in violence against women on Super Bowl Sunday proved to be a hoax make Sommers believe that domestic violence is *not* a problem in America?

2. Toward the end of the selection, Sommers mentions a recent study that shows that violence within lesbian relationships occurs at the same frequency as in heterosexual relationships. Why does she cite this particular study? Does it disprove the picture of violence against women offered by the "gender feminists"?

3. Sommers seems to accept the result of the Harris poll on domestic violence against women without questioning its results. What reason does she have to believe that the responses of women were truthful? Would the average married woman be more or less likely to say that she had been insulted by her husband? Would the average married woman be more or less likely to say that she

had been beaten by her husband? Are your predictions confirmed by the poll findings?

4. Unlike the feminists Andrea Dworkin and Gloria Steinem, Sommers rejects the idea that "battery is caused by patriarchy." How does her statistical evidence lead to her conclusion? Does she offer any theoretical reasons for her position?

5. In paragraph 40, Sommers questions how the distorted use of statistical data helps "the gender feminist in her misandrist campaign." What does the term *misandrist* mean, and what does Sommers's use of it imply about her attitude toward gender feminism? From her language in this brief passage, would you say that Sommers is herself a feminist?

FROM READING TO WRITING

6. While Sommers sees the use of "noble lies" as a particularly bad practice for feminism, other feminists believe that the end — in this case, greater attention to the problem of domestic violence — will ultimately justify the means used in attaining it. With which of these two views do you tend to agree? Write an essay in which you set forth your position. Be sure to offer reasons for your belief and, if possible, some examples from your experience that support your reasoning.

7. Try to locate in popular magazines some additional statistics about the abuse of women. If the writer cites a study in support of the statistics, attempt to locate that study. After reading the study, write an essay in which you describe how the findings were represented in the magazine article.

6

American Speech

FREEDOM · CENSORSHIP · CORRECTNESS

Americans pride themselves on their right to say whatever they want — a right they feel is guaranteed in the Bill of Rights. In recent years, however, the limits of this right have been continually tested and contested, as various groups grapple with that part of the First Amendment that prohibits Congress from making any laws "abridging the freedom of speech, or of the press." Throughout the nation's history the meaning of those few words has been hotly debated, but perhaps never before has the debate taken so many twists and represented so many different interests as it does today.

Some of the most publicized challenges to free speech have their origins in concerns that have, somewhat pejoratively, been dubbed "political correctness." Such concerns have dominated university discourse since the mid-1980s and have spilled over into the workplace and the popular media. In "The Word Police," one of America's most influential book reviewers, Michiko Kakutani, takes a lighthearted but tough-minded look at the "prohibition of certain words, phrases, and ideas . . . advanced in the cause of building a brave new world free of racism and hate."

Yet where do we draw the line between inoffensive expression and harmful epithets? As Native American activist Ward Churchill argues, if people think it's perfectly fine to call a football team the Washington Redskins, would they also approve of "an NFL team called 'Niggers' to honor Afro-Americans"? And what about, he asks, the "San Diego Spics," the "Pittsburgh Polaks," or the "Kansas City Kikes"? In "Crimes against

Humanity," Churchill reminds his readers that mass-media images of American Indians cause "real pain and real suffering to real people."

With the April 1995 bombing in Oklahoma City, the possible consequences of hate speech were horribly brought to public attention as people debated whether the excesses of talk radio could be blamed for ratcheting up the level of hostility in American society. Even prior to the bombing, some people had been worrying about the effects of angry call-in radio programs, as legal scholar and civil rights activist Patricia J. Williams indicates in her essay "Hate Radio." As she sampled a range of programs, Williams was struck by the unifying theme of intolerance — "not merely the specific intolerance on such hot topics as race and gender, but a much more general contempt for the world, a verbal stoning of anything different." In public addresses immediately after the Oklahoma City bombing, President Clinton (naming no names) worried about the "promoters of paranoia" who filled the airwaves with messages of "division and hatred."

Yet what might happen if we seriously curtail sexist, racist, prejudicial, and incendiary speech? Such speech must be strenuously protected, maintains the political journalist Jonathan Rauch, or the very people most injured by prejudice will suffer most. As Rauch puts it in his essay "In Defense of Prejudice": "An enlightened and efficient intellectual regime lets a million prejudices bloom, including many that you and I may regard as hateful or grotesque." For those who believe that incendiary forms of speech should go unprotected because they are equivalent to shouting "Fire!" in a crowded theater, the prominent criminal lawyer Alan M. Dershowitz has a discomforting answer. In "Shouting 'Fire!'" Dershowitz claims that this venerable judicial analogy, though "generally invoked, often with self-satisfaction, as an absolute argument-stopper," is seriously flawed.

Another major challenge to free speech has come from women's groups currently waging a war against pornography. Two of the country's leading antipornography figures are the activist Andrea Dworkin (see p. 390) and the legal theorist Catharine MacKinnon, who argues that pornography is *actual* (not representational) violence against women and therefore should not be protected under the free speech clause of the First Amendment. (Unfortunately, we were unable to procure permission to reprint a portion of Professor MacKinnon's important work on this issue; her position is eloquently stated in her 1995 book, *Only Words*.)

Not all feminists, however, endorse the antipornography agenda. In fact, a number of highly influential feminists vehemently disagree with the cause, arguing, as Nadine Strossen does in "Sexual Speech and the Law," that the censorship of pornography could jeopardize all free-speech precedents and eventually damage many liberal causes, including feminism and gay rights. As the first woman president of the American Civil Liberties Union, Strossen is clear on this point: "Make no mistake," she says, "if accepted, the feminist procensorship analysis would lead inevitably to the suppression of far more than pornography."

It is important to remember that the text of the First Amendment does not begin with the freedom-of-speech clause. It begins: "Congress shall make no law respecting an establishment of religion, or prohibiting the free exercise thereof." In "What to Do about the First Amendment," the controversial legal theorist and Supreme Court nominee Robert Bork discusses both parts of the amendment and reflects on their relationship to each other. His overview of the amendment provocatively covers all of the separate issues introduced in this chapter.

MICHIKO KAKUTANI

The Word Police

———————◇———————

Since the mid-1980s, academics, writers, and editors whose ideas have
been associated with the term "political correctness" have sought to pu-
rify American culture of language that gives offense to women, minorities, homosexuals, or special-interest groups like the disabled. These
efforts have influenced the subjects that are taught in schools and universities, the laws that we live under, and the language that we speak. In
response to the ascendancy of the political-correctness agenda, many
people have begun to wonder whether the fight for greater sensitivity
has begun to curtail our constitutional right to free speech.

In the following selection, journalist and cultural critic Michiko
Kakutani questions efforts by some of us to "cleanse" our native tongue
of its inherent prejudices. After graduating from Yale, Kakutani went to
work as a reporter for the *Washington Post* and later as a staff writer for
Time. In 1979, she joined the cultural news department of the *New York
Times* and has been the paper's principal book reviewer since 1983. This
selection first appeared in the *New York Times* in 1993.

SELECTED PUBLICATIONS: Kakutani's articles and reviews appear regularly in the *New York Times*.

———————————

This month's inaugural festivities, with their celebration, in Maya An-
gelou's words, of "humankind" — "the Asian, the Hispanic, the Jew/
The African, the Native American, the Sioux,/ The Catholic, the Muslim,
the French, the Greek/ The Irish, the Rabbi, the Priest, the Sheik,/ The
Gay, the Straight, the Preacher,/ The privileged, the homeless, the
Teacher" — constituted a kind of official embrace of multiculturalism
and a new politics of inclusion.

The mood of political correctness, however, has already made firm inroads into popular culture. Washington boasts a store called Politically
Correct that sells pro-whale, anti-meat, ban-the-bomb T-shirts, bumper
stickers and buttons, as well as a local cable television show called "Politically Correct Cooking" that features interviews in the kitchen with representatives from groups like People for the Ethical Treatment of Animals.

The Coppertone suntan lotion people are planning to give their longtime cover girl, Little Miss (Ms.?) Coppertone, a male equivalent, Little
Mr. Coppertone. And even Superman (Superperson?) is rumored to be
returning this spring, reincarnated as four ethnically diverse clones: an
African-American, an Asian, a Caucasian and a Latino.

Nowhere is this P.C. mood more striking than in the increasingly noisy debate over language that has moved from university campuses to the country at large — a development that both underscores Americans' puritanical zeal for reform and their unwavering faith in the talismanic power of words.

Certainly no decent person can quarrel with the underlying impulse behind political correctness: a vision of a more just, inclusive society in which racism, sexism and prejudice of all sorts have been erased. But the methods and fervor of the self-appointed language police can lead to a rigid orthodoxy — and unintentional self-parody — opening the movement to the scorn of conservative opponents and the mockery of cartoonists and late-night television hosts.

It's hard to imagine women earning points for political correctness by saying "ovarimony" instead of "testimony" — as one participant at the recent Modern Language Association convention was overheard to suggest. It's equally hard to imagine people wanting to flaunt their lack of prejudice by giving up such words and phrases as "bull market," "kaiser roll," "Lazy Susan," and "charley horse."

Several books on bias-free language have already appeared, and the 1991 edition of the *Random House Webster's College Dictionary* boasts an appendix titled "Avoiding Sexist Language." The dictionary also includes such linguistic mutations as "womyn" (women, "used as an alternative spelling to avoid the suggestion of sexism perceived in the sequence m-e-n") and "waitron" (a gender-blind term for waiter or waitress).

Many of these dictionaries and guides not only warn the reader against offensive racial and sexual slurs, but also try to establish and enforce a whole new set of usage rules. Take, for instance, *The Bias-Free Word Finder, a Dictionary of Nondiscriminatory Language* by Rosalie Maggio (Beacon Press) — a volume often indistinguishable, in its meticulous solemnity, from the tongue-in-cheek *Official Politically Correct Dictionary and Handbook* put out last year by Henry Beard and Christopher Cerf (Villard Books). Ms. Maggio's book supplies the reader intent on using kinder, gentler language with writing guidelines as well as a detailed listing of more than 5,000 "biased words and phrases."

Whom are these guidelines for? Somehow one has a tough time picturing them replacing *Fowler's Modern English Usage* in the classroom, or being adopted by the average man (sorry, individual) in the street.

The "pseudogeneric 'he,'" we learn from Ms. Maggio, is to be avoided like the plague, as is the use of the word "man" to refer to humanity. "Fellow," "king," "lord" and "master" are bad because they're "male-oriented words," and "king," "lord" and "master" are especially bad because they're also "hierarchical, dominator society terms." The politically correct lion becomes the "monarch of the jungle," new-age children play "someone on the top of the heap," and the "Mona Lisa" goes down in history as Leonardo's "acme of perfection."

As for the word "black," Ms. Maggio says it should be excised from terms with a negative spin: she recommends substituting words like "mouse" for "black eye," "ostracize" for "blackball," "payola" for "blackmail" and "outcast" for "black sheep." Clearly, some of these substitutions work better than others: somehow the "sinister humor" of Kurt Vonnegut or *Saturday Night Live* doesn't quite make it; nor does the "denouncing" of the Hollywood 10.

For the dedicated user of politically correct language, all these rules can make for some messy moral dilemmas. Whereas "battered wife" is a gender-biased term, the gender-free term "battered spouse," Ms. Maggio notes, incorrectly implies "that men and women are equally battered."

On one hand, say Francine Wattman Frank and Paula A. Treichler in their book *Language, Gender, and Professional Writing* (Modern Language Association), "he or she" is an appropriate construction for talking about an individual (like a jockey, say) who belongs to a profession that's predominantly male — it's a way of emphasizing "that such occupations are not barred to women or that women's concerns need to be kept in mind." On the other hand, they add, using masculine pronouns rhetorically can underscore ongoing male dominance in those fields, implying the need for change.

And what about the speech codes adopted by some universities in recent years? Although they were designed to prohibit students from uttering sexist and racist slurs, they would extend, by logic, to blacks who want to use the word "nigger" to strip the term of its racist connotations, or homosexuals who want to use the word "queer" to reclaim it from bigots.

In her book, Ms. Maggio recommends applying bias-free usage retroactively: she suggests paraphrasing politically incorrect quotations, or replacing "the sexist words or phrases with ellipsis dots and/or bracketed substitutes," or using "*sic*" "to show that the sexist words come from the original quotation and to call attention to the fact that they are incorrect."

Which leads the skeptical reader of *The Bias-Free Word Finder* to wonder whether "All the King's Men" should be retitled "All the Ruler's People"; "Pet Semetary," "Animal Companion Graves"; "Birdman of Alcatraz," "Birdperson of Alcatraz"; and "The Iceman Cometh," "The Ice Route Driver Cometh"?

Will making such changes remove the prejudice in people's minds? Should we really spend time trying to come up with non-male-based alternatives to "Midas touch," "Achilles' heel," and "Montezuma's revenge"? Will tossing out Santa Claus — whom Ms. Maggio accuses of reinforcing "the cultural male-as-norm system" — in favor of Belfana, his Italian female alter ego, truly help banish sexism? Can the avoidance of "violent expressions and metaphors" like "kill two birds with one stone," "sock it to 'em" or "kick an idea around" actually promote a more harmonious world?

The point isn't that the excesses of the word police are comical. The point is that their intolerance (in the name of tolerance) has disturbing implications. In the first place, getting upset by phrases like "bullish on

15

America" or "the City of Brotherly Love" tends to distract attention from the real problems of prejudice and injustice that exist in society at large, turning them into mere questions of semantics. Indeed, the emphasis currently put on politically correct usage has uncanny parallels with the academic movement of deconstruction — a method of textual analysis that focuses on language and linguistic pyrotechnics — which has become firmly established on university campuses.

In both cases, attention is focused on surfaces, on words and metaphors; in both cases, signs and symbols are accorded more importance than content. Hence, the attempt by some radical advocates to remove *The Adventures of Huckleberry Finn* from curriculums on the grounds that Twain's use of the word "nigger" makes the book a racist text — never mind the fact that this American classic (written in 1884) depicts the spiritual kinship achieved between a white boy and a runaway slave, never mind the fact that the "nigger" Jim emerges as the novel's most honorable, decent character.

Ironically enough, the P.C. movement's obsession with language is accompanied by a strange Orwellian willingness to warp the meaning of words by placing them under a high-powered ideological lens. For instance, the *Dictionary of Cautionary Words and Phrases* — a pamphlet issued by the University of Missouri's Multicultural Management Program to help turn "today's journalists into tomorrow's multicultural newsroom managers" — warns that using the word "articulate" to describe members of a minority group can suggest the opposite, "that 'those people' are not considered well educated, articulate and the like." 20

The pamphlet patronizes minority groups, by cautioning the reader against using the words "lazy" and "burly" to describe any member of such groups; and it issues a similar warning against using words like "gorgeous" and "petite" to describe women.

As euphemism proliferates with the rise of political correctness, there is a spread of the sort of sloppy, abstract language that Orwell said is "designed to make lies sound truthful and murder respectable, and to give an appearance of solidity to pure wind." "Fat" becomes "big boned" or "differently sized"; "stupid" becomes "exceptional"; "stoned" becomes "chemically inconvenienced."

Wait a minute here! Aren't such phrases eerily reminiscent of the euphemisms coined by the government during Vietnam and Watergate? Remember how the military used to speak of "pacification," or how President Richard M. Nixon's press secretary, Ronald L. Ziegler, tried to get away with calling a lie an "inoperative statement"?

Calling the homeless "the underhoused" doesn't give them a place to live; calling the poor "the economically marginalized" doesn't help them pay the bills. Rather, by playing down their plight, such language might even make it easier to shrug off the seriousness of their situation.

Instead of allowing free discussion and debate to occur, many gung-ho advocates of politically correct language seem to think that simple 25 suppression of a word or concept will magically make the problem disappear. In the *Bias-Free Word Finder*, Ms. Maggio entreats the reader not to perpetuate the negative stereotype of Eve. "Be extremely cautious in referring to the biblical Eve," she writes; "this story has profoundly contributed to negative attitudes toward women throughout history, largely because of misogynistic and patriarchal interpretations that labeled her evil, inferior, and seductive."

The story of Bluebeard, the rake (whoops! — the libertine) who killed his seven wives, she says, is also to be avoided, as is the biblical story of Jezebel. Of Jesus Christ, Ms. Maggio writes: "There have been few individuals in history as completely androgynous as Christ, and it does his message a disservice to overinsist on his maleness." She doesn't give the reader any hints on how this might be accomplished; presumably, one is supposed to avoid describing him as the Son of God.

Of course the P.C. police aren't the only ones who want to proscribe what people should say or give them guidelines for how they may use an idea; Jesse Helms and his supporters are up to exactly the same thing when they propose to patrol the boundaries of the permissible in art. In each case, the would-be censor aspires to suppress what he or she finds distasteful — all, of course, in the name of the public good.

In the case of the politically correct, the prohibition of certain words, phrases and ideas is advanced in the cause of building a brave new world free of racism and hate, but this vision of harmony clashes with the very ideals of diversity and inclusion that the multicultural movement holds dear, and it's purchased at the cost of freedom of expression and freedom of speech.

In fact, the utopian world envisioned by the language police would be bought at the expense of the ideals of individualism and democracy articulated in the "The [*sic*] Gettysburg Address": "Fourscore and seven years ago our fathers brought forth on this continent a new nation, conceived in liberty and dedicated to the proposition that all men are created equal."

Of course, the P.C. police have already found Lincoln's words hopelessly "phallocentric." No doubt they would rewrite the passage: "Fourscore and seven years ago our foremothers and forefathers brought forth on this continent a new nation, formulated with liberty, and dedicated to the proposition that all humankind is created equal." 30

PREPARING FOR DISCUSSION

1. Kakutani finds evidence of politically correct language in any number of places. Where does she find it to be most prominent? What negative consequences does she believe this language can lead to if not contained within reasonable limits? What might those reasonable limits be for Kakutani?

2. At several points in the essay, the author corrects herself in print with the use of parentheses and the P.C. term following a word like *sorry* or *whoops*. What

is her point in employing this method of self-correction? Why didn't she simply use the "correct" term in the first place?

3. Kakutani dwells on Mark Twain's use of the racist epithet *nigger* in *The Adventures of Huckleberry Finn* in paragraph 19. Even if, as Kakutani points out, "nigger" Jim turns out to be the most decent character in the novel, does this mean that the epithet is not demeaning? If great literature is universal and time-less, as Kakutani implies, then doesn't Jim remain a "nigger" everywhere and for eternity unless the epithet is deleted?

4. In paragraph 24, the author points to the word *underhoused* and asks what good this euphemism does the "homeless." Yet, in the early 1980s *homeless*, too, was a euphemism for "destitute" and even less neutral terms like "bum." Why does Kakutani believe that it is all right to use one euphemism and not another? Who is likely to have used a term like *underhoused?*

5. In paragraph 29, the author claims that the "utopian world envisioned by the language police would be bought at the expense of the ideals of individualism and democracy articulated in 'The Gettysburg Address.'" Consider her P.C. paraphrase of the opening of Lincoln's speech (paragraph 30). Has the meaning of the original changed radically? What has been lost other than the eloquence of the original?

FROM READING TO WRITING

6. Consider a hypothetical situation in which you have the choice between using P.C. language that distorts the truth in order not to hurt another person's feelings and using language that is accurate or more direct but might insult people. Which path would you choose? Write an essay explaining your decision and the reasoning that led to it.

7. Find an example of P.C. language in a major newspaper or magazine. Rewrite the sentences or paragraphs without the P.C. terms. Has the original message changed significantly? Write an essay in which you consider why the author might have chosen to use these particular words instead of other, less "correct" ones.

WARD CHURCHILL

Crimes against Humanity

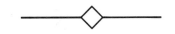

How do the terms we use to describe minority groups affect these same groups? Does the proliferation of pejorative epithets in popular culture lead to greater discrimination against the groups to which these labels refer? To answer these questions we might look at the situation of America's original peoples, who have long been the victims of such abu-sive labeling. In recent years, native peoples have begun to contest the use of such labels by sports franchises like the Kansas City Chiefs and the Washington Redskins. In the following selection, Native American rights activist and professor Ward Churchill takes on the traditional view that the use of Native American epithets to name sports franchises and commercial products is all in good fun. In doing so, he draws a chilling analogy between this practice and anti-Semitic propaganda in pre–World War II Nazi Germany.

Churchill is coordinator and associate professor of American Indian studies and communications at the University of Colorado at Boulder. A tribal member of the Keetoowah Band of Cherokee Indians, he codirects the Colorado chapter of the American Indian Movement. He is also a regular contributor to *Z Magazine* — where this selection first appeared in 1993 — and editor of the journal *New Studies on the Left*.

SELECTED PUBLICATIONS: *Fantasies of the Master Race: Literature, Cinema, and the Colonization of American Indians* (1992); *Struggle for the Land: Indigenous Resistance to Genocide, Ecocide, and Expropriation in Contemporary North America* (1993); *Indians Are Us? Culture and Genocide in Native North America* (1993); *Since the Predator Came* (1995); *Draconian Measures: A History of FBI Political Repression* (1995).

During the past couple of seasons, there has been an increasing wave of controversy regarding the names of professional sports teams like the Atlanta Braves, Cleveland Indians, Washington Redskins, and Kansas City Chiefs. The issue extends to the names of college teams like Florida State University Seminoles, University of Illinois Fighting Illini, and so on, right on down to high school outfits like the Lamar (Colorado) Savages. Also involved have been team adoption of mascots, replete with feathers, buckskins, beads, spears, and "warpaint" (some fans have opted to adorn themselves in the same fashion), and nifty little "pep" gestures like the "Indian Chant" and "Tomahawk Chop."

A substantial number of American Indians have protested that use of native names, images, and symbols as sports team mascots and the like is, by definition, a virulently racist practice. Given the historical relationship between Indians and non-Indians during what has been called the Conquest of America, American Indian Movement leader (and American Indian Anti-Defamation Council founder) Russell Means has compared the practice to contemporary Germans naming their soccer teams the "Jews," "Hebrews," and "Yids," while adorning their uniforms with grotesque caricatures of Jewish faces taken from the Nazis' anti-Semitic propaganda of the 1930s. Numerous demonstrations have occurred in conjunction with games — most notably during the November 15, 1992, matchup between the Chiefs and Redskins in Kansas City — by angry Indians and their supporters.

In response, a number of players — especially African Americans and other minority athletes — have been trotted out by professional team owners like Ted Turner, as well as university and public school officials, to announce that they mean not to insult but to honor native people. They have been joined by the television networks and most major newspapers, all of which have editorialized that Indian discomfort with the situation is "no big deal," insisting that the whole thing is just "good, clean fun." The country needs more such fun, they've argued, and "a few disgruntled Native Americans" have no right to undermine the nation's enjoyment of its leisure time by complaining. This is especially the case, some have argued, "in hard times like these." It has even been contended that Indian outrage at being systematically degraded — rather than the degradation itself — creates "a serious barrier to the sort of intergroup communication so necessary in a multicultural society such as ours."

Okay, let's communicate. We are frankly dubious that those advancing such positions really believe their own rhetoric, but, just for the sake of argument, let's accept the premise that they are sincere. If what they say is true, then isn't it time we spread such "inoffensiveness" and "good cheer" around among *all* groups so that *everybody* can participate *equally* in fostering the round of national laughs they call for? Sure it is — the country can't have too much fun or "intergroup involvement" — so the more, the merrier. Simple consistency demands that anyone who thinks the Tomahawk Chop is a swell pastime must be just as hearty in their endorsement of the following ideas — by the logic used to defend the defamation of American Indians — [and] should help us all really start yukking it up.

First, as a counterpart to the Redskins, we need an NFL team called "Niggers" to honor Afro-Americans. Halftime festivities for fans might include a simulated stewing of the opposing coach in a large pot while players and cheerleaders dance around it, garbed in leopard skins and wearing fake bones in their noses. This concept obviously goes along with the kind of gaiety attending the Chop, but also with the actions of the Kansas City Chiefs, whose team members — prominently including black team members — lately appeared on a poster looking "fierce" and "savage" by way of wearing Indian regalia. Just a bit of harmless "morale boosting," says the Chiefs's front office. You bet.

So that the newly formed Niggers sports club won't end up too out of sync while expressing the "spirit" and "identity" of Afro-Americans in the above fashion, a baseball franchise — let's call this one the "Sambos" — should be formed. How about a basketball team called the "Spearchuckers"? A hockey team called the "Jungle Bunnies"? Maybe the "essence" of these teams could be depicted by images of tiny black faces adorned with huge pairs of lips. The players could appear on TV every week or so gnawing on chicken legs and spitting watermelon seeds at one another. Catchy, eh? Well, there's "nothing to be upset about," according to those who love wearing "war bonnets" to the Super Bowl or having "Chief Illiniwik" dance around the sports arenas of Urbana, Illinois.

And why stop there? There are plenty of other groups to include. "Hispanics"? They can be "represented" by the Galveston "Greasers" and San Diego "Spics," at least until the Wisconsin "Wetbacks" and Baltimore "Beaners" get off the ground. Asian Americans? How about the "Slopes," "Dinks," "Gooks," and "Zipperheads"? Owners of the latter teams might get their logo ideas from editorial page cartoons printed in the nation's newspapers during World War II: slant eyes, buck teeth, big glasses, but nothing racially insulting or derogatory, according to the editors and artists involved at the time. Indeed, this Second World War vintage stuff can be seen as just another barrel of laughs, at least by what current editors say are their "local standards" concerning American Indians.

Let's see. Who's been left out? Teams like the Kansas City "Kikes," Hanover "Honkies," San Leandro "Shylocks," Daytona "Dagos," and Pittsburgh "Polacks" will fill a certain social void among white folk. Have a religious belief? Let's all go for the gusto and gear up the Milwaukee "Mackerel Snappers" and Hollywood "Holy Rollers." The Fighting Irish of Notre Dame can be rechristened the "Drunken Irish" or "Papist Pigs." Issues of gender and sexual preference can be addressed through creation of teams like the St. Louis "Sluts," Boston "Bimbos," Detroit "Dykes," and the Fresno "Fags." How about the Gainesville "Gimps" and Richmond "Retards," so the physically and mentally impaired won't be excluded from our fun and games?

Now, don't go getting "overly sensitive" out there. None of this is demeaning or insulting, at least not when it's being done to Indians. Just ask the folks who are doing it, or their apologists like Andy Rooney in the national media. They'll tell you — as in fact they *have* been telling you — that there's been no harm done, regardless of what their victims think, feel, or say. The situation is exactly the same as when those with precisely the same mentality used to insist that Step 'n' Fetchit was okay, or Rochester on the *Jack Benny Show*, or Amos and Andy, Charlie Chan, the Frito Bandito, or any of the other cutesy symbols making up the lexicon of American racism. Have we communicated yet?

Let's get just a little bit real here. The notion of "fun" embodied in rituals like the Tomahawk Chop must be understood for what it is. There's not a single non-Indian example used above which can be considered socially acceptable in even the most marginal sense. The reasons are obvious enough. So why is it different where American Indians are concerned? One can only conclude that, in contrast to the other groups at issue, Indians are (falsely) perceived as being too few, and therefore too weak, to defend themselves effectively against racist and otherwise offensive behavior. 10

Fortunately, there are some glimmers of hope. A few teams and their fans have gotten the message and have responded appropriately. Stanford University, which opted to drop the name "Indians" from Stanford, has experienced no resulting drop-off in attendance. Meanwhile, the local newspaper in Portland, Oregon, recently decided its long-standing editorial policy prohibiting use of racial epithets should include derogatory team names. The Redskins, for instance, are now referred to as "the Washington team," and will continue to be described in this way until the franchise adopts an inoffensive moniker (newspaper sales in Portland have suffered no decline as a result).

Such examples are to be applauded and encouraged. They stand as figurative beacons in the night, proving beyond all doubt that it is quite possible to indulge in the pleasure of athletics without accepting blatant racism into the bargain.

Nuremberg Precedents

On October 16, 1946, a man named Julius Streicher mounted the steps of a gallows. Moments later he was dead, the sentence of an international tribunal composed of representatives of the United States, France, Great Britain, and the Soviet Union having been imposed. Streicher's body was then cremated, and — so horrendous were his crimes thought to have been — his ashes dumped into an unspecified German river so that "no one should ever know a particular place to go for reasons of mourning his memory."

Julius Streicher had been convicted at Nuremberg, Germany, of what were termed "crimes against humanity." The lead prosecutor in his case — Justice Robert Jackson of the United States Supreme Court — had not argued that the defendant had killed anyone, nor that he had personally committed any especially violent act. Nor was it contended that Streicher had held any particularly important position in the German government during the period in which the so-called Third Reich had exterminated some six millions Jews, as well as several million Gypsies, Poles, Slavs, homosexuals, and other *untermenschen* ("subhumans").

The sole offense for which the accused was ordered put to death was in having served as publisher/editor of a Bavarian tabloid entitled *Der Sturmer* during the early- to mid-1930s, years before the Nazi genocide actually began. In this capacity, he had penned a long series of virulently anti-Semitic editorials and "news" stories, usually accompanied by cartoons and other images graphically depicting Jews in extraordinarily derogatory fashion. This, the prosecution asserted, had done much to "dehumanize" the targets of his distortion in the mind of the German public. In turn, such dehumanization had made it possible — or at least easier — for average Germans to later indulge in the outright liquidation of Jewish "vermin." The tribunal agreed, holding that Streicher was therefore complicit in genocide and deserving of death by hanging.

During his remarks to the Nuremberg tribunal, Justice Jackson observed that, in implementing its sentences, the participating powers were morally and legally binding themselves to adhere forever after to the same standards of conduct that were being applied to Streicher and the other Nazi leaders. In the alternative, he said, the victorious allies would have committed "pure murder" at Nuremberg — no different in substance from that carried out by those they presumed to judge — rather than establishing the "permanent benchmark for justice" which was intended.

Yet in the United States of Robert Jackson, the indigenous American Indian population had already been reduced, in a process which is ongoing to this day, from perhaps 12.5 million in the year 1500 to fewer than 250,000 by the beginning of the twentieth century. This was accomplished, according to official sources, "largely through the cruelty of [Euro-American] settlers," and an informal but clear governmental policy which had made it an articulated goal to "exterminate these red vermin," or at least whole segments of them.

Bounties had been placed on the scalps of Indians — any Indians — in places as diverse as Georgia, Kentucky, Texas, the Dakotas, Oregon, and California, and had been maintained until resident Indian populations were decimated or disappeared altogether. Entire peoples such as the Cherokee had been reduced to half their size through a policy of forced removal from their homelands east of the Mississippi River to what were then considered less preferable areas in the West.

Others, such as the Navajo, suffered the same fate while under military guard for years on end. The United States Army had also perpetrated a long series of wholesale massacres of Indians at places like Horseshoe Bend, Bear River, Sand Creek, the Washita River, the Marias River, Camp Robinson, and Wounded Knee.

Through it all, hundreds of popular novels — each competing with the next to make Indians appear more grotesque, menacing, and inhuman — were sold in the tens of millions of copies in the United States. Plainly, the Euro-American public was being conditioned to see Indians in such a way as to allow their eradication to continue. And continue it did until the Manifest Destiny of the United States — a direct precursor to what Hitler would subsequently call *Lebensraumpolitik* ("the politics of living space") — was consummated.

By 1900, the national project of "clearing" Native Americans from their land and replacing them with "superior" Anglo-American settlers was complete; the indigenous population had been reduced by as much as 98 percent while approximately 97.5 percent of their original territory had "passed" to the invaders. The survivors had been concentrated, out of sight and mind of the public, on scattered "reservations," all of them under the self-assigned "plenary" (full) power of the federal government. There was, of course, no Nuremberg-style tribunal passing judgment on those who had fostered such circumstances in North America. No. U.S. official or private citizen was ever imprisoned — never mind hanged — for implementing or propagandizing what had been done. Nor had the process of genocide afflicting Indians been completed. Instead, it merely changed form.

Between the 1880s and the 1980s, nearly half of all Native American children were coercively transferred from their own families, communities, and cultures to those of the conquering society. This was done through compulsory attendance at remote boarding schools, often hundreds of miles from their homes, where native children were kept for years on end while being systematically "decultured" (indoctrinated to think and act in the manner of Euro-Americans rather than as Indians). It was also accomplished through a pervasive foster home and adoption program — including "blind" adoptions, where children would be permanently denied information as to who they were/are and where they'd come from — placing native youths in non-Indian homes.

The express purpose of all this was to facilitate a U.S. governmental policy to bring about the "assimilation" (dissolution) of indigenous societies. In other words, Indian cultures as such were to be caused to disappear. Such policy objectives are directly contrary to the United Nations 1948 Convention on Punishment and Prevention of the Crime of Genocide, an element of international law arising from the Nuremberg proceedings. The forced "transfer of the children" of a targeted "racial, ethnical, or religious group" is explicitly prohibited as a genocidal activity under the convention's second article.

Article II of the Genocide Convention also expressly prohibits involuntary sterilization as a means of "preventing births among" a targeted population. Yet, in 1975, it was conceded by the U.S. government that its Indian Health Service (IHS), then a subpart of the Bureau of Indian Affairs (BIA), was even then conducting a secret program of involuntary sterilization that had affected approximately 40 percent of all Indian women. The program was allegedly discontinued, and the IHS was transferred to the Public Health Service, but no one was punished. In 1990, it came out that the IHS was inoculating Inuit children in Alaska with hepatitis-B vaccine. The vaccine had already been banned by the World Health Organization as having a demonstrated correlation with the HIV syndrome, which is itself correlated to AIDS. As this is written, a "field test" of hepatitis-A vaccine, also HIV-correlated, is being conducted on Indian reservations in the northern plains region.

The Genocide Convention makes it a "crime against humanity" to create conditions leading to the destruction of an identifiable human group, as such. Yet the BIA has utilized the government's plenary prerogatives to negotiate mineral leases "on behalf of" Indian peoples paying a fraction of standard royalty rates. The result has been "super profits" for a number of preferred U.S. corporations. Meanwhile, Indians, whose reservations

25

ironically turned out to be in some of the most mineral-rich areas of North America, which makes us, the nominally wealthiest segment of the continent's population, live in dire poverty.

By the government's own data in the mid-1980s, Indians received the lowest annual and lifetime per capita incomes of any aggregate population group in the United States. Concomitantly, we suffer the highest rate of infant mortality, death by exposure and malnutrition, disease, and the like. Under such circumstances, alcoholism and other escapist forms of substance abuse are endemic to the Indian community, a situation which leads both to a general physical debilitation of the population and a catastrophic accident rate. Teen suicide among Indians is several times the national average.

The average life expectancy of a reservation-based native American man is barely forty-five years; women can expect to live less than three years longer.

Such itemizations could be continued at great length, including matters like the radioactive contamination of large portions of contemporary Indian Country, the forced relocation of traditional Navajos, and so on. But the point should be made: genocide, as defined in international law, is a continuing fact of day-to-day life (and death) for North America's native peoples. Yet there has been — and is — only the barest flicker of public concern about, or even consciousness of, this reality. Absent any serious expression of public outrage, no one is punished and the process continues.

A salient reason for public acquiescence before the ongoing holocaust in Native North America has been a continuation of the popular legacy, often through more effective media. Since 1925, Hollywood has released more than two thousand films, many of them rerun frequently on television, portraying Indians as strange, perverted, ridiculous, and often dangerous things of the past. Moreover, we are habitually presented to mass audiences one-dimensionally, devoid of recognizable human motivations and emotions; Indians thus serve as props, little more. We have thus been thoroughly and systematically dehumanized.

Nor is this the extent of it. Everywhere, we are used as logos, as mascots, as jokes: Big Chief writing tablets, Red Man chewing tobacco, Winnebago campers, Navajo and Cherokee and Pontiac and Cadillac pickups and automobiles. There are the Cleveland Indians, the Kansas City Chiefs, the Atlanta Braves, and the Washington Redskins professional sports teams — not to mention those in thousands of colleges, high schools, and elementary schools across the country — each with their own degrading caricatures and parodies of Indians and/or things Indian. Pop fiction continues in the same vein, including an unending stream of New Age manuals purporting to expose the inner works of indigenous spirituality in everything from pseudophilosophical to do-it-yourself styles. Blond Yuppies from Beverly Hills amble about the country claiming to be reincarnated seventeenth-century Cheyenne Ushamans ready to perform previously secret ceremonies.

In effect, a concerted, sustained, and in some ways accelerating effort has gone into making Indians unreal. It is thus of obvious importance that the American public begin to think about the implications of such things the next time they witness a gaggle of face-painted and war-bonneted buffoons doing the Tomahawk Chop at a baseball or football game. It is necessary that they think about the implications of the grade-school teacher adorning a child in turkey feathers to commemorate Thanksgiving. Think about the significance of John Wayne or Charlton Heston killing a dozen "savages" with a single bullet the next time a western comes on TV. Think about why Land-o-Lakes finds it appropriate to market its butter with the stereotyped image of an "Indian princess" on the wrapper. Think about what it means when non-Indian academics profess — as they often do — to "know more about Indians than Indians do themselves." Think about the significance of charlatans like Carlos Castaneda and Jamake Highwater and Mary Summer Rain and Lynn Andrews churning out "Indian" best-sellers, one after the other, while Indians typically can't get into print.

Think about the real situation of American Indians. Think about Julius Streicher. Remember Justice Jackson's admonition. Understand that the treatment of Indians in American popular culture is not "cute" or "amusing" or just "good, clean fun."

Know that it causes real pain and real suffering to real people. Know that it threatens our very survival. And know that this is just as much a crime against humanity as anything the Nazis ever did. It is likely that the indigenous people of the United States will never demand that those guilty of such criminal activity be punished for their deeds. But the least we have the right to expect — indeed, to demand — is that such practices finally be brought to a halt.

PREPARING FOR DISCUSSION

1. After reviewing the use of Native American epithets as names for sports teams, Churchill generates some team names of his own. What do you make of Churchill's attempt to spread the "inoffensiveness" and "good cheer" (paragraph 4) to other racial and religious groups? Is his analogy fair? Are his made-up examples comparable to the real examples he cites at the beginning of the essay?

2. At one point in his essay, Churchill seemingly moves far from his original topic of insulting team names and takes up the Nuremberg war criminal trials. Why does he change the direction of his discussion in this way? In what ways are the trials pertinent to his argument?

3. While Churchill notes that there are over two thousand movies in which Native Americans are depicted as savage and dangerous, he nevertheless fails to mention recent movies like *Dances with Wolves, Thunderheart,* and even Disney's

Pocahontas in which the European settlers or the U.S. government and its armies are depicted in a negative light. Do these movies dehumanize Native Americans in the ways described by Churchill? Why do you think he has omitted these examples?

4. Consider Churchill's account of the trial and execution of anti-Semitic editorialist Julius Streicher at Nuremberg. What do today's depictions of Native Americans have in common with Streicher's depictions of Jews in pre–World War II Germany? Do the current portrayals of Native Americans in the media, however unflattering, breed hate or, conversely, admiration?

5. Churchill, like many other contemporary Native American writers, frequently uses the term *Indian*. He even uses it more often than *Native American*. If this is the case, why does he object to its use by the Cleveland professional baseball franchise?

FROM READING TO WRITING

6. Do you agree with Churchill that teams and products that use Native American names and logos are engaging in a form of racism? Choose a professional, college, or local team or a commercial product that uses one of these names and write an essay in which you defend or argue against the practice.

7. One assumption behind Churchill's essay is that stereotypes can hinder a minority's progress toward full civil rights and equality. Write an essay in which you analyze this premise in light of the selection and determine whether you agree with it or not. If you have been affected by stereotypes in some way, describe the ways in which you were affected. Have your own experiences made you more or less sympathetic to Churchill's position?

PATRICIA J. WILLIAMS

Hate Radio

Anyone who has listened to radio in the last few years cannot help being aware of an explosion in the number of call-in talk shows where ordinary Americans voice their opinions on politics and culture. These popular programs are generally, though not exclusively, hosted by conservative white males like Rush Limbaugh — people skilled in the art of cultivating audience outrage and anger. So pervasive has been the influence of these shows on American public opinion that they have been blamed by some with helping to foster the kind of anti-government rage that resulted in the Oklahoma City bombing in April 1995. Yet the rhetoric of these programs is not merely directed against the federal government. Increasingly, callers express anger at minorities, homosexuals, and women and blame these groups for most of America's cultural and social problems.

In the following selection, African American legal scholar Patricia J. Williams wonders if "hate radio" might not also lead to a revival of racial prejudice and an increase in hate crimes against minorities. Educated at Harvard, Williams is professor of law at Columbia University Law School. She is also a contributing editor of the *Nation* and on the board of scholars of *Ms.* magazine. She currently serves on the board of governors of the Society of American Law. This selection first appeared in *Ms.* magazine in 1994.

SELECTED PUBLICATIONS: *The Alchemy of Race and Rights* (1991); Williams's articles appear in popular publications such as the *Nation* and *Ms.*, and in professional journals such as the *Harvard Civil Rights–Civil Liberties Law Review.*

Three years ago I stood at my sink, washing the dishes and listening to the radio. I was tuned to rock and roll so I could avoid thinking about the big news from the day before — George Bush had just nominated Clarence Thomas to replace Thurgood Marshall on the Supreme Court. I was squeezing a dot of lemon Joy into each of the wineglasses when I realized that two smoothly radio-cultured voices, a man's and a woman's, had replaced the music.

"I think it's a stroke of genius on the president's part," said the female voice.

"Yeah," said the male voice. "Then those blacks, those African Americans, those Negroes — hey 'Negro' is good enough for Thurgood Marshall — whatever, they can't make up their minds [what] they want to be called. I'm gonna call them Blafricans. Black Africans. Yeah, I like it. Blafricans. Then they can get all upset because now the president appointed a Blafrican."

"Yeah, well, that's the way those liberals think. It's just crazy."

"And then after they turn down his nomination the president can say he tried to please 'em, and then he can appoint someone with some intelligence."

Back then, this conversation seemed so horrendously unusual, so singularly hateful, that I picked up a pencil and wrote it down. I was certain that a firestorm of protest was going to engulf the station and purge those foul radio mouths with the good clean soap of social outrage.

I am so naive. When I finally tuned on the radio and rolled my dial to where everyone else had been tuned while I was busy watching Cosby reruns, it took me a while to understand that there's a firestorm all right, but not of protest. In the two and a half years since Thomas has assumed his post on the Supreme Court, the underlying assumptions of the conversation I heard as uniquely outrageous have become commonplace, popularly expressed, and louder in volume. I hear the style of that snide polemicism everywhere, among acquaintances, on the street, on television in toned-down versions. It is a crude demagoguery that makes me heartsick. I feel more and more surrounded by that point of view, the assumptions of being without intelligence, the coded epithets, the "Blafrican"-like stand-ins for "nigger," the mocking angry glee, the endless tirades filled with nonspecific, nonempirically based slurs against "these people" or "those minorities" or "feminazis" or "liberals" or "scumbags" or "pansies" or "jerks" or "sleazeballs" or "loonies" or "animals" or "foreigners."

At the same time I am not so naive as to suppose that this is something new. In clearheaded moments I realize I am not listening to the radio anymore, I am listening to a large segment of white America think aloud in ever louder resurgent thoughts that have generations of historical precedent. It's as though the radio has split open like an egg, Morton Downey, Jr.'s[1] clones and Joe McCarthy's[2] ghost spilling out, broken yolks, a great collective of sometimes clever, sometimes small, but uniformly threatened brains — they have all come gushing out. Just as they were about to pass into oblivion, Jack Benny and his humble black sidekick Rochester get resurrected in the ungainly bodies of Howard Stern and his faithful black henchwoman, Robin Quivers. The culture of Amos and Andy has been revived and reassembled in Bob Grant's radio minstrelry and radio newcomer Daryl Gates's[3] sanctimonious imprecations on behalf of decent white people. And in striking imitation of Jesse Helm's nearly forgotten days as a radio host, the far Right has found its undisputed king in the personage of Rush Limbaugh — a polished demagogue with a weekly radio audience of at least twenty million, a television show that vies for ratings with the likes of Jay Leno, a newsletter with a circulation of 380,000, and two best-selling books whose combined sales are closing in on six million copies.

From Churchill to Hitler to the old Soviet Union, it's clear that radio and television have the power to change the course of history, to proselytize, and to coalesce not merely the good and the noble, but the very worst in human nature as well. Likewise, when Orson Wells made his famous radio broadcast "witnessing" the landing of a spaceship full of hos-

[1]*Morton Downey, Jr.:* Talk show host of the 1980s who ridiculed his guests and took up controversial topics.
[2]*Joe McCarthy:* U.S. Senator Joseph R. McCarthy (1909–1957), chair of the House Un-American Activities Committee, who in the 1950s hunted and prosecuted suspected Communists and Communist sympathizers.
[3]*Daryl Gates:* Los Angeles police commissioner during the Rodney King beating affair of the early 1990s.

tile Martians, the United States ought to have learned a lesson about the power of radio to appeal to mass instincts and incite mass hysteria. Radio remains a peculiarly powerful medium even today, its visual emptiness in a world of six trillion flashing images allowing one of the few remaining playgrounds for the aural subconscious. Perhaps its power is attributable to our need for an oral tradition after all, some conveying of stories, feelings, myths of ancestors, epics of alienation, and the need to rejoin ancestral roots, even ignorant bigoted roots. Perhaps the visual quiescence of radio is related to the popularity of E-mail or electronic networking. Only the voice is made manifest, unmasking worlds that cannot — or dare not? — be seen. Just yet. Nostalgia crystallizing into a dangerous future. The preconscious voice erupting into the expressed, the prime time.

What comes out of the modern radio mouth could be the *Iliad*, the   10
Rubaiyat, the griot's song of our times. If indeed radio is a vessel for the American "Song of Songs," then what does it mean that a manic, adolescent Howard Stern is so popular among radio listeners, that Rush Limbaugh's wittily smooth sadism has gone the way of prime-time television, and that both vie for the number one slot on all the best-selling book lists? What to make of the stories being told by our modern radio evangelists and their tragic unloved chorus of callers? Is it really just a collapsing economy that spawns this drama of grown people sitting around scaring themselves to death with fantasies of black feminist Mexican able-bodied gay soldiers earning $100,000 a year on welfare who are so criminally depraved that Hillary Clinton or the Antichrist-of-the-moment had no choice but to invite them onto the government payroll so they can run the country? The panicky exaggeration reminds me of a child's fear. . . . *And then, and then, a huge lion jumped out of the shadows and was about to gobble me up, and I can't ever sleep again for a whole week.*

As I spin the dial on my radio, I can't help thinking that this stuff must be related to that most poignant of fiber-optic phenomena, phone sex. Aural Sex. Radio Racism with a touch of S & M. High-priest hosts with the power and run-amok ego to discipline listeners, to smack with the verbal back of the hand, to smash the button that shuts you up once and for all. "Idiot!" shouts New York City radio demagogue Bob Grant and then the sound of droning telephone emptiness, the voice of dissent dumped out some trapdoor in aural space.

As I listened to a range of such programs what struck me as the most unifying theme was not merely the specific intolerance on such hot topics as race and gender, but a much more general contempt for the world, a verbal stoning of anything different. It is like some unusually violent game of "Simon Says," this mockery and shouting down of callers, this roar of incantations, the insistence on agreement.

But, ah, if you *will* but only agree, what sweet and safe reward, what soft enfolding by a stern and angry radio god. And as an added bonus, the invisible shield of an AM community, a family of fans who are

Exactly Like You, to whom you can express, in anonymity, all the filthy stuff you imagine "them" doing to you. The comfort and relief of being able to ejaculate, to those who understand, about the dark imagined excess overtaking, robbing, needing to be held down and taught a good lesson, needing to put it in its place before the ravenous demon enervates all that is true and good and pure in this life.

The audience for this genre of radio flagellation is mostly young, white, and male. Two thirds of Rush Limbaugh's audience is male. According to *Time* magazine, 75 percent of Howard Stern's listeners are white men. Most of the callers have spent their lives walling themselves off from any real experience with blacks, feminists, lesbians, or gays. In this regard, it is probably true, as former Secretary of Education William Bennett says, that Rush Limbaugh "tells his audience that what you believe inside, you can talk about in the marketplace." Unfortunately, what's "inside" is then mistaken for what's "outside," treated as empirical and political reality. The *National Review* extols Limbaugh's conservative leadership as no less than that of Ronald Reagan, and the Republican party provides Limbaugh with books to discuss, stories, angles, and public support. "People were afraid of censure by gay activists, feminists, environmentalists — now they are not because Rush takes them on," says Bennett.

U.S. history has been marked by cycles in which brands of this or that hatred come into fashion and go out, are unleashed and then restrained. If racism, homophobia, jingoism, and woman-hating have been features of national life in pretty much all of modern history, it rather begs the question to spend a lot of time wondering if right-wing radio is a symptom or a cause. For at least 400 years, prevailing attitudes in the West have considered African Americans less intelligent. Recent statistics show that 53 percent of people in the United States agree that blacks and Latinos are less intelligent than whites, and a majority believe that blacks are lazy, violent, welfare-dependent, and unpatriotic.

I think that what has made life more or less tolerable for "out" groups have been those moments in history when those "inside" feelings were relatively restrained. In fact, if I could believe that right-wing radio were only about idiosyncratic, singular, rough-hewn individuals thinking those inside thoughts, I'd be much more inclined to agree with Columbia University media expert Everette Dennis, who says that Stern's and Limbaugh's popularity represents the "triumph of the individual," or with *Time* magazine's bottom line that "the fact that either is seriously considered a threat . . . is more worrisome than Stern or Limbaugh will ever be." If what I were hearing had even a tad more to do with real oppressions, with real white *and* black levels of joblessness and homelessness, or with the real problems of real white men, then I wouldn't have bothered to slog my way through hours of Howard Stern's miserable obsessions.

Yet at the heart of my anxiety is the worry that Stern, Limbaugh, Grant, et al. represent the very antithesis of individualism's triumph. As the *National Review* said of Limbaugh's ascent, "It was a feat not only of the loudest voice but also of a keen political brain to round up, as Rush did, the media herd and drive them into the conservative corral." When asked about his political aspirations, Bob Grant gloated to the *Washington Post*, "I think I would make rather a good dictator."

The polemics of right-wing radio are putting nothing less than hate onto the airwaves, into the marketplace, electing it to office, teaching it in schools, and exalting it as freedom. What worries me is the increasing-to-constant commerce of retribution, control, and lashing out, fed not by fact but fantasy. What worries me is the re-emergence, more powerfully than at any time since the institution of Jim Crow, of a socio-centered self that excludes "the likes of," well, me for example, from the civic circle, and that would rob me of my worth and claim and identity as a citizen. As the *Economist* rightly observes, "Mr. Limbaugh takes a mass market — white, mainly male, middle-class, ordinary America — and talks to it as an endangered minority."

I worry about this identity whose external reference is a set of beliefs, ethics, and practices that excludes, restricts, and acts in the world on me, or mine, as the perceived if not real enemy. I am acutely aware of losing *my* mythic individualism to the surface shapes of my mythic group fearsomeness as black, as female, as left wing. "I" merge not fluidly but irretrievably into a category of "them." I become a suspect self, a moving target of loathsome properties, not merely different but dangerous. And that worries me a lot.

What happens in my life with all this translated license, this permission to be uncivil? What happens to the social space that was supposedly at the sweet mountaintop of the civil rights movement's trail? Can I get a seat on the bus without having to be reminded that I *should* be standing? Did the civil rights movement guarantee us nothing more than to use public accommodations while surrounded by raving lunatic bigots? "They didn't beat this idiot [Rodney King] enough," says Howard Stern. 20

Not long ago I had the misfortune to hail a taxicab in which the driver was listening to Howard Stern undress some woman. After some blocks, I had to get out. I was, frankly, afraid to ask the driver to turn it off — not because I was afraid of "censoring" him, which seems to be the only thing people will talk about anymore, but because the driver was stripping me too, as he leered through the rearview mirror. "Something the matter?" he demanded, as I asked him to pull over and let me out well short of my destination. (I'll spare you the full story of what happened from there — trying to get another cab, as the cabbies stopped for all the white businessmen who so much as scratched their heads near the curb; a nice young white man, seeing my plight, giving me his cab, having to thank him, he hero, me saved-but-humiliated, cabdriver pissed and surly. I fight my way to my destination, finally arriving in bad mood, militant black woman, cranky feminazi.)

When Yeltsin blared rock music at his opponents holed up in the parliament building in Moscow, in imitation of the U.S. Marines trying to torture Manual Noriega in Panama, all I could think of was that it must be like being trapped in a crowded subway car when all the portable stereos are tuned to Bob Grant or Howard Stern. With Howard Stern's voice a tinny, screeching backdrop, with all the faces growing dreamily mean as though some soporifically evil hallucinogen were gushing into their bloodstreams, I'd start begging to surrender.

Surrender to what? Surrender to the laissez-faire resegregation that is the metaphoric significance of the hundreds of "Rush rooms" that have cropped up in restaurants around the country; rooms broadcasting Limbaugh's words, rooms for your listening pleasure, rooms where bigots can capture the purity of a Rush-only lunch counter, rooms where all those unpleasant others just "choose" not to eat? Surrender to the naughty luxury of a room in which a Ku Klux Klan meeting could take place in orderly, First Amendment fashion? Everyone's "free" to come in (and a few of you outsiders do), but mostly the undesirable nonconformists are gently repulsed away. It's a high-tech world of enhanced choice. Whites choose mostly to sit in the Rush room. Feminists, blacks, lesbians, and gays "choose" to sit elsewhere. No need to buy black votes, you just pay them not to vote; no need to insist on white-only schools, you just sell the desirability of black-only schools. Just sit back and watch it work, like those invisible shock shields that keep dogs cowering in their own backyards.

How real is the driving perception behind all the Sturm und Drang of this genre of radio-harangue — the perception that white men are an oppressed minority, with no power and no opportunity in the land that they made great? While it is true that power and opportunity are shrinking for all but the very wealthy in this country (and would that Limbaugh would take that issue on), the fact remains that white men are still this country's most privileged citizens and market actors. To give just a small example, according to the *Wall Street Journal*, blacks were the only racial group to suffer a net job loss during the 1990–91 economic downturn at the companies reporting to the Equal Employment Opportunity Commission. Whites, Latinos, and Asians, meanwhile, gained thousands of jobs. While whites gained 71,144 jobs at these companies, Latinos gained 60,040, Asians gained 55,104, and blacks lost 59,479. If every black were hired in the United States tomorrow, the numbers would not be sufficient to account for white men's expanding balloon of fear that they have been specifically dispossessed by African Americans.

Given deep patterns of social segregation and general ignorance of history, particularly racial history, media remain the principal source of most ²⁵

American's knowledge of each other. Media can provoke violence or induce passivity. In San Francisco, for example, a radio show on KMEL called "Street Soldiers" has taken this power as a responsibility with great consequence: "Unquestionably," writes Ken Auletta in *The New Yorker*, "the show has helped avert violence. When a Samoan teenager was slain, apparently by Filipino gang members, in a drive-by shooting, the phones lit up with calls from Samoans wanting to tell [the hosts] they would not rest until they had exacted revenge. Threats filled the air for a couple of weeks. Then the dead Samoan's father called in, and, in a poignant exchange, the father said he couldn't tolerate the thought of more young men senselessly slaughtered. There would be no retaliation, he vowed. And there was none." In contrast, we must wonder at the phenomenon of the very powerful leadership of the Republican party, from Ronald Reagan to Robert Dole to William Bennett, giving advice, counsel, and friendship to Rush Limbaugh's passionate divisiveness.

The outright denial of the material crisis at every level of U.S. society, most urgently in black inner-city neighborhoods but facing us all, is a kind of political circus, dissembling as it feeds the frustrations of the moment. We as a nation can no longer afford to deal with such crises by *imagining* an excess of bodies, of babies, of job-stealers, of welfare mothers, of over-reaching immigrants, of too-powerful (Jewish, in whispers) liberal Hollywood, of lesbians and gays, of gang members ("gangsters" remain white, and no matter what the atrocity, less vilified than "gang members," who are black), of Arab terrorists, and uppity women. The reality of our social poverty far exceeds these scapegoats. This right-wing backlash resembles, in form if not substance, phenomena like anti-Semitism in Poland: there aren't but a handful of Jews left in that whole country, but the giant balloon of heated anti-Semitism flourishes apace, Jews blamed for the world's evils.

The overwhelming response to right-wing excesses in the United States has been to seek an odd sort of comfort in the fact that the First Amendment is working so well that you can't suppress this sort of thing. Look what's happened in Eastern Europe. Granted. So let's not talk about censorship or the First Amendment for the next ten minutes. But in Western Europe, where fascism is rising at an appalling rate, suppression is hardly the problem. In Eastern and Western Europe as well as the United States, we must begin to think just a little bit about the fiercely coalescing power of media to spark mistrust, to fan it into forest fires of fear and revenge. We must begin to think about the levels of national and social complacence in the face of such resolute ignorance. We must ask ourselves what the expected result is, not of censorship or suppression, but of so much encouragement, so much support, so much investment in the fashionability of hate. What future is it that we are designing with the devotion of such tremendous resources to the disgraceful propaganda of bigotry?

PRESIDENT WILLIAM J. CLINTON
"Words Have Consequences": In the Wake of Oklahoma City

I know that all of you are thinking about how we can serve and help the people of Oklahoma City as they work through the next stages of their tragedy. I can tell you that when Hillary and I were there on Sunday, we saw people who had not slept, who were working heroically, some at considerable risk to themselves, to try to clean out the last measure of the wreckage and to try to find those who are still unaccounted for, working in the hospitals, working on the streets. The police and firemen — many of them had not seen their families for days.

The response of our country to this bombing shows what a strong country we are when we pull together. I saw it when you had the 500-year flood here. And I thought all the top soil was going to be somewhere in the Gulf of Mexico before it got through raining. But I really saw it down there in the face of this terrible madness that those fine people have endured.

We must take away from this experience a lot of things. But we must never forget that it was a terrible thing. I will do all I can to make sure that we see the wheels of justice grind rapidly, certainly, fairly, but severely. But we must take away from this . . . we must take away from this incident a renewed determination to stand up for the fundamental constitutional rights of Americans, including the right to freedom of speech. We have to remember that freedom of speech has endured in our country for over two centuries. The First Amendment, with its freedom of speech and freedom of assembly and freedom of religion, is in many ways the most important part of what makes us Americans. But we have endured because we have exercised that freedom with responsibility and discipline.

That is what we celebrate when people come to the rural heart of America and talk about what can be done to develop it. And every speaker says, what a shame it would be if we continue to allow economic decline in rural America, where the values of work and family and community and mutual responsibility are alive and well.

I ask you on this National Day of Service to think of a personal service you can all render. Yes, stand up for freedom of speech. Yes, stand up for all of our freedoms, the freedom of assembly, the freedom to bear arms, all the freedoms we have. But remember this: with freedom — if the country is to survive and do well — comes responsibility. And that means . . . that means even as others discharge their freedom of speech, if we think they are being irresponsible, then we have the duty to stand up and say so to protect our own freedom of speech. That is our responsibility.

Words have consequences. To pretend that they do not is idle. Did Patrick Henry stand up and say, "Give me liberty or give me death," expecting it to fall on deaf ears and impact no one? Did Thomas Jefferson write, "We hold these truths to be self-evident, that all men are created equal, endowed by their Creator with certain inalienable rights, among these are life, liberty, and the pursuit of happiness," did he say that thinking the words would vanish in thin air and have no consequences? Of course not. Are you here in this great university because you think the words you stay up late at night reading, studying, have no consequence? Of course not.

We know that words have consequences. And so I say to you, even as we defend the right of people to speak freely and to say things with which we devoutly disagree, we must stand up and speak against reckless speech that can push fragile people over the edge, beyond the boundaries of civilized conduct, to take this country into a dark place.

I say that, no matter where it comes from, people are encouraging violence and lawlessness and hatred. If people are encouraging conduct that will undermine the fabric of this country, it should be spoken against whether it comes from the Left or the Right, whether it comes on radio, television, or in the movies, whether it comes in the schoolyard, or, yes, even on the college campus. The answer to hateful speech is to speak out against it in the American spirit, to speak up for freedom and responsibility.

BILL CLINTON *was sworn in as the forty-second president of the United States on January 20, 1993. These remarks were made in the aftermath of the Oklahoma City bombing in April, 1995.*

PREPARING FOR DISCUSSION

1. Williams is convinced of the power of radio to galvanize public opinion. What kinds of historical and contemporary evidence convince her of this point? In support of her claim she recalls Hitler's use of the airwaves as well as Orson Welles's "War of the Worlds" broadcast. Which of these two examples seems more relevant to Williams's argument?

2. What, according to Williams, are the unifying themes of the radio programs she examines? Does she tend to single out radio hosts with conservative or left-leaning views? How does she describe the audience for these shows? What is the appeal of such shows for that particular audience?

3. In paragraph 20, Williams asks if "the civil rights movement guarantee[d] us nothing more than to use public accommodations while surrounded by raving lunatic bigots." To whom does Williams refer to with the pronoun *us?* Does she expect more from the Constitution than the Constitution actually offers? Do you think that vocal bigotry can be legislated out of existence?

4. Williams relates an anecdote about a taxicab ride with a driver who listened to Howard Stern (paragraph 21). What is Williams's point in including the anecdote? Consider the remarks that appear in parentheses at the end of the paragraph. In what ways do these remarks relate directly to hate radio? Why does Williams choose to include them? Do they reveal anything about her attitudes toward issues other than hate speech?

5. Williams at one point accuses radio talk-show hosts of "panicky exaggeration." To what degree does she herself tend to exaggerate? When is she most

likely to use hyperbolic language? When does she tend to use more measured and reasoned tones?

6. Follow one of the talk shows that Williams mentions for a few days to a week. Is your impression of what takes place on these shows similar to or rather different from Williams's impression? Write an essay in which you consider any important similarities or differences between your views and those of Williams. What factors account for those differences?

7. Both Williams's essay and President Clinton's remarks on hate radio in the aftermath of the Oklahoma City bombing (reprinted on the pages immediately preceding these questions) suggest possible links between hate speech and violence in America. Do you consider this link to be direct, indirect, or nonexistent? Write an essay in which you agree or disagree with this proposition on the basis of a strict analysis of cause and effect.

JONATHAN RAUCH

In Defense of Prejudice

———◇———

Must offensive speech be protected at all costs? Political journalist Jonathan Rauch, best known for his attacks on both conservative and liberal efforts to limit free speech, answers yes and offers reasons for his answer in the following essay. According to Rauch, the new "purism," as he labels the current movement for greater restrictions on offensive and prejudicial speech, must lead ultimately to the egregious notion that "any criticism of any group [is a form of] prejudice." He likewise argues that while restrictions on hate speech may, in the short run, make women, homosexuals, and minorities feel less harassed in our society, in the long run, there will be nothing to prevent those in power from turning such restrictions against these formerly oppressed groups.

Rauch, a political independent, was educated at Yale. He is a fierce defender of free intellectual inquiry as the most constructive method of handling racist, sexist, and homophobic views in our society. In recent years, he has turned his attention to an examination of the "slow-action principle" in American government — one caused, he maintains, by the proliferation of special interest lobbies. A visiting fellow at the American Enterprise Institute for Public Policy for 1989–90, he has appeared on CNN, C-SPAN, and the Financial News Network. This selection first appeared in *Harper's Magazine* in 1995.

SELECTED PUBLICATIONS: *Kindly Inquisitors: The New Attacks on Free Thought* (1993); *Demosclerosis: The Silent Killer of American Government* (1994); Rausch also publishes in *Harper's Magazine* and the *Economist*.

The war on prejudice is now, in all likelihood, the most uncontroversial social movement in America. Opposition to "hate speech," formerly identified with the liberal left, has become a bipartisan piety. In the past year, groups and factions that agree on nothing else have agreed that the public expression of any and all prejudices must be forbidden. On the left, protesters and editorialists have insisted that Francis L. Lawrence resign as president of Rutgers University for describing blacks as "a disadvantaged population that doesn't have that genetic, hereditary background to have a higher average." On the other side of the ideological divide, Ralph Reed, the executive director of the Christian Coalition, responded to criticism of the religious right by calling a press conference to denounce a supposed outbreak of "name-calling, scapegoating, and religious bigotry." Craig Rogers, an evangelical Christian student at California State University, recently filed a $2.5 million sexual-harassment suit against a lesbian professor of psychology, claiming that anti-male bias in one of her lectures violated campus rules and left him feeling "raped and trapped."

In universities and on Capitol Hill, in workplaces and newsrooms, authorities are declaring that there is no place for racism, sexism, homophobia, Christian-bashing, and other forms of prejudice in public debate or even in private thought. "Only when racism and other forms of prejudice are expunged," say the crusaders for sweetness and light, "can minorities be safe and society be fair." So sweet, this dream of a world without prejudice. But the very last thing society should do is seek to utterly eradicate racism and other forms of prejudice.

I suppose I should say, in the customary I-hope-I-don't-sound-too-defensive tone, that I am not a racist and that this is not an article favoring racism or any other particular prejudice. It is an article favoring intellectual pluralism, which permits the expression of various forms of bigotry and always will. Although we like to hope that a time will come when no one will believe that people come in types and that each type belongs with its own kind, I doubt such a day will ever arrive. By all indications, *Homo sapiens* is a tribal species for whom "us versus them" comes naturally and must be continually pushed back. Where there is genuine freedom of expression, there will be racist expression. There will also be people who believe that homosexuals are sick or threaten children or — especially among teenagers — are rightful targets of manly savagery.

Homosexuality will always be incomprehensible to most people, and what is incomprehensible is feared. As for anti-Semitism, it appears to be a hardier virus than influenza. If you want pluralism, then you get racism and sexism and homophobia, and communism and fascism and xenophobia and tribalism, and that is just for a start. If you want to believe in intellectual freedom and the progress of knowledge and the advancement of science and all those other good things, then you must swallow hard and accept this: for as thickheaded and wayward an animal as us, the realistic question is how to make the best of prejudice, not how to eradicate it.

Indeed, "eradicating prejudice" is so vague a proposition as to be meaningless. Distinguishing prejudice reliably and nonpolitically from non-prejudice, or even defining it crisply, is quite hopeless. We all feel we know prejudice when we see it. But do we? At the University of Michigan, a student said in a classroom discussion that he considered homosexuality a disease treatable with therapy. He was summoned to a formal disciplinary hearing for violating the school's policy against speech that "victimizes" people based on "sexual orientation." Now, the evidence is abundant that this particular hypothesis is wrong, and any American homosexual can attest to the harm that the student's hypothesis has inflicted on many real people. But was it a statement of prejudice or of misguided belief? Hate speech or hypothesis? Many Americans who do not regard themselves as bigots or haters believe that homosexuality is a treatable disease. They may be wrong, but are they all bigots? I am unwilling to say so, and if you are willing, beware. The line between a prejudiced belief and a merely controversial one is elusive, and the harder you look the more elusive it becomes. "God hates homosexuals" is a statement of fact, not of bias, to those who believe it; "American criminals are disproportionately black" is a statement of bias, not of fact, to those who disbelieve it.

Who is right? You may decide, and so may others, and there is no need to agree. That is the great innovation of intellectual pluralism (which is to say, of post-Enlightenment science, broadly defined). We cannot know in advance or for sure which belief is prejudice and which is truth, but to advance knowledge we don't need to know. The genius of intellectual pluralism lies not in doing away with prejudices and dogmas but in channeling them — making them socially productive by pitting prejudice against prejudice and dogma against dogma, exposing all to withering public criticism. What survives at the end of the day is our base of knowledge.

What they told us in high school about this process is very largely a lie. The Enlightenment tradition taught us that science is orderly, antiseptic, rational, the province of detached experimenters and high-minded logicians. In the popular view, science stands for reason against prejudice, open-mindedness against dogma, calm consideration against passionate attachment — all personified by pop-science icons like the magisterially deductive Sherlock Holmes, the coolly analytic Mr. Spock, the genially authoritative Mr. Science (from our junior-high science films). Yet one of science's dirty secrets is that although science as a whole is as unbiased as anything human can be, scientists are just as biased as anyone else, sometimes more so. "One of the strengths of science," writes the philosopher of science David L. Hull, "is that it does not require that scientists be unbiased, only that different scientists have different biases." Another dirty secret is that, no less than the rest of us, scientists can be dogmatic and pigheaded. "Although this pigheadedness often damages the careers of individual scientists," says Hull, "it is beneficial for the manifest goal of science," which relies on people to invest years in their ideas and defend them passionately. And the dirtiest secret of all, if you believe in the antiseptic popular view of science, is that this most ostensibly rational of enterprises depends on the most irrational of motives — ambition, narcissism, animus, even revenge. "Scientists acknowledge that among their motivations are natural curiosity, the love of truth, and the desire to help humanity, but other inducements exist as well, and one of them is to 'get that son of a bitch,'" says Hull. "Time and again, scientists whom I interviewed described the powerful spur that 'showing that son of a bitch' supplied to their own research."

Many people, I think, are bewildered by this unvarnished and all too human view of science. They believe that for a system to be unprejudiced, the people in it must also be unprejudiced. In fact, the opposite is true. Far from eradicating ugly or stupid ideas and coarse or unpleasant motives, intellectual pluralism relies upon them to excite intellectual passion and redouble scientific effort. I know of no modern idea more ugly and stupid than that the Holocaust never happened, nor any idea more viciously motivated. Yet the deniers' claims that the Auschwitz gas chambers could not have worked led to closer study and, in 1993, research showing, at last, how they actually did work. Thanks to prejudice and stupidity, another opening for doubt has been shut.

An enlightened and efficient intellectual regime lets a million prejudices bloom, including many that you or I may regard as hateful or grotesque. It avoids any attempt to stamp out prejudice, because stamping out prejudice really means forcing everyone to share the same prejudice, namely that of whoever is in authority. The great American philosopher Charles Sanders Peirce wrote in 1877: "When complete agreement could not otherwise be reached, a general massacre of all who have not thought in a certain way has proved a very effective means of settling opinion in a country." In speaking of "settling opinion," Peirce was writing about one of the two or three most fundamental problems that any human society must confront and solve. For most societies down through the centuries, this problem was dealt with in the manner he described: errors were identified by the authorities — priests, politburos, dictators — or by mass opinion, and then the error-makers were eliminated along with their putative mistakes. "Let all men who reject the established belief be terrified into silence," wrote Peirce, describing this system. "This method has, from the earliest times, been one of the chief means of upholding correct theological and political doctrines."

Intellectual pluralism substitutes a radically different doctrine: we kill our mistakes rather than each other. Here I draw on another great philosopher, the late Karl Popper, who pointed out that the critical method of science "consists in letting our hypotheses die in our stead." Those who are in error are not (or are not supposed to be) banished or excommunicated or forced to sign a renunciation or required to submit to "rehabilitation" or sent for psychological counseling. It is the error we punish, not the errant. By letting people make errors — even mischievous, spiteful errors (as, for instance, Galileo's insistence on Copernicanism was taken to be in 1633) — pluralism creates room to challenge orthodoxy, think imaginatively, experiment boldly. Brilliance and bigotry are empowered in the same stroke.

Pluralism is the principle that protects and makes a place in human company for that loneliest and most vulnerable of all minorities, the minority who is hounded and despised among blacks and whites, gays and straights, who is suspect or criminal among every tribe and in every nation of the world, and yet on whom progress depends: the dissident. I am not saying that dissent is always or even usually enlightened. Most of the time it is foolish and self-serving. No dissident has the right to be taken seriously, and the fact that Aryan Nation racists or Nation of Islam anti-Semites are unorthodox does not entitle them to respect. But what goes around comes around. As a supporter of gay marriage, for example, I reject the majority's view of family, and as a Jew I reject its view of God. I try to be civil, but the fact is that most Americans regard my views on marriage as a reckless assault on the most fundamental of all institutions, and many people are more than a little discomfited by the statement "Jesus Christ was no more divine than anybody else" (which is why so few people ever say it). Trap the racists and anti-Semites, and you lay a trap for me too. Hunt for them with eradication in your mind, and you have brought dissent itself within your sights.

The new crusade against prejudice waves aside such warnings. Like earlier crusades against antisocial ideas, the mission is fueled by good (if cocksure) intentions and a genuine sense of urgency. Some kinds of error are held to be intolerable, like pollutants that even in small traces poison the water for a whole town. Some errors are so pernicious as to damage real people's lives, so wrongheaded that no person of right mind or goodwill could support them. Like their forebears of other stripe — the Church in its campaigns against heretics, the McCarthyites in their campaigns against Communists — the modern anti-racist and anti-sexist and anti-homophobic campaigners are totalists, demanding not that misguided ideas and ugly expressions be corrected or criticized but that they be eradicated. They make war not on errors but on error, and like other totalists they act in the name of public safety — the safety, especially, of minorities.

The sweeping implications of this challenge to pluralism are not, I think, well enough understood by the public at large. Indeed, the new brand of totalism has yet even to be properly named. "Multiculturalism," for instance, is much too broad. "Political correctness" comes closer but is too trendy and snide. For lack of anything else, I will call the new antipluralism "purism," since its major tenet is that society cannot be just until the last traces of invidious prejudice have been scrubbed away. Whatever you call it, the purists' way of seeing things has spread through American intellectual life with remarkable speed, so much so that many people will blink at you uncomprehendingly or even call you a racist (or sexist or homophobe, etc.) if you suggest that expressions of racism should be tolerated or that prejudice has its part to play.

The new purism sets out, to begin with, on a campaign against words, for words are the currency of prejudice, and if prejudice is hurtful then so must be prejudiced words. "We are not safe when these violent words are among us," wrote Mari Matsuda, then a UCLA law professor. Here one imagines gangs of racist words swinging chains and smashing heads in back alleys. To suppress bigoted language seems, at first blush, reasonable, but it quickly leads to a curious result. A peculiar kind of verbal shamanism takes root, as though certain expressions, like curses or magical incantations, carry in themselves the power to hurt or heal — as though words were bigoted rather than people. "Context is everything," people have always said. The use of the word "nigger" in *Huckleberry Finn* does not make the book an "act" of hate speech — or does it? In the new view, this is no longer so clear. The very utterance of the word "nigger" (at least by a non-black) is a racist act. When a *Sacramento Bee* cartoonist put the word "nigger" mockingly in the mouth of a white supremacist, there were howls of protest and 1,400 canceled subscriptions and an editorial apology, even though the word was plainly being invoked against racists, not against blacks.

Faced with escalating demands of verbal absolutism, newspapers issue lists of forbidden words. The expressions "gyp" (derived from "Gypsy") and "Dutch treat" were among the dozens of terms stricken as "offensive" in a much-ridiculed (and later withdrawn) *Los Angeles Times* speech code. The University of Missouri journalism school issued a *Dictionary of Cautionary Words and Phrases*, which included "*Buxom*: Offensive reference to a woman's chest. Do not use. See 'Woman.' *Codger*: Offensive reference to a senior citizen."

As was bound to happen, purists soon discovered that chasing   15 around after words like "gyp" or "buxom" hardly goes to the roots of the problem. As long as they remain bigoted, bigots will simply find other words. If they can't call you a kike then they will say Jewboy, Judas, or Hebe, and when all those are banned they will press words like "oven" and "lampshade" into their service. The vocabulary of hate is potentially as rich as your dictionary, and all you do by banning language used by cretins is to let them decide what the rest of us may say. The problem, some purists have concluded, must therefore go much deeper than laws: it must go to the deeper level of ideas. Racism, sexism, homophobia, and the rest must be built into the very structure of American society and American patterns of thought, so pervasive yet so insidious that, like water to a fish, they are both omnipresent and unseen. The mere existence of prejudice constructs a society whose very nature is prejudiced.

This line of thinking was pioneered by feminists, who argued that pornography, more than just being expressive, is an act by which men construct an oppressive society. Racial activists quickly picked up the argument. Racist expressions are themselves acts of oppression, they said. "All racist speech constructs the social reality that constrains the liberty of nonwhites because of their race," wrote Charles R. Lawrence III, then a law professor at Stanford. From the purist point of view, a society with even one racist is a racist society, because the idea itself threatens and demeans its targets. They cannot feel wholly safe or wholly welcome as long as racism is present. Pluralism says: There will always be some racists. Marginalize them, ignore them, exploit them, ridicule them, take pains to make their policies illegal, but otherwise leave them alone. Purists say: That's not enough. Society cannot be just until these pervasive and oppressive ideas are searched out and eradicated.

And so what is now under way is a growing drive to eliminate prejudice from every corner of society. I doubt that many people have noticed how far-reaching this anti-pluralist movement is becoming.

In universities: Dozens of universities have adopted codes proscribing speech or other expression that (this is from Stanford's policy, which is more or less representative) "is intended to insult or stigmatize an individual or a small number of individuals on the basis of their sex, race, color, handicap, religion, sexual orientation or national and ethnic origin." Some codes punish only persistent harassment of a targeted individual, but many, following the purist doctrine that even one racist is too many, go much further. At Penn, an administrator declared: "We at the University of Pennsylvania have guaranteed students and the community that they can live in a community free of sexism, racism, and homophobia." Here is the purism that gives "political correctness" its distinctive combination of puffy high-mindedness and authoritarian zeal.

In school curricula: "More fundamental than eliminating racial segregation has to be the removal of racist thinking, assumptions, symbols, and materials in the curriculum," writes theorist Molefi Kete Asante. In practice, the effort to "remove racist thinking" goes well beyond striking egregious references from textbooks. In many cases it becomes a kind of mental engineering in which students are encouraged to see prejudice everywhere; it includes teaching identity politics as an antidote to internalized racism; it rejects mainstream science as "white male" thinking; and it tampers with history, installing such dubious notions as that the ancient Greeks stole their culture from Africa or that an ancient carving of a bird is an example of "African experimental aeronautics."

In criminal law: Consider two crimes. In each, I am beaten brutally; in each, my jaw is smashed and my skull is split in just the same way. However, in the first crime my assailant calls me an "asshole"; in the second he calls me a "queer." In most states, in many localities, and, as of September 1994, in federal cases, these two crimes are treated differently: the crime motivated by bias — or deemed to be so motivated by prosecutors and juries — gets a stiffer punishment. "Longer prison terms for bigots," shrilled Brooklyn Democratic Congressman Charles Schumer, who introduced the federal hate-crimes legislation, and those are what the law now provides. Evidence that the assailant holds prejudiced beliefs, even if he doesn't actually express them while committing an offense, can serve to elevate the crime. Defendants in hate-crimes cases may be grilled on how many black friends they have and whether they have told racist jokes. To increase a prison sentence only because of the defendant's "prejudice" (as gauged by prosecutor and jury) is, of course, to try minds and punish beliefs. Purists say, Well, they are dangerous minds and poisonous beliefs.

In the workplace: Though government cannot constitutionally suppress bigotry directly, it is now busy doing so indirectly by requiring employers to eliminate prejudice. Since the early 1980s, courts and the Equal Employment Opportunity Commission have moved to bar workplace speech deemed to create a hostile or abusive working environment for minorities. The law, held a federal court in 1988, "does require that an employer take prompt action to prevent . . . bigots from expressing their opinions in a way that abuses or offends their co-workers," so as to achieve "the goal of eliminating prejudices and biases from our society." So it was, as UCLA law professor Eugene Volokh notes, that the EEOC charged that a manufacturer's ads using admittedly accurate depictions of samurai, kabuki, and sumo were "racist" and "offensive to people of Japanese origin"; that a Pennsylvania court found that an employer's printing Bible verses on paychecks was religious harassment of Jewish employees; that an employer had to desist using gender-based job titles like "foreman" and "draftsman" after a female employee sued.

On and on the campaign goes, darting from one outbreak of prejudice to another like a cat chasing flies. In the American Bar Association, activists demand that lawyers who express "bias or prejudice" be penalized. In the Education Department, the civil-rights office presses for a ban

20

on computer bulletin board comments that "show hostility toward a person or group based on sex, race or color, including slurs, negative stereotypes, jokes or pranks." In its security checks for government jobs, the FBI takes to asking whether applicants are "free of biases against any class of citizens," whether, for instance, they have told racist jokes or indicated other "prejudices." Joke police! George Orwell, grasping the close relationship of jokes to dissent, said that every joke is a tiny revolution. The purists will have no such rebellions.

The purist campaign reaches, in the end, into the mind itself. In a lecture at the University of New Hampshire, a professor compared writing to sex ("You and the subject become one"); he was suspended and required to apologize, but what was most insidious was the order to undergo university-approved counseling to have his mind straightened out. At the University of Pennsylvania, a law lecturer said, "We have ex-slaves here who should know about the Thirteenth Amendment"; he was banished from campus for a year and required to make a public apology, and he, too, was compelled to attend a "sensitivity and racial awareness" session. Mandatory re-education of alleged bigots is the natural consequence of intellectual purism. Prejudice must be eliminated!

Ah, but the task of scouring minds clean is Augean:[1] "Nobody escapes," said a Rutgers University report on campus prejudice. Bias and prejudice, it found, cross every conceivable line, from sex to race to politics: "No matter who you are, no matter what the color of your skin, no matter what your gender or sexual orientation, no matter what you believe, no matter how you behave, there is somebody out there who doesn't like people of your kind." Charles Lawrence writes: "Racism is ubiquitous. We are all racists." If he means that most of us think racist thoughts of some sort at one time or another, he is right. If we are going to "eliminate prejudices and biases from our society," then the work of the prejudice police is unending. They are doomed to hunt and hunt and hunt, scour and scour and scour.

What is especially dismaying is that the purists pursue prejudice in   25
the name of protecting minorities. In order to protect people like me (homosexual), they must pursue people like me (dissident). In order to bolster minority self-esteem, they suppress minority opinion. There are, of course, all kinds of practical and legal problems with the purists' campaign: the incursions against the First Amendment; the inevitable abuses by prosecutors and activists who define as "hateful" or "violent" whatever speech they dislike or can score points off of; the lack of any evidence that repressing prejudice eliminates rather than inflames it. But minorities, of all people, ought to remember that by definition we cannot prevail by numbers, and we generally cannot prevail by force. Against

[1]*Augean:* Cleaning out the Augean stables was one of Hercules's tasks.

the power of ignorant mass opinion and group prejudice and superstition, we have only our voices. If you doubt that minorities' voices are powerful weapons, think of the lengths to which Southern officials went to silence the Reverend Martin Luther King, Jr. (recall that the city commissioner of Montgomery, Alabama, won a $500,000 libel suit, later overturned in *New York Times v. Sullivan* [1964], regarding an advertisement in the *Times* placed by civil-rights leaders who denounced the Montgomery police). Think of how much gay people have improved their lot over twenty-five years simply by refusing to remain silent. Recall the Michigan student who was prosecuted for saying that homosexuality is a treatable disease, and notice that he was black. Under that Michigan speech code, more than twenty blacks were charged with racist speech, while no instance of racist speech by whites was punished. In Florida, the hate-speech law was invoked against a black man who called a policeman a "white cracker"; not so surprisingly, in the first hate-crimes case to reach the Supreme Court, the victim was white and the defendant black.

In the escalating war against "prejudice," the right is already learning to play by the rules that were pioneered by the purist activists of the left. [In 1994] leading Democrats, including the president, criticized the Republican Party for being increasingly in the thrall of the Christian right. Some of the rhetoric was harsh ("fire-breathing Christian radical right"), but it wasn't vicious or even clearly wrong. Never mind: when Democratic Representative Vic Fazio said Republicans were "being forced to the fringes by the aggressive political tactics of the religious right," the chairman of the Republican National Committee, Haley Barbour, said, "Christian-bashing" was "the left's preferred form of religious bigotry." Bigotry! Prejudice! "Christians active in politics are now on the receiving end of an extraordinary campaign of bias and prejudice," said the conservative leader William J. Bennett. One discerns, here, where the new purism leads. Eventually, any criticism of any group will be "prejudice."

Here is the ultimate irony of the new purism: words, which pluralists hope can be substituted for violence, are redefined by purists *as* violence. "The experience of being called 'nigger,' 'spic,' 'Jap,' or 'kike' is like receiving a slap in the face," Charles Lawrence wrote in 1990. "Psychic injury is no less an injury than being struck in the face, and it often is far more severe." This kind of talk is commonplace today. Epithets, insults, often even polite expressions of what's taken to be prejudice are called by purists "assaultive speech," "words that wound," "verbal violence." "To me, racial epithets are not speech," one University of Michigan law professor said. "They are bullets." In her speech accepting the 1993 Nobel Prize for Literature in Stockholm, Sweden, the author Toni Morrison said this: "Oppressive language does more than represent violence; it is violence."

It is not violence. I am thinking back to a moment on the subway in Washington, a little thing. I was riding home late one night and a squad of noisy kids, maybe seventeen or eighteen years old, noisily piled into the car. They yelled across the car and a girl said, "Where do we get off?"

A boy said, "Farragut North."

The girl: "*Faggot* North!"

The boy: "Yeah! Faggot North!"

General hilarity.

First, before the intellect resumes control, there is a moment of fear, an animal moment. Who are they? How many of them? How dangerous? Where is the way out? All of these things are noted preverbally and assessed by the gut. Then the brain begins an assessment: they are sober, this is probably too public a place for them to do it, there are more girls than boys, they were just talking, it is probably nothing.

They didn't notice me and there was no incident. The teenage babble flowed on, leaving me to think. I became interested in my own reaction: the jump of fear out of nowhere like an alert animal, the sense for a brief time that one is naked and alone and should hide or run away. For a time, one ceases to be a human being and becomes instead a faggot.

The fear engendered by these words is real. The remedy is as clear and as imperfect as ever: protect citizens against violence. This, I grant, is something that American society has never done very well and now does quite poorly. It is no solution to define words as violence or prejudice as oppression, and then by cracking down on words or thoughts pretend that we are doing something about violence and oppression. No doubt it is easier to pass a speech code or hate-crimes law and proclaim the streets safer than actually to make the streets safer, but the one must never be confused with the other. Every cop or prosecutor chasing words is one fewer chasing criminals. In a world rife with real violence and oppression, full of Rwandas and Bosnias and eleven-year-olds spraying bullets at children in Chicago and in turn being executed by gang lords, it is odious of Toni Morrison to say that words are violence.

Indeed, equating "verbal violence" with physical violence is a treacherous, mischievous business. Not long ago a writer was charged with viciously and gratuitously wounding the feelings and dignity of millions of people. He was charged, in effect, with exhibiting flagrant prejudice against Muslims and outrageously slandering their beliefs. "What is freedom of expression?" mused Salman Rushdie a year after the ayatollahs sentenced him to death and put a price on his head. "Without the freedom to offend, it ceases to exist." I can think of nothing sadder than that minority activists, in their haste to make the world better, should be the ones to forget the lesson of Rushdie's plight: for minorities, pluralism, not purism, is the answer. The campaigns to eradicate prejudice — all of them, the speech codes and workplace restrictions and mandatory therapy for accused bigots and all the rest — should stop, now. The whole objective of eradicating prejudice, as opposed to correcting and criticizing it, should be repudiated as a fool's errand. Salman Rushdie is right, Toni Morrison wrong, and minorities belong at his side, not hers.

PREPARING FOR DISCUSSION

1. In paragraph 2, Rauch writes that "the very last thing society should do is to seek to utterly eradicate racism and other forms of prejudice." What are his reasons for saying this? What does he think of current attempts to end racism and prejudice?

2. Early in the essay, Rauch devotes several paragraphs to the idea of "intellectual pluralism." What is his notion of this concept and how does it relate to questions of racial prejudice? Why does he include the observation about the biases of scientists toward the conclusion of this part of the essay?

3. Rauch writes against the suppression of racism and prejudice, yet he fails to make a distinction between racist thoughts and ideas and the *expression* of racist thoughts and ideas. Does Rauch's failure to make such a distinction point to the possibility that he believes that racism and prejudice could ever be eradicated? Is this a reasonable possibility in our country?

4. After noting Rauch's position on free speech on campus, consider the following: Could commitment to free speech on campus imply support for racist, sexist, and homophobic elements on campus? Does opposition to racist, sexist, and homophobic speech on campus necessarily imply a commitment to the elimination of racism, sexism, and homophobia?

5. Rauch uses the term *minority* in two different primary senses within the essay. To what groups do these senses of minority refer? In what sense are the two meanings of the term opposed to each other within the essay?

FROM READING TO WRITING

6. Virtually every college campus in America has witnessed some form of racist, sexist, or homophobic expression. Can you recall a recent incident at your own college that involved such expression? In an essay, compare your example to those in Rauch's essay. Pay special attention to the way your college administration handled the incident. Do you agree with the way that the incident was handled? Why or why not?

7. Rauch points out that the Michigan student punished for calling homosexuality a treatable disease was an African American. He likewise cites several other instances in which minorities were punished by the new speech codes prohibiting racist speech. How does Rauch explain these phenomena? How would you explain them? Write an essay in which you consider whose interests these speech codes are actually protecting.

ALAN M. DERSHOWITZ
Shouting *"Fire!"*

Whenever debates about free speech and censorship arise, someone will almost certainly try to establish the limits of free speech by claiming that no one has the right to shout "Fire!" in a crowded theater. As Alan M. Dershowitz, one of America's most distinguished trial lawyers, says, the shouting fire analogy has been "invoked so often, by so many people, in such diverse contexts, that it has become part of our national folk language." In fact, Dershowitz further states, "[it] may well be the only jurisprudential analogy that has assumed the status of a folk argument." Over the years, Dershowitz has collected numerous examples of the analogy, and in the following essay (which was selected for *The Best American Essays 1990)*, he recounts its specific origin and analyzes the ways in which it has been consistently misused both by experts and by the popular press.

The author of numerous books on legal matters, Alan M. Dershowitz is Felix Frankfurter professor of law at Harvard Law School. He has been a syndicated weekly columnist and has contributed articles to many magazines. He is considered one of the nation's preeminent criminal defense and civil liberty lawyers.

SELECTED PUBLICATIONS: *The Best Defense* (1982); *Taking Liberties* (1988); *Chutzpah* (1991); *Contrary to Public Opinion* (1992).

When the Reverend Jerry Falwell learned that the Supreme Court had reversed his $200,000 judgment against *Hustler* magazine for the emotional distress that he had suffered from an outrageous parody, his response was typical of those who seek to censor speech: "Just as no person may scream 'Fire!' in a crowded theater when there is no fire, and find cover under the First Amendment, likewise, no sleazy merchant like Larry Flynt should be able to use the First Amendment as an excuse for maliciously and dishonestly attacking public figures, as he has so often done."

Justice Oliver Wendell Holmes's classic example of unprotected speech — falsely shouting "Fire!" in a crowded theater — has been invoked so often, by so many people, in such diverse contexts, that it has become part of our national folk language. It has even appeared — most appropriately — in the theater: in Tom Stoppard's play *Rosencrantz and Guildenstern Are Dead* a character shouts at the audience, "Fire!" He then quickly explains: "It's all right — I'm demonstrating the misuse of free speech." Shouting "Fire!" in the theater may well be the only jurisprudential analogy that has assumed the status of a folk argument. A prominent historian recently characterized it as "the most brilliantly persuasive expression that ever came from Holmes' pen." But in spite of its hallowed position in both the jurisprudence of the First Amendment and the arsenal of political discourse, it is and was an inapt analogy, even in the context in which it was originally offered. It has lately become — despite, perhaps even because of, the frequency and promiscuousness of its invocation — little more than a caricature of logical argumentation.

The case that gave rise to the "Fire!"-in-a-crowded-theater analogy, *Schenck v. United States,* involved the prosecution of Charles Schenck, who was the general secretary of the Socialist party in Philadelphia, and Elizabeth Baer, who was its recording secretary. In 1917 a jury found Schenck and Baer guilty of attempting to cause insubordination among soldiers who had been drafted to fight in the First World War. They and other party members had circulated leaflets urging draftees not to "submit to intimidation" by fighting in a war being conducted on behalf of "Wall Street's chosen few."

Schenck admitted, and the Court found, that the intent of the pamphlets' "impassioned language" was to "influence" draftees to resist the draft. Interestingly, however, Justice Holmes noted that nothing in the pamphlet suggested that the draftees should use unlawful or violent means to oppose conscription: "In form at least [the pamphlet] confined itself to peaceful measures, such as a petition for the repeal of the act" and an exhortation to exercise "your right to assert your opposition to the draft." Many of its most impassioned words were quoted directly from the Constitution.

Justice Holmes acknowledged that "in many places and in ordinary times the defendants, in saying all that was said in the circular, would have been within their constitutional rights." "But," he added, "the character of every act depends upon the circumstances in which it is done." And to illustrate that truism he went on to say:

> The most stringent protection of free speech would not protect a man in falsely shouting fire in a theater, and causing a panic. It does not even protect a man from an injunction against uttering words that may have all the effect of force.

Justice Holmes then upheld the convictions in the context of a wartime draft, holding that the pamphlet created "a clear and present danger" of hindering the war effort while our soldiers were fighting for their lives and our liberty.

The example of shouting "Fire!" obviously bore little relationship to the facts of the Schenck case. The Schenck pamphlet contained a substantive political message. It urged its draftee readers to *think* about the message and then — if they so chose — to act on it in a lawful and nonviolent way. The man who shouts "Fire!" in a crowded theater is neither sending a political message nor inviting his listener to think about what he has said and decide what to do in a rational, calculated manner. On the contrary, the message is designed to force action *without* contemplation. The message "Fire!" is directed not to the mind and the conscience of the listener but, rather, to his adrenaline and his feet. It is a stimulus to immediate *action*, not thoughtful reflection. It is — as Justice Holmes recognized in his follow-up sentence — the functional equivalent of "uttering words that may have all the effect of force."

Indeed, in that respect the shout of "Fire!" is not even speech, in any meaningful sense of that term. It is a *clang* sound, the equivalent of setting off a nonverbal alarm. Had Justice Holmes been more honest about his example, he would have said that freedom of speech does not protect a kid who pulls a fire alarm in the absence of a fire. But that obviously would have been irrelevant to the case at hand. The proposition that pulling an alarm is not protected speech certainly leads to the conclusion that shouting the word "fire" is also not protected. But the core analogy is the nonverbal alarm, and the derivative example is the verbal shout. By cleverly substituting the derivative shout for the core alarm, Holmes made it possible to analogize one set of words to another — as he could not have done if he had begun with the self-evident proposition that setting off an alarm bell is not free speech.

The analogy is thus not only inapt but also insulting. Most Americans do not respond to political rhetoric with the same kind of automatic acceptance expected of schoolchildren responding to a fire drill. Not a single recipient of the Schenck pamphlet is known to have changed his mind after reading it. Indeed, one draftee, who appeared as a prosecution witness, was asked whether reading the pamphlet asserting that the draft law was unjust would make him "immediately decide that you must erase that law." Not surprisingly, he replied, "I do my own thinking." A theatergoer would probably not respond similarly if asked how he would react to a shout of "Fire!"

Another important reason why the analogy is inapt is that Holmes   10
emphasizes the factual falsity of the shout "Fire!" The Schenck pamphlet, however, was not factually false. It contained political opinions and ideas about the causes of the war and about appropriate and lawful responses to the draft. As the Supreme Court recently reaffirmed (in *Falwell v. Hustler*), "The First Amendment recognizes no such thing as a 'false' idea." Nor does it recognize false opinions about the causes of or cures for war.

A closer analogy to the facts of the Schenck case might have been provided by a person's standing outside a theater, offering the patrons a leaflet advising them that in his opinion the theater was structurally unsafe, and urging them not to enter but to complain to the building inspectors. That analogy, however, would not have served Holmes's argument for punishing Schenck. Holmes needed an analogy that would appear relevant to Schenck's political speech but that would invite the conclusion that censorship was appropriate.

Unsurprisingly, a war-weary nation — in the throes of a know-nothing hysteria over immigrant anarchists and socialists — welcomed the comparison between what was regarded as a seditious political pamphlet and a malicious shout of "Fire!" Ironically, the "Fire!" analogy is nearly all that survives from the Schenck case; the ruling itself is almost certainly not good law. Pamphlets of the kind that resulted in Schenck's imprisonment have been circulated with impunity during subsequent wars.

Over the past several years I have assembled a collection of instances — cases, speeches, arguments — in which proponents of censorship have maintained that the expression at issue is "just like" or "equivalent to" falsely shouting "Fire!" in a crowded theater and ought to be banned, "just as" shouting "Fire!" ought to be banned. The analogy is generally invoked, often with self-satisfaction, as an absolute argument-stopper. It does, after all, claim the high authority of the great Justice Oliver Wendell Holmes. I have rarely heard it invoked in a convincing, or even particularly relevant, way. But that, too, can claim lineage from the great Holmes.

Not unlike Falwell, with his silly comparison between shouting "Fire!" and publishing an offensive parody, courts and commentators have frequently invoked "Fire!" as an analogy to expression that is not an automatic stimulus to panic. A state supreme court held that "Holmes' aphorism . . . applies with equal force to pornography" — in particular to the exhibition of the movie *Carmen Baby* in a drive-in theater in close proximity to highways and homes. Another court analogized "picketing . . . in support of a secondary boycott" to shouting "Fire!" because in both instances "speech and conduct are brigaded." In the famous Skokie case one of the judges argued that allowing Nazis to march through a city where a large number of Holocaust survivors live "just might fall into the same category as one's 'right' to cry fire in a crowded theater."

Outside court the analogies become even more badly stretched. A spokesperson for the New Jersey Sports and Exposition Authority complained that newspaper reports to the effect that a large number of football players had contracted cancer after playing in the Meadowlands — a stadium atop a landfill — were the "journalistic equivalent of shouting fire in a crowded theater." An insect researcher acknowledged that his prediction that a certain amusement park might become roach-infested "may be tantamount to shouting fire in a crowded theater." The philosopher Sidney Hook, in a letter to the *New York Times* bemoaning a Supreme Court decision that required a plaintiff in a defamation action to prove that the offending statement was actually false, argued that the First

Amendment does not give the press carte blanche to accuse innocent persons "anymore than the First Amendment protects the right of someone falsely to shout fire in a crowded theater."

Some close analogies to shouting "Fire!" or setting off an alarm are, of course, available: calling in a false bomb threat; dialing 911 and falsely describing an emergency; making a loud, gunlike sound in the presence of the President; setting off a voice-activated sprinkler system by falsely shouting "Fire!" In one case in which the "Fire!" analogy was directly to the point, a creative defendant tried to get around it. The case involved a man who calmly advised an airline clerk that he was "only here to hijack the plane." He was charged, in effect, with shouting "Fire!" in a crowded theater, and his rejected defense — as quoted by the court — was as follows: "If we built fire-proof theaters and let people know about this, then the shouting of 'Fire!' would not cause panic."

Here are some more-distant but still related examples: the recent incident of the police slaying in which some members of an onlooking crowd urged a mentally ill vagrant who had taken an officer's gun to shoot the officer; the screaming of racial epithets during a tense confrontation; shouting down a speaker and preventing him from continuing his speech.

Analogies are, by their nature, matters of degree. Some are closer to the core example than others. But any attempt to analogize political ideas in a pamphlet, ugly parody in a magazine, offensive movies in a theater, controversial newspaper articles, or any of the other expressions and actions catalogued above to the very different act of shouting "Fire!" in a crowded theater is either self-deceptive or self-serving.

The government does, of course, have some arguably legitimate bases for suppressing speech which bear no relationship to shouting "Fire!" It may ban the publication of nuclear-weapon codes, of information about troop movements, and of the identity of undercover agents. It may criminalize extortion threats and conspiratorial agreements. These expressions may lead directly to serious harm, but the mechanisms of causation are very different from that at work when an alarm is sounded. One may also argue — less persuasively, in my view — against protecting certain forms of public obscenity and defamatory statements. Here, too, the mechanisms of causation are very different. None of these exceptions to the First Amendment's exhortation that the government "shall make no law . . . abridging the freedom of speech, or of the press" is anything like falsely shouting "Fire!" in a crowded theater; they all must be justified on other grounds.

A comedian once told his audience, during the stand-up routine, about the time he was standing around a fire with a crowd of people and got in trouble for yelling "Theater, theater!" That, I think, is about as clever and productive a use as anyone has ever made of Holmes's flawed analogy.

PREPARING FOR DISCUSSION

1. Dershowitz's point in this essay depends upon an understanding of what makes a proper analogy. Why does Dershowitz consider Justice Holmes's famous analogy "inapt"? In what way does the analogy's inaptness depend on Holmes having "cleverly" substituted a "derivative example" for "the core analogy"? What, according to Dershowitz, is the "core analogy"?

2. Why does Dershowitz find the analogy not only "inapt" but "insulting"? Whom does it insult? Do you think Dershowitz believes Holmes *intended* it to be insulting?

3. What is Dershowitz's attitude toward Justice Oliver Wendell Holmes? Does Dershowitz believe Holmes *deliberately* constructed a false analogy? What might have been Holmes's political motive for doing so?

4. Consider the examples of other possible analogies Dershowitz supplies. Why does he consider racial epithets among the "close analogies" but not pornographic films?

5. Does Dershowitz maintain that the shouting "fire" analogy is always a flawed analogy when applied to free speech arguments? Or are there cases in which he would find it appropriate? Explain.

FROM READING TO WRITING

6. Dershowitz says that the shouting "fire" analogy has "assumed the status of a folk argument." Consider what he means by a "folk argument," then write an essay in which you focus on another example of a flawed analogy often used in popular speech (e.g., Nazi analogies, sports analogies, military analogies, computer analogies). You can usually locate several examples in newspapers or magazines. In your essay, discuss why you think the analogy is faulty and finally unpersuasive.

7. If he were alive today, how might Justice Holmes respond to Dershowitz's attack on his famous analogy? Write an essay in which you defend the shouting "fire" analogy. You might do this either by defending the appropriateness of the analogy precisely as Holmes used it or by extending it to cover other controversial areas of free speech, such as violent pornography or obscenity. Would, for example, Holmes's analogy apply to flag burning? Would Dershowitz agree or disagree that publicly burning the American flag is equivalent to shouting "fire" in a crowded theater?

NADINE STROSSEN
Sexual Speech and the Law

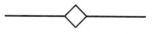

The most recent and powerful attacks on the First Amendment have been launched by feminists like Andrea Dworkin (see p. 390) and Catharine MacKinnon, who would like to make all pornography illegal. Surprisingly enough, the antipornography feminist position is most closely mirrored by the very conservatives who have traditionally been the greatest opponents to women's rights and related causes. In the following selection, Nadine Strossen, national president of the American Civil Liberties Union and professor of law at New York Law School, argues against feminists who campaign against a wide range of sexual expression. Strossen, a feminist herself, maintains that censorship poses far greater dangers to women than sexual speech and expression, even when they occur in pornography.

A graduate of Radcliffe and Harvard Law School, Strossen was in 1991 named the first woman president of the ACLU. Under her guidance, the organization continues to be the foremost defender of free expression and human rights in the United States. She has also been a member of the Council on Foreign Relations since 1994 and a founding member of Feminists for Free Expression. This selection is from her book *Defending Pornography* (1995).

SELECTED PUBLICATIONS: *Defending Pornography: Free Speech, Sex, and the Fight for Women's Rights* (1995); *Civil Liberties at Millennium's End* (1996); Strossen also publishes in *Cosmopolitan*, the *New Yorker*, the *New York Times*, the *Philadelphia Inquirer*, and *USA Today*.

Martin Luther King, Malcolm X
Freedom of speech is as good as sex.   MADONNA, performer[1]

Since Christianity . . . concentrated on sexual behavior as the root of virtue, everything pertaining to sex has been a "special case" in our culture, evoking peculiarly inconsistent attitudes.   SUSAN SONTAG, writer[2]

While Madonna believes that free speech and sex are equally good, many other Americans believe that they are equally bad — at least when the speech is *about* sex. Therefore, just as the American legal system has outlawed certain types of sexual activity — even by consenting adults in

462

private — it has outlawed certain types of sexual expression — again, even by or for consenting adults in private.

This sexual prudery in American law reflects our Puritan heritage. Garrison Keillor made this point with characteristic humor in his 1990 congressional testimony supporting the National Endowment for the Arts, which was embattled because it had funded certain sexually oriented works, including Robert Mapplethorpe's homoerotic photographs. Keillor said: "My ancestors were Puritans from England, [who] arrived here in 1648 in the hope of finding greater restrictions than were permissible under English law at the time."[3]

The First Amendment's broadly phrased free speech guarantee — "Congress shall make no law . . . abridging the freedom of speech" — contains no exception for sexual expression.[4] Nevertheless, the Supreme Court has consistently read such an exception into the First Amendment, allowing sexual speech to be restricted or even banned under circumstances in which it would not allow other types of speech to be limited. While American law is, overall, the most speech-protective in the world, it is far less protective of sexual speech than the law in some other countries. Our First Amendment jurisprudence, along with everything else in our culture, as Susan Sontag suggests, treats sex as a "special case."[5]

The very change in current law that procensorship feminists advocate — that it target sexual expression that "subordinates" or "degrades" women — highlights the important ideas that such speech conveys about significant public issues, notably, gender roles and gender-based discrimination. Consequently, the courts have recognized that the subset of sexual speech that the Dworkin-MacKinnon faction seeks to suppress, as distinct from the subset of sexual speech that is unprotected under current obscenity doctrine, is really "political" speech, which has traditionally received the highest level of legal protection.

The MacDworkinite concept of pornography, in focusing expressly on the political ideas conveyed by sexual expression, would necessarily threaten other forms of political expression, too. In contrast, the Court's concept of obscene expression focuses specifically on the alleged lack of ideas conveyed by such speech. At least in theory, then, obscenity is a self-contained category of sexual expression whose unprotected status does not directly threaten other speech. As I will explain, in practice the concept of obscenity cannot be cabined, and does threaten valuable expression. But the alternative, more expansive notion of pornography-as-discrimination even more directly threatens a broader range of speech, as well as many core free-speech principles.

If we should restrict sexually explicit speech because it purveys sexist ideas, as the feminist antipornography faction argues, then why shouldn't we restrict non–sexually explicit speech when it purveys sexist ideas? And if speech conveying sexist ideas can be restricted, then why shouldn't speech be restricted when it conveys racist, heterosexist, and other biased ideas? These logically indistinguishable applications of the feminist antipornography analysis lead many in the Dworkin-MacKinnon camp, including Dworkin and MacKinnon themselves, to advocate restricting racist and other forms of "hate" speech.[6]

Yet the Supreme Court has repeatedly held that the First Amendment protects not only speech that is *full of hate* on the speaker's part, but also speech that is *hateful* to its audience. As former justice Oliver Wendell Holmes declared, "[I]f there is any principle of the Constitution that more imperatively calls for attachment than any other it is the principle of free thought — not free thought for those who agree with us but freedom for the thought we hate."[7]

Furthermore, the Supreme Court has consistently rejected calls for censoring (nonobscene) speech when there is no demonstrable, direct causal link between the speech and immediate harm. But this is the feminist procensorship argument in a nutshell — that pornography should be suppressed based on speculation that it may lead to discrimination or violence against women in the long run, despite the lack of evidence to substantiate these fears. If we should restrict pornography on this basis, then why shouldn't we suppress any expression that might ultimately have a negative effect?

If MacDworkinism should prevail in the courts, it would jeopardize all of the foregoing free-speech precedents and principles. The government could outlaw flag burning and the teaching of Marxist doctrine because they might lead to the erosion of patriotism and our capitalist system; white supremacist and black nationalist speeches could be criminalized because they might lead to racial segregation; peaceful demonstrations for (or against) civil rights, women's rights, gay rights, and, indeed, any other potentially controversial causes could be banned because they might provoke violent counterdemonstrations; advertising for alcohol, tobacco, and innumerable other products could be prohibited because it might cause adverse health effects; feminist expression could be stifled because it might threaten "traditional family values" and the attendant domestic order and tranquility; abortion clinic advertising and other prochoice expression could be suppressed because it might lead to the termination of potential life; indeed, feminist antipornography advocacy could itself be suppressed because it could endanger cherished constitutional rights! The list is literally endless.

Make no mistake: if accepted, the feminist procensorship analysis would lead inevitably to the suppression of far more than pornography. At stake is all sexually oriented speech, any expression that allegedly subordinates or undermines the equality of any group, and any speech that may have a tendency to lead to any kind of harm. One might well ask about the feminist procensorship philosophy, not what expression would be stifled, but rather, what expression would be safe.

The "Preferred" Status of Speech in Our Hierarchy of Constitutional Rights

As noted above, the U.S. Supreme Court has relegated sexual expression to second-class status. To understand the significance of this disparity, we need first to consider the Court's rules concerning freedom of expression in general, and then to consider how the Court has refused to extend these speech-protective general rules to sexually oriented speech.

At the heart of the Supreme Court's extensive free-speech jurisprudence are two cardinal principles. The first specifies what is *not* a sufficient justification for restricting speech, and the second prescribes what *is* a sufficient justification. A Dworkin-MacKinnon–style antipornography law violates both of these core principles. Accordingly, for such a law to be upheld, the very foundations of our free-speech structure would have to be torn up.

The first of these basic principles requires "content neutrality" or "viewpoint neutrality." It holds that government may never limit speech just because any listener — or even, indeed, the majority of the community — disagrees with or is offended by its content or the viewpoint it conveys. The Supreme Court has called this the "bedrock principle" of our proud free-speech tradition under American law.[8] In recent years, the Court has steadfastly enforced this fundamental principle to protect speech that conveys ideas that are deeply unpopular with or offensive to many, if not most, Americans: for example, burning an American flag in a political demonstration against national policies,[9] and burning a cross near the home of an African-American family that had recently moved into a previously all-white neighborhood.[10]

The viewpoint-neutrality principle reflects the philosophy that, as first stated in pathbreaking opinions by former Supreme Court justices Oliver Wendell Holmes and Louis Brandeis, the appropriate response to speech with which one disagrees in a free society is not censorship but counterspeech — *more* speech, not *less*. Persuasion, not coercion, is the solution.

Rejecting this philosophy, the feminist procensorship position targets for suppression a category of sexual expression precisely because of its viewpoint — specifically, a gender-discriminatory viewpoint. Because of this fatal constitutional flaw, all Dworkin-MacKinnon–style antipornography laws will continue to be ruled unconstitutional, as were the two such laws that courts have reviewed to date, as long as our courts continue to enforce the viewpoint-neutrality principle.

The feminist antipornography laws also violate the second cardinal principle that is central to free speech law — that a restriction on speech can be justified only when necessary to prevent actual or imminent harm to an interest of "compelling" importance, such as violence or injury to others. This is often summarized as the "clear and present danger"

15

requirement. As Justice Oliver Wendell Holmes observed in a much-quoted opinion, the First Amendment would not protect someone who falsely shouted "Fire!" in a theater and caused a panic.[11]

This second core free-speech principle entails two essential prerequisites for justifying any speech restriction: that the expression will cause direct, imminent harm to a very important interest, and that only by suppressing it can we avert such harm. Each of these requirements is crucial for preserving free expression, and neither is satisfied by advocates of suppressing pornography.

The restricted speech must pose an imminent danger, not an alleged "bad tendency." Allowing speech to be curtailed on the speculative basis that it might indirectly lead to possible harm would inevitably unravel free speech protection. *All* speech might lead to potential danger at some future point. Justice Holmes recognized this fact in an important 1925 opinion. Holmes rejected the argument that pacifist and socialist ideas should be repressed because they might incite young men to resist the draft or to oppose the U.S. system of government — actions and views that many thought might ultimately undermine national interests. As Holmes noted, "Every idea is an incitement."[12]

If we banned the expression of all ideas that might lead individuals to actions that might have an adverse impact even on important interests such as national security or public safety, then scarcely any idea would be safe, and surely no idea that challenged the status quo would be. Judge Frank Easterbrook made precisely this point in holding the Indianapolis version of the Dworkin-MacKinnon model antipornography law unconstitutional. Accepting for the sake of argument the law's cornerstone assumption that "depictions of subordination tend to perpetuate subordination," Easterbrook explained:

> If pornography is what pornography does, so is other speech. . . . Efforts to suppress communist speech in the United States were based on the belief that the public acceptability of such ideas would increase the likelihood of totalitarian government. Religions affect socialization in the most pervasive way. . . . The Alien and Sedition Acts passed during the administration of John Adams rested on a sincerely held belief that disrespect for the government leads to social collapse and revolution — a belief with support in the history of many nations. . . .
>
> Racial bigotry, anti-Semitism, violence on television, reporters' biases — these and many more influence the culture and shape our socialization. . . . Yet all is protected as speech, however insidious. Any other answer leaves the government in control of all of the institutions of culture, the great censor and director of which thoughts are good for us.
>
> Sexual responses often are unthinking responses, and the association of sexual arousal with the subordination of women therefore may have a substantial effect. But almost all cultural stimuli provoke unconcious responses. Religious ceremonies condition their participants.

> Teachers convey messages by selecting what not to cover; the implicit
> message about what is off limits or unthinkable may be more powerful
> than the messages for which they present rational argument. . . . If the
> fact that speech plays a role in a process of conditioning were enough to
> permit governmental regulation, that would be the end of freedom of
> speech.[13]

While Justice Holmes rejected the so-called bad-tendency argument —
namely, that speech could be suppressed if it might have a tendency to
bring about future harm — his Supreme Court brethren accepted that argument in a series of cases during the World War I era and the ensuing
"Red Scare." In one of the low points for free speech in this country, they
allowed the imprisonment of thousands of political leaders and other citizens who did nothing more than peacefully express views critical of U.S.
participation in World War I and other government policies.

The Supreme Court has since repudiated the bad-tendency argument
in the context of what it calls "political speech," or speech about issues of
public policy. But it continues to accept that argument in the context of
sexual speech. The Court allows certain sexual expression —
"obscenity" — to be restricted merely because of its alleged tendency to
undermine community morality, without any evidence of any direct or
immediate harm.

The feminist antipornography activists seek to expand the bad-
tendency rationale to allow suppression of even more sexual speech than
is currently restricted under traditional obscenity laws. In 1992, the Canadian Supreme Court adopted the MacDworkinite bad-tendency approach. The Canadian court acknowledged that no evidence establishes a
direct causal connection between pornography and discrimination or violence against women, but it nevertheless ruled that the mere *belief* that
such a connection exists is enough to justify suppressing the speech.[14]

In contrast, the U.S. Supreme Court has rejected this censorial notion,
maintaining the crucial distinction between *advocacy* of violent or unlawful conduct, which is protected, and intentional, imminent *incitement* of
such conduct, which is not. The classic free speech dissents of justices
Holmes and Brandeis earlier in this century endorsed this critical distinction as an essential aspect of the "clear and present danger" requirement
that they also launched. The Court enshrined the distinction as a cornerstone of contemporary free speech law in a 1969 case, *Brandenburg v.
Ohio*.[15] *Brandenburg* upheld the First Amendment rights of a Ku Klux
Klan leader who addressed a rally of supporters, some of whom brandished firearms, and advocated violence and discrimination against Jews
and blacks. The Court held that this generalized advocacy was neither intended nor likely to cause immediate violent or unlawful conduct, and
therefore could not be punished.

The Supreme Court has consistently applied *Brandenburg*'s critical

20

distinction between protected advocacy and unprotected incitement to protect incendiary expression of every stripe. In 1982, it relied on this distinction to protect expression whose thrust was diametrically opposite that of the expression that had been protected in the *Brandenburg* case. The Court held that officials of the National Association for the Advancement of Colored People (NAACP) had a First Amendment right to make speeches advocating violent reprisals against individuals who violated an NAACP-organized boycott of white merchants who had allegedly engaged in racial discrimination. Even though some violence was subsequently committed against blacks who patronized white merchants, it occurred weeks or months after the inflammatory addresses. Accordingly, in a major victory for the civil rights cause, as well as for free-speech principles, the Supreme Court overturned a lower-court ruling that had declared the boycott unlawful and held the NAACP responsible for white merchants' large financial losses. The Court explained the fundamental free-speech principles at stake:

> The [NAACP leaders'] addresses generally contained an impassioned plea for black citizens to unify, to support and respect each other, and to realize the political and economic power available to them. In the course of those pleas, strong language was used. . . . Strong and effective extemporaneous rhetoric cannot be nicely channeled in purely dulcet phrases. An advocate must be free to stimulate his audience with spontaneous and emotional appeals for unity and action in a common cause. . . . To rule otherwise would ignore the "profound national commitment" that "debate on public issues should be uninhibited, robust, and wide-open."[16]

Procensorship feminists seek to eliminate the fundamental distinction between protected advocacy and unprotected incitement, arguing that sexual expression should be suppressed even if it does not expressly *advocate,* let alone *intentionally incite,* violence or discrimination against women. They want to suppress sexual words or images they interpret as consistent with views that accept violence or discrimination against women, and which might reinforce such views on the part of some audience members.

It has become fashionable among some law professors, of whom Catharine MacKinnon is a prominent example, to question the ongoing relevance of classic First Amendment principles, and I certainly endorse and engage in the constant critical reexamination of all established legal principles. Reexamining the landmark Holmes and Brandeis free-speech opinions that I have cited has left me more impressed than ever with their universal, timeless force. They remain relevant and persuasive, specifically in the context of the current pornography debate. Further, the majority rulings that these dissents so powerfully criticize stand as sobering reminders of how much freedom we would lose should we accept the procensorship feminists' call to revive the now discredited "bad-tendency" approach that these rulings reflect.

Heed the following passage from Justice Holmes's 1916 dissent in *Abrams v. United States,* in which the majority had upheld prison sentences of up to twenty years for a group of Russian immigrants who had expressed their support for the Russian Revolution and called for a general strike in the United States. It reads as if it were Justice Holmes's answer to contemporary feminists' pleas for censoring pornography — an answer that is understanding of, and even sympathetic to, their reasons for urging such censorship, but that also explains why those reasons are fundamentally at odds with a sustainable constitutional philosophy:

> Persecution for the expression of opinions seems to me perfectly logical. If you have no doubt of your premises or your power and want a certain result with all your heart you naturally express your wishes in law and sweep away all opposition. To allow opposition by speech seems to indicate that you think the speech impotent. . . . But when men have realized that time has upset many fighting faiths, they may come to believe even more than they believe the very foundations of their own conduct that the ultimate good desired is better reached by free trade in ideas — that the best test of truth is the power of the thought to get itself accepted in the competition of the market, and that truth is the only ground upon which their wishes safely can be carried out. That at any rate is the theory of our Constitution. It is an experiment, as all life is an experiment. Every year if not every day we have to wager our salvation upon some prophecy based upon imperfect knowledge. While that experiment is part of our system I think that we should be eternally vigilant against attempts to check the expression of opinions that we loathe and believe to be fraught with death, unless they so imminently threaten immediate interference with the lawful and pressing purposes of the law that an immediate check is required to save the country. . . . Only the emergency that makes it immediately dangerous to leave the correction of evil counsels to time warrants making any exception to the sweeping command, "Congress shall make no law . . . abridging the freedom of speech."[17]

Next, listen to Justice Brandeis's powerful opinion in *Whitney v. California,* a 1927 case in which the majority upheld a one- to fourteen-year prison sentence that had been imposed on Anita Whitney merely because she was a member of the Communist Labor Party, whose platform advocated the violent overthrow of the U.S. government. Although Whitney herself unsuccessfully opposed this position, and had called upon the party to pursue its goals through the political process, the Supreme Court majority held that Whitney's mere party membership warranted her criminal punishment.

While Brandeis, like Holmes, is sympathetic to fears about potential speech-induced harms, he eloquently reminds us that our constitutional philosophy reflects and requires not fear, but rather courage, in the realm of ideas. Moreover, directly responsive to the procensorship feminists' concerns about women's relatively powerless status, Brandeis presciently warns that it is precisely those who are relatively weak who will be victimized, not protected, by any fear-based repression:

> Those who won our independence . . . believed liberty to be the secret of happiness and courage to be the secret of liberty. . . . They recognized the risks to which all human institutions are subject. But they knew that order cannot be secured merely through fear of punishment for its infraction; that it is hazardous to discourage thought, hope and imagination; that fear breeds repression; that repression breeds hate; that hate menaces stable government; that the path of safety lies in the opportunity to discuss freely supposed grievances and proposed remedies; and that the fitting remedy for evil counsels is good ones. . . .
>
> Fear of serious injury cannot alone justify suppression of free speech and assembly. Men feared witches and burned women. . . .
>
> Those who won our independence by revolution were not cowards. . . . They did not exalt order at the cost of liberty. To courageous, self-reliant men, with confidence in the power of free and fearless reasoning applied through the processes of popular government, no danger flowing from speech can be deemed clear and present, unless the incidence of the evil apprehended is so imminent that it may befall before there is opportunity for full discussion. If there be time to expose through discussion the falsehood and fallacies, to avert the evil by the processes of education, the remedy to be applied is more speech, not enforced silence. Only an emergency can justify repression.[18]

In urging "courageous, self-reliant" individuals to have "confidence" in their own speech as an effective response to "evil counsels," rather than asking the government to protect them by suppressing such evil counsels, Justice Brandeis anticipates an important theme in the current feminist anticensorship movement. Rejecting the procensorship faction's emphasis on women as victims in need of governmental protection through censorship, anticensorship feminists are willing to trust our own voices — as well as those of our antipornography sister feminists — to effectively counter misogynist expression, including misogynist sexual expression. Ironically, the feminist procensorship faction apparently does not view women as capable of such self-help, but instead sees us as helpless.

Notes

1. Madonna, "Rock the Vote Video," MTV Networks, 1992.
2. Susan Sontag, "The Pornographic Imagination," in *Styles of Radical Will* (New York: Anchor Books, 1969), pp. 35–73, at p. 46.
3. Garrison Keillor, statement to the Senate Subcommittee on Education, 29 March 1990. (Testimony on NEA Grant Funding and Restrictions.)
4. Although the First Amendment expressly prohibits only congressional laws that abridge free speech, the Supreme Court has interpreted it as implicitly prohibiting any

government action that abridges free speech. Moreover, the Court has held that the First Amendment bars private citizens from invoking the legal system — for example, through private lawsuits — to suppress free speech.

5. Sontag, "Pornographic Imagination," p. 46.
6. Catharine MacKinnon, *Only Words* (Cambridge, Mass.: Harvard University Press, 1993), pp. 45–110; Andrea Dworkin and Catharine MacKinnon, *Pornography and Civil Rights: A New Day for Women's Equality* (Minneapolis: Organizing Against Pornography, 1988), p. 85.
7. *United States v. Schwimmer*, 279 U.S. 644, 654–55 (1929) (dissenting).
8. *Texas v. Johnson*, 491 U.S. 397, 414 (1989).
9. Ibid; *U.S. v. Eichman*, 496 U.S. 310 (1990).
10. *R.A.V. v. City of St. Paul*, 112 S. Ct. 2538 (1992). The Court recognized that this symbolic expression could be constitutionally prohibited under many laws, such as those prohibiting arson, vandalism, and trespass; it stressed, though, that this expression could not be prohibited under a law that focused on the ideas it conveyed — namely, a city ordinance that prohibited expression that "arouses anger, alarm or resentment . . . on the basis of race, color, creed, religion or gender."
11. *Schenck v. United States*, 249 U.S. 47, 52 (1919).
12. *Gitlow v. New York*, 268 U.S. 652, 673 (1925) (dissenting).
13. *American Booksellers Association v. Hudnut*, 771 F. 2d 323, 329–30 (1985).
14. *Butler v. the Queen*, 1 S.C.R. 452, 505 (1992, Canada) (stating that "[i]t might be suggested that proof of actual harm should be required. . . . [I]t is sufficient . . . for Parliament to have a reasonable basis for concluding that harm will result and this requirement does not demand actual proof of harm").
15. *Brandenburg v. Ohio*, 395 U.S. 444 (1969).
16. *National Association for the Advancement of Colored People (NAACP) v. Claiborne Hardware Co.*, 458 U.S. 886, 928 (1982).
17. *Abrams v. United States*, 250 U.S. 616, 630–31 (1919) (dissenting).
18. *Whitney v. California*, 274 U.S. 357, 375–77 (1927) (concurring).

PREPARING FOR DISCUSSION

1. Strossen notes that the Supreme Court has traditionally protected the expression of political ideas whereas "obscene" expression has been left unprotected. What reasons does Strossen provide for the double standard? Does she agree with the Court's distinction?

2. The author objects to any restrictions placed on sexual speech. On what legal grounds does she oppose the Supreme Court's stand on sexual speech? How does she use this argument to counter the advocates of what she calls "MacDworkinite" laws?

3. Strossen condemns the feminist procensorship position on the grounds that it "targets for suppression a category of sexual expression precisely because of its viewpoint" (paragraph 15) — grounds on which suppression cannot occur according to the Supreme Court's basic principle of free expression. Yet antipornography theorist MacKinnon argues that pornography is not speech, but an act of discrimination. In what ways does Strossen's argument remain relevant as a refutation of the feminist procensorship position? In what ways does her argument need to be modified in order to answer this position?

4. Strossen contends that the enforcement of laws against certain forms of sexual expression will inevitably come down to a matter of taste among judges

and jurors. Do you agree with Strossen's conclusion? Was the ban on 2 Live Crew's songs, for example, merely a matter of taste or were there other considerations behind these legal actions? What might these considerations have been?

5. At several points, Strossen echoes a feminist slogan "the sexual is political." What does this statement mean? Does it imply that sexual matters are always political or only that sexuality is often a political matter? For what immediate political purposes do you think the original slogan ("the *personal* is political") was invented in the first place?

FROM READING TO WRITING

6. Strossen indirectly offers women an important choice in paragraph 29. She suggests that women may either view themselves "as victims requiring government protection through censorship" or they may begin to trust their own verbal abilities to counter the implicit misogyny of most pornographic material. Write an essay in which you consider which choice is the better one for women.

7. The author notes that the Supreme Court has generally failed to provide "a clear, objective definition of proscribable obscenity." In an essay, define what you consider "proscribable obscenity" in terms that are independent of any subjective values on the part of the reader or viewer. Is it possible to formulate a definition that answers this criterion?

ROBERT H. BORK

What to Do about the First Amendment

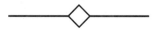

When President Reagan's Supreme Court nominee Robert Bork was rejected by Congress in 1987, many of Bork's critics cited as a reason for his rejection his desire to place greater restrictions on free expression. In the following essay, which first appeared in the neoconservative monthly *Commentary* in 1995, Bork challenges the current Supreme Court's majority position on the First Amendment and offers a new reading of our Constitution's free-speech clause. He then argues that only with restrictions on free speech can civility and self-restraint be reestablished in a country where virtually anything goes. His proposal for limited free speech is linked to his desire for greater support on the part of government for religious institutions.

Bork, widely considered to be the Right's most prominent legal theorist, was educated at the University of Chicago, where he also attended law school. He served as acting attorney general of the United States from 1973 through 1974 and as the solitor general under President Gerald Ford. For most of the 1980s, Bork was a circuit judge for the U.S. Court of Appeals. Having taught at Yale University Law School for many years, Bork accepted a position at the American Enterprise Institute for Public Policy Research as a John M. Olin scholar in legal studies.

SELECTED PUBLICATIONS: *The Antitrust Paradox: A Policy at War with Itself* (1978); *The Tempting of America: The Political Seduction of the Law* (1990).

The text of the First Amendment is quite simple: "Congress shall make no law respecting an establishment of religion, or prohibiting the free exercise thereof; or abridging the freedom of speech, or of the press, or the right of the people peaceably to assemble, and to petition the government for a redress of grievances." These are not words that would lead the uninitiated to suspect that the law, both with regard to religion and with regard to speech, could be what the Supreme Court has made of it in the past few decades.

Where religion is concerned, for example, a state may lend parochial schoolchildren geography textbooks that contain maps of the United States but may not lend them maps of the United States for use in geography class; a state may lend parochial schoolchildren textbooks on American colonial history but not a film about George Washington; a state may pay for diagnostic services conducted in a parochial school but therapeutic services must be provided in a different building.[1]

At this moment, the most prominent issue involving the religion clauses of the First Amendment stems from the decision in *Engel v. Vitale* (1962), and subsequent cases, prohibiting prayer, Bible reading, or even a moment of silence in public schools. In addition to declaring that these are all violations of the First Amendment, the Court has held unconstitutional even school practices that are neutral as among different religions on the grounds that, under the First Amendment, religion may not be preferred to irreligion. Since the vast majority of Americans are believers, these holdings are fiercely resented by most of them as attempts to impose secularism on their children, and school prayer remains a simmering political issue.

The new Speaker of the House of Representatives, Newt Gingrich, has responded to these concerns by proposing to offer a constitutional amendment to permit the prayer the Court forbids. The current draft of the amendment reads:

> Nothing in this Constitution shall be construed to prohibit individual or group prayer in public schools or other public institutions. No person

---

[1] This list comes from then-Associate Justice Rehnquist's dissent in *Wallace v. Jaffree* (1985). [Bork's note]

shall be required by the United States or by any state to participate in prayer. Neither the United States nor any state shall compose the words of any prayer to be said in public schools.

Whatever one may think of the language here and of the idea of an amendment specifically directed to school prayer, left untouched are far more serious judicial deformations of the true constitutional relationship between government and religion. For the Supreme Court has been secularizing not just the public schools but, so far as it is able, our entire culture. We have grown so accustomed to this trend that it may come as a shock to realize that it does not reflect the intention underlying the religion clauses.

The First Amendment's establishment clause — "Congress shall make no law respecting an establishment of religion" — clearly precludes recognition of an official church, and it can easily be read to prevent discriminatory aid to one or a few religions. But it hardly requires the conclusion that government may not assist religion in general or sponsor religious symbolism. An established religion is one which the state recognizes as the official religion and which it organizes by law. Typically, citizens are required to support the established church by taxation. The Congress that proposed and the states that ratified the First Amendment knew very well what an establishment of religion was, since six states had various forms of establishment at the time; ironically, one reason for the prohibition was to save these state establishments from federal interference.

The history of the formulation of the clause by Congress[2] demonstrates that it was not intended to ban government recognition of and assistance to religion; nor was it understood to require government neutrality between religion and irreligion. And as we shall see, it most certainly was not intended to erase religious references and symbolism from the actions and statements of government officials.

Had the establishment clause been read as its language and history show it should have been, the place of religion in American life would be very different from what it now is. But in modern times, the Supreme Court has developed a severe aversion to connections between government and religion. Nowhere is that more evident than in the Court's alteration of its fixed rules to allow such connections to be challenged far more easily than other claimed violations of the Constitution.

Major philosophical shifts in the law can occur through what may seem to laymen mere tinkerings with technical doctrine. Thus, the judi-

---

[2] See Walter Berns, *The First Amendment and the Future of American Democracy;* Robert Cord, *Separation of Church and State;* and C. Antieau, A. Downey, and E. Roberts, *Freedom from Federal Establishment.* [Bork's note]

ciary's power to marginalize religion in public life was vastly increased through a change in the law of what lawyers call "standing." Orthodox standing doctrine withholds the power to sue from persons alleging an interest in an issue only in their capacities as citizens or taxpayers. An individualized personal interest, some direct impact upon the plaintiff, such as the loss of money or liberty, is required. But in 1968, in *Flast v. Cohen,* the Supreme Court created the rule that taxpayers could sue under the establishment clause to enjoin federal expenditures to aid religious schools.

Though the opinion offered a strained explanation that would fit   10
some suits under other parts of the Constitution, the Court has managed to avoid allowing such suits with still more strained rationales. Every single provision of the Constitution from Article I, Section 1 to the 37th Amendment is immune from taxpayer or citizen enforcement — except one. Only under the establishment clause is an ideological interest in expunging religion sufficient to confer standing.

The unhistorical severity of establishment-clause law was codified in the Supreme Court's opinion in *Lemon v. Kurtzman* (1971). To pass muster, the Court held, a law must satisfy three criteria: (1) the statute or practice must have a secular legislative purpose; (2) its principal or primary effect must be one that neither advances nor inhibits religion; and (3) it must not foster an excessive government entanglement with religion.

So few statutes or governmental practices that brush anywhere near religion can pass all of those tests that, were they uniformly applied, they would erase all traces of religion in governmental affairs. But there are too many entrenched traditions around for *Lemon* to be applied consistently. While a case challenging the use of a paid chaplain in Nebraska's legislature was pending in the Supreme Court, the appeals court on which I then sat gathered to hear a challenge by atheists to the practice of paying the chaplains who serve Congress. We and counsel stood while a court officer intoned, "God save the United States and this honorable court," an inauspicious beginning for the plaintiffs since the ritual, followed in the Supreme Court as well, would appear to violate all three prongs of *Lemon.*

Our case was later rendered moot because the Supreme Court approved the Nebraska legislature's chaplain in *Marsh v. Chambers* (1983). Justice William Brennan, dissenting, argued that the state's practice could not pass the *Lemon* test since it hardly had a secular purpose, and the process of choosing a "suitable" chaplain who would offer "suitable" prayers involved governmental supervision and hence "entanglement" with religion. The Court majority, however, relied on the fact that employing chaplains to open legislative sessions conformed to historic precedent: not only did the Continental Congress employ a chaplain but so did both houses of the first Congress under the Constitution which also proposed the First Amendment. In fact, they also provided paid chaplains for the Army and Navy.

Presumably for that reason, Chief Justice [Warren] Burger, who had written *Lemon,* did not apply it in *Marsh.* And quite right he was. The Court often enough pays little attention to the historic meaning of the provisions of the Constitution, but it would be egregious to hold that those who sent the amendment to the states for ratification intended to prohibit what they had just done themselves.

But if the *Lemon* test should be ignored where there exists historical   15
evidence of the validity of specific practices or laws that could not other-wise pass muster, then it is a fair conclusion that the test itself contradicts the original understanding of the establishment clause and is destroying laws and practices that were not meant to be invalidated.

As matters stand, *Lemon* makes it difficult for government to give even the most harmless or beneficial forms of assistance to religious insti-tutions. New York City, for example, implemented a program, subsi-dized with federal funds, under which public-school teachers could volunteer to teach in private schools, including religious schools. The program offered instruction to educationally deprived children in reme-dial reading, mathematics, and English as a second language. The teach-ers were accountable only to the public-school system, used teaching materials selected and screened for religious content by city employees, and taught in rooms free of religious symbols. The teachers were gener-ally not members of the religious faith espoused by the schools to which they were assigned. There was no evidence that any teacher complained of interference by private-school officials or sought to teach or promote religion.

The court of appeals said this was "a program that apparently has done so much good and little, if any, detectable harm." Nevertheless, constrained by *Lemon,* that same court held the program an impermis-sible entanglement because the city, in order to be certain that the teach-ers did not inculcate religion, had to engage in some form of continuing surveillance. The Supreme Court, in *Aguilar v. Felton* (1985), affirmed on the same ground. The educationally deprived children were then re-quired to leave the school premises and receive remedial instruction in trailers.

To cite another example, the Satmar Hasidim, who observe a strict form of Orthodox Judaism, organized the village of Kiryas Joel in Orange County, New York, where only members of the sect lived. Children were educated in private religious schools which did not offer any special ser-vices to the handicapped. The handicapped pupils were thus forced to at-tend public schools outside the village. But their parents soon withdrew them because of "the panic, fear, and trauma" the children suffered in leav-ing their own community and being with people whose ways were so different and who taunted them. The New York State legislature then enacted a statute making Kiryas Joel a separate school district which ran only a secular special-education program for handicapped children; the other children of Kiryas Joel remained in the private religious schools. When the separate school district was, predictably, challenged, the trial court held that the statute violated all three criteria of *Lemon*. Dividing six to three, the Supreme Court affirmed in *Board of Education of Kiryas Joel v. Grumet* (1994), though the various opinions articulated different rationales.

Those parts of Justice David Souter's opinion in which a majority of the Court joined found an establishment-clause violation because the unusual nature of the statute gave "reason for concern whether the benefit received by the Satmar community is one that the legislature will provide equally to other religious (and nonreligious) groups" and because the statute delegated political power to a religious group. Justice [John Paul] Stevens, joined by Justices [Harry] Blackmun and [Ruth Bader] Ginsburg, concurred with the remarkable statement that in protecting the handicapped students from "panic, fear, and trauma," "the state provided official support to cement the attachment of young adherents to a particular faith."

This was only one of many decisions detecting the "establishment of religion" in the most innocuous practices. A lower court held that it was unconstitutional for a high-school football team to pray before a game that nobody be injured. Another court held that a Baltimore ordinance forbidding the sale of nonkosher foods as kosher amounted to the establishment of religion. A federal court decided that a school principal was required by the establishment clause to prevent a teacher from reading the Bible silently for his own purposes during a silent reading period because students, who were not shown to know what the teacher was reading, might, if they found out, be influenced by his choice of reading material.

The list of such decisions is almost endless, and very few receive Supreme Court review, not that that would be likely to change things. After all, the Supreme Court itself decided in *Stone v. Graham* (1980) that a public school could not display the Ten Commandments. (The school authorities were so intimidated by the current atmosphere that they attached a plaque stating that the display was intended to show our cultural heritage and not to make a religious statement; no matter, it had to come down. It also did not matter that the courtroom in which the case was heard was decorated with a painting of Moses and the Ten Commandments.)

So, too, in *Lee v. Weisman*, decided in 1992, a five-Justice majority held that a short, bland, nonsectarian prayer at a public-school commencement amounted to an establishment of religion. The majority saw government interference with religion in the fact that the school principal asked a rabbi to offer a nonsectarian prayer. Government coercion of Deborah Weisman was detected in the possibility that she might feel "peer pressure" to stand or to maintain respectful silence during the prayer. (She would, of course, have had no case had the speaker advocated Communism or genocide.) Thus was ended a long-standing tradition of prayer at school-graduation ceremonies.

The law became a parody of itself in *Lynch v. Donnelly*, a 1984 decision concerning Pawtucket, Rhode Island's inclusion of a crèche in its annual Christmas display. The Court held that the display passed muster, but only because, along with the crèche, it also included such secular features as

> a Santa Claus house, reindeer pulling Santa's sleigh, candy-striped poles, a Christmas tree, carolers, cut-out figures representing such characters as a clown, an elephant, and a teddy bear, hundreds of colored lights, and a large banner that reads "SEASON'S GREETINGS."

The display of a menorah on a public building has been subjected to a similar analysis. In other words, the question to be litigated nowadays is whether there is a sufficient number of secular symbols surrounding a religious symbol to drain the latter of its meaning.

Modern establishment-clause jurisprudence is often justified by reference to the views of Jefferson and Madison, but the truth is that their opinions on this subject were idiosyncratic among the Founders. Jefferson's often-quoted phrase about the "wall of separation" between church and state appears in a letter he wrote to the Danbury Baptist Association, and most historians agree that he was not expressing the views of those who enacted the Bill of Rights. As for Madison, the constitutional scholar Walter Berns points out:

> It is sufficient to recall that as president he vetoed a bill to grant a charter of incorporation to the Episcopal Church in Washington, D.C. [a routine practice at the time], and opposed the appointment of chaplains in the Army and Navy and the granting of tax exemptions to "Houses of Worship"; he even objected to presidential proclamations of days of thanksgiving.... The extent to which others did not share all his views is reflected in the fact that he found it necessary to yield to the pressure and issue such a proclamation.

In short, Jefferson and Madison held radical and unrepresentative positions on what constituted the establishment of religion. By following their opinions, the Supreme Court has mutilated the establishment clause as it was understood by those who made it law.

Indeed, no rigid separation of religion and government such as *Lemon* prescribes is even conceivable. For governments regularly and inevitably take actions that do not have a secular purpose, whose principal effect is to advance religion, and which entangle them with religion.

Aside from the examples already given, there are property-tax exemptions for places of worship, which do not have a secular purpose and do advance religion. Government, in the form of boards, courts, and legislatures, determines what qualifies as religion in order to award draft exemptions for conscientious objectors, aid to schools, and the like. In order to see that education is properly conducted, states must inspect and demand certain levels of performance in religious schools. Federal employees receive paid time off for Christmas, and the National Gallery preserves and displays religious paintings.

In short, our actual practices cannot be made consistent with the complete separation of religion and government.

There may be some who are dubious about the claim that the judiciary's rulings are hostile or damaging to the place of religion in society. To them, I recommend Justice Potter Stewart's dissent in *Abington School District v. Schempp*, a 1963 decision in which the majority struck down rules that required Bible reading without discussion at the beginning of each school day. Said Stewart:

> [A] compulsory state educational system so structures a child's life that if religious exercises are held to be an impermissible activity in schools, religion is placed at an artificial and state-created disadvantage. Viewed in this light, permission of such exercises for those who want them is necessary if the schools are truly to be neutral in the matter of religion. And a refusal to permit religious exercises thus is seen, not as the realization of state neutrality, but rather as the establishment of the religion of secularism, or at the least, as government support of the beliefs of those who think that religious exercises should be conducted only in private.

Similar conclusions could be drawn concerning the effects of decisions erasing religious speech and symbolism from our public life and denying nondiscriminatory aid to religious institutions. Nathan Lewin, who argued the case for the village of Kiryas Joel, wrote, justly I think:

> The *Kiryas Joel* decision proved once more that a majority of the Justices of the Supreme Court—like most judges of lower courts in the United States — are either hostile to religion or do not understand what religious observance is all about.

The case is very different with the speech and press clauses of the First Amendment.[3] Since this part of the amendment has less legislative history than the religion clauses, its plausible meaning must be deduced from other materials. But we can dispose at once of the notion that because the

---

[3] The law of the press clause is quite similar to that of the speech clause, so in the interest of brevity I will deal only with the speech clause here. [Bork's note]

First Amendment states that "Congress shall make no law . . . abridging the freedom of speech," it imposes an absolute bar to any regulation of speech. Nobody supposes that, not even judges who announce "absolute" positions. There are well-recognized exceptions of time, place, and manner: Congress, for example, can have a person prosecuted for haranguing its members from the visitors' gallery, and it has been held constitutional, under a congressionally-enacted code of military conduct, to imprison an officer for inciting troops to disobedience.

Still, the existence of the amendment implies that there is something special about speech, something that sets it apart from other human activities that are not accorded constitutional protection. Justice [Louis] Brandeis tried to specify what that something was in his impassioned concurrence in *Whitney v. California* (1927). He wrote, though more colorfully, that the benefits of speech are: (1) the development of the faculties of the individual; (2) the happiness to be derived from engaging in the activity; (3) the provision of a safety valve for society; and (4) the discovery and spread of political truth.

The list is not entirely satisfactory. The first two benefits do not distinguish speech from a myriad of other unprotected activities that develop human faculties or contribute to happiness. The safety-valve function suggests that prudence requires letting people blow off steam so they do not engage in actions that threaten stable government, yet prudence to preserve stable government is necessary in many ways, none of them important enough to be mentioned in the Constitution.

The "discovery and spread of political truth," however, does set 35 speech apart from other human activities. Only speech can deal explicitly, specifically, and directly with politics and government. In a previous writing, I too casually accepted Brandeis's qualification of the truth to be discovered and spread as "political," and I therefore mistakenly arrived at the proposition that only explicitly political speech should be protected by the speech clause.

Of course, political speech does have a special claim to protection: a representative democracy would be nonsense without it. But there is both a practical and a theoretical objection to limiting protection to explicitly political speech. The practical objection is that other forms of speech could find protection if the speaker added the admonition that we pass a law on the subject, whatever it was. The theoretical objection is that speech is both valuable and unique, whatever kind of truth it seeks to discover and spread. There is thus reason to conclude that the protection of the speech clause extends to many other types of speech that express ideas.

On the other hand, the modern Court has gone wrong, in my estimation, by accepting as a major part of the speech clause's rationale the desire of the individual to find happiness through self-expression. This is, as noted, inconsistent with the fact that many other forms of happiness-seeking are not protected. The idea that speech is the preferred form of happiness-seeking is merely an intellectual-class bias. There is no ground in constitutional law or philosophy for supposing that the fulfillment obtained through, say, dealing in financial markets is inferior to the fulfillment sought in writing a novel.

Acting on the basis of the self-expression rationale, the Court decided that a young man could not be punished for wearing into a courthouse a jacket with words on the back urging, with a four-letter verb, that an implausible sexual act be performed on the selective-service system. "One man's vulgarity," the Court opined, "is another's lyric."

The same rationale also led directly to the Court's decision in *Texas v. Johnson* (1989) that the clause protects not merely what it addresses, "speech," but actions that express moods and attitudes, such as burning the American flag. The burner could have expressed his hatred for America in as many and as eloquent words as he could muster and have been protected by the true core of the speech clause. But his lawyer said that burning the flag was important because its offensiveness drew attention in ways that mere words would not. We must await the Court's reaction when somebody, on the same theory, decides to protest the laws relating to sex by engaging in indecent exposure.

More recently, the Court wrestled with the question of whether Indiana's general ban on public nudity could be applied to naked dancing in the Kitty Kat Lounge. The answer, in *Barnes v. Glen Theatre, Inc.* (1991), was that it could, but the astonishing fact was that eight Justices thought a First Amendment question was presented because nude dancing "expresses" eroticism and sexuality. The ninth, Justice [Antonin] Scalia, thought the First Amendment was not implicated, but only because the statute was of general application and not aimed at dancing in the altogether.

In general, pornography and obscenity can hardly be thought to lie at the center of the First Amendment, but efforts by communities to limit their spread have been frustrated repeatedly by appeal to the speech clause.

To be sure, in 1973, by a vote of five to four in *Miller v. California,* the Court seemed to allow some minimal control of pornography. It stipulated that three things had to be determined before pornography could be banned or its purveyors punished:

> (a) whether the "average person, applying contemporary community standards" would find that the work, taken as a whole, appeals to the prurient interest ... , (b) whether the work depicts or describes, in a patently offensive way, sexual conduct specifically defined by the applicable state law, and (c) whether the work, taken as a whole, lacks serious literary, artistic, political, or scientific value.

Yet when Cincinnati prosecuted a museum for displaying Robert Mapplethorpe's photographs of one naked man urinating in the mouth of another and of himself naked with the butt of a bullwhip in his rectum, expert witnesses proclaimed that the pictures had serious artistic merit, and the jury acquitted. It is hard to imagine that the Supreme Court would have found fault with this verdict. In any event, *Miller* has done little to help communities that have been searching for some way to control the torrent of pornography that earlier decisions loosed upon them.

With regard to speech advocating violence and the violation of law, the Court has been no more helpful. This failure largely reflects the great influence of the famous dissents of Justices Holmes and Brandeis. The crux of their position was that such advocacy could not be punished unless there were shown a clear and present danger of success or imminent, serious harm. There is some doubt even about the provisos, for Holmes could bring himself to write, in *Gitlow v. New York* (1925), and Brandeis joined him, that,

> If in the long run the beliefs expressed in proletarian dictatorship are destined to be accepted by the dominant forces of the community, the only meaning of free speech is that they should be given their chance and have their way.

This, in a case where the defendant proposed violent action by a minority in order to impose a dictatorship. But why were the "dominant forces of the community" who wrote the law imprisoning Gitlow not permitted to have their way? How could Justices who six years earlier in *Abrams v. United States* voted to protect speech because thought should be tested in the "competition of the market" vote now to protect speech calling for violence to abolish the market? Berns sums up the matter neatly: "The only meaning of free speech turns out to mean that it is worse to suppress the advocacy of Stalinism or Hitlerism than to be ruled by Stalin or Hitler. The reasons for this are not, one might say, readily apparent."

The Holmes-Brandeis mood (it was hardly more than that) culmi- 45 nated in 1969 in *Brandenburg v. Ohio*, where the Court announced that

> the constitutional guarantees of free speech and press do not permit a state to forbid or proscribe advocacy of the use of force or law violation except where such advocacy is directed to inciting or producing imminent lawless action and is likely to incite or produce such action.

If we take seriously Brandeis's observation that speech assists the discovery and spread of political truth, however, it should be obvious that advocacy of force or the violation of law has no value. Such speech does not aim to convince a majority of a truth. Rather, it advocates violence or lawlessness to overturn the republican form of government which the Constitution embodies and guarantees to the states or to cancel the laws which legislative majorities have enacted.

The late constitutional scholar, Alexander M. Bickel, a staunch friend of the First Amendment, questioned the worth of the Holmes-Brandeis market metaphor:

> If in the long run the belief, let us say, in genocide is destined to be accepted by the dominant forces of the community, the only meaning of free speech is that it should be given its chance and have its way. Do we believe that? Do we accept it?

Bickel went on to ask

> whether the best test of the idea of proletarian dictatorship, or segregation, or genocide is really the marketplace, whether our experience has not taught us that even such ideas can get themselves accepted there.

The Brandeisian response would be that the cure for evil speech is good speech; yet to engage in debate about such ideas is to legitimate them, to say that they have their place in public discourse. As Bickel wrote, "Where nothing is unspeakable, nothing is undoable."

Bickel implicitly raised a difficult question. The advocacy of genocide, to use his example, would fall within the category of political speech, the core of the speech clause. It is preposterous, nevertheless, to suppose that those who wrote and ratified the First Amendment wanted every conceivable idea, no matter how vicious, to be proposed for a vote. The problem for judges is to draw a line between the ideas Bickel mentions and silly regulations, such as campus speech codes, that try to outlaw offensiveness. The courts have carved out exceptions to the protection even of political speech. Developments in an increasingly fragmented and angry society may force judges to rethink the legacy of Holmes and Brandeis.

Those who take the position that speech advocating violence, law violation, and forcible overthrow should be constitutionally protected often attribute their views to the Founders. But the fact is that the Founders held no such position. Jefferson and his followers took literally the amendment's statement that Congress should make no law, but they did so not on civil-libertarian grounds but out of a devotion to the sovereignty of the states. Even in the fierce debates that swirled around the Alien and Sedition Acts, the Jeffersonians' opposition to federal power was accompanied by the assertion that the states already had such laws. The Founders were clear that government had the right to punish seditious speech; they disagreed only about which government had the power to do it.

The tendencies of the Supreme Court's unhistorical applications of the First Amendment are fairly clear. The late social critic Christopher Lasch asked what accounted for our "wholesale defection from standards of personal conduct — civility, industry, self-restraint — that were once considered indispensable to democracy." He concluded that though there were a great number of influences, "the gradual decay of religion would stand somewhere near the head of the list." Despite widespread religious belief,

> Public life is thoroughly secularized. The separation of church and state, nowadays interpreted as prohibiting any public recognition of religion at all, is more deeply entrenched in America than anywhere else. Religion has been relegated to the sidelines of public debate.

As religious speech is circumscribed in the name of the First Amendment, however, the Court — in the name of that same amendment — strikes down laws by which communities attempt to require some civility, some restraint, some decency in public expression. The Ten Commandments are banned from the schoolroom, but pornographic videos are permitted. Or, as someone has quipped about the notorious sculpture by Andres Serrano, a crucifix may not be exhibited — unless it is dipped in urine, in which case it will be awarded a grant by the National Endowment for the Arts.

The result of all this is an increasingly vulgar and offensive moral and aesthetic environment, and, surely, since what is sayable is doable, an increasingly less moral, less happy, and more dangerous society.

The Supreme Court should therefore revisit and revise its First Amendment jurisprudence to conform to the original understanding of those who framed and enacted it. Religious speech and symbolism should be permissible on public property. Nondiscriminatory assistance to religious institutions should not be questioned. Communities, if they so desire, should be permitted to prefer religion to irreligion. There is no justification whatever for placing handicaps on religion that the establishment clause does not authorize.

As for the speech clause, it should be read to apply to *speech*, not to nonverbal expression, and it should protect the dissemination of ideas, not the individual's desire for self-gratification. Would this allow for greater regulation of obscenity and pornography? Probably, though there will always be a professor around, and a judge or jury to believe him, that the purest pornography has redeeming artistic merit (just as, it must be admitted, there is always the chance that genuinely meritorious works will be banned). Perhaps, too, the flood of pornography has already changed community standards and habituated us to an environment that would once have seemed unacceptable. Perhaps it is too late, perhaps there is no way back. But the Court ought not to prevent communities from trying to find one.

Finally, the wholesale protection of the advocacy of violence and law violation — a judicial construct not grounded in history — should be rescinded. The effects of incitements to violence will often be unknowable; nor need they be imminent to be dangerous. If, for example, speakers incite racial hatred and advocate violence against another race, as happens all too often nowadays, those utterances may well lead to actual violence, but it will be impossible to prove a direct connection to the speeches.

The rule of *Brandenburg* also contemplates judging the effect of each   55
particular speech. Yet even though no individual speech may have the effect of producing violence, cumulatively such speeches may have enormous influence. Whether or not it is prudent to ban all such advocacy is a different question, one that should be addressed by legislatures and prosecutors rather than courts. There is no good reason to put advocacy of violence and law violation in the marketplace of ideas.

How much chance is there that the Court will undertake such sweeping reforms? Not, it would seem, a great deal. The Court, particularly when it deals with the Constitution, and more particularly when it deals with the First Amendment, is as much a cultural and political institution as it is a legal one. It has always responded to dominant class values, and in our day that means the cultural elite: academics, clergy, entertainers, journalists, foundation staffs, bureaucrats, and the like. These folk tend to be hostile or indifferent toward religion and to sanctify the autonomous individual as against the community — precisely the attitudes underlying contemporary First Amendment jurisprudence.

That having been said, it must also be recognized that there have been strong dissents to the modern decisions, particularly to the decisions deforming the religion clauses. It is entirely possible, therefore, that we may at least expect piecemeal improvements, especially given the more conservative climate that was reflected in the 1994 elections.

PREPARING FOR DISCUSSION

1. Bork devotes the first part of his essay to a discussion of the First Amendment and state-sponsored religion. How does his treatment of this issue help him to argue in favor of limiting free speech in America? Does he notice a general pattern in the Supreme Court's decisions regarding the separation of church and state? What pattern does he notice with regard to the court's decisions regarding free speech?

2. Bork characterizes the positions of Thomas Jefferson and James Madison regarding the establishment of religion as "radical" and "unrepresentative." On what grounds does he level such a charge? What point is he making about the author of the Declaration of Independence and the man perhaps most responsible for the final form of the American Constitution? What does Bork's view of Jefferson and Madison suggest about his own view of the Constitution?

3. Consider the author's discussion of the Kiryas Joel separate-school-district decision. Why, according to Bork, were handicapped children "forced to attend public schools outside the village"? Does Bork's use of the word *forced* seem accurate here? If only Hasidic children benefited from the state-funded special-education "public" school, why does Bork suggest that government support was nondiscriminatory? Do you, like Bork, consider the establishment of a religious school with

government funds to be an "innocuous" practice or one that threatens the separation of church and state?

4. Consider Bork's anecdote of how the case in which a public school was prohibited from displaying the Ten Commandments was decided in a courtroom that was decorated with a painting of Moses and the Ten Commandments. Why does Bork relate this anecdote? Was the Ten Commandments displayed in the courtroom primarily a religious symbol or part of the iconography of justice? Do you think the school could display the Ten Commandments as part of our cultural heritage and *not* make a religious statement?

5. Bork takes as simple and unambiguous the language of the First Amendment when it comes to nondiscriminatory aid to religious institutions or the state-sponsored religious symbolism. Why does he then say that the words "Congress shall make no law . . . abridging the freedom of speech" cannot mean what they say? Why does he suggest that the language of the amendment becomes ambiguous when it comes to free speech? Does this language seem ambiguous to you?

FROM READING TO WRITING

6. Bork concurs with Christopher Lasch (see p. 195) that religion "has been relegated to the sidelines of public debate" and laments that communities have been deprived of their power to enforce civility and restraint among their citizens. Do you find either of these scenarios to be true of your own experience? Do you agree with Bork's suggestion that religion and certain restrictions on free speech are the only ways to instill morality and to restore civility? Write an essay in which you voice your agreement or disagreement with Bork.

7. Bork seems almost to agree with antipornography theorist Catharine A. MacKinnon's formula that "to say something is to do something" when he asserts that "what is sayable is doable." Would Bork go a step further and say that what is said is also *done*? Do his arguments for restricting violent speech suggest as much? Write an essay in which you test Bork's proposition. Are there things that can be said that cannot be done? Or is the saying equivalent to the doing?

Social Values

RELIGION · FAMILY · RESPONSIBILITY

Anyone who follows the American political scene knows that politics today means much more than who's in office and who isn't. A great deal of our political conflict occurs around issues that were once generally considered nonpolitical: art, education, family, religion, and moral values. In fact, our daily skirmishes over moral standards often escalate into some of our biggest and loudest battles. Not too many years ago a museum exhibit featuring the aircraft that dropped the atom bomb on Japan in 1945 would have been mounted with little objection; in 1995 such an exhibit sparked an enormous controversy. Since the provocation of public controversy is one of the most important functions of today's popular news media (perhaps more important than the factual reporting of events), topics that reflect deep-seated social and cultural conflicts are expertly selected and shaped by the media to dramatize and intensify a particular clash of values.

When the former Republican vice president Dan Quayle attacked the television sitcom *Murphy Brown* for its positive portrayal of an unwed mother's pregnancy and childbirth, Quayle angered many feminists and liberals who supported alternative family structures. In "Dan Quayle Was Right," Barbara Dafoe Whitehead, whose 1992 *Washington Post* article stimulated Quayle's attack on unwed motherhood, returns to the issue in greater detail as she examines how the rapid dissolution of the traditional two-parent family is endangering the emotional life of children.

One of the people Whitehead cites in her attempt to reestablish the normality of the two-parent family is the controversial Democratic senator from New York, Daniel Patrick Moynihan. A longtime expert on urban affairs and welfare programs, Moynihan argues in "Defining Deviancy Down" that the growing acceptability of unwed pregnancy is only one aspect of a larger social effort to view deviant behavior as normal. This is happening, Moynihan suggests, because "the amount of deviant behavior in American society has increased beyond the levels" the community can afford to acknowledge. But Moynihan gives only half the story, maintains the Pulitzer Prize–winning political commentator Charles Krauthammer in "Defining Deviancy Up." Krauthammer claims that we have not only defined deviancy down in order to explain away and normalize abnormal behavior, but we have at the same time made the normal appear to be deviant: "Normal middle-class life . . . stands exposed as the true home of violence and abuse and a whole catalog of aberrant acting and thinking."

As the question of social values continues to dominate public discourse, it begins to figure more and more prominently in the political agenda of both liberals and conservatives. The social-values debate, for example, fuels much of the Republican party's recent "Contract with America." This is apparent throughout House Speaker Newt Gingrich's program for wholesale legislative change, as he summarizes it in the selection "Contracting with America." For Gingrich, as for many combatants of what have been called America's "culture wars," the issue boils down to a fundamental vision about the moral direction of America. "I'm a history teacher by background," Gingrich says, "and I would assert and defend on any campus in this country that it is impossible to maintain civilization with twelve-year-olds having babies, with fifteen-year-olds killing each other, with seventeen-year-olds dying of AIDS, and with eighteen-year-olds ending up with diplomas they can't even read."

Whenever morality is introduced into discussion, God and religion are sure to make an appearance. The kinds of social problems alluded to by Gingrich could, according to William J. Bennett, be more properly relieved by a general spiritual renewal — a rediscovery of God. In "Revolt against God," the former secretary of education argues that "it is foolish, and futile, to rely primarily on politics to solve moral, cultural, and spiritual afflictions." How can we reverse America's social and cultural decline? Bennett offers his audience three short answers: "Do not surrender; get mad; and get in the fight."

Those short answers, of course, apply to both the Right and the Left. The award-winning journalist Barbara Ehrenreich has been unyielding, angry, and fighting for leftist causes since the early 1970s. In "Family Values," she reminds readers that the conservatives have no monopoly on what they like to call "traditional values." As she puts it, "dissent is also a 'traditional value,' and in a republic founded by revolution, a more deeply native one than smug-faced conservatism can ever be."

Despite Ehrenreich's clever appropriation of the phrase, "family values" remains a conservative or Republican initiative. This fact was made clear in Republican Senator Bob Dole's angry 1995 attack on Hollywood, in which he claimed that "one of the greatest threats to American family values is the way our popular culture ridicules them." In "Nightmares of Depravity," our reprint of his Los Angeles address, Dole insists that his fight against the entertainment industry is not a partisan battle. As an indication of this we have added "Pathways for Trash," Democratic Senator Bill Bradley's brief endorsement of Dole's remarks.

Every anthology has to end with a particular selection. In many collections the editors choose something that summarizes or effectively closes the volume. For a collection featuring a wide range of "voices across the political spectrum," however, it was impossible, for obvious reasons, to select a concluding essay that could elegantly or eloquently summarize, challenge, or represent all of today's political positions. Therefore, our final selection by world-renowned sociologist Amitai Etzioni, though it covers the broadest of topics — "A New Moral, Social, Public Order" — should be read as essentially another voice in our enormously expressive political dialogue. His optimistic, communitarian message is that Americans can effectively act on the "deterioration of private and public morality, the decline of the family, high crime rates, and the swelling of corruption in government" *without* returning the nation to a restrictive Puritanism or establishing an oppressive authoritarianism.

BARBARA DAFOE WHITEHEAD

Dan Quayle Was Right

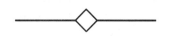

Social historian Barbara Dafoe Whitehead's essay owes its title to a now-famous incident in which former Vice President Dan Quayle condemned the popular television show *Murphy Brown* for portraying the unwed pregnancy of the sitcom's lead character in a positive light. Quayle's remarks so outraged feminists and liberals that they made the recognition and praise of alternative families a major theme of the 1992 Democratic convention that nominated Bill Clinton for president. As Whitehead points out in the following selection, however, recent studies show that not only does the two-parent family remain the healthiest environment for children to grow up in, but children raised in alternative families are likely to be less educated and more emotionally troubled than children who grow up in traditional families.

Whitehead currently serves as the vice president of the Institute for American Values, where she directs the institute's project on The Family in American Culture. She received her Ph.D. in American social history from the University of Chicago. The following selection first appeared in the *Atlantic Monthly*.

SELECTED PUBLICATIONS: *The Divorce Culture* (1996); Whitehead also publishes in the *Atlantic Monthly, Commonweal*, the *Responsive Community*, the *Los Angeles Times*, and the *Chicago Tribune*.

Divorce and out-of-wedlock childbirth are transforming the lives of American children. In the postwar generation more than 80 percent of children grew up in a family with two biological parents who were married to each other. By 1980 only 50 percent could expect to spend their entire childhood in an intact family. If current trends continue, less than half of all children born today will live continuously with their own mother and father throughout childhood. Most American children will spend several years in a single-mother family. Some will eventually live in stepparent families, but because stepfamilies are more likely to break up than intact (by which I mean two-biological-parent) families, an increasing number of children will experience family breakup two or even three times during childhood.

According to a growing body of social-scientific evidence, children in families disrupted by divorce and out-of-wedlock birth do worse than children in intact families on several measures of well-being. Children in single-parent families are six times as likely to be poor. They are also likely to stay poor longer. Twenty-two percent of children in one-parent families will experience poverty during childhood for seven years or more, as compared with only two percent of children in two-parent families. A 1988 survey by the National Center for Health Statistics found that children in single-parent families are two to three times as likely as children in two-parent families to have emotional and behavioral problems. They are also more likely to drop out of high school, to get pregnant as teenagers, to abuse drugs, and to be in trouble with the law. Compared with children in intact families, children from disrupted families are at a much higher risk for physical or sexual abuse.

Contrary to popular belief, many children do not "bounce back" after divorce or remarriage. Difficulties that are associated with family breakup often persist into adulthood. Children who grow up in single-parent or stepparent families are less successful as adults, particularly in the two domains of life — love and work — that are most essential to happiness. Needless to say, not all children experience such negative effects. However, research shows that many children from disrupted families have a harder time achieving intimacy in a relationship, forming a stable marriage, or even holding a steady job.

Despite this growing body of evidence, it is nearly impossible to discuss changes in family structure without provoking angry protest. Many people see the discussion as no more than an attack on struggling single mothers and their children: Why blame single mothers when they are doing the very best they can? After all, the decision to end a marriage or a relationship is wrenching, and few parents are indifferent to the painful burden this decision imposes on their children. Many take the perilous step toward single parenthood as a last resort, after their best efforts to hold a marriage together have failed. Consequently, it can seem particularly cruel and unfeeling to remind parents of the hardships their children might suffer as a result of family breakup. Other people believe that the dramatic changes in family structure, though regrettable, are impossible to reverse. Family breakup is an inevitable feature of American life, and anyone who thinks otherwise is indulging in nostalgia or trying to turn back the clock. Since these new family forms are here to stay, the reasoning goes, we must accord respect to single parents, not criticize them. Typical is the view expressed by a Brooklyn woman in a recent letter to *The New York Times:* "Let's stop moralizing or blaming single parents and unwed mothers, and give them the respect they have earned and the support they deserve."

Such views are not to be dismissed. Indeed, they help to explain why 5 family structure is such an explosive issue for Americans. The debate about it is not simply about the social-scientific evidence, although that is surely an important part of the discussion. It is also a debate over deeply held and often conflicting values. How do we begin to reconcile our long-standing belief in equality and diversity with an impressive body of evidence that suggests that not all family structures produce equal outcomes for children? How can we square traditional notions of public support for dependent women and children with a belief in women's right to pursue autonomy and independence in childbearing and child rearing? How do we uphold the freedom of adults to pursue individual happiness in their private relationships and at the same time respond to the needs of children for stability, security, and permanence in their family lives? What do we do when the interests of adults and children conflict? These are the difficult issues at stake in the debate over family structure.

In the past these issues have turned out to be too difficult and too politically risky for debate. In the mid-1960s Daniel Patrick Moynihan, then an assistant secretary of labor, was denounced as a racist for calling attention to the relationship between the prevalence of black single-mother families and the lower socioeconomic standing of black children. For nearly twenty years the policy and research communities backed away from the entire issue. In 1980 the Carter administration convened a historic White House Conference on Families, designed to address the growing problems of children and families in America. The result was a prolonged, publicly subsidized quarrel over the definition of "family." No president since has tried to hold a national family conference. Last year, at a time when the rate of out-of-wedlock births had reached a historic high, Vice President Dan Quayle was ridiculed for criticizing Murphy Brown. In short, every time the issue of family structure has been raised, the response has been first controversy, then retreat, and finally silence.

Yet it is also risky to ignore the issue of changing family structure. In recent years the problems associated with family disruption have grown. Overall child well-being has declined, despite a decrease in the number of children per family, an increase in the educational level of parents, and historically high levels of public spending. After dropping in the 1960s and 1970s, the proportion of children in poverty has increased dramatically, from 15 percent in 1970 to 20 percent in 1990, while the percentage of adult Americans in poverty has remained roughly constant. The teen suicide rate has more than tripled. Juvenile crime has increased and become more violent. School performance has continued to decline. There are no signs that these trends are about to reverse themselves.

If we fail to come to terms with the relationship between family structure and declining child well-being, then it will be increasingly difficult to improve children's life prospects, no matter how many new programs the federal government funds. Nor will we be able to make progress in bettering school performance or reducing crime or improving the quality of the nation's future work force — all domestic problems closely connected to family breakup. Worse, we may contribute to the problem by pursuing policies that actually increase family instability and breakup.

From Death to Divorce

Across time and across cultures, family disruption has been regarded as an event that threatens a child's well-being and even survival. This view is rooted in a fundamental biological fact: unlike the young of almost any other species, the human child is born in an abjectly helpless and immature state. Years of nurture and protection are needed before the child can achieve physical independence. Similarly, it takes years of interaction with at least one but ideally two or more adults for a child to develop into a socially competent adult. Children raised in virtual isolation from human beings, though physically intact, display few recognizably human behaviors. The social arrangement that has proved most successful in ensuring the physical survival and promoting the social development of the child is the family unit of the biological mother and father. Consequently, any event that permanently denies a child the presence and protection of a parent jeopardizes the life of the child.

The classic form of family disruption is the death of a parent. 10 Throughout history this has been one of the risks of childhood. Mothers frequently died in childbirth, and it was not unusual for both parents to die before the child was grown. As recently as the early decades of this century children commonly suffered the death of at least one parent. Almost a quarter of the children born in this country in 1900 lost one parent by the time they were fifteen years old. Many of these children lived with their widowed parent, often in a household with other close relatives. Others grew up in orphanages and foster homes.

The meaning of parental death, as it has been transmitted over time and faithfully recorded in world literature and lore, is unambiguous and essentially unchanging. It is universally regarded as an untimely and tragic event. Death permanently severs the parent-child bond, disrupting forever one of the child's earliest and deepest human attachments. It also deprives a child of the presence and protection of an adult who has a biological stake in, as well as an emotional commitment to, the child's survival and well-being. In short, the death of a parent is the most extreme and severe loss a child can suffer.

Because a child is so vulnerable in a parent's absence, there has been a common cultural response to the death of a parent: an outpouring of support from family, friends, and strangers alike. The surviving parent and child are united in their grief as well as their loss. Relatives and friends share in the loss and provide valuable emotional and financial assistance to the bereaved family. Other members of the community show sympathy for the child, and public assistance is available for those who need it. This cultural understanding of parental death has formed the basis for a tradition of public support to widows and their children. Indeed, as recently as the beginning of this century widows were the only mothers eligible for pensions in many states, and today widows with children receive more-generous welfare benefits from Survivors Insurance than do other single mothers with children who depend on Aid to Families with Dependent Children.

It has taken thousands upon thousands of years to reduce the threat of parental death. Not until the middle of the twentieth century did parental death cease to be a commonplace event for children in the United States. By then advances in medicine had dramatically reduced mortality rates for men and women.

At the same time, other forms of family disruption — separation, divorce, out-of-wedlock birth — were held in check by powerful religious, social, and legal sanctions. Divorce was widely regarded both as a deviant behavior, especially threatening to mothers and children, and as a personal lapse: "Divorce is the public acknowledgment of failure," a 1940s sociology textbook noted. Out-of-wedlock birth was stigmatized, and stigmatization is a powerful means of regulating behavior, as any smoker or overeater will testify. Sanctions against nonmarital childbirth discouraged behavior that hurt children and exacted compensatory behavior that helped them. Shotgun marriages and adoption, two common responses to nonmarital birth, carried a strong message about the risks of premarital sex and created an intact family for the child.

Consequently, children did not have to worry much about losing a   15 parent through divorce or never having had one because of nonmarital birth. After a surge in divorces following the Second World War, the rate leveled off. Only 11 percent of children born in the 1950s would by the time they turned eighteen see their parents separate or divorce. Out-of-wedlock childbirth barely figured as a cause of family disruption. In the 1950s and early 1960s, five percent of the nation's births were out of wedlock. Blacks were more likely than whites to bear children outside marriage, but the majority of black children born in the twenty years after the Second World War were born to married couples. The rate of family disruption reached a historic low point during those years.

A new standard of family security and stability was established in postwar America. For the first time in history the vast majority of the nation's children could expect to live with married biological parents throughout childhood. Children might still suffer other forms of adversity — poverty, racial discrimination, lack of educational opportunity — but only a few would be deprived of the nurture and protection of a mother and a father. No longer did children have to be haunted by the classic fears vividly dramatized in folklore and fable — that their parents would die, that they would have to live with a stepparent and stepsiblings, or that they would be abandoned. These were the years when the nation confidently boarded up orphanages and closed foundling hospitals, certain that such institutions would never again be needed. In movie theaters across the country parents and children could watch the drama of parental separation and death in the great Disney classics, secure in the knowledge that such nightmare visions as the death of Bambi's mother and the wrenching separation of Dumbo from his mother were only make-believe.

In the 1960s the rate of family disruption suddenly began to rise. After inching up over the course of a century, the divorce rate soared. Throughout the 1950s and early 1960s the divorce rate held steady at fewer than ten divorces a year per 1,000 married couples. Then, beginning in about 1965, the rate increased sharply, peaking at twenty-three divorces per 1,000 marriages by 1979. (In 1974 divorce passed death as the leading cause of family breakup.) The rate has leveled off at about twenty-one divorces per 1,000 marriages — the figure for 1991. The out-of-wedlock birth rate also jumped. It went from five percent in 1960 to 27 percent in 1990. In 1990 close to 57 percent of births among black mothers were nonmarital, and about 17 percent among white mothers. Altogether, about one out of every four women who had a child in 1990 was not married. With rates of divorce and nonmarital birth so high, family disruption is at its peak. Never before have so many children experienced family breakup caused by events other than death. Each year a million children go through divorce or separation and almost as many more are born out of wedlock.

Half of all marriages now end in divorce. Following divorce, many people enter new relationships. Some begin living together. Nearly half of all cohabiting couples have children in the household. Fifteen percent have new children together. Many cohabiting couples eventually get married. However, both cohabiting and remarried couples are more likely to break up than couples in first marriages. Even social scientists find it hard to keep pace with the complexity and velocity of such patterns. In the revised edition (1992) of his book *Marriage, Divorce, Remarriage*, the sociologist Andrew Cherlin ruefully comments: "If there were a truth-in-labeling law for books, the title of this edition should be something long and unwieldy like *Cohabitation, Marriage, Divorce, More Cohabitation, and Probably Remarriage*."

Under such conditions growing up can be a turbulent experience. In many single-parent families children must come to terms with the parent's love life and romantic partners. Some children live with cohabiting couples, either their own unmarried parents or a biological parent and a live-in partner. Some children born to cohabiting parents see their parents break up. Others see their parents marry, but 56 percent of them (as compared with 31 percent of the children born to married parents) later see their parents' marriages fall apart. All told, about three quarters of children born to cohabiting couples will live in a single-parent home at least briefly. One of every four children growing up in the 1990s will eventually enter a stepfamily. According to one survey, nearly half of all children in stepparent families will see their parents divorce again by the time they reach their late teens. Since 80 percent of divorced fathers re-marry, things get even more complicated when the romantic or marital history of the noncustodial parent, usually the father, is taken into ac-count. Consequently, as it affects a significant number of children, family disruption is best understood not as a single event but as a string of dis-ruptive events: separation, divorce, life in a single-parent family, life with a parent and live-in lover, the remarriage of one or both parents, life in one stepparent family combined with visits to another stepparent family; the breakup of one or both stepparent families. And so on. This is one reason that public schools have a hard time knowing whom to call in an emergency.

Given its dramatic impact on children's lives, one might reasonably   20
expect that this historic level of family disruption would be viewed with alarm, even regarded as a national crisis. Yet this has not been the case. In recent years some people have argued that these trends pose a serious threat to children and to the nation as a whole, but they are dismissed as declinists, pessimists, or nostalgists, unwilling or unable to accept the new facts of life. The dominant view is that the changes in family struc-ture are, on balance, positive.

A Shift in the Social Metric

There are several reasons that this is so, but the fundamental reason is that at some point in the 1970s Americans changed their minds about the meaning of these disruptive behaviors. What had once been regarded as hostile to children's best interests was now considered essential to adults' happiness. In the 1950s most Americans believed that parents should stay in an unhappy marriage for the sake of the children. The assumption was that a divorce would damage the children, and the prospect of such damage gave divorce its meaning. By the mid-1970s a majority of Ameri-cans rejected that view. Popular advice literature reflected the shift. A book on divorce published in the mid-1940s tersely asserted: "Children are entitled to the affection and *association* of two parents, not one." Thirty years later another popular divorce book proclaimed just the op-posite: "A two-parent home is not the only emotional structure within which a child can be happy and healthy. . . . The parents who take care of themselves will be best able to take care of their children." At about the same time, the long-standing taboo against out-of-wedlock childbirth also collapsed. By the mid-1970s three fourths of Americans said that it was not morally wrong for a woman to have a child outside marriage.

Once the social metric shifts from child well-being to adult well-being, it is hard to see divorce and nonmarital birth in anything but a positive light. However distressing and difficult they may be, both of these behaviors can hold out the promise of greater adult choice, freedom, and happiness. For unhappy spouses, divorce offers a way to escape a troubled or even abusive relationship and make a fresh start. For single parents, remarriage is a second try at marital happiness as well as a chance for relief from the stress, loneliness, and economic hardship of raising a child alone. For some unmarried women, nonmarital birth is a way to beat the biological clock, avoid marrying the wrong man, and experience the pleasures of motherhood. Moreover, divorce and out-of-wedlock birth involve a measure of agency and choice; they are man- and woman-made events. To be sure, not everyone exercises choice in divorce or nonmarital birth. Men leave wives for younger women, teenage girls get pregnant accidentally — yet even these unhappy events reflect the expansion of the boundaries of freedom and choice.

This cultural shift helps explain what otherwise would be inexplicable: the failure to see the rise in family disruption as a severe and troubling national problem. It explains why there is virtually no widespread public sentiment for restigmatizing either of these classically disruptive behaviors and no sense — no public consensus — that they can or should be avoided in the future. On the contrary, the prevailing opinion is that we should accept the changes in family structure as inevitable and devise new forms of public and private support for single-parent families.

The View from Hollywood

With its affirmation of the liberating effects of divorce and nonmarital childbirth, this opinion is a fixture of American popular culture today. Madison Avenue and Hollywood did not invent these behaviors, as their highly paid publicists are quick to point out, but they have played an influential role in defending and even celebrating divorce and unwed motherhood. More precisely, they have taken the raw material of demography and fashioned it into a powerful fantasy of individual renewal and rebirth. Consider, for example, the teaser for *People* magazine's cover story on Joan Lunden's divorce: "After the painful end of her 13-year marriage, the *Good Morning America* cohost is discovering a new life as a single mother — and as her own woman." *People* does not dwell on the anguish Lunden and her children might have experienced over the breakup of their family, or the difficulties of single motherhood, even for celebrity mothers. Instead, it celebrates Joan Lunden's steps toward independence and a better life. *People,* characteristically, focuses on her shopping: in the first weeks after her breakup Lunden leased "a brand-new six-bedroom, 8,000-square-foot" house and then went to Bloomingdale's, where she scooped up sheets, pillows, a toaster, dishes, seven televisions, and roomfuls of fun furniture that was "totally unlike the serious traditional pieces she was giving up."

This is not just the view taken in supermarket magazines. Even the   25 conservative bastion of the greeting-card industry, Hallmark, offers a line of cards commemorating divorce as liberation. "Think of your former marriage as a record album," says one Contemporary card. "It was full of music — both happy and sad. But what's important now is . . . YOU! the recently released HOT, NEW, SINGLE! You're going to be at the TOP OF THE CHARTS!" Another card reads: "Getting divorced can be very healthy! Watch how it improves your circulation! Best of luck! . . ." Hallmark's hip Shoebox Greetings division depicts two female praying mantises. Mantis One: "It's tough being a single parent." Mantis Two: "Yeah . . . Maybe we shouldn't have eaten our husbands."

Divorce is a tired convention in Hollywood, but unwed parenthood is very much in fashion: in the past year or so babies were born to Warren Beatty and Annette Bening, Jack Nicholson and Rebecca Broussard, and Eddie Murphy and Nicole Mitchell. *Vanity Fair* celebrated Jack Nicholson's fatherhood with a cover story (April, 1992) called "Happy Jack." What made Jack happy, it turned out, was no-fault fatherhood. He and Broussard, the twenty-nine-year-old mother of his children, lived in separate houses. Nicholson said, "It's an unusual arrangement, but the last twenty-five years or so have shown me that I'm not good at cohabitation. . . . I see Rebecca as much as any other person who is cohabiting. And *she* prefers it. I think most people would in a more honest and truthful world." As for more-permanent commitments, the man who is not good at cohabitation said: "I don't discuss marriage much with Rebecca. Those discussions are the very thing I'm trying to avoid. I'm after this immediate real thing. That's all I believe in." (Perhaps Nicholson should have had the discussion. Not long after the story appeared, Broussard broke off the relationship.)

As this story shows, unwed parenthood is thought of not only as a way to find happiness but also as a way to exhibit such virtues as honesty and courage. A similar argument was offered in defense of Murphy Brown's unwed motherhood. Many of Murphy's fans were quick to point out that Murphy suffered over her decision to bear a child out of wedlock. Faced with an accidental pregnancy and a faithless lover, she agonized over her plight and, after much mental anguish, bravely decided to go ahead. In short, having a baby without a husband represented a higher level of maternal devotion and sacrifice than having a baby with a husband. Murphy was not just exercising her rights as a woman; she was exhibiting true moral heroism.

On the night Murphy Brown became an unwed mother, 34 million Americans tuned in, and CBS posted a 35 percent share of the audience. The show did not stir significant protest at the grass roots and lost none of its advertisers. The actress Candice Bergen subsequently appeared on the cover of nearly every women's and news magazine in the country and received an honorary degree at the University of Pennsylvania as well as an Emmy award. The show's creator, Diane English, popped up in Hanes stocking ads. Judged by conventional measures of approval, Murphy Brown's motherhood was a hit at the box office.

Increasingly, the media depicts the married two-parent family as a source of pathology. According to a spate of celebrity memoirs and interviews, the married-parent family harbors terrible secrets of abuse, violence, and incest. A bumper sticker I saw in Amherst, Massachusetts, read UNSPOKEN TRADITIONAL FAMILY VALUES: ABUSE, ALCOHOLISM, INCEST. The pop therapist John Bradshaw explains away this generation's problems with the dictum that 96 percent of families are dysfunctional, made that way by the addicted society we live in. David Lynch creates a new aesthetic of creepiness by juxtaposing scenes of traditional family life with images of seduction and perversion. A Boston-area museum puts on an exhibit called "Goodbye to Apple Pie," featuring several artists' visions of child abuse, including one mixed-media piece with knives poking through a little girl's skirt. The piece is titled *Father Knows Best*.

No one would claim that two-parent families are free from conflict, violence, or abuse. However, the attempt to discredit the two-parent family can be understood as part of what Daniel Patrick Moynihan has described as a larger effort to accommodate higher levels of social deviance. "The amount of deviant behavior in American society has increased beyond the levels the community can 'afford to recognize,'" Moynihan argues. One response has been to normalize what was once considered deviant behavior, such as out-of-wedlock birth. An accompanying response has been to detect deviance in what once stood as a social norm, such as the married-couple family. Together these responses reduce the acknowledged levels of deviance by eroding earlier distinctions between the normal and the deviant. 30

Several recent studies describe family life in its postwar heyday as the seedbed of alcoholism and abuse. According to Stephanie Coontz, the author of the book *The Way We Never Were: American Families and the Nostalgia Trap,* family life for married mothers in the 1950s consisted of "booze, bowling, bridge, and boredom." Coontz writes: "Few would have guessed that radiant Marilyn Van Derbur, crowned Miss America in 1958, had been sexually violated by her wealthy, respectable father from the time she was five until she was eighteen, when she moved away to college." Even the budget-stretching casserole comes under attack as a sign of culinary dysfunction. According to one food writer, this homely staple of postwar family life brings back images of "the good mother of the '50s . . . locked in Ozzie and Harriet land, unable to move past the canvas of a Corning Ware dish, the palette of a can of Campbell's soup, the mushy dominion of which she was queen."

Nevertheless, the popular portrait of family life does not simply reflect the views of a cultural elite, as some have argued. There is strong support at the grass roots for much of this view of family change. Survey after survey shows that Americans are less inclined than they were a

generation ago to value sexual fidelity, lifelong marriage, and parenthood as worthwhile personal goals. Motherhood no longer defines adult
womanhood, as everyone knows; equally important is the fact that fatherhood has declined as a norm for men. In 1976 less than half as many
fathers as in 1957 said that providing for children was a life goal. The
proportion of working men who found marriage and children burdensome and restrictive more than doubled in the same period. Fewer than
half of all adult Americans today regard the idea of sacrifice for others as
a positive moral virtue.

Dinosaurs Divorce

It is true that many adults benefit from divorce or remarriage. According
to one study, nearly 80 percent of divorced women and 50 percent of divorced men say they are better off out of the marriage. Half of divorced
adults in the same study report greater happiness. A competent self-help
book called *Divorce and New Beginnings* notes the advantages of single
parenthood: single parents can "develop their own interests, fulfill their
own needs, choose their own friends and engage in social activities of
their choice. Money, even if limited, can be spent as they see fit." Apparently, some women appreciate the opportunity to have children out of
wedlock. "The real world, however, does not always allow women who
are dedicated to their careers to devote the time and energy it takes to
find — or be found by — the perfect husband and father wanna-be," one
woman said in a letter to *The Washington Post*. A mother and chiropractor
from Avon, Connecticut, explained her unwed maternity to an interviewer this way: "It is selfish, but this was something I needed to do
for me."

There is very little in contemporary popular culture to contradict this
optimistic view. But in a few small places another perspective may be
found. Several racks down from its divorce cards, Hallmark offers a line
of cards for children — To Kids with Love. These cards come six to a
pack. Each card in the pack has a slightly different message. According to
the package, the "thinking of you" messages will let a special kid "know
how much you care." Though Hallmark doesn't quite say so, it's clear
these cards are aimed at divorced parents. "I'm sorry I'm not always
there when you need me but I hope you know I'm always just a phone
call away." Another card reads: "Even though your dad and I don't live
together anymore, I know he's still a very special part of your life. And as
much as I miss you when you're not with me, I'm still happy that you
two can spend time together."

Hallmark's messages are grounded in a substantial body of well-   35
funded market research. Therefore it is worth reflecting on the diver-
gence in sentiment between the divorce cards for adults and the divorce

cards for kids. For grown-ups, divorce heralds new beginnings (A HOT NEW SINGLE). For children, divorce brings separation and loss ("I'm sorry I'm not always there when you need me").

An even more telling glimpse into the meaning of family disruption can be found in the growing children's literature on family dissolution. Take, for example, the popular children's book *Dinosaurs Divorce: A Guide for Changing Families* (1986), by Laurene Krasny Brown and Marc Brown. This is a picture book, written for very young children. The book begins with a short glossary of "divorce words" and encourages children to "see if you can find them" in the story. The words include "family counselor," "separation agreement," "alimony," and "child custody." The book is illustrated with cartoonish drawings of green dinosaur parents who fight, drink too much, and break up. One panel shows the father dinosaur, suitcase in hand, getting into a yellow car.

The dinosaur children are offered simple, straightforward advice on what to do about the divorce. *On custody decisions:* "When parents can't agree, lawyers and judges decide. Try to be honest if they ask you questions; it will help them make better decisions." *On selling the house:* "If you move, you may have to say good-bye to friends and familiar places. But soon your new home will feel like the place you really belong." *On the economic impact of divorce:* "Living with one parent almost always means there will be less money. Be prepared to give up some things." *On holidays:* "Divorce may mean twice as much celebrating at holiday times, but you may feel pulled apart." *On parents' new lovers:* "You may sometimes feel jealous and want your parent to yourself. Be polite to your parents' new friends, even if you don't like them at first." *On parents' remarriage:* "Not everyone loves his or her stepparents, but showing them respect is important."

These cards and books point to an uncomfortable and generally unacknowledged fact: what contributes to a parent's happiness may detract from a child's happiness. All too often the adult quest for freedom, independence, and choice in family relationships conflicts with a child's developmental needs for stability, constancy, harmony, and permanence in family life. In short, family disruption creates a deep division between parents' interests and the interests of children.

One of the worst consequences of these divided interests is a withdrawal of parental investment in children's well-being. As the Stanford economist Victor Fuchs has pointed out, the main source of social investment in children is private. The investment comes from the children's parents. But parents in disrupted families have less time, attention, and money to devote to their children. The single most important source of disinvestment has been the widespread withdrawal of financial support and involvement by fathers. Maternal investment, too, has declined, as women try to raise families on their own and work outside the home.

Moreover, both mothers and fathers commonly respond to family breakup by investing more heavily in themselves and in their own personal and romantic lives.

Sometimes the tables are completely turned. Children are called   40 upon to invest in the emotional well-being of their parents. Indeed, this seems to be the larger message of many of the children's books on divorce and remarriage. *Dinosaurs Divorce* asks children to be sympathetic, understanding, respectful, and polite to confused, unhappy parents. The sacrifice comes from the children: "Be prepared to give up some things." In the world of divorcing dinosaurs, the children rather than the grownups are the examplars of patience, restraint, and good sense.

Three Seventies Assumptions

As it first took shape in the 1970s, the optimistic view of family change rested on three bold new assumptions. At that time, because the emergence of the changes in family life was so recent, there was little hard evidence to confirm or dispute these assumptions. But this was an expansive moment in American life.

The first assumption was an economic one: that a woman could now afford to be a mother without also being a wife. There were ample grounds for believing this. Women's work-force participation had been gradually increasing in the postwar period, and by the beginning of the 1970s women were a strong presence in the workplace. What's more, even though there was still a substantial wage gap between men and women, women had made considerable progress in a relatively short time toward better-paying jobs and greater employment opportunities. More women than ever before could aspire to serious careers as business executives, doctors, lawyers, airline pilots, and politicians. This circumstance, combined with the increased availability of child care, meant that women could take on the responsibilities of a breadwinner, perhaps even a sole breadwinner. This was particularly true for middle-class women. According to a highly regarded 1977 study by the Carnegie Council on Children, "The greater availability of jobs for women means that more middle-class children today survive their parents' divorce without a catastrophic plunge into poverty."

Feminists, who had long argued that the path to greater equality for women lay in the world of work outside the home, endorsed this assumption. In fact, for many, economic independence was a steppingstone toward freedom from both men and marriage. As women began to earn their own money, they were less dependent on men or marriage, and marriage diminished in importance. In Gloria Steinem's memorable words, "A woman without a man is like a fish without a bicycle."

This assumption also gained momentum as the meaning of work changed for women. Increasingly, work had an expressive as well as an economic dimension: being a working mother not only gave you an income but also made you more interesting and fulfilled than a stay-at-home mother. Consequently, the optimistic economic scenario was driven by a cultural imperative. Women would achieve financial independence because, culturally as well as economically, it was the right thing to do.

The second assumption was that family disruption would not cause 45
lasting harm to children and could actually enrich their lives. *Creative Divorce: A New Opportunity for Personal Growth,* a popular book of the seventies, spoke confidently to this point: "Children can survive any family crisis without permanent damage — and grow as human beings in the process. . . . " Moreover, single-parent and stepparent families created a more extensive kinship network than the nuclear family. This network would envelop children in a web of warm and supportive relationships. "Belonging to a stepfamily means there are more people in your life," a children's book published in 1982 notes. "More sisters and brothers, including the step ones. More people you think of as grandparents and aunts and uncles. More cousins. More neighbors and friends. . . . Getting to know and like so many people (and having them like you) is one of the best parts of what being in a stepfamily . . . is all about."

The third assumption was that the new diversity in family structure would make America a better place. Just as the nation has been strengthened by the diversity of its ethnic and racial groups, so it would be strengthened by diverse family forms. The emergence of these brave new families was but the latest chapter in the saga of American pluralism.

Another version of the diversity argument stated that the real problem was not family disruption itself but the stigma still attached to these emergent family forms. This lingering stigma placed children at psychological risk, making them feel ashamed or different; as the ranks of single-parent and stepparent families grew, children would feel normal and good about themselves.

These assumptions continue to be appealing, because they accord with strongly held American beliefs in social progress. Americans see progress in the expansion of individual opportunities for choice, freedom, and self-expression. Moreover, Americans identify progress with growing tolerance of diversity. Over the past half century, the pollster Daniel Yankelovich writes, the United States has steadily grown more open-minded and accepting of groups that were previously perceived as alien, untrustworthy, or unsuitable for public leadership or social esteem. One such group is the burgeoning number of single-parent and stepparent families.

The Education of Sara McLanahan

In 1981 Sara McLanahan, now a sociologist at Princeton University's Woodrow Wilson School, read a three-part series by Ken Auletta in *The New Yorker.* Later published as a book titled *The Underclass,* the series presented a vivid portrait of the drug addicts, welfare mothers, and school dropouts who took part in an education-and-training program in New York City. Many were the children of single mothers, and it was Auletta's clear implication that single-mother families were contributing to the growth of an underclass. McLanahan was taken aback by this notion. "It struck me as strange that he would be viewing single mothers at that level of pathology."

"I'd gone to graduate school in the days when the politically correct argument was that single-parent families were just another alternative family form, and it was fine," McLanahan explains, as she recalls the state of social-scientific thinking in the 1970s. Several empirical studies that were then current supported an optimistic view of family change. (They used tiny samples, however, and did not track the well-being of children over time.)

One, *All Our Kin*, by Carol Stack, was required reading for thousands of university students. It said that single mothers had strengths that had gone undetected and unappreciated by earlier researchers. The single-mother family, it suggested, is an economically resourceful and socially embedded institution. In the late 1970s McLanahan wrote a similar study that looked at a small sample of white single mothers and how they coped. "So I was very much of that tradition."

By the early 1980s, however, nearly two decades had passed since the changes in family life had begun. During the intervening years a fuller body of empirical research had emerged: studies that used large samples, or followed families through time, or did both. Moreover, several of the studies offered a child's-eye view of family disruption. The National Survey on Children, conducted by the psychologist Nicholas Zill, had set out in 1976 to track a large sample of children aged seven to eleven. It also interviewed the children's parents and teachers. It surveyed its subjects again in 1981 and 1987. By the time of its third round of interviews the eleven-year-olds of 1976 were the twenty-two-year-olds of 1987. The California Children of Divorce Study, directed by Judith Wallerstein, a clinical psychologist, had also been going on for a decade. E. Mavis Hetherington, of the University of Virginia, was conducting a similar study of children from both intact and divorced families. For the first time it was possible to test the optimistic view against a large and longitudinal body of evidence.

It was to this body of evidence that Sara McLanahan turned. When she did, she found little to support the optimistic view of single motherhood. On the contrary. When she published her findings with Irwin Garfinkel in a 1986 book, *Single Mothers and Their Children*, her portrait of single motherhood proved to be as troubling in its own way as Auletta's.

One of the leading assumptions of the time was that single motherhood was economically viable. Even if single mothers did face economic trials, they wouldn't face them for long, it was argued, because they wouldn't remain single for long: single motherhood would be a brief phase of three to five years, followed by marriage. Single mothers would be economically resilient: if they experienced setbacks, they would recover quickly. It was also said that single mothers would be supported by informal networks of family, friends, neighbors, and other single mothers. As McLanahan shows in her study, the evidence demolishes all these claims.

For the vast majority of single mothers, the economic spectrum turns out to be narrow, running between precarious and desperate. Half the single mothers in the United States live below the poverty line. (Currently, one out of ten married couples with children is poor.) Many others live on the edge of poverty. Even single mothers who are far from poor are likely to experience persistent economic insecurity. Divorce almost always brings a decline in the standard of living for the mother and children.

Moreover, the poverty experienced by single mothers is no more brief than it is mild. A significant number of all single mothers never marry or remarry. Those who do, do so only after spending roughly six years, on average, as single parents. For black mothers the duration is much longer. Only 33 percent of African-American mothers had remarried within ten years of separation. Consequently, single motherhood is hardly a fleeting event for the mother, and it is likely to occupy a third of the child's childhood. Even the notion that single mothers are knit together in economically supportive networks is not borne out by the evidence. On the contrary, single parenthood forces many women to be on the move, in search of cheaper housing and better jobs. This need-driven restless mobility makes it more difficult for them to sustain supportive ties to family and friends, let alone other single mothers.

Single-mother families are vulnerable not just to poverty but to a particularly debilitating form of poverty: welfare dependency. The dependency takes two forms: First, single mothers, particularly unwed mothers, stay on welfare longer than other welfare recipients. Of those never-married mothers who receive welfare benefits, almost 40 percent remain on the rolls for ten years or longer. Second, welfare dependency tends to be passed on from one generation to the next. McLanahan says, "Evidence on intergenerational poverty indicates that, indeed, offspring from [single-mother] families are far more likely to be poor and to form mother-only families than are offspring who live with two parents most of their pre-adult life." Nor is the intergenerational impact of single motherhood limited to African-Americans, as many people seem to believe. Among white families, daughters of single parents are 53 percent more likely to marry as teenagers, 111 percent more likely to have children as teenagers, 164 percent more likely to have a premarital birth, and

92 percent more likely to dissolve their own marriages. All these inter-generational consequences of single motherhood increase the likelihood of chronic welfare dependency.

McLanahan cites three reasons that single-mother families are so vulnerable economically. For one thing, their earnings are low. Second, unless the mothers are widowed, they don't receive public subsidies large enough to lift them out of poverty. And finally, they do not get much support from family members — especially the fathers of their children. In 1982 single white mothers received an average of $1,246 in alimony and child support, black mothers an average of $322. Such payments accounted for about 10 percent of the income of single white mothers and for about 3.5 percent of the income of single black mothers. These amounts were dramatically smaller than the income of the father in a two-parent family and also smaller than the income from a second earner in a two-parent family. Roughly 60 percent of single white mothers and 80 percent of single black mothers received no support at all.

Until the mid-1980s, when stricter standards were put in place, child-support awards were only about half to two-thirds what the current guidelines require. Accordingly, there is often a big difference in the living standards of divorced fathers and of divorced mothers with children. After divorce the average annual income of mothers and children is $13,500 for whites and $9,000 for nonwhites, as compared with $25,000 for white nonresident fathers and $13,600 for nonwhite nonresident fathers. Moreover, since child-support awards account for a smaller portion of the income of a high-earning father, the drop in living standards can be especially sharp for mothers who were married to upper-level managers and professionals.

Unwed mothers are unlikely to be awarded any child support at all, 60 partly because the paternity of their children may not have been established. According to one recent study, only 20 percent of unmarried mothers receive child support.

Even if single mothers escape poverty, economic uncertainty remains a condition of life. Divorce brings a reduction in income and standard of living for the vast majority of single mothers. One study, for example, found that income for mothers and children declines on average about 30 percent, while fathers experience a 10 to 15 percent increase in income in the year following a separation. Things get even more difficult when fathers fail to meet their child-support obligations. As a result, many divorced mothers experience a wearing uncertainty about the family budget: whether the check will come in or not; whether new sneakers can be bought this month or not; whether the electric bill will be paid on time or not. Uncertainty about money triggers other kinds of uncertainty. Mothers and children often have to move to cheaper housing after a divorce. One study shows that about 38 percent of divorced mothers and their children move during the first year after a divorce. Even several years later the rate of moves for single mothers is about a third higher than the rate for two-parent families. It is also common for a mother to change her job or increase her working hours or both following a divorce. Even the composition of the household is likely to change, with other adults, such as boyfriends or babysitters, moving in and out.

All this uncertainty can be devastating to children. Anyone who knows children knows that they are deeply conservative creatures. They like things to stay the same. So pronounced is this tendency that certain children have been known to request the same peanut-butter-and-jelly sandwich for lunch for years on end. Children are particularly set in their ways when it comes to family, friends, neighborhoods, and schools. Yet when a family breaks up, all these things may change. The novelist Pat Conroy has observed that "each divorce is the death of a small civilization." No one feels this more acutely than children.

Sara McLanahan's investigation and others like it have helped to establish a broad consensus on the economic impact of family disruption on children. Most social scientists now agree that single motherhood is an important and growing cause of poverty, and that children suffer as a result. (They continue to argue, however, about the relationship between family structure and such economic factors as income inequality, the loss of jobs in the inner city, and the growth of low-wage jobs.) By the mid-1980s, however, it was clear that the problem of family disruption was not confined to the urban underclass, nor was its sole impact economic. Divorce and out-of-wedlock childbirth were affecting middle- and upper-class children, and these more privileged children were suffering negative consequences as well. It appeared that the problems associated with family breakup were far deeper and far more widespread than anyone had previously imagined.

The Missing Father

Judith Wallerstein is one of the pioneers in research on the long-term psychological impact of family disruption on children. The California Children of Divorce Study, which she directs, remains the most enduring study of the long-term effects of divorce on children and their parents. Moreover, it represents the best-known effort to look at the impact of divorce on middle-class children. The California children entered the study without pathological family histories. Before divorce they lived in stable, protected homes. And although some of the children did experience economic insecurity as the result of divorce, they were generally free from the most severe forms of poverty associated with family breakup. Thus the study and the resulting book (which Wallerstein wrote with Sandra Blakeslee), *Second Chances: Men, Women, and Children a Decade after Divorce*

(1989), provide new insight into the consequences of divorce which are not associated with extreme forms of economic or emotional deprivation.

When, in 1971, Wallerstein and her colleagues set out to conduct clin-   65
ical interviews with 131 children from the San Francisco area, they thought they were embarking on a short-term study. Most experts believed that divorce was like a bad cold. There was a phase of acute discomfort, and then a short recovery phase. According to the conventional wisdom, kids would be back on their feet in no time at all. Yet when Wallerstein met these children for a second interview more than a year later, she was amazed to discover that there had been no miraculous recovery. In fact, the children seemed to be doing worse.

The news that children did not "get over" divorce was not particularly welcome at the time. Wallerstein recalls, "We got angry letters from therapists, parents, and lawyers saying we were undoubtedly wrong. They said children are really much better off being released from an unhappy marriage. Divorce, they said, is a liberating experience." One of the main results of the California study was to overturn this optimistic view. In Wallerstein's cautionary words, "Divorce is deceptive. Legally it is a single event, but psychologically it is a chain — sometimes a never-ending chain — of events, relocations, and radically shifting relationships strung through time, a process that forever changes the lives of the people involved."

Five years after divorce more than a third of the children experienced moderate or severe depression. At ten years a significant number of the now young men and women appeared to be troubled, drifting, and underachieving. At fifteen years many of the thirtyish adults were struggling to establish strong love relationships of their own. In short, far from recovering from their parents' divorce, a significant percentage of these grownups were still suffering from its effects. In fact, according to Wallerstein, the long-term effects of divorce emerge at a time when young adults are trying to make their own decisions about love, marriage, and family. Not all children in the study suffered negative consequences. But Wallerstein's research presents a sobering picture of divorce. "The child of divorce faces many additional psychological burdens in addition to the normative tasks of growing up," she says.

Divorce not only makes it more difficult for young adults to establish new relationships. It also weakens the oldest primary relationship: that between parent and child. According to Wallerstein, "Parent-child relationships are permanently altered by divorce in ways that our society has not anticipated." Not only do children experience a loss of parental attention at the onset of divorce, but they soon find that at every stage of their development their parents are not available in the same way they once were. "In a reasonably happy intact family," Wallerstein observes, "the child gravitates first to one parent and then to the other, using skills and attributes from each in climbing the developmental ladder." In a divorced family, children find it "harder to find the needed parent at needed times." This may help explain why very young children suffer the most as the result of family disruption. Their opportunities to engage in this kind of ongoing process are the most truncated and compromised.

The father-child bond is severely, often irreparably, damaged in disrupted families. In a situation without historical precedent, an astonishing and disheartening number of American fathers are failing to provide financial support to their children. Often, more than the father's support check is missing. Increasingly, children are bereft of any contact with their fathers. According to the National Survey of Children, in disrupted families only one child in six, on average, saw his or her father as often as once a week in the past year. Close to half did not see their father at all in the past year. As time goes on, contact becomes even more infrequent. Ten years after a marriage breaks up, more than two thirds of children report not having seen their father for a year. Not surprisingly, when asked to name the "adults you look up to and admire," only 20 percent of children in single-parent families named their father, as compared with 52 percent of children in two-parent families. A favorite complaint among Baby Boom Americans is that their fathers were emotionally remote guys who worked hard, came home at night to eat supper, and didn't have much to say to or do with the kids. But the current generation has a far worse father problem: many of their fathers are vanishing entirely.

Even for fathers who maintain regular contact, the pattern of father-child relationships changes. The sociologists Andrew Cherlin and Frank Furstenberg, who have studied broken families, write that the fathers behave more like other relatives than like parents. Rather than helping with homework or carrying out a project with their children, nonresidential fathers are likely to take the kids shopping, to the movies, or out to dinner. Instead of providing steady advice and guidance, divorced fathers become "treat" dads. 70

Apparently — and paradoxically — it is the visiting relationship itself, rather than the frequency of visits, that is the real source of the problem. According to Wallerstein, the few children in the California study who reported visiting with their fathers once or twice a week over a ten-year period still felt rejected. The need to schedule a special time to be with the child, the repeated leave-takings, and the lack of connection to the child's regular, daily schedule leaves many fathers adrift, frustrated, and confused. Wallerstein calls the visiting father a parent without portfolio.

The deterioration in father-child bonds is most severe among children who experience divorce at an early age, according to a recent study. Nearly three quarters of the respondents, now young men and women, report having poor relationships with their fathers. Close to half have received psychological help, nearly a third have dropped out of high school, and about a quarter report having experienced high levels of problem behavior or emotional distress by the time they became young adults.

Long-Term Effects

Since most children live with their mothers after divorce, one might expect that the mother-child bond would remain unaltered and might even be strengthened. Yet research shows that the mother-child bond is also weakened as the result of divorce. Only half of the children who were close to their mothers before a divorce remained equally close after the divorce. Boys, particularly, had difficulties with their mothers. Moreover, mother-child relationships deteriorated over time. Whereas teenagers in disrupted families were no more likely than teenagers in intact families to report poor relationships with their mothers, 30 percent of young adults from disrupted families have poor relationships with their mothers, as compared with 16 percent of young adults from intact families. Mother-daughter relationships often deteriorate as the daughter reaches young adulthood. The only group in society that derives any benefit from these weakened parent-child ties is the therapeutic community. Young adults from disrupted families are nearly twice as likely as those from intact families to receive psychological help.

Some social scientists have criticized Judith Wallerstein's research because her study is based on a small clinical sample and does not include a control group of children from intact families. However, other studies generally support and strengthen her findings. Nicholas Zill has found similar long-term effects on children of divorce, reporting that "effects of marital discord and family disruption are visible twelve to twenty-two years later in poor relationships with parents, high levels of problem behavior, and an increased likelihood of dropping out of high school and receiving psychological help." Moreover, Zill's research also found signs of distress in young women who seemed relatively well adjusted in middle childhood and adolescence. Girls in single-parent families are also at much greater risk for precocious sexuality, teenage marriage, teenage pregnancy, nonmarital birth, and divorce than are girls in two-parent families.

Zill's research shows that family disruption strongly affects school 75 achievement as well. Children in disrupted families are nearly twice as likely as those in intact families to drop out of high school; among children who do drop out, those from disrupted families are less likely eventually to earn a diploma or a GED. Boys are at greater risk for dropping out than girls, and are also more likely to exhibit aggressive, acting-out behaviors. Other research confirms these findings. According to a study by the National Association of Elementary School Principals, 33 percent of two-parent elementary school students are ranked as high achievers, as compared with 17 percent of single-parent students. The children in single-parent families are also more likely to be truant or late or to have disciplinary action taken against them. Even after controlling for race, income, and religion, scholars find significant differences in educational attainment between children who grow up in intact families and children who do not. In his 1992 study *America's Smallest School: The Family*, Paul Barton shows that the proportion of two-parent families varies widely from state to state and is related to variations in academic achievement. North Dakota, for example, scores highest on the math-proficiency test and second highest on the two-parent-family scale. The District of Columbia is second lowest on the math test and lowest in the nation on the two-parent-family scale.

Zill notes that "while coming from a disrupted family significantly increases a young adult's risks of experiencing social, emotional or academic difficulties, it does not foreordain such difficulties. The majority of young people from disrupted families have successfully completed high school, do *not* currently display high levels of emotional distress or problem behavior, and enjoy reasonable relationships with their mothers." Nevertheless, a majority of these young adults do show maladjustment in their relationships with their fathers.

These findings underscore the importance of both a mother and a father in fostering the emotional well-being of children. Obviously, not all children in two-parent families are free from emotional turmoil, but few are burdened with the troubles that accompany family breakup. Moreover, as the sociologist Amitai Etzioni explains in *The Spirit of Community*, two parents in an intact family make up what might be called a mutually supportive education coalition. When both parents are present, they can play different, even contradictory, roles. One parent may goad the child to achieve, while the other may encourage the child to take time out to daydream or toss a football around. One may emphasize taking intellectual risks, while the other may insist on following the teacher's guidelines. At the same time, the parents regularly exchange information about the child's school problems and achievements, and have a sense of the overall educational mission. However, Etzioni writes,

> The sequence of divorce followed by a succession of boy or girlfriends, a second marriage, and frequently another divorce and another turnover of partners often means a repeatedly disrupted educational coalition. Each change in participants involves a change in the educational agenda for the child. Each new partner cannot be expected to pick up the previous one's educational post and program. . . . As a result, changes in parenting partners mean, at best, a deep disruption in a child's education, though of course several disruptions cut deeper into the effectiveness of the educational coalition than just one.

The Bad News about Stepparents

Perhaps the most striking, and potentially disturbing, new research has to do with children in stepparent families. Until quite recently the optimistic assumption was that children saw their lives improve when they became part of a stepfamily. When Nicholas Zill and his colleagues began to study the effects of remarriage on children, their working hypothesis was that stepparent families would make up for the shortcomings of the single-parent family. Clearly, most children are better off economically when they are able to share in the income of two adults. When a second adult joins the household, there may be a reduction in the time and work pressures on the single parent.

The research overturns this optimistic assumption, however. In general the evidence suggests that remarriage neither reproduces nor restores the intact family structure, even when it brings more income and a second adult into the household. Quite the contrary. Indeed, children living with stepparents appear to be even more disadvantaged than children living in a stable single-parent family. Other difficulties seem to offset the advantages of extra income and an extra pair of hands. However much our modern sympathies reject the fairy-tale portrait of stepparents, the latest research confirms that the old stories are anthropologically quite accurate. Stepfamilies disrupt established loyalties, create new uncertainties, provoke deep anxieties, and sometimes threaten a child's physical safety as well as emotional security.

Parents and children have dramatically different interests in and expectations for a new marriage. For a single parent, remarriage brings new commitments, the hope of enduring love and happiness, and relief from stress and loneliness. For a child, the same event often provokes confused feelings of sadness, anger, and rejection. Nearly half the children in Wallerstein's study said they felt left out in their stepfamilies. The National Commission on Children, a bipartisan group headed by Senator John D. Rockefeller, of West Virginia, reported that children from stepfamilies were more likely to say they often felt lonely or blue than children from either single-parent or intact families. Children in stepfamilies were the most likely to report that they wanted more time with their mothers. When mothers remarry, daughters tend to have a harder time adjusting than sons. Evidently, boys often respond positively to a male presence in the household, while girls who have established close ties to their mother in a single-parent family often see the stepfather as a rival and an intruder. According to one study, boys in remarried families are less likely to drop out of school than boys in single-parent families, while the opposite is true for girls.

A large percentage of children do not even consider stepparents to be part of their families, according to the National Survey on Children. The NSC asked children, "When you think of your family, who do you include?" Only 10 percent of the children failed to mention a biological parent, but a third left out a stepparent. Even children who rarely saw their noncustodial parents almost always named them as family members. The weak sense of attachment is mutual. When parents were asked the same question, only one percent failed to mention a biological child, while 15 percent left out a stepchild. In the same study stepparents with both natural children and stepchildren said that it was harder for them to love their stepchildren than their biological children and that their children would have been better off if they had grown up with two biological parents.

One of the most severe risks associated with stepparent-child ties is the risk of sexual abuse. As Judith Wallerstein explains, "The presence of a stepfather can raise the difficult issue of a thinner incest barrier." The incest taboo is strongly reinforced, Wallerstein says, by knowledge of paternity and by the experience of caring for a child since birth. A stepfather enters the family without either credential and plays a sexual role as the mother's husband. As a result, stepfathers can pose a sexual risk to the children, especially to daughters. According to a study by the Canadian researchers Martin Daly and Margo Wilson, preschool children in stepfamilies are forty times as likely as children in intact families to suffer physical or sexual abuse. (Most of the sexual abuse was committed by a third party, such as a neighbor, a stepfather's male friend, or another nonrelative.) Stepfathers discriminate in their abuse: they are far more likely to assault nonbiological children than their own natural children.

Sexual abuse represents the most extreme threat to children's well-being. Stepfamilies also seem less likely to make the kind of ordinary investments in the children that other families do. Although it is true that the stepfamily household has a higher income than the single-parent household, it does not follow that the additional income is reliably available to the children. To begin with, children's claim on stepparents' resources is shaky. Stepparents are not legally required to support stepchildren, so their financial support of these children is entirely voluntary. Moreover, since stepfamilies are far more likely to break up than intact families, particularly in the first five years, there is always the risk — far greater than the risk of unemployment in an intact family — that the second income will vanish with another divorce. The financial commitment to a child's education appears weaker in stepparent families, perhaps because the stepparent believes that the responsibility for educating the child rests with the biological parent.

Similarly, studies suggest that even though they may have the time, the parents in stepfamilies do not invest as much of it in their children as the parents in intact families or even single parents do. A 1991 survey by the National Commission on Children showed that the parents in stepfamilies were less likely to be involved in a child's school life, including involvement in extracurricular activities, than either intact-family parents or single parents. They were the least likely to report being involved in such time-consuming activities as coaching a child's team, accompanying class trips, or helping with school projects. According to McLanahan's research, children in stepparent families report lower educational aspirations on the part of their parents and lower levels of parental involvement with schoolwork. In short, it appears that family income and the number of adults in the household are not the only factors affecting children's well-being.

Diminishing Investments

There are several reasons for this diminished interest and investment. In the law, as in the children's eyes, stepparents are shadowy figures. According to the legal scholar David Chambers, family law has pretty much ignored stepparents. Chambers writes, "In the substantial majority of states, stepparents, even when they live with a child, have no legal obligation to contribute to the child's support; nor does a stepparent's presence in the home alter the support obligations of a noncustodial parent. The stepparent also has . . . no authority to approve emergency medical treatment or even to sign a permission slip. . . ." When a marriage breaks up, the stepparent has no continuing obligation to provide for a stepchild, no matter how long or how much he or she has been contributing to the support of the child. In short, Chambers says, stepparent relationships are based wholly on consent, subject to the inclinations of the adult and the child. The only way a stepparent can acquire the legal status of a parent is through adoption. Some researchers also point to the cultural ambiguity of the stepparent's role as a source of diminished interest, while others insist that it is the absence of a blood tie that weakens the bond between stepparent and child.

Whatever its causes, the diminished investment in children in both single-parent and stepparent families has a significant impact on their life chances. Take parental help with college costs. The parents in intact families are far more likely to contribute to children's college costs than are those in disrupted families. Moreover, they are usually able to arrive at a shared understanding of which children will go to college, where they will go, how much the parents will contribute, and how much the children will contribute. But when families break up, these informal understandings can vanish. The issue of college tuition remains one of the most contested areas of parental support, especially for higher-income parents.

The law does not step in even when familial understandings break down. In the 1980s many states lowered the age covered by child-support agreements from twenty-one to eighteen, thus eliminating college as a cost associated with support for a minor child. Consequently, the question of college tuition is typically not addressed in child-custody agreements. Even in states where the courts do require parents to contribute to college costs, the requirement may be in jeopardy. In a recent decision in Pennsylvania the court overturned an earlier decision ordering divorced parents to contribute to college tuition. This decision is likely to inspire challenges in other states where courts have required parents to pay for college. Increasingly, help in paying for college is entirely voluntary.

Judith Wallerstein has been analyzing the educational decisions of the college-age men and women in her study. She reports that "a full 42 percent of these men and women from middle class families appeared to have ended their educations without attempting college or had left college before achieving a degree at either the two-year or the four-year level." A significant percentage of these young people have the ability to attend college. Typical of this group are Nick and Terry, sons of a college professor. They had been close to their father before the divorce, but their father remarried soon after the divorce and saw his sons only occasionally, even though he lived nearby. At age nineteen Nick had completed a few junior-college courses and was earning a living as a salesman. Terry, twenty-one, who had been tested as a gifted student, was doing blue-collar work irregularly.

Sixty-seven percent of the college-age students from disrupted families attended college, as compared with 85 percent of other students who attended the same high schools. Of those attending college, several had fathers who were financially capable of contributing to college costs but did not.

The withdrawal of support for college suggests that other customary forms of parental help-giving, too, may decline as the result of family breakup. For example, nearly a quarter of first-home purchases since 1980 have involved help from relatives, usually parents. The median amount of help is $5,000. It is hard to imagine that parents who refuse to contribute to college costs will offer help in buying first homes, or help in buying cars or health insurance for young adult family members. And although it is too soon to tell, family disruption may affect the generational transmission of wealth. Baby Boomers will inherit their parents' estates, some substantial, accumulated over a lifetime by parents who lived and saved together. To be sure, the postwar generation benefited from an expanding economy and a rising standard of living, but its ability to accumulate wealth also owed something to family stability. The lifetime assets, like the marriage itself, remained intact. It is unlikely that the children of disrupted families will be in so favorable a position.

Moreover, children from disrupted families may be less likely to help their aging parents. The sociologist Alice Rossi, who has studied intergenerational patterns of help-giving, says that adult obligation has its roots in early-childhood experience. Children who grow up in intact families experience higher levels of obligation to kin than children from broken families. Children's sense of obligation to a nonresidential father is particularly weak. Among adults with both parents living, those separated from their father during childhood are less likely than others to see the father regularly. Half of them see their father more than once a year, as compared with nine out of ten of those whose parents are still married. Apparently a kind of bitter justice is at work here. Fathers who do not

90

support or see their young children may not be able to count on their adult children's support when they are old and need money, love, and attention.

In short, as Andrew Cherlin and Frank Furstenburg put it, "Through divorce and remarriage, individuals are related to more and more people, to each of whom they owe less and less." Moreover, as Nicholas Zill argues, weaker parent-child attachments leave many children more strongly exposed to influences outside the family, such as peers, boyfriends or girlfriends, and the media. Although these outside forces can sometimes be helpful, common sense and research opinion argue against putting too much faith in peer groups or the media as surrogates for Mom and Dad.

Poverty, Crime, Education

Family disruption would be a serious problem even if it affected only individual children and families. But its impact is far broader. Indeed, it is not an exaggeration to characterize it as a central cause of many of our most vexing social problems. Consider three problems that most Americans believe rank among the nation's pressing concerns: poverty, crime, and declining school performance.

More than half of the increase in child poverty in the 1980s is attributable to changes in family structure, according to David Eggebeen and Daniel Lichter, of Pennsylvania State University. In fact, if family structure in the United States had remained relatively constant since 1960, the rate of child poverty would be a third lower than it is today. This does not bode well for the future. With more than half of today's children likely to live in single-parent families, poverty and associated welfare costs threaten to become even heavier burdens on the nation.

Crime in American cities has increased dramatically and grown more   95
violent over recent decades. Much of this can be attributed to the rise in disrupted families. Nationally, more than 70 percent of all juveniles in state reform institutions come from fatherless homes. A number of scholarly studies find that even after the groups of subjects are controlled for income, boys from single-mother homes are significantly more likely than others to commit crimes and to wind up in the juvenile justice, court, and penitentiary systems. One such study summarizes the relationship between crime and one-parent families in this way: "The relationship is so strong that controlling for family configuration erases the relationship between race and crime and between low income and crime. This conclusion shows up time and again in the literature." The nation's mayors, as well as police officers, social workers, probation officers, and court officials, consistently point to family breakup as the most important source of rising rates of crime.

Terrible as poverty and crime are, they tend to be concentrated in inner cities and isolated from the everyday experience of many Americans. The same cannot be said of the problem of declining school performance. Nowhere has the impact of family breakup been more profound or widespread than in the nation's public schools. There is a strong consensus that the schools are failing in their historic mission to prepare every American child to be a good worker and a good citizen. And nearly everyone agrees that the schools must undergo dramatic reform in order to reach that goal. In pursuit of that goal, moreover, we have suffered no shortage of bright ideas or pilot projects or bold experiments in school reform. But there is little evidence that measures such as curricular reform, school-based management, and school choice will address, let alone solve, the biggest problem schools face: the rising number of children who come from disrupted families.

The great educational tragedy of our time is that many American children are failing in school not because they are intellectually or physically impaired but because they are emotionally incapacitated. In schools across the nation principals report a dramatic rise in the aggressive, acting-out behavior characteristic of children, especially boys, who are living in single-parent families. The discipline problems in today's suburban schools — assaults on teachers, unprovoked attacks on other students, screaming outbursts in class — outstrip the problems that were evident in the toughest city schools a generation ago. Moreover, teachers find many children emotionally distracted, so upset and preoccupied by the explosive drama of their own family lives that they are unable to concentrate on such mundane matters as multiplication tables.

In response, many schools have turned to therapeutic remediation. A growing proportion of many school budgets is devoted to counseling and other psychological services. The curriculum is becoming more therapeutic: children are taking courses in self-esteem, conflict resolution, and aggression management. Parental advisory groups are conscientiously debating alternative approaches to traditional school discipline, ranging from teacher training in mediation to the introduction of metal detectors and security guards in the schools. Schools are increasingly becoming emergency rooms of the emotions, devoted not only to developing minds but also to repairing hearts. As a result, the mission of the school, along with the culture of the classroom, is slowly changing. What we are seeing, largely as a result of the new burdens of family disruption, is the psychologization of American education.

Taken together, the research presents a powerful challenge to the prevailing view of family change as social progress. Not a single one of the assumptions underlying that view can be sustained against the empirical evidence. Single-parent families are not able to do well economically on a mother's income. In fact, most teeter on the economic brink, and many fall into poverty and welfare dependency. Growing up in a disrupted family does not enrich a child's life or expand the number of adults committed to the child's well-being. In fact, disrupted families threaten the psychological well-being of children and diminish the investment of adult time and money in them. Family diversity in the form of increasing numbers of single-parent and stepparent families does not strengthen the social fabric. It dramatically weakens and undermines society, placing new burdens on schools, courts, prisons, and the welfare system. These new families are not an improvement on the nuclear family, nor are they even just as good, whether you look at outcomes for children or outcomes for society as a whole. In short, far from representing social progress, family change represents a stunning example of social regress.

The Two-Parent Advantage

All this evidence gives rise to an obvious conclusion: growing up in an   100
intact two-parent family is an important source of advantage for American children. Though far from perfect as a social institution, the intact family offers children greater security and better outcomes than its fast-growing alternatives: single-parent and stepparent families. Not only does the intact family protect the child from poverty and economic insecurity; it also provides greater noneconomic investments of parental time, attention, and emotional support over the entire life course. This does not mean that all two-parent families are better for children than all single-parent families. But in the face of the evidence it becomes increasingly difficult to sustain the proposition that all family structures produce equally good outcomes for children.

Curiously, many in the research community are hesitant to say that two-parent families generally promote better outcomes for children than single-parent families. Some argue that we need finer measures of the extent of the family-structure effect. As one scholar has noted, it is possible, by disaggregating the data in certain ways, to make family structure "go away" as an independent variable. Other researchers point to studies that show that children suffer psychological effects as a result of family conflict preceding family breakup. Consequently, they reason, it is the conflict rather than the structure of the family that is responsible for many of the problems associated with family disruption. Others, including Judith Wallerstein, caution against treating children in divorced families and children in intact families as separate populations, because doing so tends to exaggerate the differences between the two groups. "We have to take this family by family," Wallerstein says.

Some of the caution among researchers can also be attributed to ideological pressures. Privately, social scientists worry that their research may serve ideological causes that they themselves do not support, or that their work may be misinterpreted as an attempt to "tell people what to do." Some are fearful that they will be attacked by feminist colleagues, or, more generally, that their comments will be regarded as an effort to turn back the clock to the 1950s — a goal that has almost no constituency in the academy. Even more fundamental, it has become risky for anyone — scholar, politician, religious leader — to make normative statements today. This reflects not only the persistent drive toward "value neutrality" in the professions but also a deep confusion about the purposes of public discourse. The dominant view appears to be that social criticism, like criticism of individuals, is psychologically damaging. The worst thing you can do is to make people feel guilty or bad about themselves.

When one sets aside these constraints, however, the case against the two-parent family is remarkably weak. It is true that disaggregating data can make family structure less significant as a factor, just as disaggregating Hurricane Andrew into wind, rain, and tides can make it disappear as a meteorological phenomenon. Nonetheless, research opinion as well as common sense suggests that the effects of changes in family structure are great enough to cause concern. Nicholas Zill argues that many of the risk factors for children are doubled or more than doubled as the result of family disruption. "In epidemiological terms," he writes, "the doubling of a hazard is a substantial increase. . . . [T]he increase in risk that dietary cholesterol poses for cardiovascular disease, for example, is far less than double, yet millions of Americans have altered their diets because of the perceived hazard."

The argument that family conflict, rather than the breakup of parents, is the cause of children's psychological distress is persuasive on its face. Children who grow up in high-conflict families, whether the families stay together or eventually split up, are undoubtedly at great psychological risk. And surely no one would dispute that there must be societal measures available, including divorce, to remove children from families where they are in danger. Yet only a minority of divorces grow out of pathological situations; much more common are divorces in families unscarred by physical assault. Moreover, an equally compelling hypothesis is that family breakup generates its own conflict. Certainly, many families exhibit more conflictual and even violent behavior as a consequence of divorce than they did before divorce.

Finally, it is important to note that clinical insights are different from sociological findings. Clinicians work with individual families, who cannot and should not be defined by statistical aggregates. Appropriate to a clinical approach, moreover, is a focus on the internal dynamics of family functioning and on the immense variability in human behavior. Nevertheless, there is enough empirical evidence to justify sociological statements about the causes of declining child well-being and to demonstrate that despite the plasticity of human response, there are some useful rules of thumb to guide our thinking about and policies affecting the family.

For example, Sara McLanahan says, three structural constants are commonly associated with intact families, even intact families who would not win any "Family of the Year" awards. The first is economic. In intact families, children share in the income of two adults. Indeed, as a number of analysts have pointed out, the two-parent family is becoming more rather than less necessary, because more and more families need two incomes to sustain a middle-class standard of living.

McLanahan believes that most intact families also provide a stable authority structure. Family breakup commonly upsets the established boundaries of authority in a family. Children are often required to make decisions or accept responsibilities once considered the province of parents. Moreover, children, even very young children, are often expected to behave like mature adults, so that the grown-ups in the family can be free to deal with the emotional fallout of the failed relationship. In some instances family disruption creates a complete vacuum in authority; everyone invents his or her own rules. With lines of authority disrupted or absent, children find it much more difficult to engage in the normal kinds of testing behavior, the trial and error, the failing and succeeding, that define the developmental pathway toward character and competence. McLanahan says, "Children need to be the ones to challenge the rules. The parents need to set the boundaries and let the kids push the boundaries. The children shouldn't have to walk the straight and narrow at all times."

Finally, McLanahan holds that children in intact families benefit from stability in what she neutrally terms "household personnel." Family disruption frequently brings new adults into the family, including stepparents, live-in boyfriends or girlfriends, and casual sexual partners. Like stepfathers, boyfriends can present a real threat to children's, particularly to daughters', security and well-being. But physical or sexual abuse represents only the most extreme such threat. Even the very best of boyfriends can disrupt and undermine a child's sense of peace and security, McLanahan says. "It's not as though you're going from an unhappy marriage to peacefulness. There can be a constant changing until the mother finds a suitable partner."

McLanahan's argument helps explain why children of widows tend to do better than children of divorced or unmarried mothers. Widows differ from other single mothers in all three respects. They are economically more secure, because they receive more public assistance through Survivors Insurance, and possibly private insurance or other kinds of support from family members. Thus widows are less likely to leave the neighborhood in search of a new or better job and a cheaper house or apartment. Moreover, the death of a father is not likely to disrupt the authority structure radically. When a father dies, he is no longer physically present, but his death does not dethrone him as an authority figure in the child's life. On the contrary, his authority may be magnified through death. The mother can draw on the powerful memory of the departed father as a way of intensifying her parental authority: "Your father would have wanted it this way." Finally, since widows tend to be older than divorced mothers, their love life may be less distracting.

Regarding the two-parent family, the sociologist David Popenoe, 110
who has devoted much of his career to the study of families, both in the
United States and in Scandinavia, makes this straightforward assertion:

> Social science research is almost never conclusive. There are always
> methodological difficulties and stones left unturned. Yet in three
> decades of work as a social scientist, I know of few other bodies of data
> in which the weight of evidence is so decisively on one side of the issue:
> on the whole, for children, two-parent families are preferable to single-
> parent and stepfamilies.

The Regime Effect

The rise in family disruption is not unique to American society. It is evident in virtually all advanced nations, including Japan, where it is also shaped by the growing participation of women in the work force. Yet the United States has made divorce easier and quicker than in any other Western nation with the sole exception of Sweden — and the trend toward solo motherhood has also been more pronounced in America. (Sweden has an equally high rate of out-of-wedlock birth, but the majority of such births are to cohabiting couples, a long-established pattern in Swedish society.) More to the point, nowhere has family breakup been greeted by a more triumphant rhetoric of renewal than in America.

What is striking about this rhetoric is how deeply it reflects classic themes in American public life. It draws its language and imagery from the nation's founding myth. It depicts family breakup as a drama of revolution and rebirth. The nuclear family represents the corrupt past, an institution guilty of the abuse of power and the suppression of individual freedom. Breaking up the family is like breaking away from Old World tyranny. Liberated from the bonds of the family, the individual can achieve independence and experience a new beginning, a fresh start, a new birth of freedom. In short, family breakup recapitulates the American experience.

This rhetoric is an example of what the University of Maryland political philosopher William Galston has called the "regime effect." The founding of the United States set in motion a new political order based to an unprecedented degree on individual rights, personal choice, and egalitarian relationships. Since then these values have spread beyond their original domain of political relationships to define social relationships as well. During the past twenty-five years these values have had a particularly profound impact on the family.

Increasingly, political principles of individual rights and choice shape our understanding of family commitment and solidarity. Family relationships are viewed not as permanent or binding but as voluntary and easily terminable. Moreover, under the sway of the regime effect the family loses its central importance as an institution in the civil society, accomplishing certain social goals such as raising children and caring for its members, and becomes a means to achieving greater individual happiness — a lifestyle choice. Thus, Galston says, what is happening to the American family reflects the "unfolding logic of authoritative, deeply American moral-political principles."

One benefit of the regime effect is to create greater equality in adult   115
family relationships. Husbands and wives, mothers and fathers, enjoy relationships far more egalitarian than past relationships were, and most Americans prefer it that way. But the political principles of the regime effect can threaten another kind of family relationship — that between parent and child. Owing to their biological and developmental immaturity, children are needy dependents. They are not able to express their choices according to limited, easily terminable, voluntary agreements. They are not able to act as negotiators in family decisions, even those that most affect their own interests. As one writer has put it, "a newborn does not make a good 'partner.'" Correspondingly, the parental role is antithetical to the spirit of the regime. Parental investment in children involves a diminished investment in self, a willing deference to the needs and claims of the dependent child. Perhaps more than any other family relationship, the parent-child relationship — shaped as it is by patterns of dependency and deference — can be undermined and weakened by the principles of the regime.

More than a century and a half ago Alexis de Tocqueville made the striking observation that an individualistic society depends on a communitarian institution like the family for its continued existence. The family cannot be constituted like the liberal state, nor can it be governed entirely by that state's principles. Yet the family serves as the seedbed for the virtues required by a liberal state. The family is responsible for teaching lessons of independence, self-restraint, responsibility, and right conduct, which are essential to a free, democratic society. If the family fails in these tasks, then the entire experiment in democratic self-rule is jeopardized.

To take one example: independence is basic to successful functioning in American life. We assume that most people in America will be able to work, care for themselves and their families, think for themselves, and inculcate the same traits of independence and initiative in their children. We depend on families to teach people to do these things. The erosion of the two-parent family undermines the capacity of families to impart this knowledge; children of long-term welfare-dependent single parents are far more likely than others to be dependent themselves. Similarly, the children in disrupted families have a harder time forging bonds of trust with others and giving and getting help across the generations. This, too, may lead to greater dependency on the resources of the state.

Over the past two and a half decades Americans have been conducting what is tantamount to a vast natural experiment in family life. Many would argue that this experiment was necessary, worthwhile, and long overdue. The results of the experiment are coming in, and they are clear. Adults have benefited from the changes in family life in important ways, but the same cannot be said for children. Indeed, this is the first generation in the nation's history to do worse psychologically, socially, and economically than its parents. Most poignantly, in survey after survey the children of broken families confess deep longings for an intact family.

Nonetheless, as Galston is quick to point out, the regime effect is not an irresistible undertow that will carry away the family. It is more like a swift current, against which it is possible to swim. People learn; societies can change, particularly when it becomes apparent that certain behaviors damage the social ecology, threaten the public order, and impose new burdens on core institutions. Whether Americans will act to overcome the legacy of family disruption is a crucial but as yet unanswered question.

PREPARING FOR DISCUSSION

1. Whitehead notes that recent attempts to examine changes in family structure are usually met with fierce protests. How does she account for these protests? What kinds of people tend to make up the protesting faction?

2. What is Whitehead's attitude toward the stigma about divorce in America? Does the stigma against divorce show any signs of having been lifted?

3. Does Whitehead concern herself with the problems that divorced parents and unwed mothers face? Is it possible that what is better for the parent might sometimes be better for the child as well?

4. Whitehead argues against the view that "value neutrality" is necessary to keep academic studies from psychologically damaging the people or groups under study. On what grounds does she reject this view?

5. In the final section of the essay, Whitehead resorts to political and even revolutionary metaphors to describe the recent liberal rhetoric about families. What particular words and phrases does she use in her description? Why has she chosen this metaphor? What effect does it have on readers?

FROM READING TO WRITING

6. Whitehead has observed within popular culture both tacit and express approval of divorce and single motherhood. Do you find similar instances of such

approval on television and in movies? Write an essay in which you describe such
an instance. What was the context of the divorce? Do you feel it was justified?

7. Consider your own attitudes about unwed motherhood and divorce. To
what extent do you agree with Whitehead's position and accept her analysis of
the figure on child welfare that she includes in her essay? In an essay, explore
your own sense of the impact of two-parent families on a child's development.
Have you noticed a major difference in children raised in one-parent families as
opposed to two-parent families?

DANIEL PATRICK MOYNIHAN

Defining Deviancy Down

The rise in crime, the rapidly increasing number of broken homes, and
the explosion of homelessness are just a few of the social ills that have
ravaged American society during the last three decades. Yet for many
Americans, the best way to deal with this crisis is simply to deny that
anything unusual has occurred. One method of denial — the one explored in the following selection — is that of defining deviancy down, a
process by which behavior formerly deemed unacceptable in civil society is now viewed as normal. Daniel Patrick Moynihan, the senior U.S.
senator from New York, questions the lowering of standards by which
we classify behaviors as deviant.

Moynihan attended the City College of New York and Tufts University and received his Ph.D. from the Fletcher School of Law and Foreign Policy. A member of the cabinet or subcabinet of Presidents
Kennedy, Johnson, Nixon, and Ford, Moynihan is the only person in
American history to serve in four successive administrations. He was
the U.S. ambassador to India from 1973 to 1975 and the U.S. representative to the United Nations from 1975 to 1976. He is a former director of
the joint Center for Urban Studies at the Massachusetts Institute of Technology and Harvard University. This selection first appeared in the
American Scholar in 1993.

SELECTED PUBLICATIONS: *Perspectives on Poverty* (1969); *Toward a National Urban Policy* (1970); *Counting Our Blessings: Reflections on the Future
of America* (1980); *Family and Nation* (1986); *Came the Revolution: Argument
in the Reagan Era* (1988); *Pandaemonium: Ethnicity in International Politics*
(1993).

In one of the founding texts of sociology, *The Rules of Sociological Method* (1895), Emile Durkheim set it down that "crime is normal." "It is," he wrote, "completely impossible for any society entirely free of it to exist." By defining what is deviant, we are enabled to know what is not, and hence to live by shared standards. This aperçu appears in the chapter entitled "Rules for the Distinction of the Normal from the Pathological." Durkheim writes:

> From this viewpoint the fundamental facts of criminology appear to us in an entirely new light. . . . [T]he criminal no longer appears as an utterly unsociable creature, a sort of parasitic element, a foreign, inassimilable body introduced into the bosom of society. He plays a normal role in social life. For its part, crime must no longer be conceived of as an evil which cannot be circumscribed closely enough. Far from there being cause for congratulation when it drops too noticeably below the normal level, this apparent progress assuredly coincides with and is linked to some social disturbance.

Durkheim suggests, for example, that "in times of scarcity" crimes of assault drop off. He does not imply that we ought to approve of crime — "[p]ain has likewise nothing desirable about it" — but we need to understand its function. He saw religion, in the sociologist Randall Collins's terms, as "fundamentally a set of ceremonial actions, assembling the group, heightening its emotions, and focusing its members on symbols of their common belongingness." In this context "a punishment ceremony creates social solidarity."

The matter was pretty much left at that until seventy years later when, in 1965, Kai T. Erikson published *Wayward Puritans*, a study of "crime rates" in the Massachusetts Bay Colony. The plan behind the book, as Erikson put it, was "to test [Durkheim's] notion that the number of deviant offenders a community can afford to recognize is likely to remain stable over time." The notion proved out very well indeed. Despite occasional crime waves, as when itinerant Quakers refused to take off their hats in the presence of magistrates, the amount of deviance in this corner of seventeenth-century New England fitted nicely with the supply of stocks and whipping posts. Erikson remarks:

> It is one of the arguments of the . . . study that the amount of deviation a community encounters is apt to remain fairly constant over time. To start at the beginning, it is a simple logistic fact that the number of deviancies which come to a community's attention are limited by the kinds of equipment it uses to detect and handle them, and to that extent the rate of deviation found in a community is at least in part a function of the size and complexity of its social control apparatus. A community's capacity for handling deviance, let us say, can be roughly estimated by counting its prison cells and hospital beds, its policemen and psychiatrists, its courts and clinics. Most communities, it would seem, operate with the expectation that a relatively constant number of control agents

is necessary to cope with a relatively constant number of offenders. The amount of men, money, and material assigned by society to "do something" about deviant behavior does not vary appreciably over time, and the implicit logic which governs the community's efforts to man a police force or maintain suitable facilities for the mentally ill seems to be that there is a fairly stable quota of trouble which should be anticipated.

In this sense, the agencies of control often seem to define their job as that of keeping deviance within bounds rather than that of obliterating it altogether. Many judges, for example, assume that severe punishments are a greater deterrent to crime than moderate ones, and so it is important to note that many of them are apt to impose harder penalties when crime seems to be on the increase and more lenient ones when it does not, almost as if the power of the bench were being used to keep the crime rate from getting out of hand.

Erikson was taking issue with what he described as "a dominant strain in sociological thinking" that took for granted that a well-structured society "is somehow designed to prevent deviant behavior from occurring." In both authors, Durkheim and Erikson, there is an undertone that suggests that, with deviancy, as with most social goods, there is the continuing problem of demand exceeding supply. Durkheim invites us to

> imagine a society of saints, a perfect cloister of exemplary individuals. Crimes, properly so called, will there be unknown; but faults which appear venial to the layman will create there the same scandal that the ordinary offense does in ordinary consciousness. If, then, this society has the power to judge and punish, it will define these acts as criminal and will treat them as such.

Recall Durkheim's comment that there need be no cause for congratulations should the amount of crime drop "too noticeably below the normal level." It would not appear that Durkheim anywhere contemplates the possibility of too much crime. Clearly his theory would have required him to deplore such a development, but the possibility seems never to have occurred to him.

Erikson, writing much later in the twentieth century, contemplates both possibilities. "Deviant persons can be said to supply needed services to society." There is no doubt a tendency for the supply of any needed thing to run short. But he is consistent. There can, he believes, be *too much* of a good thing. Hence "the number of deviant offenders a community *can afford* to recognize is likely to remain stable over time" [my emphasis].

Social scientists are said to be on the lookout for poor fellows getting   5
a bum rap. But here is a theory that clearly implies that there are circumstances in which society will choose *not* to notice behavior that would be otherwise controlled, or disapproved, or even punished.

It appears to me that this is in fact what we in the United States have been doing of late. I proffer the thesis that, over the past generation, since the time Erikson wrote, the amount of deviant behavior in American society has increased beyond the levels the community can "afford to recognize" and that, accordingly, we have been re-defining deviancy so as to exempt much conduct previously stigmatized, and also quietly raising the "normal" level in categories where behavior is now abnormal by any earlier standard. This redefining has evoked fierce resistance from defenders of "old" standards, and accounts for much of the present "cultural war" such as proclaimed by many at the 1992 Republican National Convention.

Let me, then, offer three categories of redefinition in these regards: the *altruistic*, the *opportunistic*, and the *normalizing*.

The first category, the *altruistic*, may be illustrated by the deinstitutionalization movement within the mental health profession that appeared in the 1950s. The second category, the *opportunistic*, is seen in the interest group rewards derived from the acceptance of "alternative" family structures. The third category, the *normalizing*, is to be observed in the growing acceptance of unprecedented levels of violent crime.

It happens that I was present at the beginning of the deinstitutionalization movement. Early in 1955 Averell Harriman, then the new governor of New York, met with his new commissioner of mental hygiene, Dr. Paul Hoch, who described the development, at one of the state mental hospitals, of a tranquilizer derived from rauwolfia. The medication had been clinically tested and appeared to be an effective treatment for many severely psychotic patients, thus increasing the percentage of patients discharged. Dr. Hoch recommended that it be used systemwide; Harriman found the money. That same year Congress created a Joint Commission on Mental Health and Illness whose mission was to formulate "comprehensive and realistic recommendations" in this area, which was then a matter of considerable public concern. Year after year, the population of mental institutions grew. Year after year, new facilities had to be built. Never mind the complexities: population growth and such like matters. There was a general unease. Durkheim's constant continued to be exceeded. (In *Spanning the Century: The Life of W. Averell Harriman,* Rudy Abramson writes: "New York's mental hospitals in 1955 were overflowing warehouses, and new patients were being admitted faster than space could be found for them. When he was inaugurated, 94,000 New Yorkers were confined to state hospitals. Admissions were running at more than 2,500 a year and rising, making the Department of Mental Hygiene the fastest-growing, most-expensive, most-hopeless department of state government.")

The discovery of tranquilizers was adventitious. Physicians were [10] seeking cures for disorders that were just beginning to be understood. Even a limited success made it possible to believe that the incidence of this particular range of disorders, which had seemingly required persons to be confined against their will or even awareness, could be greatly reduced. The Congressional Commission submitted its report in 1961; it proposed a nationwide program of deinstitutionalization.

Late in 1961, President Kennedy appointed an interagency committee to prepare legislative recommendations based upon the report. I represented Secretary of Labor Arthur J. Goldberg on this committee and drafted its final submission. This included the recommendation of the National Institute of Mental Health that 2,000 community mental health centers (one per 100,000 of population) be built by 1980. A buoyant Presidential Message to Congress followed early in 1963. "If we apply our medical knowledge and social insights fully," President Kennedy pronounced, "all but a small portion of the mentally ill can eventually achieve a wholesome and a constructive social adjustment." A "concerted national attack on mental disorders [was] now possible and practical." The president signed the Community Mental Health Centers Construction Act on October 31, 1963, his last public bill-signing ceremony. He gave me a pen.

The mental hospitals emptied out. At the time Governor Harriman met with Dr. Hoch in 1955, there were 93,314 adult residents of mental institutions maintained by New York State. As of August 1992, there were 11,363. This occurred across the nation. However, the number of community mental health centers never came near the goal of the 2,000 proposed community centers. Only some 482 received federal construction funds between 1963 and 1980. The next year, 1981, the program was folded into the Alcohol and Other Drug Abuse block grant and disappeared from view. Even when centers were built, the results were hardly as hoped for. David F. Musto of Yale writes that the planners had bet on improving national mental health "by improving the quality of general community life through expert knowledge, not merely by more effective treatment of the already ill." There was no such knowledge.

However, worse luck, the belief that there *was* such knowledge took hold within sectors of the profession that saw institutionalization as an unacceptable mode of social control. These activists subscribed to a redefining mode of their own. Mental patients were said to have been "labeled," and were not to be drugged. Musto says of the battles that followed that they were "so intense and dramatic precisely because both sides shared the fantasy of an omnipotent and omniscient mental health technology which could thoroughly reform society; the prize seemed eminently worth fighting for."

But even as the federal government turned to other matters, the mental institutions continued to release inmates. Professor Fred Siegel of Cooper Union observes: "In the great wave of moral deregulation that began in the mid-1960s, the poor and the insane were freed from the fetters of middle-class mores." They might henceforth sleep in doorways as often as they chose. The problem of the homeless appeared, characteristically defined as persons who lacked "affordable housing."

The *altruistic* mode of redefinition is just that. There is no reason to believe that there was any real increase in mental illness at the time deinstitutionalization began. Yet there was such a perception, and this enabled good people to try to do good, however unavailing in the end.

Our second, or *opportunistic,* mode of re-definition reveals at most a nominal intent to do good. The true object is to do well, a long-established motivation among mortals. In this pattern, a growth in deviancy makes possible a transfer of resources, including prestige, to those who control the deviant population. This control would be jeopardized if any serious effort were made to reduce the deviancy in question. This leads to assorted strategies for re-defining the behavior in question as not all that deviant, really.

In the years from 1963 to 1965, the Policy Planning Staff of the U.S. Department of Labor picked up the first tremors of what Samuel H. Preston, in the 1984 Presidential Address to the Population Association of America, would call "the earthquake that shuddered through the American family in the past twenty years." *The New York Times* recently provided a succinct accounting of Preston's point:

> Thirty years ago, 1 in every 40 white children was born to an unmarried mother; today it is 1 in 5, according to Federal data. Among blacks, 2 of 3 children are born to an unmarried mother; 30 years ago the figure was 1 in 5.

In 1991, Paul Offner and I published longitudinal data showing that, of children born in the years 1967–69, some 22.1 percent were dependent on welfare — that is to say, Aid to Families with Dependent Children — before reaching age 18. This broke down as 15.7 percent for white children, 72.3 percent for black children. Projections for children born in 1980 gave rates of 22.2 percent and 82.9 percent, respectively. A year later, a *New York Times* series on welfare and poverty called this a "startling finding . . . a symptom of vast social calamity."

And yet there is little evidence that these facts are regarded as a calamity in municipal government. To the contrary, there is general acceptance of the situation as normal. Political candidates raise the subject, often to the point of dwelling on it. But while there is a good deal of demand for symbolic change, there is none of the marshaling of resources that is associated with significant social action. Nor is there any lack of evidence that there is a serious social problem here.

Richard T. Gill writes of "an accumulation of data showing that intact biological parent families offer children very large advantages compared to any other family or non-family structure one can imagine." Correspondingly, the disadvantages associated with single-parent families spill over into other areas of social policy that now attract great public concern. Leroy L. Schwartz, M.D., and Mark W. Stanton argue that the real quest regarding a government-run health system such as that of Canada or Germany is whether it would work "in a country that has social problems that countries like Canada and Germany don't share to the same extent." Health problems reflect ways of living. The way of life associated with "such social pathologies as the breakdown of the family structure" lead to medical pathologies. Schwartz and Stanton conclude: "The United States is paying dearly for its social and behavioral problems," for they have now become medical problems as well.

To cite another example, there is at present no more vexing problem of social policy in the United States than that posed by education. A generation of ever-more ambitious statutes and reforms have produced weak responses at best and a fair amount of what could more simply be called dishonesty. ("Everyone knows that Head Start works." By the year 2000, American students will "be first in the world in science and mathematics.") None of this should surprise us. The 1966 report *Equality of Educational Opportunity* by James S. Coleman and his associates established that the family background of students played a much stronger role in student achievement relative to variations in the ten (and still standard) measures of school quality.

In a 1992 study entitled *America's Smallest School: The Family*, Paul Barton came up with the elegant and persuasive concept of the parent-pupil ratio as a measure of school quality. Barton, who was on the policy planning staff in the Department of Labor in 1965, noted the great increase in the proportion of children living in single-parent families since then. He further noted that the proportion "varies widely among the states" and is related to "variation in achievement" among them. The correlation between the percentage of eighth graders living in two-parent families and average mathematics proficiency is a solid .74. North Dakota, highest on the math test, is second highest on the family compositions scale — that is, it is second in the percentage of kids coming from two-parent homes. The District of Columbia, lowest on the family scale, is second lowest in the test score.

A few months before Barton's study appeared, I published an article showing that the correlation between eighth-grade math scores and distance of state capitals from the Canadian border was .522, a respectable showing. By contrast, the correlation with per pupil expenditure was a derisory .203. I offered the policy proposal that states wishing to improve their schools should move closer to Canada. This would be difficult, of course, but so would it be to change the parent-pupil ratio. Indeed, the 1990 Census found that for the District of Columbia, apart from Ward 3 west of Rock Creek Park, the percentage of children living in single-parent families in the seven remaining wards ranged from a low of 63.6 percent to a high of 75.7. This being a one-time measurement, over time the proportions become asymptotic. And this in the nation's capital. No demand for change comes from that community — or as near to no demand as makes no matter. *For there is good money to be made out of bad schools.* This is a statement that will no doubt please many a hard heart, and displease many genuinely concerned to bring about change. To the latter, a group in which I would like to include myself, I would only say that we are obliged to ask why things do not change.

For a period there was some speculation that, if family structure got bad enough, this mode of deviancy would have less punishing effects on children. In 1991 Deborah A. Dawson, of the National Institutes of Health, examined the thesis that "the psychological effects of divorce and single parenthood on children were strongly influenced by a sense of shame in being 'different' from the norm." If this were so, the effect should have fallen off in the 1980s, when being from a single-parent home became much more common. It did not. "The problems associated with task overload among single parents are more constant in nature," Dawson wrote, adding that since the adverse effects had not diminished, they were "not based on stigmatization but rather on inherent problems in alternative family structures" — *alternative* here meaning other than two-parent families. We should take note of such candor. Writing in the *Journal of Marriage and the Family* in 1989, Sara McLanahan and Karen Booth noted: "Whereas a decade ago the prevailing view was that single motherhood had no harmful effects on children, recent research is less optimistic."

The year 1990 saw more of this lesson. In a paper prepared for the Progressive Policy Institute, Elaine Ciulla Kamarck and William A. Galston wrote that "if the economic effects of family breakdown are clear, the psychological effects are just now coming into focus." They cite Karl Zinsmeister:

> There is a mountain of scientific evidence showing that when families disintegrate children often end up with intellectual, physical, and emotional scars that persist for life. . . . We talk about the drug crisis, the education crisis, and the problems of teen pregnancy and juvenile crime. But all these ills trace back predominantly to one source: broken families.

As for juvenile crime, they cite Douglas Smith and G. Roger Jarjoura: "Neighborhoods with larger percentages of youth (those aged 12 to 20) and areas with higher percentages of single-parent households also have higher rates of violent crime." They add: "The relationship is so strong that controlling for family configuration erases the relationship between race and crime and between low income and crime. This conclusion shows up time and time again in the literature; poverty is far from the sole determinant of crime." But the large point is avoided. In a 1992 essay "The Expert's Story of Marriage," Barbara Dafoe Whitehead examined "the story of marriage as it is conveyed in today's high school and college textbooks." Nothing amiss in this tale.

It goes like this:

The life course is full of exciting options. The lifestyle options available to individuals seeking a fulfilling personal relationship include living a heterosexual, homosexual, or bisexual single lifestyle; living in a commune; having a group marriage; being a single parent; or living together. Marriage is yet another lifestyle choice. However, before choosing marriage, individuals should weigh its costs and benefits against other lifestyle options and should consider what they want to get out of their intimate relationships. Even within marriage, different people want different things. For example, some people marry for companionship, some marry in order to have children, some marry for emotional and financial security. Though marriage can offer a rewarding path to personal growth, it is important to remember that it cannot provide a secure or permanent status. Many people will make the decision between marriage and singlehood many times throughout their life.

Divorce represents part of the normal family life cycle. It should not be viewed as either deviant or tragic, as it has been in the past. Rather, it establishes a process for "uncoupling" and thereby serves as the foundation for individual renewal and "new beginnings."

History commences to be rewritten. In 1992, the Select Committee on Children, Youth, and Families of the U.S. House of Representatives held a hearing on "Investing in Families: A Historical Perspective." A fact sheet prepared by committee staff began:

"INVESTING IN FAMILIES: A HISTORICAL PERSPECTIVE"
FACT SHEET
*HISTORICAL SHIFTS IN FAMILY COMPOSITION
CHALLENGING CONVENTIONAL WISDOM*

While in modern times the percentage of children living with one parent has increased, more children lived with just one parent in Colonial America.

The fact sheet proceeded to list program on program for which federal funds were allegedly reduced in the 1980s. We then come to a summary.

Between 1970 and 1991, the value of AFDC [Aid to Families with Dependent Children] benefits decreased by 41%. In spite of proven success of Head Start, only 28% of eligible children are being served. As of 1990, more than $18 billion in child support went uncollected. At the same time, the poverty rate among single-parent families with children under 18 was 44%. Between 1980 and 1990, the rate of growth in the total Federal budget was four times greater than the rate of growth in children's programs.

In other words, benefits paid to mothers and children have gone down steadily, as indeed they have done. But no proposal is made to restore benefits to an earlier level, or even to maintain their value, as is the case with other "indexed" Social Security programs. Instead we go directly to the subject of education spending.

Nothing new. In 1969, President Nixon proposed a guaranteed income, the Family Assistance Plan. This was described as an "income strategy" as against a "services strategy." It may or may not have been a good idea, but it was a clear one, and the resistance of service providers to it was equally clear. In the end it was defeated, to the huzzahs of the advocates of "welfare rights." What is going on here is simply that a large increase in what once was seen as deviancy has provided opportunity to a wide spectrum of interest groups that benefit from re-defining the problem as essentially normal and doing little to reduce it.

Our *normalizing* category most directly corresponds to Erikson's proposition that "the number of deviant offenders a community can afford to recognize is likely to remain stable over time." Here we are dealing with the popular psychological notion of "denial." In 1965, having reached the conclusion that there would be a dramatic increase in single-parent families, I reached the further conclusion that this would in turn lead to a dramatic increase in crime. In an article in *America*, I wrote:

> From the wild Irish slums of the 19th century Eastern seaboard to the riot-torn suburbs of Los Angeles, there is one unmistakable lesson in American history: a community that allows a large number of young men to grow up in broken families, dominated by women, never acquiring any stable relationship to male authority, never acquiring any set of rational expectations about the future — that community asks for and gets chaos. Crime, violence, unrest, unrestrained lashing out at the whole social structure — that is not only to be expected; it is very near to inevitable.

The inevitable, as we now know, has come to pass, but here again our response is curiously passive. Crime is a more or less continuous subject of political pronouncement, and from time to time it will be at or near the top of opinion polls as a matter of public concern. But it never gets much further than that. In the words spoken from the bench, Judge Edwin Torres of the New York State Supreme Court, Twelfth Judicial District, described how "the slaughter of the innocent marches unabated: subway riders, bodega owners, cab drivers, babies; in laundromats, at cash machines, on elevators, in hallways." In personal communication, he writes: "This numbness, this near narcoleptic state can diminish the human condition to the level of combat infantrymen, who, in protracted campaigns, can eat their battlefield rations seated on the bodies of the fallen, friend and foe alike. A society that loses its sense of outrage is doomed to extinction." There is no expectation that this will change, nor any efficacious public insistence that it do so. The crime level has been *normalized*.

Consider the St. Valentine's Day Massacre. In 1929 in Chicago during   30
Prohibition, four gangsters killed seven gangsters on February 14. The
nation was shocked. The event became legend. It merits not one but two
entries in the *World Book Encyclopedia*. I leave it to others to judge, but it
would appear that the society in the 1920s was simply not willing to put
up with this degree of deviancy. In the end, the Constitution was
amended, and Prohibition, which lay behind so much gangster violence,
ended.

In recent years, again in the context of illegal traffic in controlled sub-
stances, this form of murder has returned. But it has done so at a level
that induces denial. James Q. Wilson comments that Los Angeles has the
equivalent of a St. Valentine's Day Massacre every weekend. Even the
most ghastly reenactments of such human slaughter produce only moderate responses. On the morning after the close of the Democratic National Convention in New York City in July, there was such an account in
the second section of the *New York Times*. It was not a big story; bottom of
the page, but with a headline that got your attention. "3 Slain in Bronx
Apartment, but a Baby is Saved." A subhead continued: "A mother's last
act was to hide her little girl under the bed." The article described a drug
execution; the now-routine blindfolds made from duct tape; a man and a
woman and a teenager involved. "Each had been shot once in the head."
The police had found them a day later. They also found, under a bed, a
three-month-old baby, dehydrated but alive. A lieutenant remarked of
the mother, "In her last dying act she protected her baby. She probably
knew she was going to die, so she stuffed the baby where she knew it
would be safe." But the matter was left there. The police would do their
best. But the event passed quickly; forgotten by the next day, it will never
make *World Book*.

Nor is it likely that any great heed will be paid to an uncanny reen-
actment of the Prohibition drama a few months later, also in the Bronx:
The *Times* story, page B3, reported:

9 Men Posing as Police
Are Indicted in 3 Murders
Drug Dealers Were Kidnapped for Ransom

The *Daily News* story, same day, page 17, made it *four* murders,
adding nice details about torture techniques. The gang members posed
as federal Drug Enforcement Administration agents, real badges and all.
The victims were drug dealers, whose families were uneasy about calling
the police. Ransom seems generally to have been set in the $650,000
range. Some paid. Some got it in the back of the head. So it goes.

Yet, violent killings, often random, go on unabated. Peaks continue
to attract some notice. But these are peaks above "average" levels that
thirty years ago would have been thought epidemic.

LOS ANGELES, AUG. 24 (Reuters) Twenty-two people were killed in Los Angeles over the weekend, the worst period of violence in the city since it was ravaged by riots earlier this year, the police said today.

Twenty-four others were wounded by gunfire or stabbings, including a 19-year old woman in a wheelchair who was shot in the back when she failed to respond to a motorist who asked for directions in south Los Angeles.

["The guy stuck a gun out of the window and just fired at her," said a police spokesman, Lieut. David Rock. The woman was later described as being in stable condition.

Among those who died was an off-duty officer, shot while investigating reports of a prowler in a neighbor's yard, and a Little League baseball coach who had argued with the father of a boy he was coaching.]

The police said at least nine of the deaths were gang-related, including that of a 14-year old girl killed in a fight between rival gangs.

Fifty-one people were killed in three days of rioting that started April 29 after the acquittal of four police officers in the beating of Rodney G. King.

Los Angeles usually has above-average violence during August, but the police were at a loss to explain the sudden rise. On an average weekend in August, 14 fatalities occur.

Not to be outdone, two days later the poor Bronx came up with a near record, as reported in *New York Newsday:*   35

Armed with 9-mm. pistols, shotguns and M-16 rifles, a group of masked men and women poured out of two vehicles in the South Bronx early yesterday and sprayed a stretch of Longwood Avenue with a fusillade of bullets, injuring 12 people.

A Kai Erikson of the future will surely need to know that the Department of Justice in 1990 found that Americans reported only about 38 percent of all crimes and 48 percent of violent crimes. This, too, can be seen as a means of *normalizing* crime. In much the same way, the vocabulary of crime reporting can be seen to move toward the normal-seeming. A teacher is shot on her way to class. The *Times* subhead reads: "Struck in the Shoulder in the Year's First Shooting Inside a School." First of the season.

It is too early, however, to know how to regard the arrival of the doctors on the scene declaring crime a "public health emergency." The June 10, 1992, issue of the *Journal of the American Medical Association* was devoted entirely to papers on the subject of violence, principally violence associated with firearms. An editorial in the issue signed by former Surgeon General C. Everett Koop and Dr. George D. Lundberg is entitled: "Violence in America: A Public Health Emergency." Their proposition is admirably succinct.

> Regarding violence in our society as purely a sociological matter, or one of law enforcement, has led to unmitigated failure. It is time to test further whether violence can be amenable to medical/public health interventions.
>
> We believe violence in America to be a public health emergency, largely unresponsive to methods thus far used in its control. The solutions are very complex, but possible.

The authors cited the relative success of epidemiologists in gaining some jurisdiction in the area of motor vehicle casualties by re-defining what had been seen as a law enforcement issue into a public health issue. Again, this process began during the Harriman administration in New York in the 1950s. In the 1960s the morbidity and mortality associated with automobile crashes was, it could be argued, a major public health problem; the public health strategy, it could also be argued, brought the problem under a measure of control. Not in "the 1970s and 1980s," as the *Journal of the American Medical Association* would have us think: the federal legislation involved was signed in 1965. Such a strategy would surely produce insights into the control of violence that elude law enforcement professionals, but whether it would change anything is another question.

For some years now I have had legislation in the Senate that would prohibit the manufacture of .25 and .32 caliber bullets. These are the two calibers most typically used with the guns known as Saturday Night Specials. "Guns don't kill people," I argue, "bullets do."

Moreover, we have a two-century supply of handguns but only a four-year supply of ammunition. A public health official would immediately see the logic of trying to control the supply of bullets rather than of guns.

Even so, now that the doctor has come, it is important that criminal   40
violence not be defined down by epidemiologists. Doctors Koop and Lundberg note that in 1990 in the state of Texas "deaths from firearms, for the first time in many decades, surpassed deaths from motor vehicles, by 3,443 to 3,309." A good comparison. And yet keep in mind that the number of motor vehicle deaths, having leveled off since the 1960s, is now pretty well accepted as normal at somewhat less than 50,000 a year, which is somewhat less than the level of the 1960s — the "carnage," as it once was thought to be, is now accepted as normal. This is the price we pay for high-speed transportation: there is a benefit associated with it. But there is no benefit associated with homicide, and no good in getting

used to it. Epidemiologists have powerful insights that can contribute to lessening the medical trauma, but they must be wary of normalizing the social pathology that leads to such trauma.

The hope — if there be such — of this essay has been twofold. It is, first, to suggest that the Durkheim constant, as I put it, is maintained by a dynamic process which adjusts upwards and *downwards*. Liberals have traditionally been alert for upward redefining that does injustice to individuals. Conservatives have been correspondingly sensitive to downward redefining that weakens societal standards. Might it not help if we could all agree that there is a dynamic at work here? It is not revealed truth, nor yet a scientifically derived formula. It is simply a pattern we observe in ourselves. Nor is it rigid. There may once have been an unchanging supply of jail cells which more or less determined the number of prisoners. No longer. We are building new prisons at a prodigious rate. Similarly, the executioner is back. There is something of a competition in Congress to think up new offenses for which the death penalty is deemed the only available deterrent. Possibly also modes of execution, as in "fry the kingpins." Even so, we are getting used to a lot of behavior that is not good for us.

As noted earlier, Durkheim states that there is "nothing desirable" about pain. Surely what he meant was that there is nothing pleasurable. Pain, even so, is an indispensable warning signal. But societies under stress, much like individuals, will turn to pain killers of various kinds that end up concealing real damage. There is surely nothing desirable about *this*. If our analysis wins general acceptance, if, for example, more of us came to share Judge Torres's genuine alarm at "the trivialization of the lunatic crime rate" in his city (and mine), we might surprise ourselves at how well we respond to the manifest decline of the American civic order. Might.

PREPARING FOR DISCUSSION

1. Moynihan offers a view of deviancy in American culture. How does he define the term *deviancy*? How, according to Moynihan, do most communities tend to react to deviancy? What accounts for this reaction?

2. Moynihan believes that "deviancy" has been redefined in three different ways. What are the three categories of redefinition he describes? Which of these three kinds of redefinition, according to Moynihan, are motivated by the desire to do good? What are the motivations for the other two types of redefinition?

3. Moynihan argues that Americans are now less likely to be shocked or outraged by violence than in previous decades. Yet he also notes that news stories about urban violence are often "buried" in the back pages of newspapers. What effect might the placement of such stories have on the capacity of Americans to

tolerate violence? Does Moynihan underestimate the power of the press to influence public opinion?

4. Does Moynihan seem optimistic that a realistic view of deviant social behavior will allow us to correct these behaviors? Where in the essay do you detect such optimism? Does understanding a problem for what it is rather than denying it mean that the problem may be solved as well?

5. According to the author, the term *alternative* has been adopted to describe families whose structure is based on something other than the two-parent model. Why do you think this term has been increasingly applied to nontraditional family arrangements? Do you believe that the use of such a term might actually be damaging to the institution of family?

FROM READING TO WRITING

6. Moynihan argues that certain behaviors that once would have been viewed as unacceptable are now accepted as "normal." Write an essay in which you describe a behavior that is now considered normal that was once thought socially unacceptable. What are the reasons for this acceptance? Are the reasons you provide consistent with Moynihan's argument?

7. Collect news stories about recent crimes in your area. Which of these stories are particularly upsetting? Which are not? Write an essay in which you evaluate the news stories you have chosen. What kinds of details tend to bother you most? What kinds of details do not bother you? Can you find examples of what Moynihan calls "normalization" in your reactions?

CHARLES KRAUTHAMMER

Defining Deviancy Up

—————◇—————

Along with society's tendency to accept or even to praise lifestyles and values previously regarded as deviant, award-winning journalist Charles Krauthammer observes an equally strong tendency to denigrate the American middle class and its values. This indictment, as he argues in the following selection, extends not merely to the idea of family and the practice of heterosexual courtship, but even to the thoughts of average Americans that some believe to be dangerous and in need of correction.

Krauthammer's weekly columns on national politics for the *Washington Post* and monthly columns for *Time* have been called "independent and hard to peg politically." He was educated at McGill University and Oxford, where he studied political science and economics. He later attended Harvard Medical School and served as chief resident in psychiatry at Massachusetts General Hospital. In 1978, he left practicing medicine to direct planning in psychiatric research for the Carter administration. After serving as a speech writer for Vice President Walter Mondale in the 1980 presidential campaign, he joined the *New Republic* (where this selection first appeared in 1993) as a writer and editor. In 1984, he won the National Magazine Award for his essays published in that magazine. He also won the Pulitzer Prize in 1987 for distinguished commentary.

SELECTED PUBLICATIONS: *Cutting Edge: Making Sense of the Eighties* (1985); Krauthammer also publishes regularly with the *Washington Post*, *Time* magazine, and the *New Republic*.

In a recent essay in *The American Scholar* titled "Defining Deviancy Down," Daniel Patrick Moynihan offers an arresting view of the epidemic of deviancy — of criminality, family breakdown, mental illness — that has come to characterize the American social landscape. Deviancy has reached such incomprehensible proportions, argues Moynihan, that we have had to adopt a singular form of denial: we deal with the epidemic simply by defining away most of the disease. We lower the threshold for what we are prepared to call normal in order to keep the volume of deviancy — redefined deviancy — within manageable proportions.

For example. Since 1960 the incidence of single parenthood has more than tripled. Almost 30 percent of all American children are now born to unmarried mothers. The association of fatherlessness with poverty, welfare dependency, crime and other pathologies points to a monstrous social problem. Yet, as the problem has grown, it has been systematically redefined by the culture — by social workers, intellectuals and most famously by the mass media — as simply another lifestyle choice. Dan Quayle may have been right, but Murphy Brown won the ratings war.

Moynihan's second example is crime. We have become totally inured to levels of criminality that would have been considered intolerable thirty years ago. The St. Valentine's Day massacre, which caused a national uproar and merited two entries in the *World Book Encyclopedia*, involved four thugs killing seven other thugs. An average weekend in today's Los Angeles, notes James Q. Wilson. More than half of all violent crimes are not even reported. We have come to view homicide as ineradicable a part of the social landscape as car accidents.

And finally there is mental illness. Unlike family breakdown and criminality, there has probably been no increase in mental illness over the last thirty years. Rates of schizophrenia do not change, but the rate of hospitalization for schizophrenia and other psychoses has changed. The mental hospitals have been emptied. In 1955 New York state asylums had 93,000 patients. Last year they had 11,000. Where have the remaining 82,000 and their descendants gone? Onto the streets mostly. In one generation, a flood of pathetically ill people has washed onto the streets of America's cities. We now step over these wretched and abandoned folk sleeping in doorways and freezing on grates. They, too, have become accepted as part of the natural landscape. We have managed to do that by redefining them as people who simply lack affordable housing. They are not crazy or sick, just very poor — as if anyone crazy and sick and totally abandoned would not end up very poor.

Moynihan's powerful point is that with the moral deregulation of the   5 1960s, we have had an explosion of deviancy in family life, criminal behavior and public displays of psychosis. And we have dealt with it in the only way possible: by redefining deviancy down so as to explain away and make "normal" what a more civilized, ordered and healthy society long ago would have labeled — and long ago did label — deviant.

Moynihan is right. But it is only half the story. There is a complementary social phenomenon that goes with defining deviancy down. As part of the vast social project of moral leveling, it is not enough for the deviant to be normalized. The normal must be found to be deviant. Therefore, while for the criminals and the crazies deviancy has been defined down (the bar defining normality has been lowered), for the ordinary bourgeois deviancy has been defined up (the bar defining normality has been raised). Large areas of ordinary behavior hitherto considered benign have had their threshold radically redefined up, so that once innocent behavior now stands condemned as deviant. Normal middle-class life then stands exposed as the true home of violence and abuse and a whole catalog of aberrant acting and thinking.

As part of this project of moral leveling, entirely new areas of deviancy — such as date rape and politically incorrect speech — have been discovered. And old areas — such as child abuse — have been amplified by endless reiteration in the public presses and validated by learned reports of their astonishing frequency. The net effect is to show that deviancy is not the province of criminals and crazies but thrives in the heart of the great middle class. The real deviants of society stand unmasked. Who are they? Not Bonnie and Clyde but Ozzie and Harriet. True, Ozzie and Harriet have long been the object of ridicule. Now, however, they are under indictment.

The moral deconstruction of middle-class normality is a vast project. Fortunately, thousands of volunteers are working the case. By defining deviancy up they have scored some notable successes. Three, in particular. And in precisely the areas Moynihan identified: family life, crime and thought disorders.

First, family life. Under the new dispensation it turns out that the ordinary middle-class family is not a warm, welcoming fount of "family values," not a bedrock of social and psychic stability as claimed in conservative propaganda. It is instead a caldron of pathology, a teeming source of the depressions, alienations and assorted dysfunctions of adulthood. Why? Because deep in the family lies the worm, the 1990s version of original sin: child abuse.

Child abuse is both a crime and a tragedy, but is it nineteen times   10
more prevalent today than it was thirty years ago? That is what the statistics offer. In 1963: 150,000 reported cases. In 1992: 2.9 million.

Now, simply considering the historical trajectory of the treatment of children since the nineteenth century, when child labor — even child slavery — was common, it is hard to believe that the tendency toward improved treatment of children has been so radically reversed in one generation.

Plainly it hasn't. What happened then? The first thing that happened was an epidemic of over-reporting. Douglas Besharov points out that whereas in 1975 about one-third of child abuse cases were dismissed for lack of evidence, today about two-thirds are dismissed. New York State authorities may have considered it a great social advance that between 1979 and 1983, for example, reported cases of child abuse increased by almost 50 percent. But over the same period, the number of substantiated cases actually declined. In other words, the 22,000 increase of reported cases yielded a net decrease of real cases.

Note the contrast. For ordinary crime, to which we have become desensitized, we have defined deviancy down. One measure of this desensitization is under-reporting: nearly two out of every three ordinary crimes are never even reported. Child abuse is precisely the opposite. For child abuse, to which we have become exquisitely oversensitized, deviancy has been correspondingly defined up. One of the measures of oversensitization is over-reporting: whereas two out of three ordinary crimes are never reported, two out of three reported cases of child abuse are never shown to have occurred.

The perceived epidemic of child abuse is a compound of many factors. Clearly, over-reporting is one. Changing societal standards regarding corporal punishment is another. But beyond the numbers and definitions there is a new ideology of child abuse. Under its influence, the helping professions, committed to a belief in endemic abuse, have encouraged a massive search to find cases, and where they cannot be found, to invent them.

Consider this advice from one of the more popular self-help books on   15
sex abuse, *Courage to Heal.* "If you are unable to remember any specific instances [of childhood sex abuse] . . . but still have a feeling that something abusive happened to you, it probably did." And "if you think you were abused and your life shows the symptoms, then you were."

If your life shows the symptoms. In a popular culture saturated with tales of child abuse paraded daily on the airwaves, it is not hard to suggest to vulnerable people that their problems — symptoms—are caused by long-ago abuse, indeed, even unremembered abuse. Hence the reductio ad absurdum[1] of the search for the hidden epidemic: adults who present themselves suddenly as victims of child abuse after decades of supposed amnesia — the amnesia reversed and the memory reclaimed thanks to the magic of intensive psychotherapy.

Now, the power of therapeutic suggestion is well-known. Dr. George Ganaway of Emory University points out — and, as a retired psychiatrist, I well remember — how fiction disguised as memory can be created at the suggestion of a trusted therapist whom the patient wants to please.

Why should memories of child abuse please the therapist? Because it fits the new ideology of neurosis. For almost a century Freudian ideology located the source of adult neuroses in the perceived psychosexual traumas of childhood. But Freud concluded after initial skepticism that these psychosexual incidents were fantasy.

Today Freud's conclusion is seen either as a great error or, as Jeffrey Masson and other anti-Freudian crusaders insist, as a great betrayal of what he knew to be the truth. Today's fashion, promoted by a vanguard of therapists and researchers, is that the fantasies are true. When the patient presents with depression, low self-esteem or any of the common ailments of modern life, the search begins for the underlying childhood sexual abuse. "Some contemporary therapists," writes Elizabeth Loftus, professor of psychology at the University of Washington, "have been known to tell patients, on the basis of a suggestive history or 'symptom profile,' that they definitely had a traumatic experience. The therapist then urges the patient to pursue the recalcitrant memories."

This new psychology is rooted in and reinforces current notions about the pathology of ordinary family life. Rather than believing, as we did for a hundred years under the influence of Freud, that adult neurosis results from the inevitable psychological traumas of sexual maturation, compounded by parental error and crystallized in the (literally) fantastic memories of the patient, today there is a new dispensation. Nowadays neurosis is the outcome not of innocent errors but of criminal acts occurring in the very bosom of the ordinary-looking family. Seek and ye shall find: the sins of the fathers are visible in the miserable lives of the children. Child abuse is the crime waiting only to be discovered with, of course, the proper therapeutic guidance and bedtime reading. It is the dirty little secret behind the white picket fence. And beside this offense, such once-regarded deviancies of family life as illegitimacy appear benign.

[1] *reductio ad absurdum:* "Reduction to the point of absurdity" (Latin).

So much for the family. Let us look now at a second pillar of everyday bourgeois life: the ordinary heterosexual relationship. A second vast category of human behavior that until recently was considered rather normal has had its threshold for normality redefined up so as to render much of it deviant. Again we start with a real offense: rape. It used to be understood as involving the use of or threat of force. No longer. It has now been expanded by the concept of date rape to encompass an enormous continent of behavior that had long been viewed as either normal or ill-mannered, but certainly not criminal.

"Some 47 percent of women are victims of rape or attempted rape . . . and 25 percent of women are victims of completed rape." So asserts Catharine MacKinnon on a national television news special. Assertions of this sort are commonplace. A Stanford survey, for example, claims that a third of its women have suffered date rape. The most famous and widely reported study of the rape epidemic is the one done by Mary Koss (and published, among other places, in *Ms.* magazine). Her survey of 6,159 college students found that 15 percent had been raped and another 12 percent subjected to attempted rape. She also reported that in a single year 3,187 college females reported 886 incidents of rape or attempted rape. That is more than one incident for every four women per year. At that rate, about three out of every four undergraduate women would be victims of rape or attempted rape by graduation day.

If those numbers sound high, they are. As Neil Gilbert points out in *The Public Interest,* the numbers compiled by the FBI under the Unified Crime Reporting Program and suitably multiplied to account for presumed unreported cases, yield an incidence of rape somewhere around one in a thousand. As for the college campus, reports from 2,400 campuses mandated by the Student Right-to-Know and Campus Security Act of 1990 showed fewer than 1,000 rapes for 1991. That is about one-half a rape per campus per year. Barnard College, a hotbed of anti-rape and Take Back the Night activity, released statistics in 1991 showing no reports of rape, date or otherwise, among its 2,200 students. Same for Harvard, Yale, Princeton, Brown — and Antioch, author of the strictest, most hilarious sexual correctness code in American academia.

How does one explain the vast discrepancy — 1 in 2 differs from 1 in 1,000 by a factor of 500 — between the real numbers and the fantastic numbers that have entered the popular imagination? Easy. Deviancy has again been redefined — up. Rape has been expanded by Koss and other researchers to include behavior that you and I would not recognize as rape. And not just you and I — the supposed victims themselves do not recognize it as rape. In the Koss study, 73 percent of the women she labeled as rape victims did not consider themselves to have been raped. Fully 42 percent had further sexual relations with the so-called rapist.

Now, women who have been raped are not generally known for   25 going back for more sex with their assailants. Something is wrong here. What is wrong is the extraordinarily loose definition of sexual coercion and rape. Among the questions Koss asked her subjects were these: "Have you given in to sexual intercourse when you didn't want to because you were overwhelmed by a man's continual arguments and pressure?" and "Have you had sexual intercourse when you didn't want to because a man gave you alcohol or drugs?" The Stanford study, the one that turned up one out of three female students as victims of date rape, rests on respondents' self-report of "full sexual activity when they did not want to."

It is a common enough experience for people (both men and women) to be of two minds about having sex, and yet decide, reluctantly but certainly freely, to go ahead even though they do not really want to. Call that rape and there are few who escape the charge.

The cornerstone of this new and breathtakingly loose definition is the idea of verbal coercion. Consider this definition from the "Nonviolent Sexual Coercion" chapter in *Acquaintance Rape: The Hidden Crime* (John Wiley, 1991): "We define verbal sexual coercion as a woman's consenting to unwanted sexual activity because of a man's verbal arguments, not including verbal threats of physical force." With rape so radically defined up — to include offering a drink or being verbally insistent — it is no surprise that the result is an epidemic of sexual deviancy.

Of course, behind these numbers is an underlying ideology about the inherent aberrancy of all heterosexual relations. As Andrea Dworkin once said, "Romance . . . is rape embellished with meaningful looks." The date rape epidemic is just empirical dressing for a larger theory which holds that because relations between men and women are inherently unequal, sex can never be truly consensual. It is always coercive.

"The similarity between the patterns, rhythms, roles and emotions, not to mention acts, which make up rape (and battery) on the one hand and intercourse on the other . . . ," writes MacKinnon, "makes it difficult to sustain the customary distinctions between pathology and normalcy, violence and sex." And "Compare victims' reports of rape with women's reports of sex. They look a lot alike. . . . In this light, the major distinction between intercourse (normal) and rape (abnormal) is that the normal happens so often that one cannot get anyone to see anything wrong with it." Or as Susan Estrich puts it, "Many feminists would argue that so long as women are powerless relative to men, viewing 'yes' as a sign of true consent is misguided." But if "yes" is not a sign of true consent, then what is? A notarized contract?

And if there is no such thing as real consent, then the radical feminist   30
ideal is realized: all intercourse is rape. Who needs the studies? The incidence of rape is not 25 percent or 33 or 50. It is 100 percent. Then Naomi Wolf can write in *The Beauty Myth* that we have today "a situation among

the young in which boys rape and girls get raped *as a normal course of events.*" (Her italics.)

Date rape is only the most extreme example of deviancy redefined broadly enough to catch in its net a huge chunk of normal, everyday behavior. It is the most extreme example because it is criminal. But then there are the lesser offenses, a bewildering array of transgressions that come under the rubric of sexual harassment, the definition of which can be equally loose and floating but is always raised high enough to turn innocent behavior into deviancy. As Allan Bloom wrote, "What used to be understood as modes of courtship are now seen as modes of male intimidation."

So much then for the family and normal heterosexual relations. On now to the third great area of the new deviancy: thought crimes.

This summer, I was visited by an FBI agent doing a routine background check on a former employee of mine now being considered for some high administration post. The agent went through the usual checklist of questions that I had heard many times before: questions about financial difficulties, drug abuse, alcoholism. Then he popped a new one: Did this person ever show any prejudice to a group based on race, ethnicity, gender, national origin, etc.? I assumed that he was not interested in whether the person had been involved in any racial incident. The FBI would have already known about that. What he wanted to know about was my friend's deeper thoughts, feelings he might have betrayed only to someone with whom he had worked intimately for two years. This was the point in the interview at which I was supposed to testify whether I had heard my friend tell any sexist or racist jokes or otherwise show signs of hidden prejudice. That is when it occurred to me that insensitive speech had achieved official status as a thought crime.

Now, again we start with real deviance — racial violence of the kind once carried out by the Klan or today by freelancers like the two men in Tampa recently convicted of a monstrous racial attack on a black tourist. These are outlawed and punished. So are the more benign but still contemptible acts of nonviolent racial discrimination, as in housing, for example. But now that overt racial actions have been criminalized and are routinely punished, the threshold for deviancy has been ratcheted up. The project now is to identify prejudiced thinking, instincts, anecdotes, attitudes.

The great arena for this project is the American academy. The proliferation of speech codes on campuses, restrained only by their obvious unconstitutionality, was an attempt by universities to curtail speech that may cause offense to groups designated for special protection. A University of Michigan student, for example, offers the opinion *in class* that homosexuality is an illness, and finds himself hauled before a formal

35

university hearing on charges of harassing students on the basis of sexual orientation.

The irony here is quite complete. It used to be that homosexuality was considered deviant. But now that it has been declared a simple lifestyle choice, those who are not current with the new definitions, and have the misfortune to say so in public, find themselves suspected of deviancy.

There is, of course, the now-famous case of the Israeli-born University of Pennsylvania student who called a group of rowdy black sorority sisters making noise outside his dorm in the middle of the night "water buffaloes" (his rough translation from the Hebrew _behema_). He was charged with racial harassment. A host of learned scholars was assigned the absurd task of locating the racial antecedents of the term. They could find none. (They should have asked me. I could have saved them a lot of trouble. My father called me behemah so many times it almost became a term of endearment. I don't think he was racially motivated.) Nonetheless, the university, convinced that there was some racial animus behind that exotic term and determined not to let it go unpunished, tried to pressure the student into admitting his guilt. Penn offered him a plea bargain. Proceedings would be stopped if he confessed and allowed himself to be re-educated through a "program for living in a diverse community environment."

Consider: the psychotic raving in the middle of Broadway is free to rave. No one will force him into treatment. But a student who hurls "water buffalo" at a bunch of sorority sisters is threatened with the ultimate sanction at the disposal of the university — expulsion — unless he submits to treatment to correct his deviant thinking.

This may seem ironic but it is easily explained. Under the new dispensation it is not insanity but insensitivity that is the true sign of deviant thinking, requiring thought control and re-education. One kind of deviancy we are prepared to live with; the other, we are not. Indeed, one kind, psychosis, we are hardly prepared to call deviancy at all. As Moynihan points out, it is now part of the landscape.

The mentally ill are not really ill. They just lack housing. It is the rest 40 of us who are guilty of disordered thinking for harboring — beneath the bland niceties of middle-class life — racist, misogynist, homophobic and other corrupt and corrupting insensitivities.

Ordinary criminality we are learning to live with. What we are learning we cannot live with is the heretofore unrecognized violence against women that lurks beneath the facade of ordinary, seemingly benign, heterosexual relations.

The single-parent and broken home are now part of the landscape. It is the Ozzie and Harriet family, rife with abuse and molestation, that is the seedbed of deviance.

The rationalization of deviancy reaches its logical conclusion. The deviant is declared normal. And the normal is unmasked as deviant. That, of course, makes us all that much more morally equal. The project is complete. What real difference is there between us?

And that is the point. Defining deviancy up, like defining deviancy down, is an adventure in moral equivalence. As such, it is the son of an old project that met its demise with the end of the Soviet empire. There once was the idea of moral equivalence between the East and the West. Even though the Soviets appeared to be imperialist and brutal and corrupt and rapacious, we were really as bad as they were. We could match them crime for crime throughout the world.

Well, this species of moral equivalence is now dead. The liberation of the Communist empire, the opening of the archives, the testimony of the former inmates — all these have made a mockery of this version of moral equivalence.

But ideology abhors a vacuum. So we have a new version of moral equivalence: the moral convergence within Western society of the normal and the deviant. It is a bold new way to strip the life of the bourgeois West of its moral sheen. Because once it becomes, to use MacKinnon's words, "difficult to sustain the customary distinctions between pathology and normalcy," the moral superiority to which bourgeois normalcy pretends vanishes.

And the perfect vehicle for exposing the rottenness of bourgeois life is defining deviancy up. After all, the law-abiding middle classes define their own virtue in contrast to the deviant, a contrast publicly dramatized by opprobrium, ostracism and punishment. And now it turns out that this great contrast between normality and deviance is a farce. The real deviants, mirabile dictu,[2] are those who carry the mask of sanity, the middle classes living on their cozy suburban streets, abusing their children, violating their women and harboring deep inside them the most unholy thoughts.

Defining deviancy up is a new way of satisfying an old ideological agenda. But it also fills a psychological need. The need was identified by Moynihan: How to cope with the explosion of real deviancy? One way is denial: defining real deviancy down creates the pretense that deviance has disappeared because it has been redefined as normal. Another strategy is distraction: defining deviancy up creates brand-new deviancies that we can now go off and fight. That distracts us from real deviancy and gives us the feeling that, despite the murder and mayhem and madness around us, we are really preserving and policing our norms.

Helpless in the face of the explosion of real criminality, for example, we satisfy our crime-fighting needs with a crusade against date rape. Like looking for your lost wallet under the street lamp even though you lost it elsewhere, this job is easier even if not terribly relevant to the problem at hand. Defining deviancy up creates a whole new universe of behavior to

[2] *mirabile dictu:* "Wonderful to relate" (Latin).

police, and — a bonus — a higher class of offender. More malleable, too: the guilt-ridden bourgeois, the vulnerable college student, is a far easier object of social control than the hardened criminal or the raving lunatic.

These new crusades do nothing, of course, about real criminality or lunacy. But they make us feel that we are making inroads on deviancy nonetheless. A society must feel that it is policing its norms by combating deviancy. Having given up fighting the real thing, we can't give up the fight. So we fight the new deviancy with satisfying vigor. That it is largely a phantom and a phony seems not to matter at all.

50

PREPARING FOR DISCUSSION

1. Krauthammer describes "a complimentary social phenomenon that goes with [Moynihan's concept] of defining deviancy down." Describe that phenomenon. Why does the author view it as an assault on middle-class life in America?

2. How does Krauthammer explain the rise in reported cases of child abuse? How does he use this explanation to illustrate the phenomenon of "defining deviancy up"? What other instances of the phenomenon does he provide?

3. Krauthammer makes a connection between the date-rape epidemic and the assault on traditional heterosexual arrangements like marriage. On what grounds does he make this connection? Do you agree with him that oversensitization to date rape and sexual harassment has undermined the social practices that lead to marriage? What evidence would you offer against Krauthammer's conclusion?

4. After noting that homosexuality is now considered "a simple lifestyle choice" rather than a "deviant" behavior, the author comments that "those who are not current with the new definitions . . . [may] find themselves suspected of deviancy" (paragraph 36). Do you think that Krauthammer places too much emphasis on "being current with the new definitions"? Does not knowing these new definitions necessarily imply attitudes that are "politically incorrect," as Krauthammer suggests they might?

5. Krauthammer calls "thought crimes" a "third great area of the new deviancy." The phrase "thought crime" makes its first major appearance in George Orwell's *Nineteen Eighty-four,* a novel that depicts life within a totalitarian state in which all aspects of a person's life come under government scrutiny. Why do you think Krauthammer chose to adopt Orwell's phrase for use in his essay? What kinds of connections does he intend to make between Orwell's fictional society and our own?

FROM READING TO WRITING

6. Can you think of some other examples from everyday life that might illustrate Krauthammer's concept of "defining deviancy up"? Write an essay in which you record your findings and explain as precisely as possible what middle-class value is under attack. What deviant behavior is being promoted as "normal"?

7. Krauthammer believes that the incidence of child abuse and date rape in this country has been blown out of all proportion. Write an essay in which you state your opinion on either of these issues. If you believe there is a crisis, what kinds of facts and figures would you need to refute Krauthammer's statistics? If you think the issue has been exaggerated, who is responsible for the exaggeration, and why have they exaggerated? Who most stands to suffer from such an exaggeration? If you think the problem lies somewhere in between, how do you distinguish the real crisis from the hype?

NEWT GINGRICH

Contracting with America

———————◇———————

The congressional elections of November 1994 resulted in what House Speaker Newt Gingrich called at the time "the most shatteringly one-sided Republican victory since 1946." In fact, Gingrich credits his own *Contract with America* and its being embraced by more than three hundred lawmakers and congressional candidates for the Republican victory. The *Contract*, a program of sweeping conservative legislation, was the basis for most congressional activity during the first half of 1995. At its heart lay the traditional conservative emphasis on reduced government spending and lower taxation. Yet, as the following selection shows, the *Contract* also stands firm on empowering average American families in their pursuit of happiness.

Newt Gingrich, now serving his ninth term in Congress as a representative from Georgia, became Speaker of the House of Representatives in January 1995. Gingrich received his bachelor's degree from Emory University and his Ph.D. from Tulane University in modern European history. Before being elected to Congress in 1978, he taught at West Georgia College for eight years. The following selection was originally delivered as an address to the Washington Research Group Symposium on November 11, 1994, and appeared as an appendix to *Contract with America*.

SELECTED PUBLICATIONS: *Window of Opportunity* (1984); *Contract with America* (1994); *To Renew America* (1995).

———————————————

Seventy-six years today the armistice was declared at the eleventh hour of the eleventh day of the eleventh month in what was then called the Great War. Indirectly, that had an enormous impact on my life because it was while my dad was stationed with the Army in Europe and I was a fourteen-year-old freshman in high school that we went to the battlefield in Verdun, which was the largest battlefield in the Western front of that war. We spent a weekend with a friend of his who had been on a death march in the Philippines and served three years in a Japanese prison camp. The Great War was both an example of what happens when leadership fails and societies collide and it was an example in its aftermath of what happens when people lie to themselves about the objective realities of the human condition. Because instead of leading to world peace as Woodrow Wilson had so devoutly hoped, it, in fact, ultimately led to the Second World War. And instead of leading to greater freedom for all human beings, as Woodrow Wilson's Fourteen Points had hoped, it led to Nazism and the Soviet empire, the Gulag, and Auschwitz.

And so it is both good for us today to remember the cost paid by those who believe enough in freedom to have died for it and useful to remind ourselves that that price has to be paid every year and every week and that it is better by far to pay that price in peacetime by being vigilant and by trying to do that which is right than it is to allow your society to decay or to have inadequate leadership and drift into a cataclysm comparable to the First and Second World Wars.

And that's not just a foreign policy or national defense battle cry. What is ultimately at stake in our current environment is literally the future of American civilization as it has existed for the last several hundred years. I'm a history teacher by background, and I would assert and defend on any campus in this country that it is impossible to maintain civilization with twelve-year-olds having babies, with fifteen-year-olds killing each other, with seventeen-year-olds dying of AIDS, and with eighteen-year-olds ending up with diplomas they can't even read. What is at issue is literally not Republican or Democrat or liberal or conservative, but the question of whether or not our civilization will survive.

Since the election, the article which has most accurately captured its essence is Charles Krauthammer's column this morning in *The Washington Post*, which makes the correct point that you have the most explicitly ideologically committed House Republican Party in modern history. That we held an event on September 27 on the Capitol steps that over 300 members signed or candidates signed up for. That we told the country in a full-page ad in *TV Guide* where we were going and the direction we would take. That President Clinton and Tony Coelho took up the challenge. That the Democratic National Committee ran $2 million of ads attacking the *Contract with America*. That the President personally attacked the *Contract* virtually everywhere he went. And that in the end there was the most shatteringly one-sided Republican victory since 1946.

Since then, there's been an enormous effort by the Washington elite to avoid the reality that this lesson was actually about some fairly big ideas — Which direction do you want to go in? — and that those who argued for counterculture values, bigger government, redistributionist economics, and bureaucracies deciding how you should spend your money, were on the losing end in virtually every part of the country.

When in Georgia we elect five statewide elected officials, we have a majority seven to four in the House delegation, there may be something that's a message. And you can either say, well, but that's those Southern Christian religious groups. Fine. In Washington state we went from seven to one Democrat to six to two Republican. You can hardly argue that it's Southern fundamentalism that swept Washington state. And yet I've seen talk shows where learned experts who were totally wrong a week ago are equally wrong now. It's amazing how often we can watch experts who had no idea what was about to happen explain to us afterwards what it meant. Part of the problem is stereotyping.

Let me discuss several stereotypes that I think are very important — or several things that break out of the stereotype. Part of our problem is the level at which we think. I use a planning model and a leadership model that is very explicit. The planning model is derived from how George Marshall and Dwight Eisenhower and Franklin Roosevelt managed the Second World War, which was the most complex, large human activity ever undertaken. Essentially, they had a four-layer model, and it's a hierarchy. The top of it was vision, and after you understood your vision of what you're doing you designed strategies, and once you have your vision and strategies clear you designed projects which were the building blocks of your strategies, and inside the context of those projects you delegated dramatically an entrepreneurial model in which a project was a definable, delegatable achievement. Eisenhower's job was to invade the continent of Europe, defeat the German army and occupy the German heartland. His actual order from the combined chiefs was two paragraphs, all the rest was detail. That's delegation on a fairly grand scale.

At the bottom of the model is tactics, what you do every day. Washington, D.C., is a city so consumed by its own tactical self-amusement that it's very hard for the city to have any sense of projects, and the concept of vision and strategies is almost beyond its comprehension.

The second model is a leadership model that is a process. That is, they're not a hierarchy, all the words that define this model are equally important, but there's a sequence that matters. It's a very direct sequence: Listen, learn, help, and lead. You listen to the American people, you learn from the American people, you help the American people; and in a rational society, if people know you'll listen to them, learn from them and help them, they want you to lead them.

So the job of a leader is first of all to think about things, develop a vision and strategies and projects and tactics, and then go back out and 10 listen to the people and find out whether or not in fact they're on the same wavelength. And if not, to assume that there's at least a better than even chance that it is the people and not the elite who are right.

That's a very specific model. You may disagree with it or not like it but it's a very specific model and if you want to understand what the next Speaker of the House is going to function like, it's a model that will in fact be fairly predictive.

It's very hard for the Washington elite to come to grips with the reality that there's now a national Republican Party. That's the biggest single message of this election. That for the first time in history, the civil war, in effect, is over, and Republicans were able to run everywhere simultaneously. And, standing on Ronald Reagan's shoulders, the Republican Party now has enough recruits and enough resources and enough leaders to actually be capable of running everywhere. And it was literally the first election in history where there were fewer Democrats without opposition than Republicans. We had more Republicans running unopposed for the House in 1994 than there were Democrats. That has never, ever, in the history of the two parties, for 140 years, been true. And, we won, which makes it even more historic.

This was clearly a historic election which clearly had a mandate. And that's outside the Washington elite's view, and they don't want to believe that because it's not the mandate they wanted.

I want to draw a distinction between two words, because we're going to get into a lot of confusion at the vision level about these two words. I am very prepared to cooperate with the Clinton administration. I am not prepared to compromise. The two words are very different. On everything on which we can find agreement, I will cooperate.

On those things that are at the core of our *Contract*, those things   15
which are at the core of our philosophy, and on those things where we believe we represent the vast majority of Americans, there will be no compromise. So let me draw the distinction: Cooperation, yes; compromise, no.

People have been trying to figure out how to put me in a box, and it's very hard because I don't fit boxes very well. The best description of me is that I'm a conservative futurist. For a long time, I have been friends with Alvin and Heidi Toffler, the authors of *Future Shock* and *The Third Wave*. I really believe it's useful to think about the twenty-first century. On the other hand, I believe the most powerful single doctrine for the leadership of human beings and for their opportunity to pursue happiness is the *Federalist Papers*, Tocqueville's *Democracy in America*, the Declaration of Independence, and the Constitution. I also recommend to all the congressional staffs that they buy Peter Drucker's *Effective Executive*, study W. Edwards Deming's concepts of quality, look at the new Progress and Freedom Foundation's report on Alvin Toffler's works. I also suggest immersing yourself in the Founding Fathers. These people thought a long time about the nature of being human, about the problems of power, about how to organize a free society so it could sustain freedom. And if you can combine the two, you can begin to create an opportunity for every American to participate in ways that will prove to be quite remarkable.

Now, that obviously doesn't fit anybody's current word processor. We want to get to the twenty-first century, and we want to do so in a way that's effective.

There are five large changes we have to go through. First, we have to accelerate the transition from a second wave mechanical, bureaucratic society to a third wave information society, to use Alvin Toffler's model. Two simple examples: One, imagine the speed and ease with which you use a bank teller card anywhere on the planet and electronically verify your account and get money; second, imagine what happens when you call the federal government about a case. There's no objective reason that institutions of government have to be two or three generations behind the curve in information systems and management, but they are. And that means, for example, if we're really serious about distance medicine and about distance learning and about distance work, we could revolutionize the quality of life in rural America and create the greatest explosion of new opportunity for rural America in history. And yet, we're currently moving in the opposite direction so that at a time when the IRS should be making it easier to have a home office, they make it harder. Now that's foolish. It's exactly the wrong direction.

Second, we will change the rules of the House to require that all documents and all conference reports and all committee reports be filed electronically as well as in writing and that they cannot be filed until they are available to any citizen who wants to pull them up. Thus, information will be available to every citizen in the country at the same moment that it is available to the highest paid Washington lobbyist. Over time, that will change the entire flow of information and the entire quality of knowledge in the country and it will change the way people will try to play games in the legislative process.

Third, we need to recognize the objective reality of the world market, to realize that we create American jobs through world sales and that we need to make a conscious national decision that we want to have the highest value added jobs on the planet with the greatest productivity so we can have the highest take-home pay and the greatest range of choices in lifestyles. In order to do that we have to literally rethink the assumptions that grew up in a self-indulgent national economy and we have to recognize that litigation, taxation, regulation, welfare, education, the very structure of government, the structure of health — all those things have to be reexamined from the standpoint of what will make us the most competitive society on the planet, the most desirable place to invest to create jobs, and the place with the best trained and most entrepreneurial work force, most committed to Deming's concepts of quality.

That's a big challenge. One step, frankly, has to be that every child in America should be required to do at least two hours of homework a night or they're being cheated for the rest of their lives in their ability to compete with the Germans and the Japanese and the Chinese. Now, one of the differences I would suggest between where we are going and where our friends on the left would go, is I do not derive from that a belief that we need a federal department of homework checkers. I believe that we should say to every parent in the country, "Your child ought to be doing two hours of homework. If they're not, go see the teacher. If you can't convince the teacher, get a better teacher, and in the interim assign it yourself." I was taught to read by my grandmother. General George Marshall was taught to read by his aunt. The objective fact is, historically this was a country that got the job done, not a country that found scapegoats for failure. And so we've simply got to reassert a level of civic responsibility we're not used to.

Fourth, we have to replace the welfare state with an opportunity society. It is impossible to take the Great Society structure of bureaucracy, the redistributionist model of how wealth is acquired, and the counterculture value system that now permeates the way we deal with the poor, and have any hope of fixing them. They are a disaster. They ruin the poor, they create a culture of poverty and a culture of violence which is destructive of this civilization, and they have to be replaced thoroughly from the ground up.

This should be done in cooperation with the poor. The people who have the most to gain from eliminating the culture of poverty and replacing it with a culture of productivity are the people currently trapped in a nightmare, living in public housing projects with no one going to work, living in neighborhoods with no physical safety, their children forced to walk into buildings where there will be no learning, and living in a community where taxes and red tape and regulation destroy their hope of creating new entrepreneurial small businesses and doing what every other generation of poor Americans have done, which is to leave poverty behind by acquiring productivity.

We simply need to reach out and erase the slate and start over, and we need to start with the premise that every American is endowed by their Creator with certain inalienable rights, among which are life, liberty, and the pursuit of happiness, and that extends to the poorest child in Washington, D.C., and the poorest child in West Virginia, and the poorest child in American Indian reservations. And we have been failing all of them because we have lacked the courage to be mentally tough enough to get the job done. I think it can be done, but I think it's very deep and represents a very bold change.

We have to recognize that American exceptionalism — to use Everett   25
Carl Ladd's phrase — is real; that this has been the most successful civilization in the history of the human race at liberating people to pursue

happiness. There is no other society in history where as many people from as many cultures speaking as many languages could come together and become a nation, and where they could then be liberated to go off and be who they wanted to be. This is a country where Colin Powell and John Shalikashvili can both be chairman of the Joint Chiefs and nobody even thinks about the remarkable difference in ethnicity because they're Americans, and that's the way it should be.

That means we have to say to the counterculture: Nice try, you failed, you're wrong. And we have to simply, calmly, methodically reassert American civilization and reestablish the conditions, which I believe starts with the work ethic. You cannot study 300 years of American civilization without coming to the conclusion that working and being expected to work and being involved — and work may be for money or it may be at home, it may be a hobby that you pursue, but the sense of energy, the pursuit of happiness, which is not — it's an active verb — not happiness stamps, not a department of happiness, not therapy for happiness. Pursuit. This is also a muscular society and we've been kidding ourselves about it. The New Hampshire slogan is "Live free or die." It is not "Live free or whine." And so we have to think through what are the deeper underlying cultural meanings of being American and how do we reassert them.

Fifth, and lastly, and this is one where I, frankly, became more radical all fall. I realized as I would talk to audiences — I was in 127 districts in the last two years, and I realized as I would talk to audiences that there was an enormous danger that they were going to say, "Terrific speech, let's elect Gingrich Speaker, let's elect our local candidate to the House, they'll do the job." And let me tell all of you flatly, the long experiment in professional politicians and professional government is over, and it failed. You cannot hire a teacher to teach your child and walk off and then blame the teacher. You cannot hire a policeman to protect your neighborhood and then walk off and blame the police. You cannot hire a public health service to protect your health and then walk off and blame the public health service.

We have to reestablish — and I particularly want to thank Gordon Wood, who will probably get in a lot of trouble at Brown University for my using his name, but Gordon Wood's understanding of the origins of the American Revolution and his understanding of the core intent of Jeffersonian politics was for me a liberating moment because it's his argument that what Jefferson understood was that you had to have limited but effective government precisely in order to liberate people to engage in civic responsibility, and that the larger government grew, the more you would crowd out civic responsibility.

Now, this means that my challenge to the American people is simple. You really want to dramatically reduce power in Washington? You have to be willing to take more responsibility back home. You really want to reduce the bureaucracy of the welfare state? You have to accept greater responsibility back home. We are going to have to be partners. This is going to have to be a team in which we work together to renew American civilization, which is frankly why I teach the course I do on videotape and we make it available across the country. In fact, I will shamelessly tell you we use an 800 number. I hope all of you will call. And I'm very serious about it. I mean, if you're not going to take the time to learn about ideas, why should you think we'll change? The things that are wrong in America are not wrong because of money or lack of money; they're wrong because we've had a bad set of ideas that haven't worked and we need to replace them with a good set of ideas. And you can actually call. It's 1-800-TO RENEW — T-O-R-E-N-E-W.

The event on September 27 was designed as a subset of these big   30 principles. The Capitol steps event basically said, Look, we are a team, we are going to go in a dramatically different direction, we're going to give you eight reforms on the opening day, starting with the Shays Act, which will apply to the Congress every law it applies to the rest of the country so congressmen will learn all the problems they've imposed on everybody else.

We are going to cut the number of congressional committee staffs by a third, and we sent a letter to that effect to Speaker Tom Foley on Wednesday, frankly in order to allow the Democratic staff to know that a substantial number of them ought to be looking for jobs, because we thought that was the most decent and most correct way to deal with it. We are going to cut the number of congressional committees. We are going to eliminate the current services budget and replace it with a straight line budget, where if you have a dollar increase it counts as a dollar increase. This is the only place in the world where you can increase spending massively and it counts as a cut. And it has been a major source of the problem of dealing with the deficit because you create a linguistic barrier to honesty. And so we're simply going to eliminate it. You're not going to get a current services budget in this Congress — not on the House side.

Now, at the end of the opening day, we will introduce the ten bills we described in the *Contract*. We will read the *Contract* as the opening item of business every day for the first hundred days, and at the end of the first hundred days the American people, at Easter, will be able to say they saw a group of people who actually said what they were going to do and then kept their word. Now, we don't guarantee we'll pass all ten, and it's very clear in the *Contract* that what — some of these are very controversial — litigation reform, including malpractice, product liability and strike law firms is one item; a balanced budget amendment to the Constitution; a vote on term limits; an effective, enforceable death penalty with a one-time unified appeal; beginning to phase-out the marriage penalty in the tax code;

allowing senior citizens to earn up to $39,000 a year without penalty from Social Security; a capital gains cut and indexing. These are not small things, but they move in the right direction. Welfare reform, emphasizing work and family. A line-item veto, including frankly, a line-item veto for this president, so that we as Republican conservatives are prepared to give to President Clinton a line-item veto because we think it's right for America. These are real changes. It's going to be real hard to do and it's going to take a lot of people helping.

Let me say one last thing: If this just degenerates after an historic election back into the usual baloney of politics in Washington and pettiness in Washington, then the American people I believe will move toward a third party in a massive way. I think they are fed up with Washington, they are fed up with its games, they are fed up with petty partisanship. I don't think they mind grand partisanship, and there's a big difference. To have a profound disagreement over the direction of your country or over the principles by which your economy works, or over the manner in which your government should structure resources, that is legitimate and the American people believe in that level of debate and relish it.

The question will be over the next six months, can we reach out to the American people, can we recruit enough of them — notice I didn't say "Republicans" — the American people. Can we reach out to enough Democrats? Jack Kemp had a very encouraging talk with a leading member of the Black Caucus about working together and developing a program that is very bold and very dramatic in terms of helping the poor create jobs and helping those who want to rise have a real opportunity to acquire wealth and to create a better future for themselves. Now, if we can reach out and truly try to do this — and remember what I quoted on the Capitol steps, which was Franklin Delano Roosevelt, on March 4, 1933, standing in his braces at a time when it was inconceivable that somebody who had polio could be elected to major office, and standing there and saying on a wintry, overcast day in the middle of the Great Depression that we had nothing to fear but fear itself.

When you hear gunshots in your nation's capital at night and you know that young Americans have died needlessly, then I would suggest to you that we have every reason to have the moral courage to confront every weakness of the current structure and to replace it, and if the first wave of experiments fail, to have the courage to say, "Well, that one didn't work," and have a second one and a third one and a fourth one. And the Monday morning we wake up and we can look on the morning news and no young American was killed anywhere in America, and we can know that every one of them is going to a school where they're actually learning how to read, and we know that they live under a tax code where if they want to it's easy to start creating jobs and to have your own

35

business, and it's easy to start accumulating a little money to create a better future, that morning I think we can say, "Okay, this journey has been worth it." But until that day, it just stays politics.

We have an enormous amount of work to do. All I can promise you on the side of the House Republicans is that we're going to be open to working with everyone, that we will cooperate with anyone, and we will compromise with no one, and that's the base of where we're going and that's what we believe this election is all about.

PREPARING FOR DISCUSSION

1. Gingrich begins his talk with a discussion of the lessons of World War I. Why does he choose World War I as an appropriate topic with which to begin his remarks? What, according to Gingrich, are the lessons of World War I?

2. In paragraphs 22 and 26, Gingrich refers to the failure of the counterculture to change the ways Americans think about government. What elements in our society make up the counterculture and what values does it represent? Why does Gingrich say that the counterculture failed?

3. Why does Gingrich mention that he is a history teacher by background when holding that "it is impossible to maintain civilization with twelve-year-olds having babies, with fifteen-year-olds killing each other, with seventeen-year-olds dying of AIDS, and with eighteen-year-olds ending up with diplomas they can't even read" (paragraph 3)? Does he cite any historical precedent for his observations as a teacher of history?

4. Gingrich notes that an "understanding of the core intent of Jeffersonian politics was for [him] a liberating moment" since Jefferson believed in "limited but effective government." Yet Jeffersonian political theory was precisely the theory of government that James Madison and Alexander Hamilton argued against in the *Federalist Papers*. Madison and Hamilton believed in a powerful federal government, and the *Federalist Papers* are now viewed as the basis of our Constitution. Does Gingrich's embrace of Jeffersonian principles of government make him an opponent to the American Constitution as the founders framed it? On the basis of his speech, how would you describe Gingrich's attitude toward the Constitution?

5. In paragraph 26, Gingrich describes American society as "muscular." What does he mean by this adjective? Does it refer to the sense of work he develops earlier in the paragraph or to something else? Does he intend *muscular* as a gendered term or as one that is gender neutral? How does his parody of the New Hampshire state slogan as "Live free or whine" create a larger context for his use of the term *muscular?*

FROM READING TO WRITING

6. At one point in the speech, Gingrich introduces a brief summary of most of the ten bills that appeared in the *Contract with America* and that he intends to bring to a vote in Congress. In an essay, select one of Gingrich's proposed re-

forms and argue for or against it on the basis of your understanding of contemporary American politics.

7. Gingrich argues that the way that government currently works prevents citizens from fulfilling their civic responsibility. Do you agree or disagree? Write an essay in which you explain your position. If you agree with Gingrich, how has government prevented you from acting as a responsible citizen? If you disagree with Gingrich, in what ways have you fulfilled your civic responsibility as a citizen?

WILLIAM J. BENNETT

Revolt against God: America's Spiritual Despair

———————◇———————

Is America in the midst of a spiritual crisis? If so, what can be done to remedy this despair? In the following selection, former U.S. Secretary of Education William J. Bennett argues for the spiritual renewal of America. He sees an American public plagued by self-doubt, exhaustion, boredom, negative thinking, and materialism, all symptoms of what he calls "a corruption of the heart, a turning away in the soul." Bennett believes, moreover, that the spiritual health of America can only be restored through public policies "that once again make a connection between our deepest beliefs and our legislative agenda."

Bennett was educated at Williams College, the University of Texas, where he earned a doctorate in philosophy, and Harvard Law School. He taught at a number of leading universities, including the University of North Carolina, before being selected by President Ronald Reagan as the chairman of the National Endowment for the Humanities in 1981. Under Reagan he also served as secretary of education from 1985 to 1988. Later President George Bush appointed him "drug czar" under his administration. In 1986, Bennett, a life-long Democrat, changed his political affiliation to Republican. He currently serves as codirector of Empower America, an organization dedicated to promoting conservative values. Bennett is also the John M. Olin Distinguished Fellow in Cultural Policy Studies at the Heritage Foundation and a senior editor at the *National Review*. This selection was adapted from an address Bennett delivered on the Heritage Foundation's twentieth anniversary in 1994.

SELECTED PUBLICATIONS: *American Education: Making It Work: A Report to the President and the American People* (1988); *Our Children and Our Country: Improving America's Schools and Affirming the Common Culture*

(1988); *The De-Valuing of America: The Fight for Our Culture and Our Children* (1992); *The Book of Virtues* (1994).

We gather in a spirit of celebration. But tonight I speak out of a spirit of concern — for this evening my task is to provide an assessment of the social and cultural condition of modern American society. And while many people agree that there is much to be concerned about these days, I don't think that people fully appreciate the depth, or even the nature, of what threatens us — and, therefore, we do not yet have a firm hold on what it will take to better us. We need to have an honest conversation about these issues.

A few months ago I had lunch with a friend of mine, a man who has written for a number of political journals and who now lives in Asia. During our conversation the topic turned to America — specifically, America as seen through the eyes of foreigners.

During our conversation, he told me what he had observed during his travels: that while the world still regards the United States as the leading economic and military power on earth, this same world no longer beholds us with the moral respect it once did. When the rest of the world looks at America, he said, they see no longer a "shining city on a hill." Instead, they see a society in decline, with exploding rates of crime and social pathologies. We all know that foreigners often come here in fear — and once they are here, they travel in fear. It is our shame to realize that they have good reason to fear; a record number of them get killed here.

Today, many who come to America believe they are visiting a degraded society. Yes, America still offers plenty of jobs, enormous opportunity, and unmatched material and physical comforts. But there is a growing sense among many foreigners that when they come here, they are slumming. I have, like many of us, an instinctive aversion to foreigners harshly judging my nation; yet I must concede that much of what they think is true.

"You're Becoming American"

I recently had a conversation with a D.C. cab driver who is doing graduate work at American University. He told me that once he receives his masters degree he is going back to Africa. His reason? His children. He doesn't think they are safe in Washington. He told me that he didn't want them to grow up in a country where young men will paw his daughter and expect her to be an "easy target," and where his son might be a different kind of target — the target of violence from the hands of other young males. "It is more civilized where I come from," said this

5

man from Africa. I urged him to move outside of Washington; things should improve.

But it is not only violence and urban terror that signal decay. We see it in many forms. *Newsweek* columnist Joe Klein recently wrote about Berenice Belizaire, a young Haitian girl who arrived in New York in 1987. When she arrived in America she spoke no English and her family lived in a cramped Brooklyn apartment. Eventually Berenice enrolled at James Madison High School, where she excelled. According to Judith Khan, a math teacher at James Madison, "[The immigrants are] why I love teaching in Brooklyn. They have a drive in them that we no longer seem to have." And far from New York City, in the beautiful Berkshire mountains where I went to school, Philip Kasinitz, an assistant professor of sociology at Williams College, has observed that Americans have become the object of ridicule among immigrant students on campus. "There's an interesting phenomenon. When immigrant kids criticize each other for getting lazy or loose, they say, 'You're becoming American,'" Kasinitz says. "Those who work hardest to keep American culture at bay have the best chance of becoming American success stories."

Last year an article was published in the *Washington Post* which pointed out how students from other countries adapt to the lifestyle of most American teens. Paulina, a Polish high school student studying in the United States, said that when she first came here she was amazed by the way teens spent their time. According to Paulina:

> In Warsaw, we would talk to friends after school, go home and eat with our parents and then do four or five hours of homework. When I first came here, it was like going into a crazy world, but now I am getting used to it. I'm going to Pizza Hut and watching TV and doing less work in school. I can tell it is not a good thing to get used to.

Think long and hard about these words, spoken by a young Polish girl about America: "When I first came here it was like going into a crazy world, but now I am getting used to it." And, "I can tell it is not a good thing to get used to."

Something has gone wrong with us.

Social Regression

This is a conclusion which I come to with great reluctance. During the late 1960s and 1970s, I was one of those who reacted strongly to criticisms of America that swept across university campuses. I believe that many of those criticisms — "Amerika" as an inherently repressive, imperialist, and racist society — were wrong then, and they are wrong now. But intellectual honesty demands that we accept facts that we would sometimes like to wish away. Hard truths are truths nonetheless. And the hard truth is that something has gone wrong with us.

10

America is not in danger of becoming a third world country; we are too rich, too proud and too strong to allow that to happen. It is not that we live in a society completely devoid of virtue. Many people live well, decently, even honorably. There are families, schools, churches and neighborhoods that work. There are places where virtue is taught and learned. But there is a lot less of this than there ought to be. And we know it. John Updike put it this way: "The fact that . . . we still live well cannot ease the pain of feeling that we no longer live nobly."

Let me briefly outline some of the empirical evidence that points to cultural decline, evidence that while we live well materially, we don't live nobly. Earlier this year I released, through the auspices of the Heritage Foundation, *The Index of Leading Cultural Indicators,* the most comprehensive statistical portrait available of behavioral trends over the last thirty years. Among the findings: since 1960, the population has increased 41 percent; the Gross Domestic Product has nearly tripled; and total social spending by all levels of government (measured in constant 1990 dollars) has risen from $142.7 billion to $787 billion — more than a five-fold increase.

But during the same thirty-year period, there has been a 560 percent increase in violent crime; more than a 400 percent increase in illegitimate births; a quadrupling in divorces; a tripling of the percentage of children living in single-parent homes; more than a 200 percent increase in the teenage suicide rate; and a drop of 75 points in the average S.A.T. scores of high-school students.

These are not good things to get used to.

Today 30 percent of all births and 68 percent of black births are illegitimate. By the end of the decade, according to the most reliable projections, 40 percent of all American births and 80 percent of minority births will occur out of wedlock.   15

These are not good things to get used to.

And then there are the results of an ongoing teacher survey. Over the years teachers have been asked to identify the top problems in America's schools. In 1940 teachers identified them as talking out of turn; chewing gum; making noise; running in the hall; cutting in line; dress code infractions; and littering. When asked the same question in 1990, teachers identified drug use; alcohol abuse; pregnancy; suicide; rape; robbery; and assault. These are not good things to get used to, either.

Consider, too, where the United States ranks in comparison with the rest of the industrialized world. We are at or near the top in rates of abortions, divorces, and unwed births. We lead the industrialized world in murder, rape and violent crime. And in elementary and secondary education, we are at or near the bottom in achievement scores.

These facts alone are evidence of substantial social regression. But there are other signs of decay, ones that do not so easily lend themselves to quantitative analyses (some of which I have already suggested in my opening anecdotes). What I am talking about is the moral, spiritual and aesthetic character and habits of a society — what the ancient Greeks referred to as its *ethos*. And here, too, we are facing serious problems. For there is a coarseness, a callousness, a cynicism, a banality, and a vulgarity to our time. There are just too many signs of de-civilization — that is, civilization gone rotten. And the worst of it has to do with our children. Apart from the numbers and the specific facts, there is the ongoing, chronic crime against children: the crime of making them old before their time. We live in a culture which at times seems almost dedicated to the corruption of the young, to assuring the loss of their innocence before their time.

This may sound overly pessimistic or even alarmist, but I think this is the way it is. And my worry is that people are not unsettled enough; I don't think we are angry enough. We have become inured to the cultural rot that is setting in. Like Paulina, we are getting used to it, even though it is not a good thing to get used to. People are experiencing atrocity overload, losing their capacity for shock, disgust, and outrage. A few weeks ago eleven people were murdered in New York City within ten hours — and as far as I can tell, it barely caused a stir. 20

Two weeks ago a violent criminal, who mugged and almost killed a 72-year-old man and was shot by a police officer while fleeing the scene of the crime, was awarded $4.3 million. Virtual silence.

And during last year's Los Angeles riots, Damian Williams and Henry Watson were filmed pulling an innocent man out of a truck, crushing his skull with a brick, and doing a victory dance over his fallen body. Their lawyers then built a successful legal defense on the proposition that people cannot be held accountable for getting caught up in mob violence. ("They just got caught up in the riot," one juror told the *New York Times*. "I guess maybe they were in the wrong place at the wrong time.") When the trial was over and these men were found not guilty on most counts, the sound you heard throughout the land was relief. We are "defining deviancy down," in Senator Moynihan's memorable phrase. And in the process we are losing a once-reliable sense of civic and moral outrage.

Urban Surrender

Listen to this story from former New York City Police Commissioner Raymond Kelly:

> A number of years ago there began to appear, in the windows of automobiles parked on the streets of American cities, signs which read: "No radio." Rather than express outrage, or even annoyance at the possibility of a car break-in, people tried to communicate with the potential thief in conciliatory terms. The translation of "no radio" is: "Please break into someone else's car, there's nothing in mine." These "no radio" signs are

flags of urban surrender. They are hand-written capitulations. Instead of "no radio," we need new signs that say "no surrender."

And what is so striking today is not simply the increased *number* of violent crimes, but the *nature* of those crimes. It is no longer "just" murder we see, but murders with a prologue, murders accompanied by acts of unspeakable cruelty and inhumanity.

From pop culture, with our own ears, we have heard the terrible de-   25
basement of music. Music, harmony and rhythm find their way into the soul and fasten mightily upon it, Plato's *Republic* teaches us. Because music has the capacity to lift us up or to bring us down, we need to pay more careful attention to it. It is a steep moral slide from Bach, and even Buddy Holly, to Guns 'n Roses and 2 Live Crew. This week an indicted murderer, Snoop Doggy Dogg, saw his rap album, *Doggystyle*, debut at number one. It may be useful for you to read, as I have, some of his lyrics and other lyrics from heavy metal and rap music, and then ask yourself: how much worse could it possibly get? And then ask yourself: what will happen when young boys who grow up on mean streets, without fathers in their lives, are constantly exposed to music which celebrates the torture and abuse of women?

There is a lot of criticism directed at television these days — the casual cruelty, the rampant promiscuity, the mindlessness of sit-coms and soap operas. Most of the criticisms are justified. But this is not the worst of it. The worst of television is the daytime television talk shows, where indecent exposure is celebrated as a virtue. It is hard to remember now, but there was once a time when personal failures, subliminal desires, and perverse taste were accompanied by guilt or embarrassment, at least by silence.

Today these are a ticket to appear as a guest on the *Sally Jessy Raphael Show*, or one of the dozens or so shows like it. I asked my staff to provide me with a list of some of the daytime talk-show topics from only the last two weeks. They include: cross-dressing couples; a three-way love affair; a man whose chief aim in life is to sleep with women and fool them into thinking that he is using a condom during sex; women who can't say no to cheating; prostitutes who love their jobs; a former drug dealer; and an interview with a young girl caught in the middle of a bitter custody battle. These shows present a two-edged problem to society: the first edge is that some people want to appear on these shows in order to expose themselves. The second edge is that lots of people are tuning in to watch them expose themselves. This is not a good thing to get used to.

Who's to blame? Here I would caution conservatives against the tendency to blame liberals for our social disorders. Contemporary liberalism does have a lot for which to answer; many of its doctrines have wrought a lot of damage. Universities, intellectuals, think tanks, and government departments have put a lot of poison into the reservoirs of national discourse. But to simply point the finger of blame at liberals and elites is wrong. The hard fact of the matter is that this was not something done to us; it is also something we have done to ourselves. Liberals may have been peddling from an empty wagon, but we were buying.

Much of what I have said is familiar to many of you. Why is this happening? What is behind all this? Intelligent arguments have been advanced as to why these things have come to pass. Thoughtful people have pointed to materialism and consumerism; an overly permissive society; the writings of Rousseau, Marx, Freud, Nietzsche; the legacy of the 1960s; and so on. There is truth in almost all of these accounts. Let me give you mine.

Spiritual Acedia

I submit to you that the real crisis of our time is spiritual. Specifically, our problem is what the ancients called *acedia*. *Acedia* is the sin of sloth. But *acedia*, as understood by the saints of old, is *not* laziness about life's affairs (which is what we normally think sloth to be). *Acedia* is something else; properly understood, *acedia* is an aversion to and a negation of *spiritual* things. *Acedia* reveals itself as an undue concern for external affairs and worldly things. *Acedia* is spiritual torpor; an absence of zeal for divine things. And it brings with it, according to the ancients, "a sadness, a sorrow of the world."

Acedia manifests itself in man's "joyless, ill-tempered, and self-seeking rejection of the nobility of the children of God." The slothful man *hates* the spiritual, and he wants to be free of its demands. The old theologians taught that *acedia* arises from a heart steeped in the worldly and carnal, and from a *low esteem* of divine things. It eventually leads to a hatred of the good altogether. With hatred comes more rejection, more ill-temper, more sadness, and sorrow.

Spiritual *acedia* is not a new condition, of course. It is the seventh capital sin. But today it is in ascendance. In coming to this conclusion, I have relied on two literary giants — men born on vastly different continents, the product of two completely different worlds, and shaped by wholly different experiences — yet writers who possess strikingly similar views, and who have had a profound impact on my own thinking. It was an unusual and surprising moment to find their views coincident.

When the late novelist Walker Percy was asked what concerned him most about the future of America, he answered:

> Probably the fear of seeing America, with all its great strength and beauty and freedom . . . gradually subside into decay through default and be defeated, not by the Communist movement . . . but from within by weariness, boredom, cynicism, greed and in the end helplessness before its great problems.

And here are the words of the prophetic Aleksandr Solzhenitsyn (echoing his 1978 Harvard commencement address in which he warned of the West's "spiritual exhaustion"):

> In the United States the difficulties are not a Minotaur or a dragon — not imprisonment, hard labor, death, government harassment and censorship — but cupidity, boredom, sloppiness, indifference. Not the acts of a mighty all-pervading repressive government but the failure of a listless public to make use of the freedom that is its birthright.

What afflicts us, then, is a corruption of the heart, a turning away in 35 the soul. Our aspirations, our affections and our desires are turned toward the wrong things. And only when we turn them toward the right things — toward enduring, noble, spiritual things — will things get better.

Lest I leave the impression of bad news on all fronts, I do want to be clear about the areas where I think we have made enormous gains: material comforts, economic prosperity and the spread of democracy around the world. The American people have achieved a standard of living unimagined 50 years ago. We have seen extraordinary advances in medicine, science and technology. Life expectancy has increased more than 20 years during the last six decades. Opportunity and equality have been extended to those who were once denied them. And of course America prevailed in our "long, twilight struggle" against communism. Impressive achievements, all.

Yet even with all of this, the conventional analysis is still that this nation's major challenges have to do with getting more of the same: achieving greater economic growth, job creation, increased trade, health care, or more federal programs. Some of these things are desirable, such as greater economic growth and increased trade; some of them are not, such as more federal programs. But to look to any or all of them as the solution to what ails us is akin to assigning names to images and shadows, it so widely misses the mark.

If we have full employment and greater economic growth — if we have cities of gold and alabaster — but our children have not learned how to walk in goodness, justice, and mercy, then the American experiment, no matter how gilded, will have failed.

I realize I have laid down strong charges, a tough indictment. Some may question them. But if I am wrong, if my diagnosis is not right, then someone must explain to me this: why do Americans feel so bad when things are economically, militarily and materially so good? Why amidst this prosperity and security are enormous numbers of people — almost 70 percent of the public — saying that we are off track? This paradox is described in the Scottish author John Buchan's work. Writing a half-century ago, he described the "coming of a too garish age, when life would be lived in the glare of neon lamps and the spirit would have no solitude." Here is what Buchan wrote about his nightmare world:

> In such a [nightmare] world everyone would have leisure. But everyone would be restless, for there would be no spiritual discipline in life. . . . It would be a feverish, bustling world, self-satisfied and yet malcontent, and under the mask of a riotous life there would be death at the heart. In the perpetual hurry of life there would be no chance of quiet for the soul. . . . In such a bagman's paradise, where life would be rationalised and padded with every material comfort, there would be little satisfaction for the immortal part of man.

During the last decade of the twentieth century, many have achieved   40
this bagman's paradise. And this is not a good thing to get used to.

In identifying spiritual exhaustion as the central problem, I part company with many. There *is* a disturbing reluctance in our time to talk seriously about matters spiritual and religious. Why? Perhaps it has to do with the modern sensibility's profound discomfort with the language and the commandments of God. Along with other bad habits, we have gotten used to not talking about the things which matter most — and so, we don't.

One will often hear that religious faith is a private matter that does not belong in the public arena. But this analysis does not hold — at least on some important points. Whatever your faith — or even if you have none at all — it is a fact that when millions of people stop believing in God, or when their belief is so attenuated as to be belief in name only, enormous public consequences follow. And when this is accompanied by an aversion to spiritual language by the political and intellectual class, the public consequences are even greater. How could it be otherwise? In modernity, *nothing* has been more consequential, or more public in its consequences, than large segments of American society privately turning away from God, or considering Him irrelevant, or declaring Him dead. Dostoyevsky reminded us in *Brothers Karamazov* that "if God does not exist, everything is permissible." We are now seeing "everything." And much of it is not good to get used to.

Social Regeneration

What can be done? First, here are the short answers: do not surrender; get mad; and get in the fight. Now, let me offer a few, somewhat longer, prescriptions.

1. At the risk of committing heresy before a Washington audience, let me suggest that our first task is to recognize that, in general, we place too much hope in politics. I am certainly not denying the impact (for good and for ill) of public policies. I would not have devoted the past decade

of my life to public service — and I could not work at the Heritage Foundation — if I believed that the work with which I was engaged amounted to nothing more than striving after wind and ashes. But it is foolish, and futile, to rely primarily on politics to solve moral, cultural, and spiritual afflictions.

The last quarter-century has taught politicians a hard and humbling 45 lesson: there are intrinsic limits to what the state can do, particularly when it comes to imparting virtue, and forming and forging character, and providing peace to souls. Samuel Johnson expressed this (deeply conservative and true) sentiment when he wrote, "How small, of all that human hearts endure, That part which laws or kings can cause or cure!"

King Lear was a great king — sufficient to all his political responsibilities and obligations. He did well as king, but as a father and a man, he messed up terribly. The great king was reduced to the mud and ignominy of the heath, cursing his daughters, his life, his gods. Politics *is* a great adventure; it is greatly important; but its proper place in our lives has been greatly exaggerated. Politics — especially inside the Beltway politics — has too often become the graven image of our time.

2. We must have public policies that once again make the connection between our deepest beliefs and our legislative agenda. Do we Americans, for example, believe that man is a spiritual being with a potential for individual nobility and moral responsibility? Or do we believe that his ultimate fate is to be merely a soulless cog in the machine of state? When we teach sex-education courses to teenagers, do we treat them as if they are young animals in heat? Or, do we treat them as children of God?

In terms of public policy, the failure is not so much intellectual; it is a failure of will and courage. Right now we are playing a rhetorical game: we say one thing and we do another. Consider the following:

- We say that we desire from our children more civility and responsibility, but in many of our schools we steadfastly refuse to teach right and wrong.
- We say that we want law and order in the streets, but we allow criminals, including violent criminals, to return to those same streets.
- We say that we want to stop illegitimacy, but we continue to subsidize the kind of behavior that virtually guarantees high rates of illegitimacy.
- We say that we want to discourage teenage sexual activity, but in classrooms all across America educators are more eager to dispense condoms than moral guidance.
- We say that we want more families to stay together, but we liberalize divorce laws and make divorce easier to attain.
- We say that we want to achieve a color-blind society and judge

people by the content of their character, but we continue to count by race, skin and pigment.

- We say that we want to encourage virtue and honor among the young, but it has become a mark of sophistication to shun the language of morality.

3. We desperately need to recover a sense of the fundamental purpose of education, which is to provide for the intellectual *and* moral education of the young. From the ancient Greeks to the founding fathers, moral instruction was *the* central task of education. "If you ask what is the good of education," Plato said, "the answer is easy — that education makes good men, and that good men act nobly." Jefferson believed that education should aim at improving one's "morals" and "faculties." And of education, John Locke said this: "'Tis virtue that we aim at, hard virtue, and not the subtle arts of shifting." Until a quarter-century or so ago, this consensus was so deep as to go virtually unchallenged. Having departed from this time-honored belief, we are now reaping the whirlwind. And so we talk not about education as the architecture of souls, but about "skills facilitation" and "self-esteem" and about being "comfortable with ourselves."

4. As individuals and as a society, we need to return religion to its proper place. Religion, after all, provides us with moral bearings. And if I am right and the chief problem we face is spiritual impoverishment, then the solution depends, finally, on spiritual renewal. I am not speaking here about coerced spiritual renewal — in fact, there is no such thing — but about renewal freely taken. 50

The enervation of strong religious beliefs — *in both our private lives as well as our public conversations* — has de-moralized society. We ignore religion and its lessons at our peril. But instead of according religion its proper place, much of society ridicules and disdains it, and mocks those who are serious about their faith. In America today, the only respectable form of bigotry is bigotry directed against religious people. This antipathy toward religion cannot be explained by the well-publicized moral failures and financial excesses of a few leaders or charlatans, or by the censoriousness of some of their followers. No, the reason for hatred of religion is because it forces modern man to confront matters he would prefer to ignore.

Every serious student of American history, familiar with the writings of the founders, knows the civic case for religion. It provides society with a moral anchor — and nothing else has yet been found to substitute for it. Religion tames our baser appetites, passions, and impulses. And it helps us to thoughtfully sort through the "ordo amoris," the order of the loves.

But remember, too, that for those who believe, it is a mistake to treat religion merely as a useful means to worldly ends. Religion rightly demands that we take seriously not only the commandments of the faith, but that we also take seriously the object of the faith. Those who believe know that although we are pilgrims and sojourners and wanderers in this earthly kingdom, ultimately we are citizens of the City of God — a City which man did not build and cannot destroy, a City where there is no sadness, where the sorrows of the world find no haven, and where there is peace the world cannot give.

Pushing Back

Let me conclude. In his 1950 Nobel Prize acceptance speech, William Faulkner declared, "I decline to accept the end of man." Man will not merely endure but prevail because, as Faulkner said, he alone among creatures "has a soul, a spirit capable of compassion and sacrifice and endurance."

Today we must in the same way decline to accept the end of moral   55
man. We must carry on the struggle, for our children. We will push back hard against an age that is pushing hard against us. When we do, we will emerge victorious against the trials of our time. When we do, we will save our children from the decadence of our time.

We have a lot of work to do. Let's get to it.

PREPARING FOR DISCUSSION

1. Bennett argues that America is undergoing a process of cultural decline. What evidence does he cite for the decline? Do you agree with him that these are all symptoms of such a phenomenon?

2. What are the paradoxes that Bennett perceives in American society? Why does he believe that many of these paradoxes can be resolved through a greater emphasis on moral and religious education?

3. Bennett stresses the need for moral education throughout his essay. Does he make any distinction between moral and religious education? Do you believe that moral values can be instilled without the help of religion? Does the concept of soul belong exclusively to religious discourse?

4. Bennett maintains that the "only respectable form of bigotry is directed against religious people" (paragraph 51). Do you think he means all religious people or only those referred to as fundamentalist? What reasons does Bennett suggest for the prejudicial attitudes that he believes are being directed toward orthodox religious groups? Can such intolerance be traced to those groups' own intolerance for secular values?

5. Bennett blames contemporary liberalism for putting "a lot of poison into the reservoirs of national discourse." What does his analogy suggest about his attitude toward liberalism? What does his analogy suggest about the nature of public discourse?

FROM READING TO WRITING

6. Placing constitutional considerations aside for a moment, would you personally like to see a greater emphasis on moral and religious teaching in schools and universities? Write an essay in which you state your view and the reasons that you hold it. Would recalling the Constitution's position on the separation of church and state alter your view in any way?

7. Bennett reports that students born in other nations often thrive in American schools and universities. How does he account for their success? Write an essay in which you consider why foreign students, many of whom know little English, tend to do so well in the American educational system. To what extent may their success be traced to the values they hold?

BARBARA EHRENREICH

Family Values

———◇———

While the conservative initiative to praise and foster "family values" has been well received by some Americans, it is still unclear to many others just what these values are. Conservatives are fond of pointing to "traditional" two-parent families that play and pray together as the backbone of our country. Yet critics of the "family values" initiative have condemned it as merely another right-wing attempt to undo the gains of civil rights, feminism, and the gay liberation movement. Feminist and socialist party leader Barbara Ehrenreich draws on her own family history to present an "alternative" yet "traditional" set of family values.

Ehrenreich attended Reed College and earned her doctorate at Rockefeller University. For several years in the 1970s, she worked for the Health Policy Advisory Center, exposing inefficiency and corruption in the American health-care system. She is currently a fellow at the Institute for Policy Studies in Washington, D.C. The selection that follows is the introduction to her 1989 book, *Fear of Falling: The Inner Life of the Middle Class.*

SELECTED PUBLICATIONS: *Fear of Falling: The Inner Life of the Middle Class* (1989); *The Worst Years of Our Lives: Irreverent Notes from a Decade of Greed* (1990); *The Snarling Citizen: Essays* (1995); Ehrenreich also publishes with *Ms., Mother Jones,* the *Nation,* the *New York Times,* and the *New Republic.*

Sometime in the eighties, Americans had a new set of "traditional values" installed. It was part of what may someday be known as the "Reagan renovation," that finely balanced mix of cosmetic refinement and moral coarseness which brought $200,000 china to the White House dinner table and mayhem to the beleaguered peasantry of Central America. All of the new traditions had venerable sources. In economics, we borrowed from the Bourbons; in foreign policy, we drew on themes fashioned by the nomad warriors of the Eurasian steppes. In spiritual matters, we emulated the braying intolerance of our archenemies and esteemed customers, the Shi'ite fundamentalists.

A case could be made, of course, for the genuine American provenance of all these new "traditions." We've had our own robber barons, military adventurers, and certainly more than our share of enterprising evangelists promoting ignorance and parochialism as a state of grace. From the vantage point of the continent's original residents, or, for example, the captive African laborers who made America a great agricultural power, our "traditional values" have always been bigotry, greed, and belligerence, buttressed by wanton appeals to a God of love.

The kindest — though from some angles most perverse — of the era's new values was "family." I could have lived with "flag" and "faith" as neotraditional values — not happily, but I could have managed — until "family" was press-ganged into joining them. Throughout the eighties, the winning political faction has been aggressively "profamily." They have invoked "the family" when they trample on the rights of those who hold actual families together, that is, women. They have used it to justify racial segregation and the formation of white-only, "Christian" schools. And they have brought it out, along with flag and faith, to silence any voices they found obscene, offensive, disturbing, or merely different.

Now, I come from a family — was raised in one, in fact — and one salubrious effect of right-wing righteousness has been to make me hew ever more firmly to the traditional values of my own progenitors. These were not people who could be accused of questionable politics or ethnicity. Nor were they members of the "liberal elite" so hated by our current conservative elite. They were blue-eyed, Scotch-Irish Democrats. They were small farmers, railroad workers, miners, shopkeepers, and migrant farm workers. In short, they fit the stereotype of "real" Americans; and their values, no matter how unpopular among today's opinion-shapers, are part of America's tradition, too. To my mind, of course, the finest part.

But let me introduce some of my family, beginning with my father,   5
who was, along with my mother, the ultimate source of much of my radicalism, feminism, and, by the standards of the eighties, all-around bad attitude.

One of the first questions in a test of mental competency is "Who is the president of the United States?" Even deep into the indignities of Alzheimer's disease, my father always did well on that one. His blue eyes would widen incredulously, surprised at the neurologist's ignorance, then he would snort in majestic indignation, "Reagan, that dumb son of a bitch." It seemed to me a good deal — two people tested for the price of one.

Like so many of the Alzheimer's patients he came to know, my father enjoyed watching the president on television. Most programming left him impassive, but when the old codger came on, his little eyes twinkling piggishly above the disciplined sincerity of his lower face, my father would lean forward and commence a wickedly delighted cackle. I think he was prepared, more than the rest of us, to get the joke.

But the funniest thing was Ollie North. For an ailing man, my father did a fine parody. He would slap his hand over his heart, stare rigidly at attention, and pronounce, in his deepest bass rumble, "God Bless Am-ar-ica!" I'm sure he couldn't follow North's testimony — who can honestly say that they did? — but the main themes were clear enough in pantomime: the watery-eyed patriotism, the extravagant self-pity, the touching servility toward higher-ranking males. When I told my father that many people considered North a hero, a representative of the finest American traditions, he scowled and swatted at the air. Ollie North was the kind of man my father had warned me about, many years ago, when my father was the smartest man on earth.

My father had started out as a copper miner in Butte, Montana, a tiny mountain city famed for its bars, its brawls, and its distinctly unservile work force. In his view, which remained eagle-sharp even after a stint of higher education, there were only a few major categories of human beings. There were "phonies" and "decent" people, the latter group having hardly any well-known representatives outside of Franklin Delano Roosevelt and John L. Lewis, the militant and brilliantly eloquent leader of the miners' union. "Phonies," however, were rampant, and, for reasons I would not understand until later in life, could be found clustered especially thick in the vicinity of money or power.

Well before he taught me other useful things, like how to distinguish 10
fool's gold, or iron pyrite, from the real thing, he gave me some tips on the detection of phonies. For one thing, they broadened the *e* in "America" to a reverent *ahh*. They were the first to leap from their seats at the playing of "The Star Spangled Banner," the most visibly moved participants in any prayer. They espoused clean living and admired war. They preached hard work and paid for it with nickels and dimes. They loved their country above all, but despised the low-paid and usually invisible men and women who built it, fed it, and kept it running.

Two other important categories figured in my father's scheme of things. There were dumb people and smart ones: a distinction which had nothing to do with class or formal education, the dumb being simply all those who were taken in by the phonies. In his view, dumbness was rampant, and seemed to increase in proportion to the distance from Butte, where at least a certain hard-boiled irreverence leavened the atmosphere. The best prophylactic was to study and learn all you could, however you could, and, as he adjured me over and over: always ask *why*.

Finally, there were the rich and the poor. While poverty was not seen as an automatic virtue — my parents struggled mightily to escape it — wealth always carried a presumption of malfeasance. I was instructed that, in the presence of the rich, it was wise to keep one's hand on one's wallet. "Well," my father fairly growled, "how do you think they got their money in the first place?"

It was my mother who translated these lessons into practical politics. A miner's daughter herself, she offered two overarching rules for comportment: never vote Republican and never cross a union picket line. The pinnacle of her activist career came in 1964, when she attended the Democratic Convention as an alternate delegate and joined the sit-in staged by civil rights leaders and the Mississippi Freedom Democratic Party. This was not the action of a "guilt-ridden" white liberal. She classified racial prejudice along with superstition and other manifestations of backward thinking, like organized religion and overcooked vegetables. The worst thing she could find to say about a certain in-law was that he was a Republican and a churchgoer, though when I investigated these charges later in life, I was relieved to find them baseless.

My mother and father, it should be explained, were hardly rebels. The values they imparted to me had been "traditional" for at least a generation before my parents came along. According to my father, the first great steps out of mental passivity had been taken by his maternal grandparents, John Howes and Mamie O'Laughlin Howes, sometime late in the last century. You might think their rebellions small stuff, but they provided our family with its "myth of origins" and a certain standard to uphold.

I knew little about Mamie O'Laughlin except that she was raised as a   15
Catholic and ended up in western Montana sometime in the 1880s. Her father, very likely, was one of those itinerant breadwinners who went west to prospect and settled for mining. At any rate, the story begins when her father lay dying, and Mamie dutifully sent to the next town for a priest. The message came back that the priest would come only if twenty-five dollars was sent in advance. This being the West at its wildest, he may have been justified in avoiding house calls. But not in the price, which was probably more cash than my great-grandmother had ever had at one time. It was on account of its greed that the church lost the souls of Mamie O'Laughlin and all of her descendents, right down to the present time. Furthermore, whether out of filial deference or natural intelligence, most of us have continued to avoid organized religion, secret societies, astrology, and New Age adventures in spiritualism.

As the story continues, Mamie O'Laughlin herself lay dying a few years later. She was only thirty-one, the mother of three small children, one of them an infant whose birth, apparently, led to a mortal attack of pneumonia. This time, a priest appeared unsummoned. Because she was too weak to hold the crucifix, he placed it on her chest and proceeded to administer the last rites. But Mamie was not dead yet. She pulled herself together at the last moment, flung the crucifix across the room, fell back, and died.

This was my great-grandmother. Her husband, John Howes, is a figure of folkloric proportions in my memory, well known in Butte many decades ago as a powerful miner and a lethal fighter. There are many stories about John Howes, all of which point to a profound inability to accept authority in any of its manifestations, earthly or divine. As a young miner, for example, he caught the eye of the mine owner for his skill at handling horses. The boss promoted him to an aboveground driving job, which was a great career leap for the time. Then the boss committed a foolish and arrogant error. He asked John to break in a team of horses for his wife's carriage. Most people would probably be flattered by such a request, but not in Butte, and certainly not John Howes. He declared that he was no man's servant, and quit on the spot.

Like his own wife, John Howes was an atheist or, as they more likely put it at the time, a freethinker. He, too, had been raised as a Catholic — on a farm in Ontario — and he, too, had had a dramatic, though somehow less glorious, falling out with the local clergy. According to legend, he once abused his position as an altar boy by urinating, covertly of course, in the holy water. This so enhanced his enjoyment of the Easter communion service that he could not resist letting a few friends in on the secret. Soon the priest found out and young John was defrocked as an altar boy and condemned to eternal damnation.

The full weight of this transgression hit a few years later, when he became engaged to a local woman. The priest refused to marry them and forbade the young woman to marry John anywhere, on pain of excommunication. There was nothing to do but head west for the Rockies, but not before settling his score with the church. According to legend, John's last act in Ontario was to drag the priest down from his pulpit and slug him, with his brother, presumably, holding the scandalized congregation at bay.

I have often wondered whether my great-grandfather was caught up [20] in the radicalism of Butte in its heyday: whether he was an admirer of Joe Hill, Big Bill Haywood, or Mary "Mother" Jones, all of whom passed through Butte to agitate, and generally left with the Pinkertons on their tails. But the record is silent on this point. All I know is one last story about him, which was told often enough to have the ring of another "traditional value."

According to my father, John Howes worked on and off in the mines after his children were grown, eventually saving enough to buy a small plot of land and retire to farming. This was his dream, anyway, and a powerful one it must have been for a man who had spent so much of his life underground in the dark. So he loaded up a horse-drawn cart with all his money and belongings and headed downhill, toward Montana's eastern plains. But along the way he came to an Indian woman walking with a baby in her arms. He offered her a lift and ascertained, pretty easily, that she was destitute. So he gave her his money, all of it, turned the horse around, and went back to the mines.

Far be it from me to interpret this gesture for my great-grandfather, whom I knew only as a whiskery, sweat-smelling, but straight-backed old man in his eighties. Perhaps he was enacting his own uncompromising version of Christian virtue, even atoning a little for his youthful offenses to the faithful. But at another level I like to think that this was one more gesture of defiance of the mine owners who doled out their own dollars so grudgingly — a way of saying, perhaps, that whatever they had to offer, he didn't really need all that much.

So these were the values, sanctified by tradition and family loyalty, that I brought with me to adulthood. Through much of my growing-up, I thought of them as some mutant strain of Americanism, an idiosyncracy which seemed to grow rarer as we clambered into the middle class. Only in the sixties did I begin to learn that my family's militant skepticism and oddball rebelliousness were part of a much larger stream of American dissent. I discovered feminism, the antiwar movement, the civil rights movement. I learned that millions of Americans, before me and around me, were "smart" enough, in my father's terms, to have asked "Why?" — and, beyond that, the far more radical question, "Why not?"

These are also the values I brought into the Reagan-Bush era, when all the dangers I had been alerted to as a child were suddenly realized. The "phonies" came to power on the strength, aptly enough, of a professional actor's finest performance. The "dumb" were being led and abetted by low-life preachers and intellectuals with expensively squandered educations. And the rich, as my father predicted, used the occasion to dip deep into the wallets of the desperate and the distracted.

It's been hard times for a traditionalist of my persuasion. Long- 25 standing moral values — usually claimed as "Judeo-Christian" but actually of much broader lineage — were summarily tossed, along with most familiar forms of logic. We were told, at one time or another, by the president or his henchpersons, that trees cause pollution, that welfare causes poverty, and that a bomber designed for mass destruction may be aptly named the *Peacemaker*. "Terrorism" replaced missing children to become our national bugaboo and — simultaneously — one of our most potent instruments of foreign policy. At home, the poor and the middle class where shaken down, and their loose change funneled blithely upwards to the already overfed.

Greed, the ancient lubricant of commerce, was declared a wholesome stimulant. Nancy Reagan observed the deep recession of '82 and '83 by redecorating the White House, and continued with this Marie Antoinette theme while advising the underprivileged, the alienated, and the addicted to "say no." Young people, mindful of their elders' Wall Street capers, abandoned the study of useful things for finance banking and other occupations derived, ultimately, from three-card monte. While the poor donned plastic outerware and cardboard coverings, the affluent ran nearly naked through the streets, working off power meals of goat cheese, walnut oil, and crème fraîche.

Religion, which even I had hoped would provide a calming influence and reminder of mortal folly, decided to join the fun. In an upsurge of piety, millions of Americans threw their souls and their savings into evangelical empires designed on the principle of pyramid scams. Even the sleazy downfall of our telemessiahs — caught masturbating in the company of ten-dollar prostitutes or fornicating in their Christian theme parks — did not discourage the faithful. The unhappily pregnant were mobbed as "baby-killers"; sexual nonconformists — gay and lesbian — were denounced as "child molesters"; atheists found themselves lumped with "Satanists," Communists, and consumers of human flesh.

Yet somehow, despite it all, a trickle of dissent continued. There were homeless people who refused to be shelved in mental hospitals for the crime of poverty, strikers who refused to join the celebration of unions in faraway countries and scabs at home, women who insisted that their lives be valued above those of accidental embryos, parents who packed up their babies and marched for peace, students who protested the ongoing inversion of normal, nursery-school-level values in the name of a more habitable world.

I am proud to add my voice to all these. For dissent is also a "traditional value," and in a republic founded by revolution, a more deeply native one than smug-faced conservatism can ever be. Feminism was practically invented here, and ought to be regarded as one of our proudest exports to the world. Likewise, it tickles my sense of patriotism that Third World insurgents have often borrowed the ideas of our own African-American movement. And in what ought to be a source of shame to some and pride to others, our history of labor struggle is one of the hardest-fought and bloodiest in the world.

No matter that patriotism is too often the refuge of scoundrels. Dissent, rebellion, and all-around hell-raising remain the true duty of patriots.

ROBERT DOLE
Nightmares of Depravity

I want to talk about a specific matter tonight. I may not win an Oscar, but I'll talk about it anyway. I want to talk to you tonight about the future of America — about issues of moral importance, matters of social consequence.

Last month, during my announcement tour, I gave voice to concerns held across this country about what is happening to our popular culture. I made what I thought was an obvious point, a point that worries countless American parents: that one of the greatest threats to American family values is the way our popular culture ridicules them. Our music, movies, television and advertising regularly push the limits of decency, bombarding our children with destructive messages of casual violence and even more casual sex. And I concluded that we must hold Hollywood and the entire entertainment industry accountable for putting profit ahead of common decency.

So here I am in California — the home of the entertainment industry and to many of the people who shape our popular culture. And I'm asking for their help. I believe our country is crying out for leaders who will call us as a people to our better nature, not to profit from our weaknesses; who will bring back our confidence in the good, not play on our fears of life's dark corners. This is true for those of us who seek public office. And it is true for those who are blessed with the talent to lead America's vaunted entertainment industry.

Actors and producers, writers and directors, people of talent around the world dream of coming to Hollywood. Because if you are the best, this is where you are. Americans were pioneers in film, and dominate world-wide competition today. The American entertainment industry is at the cutting edge of creative excellence, but also too often the leading edge of a culture becoming dangerously coarse.

I have two goals tonight. One is to make crystal clear to you the effect this industry has on America's children, in the hope that it will rise to their defense. And the other is to speak more broadly to America about the corporate executives who hide behind the lofty language of free speech in order to profit from the debasing of America.

There is often heard in Hollywood a kind of "aw shucks" response to attempts to link societal effects with causes in the culture. It's the "we just make movies people want" response. I'll take that up in a minute. But when they go to work tomorrow, when they sift through competing proposals for their time and their money, when they consider how badly they need the next job, I want the leaders of the entertainment industry to think about the influence they have on America's children.

Let there be no mistake: televisions and movie screens, boomboxes and headsets are windows on the world for our children. If you are too old, or too sophisticated, or too close to the problem, just ask a parent. What to some is art, to our children is a nightly news report on the world outside their limited experience. What to some is make-believe, to

578

them is the "real skinny" on the adult world they are so eager to experience. Kids know firsthand what they see in their families, their schools, their immediate communities. But our popular culture shapes their view of the "real world." Our children believe those paintings in celluloid are reflections of reality. But I don't recognize America in much of what I see.

My voice and the rising voices of millions of other Americans who share this view represent more than the codgy old attempt of one generation to steal the fun of another. A line has been crossed — not just of taste, but of human dignity and decency. It is crossed every time sexual violence is given a catchy tune. When teen suicide is set to an appealing beat. When Hollywood's dream factories turn out nightmares of depravity.

You know what I mean. I mean *Natural Born Killers. True Romance.* Films that revel in mindless violence and loveless sex. I'm talking about groups like Cannibal Corpse, Geto Boys and 2 Live Crew. About a culture business that makes money from "music" extolling the pleasures of raping, torturing and mutilating women; from "songs" about killing policemen and rejecting law. The mainstreaming of deviancy must come to an end, but it will only stop when the leaders of the entertainment industry recognize and shoulder their responsibility.

But let me be very clear: I am not saying that our growing social problems are entirely Hollywood's fault. They are not. People are responsible for their actions. Movies and music do not make children into murderers. But a numbing exposure to graphic violence and immorality does steal away innocence, smothering our instinct for outrage. And I think we have reached the point where our popular culture threatens to undermine our character as a nation.

Which brings me to my second point tonight. Our freedom is precious. I have risked my life to defend it, and would do so again. We must always be proud that in America we have the freedom to speak without Big Brother's permission. Our freedom to reap the rewards of our capitalist system has raised the standard of living around the world. The profit motive is the engine of that system, and is honorable. But those who cultivate moral confusion for profit should understand this: we will name their names and shame them as they deserve to be shamed. We will contest them for the heart and soul of every child, in every neighborhood. For we who are outraged also have the freedom to speak. If we refuse to condemn evil, it is not tolerance but surrender. And we will never surrender.

Let me be specific. One of the companies on the leading edge of coarseness and violence is Time Warner. It is a symbol of how much we have lost. In the 1930s its corporate predecessor, Warner Brothers, made a series of movies, including *G-Men,* for the purpose of restoring "dignity and public confidence in the police." It made movies to help the war effort in the early 1940s. Its company slogan, put on a billboard across from the studio, was "Combining Good Citizenship with Good Picture Making."

Today Time Warner owns a company called Interscope Records which columnist John Leo called the "cultural equivalent of owning half the world's mustard gas factories." Ice-T of "Cop Killer" fame is one of Time Warner's "stars." I cannot bring myself to repeat the lyrics of some of the "music" Time Warner promotes. But our children do. There is a difference between the description of evil through art, and the marketing of evil through commerce. I would like to ask the executives of Time Warner a question: Is this what you intended to accomplish with your careers? Must you debase our nation and threaten our children for the sake of corporate profits?

And please don't answer that you are simply responding to the market. Because that is not true. In the movie business, as Michael Medved points out, the most profitable films are the ones most friendly to the family. Last year, the top five grossing films were the blockbusters *The Lion King, Forrest Gump, True Lies, The Santa Clause* and *The Flintstones*. To put it in perspective, it has been reported that *The Lion King* made six times as much money as *Natural Born Killers*.

The corporate executives who dismiss my criticism should not misunderstand. Mine is not the objection of some tiny group of zealots or an ideological fringe. From inner-city mothers to suburban mothers to families in rural America — parents are afraid, and growing angry. There once was a time when parents felt the community of adults was on their side. Now they feel surrounded by forces assaulting their children and their code of values.

This is not a partisan matter. I am a conservative Republican, but I am joined in this fight by moderates, independents and liberal Democrats. Senator Bill Bradley has spoken eloquently on this subject, as has Senator Paul Simon, who talks of our nation's "crisis of glamorized violence." And leaders of the entertainment industry are beginning to speak up, as well.

Mark Canton, the president of Universal Pictures, said, "Any smart business person can see what we must do — make more 'PG'-rated films." He said, "Together . . . we can make the needed changes. If we don't, this decade will be noted in the history books as the embarrassing legacy of what began as a great art form. We will be labeled, 'the decline of an empire.'"

Change is possible — in Hollywood, and across the entertainment industry. There are few national priorities more urgent. I know that good and caring people work in this industry. If they are deaf to the concerns I have raised tonight, it must be because they do not fully understand what is at stake. But we must make them understand. We must make it clear that tolerance does not mean neutrality between love and cruelty, between peace and violence, between right and wrong. Ours is not a crusade for censorship, it is a call for good citizenship.

When I announced I was running for president, I said that my mission is to rein in our government, to reconnect the powerful with the values which have made America strong and to reassert America's place as a great nation in the world. Tonight I am speaking beyond this room to some of the most powerful arbiters of our values. Tonight my challenge to the entertainment industry is to accept a calling above and beyond the bottom line — to fulfill a duty to the society which provides its profits. Help our nation maintain the innocence of its children. Prove to us that courage and conscience are alive and well in Hollywood.

Republican BOB DOLE *is currently Senate Majority Leader and U.S. Senator for Kansas. These remarks were delivered in Los Angeles, California on May 31, 1995.*

BILL BRADLEY
"Pathways for Trash": A Response to Dole

I applaud Senator Dole. Almost by any measure, the airwaves have become the pathways for too much trash. Violence without context and sex without attachment come into our homes too frequently in ways that we cannot control unless we are monitoring the television constantly.

Studies show that by the time a kid reaches 18, he's seen 26,000 murders on TV. That has implications. It creates a sense of unreality about the finality, pain, suffering and inhumanity of brutal violence. The question really is, What is government's role? The answer has got to be more citizenship in the boardroom, not censorship. The public has got to hold boards of directors, executives and corporations accountable for making money out of trash.

For example, if you see something that offends you, find out who the sponsor is, find out who's on its board of directors, find out where they live, who their neighbors are, their local clubs, churches and synagogues. Send a letter to the members of the board at their homes and ask whether they realize they are making huge profits from the brutal degradation of other human beings. Then send a copy of that letter to all of their neighbors and friends. You can also begin to put economic pressure on a corporation. Because the market that the economic conservative champions undermines the moral character that the social conservative desires, you have to try to introduce into the functioning of the market a moral sensibility that is usually absent.

BILL BRADLEY, *a Democrat, is the senior U.S. Senator from New Jersey. His remarks appeared in* Time *on June 12, 1995.*

PREPARING FOR DISCUSSION

1. To what social and cultural factors does Ehrenreich attribute the rise of "family values"? Why does she object to the notion of "family values" as it is currently understood? How, according to Ehrenreich, has the appeal to "family values" affected American culture?

2. What point does Ehrenreich hope to make by narrating her own family's

history and values? How do these values differ from those currently covered by the Bush-era phrase "family values"? Describe these values and the ones to which they are opposed.

3. At several points in the essay, Ehrenreich refers to the legendary or folkloric aspect of many of the family anecdotes she relates. Does this aspect of Ehrenreich's narrative in any way undermine the force of her attack on the new "family values"? Would the historical verification of the stories she relates strengthen her position?

4. Ehrenreich writes that "it was my mother who translated [my father's] lessons into practical politics": "never vote Republican and never cross a union picket line." Review the political lessons taught Ehrenreich by her father and then consider whether her mother's translation of those lessons into practical politics is an accurate one. How does such a translation take place? Do you think that Ehrenreich is using the term *translation* literally or in some other way?

5. Consider Ehrenreich's father's distinction between "smart" and "dumb" people. What are the senses of these words to him? Does he define these terms in the usual sense? Would he call most Americans today "smart" or "dumb"?

FROM READING TO WRITING

6. Examine your family's history and the values that have been passed down to you. Write an essay in which you trace the origins of those values and how they have been transmitted through the generations. Have there been any historical or cultural changes that forced your family to alter or abandon these values?

7. Do the values that Ehrenreich attributes to her family strike you as "traditional"? Write an essay in which you explain your view. What kinds of family values do you find "traditional"? Do you generally believe that "traditional" values are superior to others? Why or why not?

AMITAI ETZIONI

A New Moral, Social, Public Order

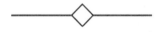

One of the most influential political movements to emerge in recent years is the communitarian movement. This centrist movement encourages ordinary Americans to sacrifice some of their civil liberty and self-interest in the name of the community and the public good. In keeping with the movement's emphasis on civic responsibility over individual rights, communitarians propose, among other public-minded measures, mandatory public service for high school and college students, courses in moral education in public schools, and tougher divorce laws to encourage couples with children to stay together. In the following selection, sociologist and founder of the communitarian movement Amitai Etzioni sets out the theory behind such proposals.

Etzioni was born in Germany and raised in Israel. He came to the United States in the late 1950s to work on his doctorate in sociology, which he received from the University of California at Berkeley. For twenty years, beginning in 1958, he served as a professor of sociology at Columbia University. Since 1980, he has taught at George Washington University, where he was named the first University Professor in that institution's history. He also served as senior adviser in the White House from 1979 to 1980 and is the founder and editor of *The Responsive Community: Rights and Responsibilities,* a communitarian quarterly. This selection is from his 1993 book, *The Spirit of Community.*

SELECTED PUBLICATIONS: *The Active Society: A Theory of Societal and Political Processes* (1968); *Social Problems* (1983); *An Immodest Agenda: Rebuilding America before the 21st Century* (1983); *The Moral Dimension: Toward a New Economics* (1988); *The Spirit of Community: Rights, Responsibilities, and the Communitarian Agenda* (1993).

We Hold These Truths

We hold that a moral revival in these United States is possible without puritanism; that is, without busybodies meddling into our personal affairs, without thought police controlling our intellectual life. We *can* attain a recommitment to moral values — without puritanical excesses.

We hold that law and order can be restored without turning this country of the free into a police state, as long as we grant public authorities some carefully crafted and circumscribed new powers.

We hold that the family — without which no society has ever survived, let alone flourished — can be saved, without forcing women to stay at home or otherwise violating their rights.

We hold that schools *can* provide essential moral education — without indoctrinating young people.

We hold that people can again live in communities without turning into vigilantes or becoming hostile to one another.

We hold that our call for increased social responsibilities is not a call for curbing rights. On the contrary, *strong rights presume strong responsibilities.*

We hold that the pursuit of self-interest can be balanced by a commitment to the community, without requiring us to lead a life of austerity, altruism, or self-sacrifice. Furthermore, unbridled greed can be replaced by legitimate opportunities and socially constructive expressions of self-interest.

We hold that powerful special-interest groups in the nation's capital, and in many statehouses and city halls, can be curbed without limiting the constitutional right of the people to lobby and petition those who govern. The public interest *can* reign, without denying the legitimate interests and the right to lobby of the various constituencies that make up America.

We hold these truths as Communitarians, as people committed to creating a new moral, social, and public order based on restored communities, without allowing puritanism or oppression.

The Communitarian Thesis

The Communitarian assertions rest upon a single core thesis: Americans — who have long been concerned with the deterioration of private and public morality, the decline of the family, high crime rates, and the swelling of corruption in government — can now act without fear. We can act without fear that attempts to shore up our values, responsibilities, institutions, and communities will cause us to charge into a dark tunnel of moralism and authoritarianism that leads to a church-dominated state or a right-wing world.

Let me introduce the Communitarian approach by way of an example: Airline pilots, school bus drivers, and others who directly hold people's lives in their hands can be required to be tested for drug and alcohol use. This would significantly enhance our safety, without testing every Dick, Jane, and Harry, from employees of the Weather Bureau to children in kindergarten. Beyond the important details (such as, should police officers also be tested? will the samples be collected in the presence of others?) are matters of principle, such as how we can restore a civil society (in this case, enhance public safety) while upholding our constitutional rights and moral traditions.

The Communitarian movement — which is an environmental movement dedicated to the betterment of our moral, social, and political environment — seeks to sort out these principles. And Communitarians are dedicated to working with our fellow citizens to bring about the changes in values, habits, and public policies that will allow us to do for society what the environmental movement seeks to do for nature: to safeguard and enhance our future.

America in the Early Nineties

From time to time there's a finding of social science that may by itself be of limited importance but illuminates a major conundrum: A study has shown that young Americans expect to be tried before a jury of their peers but are rather reluctant to serve on one. This paradox highlights a major aspect of contemporary American civic culture: a strong sense of entitlement — that is, a demand that the community provide more services and strongly uphold rights — coupled with a rather weak sense of obligation to the local and national community. Thus, most Americans applauded the show of force in Grenada, Panama, and in the Persian Gulf, but many were reluctant to serve in the armed forces or see their sons and daughters called up.

First prize for capturing this anticommunitarian outlook should be awarded to a member of a television audience who exclaimed during a show on the savings and loan mess, "The taxpayers should not have to pay for this; the government should," as if there really were an Uncle Sam who could pick up the tab for us all.

A 1989 study by People for the American Way notes:

> *Young people have learned only half of America's story.* Consistent with the priority they place on personal happiness, young people reveal notions of America's unique character that emphasize freedom and license almost to the complete exclusion of service or participation. Although they clearly appreciate the democratic freedoms that, in their view, make theirs the "best country in the world to live in," they fail to perceive a need to reciprocate by exercising the duties and responsibilities of good citizenship.

Only one out of eight (12 percent) of the respondents felt that voting was part of what makes a good citizen. When asked what was special about the United States, young people responded: "Individualism and the fact that it is a democracy and you can do whatever you want." And: "We really don't have any limits."

The imbalance between rights and responsibilities has existed for a long time. Indeed, some argue that it is a basic trait of the American character. However, America's leaders have exacerbated this tendency in recent years. In 1961 President John F. Kennedy could still stir the nation when he stated: "Ask not what your country can do for you. Ask what you can do for your country." But Presidents Ronald Reagan and George Bush, backed up by some Democrats in Congress, proposed a much less onerous course: they suggested that ever-increasing economic growth would pay for government services, and taxpayers would be expected to shell out less — implying that Americans could have their cake and eat it, too.

In many other areas, from public education to the war on illegal drugs, facile, nontaxing "solutions" have been offered. Thus it has been suggested that we can improve our education system without additional expenditures simply by increasing parental choices among schools. Choice, it is claimed, will "drive the bad schools out of business." And how should we deal with the demand for illicit drugs? "Just say no."

Harvard legal historian Lawrence Friedman points to a particularly troubling mismatch of rights and responsibilities: a tendency among

Americans in recent years to claim rights for themselves and to leave responsibilities to the government. It is therefore necessary to reiterate that
sooner or later the responsibilities we load on the government end up on
our shoulders or become burdens we bequeath to our children.

A Four-Point Agenda on Rights and Responsibilities

Correcting the current imbalance between rights and responsibilities requires a four-point agenda: a moratorium on the minting of most, if not
all, new rights; reestablishing the link between rights and responsibilities;
recognizing that some responsibilities do not entail rights; and, most
carefully, adjusting some rights to the changed circumstances. These pivotal points deserve some elaboration.

A Moratorium. We should, for a transition period of, say, the next   20
decade, put a tight lid on the manufacturing of new rights. The incessant
issuance of new rights, like the wholesale printing of currency, causes a
massive inflation of rights that devalues their moral claims.

When asked whether certain things are "a privilege that a person
should have to earn, or a right to which he is entitled as a citizen," most
Americans (81 percent) considered health care a right (versus 16 percent
who said it was a privilege). Two-thirds (66 percent) considered adequate housing a right (as opposed to 31 percent who called it a privilege).
Indeed, why not? Until one asks, as there are no free lunches, who will
pay for unlimited health care and adequate housing for all? The champions of rights are often quite mum on this question, which if left unanswered makes the claim for a right a rather empty gesture.

Tajel Shah, the president of the U.S. Student Association, claims that
higher education "is a right, not a privilege." A fine sentiment indeed. It
would, however, be more responsible if she at least hinted at how this
right is to be paid for — in whose ledger the entailed obligation is to be
entered.

In Santa Monica, California, men were found dealing drugs in public
women's rooms on the beaches and in parks. To combat the abuse, the
city council passed an ordinance that prohibited men and women from
using the opposite sex's facilities unless they were in urgent need (which
was defined as a line of three or more in front of them). This did not satisfy a local activist, Gloria Allred, who saw in the ordinance a violation of
a woman's right to urinate in any public facility, at any time. Referring to
a similar ordinance in Houston, Texas, she stated: "Little did I know that
such a nightmare might soon be reenacted in this fair city." Ms. Allred
warned: "This is the first step down a long dark road of restricting
women's rights in the name of public safety."

Death-row inmates at San Quentin have sued to protect their reproductive "rights" through artificial insemination. An attorney in the case

reports that "these inmates believe that they are being subjected to cruel and unusual punishment because not only are they being sentenced to die, but future generations of their family are being executed also. . . ."

Lisa Dangler, a mother in Yorktown, New York, sued the local school 25
district for not admitting her son into the high school honor society. She argued that his rejection reduced his chances of being accepted by a select college and medical school. She further claimed that he was being punished because the Danglers were outspoken critics of the school — and hence his rejection was actually a violation of the family's right of free speech. A jury rejected her suit. The presiding judge stated that if the jury had ruled in Ms. Dangler's favor, he would have overturned the verdict. He added: "By attempting to elevate mere personal desires into constitutional rights and claiming denial of their civil rights whenever their desires are not realized, these persons are demeaning the essential rights and procedures that protect us all."

The American Bankers Association took out a full-page ad in *The Washington Post* (when Congress was considering putting a cap on the interest banks may charge credit-card holders) that bore the headline WILL CONGRESS DENY MILLIONS OF AMERICANS THE RIGHT TO KEEP THEIR CREDIT CARDS?

Once, rights were very solemn moral/legal claims, ensconced in the Constitution and treated with much reverence. We all lose if the publicity department of every special interest can claim that someone's rights are violated every time they don't get all they want. Suspending for a while the minting of new rights, unless there are unusually compelling reasons to proceed, will serve to restore the special moral standing and suasion of rights.

We need to remind one another that *each newly minted right generates a claim on someone.* In effect, new rights often arouse or play upon feelings of guilt in others. There is a limited amount of guilt, however, that one can lay upon other people before they balk. Unless we want to generate a universal backlash against rights, we need to curb rights inflation and protect the currency of rights from being further devalued.

Moreover, the expression of ever more wants, many quite legitimate, in the language of rights makes it difficult to achieve compromises and to reach consensus, processes that lie at the heart of democracy. A society that is studded with groups of true believers and special-interest groups, each brimming with rights, inevitably turns into a society overburdened with conflicts. Columnist John Leo of *U.S. News & World Report* declares: "Rights talk polarizes debate; it tends to suppress moral discussion and consensus building. Once an agenda is introduced as a 'right,' sensible discussion and moderate positions tend to disappear."

Even if lawyers and judges realize among themselves that individual 30
rights are limited by the rights of others and the needs of the community, as the language of rights penetrates into everyday discourse, the discourse

becomes impoverished and confrontational. It is one thing to claim that you and I have different interests and see if we can work out a compromise; or, better yet, that we both recognize the merit or virtue of a common cause, say, a cleaner environment. The moment, however, that I claim a *right* to the same piece of land or property or public space as you, we start to view one another like the Catholics and Protestants in Northern Ireland or the Palestinians and Israelis in the Middle East.

A return to a language of social virtues, interests, and, above all, social responsibilities will reduce contentiousness and enhance social cooperation.

People treat rights-based arguments, unlike many others, as "trump cards" that neutralize all other positions. Cass R. Sunstein, professor of jurisprudence at the University of Chicago, put it well when he pointed out that rights can "be conclusions masquerading as reasons." For example, he writes, those who defend even the most extreme kinds of what he labels violent pornography state that it is a form of free speech, period. Sunstein suggests that perhaps a person is entitled to this particularly abusive form of speech. But, he argues, an individual's entitlement should be established in detailed argumentation that would weigh the right at issue against the rights of those who are hurt by the given act, rather than simply asserting that it is a right, as if its evocation closed off all debate.

Mary Ann Glendon, a Harvard Law professor and leading Communitarian, shows that we treat many rights the way we treat property, which we tend to view as intrinsically "ours" and which we are therefore free to do with as we wish. Actually, we readily accept that there are many things we may not do with things we own, such as burning leaves, which may endanger others, or playing the stereo loud enough to be heard five blocks away. To put it differently, we all know on one level that our liberties are limited by those of others and that we can do what we want only *as long as we do not harm others.* Rights talk, however, pushes us to disregard this crucial qualification, the concern for one another and for the community. Soon "I can do what I want as long as I do not hurt others" becomes "I can do what I want, because I have a right to do it."

A telling case in point is the opposition to seat belts and motorcycle helmets. Libertarians have long argued adamantly that the government should not require people to use these safety devices. They blocked the introduction of seat belt and motorcycle helmet laws in many jurisdictions and ensured the repeal of such regulations in several localities where they had been in place. The main libertarian argument is that people have a right to do with their lives what they wish, including endangering them. People are said to be the best judges of what is good for them, because they will have to live with the consequences of their acts. Therefore we should treat people as adults and not as children, without paternalism. (Some libertarians apply the same idea to the use of narcotics.)

Reckless individuals, however, do not absorb many of the conse-   35
quences of their acts. Drivers without seat belts are more likely than those wearing belts to lose control of their cars in an accident and hurtle into others. They are also more likely to die and leave their children for society to attend to and pick up the pieces. And, of course, they draw on our community resources, from ambulance services to hospitals, when they are involved in accidents, for which they pay at best a fraction of the cost. To insist that people drive safely and responsibly is hence a concern for the needs of others and the community; there is no individual right that automatically trumps these considerations.

Aside from a temporary suspension in the minting of new rights, *there are several rights,* some recently generated and some of long standing, *that deserve reexamination.* It makes little sense, for example, to refer to rights of inanimate objects, as law professor Christopher Stone did some years back in an environmental flourish:

> It is no answer to say that streams and forests . . . cannot speak. Corporations cannot speak either; nor can states, estates, infants, incompetents, municipalities or universities. . . . One ought, I think, to handle the legal problems of natural objects as one does the problem of legal incompetents — human beings who have become vegetable. . . . On a parity of reasoning, we should have a system in which, when a friend of a natural object perceives it to be endangered, he can apply to a court for the creation of a guardianship.

Others have pointed out that many builders use sand from beaches, that cities cut into them to create new harbors, and that utilities use them for their power plants — all of them benefiting from beaches and contributing to their erosion. But instead of turning to the language of responsibility to protect beaches, legal scholars, among them a Los Angeles lawyer who specializes in the environment, have advanced the notion that sand has rights! It is difficult to imagine a way to trivialize rights more than to claim that they are as common as sand.

Stone is correct that one can find a way to appoint a lawyer not merely for everybody, but also for everything, and surely many objects — say, a majestic mountain — deserve some protection, even command some respect. (Corporations are different because they are combinations of humans and hence are more akin to communities than to animals or stones.) None of this, however, proves that we have to consider them as if they command rights. The difference between granting them some consideration versus rights is that to grant them rights puts them on the same plane as humans — and we should grant humans a higher moral standing than brooks and sand. Note that *consideration for the objects themselves is secondary.* The stunning mountain requires protection so that other humans may find it stunning, and not for its own sake. Therefore we have an *interest* in protecting it; but to accord it the higher status of commanding a right interferes with our dealing with it in a dispassionate way. We must and can find ways to recognize the value of things and to respect them without imbuing them with rights. Let's just say that they deserve our respect and command our care.

Rights Presume Responsibilities.   Claiming rights without assuming responsibilities is unethical and illogical. Mary Ann Glendon puts it well: "Buried deep in our rights dialect," she writes, "is an unexpressed premise that we roam at large in a land of strangers, where we presumptively have no obligations toward others except to avoid the active infliction of harm." She notes in *Rights Talk:*

> Try, for example, to find in the familiar language of our Declaration of Independence or Bill of Rights anything comparable to the statements in the Universal Declaration of Human Rights that "everyone has duties to the community," and that everyone's rights and freedoms are subject to limitations "for the purposes of securing due recognition and respect for the rights and freedoms of others and of meeting the just requirements of morality, public order and the general welfare in a democratic society."

The Constitution, while not nearly as explicit on obligations to the community as the other documents cited, does open with the quest "to form a more perfect Union" and speaks of the need to "promote the general welfare" for that purpose.

To take and not to give is an amoral, self-centered predisposition that   40
ultimately no society can tolerate. To revisit the finding that many try to evade serving on a jury, which, they claim, they have a right to be served by, is egotistical, indecent, and in the long run impractical. Hence, *those most concerned about rights ought to be the first ones to argue for the resumption of responsibilities.* One presumes the other. Much of the following discussion about the conditions under which moral commitments can be strengthened in the family, schools, and in communities speaks directly to the shoring up of our responsibilities. Indeed, many of our core values entail concern for others and the commons we share. As we restore the moral voice of communities (and the web of social bonds, the Communitarian nexus, that enables us to speak as a community), we will also be more able to encourage one another to live up to our social responsibilities.

Responsibilities without Rights.   Although it is difficult to imagine rights without corollary responsibilities, we must recognize that we have some duties that lay moral claims on us from which we derive no immediate benefit or even long-term payoff. Our commitment to a shared future, especially our responsibility to the environment, is a case in point. We are to care for the environment not only or even mainly for our own sakes (although we may desire some assurance of potable water, breathable air, and protection from frying because the ozone layer is thinning out). We have a moral commitment to leave for future generations a livable environment, even perhaps a better one than the one we inherited, certainly not one that has been further depleted. *The same observations hold true for our responsibility to our moral, social, and political environment.*

Careful Adjustments.   Finally, some areas in which legal rights have been interpreted in ways that hobble public safety and health are to be reinterpreted. Thus, the Fourth Amendment outlaws *unreasonable* searches and seizures. The question of what is deemed reasonable versus unreasonable is subject to change over time. In several areas of public life, the times now call for a modest increase in what we can reasonably be asked to do for the sake of the community, for public safety and public health.

Radical Individualists, such as libertarians and the American Civil Liberties Union (ACLU), have effectively blocked many steps to increase public safety and health. Among the measures they systematically oppose are sobriety checkpoints (which can play an important role in reducing slaughter on the highways), *all* drug testing (even of those who have the lives of others directly in their control), and limiting the flood of private money into the pockets, drawers, and war chests of local and national elected representatives.

Having presented this fourth part of the Communitarian agenda before scores of groups, my colleagues and I have learned that this element of balancing rights and responsibilities is the most controversial. Yet such adjustments can be made without opening the floodgates to a police state or excessive intrusion by public health departments. On the contrary, *the best way to curb authoritarianism and right-wing tendencies is to stop the anarchic drift by introducing carefully calibrated responses to urgent and legitimate public concerns* about safety and the control of epidemics.

Moral Reconstruction

Social responsibility is but one of the core virtues that need reaffirmation.   45
We require a general *shoring up of our moral foundations*. Since the early sixties, many of our moral traditions, social values, and institutions have been challenged, often for valid reasons. The end result is that we live in a state of increasing moral confusion and social anarchy. Once we were quite clear about what young couples were supposed to do — and refrain from doing — even if many of them did not fully live up to these expectations. The trouble now is not that the traditional family was undermined; it did deserve a critical going-over. The trouble is that no new concept of the family — of responsibility to children, of intimacy, and of

commitment to one another — has emerged to replace the traditional form. (The fate of two books by Betty Friedan illustrates the difference: *The Feminine Mystique*, which was critical of the traditional family, was all the rage in the 1960s and early 1970s. Her second book, *The Second Stage*, published in 1981, which advocated the restructuring of the family, fell on deaf ears.) Moral transitions often work this way: destruction comes quickly. A vacuum prevails. Reconstruction is slow. This is where we are now: it is time to reconstruct, in the full sense of the term — not to return to the traditional, but to return to a moral affirmation, reconstructed but firmly held.

Once schools transmitted the moral and social values of previous generations to the young. Granted, these values were complacent, a bit authoritarian, and rather discriminatory. Did we shake them up! But this was the easy part, as destruction often is. Now we are all too often left with educational rubble. Schools are so overwhelmed simply by maintaining order and passing on elementary knowledge and skills that they have neither the time nor the inclination to attend to their most important mission: transmitting a core of values to the next generation.

In the fifties we were quite clear what our attitude toward authority figures should be: a great deal of respect and only a modicum of questioning. Parents, ministers, doctors, labor leaders, presidents — all commanded a fair amount of unchallenged moral authority to tell right from wrong, to guide the young and perplexed. The silent generation may well have been too silent and too compliant. It was largely blind to racial and gender discrimination, and it seems to have been genuinely unaware that millions of Americans lived in abject poverty. (It would take the undeniable data in Michael Harrington's *The Other America*, which was heralded by President John F. Kennedy, for poverty in America to be discovered.)

Since the 1950s we have cut our authority figures down to size. In the mid-sixties still nearly one-half of Americans expressed high confidence in the leaders of most institutions, from the military to Congress and from the press to corporations. Over the past twenty-five years, however, the proportion of Americans who have confidence in their leaders has dropped significantly. Public officials are daily skewered in the press. Once a venerated figure, Christopher Columbus has been brought down from his pedestal to be tried in the court of public opinion. Is he a national hero or a conquering murderer? asked *The New York Times* on Columbus Day 1991. Others, from George Washington to Martin Luther King, Jr., are being treated less kindly. Public opinion polls show that a majority of Americans believe that those in power do not care about their constituents. We are bereft of clear leadership in most matters, especially moral matters.

Liberal friends, who read a draft version of *The Spirit of Community*, expressed concern about the use of the term *moral*. Americans don't like to be told about morals, said one, and it sounds like preaching. Another suggested that the term reminds him of the Moral Majority. I do not mean to preach, but to share a concern and perhaps an agenda. I am sorry if I remind people of the Moral Majority, because I believe that although they raised the right questions they provided the wrong, largely authoritarian and dogmatic, answers. However, one of the purposes of *The Spirit of Community* is to retrieve for the realm of democratic discourse good, basic terms that we have allowed to become the political slogans of archconservatives and the right wing. Just because a Pat Robertson talked about family values, community, and morality when he tried to keep social conservatives in the Bush camp during election campaigns should not mean that the rest of us should shy away from applying these pivotal social concepts. And just because some abuse these terms to foment divisiveness and hate, and to attack all intellectuals or liberals as if they were one "cultural elite," hostile to all that is good in America, should not lead us implicitly to accept this notion. Just as we should not give up on patriotism because some politicians wrap themselves with the flag when it suits their narrow purposes, so should we not give up on morality because some abuse it to skewer their fellow community members.

As rights exploded and responsibilities receded, as the moral infrastructure crumbled, so did the public interest. True, special interests have always been with us. Moreover, pluralism — the rich fabric of various groupings, subcultures, and viewpoints — is a major foundation of the freedom that is the proud hallmark of this country, a country that was created by people fleeing enforced homogeneity. 50

But since the sixties, the forces that combined all the plurals into one mosaic — one society and one nation — have waned. The notion of a shared community or public interest, which balances but does not replace the plurality of particular interests, has been eroded. Political parties, vying over their conception of the public good, have been largely pushed aside; they have been replaced on center stage by myriad special interests and a Congress that is deeply indebted to them. Now all too often the dominant interests are not those of major segments of the population, such as consumers, workers, and industrialists. Instead they are those of groups that represent narrow, self-serving goals, such as parking lot owners seeking a special tax deduction, beehive owners in quest of a government subsidy, and organizations of sugar farmers, office equipment makers, and thousands of others. Their subsidies, tax concessions, special credits, and such consume large chunks of the public budget. Among them they are eating up the country's wealth and sapping its energy, leaving little for the projects that serve the commonweal — that is, all of us and our shared future.

PREPARING FOR DISCUSSION

1. What, according to Etzioni, is the central paradox of civic culture in America? What does he think is the best way to resolve such a conflict?

2. What does the author believe to be a proper balance between rights and responsibilities? How does he propose to achieve this balance? What kinds of sacrifices will American citizens have to make in order to achieve this balance?

3. Many of Etzioni's critics consider communitarianism to be little more than an attempt to restrict individual rights in response to the authoritarian elements in our country who would seek even greater restrictions on our liberties. In what sense might Etzioni's vision for our nation be said to be opposed to traditional American political values? What are these values and why do Etzioni's ideas pose a threat to them?

4. In paragraph 28, Etzioni writes that "unless we want to generate a universal backlash against rights, we need to curb rights inflation and protect the currency of rights from being further devalued." Why does he use these economic analogies to the current "rights" situation? Do you think that monetary analogies are appropriate for the discussion of our rights as American citizens?

5. In the opening paragraphs of his essay, Etzioni partly echoes the language of The Declaration of Independence. Why does he choose to echo this document? How do the political values represented in the opening paragraphs of the essay compare with the values of the document it echoes?

FROM READING TO WRITING

6. Etzioni offers his view of the proper balance between rights and responsibilities in American society. Write an essay in which you describe your own sense of what that balance should be. Does it differ greatly from Etzioni's? If so, in what ways does it differ? If not, did you arrive at a similar conclusion through reasoning similar to or different from Etzioni's?

7. Consider Etzioni's statement that "the best way to curb authoritarianism and right-wing tendencies is to stop anarchic drift by introducing carefully calibrated responses to urgent and legitimate public concerns about safety and the control of epidemics" (paragraph 44). What does Etzioni mean by "carefully calibrated responses"? Do you agree or disagree with Etzioni on the best way to avoid authoritarian government? Write an essay in which you consider whether it is necessary to sacrifice some rights to save the democratic process.

Appendix

The Constitution of the United States of America[1]

––––––––––◇––––––––––

We the People of the United States, in Order to form a more perfect Union, establish Justice, insure domestic Tranquility, provide for the common defence, promote the general Welfare, and secure the Blessings of Liberty to ourselves and our Posterity, do ordain and establish this Constitution for the United States of America.

Article. I.

Section. 1. All legislative Powers herein granted shall be vested in a Congress of the United States, which shall consist of a Senate and House of Representatives.

Section. 2. The House of Representatives shall be composed of Members chosen every second Year by the People of the several States, and the Electors in each State shall have the Qualifications requisite for Electors of the most numerous Branch of the State Legislature.

No Person shall be a Representative who shall not have attained to the Age of twenty five Years, and been seven Years a Citizen of the United States, and who shall not, when elected, be an Inhabitant of that State in which he shall be chosen.

Representatives and direct Taxes[2] shall be apportioned among the several States which may be included within this Union, according to their respective Numbers, which shall be determined by adding to the

---

[1] From the engrossed copy in the National Archives. Original spelling, capitalization, and punctuation have been retained.
[2] Modified by the Sixteenth Amendment.

whole Number of free Persons, including those bound to Service for a Term of Years, and excluding Indians not taxed, three fifths of all other Persons.[3] The actual Enumeration shall be made within three Years after the first Meeting of the Congress of the United States, and within every subsequent Term of ten Years, in such Manner as they shall by Law direct. The Number of Representatives shall not exceed one for every thirty Thousand, but each State shall have at Least one Representative; and until such enumeration shall be made, the State of New Hampshire shall be entitled to chuse three; Massachusetts eight; Rhode Island and Providence Plantations one; Connecticut five; New York six; New Jersey four; Pennsylvania eight; Delaware one; Maryland six; Virginia ten; North Carolina five; South Carolina five; and Georgia three.

When vacancies happen in the Representation from any State, the Executive Authority thereof shall issue Writs of Election to fill such Vacancies.

The House of Representatives shall chuse their Speaker and other Officers; and shall have the sole Power of Impeachment.

Section. 3. The Senate of the United States shall be composed of two Senators from each State, chosen by the Legislature thereof, for six Years; and each Senator shall have one Vote.[4]

Immediately after they shall be assembled in Consequence of the first Election, they shall be divided as equally as may be into three Classes. The Seats of the Senators of the first Class shall be vacated at the Expiration of the second Year, of the second Class at the Expiration of the fourth Year, and of the third Class at the Expiration of the sixth Year, so that one third may be chosen every second Year; and if Vacancies happen by Resignation, or otherwise, during the Recess of the Legislature of any State, the Executive thereof may make temporary Appointments until the next Meeting of the Legislature, which shall then fill such Vacancies.[5]

No Person shall be a Senator who shall not have attained to the Age of thirty Years, and been nine Years a Citizen of the United States, and who shall not, when elected, be an Inhabitant of that State for which he shall be chosen.

The Vice President of the United States shall be President of the Senate, but shall have no Vote, unless they be equally divided.

The Senate shall chuse their other Officers, and also a President pro tempore, in the Absence of the Vice President, or when he shall exercise the Office of President of the United States.

The Senate shall have the sole Power to try all Impeachments. When sitting for that Purpose, they shall be on Oath or Affirmation. When the

---

[3] Replaced by the Fourteenth Amendment.
[4] Superseded by the Seventeenth Amendment.
[5] Modified by the Seventeenth Amendment.

President of the United States is tried, the Chief Justice shall preside: And no Person shall be convicted without the Concurrence of two thirds of the Members present.

Judgment in Cases of Impeachment shall not extend further than to removal from Office, and disqualification to hold and enjoy any Office of honor, Trust or Profit under the United States: but the Party convicted shall nevertheless be liable and subject to Indictment, Trial, Judgment and Punishment, according to Law.

Section. 4. The Times, Places and Manner of holding Elections for Senators and Representatives, shall be prescribed in each State by the Legislature thereof, but the Congress may at any time by Law make or alter such Regulation, except as to the Places of chusing Senators.

The Congress shall assemble at least once in every Year, and such Meeting shall be on the first Monday in December, unless they shall by Law appoint a different Day.[6]

Section. 5. Each House shall be the Judge of the Elections, Returns and Qualifications of its own Members, and a Majority of each shall constitute a Quorum to do Business; but a smaller Number may adjourn from day to day, and may be authorized to compel the Attendance of absent Members, in such Manner, and under such Penalties as each House may provide.

Each House may determine the Rules of its Proceedings, punish its Members for disorderly Behaviour, and, with the Concurrence of two thirds, expel a Member.

Each House shall keep a Journal of its Proceedings, and from time to time publish the same, excepting such Parts as may in their Judgment require Secrecy; and the Yeas and Nays of the Members of either House on any question shall, at the Desire of one fifth of those Present, be entered on the Journal.

Neither House, during the Session of Congress, shall, without the Consent of the other, adjourn for more than three days, nor to any other Place than that in which the two Houses shall be sitting.

Section. 6. The Senators and Representatives shall receive a Compensation for their Services, to be ascertained by Law, and paid out of the Treasury of the United States. They shall in all Cases, except Treason, Felony and Breach of the Peace, be privileged from Arrest during their Attendance at the Session of their respective Houses, and in going to and returning from the same; and for any Speech or Debate in either House, they shall not be questioned in any other Place.

No Senator or Representative shall, during the Time for which he was elected, be appointed to any civil Office under the Authority of the United States, which shall have been created, or the Emoluments whereof

[6] Superseded by the Twentieth Amendment.

shall have been encreased during such time; and no Person holding any Office under the United States, shall be a Member of either House during his Continuance in Office.

Section. 7. All Bills for raising Revenue shall originate in the House of Representatives; but the Senate may propose or concur with Amendments as on other Bills.

Every Bill which shall have passed the House of Representatives and the Senate shall, before it become a Law, be presented to the President of the United States; If he approve he shall sign it, but if not he shall return it, with his Objections to that House in which it shall have originated, who shall enter the Objections at large on their Journal, and proceed to reconsider it. If after such Reconsideration two thirds of that House shall agree to pass the Bill, it shall be sent, together with the Objections, to the other House, by which it shall likewise be reconsidered, and if approved by two thirds of that House, it shall become a Law. But in all such Cases the Votes of both Houses shall be determined by yeas and Nays, and the Names of the Persons voting for and against the Bill shall be entered on the Journal of each House respectively. If any Bill shall not be returned by the President within ten Days (Sundays excepted) after it shall have been presented to him, the Same shall be a Law, in like Manner as if he had signed it, unless the Congress by their Adjournment prevent its Return, in which Case it shall not be a Law.

Every Order, Resolution, or Vote to which the Concurrence of the Senate and House of Representatives may be necessary (except on a question of Adjournment) shall be presented to the President of the United States; and before the Same shall take Effect, shall be approved by him, or being disapproved by him shall be repassed by two thirds of the Senate and House of Representatives, according to the Rules and Limitations prescribed in the Case of a Bill.

Section. 8. The Congress shall have Power To lay and collect Taxes, Duties, Imposts and Excises, to pay the Debts and provide for the common Defence and general Welfare of the United States; but all Duties, Imposts and Excises shall be uniform throughout the United States;

To borrow Money on the credit of the United States;

To regulate Commerce with foreign Nations, and among the several States, and with the Indian Tribes;

To establish an uniform Rule of Naturalization, and uniform Laws on the subject of Bankruptcies throughout the United States;

To coin Money, regulate the Value thereof, and of foreign Coin, and fix the Standard of Weights and Measures;

To provide for the Punishment of counterfeiting the Securities and current Coin of the United States;

To establish Post Offices and post Roads;

To promote the Progress of Science and useful Arts, by securing for limited Times to Authors and Inventors the exclusive Right to their respective Writings and Discoveries;

To constitute Tribunals inferior to the supreme Court;

To define and punish Piracies and Felonies committed on the high Seas, and Offences against the Law of Nations;

To declare War, grant Letters of Marque and Reprisal, and make Rules concerning Captures on Land and Water;

To raise and support Armies, but no Appropriation of Money to that Use shall be for a longer Term than two Years;

To provide and maintain a Navy;

To make Rules for the Government and Regulation of the land and naval Forces;

To provide for calling forth the Militia to execute the Laws of the Union, suppress Insurrections and repel Invasions;

To provide for organizing, arming, and disciplining, the Militia, and for governing such Part of them as may be employed in the Service of the United States, reserving to the States respectively, the Appointment of the Officers, and the Authority of training the Militia according to the discipline prescribed by Congress;

To exercise exclusive Legislation in all Cases whatsoever, over such District (not exceeding ten Miles square) as may, by Cession of particular States, and the Acceptance of Congress, become the Seat of the Government of the United States, and to exercise like Authority over all Places purchased by the Consent of the Legislature of the State in which the Same shall be, for the Erection of Forts, Magazines, Arsenals, dock-Yards, and other needful Buildings; — And

To make all Laws which shall be necessary and proper for carrying into Execution the foregoing Powers, and all other Powers vested by this Constitution in the Government of the United States, or in any Department or Officer thereof.

Section. 9. The Migration or Importation of such Persons as any of the States now existing shall think proper to admit, shall not be prohibited by the Congress prior to the Year one thousand eight hundred and eight, but a Tax or duty may be imposed on such Importation, not exceeding ten dollars for each Person.

The Privilege of the Writ of Habeas Corpus shall not be suspended, unless when in Cases of Rebellion or Invasion the public Safety may require it.

No Bill of Attainder or ex post facto Law shall be passed.

No Capitation, or other direct, Tax shall be laid, unless in Proportion to the Census or Enumeration herein before directed to be taken.

No Tax or Duty shall be laid on Articles exported from any State.

No Preference shall be given by any Regulation of Commerce or Revenue to the Ports of one State over those of another: nor shall Vessels bound to, or from, one State, be obliged to enter, clear, or pay Duties in another.

No Money shall be drawn from the Treasury, but in Consequence of Appropriations made by Law, and a regular Statement and Account of the Receipts and Expenditures of all public Money shall be published from time to time.

No Title of Nobility shall be granted by the United States: And no Person holding any Office of Profit or Trust under them, shall, without the Consent of the Congress, accept of any present, Emolument, Office, or Title, of any kind whatever, from any King, Prince, or foreign State.

Section. 10. No State shall enter into any Treaty, Alliance, or Confederation; grant Letters of Marque and Reprisal; coin Money; emit Bills of Credit; make any Thing but gold and silver Coin a Tender in Payment of Debts; pass any Bill of Attainder, ex post facto Law, or Law impairing the Obligation of Contracts, or grant any Title of Nobility.

No State shall, without the Consent of the Congress, lay any Imposts or Duties on Imports or Exports, except what may be absolutely necessary for executing its inspection Laws: and the net Produce of all Duties and Imposts, laid by any State on Imports or Exports, shall be for the Use of the Treasury of the United States; and all such Laws shall be subject to the Revision and Controul of the Congress.

No State shall, without the Consent of Congress, lay any Duty of Tonnage, keep Troops, or Ships of War in time of Peace, enter into any Agreement or Compact with another State, or with a foreign Power, or engage in War, unless actually invaded, or in such imminent Danger as will not admit of delay.

Article. II.

Section. 1. The executive Power shall be vested in a President of the United States of America. He shall hold his Office during the Term of four Years, and, together with the Vice President, chosen for the same Term, be elected, as follows:

Each State shall appoint, in such Manner as the Legislature thereof may direct, a Number of Electors, equal to the whole Number of Senators and Representatives to which the State may be entitled in the Congress: but no Senator or Representative, or Person holding an Office of Trust or Profit under the United States, shall be appointed an Elector.

The Electors shall meet in their respective States, and vote by Ballot for two Persons, of whom one at least shall not be an Inhabitant of the same State with themselves. And they shall make a List of all the Persons voted for, and of the Number of Votes for each; which List they shall sign and certify, and transmit sealed to the Seat of the Government of the United States, directed to the President of the Senate. The President of the Senate shall, in the Presence of the Senate and House of Representatives, open all the Certificates, and the Votes shall then be counted. The Person having the greatest Number of Votes shall be the President, if such Number be a Majority of the whole Number of Electors appointed; and if there be more than one who have such Majority, and have an equal Number of Votes, then the House of Representatives shall immediately chuse by Ballot one of them for President; and if no Person have a Majority, then from the five highest on the List the said House shall in like Manner chuse the President. But in chusing the President, the Votes shall be taken by States, the Representation from each State having one Vote; A quorum for this Purpose shall consist of a Member or Members from two thirds of the States, and a Majority of all the States shall be necessary to a Choice. In every Case, after the Choice of the President, the Person having the greatest Number of Votes of the Electors shall be the Vice President. But if there should remain two or more who have equal Votes, the Senate shall chuse from them by Ballot the Vice President.[7]

The Congress may determine the Time of chusing the Electors, and the Day on which they shall give their Votes; which Day shall be the same throughout the United States.

No Person except a natural born Citizen, or a Citizen of the United States, at the time of the Adoption of this Constitution, shall be eligible to the Office of President, neither shall any Person be eligible to that Office who shall not have attained to the Age of thirty five Years, and been fourteen Years a Resident within the United States.

In Case of the Removal of the President from Office, or of his Death, Resignation, or Inability to discharge the Powers and Duties of the said Office, the Same shall devolve on the Vice President, and the Congress may by Law provide for the Case of Removal, Death, Resignation or Inability, both of the President and Vice President, declaring what Officer shall then act as President, and such Officer shall act accordingly, until the Disability be removed, or a President shall be elected.[8]

The President shall, at stated Times, receive for his Services, a Compensation, which shall neither be encreased nor diminished during the Period for which he shall have been elected, and he shall not receive within that Period any other Emolument from the United States, or any of them.

Before he enter on the Execution of his Office, he shall take the following Oath or Affirmation: — "I do solemnly swear (or affirm) that I will faithfully execute the Office of President of the United States, and will to the best of my Ability, preserve, protect and defend the Constitution of the United States."

Section. 2. The President shall be Commander in Chief of the Army and Navy of the United States, and of the Militia of the several States,

---

[7] Superseded by the Twelfth Amendment.
[8] Modified by the Twenty-fifth Amendment.

when called into the actual Service of the United States; he may require the Opinion, in writing, of the principal Officer in each of the executive Departments, upon any Subject relating to the Duties of their respective Offices, and he shall have Power to grant Reprieves and Pardons for Offences against the United States, except in Cases of Impeachment.

He shall have Power, by and with the Advice and Consent of the Senate, to make Treaties, provided two thirds of the Senators present concur; and he shall nominate, and by and with the Advice and Consent of the Senate, shall appoint Ambassadors, other public Ministers and Consuls, Judges of the supreme Court, and all other Officers of the United States, whose Appointments are not herein otherwise provided for, and which shall be established by Law; but the Congress may by Law vest the Appointment of such inferior Officers, as they think proper, in the President alone, in the Courts of Law, or in the Heads of Departments.

The President shall have Power to fill up all Vacancies that may happen during the Recess of the Senate, by granting Commissions which shall expire at the End of their next Session.

Section. 3. He shall from time to time give to the Congress Information of the State of the Union, and recommend to their Consideration such Measures as he shall judge necessary and expedient; he may, on extraordinary Occasions, convene both Houses, or either of them, and in Case of Disagreement between them, with Respect to the Time of Adjournment, he may adjourn them to such Time as he shall think proper; he shall receive Ambassadors and other public Ministers; he shall take Care that the Laws be faithfully executed, and shall Commission all the Officers of the United States.

Section. 4. The President, Vice President and all civil Officers of the United States, shall be removed from Office on Impeachment for, and Conviction of, Treason, Bribery, or other high Crimes and Misdemeanors.

Article. III.

Section. 1. The judicial Power of the United States, shall be vested in one supreme Court, and in such inferior Courts as the Congress may from time to time ordain and establish. The Judges, both of the supreme and inferior Courts, shall hold their Offices during good Behaviour, and shall, at stated Times, receive for their Services, a Compensation, which shall not be diminished during their Continuance in Office.

Section. 2. The judicial Power shall extend to all Cases, in Law and Equity, arising under this Constitution, the Laws of the United States, and Treaties made, or which shall be made, under their Authority; — to all Cases affecting Ambassadors, other public Ministers and Consuls; — to all Cases of admiralty and maritime Jurisdiction; — to Controversies to which the United States shall be a Party; — to Controversies between two or more States; — between a State and Citizens of another State;[9] — between Citizens of different States, — between Citizens of the same State claiming Lands under Grants of different States, and between a State, or the Citizens thereof, and foreign States, Citizens or Subjects.

In all Cases affecting Ambassadors, other public Ministers and Consuls, and those in which a State shall be Party, the supreme Court shall have original Jurisdiction. In all the other Cases before mentioned, the supreme Court shall have appellate Jursidiction, both as to Law and Fact, with such Exceptions, and under such Regulations as the Congress shall make.

The Trial of all Crimes, except in Cases of Impeachment, shall be by Jury; and such Trial shall be held in the State where the said Crimes shall have been committed; but when not committed within any State, the Trial shall be at such Place or Places as the Congress may by Law have directed.

Section. 3. Treason against the United States, shall consist only in levying War against them, or in adhering to their Enemies, giving them Aid and Comfort. No Person shall be convicted of Treason unless on the Testimony of two Witnesses to the same overt Act, or on Confession in open Court.

The Congress shall have Power to declare the Punishment of Treason, but no Attainder of Treason shall work Corruption of Blood, or Forfeiture except during the Life of the Person attainted.

Article. IV.

Section. 1. Full Faith and Credit shall be given in each State to the public Acts, Records, and judicial Proceedings of every other State. And the Congress may by general Laws prescribe the Manner in which such Acts, Records and Proceedings shall be proved, and the Effect thereof.

Section. 2. The Citizens of each State shall be entitled to all Privileges and Immunities of Citizens in the several States.

A Person charged in any State with Treason, Felony, or other Crime, who shall flee from Justice, and be found in another State, shall on Demand of the executive Authority of the State from which he fled, be delivered up, to be removed to the State having Jurisdiction of the Crime.

No Person held to Service or Labour in one State, under the Laws thereof, escaping into another, shall, in Consequence of any Law or Regulation therein, be discharged from such Service or Labour, but shall be delivered up on Claim of the Party to whom such Service or Labour may be due.

---

[9] Modified by the Eleventh Amendment.

Section. 3. New States may be admitted by the Congress into this Union; but no new State shall be formed or erected within the Jurisdiction of any other State, nor any State be formed by the Junction of two or more States, or Parts of States, without the Consent of the Legislatures of the States concerned as well as of the Congress.

The Congress shall have Power to dispose of and make all needful Rules and Regulations respecting the Territory or other Property belonging to the United States; and nothing in this Constitution shall be so construed as to Prejudice any Claims of the United States, or of any particular State.

Section. 4. The United States shall guarantee to every State in this Union a Republican Form of Government, and shall protect each of them against Invasion; and on Application of the Legislature, or of the Executive (when the Legislature cannot be convened) against domestic Violence.

Article. V.

The Congress, whenever two thirds of both Houses shall deem it necessary, shall propose Amendments to this Constitution, or, on the Application of the Legislatures of two thirds of the several States, shall call a Convention for proposing Amendments, which, in either Case, shall be valid to all Intents and Purposes, as Part of this Constitution, when ratified by the Legislatures of three fourths of the several States, or by Conventions in three fourths thereof, as the one or the other Mode of Ratification may be proposed by the Congress; Provided that no Amendment which may be made prior to the Year One thousand eight hundred and eight shall in any Manner affect the first and fourth Clauses in the Ninth Section of the first Article; and that no State, without its Consent, shall be deprived of its equal Suffrage in the Senate.

Article. VI.

All Debts contracted and Engagements entered into, before the Adoption of this Constitution, shall be as valid against the United States under this Constitution, as under the Confederation.

This Constitution, and the Laws of the United States which shall be made in Pursuance thereof; and all Treaties made, or which shall be made, under the Authority of the United States, shall be the supreme Law of the Land; and the Judges in every State shall be bound thereby, any Thing in the Constitution or Laws of any State to the Contrary notwithstanding.

The Senators and Representatives before mentioned, and the Members of the several State Legislatures, and all executive and judicial Officers, both of the United States and of the several States, shall be bound by

Oath or Affirmation, to support this Constitution; but no religious Test shall ever be required as a Qualification to any Office or public Trust under the United States.

Article. VII.

The Ratification of the Conventions of nine States, shall be sufficient for the Establishment of this Constitution between the States so ratifying the Same.

done in Convention by the Unanimous Consent of the States present the Seventeenth Day of September in the Year of our Lord one thousand seven hundred and Eighty seven and of the Independence of the United States of America the Twelfth. *In witness* whereof We have hereunto subscribed our Names,

Articles in Addition to, and Amendment of, the Constitution of the United States of America, Proposed by Congress, and Ratified by the Legislatures of the Several States, Pursuant to the Fifth Article of the Original Constitution.

Amendment I[10]

Congress shall make no law respecting an establishment of religion, or prohibiting the free exercise thereof; or abridging the freedom of speech, or of the press; or the right of the people peaceably to assemble, and to petition the Government for a redress of grievances.

Amendment II

A well regulated Militia, being necessary to the security of a free State, the right of the people to keep and bear Arms shall not be infringed.

Amendment III

No Soldier shall, in time of peace, be quartered in any house, without the consent of the Owner, nor in time of war, but in a manner to be prescribed by law.

Amendment IV

The right of the people to be secure in their persons, houses, papers, and effects, against unreasonable searches and seizures, shall not be violated, and no Warrants shall issue, but upon probable cause, supported by

---

[10] The first ten amendments were passed by Congress September 25, 1789. They were ratified by three-fourths of the states December 15, 1791.

Oath or affirmation, and particularly describing the place to be searched, and the persons or things to be seized.

Amendment V

No person shall be held to answer for a capital or otherwise infamous crime, unless on a presentment or indictment of a Grand Jury, except in cases arising in the land or naval forces, or in the Militia, when in actual service in time of War or public danger; nor shall any person be subject for the same offence to be twice put in jeopardy of life or limb; nor shall be compelled in any criminal case to be a witness against himself, nor be deprived of life, liberty, or property, without due process of law; nor shall private property be taken for public use, without just compensation.

Amendment VI

In all criminal prosecutions, the accused shall enjoy the right to a speedy and public trial, by an impartial jury of the State and district wherein the crime shall have been committed, which district shall have been previously ascertained by law, and to be informed of the nature and cause of the accusation; to be confronted with the witnesses against him; to have compulsory process for obtaining witnesses in his favor, and to have the Assistance of Counsel for his defence.

Amendment VII

In suits at common law, where the value in controversy shall exceed twenty dollars, the right of trial by jury shall be preserved, and no fact tried by a jury, shall be otherwise reexamined in any Court of the United States, than according to the rules of the common law.

Amendment VIII

Excessive bail shall not be required, nor excessive fines imposed, nor cruel and unusual punishments inflicted.

Amendment IX

The enumeration in the Constitution, of certain rights, shall not be construed to deny or disparage others retained by the people.

Amendment X

The powers not delegated to the United States by the Constitution; nor prohibited by it to the States, are reserved to the States respectively, or to the people.

Amendment XI[11]

The Judicial power of the United States shall not be construed to extend to any suit in law or equity, commenced or prosecuted against one of the United States by Citizens of another State, or by Citizens or Subjects of any Foreign State.

Amendment XII[12]

The Electors shall meet in their respective States and vote by ballot for President and Vice-President, one of whom, at least, shall not be an inhabitant of the same State with themselves; they shall name in their ballots the person voted for as President, and in distinct ballots the person voted for as Vice-President, and they shall make distinct lists of all persons voted for as President, and of all persons voted for as Vice-President, and of the number of votes for each, which lists they shall sign and certify, and transmit sealed to the seat of the government of the United States, directed to the President of the Senate; — The President of the Senate shall, in the presence of the Senate and House of Representatives, open all the certificates and the votes shall then be counted; — The person having the greatest number of votes for President, shall be the President, if such number be a majority of the whole number of Electors appointed; and if no person have such majority, then from the persons having the highest numbers not exceeding three on the list of those voted for as President, the House of Representatives shall choose immediately, by ballot, the President. But in choosing the President, the votes shall be taken by states, the representation from each state having one vote; a quorum for this purpose shall consist of a member or members from two-thirds of the states, and a majority of all the states shall be necessary to a choice. And if the House of Representatives shall not choose a President whenever the right of choice shall devolve upon them, before the fourth day of March next following, then the Vice-President shall act as President, as in the case of the death or other constitutional disability of the President. — The person having the greatest number of votes as Vice-President, shall be the Vice-President, if such number be a majority of the whole number of Electors appointed, and if no person have a majority, then from the two highest numbers on the list, the Senate shall choose the Vice-President; a quorum for the purpose shall consist of two-thirds of the whole number of Senators, and a majority of the whole number shall be necessary to a choice. But no person constitutionally ineligible to the office of President shall be eligible to that of Vice-President of the United States.

[11] Passed March 4, 1794. Ratified January 23, 1795.
[12] Passed December 9, 1803. Ratified June 15, 1804.

Amendment XIII[13]

SECTION 1. Neither slavery nor involuntary servitude, except as a punishment for crime whereof the party shall have been duly convicted, shall exist within the United States, or any place subject to their jurisdiction.

SECTION 2. Congress shall have power to enforce this article by appropriate legislation.

Amendment XIV[14]

SECTION 1. All persons born or naturalized in the United States, and subject to the jurisdiction thereof, are citizens of the United States and of the State wherein they reside. No State shall make or enforce any law which shall abridge the privileges or immunities of citizens of the United States; nor shall any State deprive any person of life, liberty, or property, without due process of law; nor deny to any person within its jurisdiction the equal protection of the laws.

SECTION 2. Representatives shall be apportioned among the several States according to their respective numbers, counting the whole number of persons in each State, excluding Indians not taxed. But when the right to vote at any election for the choice of electors for President and Vice-President of the United States, Representatives in Congress, the Executive and Judicial officers of a State, or the members of the Legislature thereof, is denied to any of the male inhabitants of such State, being twenty-one years of age, and citizens of the United States, or in any way abridged, except for participation in rebellion, or other crime, the basis of representation therein shall be reduced in the proportion which the number of such male citizens shall bear to the whole number of male citizens twenty-one years of age in such State.

SECTION 3. No person shall be a Senator or Representative in Congress, or elector of President and Vice-President, or hold any office, civil or military, under the United States, or under any State, who, having previously taken an oath, as a member of Congress, or as an officer of the United States, or as a member of any State legislature, or as an executive or judicial officer of any State, to support the Constitution of the United States, shall have engaged in insurrection or rebellion against the same, or given aid or comfort to the enemies thereof. But Congress may by a vote of two-thirds of each House, remove such disability.

SECTION 4. The validity of the public debt of the United States, authorized by law, including debts incurred for payment of pensions and bounties for services in suppressing insurrection or rebellion, shall not be questioned. But neither the United States nor any State shall assume or pay

[13] Passed January 31, 1865. Ratified December 6, 1865.
[14] Passed June 13, 1866. Ratified July 8, 1868.

any debt or obligation incurred in aid of insurrection or rebellion against the United States, or any claim for the loss or emancipation of any slave; but all such debts, obligations, and claims shall be held illegal and void.

SECTION 5. The Congress shall have the power to enforce, by appropriate legislation, the provisions of this article.

Amendment XV[15]

SECTION 1. The right of citizens of the United States to vote shall not be denied or abridged by the United States or by any State on account of race, color, or previous condition of servitude —

SECTION 2. The Congress shall have power to enforce this article by appropriate legislation.

Amendment XVI[16]

The Congress shall have power to lay and collect taxes on incomes, from whatever source derived, without apportionment among the several States, and without regard to any census or enumeration.

Amendment XVII[17]

The Senate of the United States shall be composed of two Senators from each State, elected by the people thereof, for six years; and each Senator shall have one vote. The electors in each State shall have the qualifications requisite for electors of the most numerous branch of the State legislatures.

When vacancies happen in the representation of any State in the Senate, the executive authority of such State shall issue writs of election to fill such vacancies: *Provided,* That the legislature of any State may empower the executive thereof to make temporary appointments until the people fill the vacancies by election as the legislature may direct.

This amendment shall not be so construed as to affect the election or term of any Senator chosen before it becomes valid as part of the Constitution.

Amendment XVIII[18]

SECTION 1. After one year from the ratification of this article the manufacture, sale, or transportation of intoxicating liquors within, the importation thereof into, or the exportation thereof from the United States and all

---

[15] Passed February 26, 1869. Ratified February 2, 1870.
[16] Passed July 12, 1909. Ratified February 3, 1913.
[17] Passed May 13, 1912. Ratified April 8, 1913.
[18] Passed December 18, 1917. Ratified January 16, 1919.

territory subject to the jurisdiction thereof for beverage purposes is hereby prohibited.

SECTION 2. The Congress and the several States shall have concurrent power to enforce this article by appropriate legislation.

SECTION 3. This article shall be inoperative unless it shall have been ratified as an amendment to the Constitution by the legislatures of the several States, as provided in the Constitution, within seven years from the date of the submission hereof to the States by the Congress.

Amendment XIX[19]

The right of citizens of the United States to vote shall not be denied or abridged by the United States or by any State on account of sex.

Congress shall have power to enforce this article by appropriate legislation.

Amendment XX[20]

SECTION 1. The terms of the President and Vice-President shall end at noon on the 20th day of January, and the terms of Senators and Representatives at noon on the 3d day of January, of the years in which such terms would have ended if this article had not been ratified; and the terms of their successors shall then begin.

SECTION 2. The Congress shall assemble at least once in every year, and such meeting shall begin at noon on the 3d day of January, unless they shall by law appoint a different day.

SECTION 3. If, at the time fixed for the beginning of the term of the President, the President elect shall have died, the Vice-President elect shall become President. If a President shall not have been chosen before the time fixed for the beginning of his term, or if the President elect shall have failed to qualify, then the Vice-President elect shall act as President until a President shall have qualified; and the Congress may by law provide for the case wherein neither a President elect nor a Vice-President elect shall have qualified, declaring who shall then act as President, or the manner in which one who is to act shall be selected, and such person shall act accordingly until a President or Vice-President shall have qualified.

SECTION 4. The Congress may by law provide for the case of the death of any of the persons from whom the House of Representatives may choose a President whenever the right of choice shall have devolved upon them, and for the case of the death of any of the persons from whom the Senate may choose a Vice-President whenever the right of choice shall have devolved upon them.

[19] Passed June 4, 1919. Ratified August 18, 1920.
[20] Passed March 2, 1932. Ratified January 23, 1933.

SECTION 5. Sections 1 and 2 shall take effect on the 15th day of October following the ratification of this article.

SECTION 6. This article shall be inoperative unless it shall have been ratified as an amendment to the Constitution by the legislatures of three-fourths of the several States within seven years from the date of its submission.

Amendment XXI[21]

SECTION 1. The eighteenth article of amendment to the Constitution of the United States is hereby repealed.

SECTION 2. The transportation or importation into any State, Territory, or possession of the United States for delivery or use therein of intoxicating liquors, in violation of the laws thereof, is hereby prohibited.

SECTION 3. This article shall be inoperative unless it shall have been ratified as an amendment to the Constitution by conventions in the several States, as provided in the Constitution, within seven years from the date of the submission hereof to the States by the Congress.

Amendment XXII[22]

No person shall be elected to the office of the President more than twice, and no person who has held the office of President, or acted as President, for more than two years of a term to which some other person was elected President shall be elected to the office of the President more than once.

But this Article shall not apply to any person holding the office of President when this Article was proposed by the Congress, and shall not prevent any person who may be holding the office of President, or acting as President, during the term within which this Article becomes operative from holding the office of President or acting as President during the remainder of such term.

Amendment XXIII[23]

SECTION 1. The District constituting the seat of Government of the United States shall appoint in such manner as the Congress may direct:

A number of electors of President and Vice President equal to the whole number of Senators and Representatives in Congress to which the District would be entitled if it were a State, but in no event more than the least populous State; they shall be in addition to those appointed by the States, but

[21] Passed February 20, 1933. Ratified December 5, 1933.
[22] Passed March 12, 1947. Ratified March 1, 1951.
[23] Passed June 16, 1960. Ratified April 3, 1961.

they shall be considered, for the purposes of the election of President and Vice President, to be electors appointed by the State; and they shall meet in the District and perform such duties as provided by the twelfth article of amendment.

SECTION 2. The Congress shall have power to enforce this article by appropriate legislation.

Amendment XXIV[24]

SECTION 1. The right of citizens of the United States to vote in any primary or other election for President or Vice President, or for Senator or Representative in Congress, shall not be denied or abridged by the United States or any State by reason of failure to pay any poll tax or other tax.

SECTION 2. The Congress shall have power to enforce this article by appropriate legislation.

Amendment XXV[25]

SECTION 1. In case of the removal of the President from office or of his death or resignation, the Vice President shall become President.

SECTION 2. Whenever there is a vacancy in the office of the Vice President, the President shall nominate a Vice President who shall take office upon confirmation by a majority vote of both Houses of Congress.

SECTION 3. Whenever the President transmits to the President pro tempore of the Senate and the Speaker of the House of Representatives his written declaration that he is unable to discharge the powers and duties of his office, and until he transmits to them a written declaration to the contrary, such powers and duties shall be discharged by the Vice President as Acting President.

SECTION 4. Whenever the Vice President and a majority of either the principal officers of the executive department or of such other body as Congress may by law provide, transmit to the President pro tempore of the Senate and the Speaker of the House of Representatives their written declaration that the President is unable to discharge the powers and duties of his office, the Vice President shall immediately assume the powers and duties of the office of Acting President.

Thereafter, when the President transmits to the President pro tempore of the Senate and the Speaker of the House of Representatives his written declaration that no inability exists, he shall resume the powers and duties of his office unless the Vice President and a majority of either the principal officers of the executive department or of such other body as Congress may by law provide, transmit within four days to the Presi-

[24]Passed August 27, 1962. Ratified January 23, 1964.
[25]Passed July 6, 1965. Ratified February 11, 1967.

dent pro tempore of the Senate and the Speaker of the House of Representatives their written declaration that the President is unable to discharge the powers and duties of his office. Thereupon Congress shall decide the issue, assembling within forty-eight hours for that purpose if not in session. If the Congress, within twenty-one days after receipt of the latter written declaration, or, if Congress is not in session, within twenty-one days after Congress is required to assemble, determines by two-thirds vote of both Houses that the President is unable to discharge the powers and duties of his office, the Vice President shall continue to discharge the same as Acting President; otherwise, the President shall resume the powers and duties of his office.

Amendment XXVI[26]

SECTION 1. The right of citizens of the United States, who are eighteen years of age or older, to vote shall not be denied or abridged by the United States or by any State on account of age.

SECTION 2. The Congress shall have power to enforce this article by appropriate legislation.

---

[26] Passed March 23, 1971. Ratified July 5, 1971.

The Bill of Rights

————————◇————————

ARTICLES IN ADDITION TO, and Amendment of the Constitution of the United States of America, proposed by Congress, and ratified by the Legislatures of the several States, pursuant to the fifth Article of the original Constitution.

Art. I

Congress shall make no law respecting an establishment of religion, or prohibiting the free exercise thereof; or abridging the freedom of speech, or of the press; or the right of the people peaceably to assemble, and to petition the government for a redress of grievances.

Art. II

A well regulated Militia, being necessary to the security of a free State, the right of the people to keep and bear Arms, shall not be infringed.

Art. III

No Soldier shall, in time of peace be quartered in any house, without the consent of the Owner, nor in time of war, but in a manner to be prescribed by law.

Art. IV

The right of the people to be secure in their persons, houses, papers, and effects, against unreasonable searches and seizures, shall not be violated, and no Warrants shall issue, but upon probable cause, supported by Oath or affirmation, and particularly describing the place to be searched, and the persons or things to be seized.

Art. V

No person shall be held to answer for a capital, or otherwise infamous crime, unless on a presentment or indictment of a Grand Jury, except in cases arising in the land or naval forces, or in the Militia, when in actual service in time of War or public danger; nor shall any person be subject for the same offence to be twice put in jeopardy of life or limb; nor shall be compelled in any criminal case to be a witness against himself, nor be deprived of life, liberty, or property, without due process of law; nor shall private property be taken for public use, without just compensation.

Art. VI

In all criminal prosecutions, the accused shall enjoy the right to a speedy and public trial, by an impartial jury of the State and district wherein the crime shall have been committed, which district shall have been previously ascertained by law, and to be informed of the nature and cause of the accusation; to be confronted with the witnesses against him; to have compulsory process for obtaining witnesses in his favor, and to have the Assistance of Counsel for his defence.

Art. VII

In Suits at common law, where the value in controversy shall exceed twenty dollars, the right of trial by jury shall be preserved, and no fact tried by a jury, shall be otherwise re-examined in any Court of the United States, than according to the rules of the common law.

Art. VIII

Excessive bail shall not be required, nor excessive fines imposed, nor cruel and unusual punishments inflicted.

Art. IX

The enumeration in the Constitution, of certain rights, shall not be construed to deny or disparage others retained by the people.

Art. X

The powers not delegated to the United States by the Constitution, nor prohibited by it to the States, are reserved to the States respectively, or to the people.

Jordan, June. "A New Politics of Sexuality." From *Technical Difficulties* by June Jordan. Copyright © 1992 by June Jordan. Reprinted by permission of Pantheon Books, a Division of Random House, Inc.

Kakutani, Michiko. "The Word Police." © 1993 by The New York Times Company. Reprinted by permission.

Kaminer, Wendy. "Feminism's Identity Crisis" by Wendy Kaminer. First published in *The Atlantic Monthly*, October 1993. Copyright © 1993 by Wendy Kaminer. Reprinted by permission of the author.

Kennedy, Randall. "The Phony War" by Randall Kennedy. First published in *The New Republic*, October 1994. Copyright © 1995 by Randall M. Kennedy. Reprinted by permission of the author.

Krauthammer, Charles. "Defining Deviancy Up." Reprinted by permission (Copyright © 1993) *The New Republic*, Inc.

Lasch, Christopher. "Revolt of the Elites." Adapted from *The Revolt of the Elites* by Christopher Lasch, with the permission of W. W. Norton & Company, Inc. Originally appeared in *Harper's* (November 1994). Copyright © 1994, 1995 by the Estate of Christopher Lasch.

Limbaugh, Rush. "To Ogle or Not to Ogle." From *The Way Things Ought to Be* by Rush Limbaugh. Reprinted with the permission of Pocket Books, a Division of Simon & Schuster Inc. © 1992 by Rush Limbaugh.

Lind, Michael. "To Have and Have Not: Notes on the Progress of the American Class War." Reprinted with the permission of The Free Press, an imprint of Simon & Schuster Inc. from *The Next American Nation: The New Nationalism and the Fourth American Revolution* by Michael Lind. Copyright © 1995 by Michael Lind.

Loury, Glenn. "Black Dignity and the Common Good." From *One by One from the Inside Out*. Copyright © 1995 by Glenn C. Loury. First published in *First Things* 4 (June/July 1990): pp. 12–19. Reprinted by permission of the author and *First Things*.

Martínez, Elizabeth. "Seeing More Than Black & White." First published in Z Magazine, November 1990. Reprinted by permission of the author.

Moynihan, Daniel Patrick. "Defining Deviancy Down." Reprinted from *The American Scholar*, Volume 62, No. 1, Winter 1993. Copyright © 1992 by the author.

Paglia, Camille. "Sex Crime: Rape." From *Vamps and Tramps* by Camille Paglia. Copyright © 1994 by Camille Paglia. Reprinted by permission of Vintage Books, a Division of Random House, Inc.

Pollitt, Katha. "Feminism at the Crossroads." First published in *Dissent* Magazine, Spring 1994. Katha Pollitt is the author of *Reasonable Creatures: Essays on Women & Feminism*. She writes a bimonthly column for *The Nation*. Reprinted by permission of the author.

Rauch, Jonathan. "In Defense of Prejudice." Copyright © 1995 by *Harper's Magazine*. All rights reserved. Reproduced from the May 1995 issue by special permission.

Reich, Robert. "Class Anxieties." Copyright © 1995 by *Harper's Magazine*. All rights reserved. Reproduced from the February issue by special permission.

Rubin, Lillian B. "People Don't Know Right from Wrong Anymore." Reprinted from *Tikkun Magazine*, a bi-monthly Jewish Critique of Politics, Culture, and Society. Subscriptions are $31.00 per year from *Tikkun*, 251 West 100th Street, 5th floor, New York, NY 10025.

Rushton, J. Philippe. "Race and Crime: An International Dilemma" by J. Philippe Rushton, *Society*, January/February 1995. Reprinted by permission of Freedom House. Copyright © 1995 by Freedom House; all rights reserved.

Schlesinger Jr., Arthur. "Forward" to *The Disuniting of America*. W. W. Norton, 1992. Reprinted by permission of the author.

Sommers, Christina Hoff. "Noble Lies" reprinted with the permission of Simon & Schuster Inc. From *Who Stole Feminism?* by Christina Hoff Sommers. © 1994 by Christina Sommers.

Sowell, Thomas. "A World View of Cultural Diversity" by Thomas Sowell, *Society*, November/December 1991. Reprinted by permission of Transaction Publishers. Copyright © 1991 Transaction Publishers; all rights reserved.

Steele, Shelby. "On Being Black and Middle Class" by Shelby Steele. Copyright © 1990 by Shelby Steele. From *The Content of Our Character* reprinted with permission from St. Martin's Press, New York, NY. First appeared in *Commentary*, January 1988; by permission; all rights reserved.

Strossen, Nadine. "Sexual Speech and the Law" reprinted with the permission of Scribner, a division of Simon & Schuster Inc. from *Defending Pornography* by Nadine Strossen. © 1994 Nadine Strossen.

Sullivan, Andrew. "The Politics of Homosexuality." Reprinted by permission. Copyright © 1993, *The New Republic*, Inc.

Tannen, Deborah. "Put Down that Paper and Talk to Me!" From *You Just Don't Understand* by Deborah Tannen, Ph.D. Copyright © 1990 by permission of William Morrow & Company, Inc.

Walzer, Michael. "Multiculturalism and Individualism." First published in the Spring 1994 issue of *Dissent*. Copyright © 1994 by *Dissent*. Reprinted by permission of the magazine.

West, Cornel. "Diverse New World." Cornel West is a Professor of Black Studies at Harvard University. He is the author of, among other works, *Race Matters, The American Evasion of Philosophy*, and *Keeping Faith*. He is an Honorary Chair of the Democratic Socialists of America, in whose publication *Democratic Left* this essay originally appeared.

Whitehead, Barbara Dafoe. "Dan Quayle Was Right." © 1993 Barbara Dafoe Whitehead, as first published in *The Atlantic Monthly*.

Williams, Patricia. "Hate Radio." Reprinted by permission of *Ms.* Magazine, © 1994.

Wilson, James Q. "Gender." Reprinted with the permission of The Free Press, an imprint of Simon & Schuster, Inc. from *The Moral Sense* by James Q. Wilson. Copyright © 1993 by James Q. Wilson.

Wilson, William Julius. "Cycles of Deprivation and the Ghetto Underclass Debate." From *The Truly Disadvantaged* by William Julius Wilson. Copyright © 1987 by the University of Chicago. All rights reserved.

Wolf, Naomi. "Are Opinions Male?" Reprinted by permission. Copyright © 1993, *The New Republic*, Inc.

Index of Authors
and Titles